Tilting a

An Interview wi

and Jim McCarty

By
Gary Bean

L/L Research
Louisville, Kentucky
© 2016

Tilting at Windmills: An Interview with Carla L. Rueckert and Jim McCarty

Copyright © 2016 L/L Research

ISBN: 978-0-945007-39-5

This printing is a second edition. 40 small updates were made, including fixing typos, errors, and adding new content—April, 2017.

Published by L/L Research
Box 5195
Louisville, Kentucky 40255-0195, USA
www.llresearch.org

Cover and chapter header credit: John Hodapp, www.johnhodapp.net

Dedication

Carla Lisbeth Rueckert and James Allen McCarty, to whom but you could I dedicate this book? Thank you for green-lighting and embracing this project. In a life where you've always stressed your secondary importance to the material itself I know that you were initially concerned that this interview would make you more important than the work. I hope that my care in writing the questions, making disclaimers, and keeping perspective has struck the right balance.

When I first crossed paths with you as a young person my mindset was one that lifted you to an elevated status. Through many years of knowing and working with you that veneer washed away revealing your full, ordinary, everyday humanhood: blind spots, shortcomings, weaknesses, warts and all.

But as the image I had constructed faded, and your actual and authentic natures became apparent, my crest was not fallen. On the contrary, my respect for you only increased as I witnessed ordinary humans with extraordinary strength of heart living a life of magic, beauty, seeking and service through the dirt and grime of the third-density experience.

One can view our collective human situation here on planet Earth as being somewhat lost in a thick jungle of our own confusions. In lieu of understanding who and what we really are, we cling to scientific, religious, or socio-cultural truths and myths in order to help us make sense of this mystery. All of these sources do—when viewed through the right lens—reveal some aspect of the truth (isn't everything the Creator meeting the Creator?), especially the heart of religious teaching. *Taken at face value*, though, many of these threads of human thought obscure and distort the unified nature of reality.

Maps are needed. And while our human heritage preserves a handful of impeccable maps passed down to us by mystical sources who have experienced the truth of our situation, most maps are, by varying degrees, misguided and replete with misunderstanding. They do not empower the seeker with responsibility and authority for their own creation and evolution. They do not encourage the seeker to seek the truth for him or herself, to discover who he or she *already* really is. They do not establish a framework that reconciles the many to the One (insofar as words are able). And they generally do not present themselves as humble maps only, of aid strictly as a tool to the seeker who must him or herself walk the terrain. Though each of course must make that assessment for themselves—what is a faulty map for me may be perfect for another.

It is within this wilderness that you helped bring forth one of the most reliable, trustworthy, clear, beautiful and profound maps of which I'm aware. In conjunction with Don Elkins you made contact with those humble messengers who are in a position to lend some clarity to our conflicted human situation, thereby carving out a uniquely novel and direct path through the mazed terrain, one that hadn't quite existed prior to your work. One that has every potential to endure as it concerns itself with timeless principles in the seeking of eternity and infinity.

The path is always within and awaiting the seeker's efforts, of course—your work and its message can be no more than the signpost pointing to the ocean—but the philosophy you brought to this world is among the clearest signpost orienting the seeker to that inner work and to the infinite possibilities when the faculties of will and faith intersect in the seeking of the Creator. Of course you cannot take credit for all the content, but you can take credit for the fidelity with which you preserved and shared this information, and for being faithful instruments that have allowed the Creator to pluck harmony and song from your seven-stringed selves, with acceptable amounts of distortion.

To those for whom this material resonates your work has been a gift. Your life has been a gift. But whatever roles we may each seem to play upon the incarnational stage we are all only one thing: the Creator interacting with and knowing Itself. May we each reveal to each other who and what we really are, and go forth rejoicing in the One Infinite Creator.

And from the bottom of my heart may I thank you, Carla and Jim.

Those who know me may wonder at this image, but it is my favorite photo of myself. It was made when I was at Noyes Camp, a dancing camp in Connecticut, at a very early age, when my body had no limitations. No matter how limited I may become, this figure expresses my essence. Fly with me! – Carla L. Rueckert

Table of Contents

Part IV: Reflections & The Horizon

DAY 5

Part V: Spiritual Principles & Channeling

DAY 6

Part VI: Personal Biography

DAY 7

Appendices

Acknowledgements

I'm always amazed when I read the acknowledgements page in a book, especially non-fiction. The author tends to thank enough people sufficient to invade mainland Europe. I think to myself *how does he/she even know that many people much less having managed to rope them into helping.*

Though it required less people, this book was no exception to the immutable law which states that it takes a village to raise a book. Each who brought this book into manifestation generously, graciously, and freely volunteered their time, energy, and in some cases buckets of sweat. They include:

Aaron Turner, Michelle Holt, Linda Hoagland, and Kimberly Thompson for listening to the audio recordings of this interview and translating the spoken word into text through the art of transcription. If you've ever attempted transcription of the spoken word, not to mention at the speed of conversation, not to mention with dialogue including interruptions and some simultaneous speakings, you'll know it's none-too-easy a task. To Aaron Turner especially I owe my gratitude in this category for carrying the lion's share of that load.

Though given homage in the Dedications page, and thanked by way of the book itself, **Jim McCarty** for performing a read-through of the material before publication and making himself available to the multitudes of questions I had *after* the interview while editing and building footnotes and endnotes.

Tobey Wheelock for his years of proactively initiated volunteer effort in building and maintaining www.lawofone.info—not for L/L Research, and not for this book (as it was done years before this came into being), but for the benefit of the student of *The Law of One*, of which I am self-avowedly one for life. The way he numbered the Q&As of the Ra contact and entered the material into a database in order to make it searchable made my research for this project to create over 400 questions exponentially more efficient, and the book significantly richer. And the endnotes a lot longer. Sorry about that.

John Hodapp for calling upon some great magic in order to create what probably caught your eye more than the title or the book's description: its cover art. John went above and beyond investing himself into and believing in this project, doing his utmost to cooperate with my non-artistic-lucky-if-I-can-draw-a-circle vision of a Quixotesque cover, and windmills for chapter headers. Outside of the photo gallery, and the (*obviously*) artful formatting of the text, his is the only contribution that gives this great labor of love a visual aesthetic. I've gazed so long at the cover artwork that it is by this point burned into my retinas. It is sublime and perfect. Please visit John's webpage at www.johnhodapp.net.

Ken Wendt for being not only the officiant of my wedding (having been ordained by the Church of Latter-Day Dude, a *Big Lebowski* offshoot), but also (to speak to something actually relevant to this book) for traveling to Louisville and giving a full week of his life to film the seven-day interview. In another age when more than ten people are interested in the work of L/L Research (say, after the ETs have landed, or we are in a new density, or HBO makes a miniseries), there will exist this wonderful archival footage of two humble people reflecting upon their work and their unique mission.

Jeremy Weiland for being on the other end of the red phone (you know, like the US and Russia share) who answered the urgent call with me shouting *NEED EDITING NOW!* Providing me very useful and detailed feedback on the introduction, dedication, and epilogue pieces. And, while I'm here, for being one of my longest-standing friends in the new incarnation that began upon awakening to spiritual seeking.

Lane Ratchford who responded to my call seeking an editor for the second half of the book after the first editor became physically unable. Despite being afflicted with that which curses everyone these days, an overly busy life, she squeaked out the time to navigate through the reams of digital files with instructions and editing notes in order to apply her "nerd grammar" to editing the second half of the book. Also for sharing questions and insights from her standpoint as a mental health professional that prompted me to write the needed endnotes to Chapter 27 regarding Don Elkins' final years.

An individual who wished to remain anonymous for doling out tons of time and labor to help refine our existing editing/formatting standards, raising the bar and setting us on a course to bring the book into a professional aesthetic that we might otherwise not achieved on our own. Thank you *you know who you are.*

Austin Bridges for carrying out and then undertaking the journey with me to further develop those standards in formatting the entire book for publication *after* performing the final round of edits to the remaining two-thirds of the books (effectively becoming a book publisher), for navigating the self-publishing world, and for scanning hundreds of negatives, slides, and photos both for preservation and so that I could build the photo gallery of this book. Together we proved that we could publish a book! Also for being my constant companion in the office who held down the fort as I conducted the interview, who puts up with my daily interruptions to his work as I turn to him with questions both important and inane, and who is as steady and rock-like in everything he does as his beard is long. Austin has been a crucial ingredient in amplifying what L/L Research has been able to accomplish and in assisting in, shall we say, *bridging* L/L Research into its next evolutionary phase of service.

Don Elkins for being the one person I have not personally met who has most directly and powerfully affected my life. His work would never have achieved or even come close to the mountaintop without the synergistic, mutually supportive and sacrificial group work that Carla and Jim undertook with him, but that effort grew out of his own personal drive to question, to seek, to know, to understand. He was the leader that drove the spearhead profoundly and deeply into the unknown, returning with treasures for the rest of us that will, if the work survives, redound to countless generations of spiritual seekers, rippling outward through metaphysical waters into places of eternity we can scarce imagine.

And finally, **Michelle Holt** for transcribing, editing, counseling, drafting the house standards, and for doing everything she did while walking the long and arduous journey of recovering from the catalyst of cancer. Though this book could not have been accomplished without the combined efforts of everyone listed, especially Austin Bridges' home runs in the book's latter stages, (and presumably a healthy dose of unseen support), if I had to name one angel most vital to the project it would be Michelle. After transcribing multiple sessions she then selflessly volunteered for the critical first editor role, in so doing helping to lay the foundation of the standards and helping us to take a giant, self-empowering step forward in transitioning from the loss of L/L's volunteer editor of 17 years by developing L/L Research's first ever articulated house standards document—something that helps us to define our standards of editing and publishing for this and all future publications. And when reviews were needed of other pieces, or questions appeared in the mind, Michelle made herself available to the need with palpable gifts of grace, support, and infusions of love. Thank you, Michelle.

This book has largely been a labor of love. Even roughly seventy percent of my own part in its development took place outside of the L/L Research office, often late at night on my personal computer. But to those aforementioned beautiful souls who gave of themselves to this book, I ask that you rise now for a private standing ovation (provided you are not in a public space as this would call suspicion on you).

To everyone I mentioned here I owe a debt of gratitude that words cannot repay. Hopefully I am not karmically bound to you to pay off this off in future lives. In which case may I instead send you gift cards to chain restaurants now in order to absolve me of any outstanding karmic debt?

Thank you, my friends. Thank you for helping me get this supplementary but wonderful material of Carla, Jim, and Don's into the hands of spiritual seekers. Hopefully it may help deepen their understanding of the philosophy and the context of how it came to be. Hopefully it may assist in some small way in their own journey of self-realization. And if not then at least give them something that might net 50¢ at the next yard sale.

Introduction

Background

The book you're holding in your hands, or your robotic arms managed by your AI brain (depending on the year you read this), contains the transcripts from a seven-day, 30-hour, 400+ question interview with Carla L. Rueckert and Jim McCarty. This book is intended to be secondary and supplementary to their channeled and written work, but in the event you've started here we'll begin with a brief explanation regarding who these two are.

Carla L. Rueckert and James McCarty are two of the original three founders of the non-profit organization L/L Research. L/L Research was officially formed in 1970, but was an outgrowth of the research efforts begun in 1955 by Donald Tully Elkins. Over the course of five decades, eleven published books, fifteen hundred transcripts, and one cassette labeled "Best Jams Mixtape Vol. 1," L/L Research has produced a considerable library of information on matters of spirituality, philosophy, and metaphysics, the heart of which was informed by experiments in channeling. As an ethical choice and matter of policy, L/L Research has, from the beginning, even before the internet, made its work available for free as a resource for the interested spiritual seeker. You can access this material at the archive website www.llresearch.org.

Purpose of the Interview

The interview is largely an investigation into the story of L/L Research's birth, growth, and journey, along with the personal journeys of Carla, Jim, and Don. The organization's biography and the personal journeys are two categories which overlap, intertwine, and merge in so many places that extricating one from the other is challenging. Better it is to take in the scope of both, for to understand their story is to better understand the story of L/L Research.

Some of this book explores philosophy, metaphysics, and channeling. Other parts examine spiritual principles, emphasizing how they manifest both in an organization and in one's personal life. Much of it simply documents events that happened, decisions that were made, emotions that were felt, people who participated, and other biographical information.

This story and material will certainly be interesting to some, but not *objectively* interesting to all. Neither here nor at any point do I attempt to convey that You Should Pay Attention to These People and Their Work. This book is intended neither to persuade nor to entertain the reader; it was written as a simple record built from the available evidence.* The book also presupposes that you, the reader, are already familiar with the work of L/L Research. Though it can be picked up, read, and understood by anyone, the first 15 chapters are less a pure biography and more biographical *context*, or backstory, for the reader who has first read the material and wants to understand what happened and how it came to be. For the new reader, the backstory in the first 19 chapters does not necessarily convey the elegant, profound, and beautiful heart of the philosophy. This can only be discovered by going directly to the material itself.

A good deal of the ground this book covers has already been addressed quite well elsewhere in the L/L Research library, beginning with the Commentary of the original Book V and the Introduction to the original Book I of *The Law of One* material. Various other writings, interviews, and speeches by Carla and Jim have spoken to different portions of this book's subject matter as well. The goal of this project is to collect the story of L/L Research and their work in a single, streamlined place. Therefore, though there is much new ground that is broken, a bit of overlap is likely.

The work has been divided into four categories, plus appendices:

- **Chapters 1–19:** the biography of L/L Research, with twelve chapters focusing upon the Ra contact.
- **Chapters 20–22:** reflections and hopes for the future.
- **Chapters 23–25:** the theory and practice of both spiritual principles and channeling.
- **Chapters 26–30:** investigations into their personal journey(s).
- **Appendices:** investigation into sacred sexuality, discussion of Carla's passing and Jim's transformation, an essay on the book's title, and L/L Research's first timeline.

---

* This historical record was made, as well, for those who may carry the L/L Research torch when we are dust, or cryogenically frozen meat bags. Those future torch-bearers, and interested readers, can look back and see: *This is what they intended; this is who they felt they were; this is what they were trying to do.* And subsequently choose either to honor, amend, or deviate from the principles that motivated their lives.

This book places special focus upon what you might call the magnum opus of Don, Carla, Jim's, and outer service: the Ra contact. The transcripts of which became the original five *The Law of One* volumes as well as a forthcoming book titled *The Ra Contact: Teaching the Law of One*.

My Relationship with Jim and Carla

I met Carla and Jim fourteen years ago in 2002, relocated to Louisville to participate in spiritual community in their home in 2003, became Administrative Assistant to Carla at her invitation and insistence in 2005, transitioned to Administrator of L/L Research (more or less running the organization) at some point in there, and became Director of L/L Research in 2015. I've spent some of those years living with them, and all of those years knowing them, learning from them, and working alongside them in a spirit of shared mission and service.

Carla and Jim are many things to me, of which I could write a great deal. Most significantly, they are friends and fellow travelers of importance along the dusty path of spiritual seeking. They are two people I genuinely love. This does not mean I never disagree with them, rather that I see and cherish Carla and Jim for who they are. This is stated up front so that you, the reader, understand wherefrom I, the interviewer, come. On one hand my personal familiarity is a great strength—no one else has stood for so long at the very point where L/L Research, the Law of One philosophy, their work, and their personal lives intersect. On the other hand an interviewer with a more detached journalistic approach may have questioned more insightfully, or critically, or in directions I didn't think to pursue.

Further, I did not ask questions from the position of a skeptic. Though I feel the heart of L/L Research's information is exquisitely congruent with the message of oneness or non-duality that all mystics have unanimously and consistently reported throughout the ages, I understand that some of the claims within this body of work about the way the universe works simply cannot be proven by present means of verification.

My aim, therefore, was not to ask with an intent to challenge Carla and Jim to prove anything, nor to convince anyone of the veracity of the content or the truth of what transpired in their lives. I interviewed two people in order that they might share the stories of the lives they actually lived and the work they actually undertook for the benefit of the *already interested* reader, both new and old, and myself as I find their work of great personal significance on my spiritual journey.

Their Replies

Any who have read Carla's writing or heard her talk will know almost immediately what a powerful and eloquent thinker, writer, and speaker she was. Carla seemed to sit atop a bottomless well of inspiration that took only the slightest provocation for its clear waters to stream forth through her communication, written or spoken. Though that clarity still shines in this interview, these transcripts do not represent Carla at the height of her powers. By this point she had been bound to a hospital bed for three years with a painful open wound on her lower back from a spinal fusion surgery that refused to heal. In a different time I think some of Carla's replies might have been stronger than they are in this interview. But if you don't notice any diminishment then this speaks to just how good she really was.

Generally speaking Carla and Jim gave outstanding replies in spite of any obstacles. Not always complete, or always the most precise, or always the deepest possible answer, or always, by whatever your criteria of measurement, the "best." But I was nevertheless blown away and humbled by their replies. I'm grateful beyond words that they were able to offer something so substantive and insightful to questions that were often, by my measure, lackluster. Their output was so much greater than my input. It's as if I gave them a few dehydrated beans and they returned a succulent stew steaming with aromas that excite the senses and warm the belly with life-giving properties.

Mechanics of the Interview and Editing Notes

The interview was one long conversation that took place in one take. No redo's, no mulligans, no scripting of any replies; just an organized Q&A. Jim did a quick read through of the questions before I asked them. Carla, on the other hand, had no advanced knowledge of the questions. This was both a strength and a weakness. Her spontaneity sometimes soared. At other times I wished she *had* considered the question prior to its being vocalized.

Beginning on Monday, July 21, 2014, we met in Carla's and Jim's bedroom—Carla in her hospital bed, Jim sitting alongside her in the same hardback wooden chair he sat in for the Ra contact. With the summer sun streaming through the windows we progressed through the questions over the course of seven consecutive days. Most of the questions were devised in the couple of weeks leading up to the interview, but many times questions were asked impromptu. The entire thing was captured with a digital audio recorder and was filmed by our good friend and videographer, Ken Wendt.

Afterward the audio was sent to a few volunteer transcribers. After the transcripts were returned they went through a several rounds of re-listening and editing to ensure accuracy as well as to make the text more legible for the reader.[†] Some sentences have been slightly altered to increase readability (especially my own sometimes bumbling questions) while retaining the meaning and intent of what was said. For instance, the following sentence from Carla:

> *He pursued any and all angles, and the Mantell case was that which focused him more on UFOs, and he really was triggered into a lot more UFO research because of the Mantell case.*

Became:

> *He pursued any and all angles. The Mantell case was that which triggered and focused his research into UFOs.*

And a final note about laughter. Everyone knows, at least intuitively if not always consciously, that laughter plays an important role in human communication. Whether one is producing or hearing the guffaw it signals any number of different things, from *that was funny*, to *I approve of you*, to *I will now destroy your city* (in the diabolical variety).

Carla and Jim laugh easily. Their belly rumbles were frequent visitors to the conversation. That laughter conveyed a great deal about the light heart with which Carla and Jim take these serious matters, along with their own spirit of play and joy in their very disciplined lives. The one listening to the interview would obviously gain the benefit of experiencing this whereas the reader would not; *unless*, that is, we included indications of laughter.

Laughter, however, does not translate into print very well. Some people fervently reject any inclusion of representations of laughter in their written communication while others heap it on like three helpings of gravy over one helping of mashed potatoes. I attempted to include most mo-

---

[†] See Acknowledgements for debts of gratitude paid in words too poor to do justice to the volunteers who made this possible.

ments of laughter in the text as judiciously as possible. Rest assured that I did not use "LOL" to denote this. Though I am sorely tempted to do so now . . .

Experience of the interview

When the interview was over I sat in wonder that the seven days even happened. Personally it was one of the greatest things I've ever had the honor of doing. Not great in scale—as it is of secondary/supplementary interest to L/L's primary work, and will be read by very few—but great in terms of depth of meaning for me and a fulfillment of a portion of my incarnational mission. Though it often seems such as an abstract concept in the Law of One philosophy, I felt the *positive polarity* acutely and viv-idly during this process. Being with other open-hearted people in so intensive and focused a way: fully present, no distractions, no dissipation of energy, attention placed completely upon the other, all friction and most barriers absent—that alone is a profound heart opener into the ex-perience of the Creator. Though often exhausting (as I was conducting this interview while performing my normal workday duties), I left a few of the sessions, especially the final one, wanting jubilantly to embrace the world.[‡]

I wasn't sure that Jim and Carla would accept the project given its scope and the time/energy necessary to complete it, much less that, upon ac-cepting, getting through it would be daunting. But everything seemed to come together perfectly, and we moved forward question by question. I'm so excited by it all, especially that these two people (who have been the most significant influences upon my spiritual and adult life) can be shared with the world in a light which approaches something of the perspective I've been privileged to know.

No, this isn't to glorify. It is not to direct attention to personality but to the love shining through the eyes, the light in the wisdom of their reflec-tions, the unity underlying the path they have walked, and the desire to serve which motivates Carla and Jim's efforts to be as instruments for that particular vibration or wavelength of love and light known as the Law of One. And it is to tell the story of their work and organization, L/L Re-search. It is good history, good supplementary info, good probing of spiritual principles, and good reminders of who we are and what we're all

---

[‡] Carla and Jim also liked it too. They said it was the best seven-day, 30-hour, 400+ question interview they had ever done in their lives.

doing here. And it looks good on a book shelf, quite frankly. I am so happy with all of it. But, its "goodness" is something for you to determine. And about that . . .

L/L Disclaimer: Your Relationship with the Material

Though this book can stand independent in its own right, it is designed to fulfill the need for context for readers already familiar with the philosophy. More importantly, throughout the course of this interview we ask you to please be mindful that this interview does not intend to uphold Carla, Jim, or Don as perfect beings who should be placed upon a pedestal and emulated. Where we move into their personal interpretation and application of the material during this discussion remember that what is shared is opinion only and is not to be construed as infallible or the final word on the subject.

It is not to their personalities that they would direct your attention but rather to the principles contained within the Law of One philosophy. Those principles encourage the authentic discovery of who you really are, as Eckhart Tolle would say, *beyond name and form*.

The fundamental tenet of the Law of One is that "self" and "Creator" are two ways of saying the same thing. In other words, and in accordance with the vision disclosed to mystics, all is one.

But words and intellectual formulations can *never*—no matter how precise, profound, or perfect—capture or contain the truth. That is the case whether from Confederation sources, Jesus, Buddha, or other enlightened beings. Why? Because *you* are the living truth that you seek. *You* are beingness itself. *You* are the mystery. *You* are the Creator; you always have been. Consequently L/L Research's desire is not that the information in this or any of its books become dogma. It is only offered that it may be of some small aid to you as a resource on your own journey of seeking.

The dispassionate spirit with which they have always offered this information is one of non-coercion and non-proselytism. Carla, Jim, Don, and the Confederation sources have always encouraged the seeker's own discrimination. Naturally they would be delighted if the information was of any help to you but suggest leaving it behind without a second thought if there is no resonance. They emphasize the relative unimportance of this interview in light of the grand mystery which beckons each of us onward in the seeking of truth.

CHAPTER 1

The Beginning

GARY To begin our investigation into the story of L/L Research, I've chosen a moment in 1948 that was pivotal in the life of Don Elkins: Carla and Jim, what sparked Don Elkins' interest in researching the UFO phenomena and the paranormal? How old was he then?

JIM Well, he was 17 years old, and it was an actual UFO case that occurred right here in Louisville, Kentucky. It was one of the first reported across the country. Don had been taking flying lessons from the Elkins-Mantell Flying School.[1] (The Elkins at the school was a distant relative.)

Thomas Mantell was a captain in the Kentucky Air National Guard.[2] On that particular day he was en route from Marietta, Georgia, to Louisville's airport, Standiford Field, with three other pilots, each flying a P-51, former World War II fighter planes. They got a call from the control tower at Godman Field, Ft. Knox, saying there had been sightings of a UFO over Maysville, Kentucky, and could they alter their course and investigate to see what was going on.

So they that did that. One of them was low on fuel so he went on to Standiford Field. The two wingmen and Captain Mantell continued on, and within about 30 minutes they made contact with the UFO and discovered that it was huge, it was metallic, and it was shaped like an inverted ice cream cone with a point on top and a big round ball at the bottom. Captain Mantell said he was going to close in to try to get a better look, and as he did this, the craft shot straight up at an incredible rate of speed. Captain Mantell said that he had seen entities[3] in the craft and that he was going to follow, because he wanted to find out more about what was going on and who this was.

As he passed through about 20,000 feet, he passed out because his plane, being a World War II vintage, did not have oxygen. His brain suffered hypoxia and he augered in and crashed near the Kentucky-Tennessee border. This of course killed him, and it did two things: it got interest nationally in UFOs (which had been pooh-poohed before that quite a lot—no one really thought they were real), and the second thing it did was it got Don Elkins interested in UFOs.

CARLA He had been interested since he sort of woke up the way teenagers do—but not so much with rebelling against what his parents did, which he approved of. His mom was a reader in the Church of Christ, Scientist, what is normally called the Christian Science Church.[4] From the age of nine onward he didn't go in; instead he would wait in the car while the family went in and worshipped. He didn't believe in that,[5] but he thought that the theory was good. However when he got to a certain point in school, he studied the first things about science which indicated that we did not know what light and gravity were. We were using these values and a lot was depending on them, but we actually didn't know why they worked. He became interested in what was going on and why. Just the question of *why?* He pursued any and all angles. The Mantell case was that which triggered and focused his research into UFOs.

GARY So prior to Mantell, he was pursuing his own truth? Asking questions . . .

CARLA Yes, definitely.

GARY Once his interest was awakened to the UFO phenomena due to the Mantell case, how did he pursue and manifest his passion?[6]

CARLA Don did everything he could think of. He learned how to fly, and using small planes he flew to different places to interview people like—who was the guy[7] that did those flash cards, the stars, and all the early work in telepathy? Anyway, he was famous at the time, and Don went to see him and talk to him about it. He went to see anybody he thought might have any answers. He went to séances, he went to chan-neling sessions—he investigated anything that was other than normal science.

GARY So what set him on this trajectory, prior to the Mantell case, was a distinct understanding on his part of the limitations of current knowledge. He saw that there was much more beyond what we presently understood.

CARLA That's right.

GARY Do you know what Don's preliminary thoughts were on UFOs in the beginning phases of his investigation? Had he considered UFOs or similar matters before this event?

CARLA Before the Mantell case he'd considered them but only generally.

After the Mantell case, as I said, he learned to fly, and he interviewed quite a big series of people that had UFO experiences—not people that thought they might have seen something, but people who had had an ex-perience: *so-and-so came down and they had such-and-such discussion and they got on board and they went to such-and-such a place,* and so forth.[8]

So, from the very beginning he knew that UFOs were an actuality of our experience on planet Earth and that a lot of people had had UFO experi-ences. He was interested first, I think, in gathering his research, and secondly in helping people to become aware that there was more to life than met the eye. He was very big on sharing this information any way that he could. He did a lot of talking to people.

GARY So you said that from the onset of his investigation into UFOs, he felt that they were an actuality on Earth. By "actuality," does that mean that Don had reached the conclusion that UFOs were occupied and op-erated by intelligences from outside of Earth?

CARLA That's right.

GARY Because some who study the phenomena posit that they may be manifestations of the collective unconscious, that they're not real in the outer [objective and empirical] sense.

CARLA He thought that the people that had proposed those theories were very interesting, but as far as he himself was concerned, UFOs were real—as someone like Orfeo Angelucci[9] or any number of those that he interviewed at the time would attest. They were seemingly occupied by human-like people that seemed to be very well-intentioned and kindly towards Earth.

He began to be interested in why they were here, not just that they were here but precisely why. It wasn't until later that he gathered enough material to start separating things into positively oriented and possibly negatively oriented entities out there.

GARY What would you say were Don Elkins' driving questions? What puzzle was he attempting to solve or penetrate?

CARLA There was nothing for Don but the biggest, the widest, the deepest. His mind would not be satisfied with a segment of the answer. He wanted to know the answer to the puzzle of why everything worked. He thought that UFOs might have part of it so he investigated. He thought seeing ghosts and finding out things like . . . He learned how to do hypnotic regression and found out that he seemed to be able to regress people beyond this Earth experience to other experiences on and off this Earth, and so he discovered, he felt, that part of the lesson lay in—part of the puzzle pieces lay in reincarnation. He was interested in whatever—[*sounds of kitty throwing up a fur ball*]—whatever makes Pickwick throw up. [*laughs*] Sorry guys, our cats are expressing stage fright, I guess. Is Pickwick okay?

GARY Dan-D, actually.

CARLA Dan-D, okay. Poor Dan-D.[10]

Anyway, anything and everything. But he soon narrowed it down, basically, to investigations into reincarnation and investigations into channeling. He felt that channeled messages consisted of messages from elsewhere of a positive nature, and also messages from people that had incarnated before and were no longer incarnate, like Tom Edison. He was very interested in a series of channelings by a lady in Chicago who channeled Tom Edison. Don was looking at any material that would give him more puzzle pieces to put into the puzzle.

GARY Did he have a vision of what that big picture was? Or was it completely unknown to him—all these various leads providing another piece and another piece and another?

CARLA I think that it was the latter. I think that it took him a long, long time to settle down to one way of seeking the answer. I was his research partner all through the '70s until the Ra contact began in '80. We investigated hard UFO cases, cases around here and in Tennessee where he could get to with his rented airplane. I went to séances with him. And then I did quite a few hypnotic regressions with him. (I mean I was there when he did quite a few hypnotic regressions.) So he had narrowed it down to those methods of investigating the truth.

He felt from the very beginning that the truth did involve many of his mother's most cherished beliefs, and that, as Christian Science believes, this is all an illusion and that spirit is the reality. (That was why Christian Science healing works, because you simply sit there and you know that what you're looking at is an illusion, the sickness is an illusion, and you know that it doesn't have to be there. It's only there because your thinking is messed up. So you can make a healing that way. That's what Christian Science practitioners do for you. Instead of doctoring physically they doctor metaphysically, and many healings have been done that way.)

So he felt that the illusory nature of the material world was the basic thing, and that reincarnation showed you were here but then you weren't here, but you still existed. And then you came back and you were here again. He thought that the channeling was interesting because it indicated that there were others from elsewhere that had kindly thoughts toward us. It was a long time before he was able to admit that there were negatively oriented UFOs. He thought they were all nice guys. Some of them *are* very nice guys. But there is a segment of those who wish us active harm.

GARY And we have a very substantial section devoted to just that topic further on in the interview.

So it seems that the big picture gradually, incrementally disclosed itself to Don's investigative efforts. You mentioned that conducting past-life regressions was among his primary modes of investigation. When did he cross paths with this technique and how did he learn to conduct it himself?

CARLA I don't know just when or where he did because it was before I knew him. When I met him in 1962, he was already conducting hypnotic regressions. In his investigative efforts he just ran across it. He got interested and he thought, "Hey, I can do this myself." So he learned how. And he learned very carefully. I've never seen anybody do it better.

GARY Don, born in 1930, was 18 years old when the Mantell case happened. And you had mentioned that prior to the Mantel crash he had become aware that humanity was a species that knew very little—that there was much more. Do you know about what age that was for Don?

CARLA I don't know. I would guess whenever the first time it is that you take a class where—probably physics, probably physics. He was in a college track at Male High School in Louisville, Kentucky, and he would have run across that pretty early, probably at the age of 14 or 15.

GARY Okay. In his efforts to find this big picture he discovered channeling. Do you know at what point channeled information entered the scene?

CARLA I don't. He was already doing the channeling thing when I met him. I met him in '62—in '61, actually. He was one of my then-fiancé's teachers at engineering school. He was a physics teacher. He got a group together late in '61, and we started in January of '62.

GARY Okay. Do you know what his initial response to channeling was? Sounds like he was pretty open to considering everything . . .

CARLA That's right. He wanted to investigate further. His basic feeling was that if you have a non-provable area of investigation your best bet is thickness of information, so gather a great deal of information.

GARY Do you know specifically how he incorporated the information coming through channels into his developing theory?

CARLA No, I really think that it was a cumulative effect rather than a specific one. I think that, thinking about it, he figured that if he was able to do this, if people were able to channel then there must be something that they were channeling. There was an end result. So he was aiming for the result—he was aiming for who the source was and what they had to say that would help him with his puzzle.

GARY It seems like he was someone who wasn't afraid to stand apart from the crowd.

CARLA Don was completely fearless. He had no interest whatsoever in following any crowd—none.

GARY So in the course of his efforts, he at some point learned of a group in Detroit, Michigan, that was channeling messages from alleged occupants of UFOs. How did Don first learn about this group?

CARLA It was odd. Don had been called in on perhaps half a dozen cases—whenever somebody called the University of Louisville with a case, the University called Don. One of these cases was the Hoagland case that is written about in *The Secrets of the UFO*. So shortly after this case was investigated and recorded and written about . . . [*hesitates*] no, I'm wrong there. It was somebody at the university who knew of Don's interest in UFOs, and this person also became aware of someone who had been a part of a UFO group in Detroit and had moved to Louisville to work at the Ford plant.

So they got Don and Hal together. Hal Price was the name of the guy. He was a checker at Ford, a very responsible position. You never met a more upright man of probity[11]—a marvelous, dignified fellow—but totally open to the possibility of channeled information because of personal experience.

Hal had been part of a channeling group: he'd seen it happen. So Hal had ahold of a body of material channeled by this group including something called *The Brown Notebook*.[12] (*The Brown Notebook* must have been originally written down by hand in a brown-colored notebook.)

It was a series of short channelings to this other guy in the channeling group. One of the channelings was concerning how you could start a group like it. They explained that you got the group together regularly, weekly at least, and you sat and meditated and you waited and sooner or later the invitation would bring some channeled material. So Don got together a group of the students to do the same, and I found out about it and asked to be part of it.

GARY So Hal Price comes down from Detroit. Hal Price was part of the Detroit Group. Hal, through a mutual friend, introduces Don to this material, and Don obviously finds some value in it. Don then visits the Detroit Group—is that right? And if so, what happened then?

CARLA I imagine he did visit the Detroit Group, but I think that the important thing that happened was Don's reading of that *Brown Notebook*, because it was the material in that notebook where it said you can receive your own messages which made Don think, *well, ya know, that would be a really good thing to try*. And so he felt all along that he could bring volunteers together to conduct a scientific experiment in channeling.

He did not, at first, tell anybody that the idea was not simply to meditate but to channel. So nothing happened right at first. The significant thing that turned the group around was that Walt Rogers from the Detroit Group came down and channeled for this group (the Louisville Group) and said while channeling, "Why in the world—we've been trying to get ahold of you but we've been unable to penetrate your reluctance to speak. If you would simply open up and allow us to speak through you, we would offer you information."

After that, the 12 guys all started opening up and trying to get information, and for a few months you heard a lot of [*Carla makes unusual clucking and clicking noises*] and it was so funny. It sounded like there was a whole room full of flapping window shades. But eventually they began to produce some material, and Don began to get some meager but satisfying results.

GARY So these initial 12 people were students of his, correct?

CARLA Uh-huh.

GARY How in the world did he attract them to this particular experiment?

CARLA Don had an incredible amount of charisma. I think any one of his students would have done anything he suggested because it was Don and it was cool. It was as simple as that.

GARY And once it was clear what they were attempting to do, they stayed on board and continued with the experiment as long as they were in school?

CARLA Most of them did, as long as they were in school. You have to remember that, as it happened, this was the hippie era and it was very fashionable to meditate. So there was not something in the culture of the peer group that was, *why are you doing that?* It was like, *oh, cool, can I do that too?* So we ended up sometimes having quite a large group.

GARY So, quick mechanical question: How often would the group meet, and when would they meet?

CARLA It met on Sunday night at eight o'clock, once a week.

GARY Were their objectives clear? Did Don make clear this is what we're doing, and this is why we are doing it?

CARLA No, he just said he thought it would be interesting if we got together and had silent meditation, and I joined it because it was silent meditation and not for anything more.

GARY While conducting these experiments, did Don or others receive any negative feedback from the community, from his professional colleagues, or from family members of the students, or from neighbors, etc.?

CARLA If he did, I don't know about it. You have to, again, always remember that Don was an incredibly pleasant, affable, charming, wonderfully sociable guy. He knew how to be with people, talk to people, and teach people; and generally he was so well-thought-of that it was basically, *well, you know he's a little strange, but he's really interesting.* That was the reaction that people had, rather than condemning him or telling him he was crazy. I'm sure people did, but I just didn't hear about it.

GARY Even nowadays we live in a Western world with a much more accepting, tolerant society, but nevertheless it's still difficult now to stand apart from the crowd. In that time it must have been much more so. It sounds like he inspired some trust and confidence in other people.

CARLA He did indeed.

GARY How did Don refer to these sources being channeled, and did he develop anything resembling a friendship or a sense of familiarity with these sources?

CARLA To reply to the first part of the question: He was always extremely careful to refer to and treat the information as part of a scientific investigation. He never tried to tell anybody anything. He would just share information if asked. When he did open up it was because somebody asked him to, so he didn't put himself in the position of banging on the door of popular belief. He simply would tell people what he was investigating when asked. He was always very careful to keep it scientific, saying "allegedly this" and "possibly that."

Now as to the second part of the question, in having a personal relationship with them: I think that he did. I think he identified with those entities from the Detroit Group who spoke of love being the answer and that we are all—again like his childhood teachings—we are all illusions. This is all a grand illusion, and we're not really here. We're really spiritual—that's our actual reality. And I think that was something that was his first piece in the puzzle: his realization that the information he sought wasn't going to come from here because this was all an illusion. It was necessary to seek beyond scientific limits.

GARY In session 12, question 11 of the Ra contact,[13] Don asked which group was contacting his channeling group in 1962. Ra replies saying that it was the Confederation. Do you know if Don is referring to his or to the Detroit Group's formal channeling experiments, or to another incident at that time?

CARLA No, it was the Detroit Group's channeling.

GARY That completes our section of Don's life and work up to the point of meeting you [Carla]. Now we focus on your meeting and beyond.

---

[1] "Capt. Thomas Mantell started in business [on March 21, 1947] as part owner of a GI flying school. Elkins-Mantell Flying School, Bowman Field, Louisville, KY. He was federally recognized in the Air National Guard about the 16th of February, 1947. He started flying the P-51 about May of 1947 and built his time to around 70 hours up until his death. He was a flight leader. His military time was approximately 2,300 hours, his civilian time was around 700 hours."

"Tyler's Report pp 36–39," National Investigations Committee on Aerial Phenomena, accessed September 1, 2015, www.nicap.org/docs/mantell/mantell_accrep_tyler.pdf.

[2] "Captain Thomas Francis Mantell Jr. (30 June 1922 – 7 January 1948) was a United States Air Force serviceman and a World War II veteran. Mantell was awarded the Distinguished Flying Cross for courageous action during the Normandy landings, and an Air Medal with three Oak leaf clusters for heroism.... On 16 June 1942, Mantell joined the U.S. Army Air Corps, finishing Flight School on 30 June 1943. During World War II, he was assigned to the 440th Troop Carrier Group which air dropped the 101st Airborne Division into Normandy, France on 6 June 1944. After the war, Mantell returned to Louisville, joining the newly formed Kentucky Air National Guard on 16 February 1947."

Wikipedia, The Free Encyclopedia, s.v. "Mantell UFO Incident," accessed September 1, 2015, https://en.wikipedia.org/wiki/Mantell_UFO_incident.

[3] "Richard T. Miller, who was in the Operations Room of Scott Air Force Base in Belleville, Illinois, also made several profound statements regarding the crash. He was monitoring the radio talk between Mantell and Godman Tower, and heard this statement very clearly: 'My God, I see people in this thing!' Miller added that on the morning after the crash, at a briefing, investigators had stated that Mantell died 'pursuing an intelligently controlled unidentified flying object.'"

"1948, The Death of Thomas Mantell," UFO Casebook.com, accessed February 9, 2016, www.ufocasebook.com/Mantell.html.

[4]

Founded in 1879, Boston, Christian Science has been described by its discoverer and founder, Mary Baker Eddy, as a return to "primitive Christianity and its lost element of healing." Adherents subscribe to a radical form of philosophical idealism, believing that reality is purely spiritual and the material world an illusion. This includes the view that disease is a mental error rather than physical disorder, and that the sick should be treated by a form of prayer that seeks to correct the beliefs responsible for the illusion of ill health. In Christian Science, sickness is viewed as absence of "right thinking" or failure to connect to Divine Mind.

(An endnote written by our good friend Sam Womelsdorf, heavily borrowed from the wiki article cited below.)

Wikipedia, The Free Encyclopedia, s.v. "Church of Christ, Scientist," accessed September 1, 2015,
https://en.wikipedia.org/wiki/Church_of_Christ,_Scientist.

[5]

In this paragraph, Carla seems to indicate that Don did agree with the church doctrine (which includes the tenet that all illnesses are caused by improper thinking), but that he did not believe in their methods or practices or forms of worship. Jim adds, "His mother, as a reader, would have been in charge of preaching this church doctrine and combining it with Scripture. I think that is where Don got his idea about the mental aspect of experiencing reality. He just didn't associate it with anything in the Bible."

[6]

To read more about Elkins developing study of UFOs, see the June 4, 1978 interview he gave Louisville's *Courier Journal* newspaper. An excerpt:

> When I first started checking out the contactee reports, I must admit that my sympathies were very much with orthodox scientists: I suspected the early contactees were charlatans because I did not have enough background in the study of "Ufology" to think differently. Their stories didn't "compute" in any orthodox sense.

> But the more contactee reports I read from people all over the world—people who did not know each other and had shown no previous desire for publicity—the more I was struck by the similarity of the messages the contactees said they had received.

The Courier Journal – "UFO Prober", Bruce Swain with Don Elkins, L/L Research, June 4, 1978, www.llresearch.org/interviews/interview_1978_0604.aspx

[7]

It was J.B. Rhine, the "father of parapsychology" from Duke University.

[8]

In a lecture Don Elkins gave at Jefferson Community College on April 21, 1981, he said:

> I've been at this business for a long time. I got interested in UFOs in

1948. Maybe some of you remember Tom Mantell, who was killed flying an F-51 because a UFO was sighted flying near Fort Knox. I was a student pilot in the Elkins Mantell Flying School at Bowman Field when he got killed. So I was greatly interested in UFOs starting in 1948. I didn't really get to devote much time to research in that area, and related areas, until 1955. In 1955 I really went to it and I've been researching the subject ever since.

In a footnote to the transcript of Elkins' lecture, Carla added, "Getting his degree as a Mechanical Engineer and serving in the Korean War took up his time for a few years."

"The Spiritual Significance of UFOs," Don Elkins, April 21, 1981, www.llresearch.org/speeches/speech_1981_0421.aspx.

[9] "Orfeo Matthew Angelucci (Orville Angelucci), (June 25, 1912 – July 24, 1993) was one of the most unusual of the mid-1950s so-called 'contactees' who claimed to be in contact with extraterrestrials."

Wikipedia, The Free Encyclopedia, s.v. "Orfeo Angelucci," accessed September 1, 2015, http://en.wikipedia.org/wiki/Orfeo_Angelucci.

[10] In 2016 Jim added:

Pickwick is our 19-year-old orange tabby kitty who still chases his tail but has no chance of catching it because it is too short. He loves everybody and is our goodwill ambassador.

Chloe is our nine-year-old black cat with shiny fur. She is our hermit cat who really doesn't like company.

Chloe's brother is Dan D. Lion, also nine-years-old, and is a grey tabby kitty with no tail because of a run-in with a raccoon five years ago. He is a lover with a huge purr."

[11] Carla's way of speaking highly of another often involved superlatives.

[12] Hal Price reported that Don's response to *The Brown Notebook* went something along the lines of, "This is the glue that puts it all together for me."

The Brown Notebook is available in the "Origins" section of LLResearch.org http://www.llresearch.org/origins/origins_toc.aspx.

L/L Research hopes to eventually publish a conversation with Hal Price from a chance meet-up in 2013.

[13] From this point forward all references to particular session and question numbers from the Ra contact will be in the format of "session number.question number" (e.g., 12.11). This format was first implemented by Tobey Wheelock.

CHAPTER 2

Don Meets Carla

GARY Okay, Carla, when did you and Don meet and through what circumstance?

CARLA I met Don by being the girlfriend of Jim D.,* who was a student of Don's at Speed Scientific School. Jim introduced me to him in the course of lunch one day. We were eating at the same place.

GARY Did that meeting strike you as unusual? Did you feel that you had just met an important person in your life?

CARLA No, I really didn't; I thought he was a very interesting cat, and I wanted to get to know him better. Don tells me now—or told me later on [*laughs*], much later on (after a marriage and a divorce, and he and I had gotten together and spent quite a bit of time together), sometime in the '70s he said—"Well, I knew the first time that I met you that I would be with you."

GARY So at that lunch Don had that realization, but didn't communicate it . . .

CARLA Not a bit of it. Of course Don never communicated.

---

* Jim D. and Jim McCarty (the Jim in this interview) are two different Jims. The latter Carla would meet in 1978 and marry in 1987.

GARY That would be an odd thing to communicate to somebody the first time you met.

CARLA Well, it would unless you had an object to pursue.

GARY I have a series of questions now about your relationship with Don that we'll explore in more depth in the personal biography section. I leave these questions in this section as well, because these dynamics had a direct impact on the success, and eventual end, of the Ra contact.

Just to briefly touch on the highlights: You and Don did not join upon first meeting; instead, you had a four-year detour. Can you briefly describe that?

CARLA Surely. Jim D. was an excellent guitar player and singer, and he had been part of a Kingston Trio knockoff, the Jamaican Trio (or something like that), in high school with some of his high school buddies. And when he found out that I had a higher score than he did on an IQ test that everybody took at the school we both went to, he said, "I've got to meet her," because I was the only person who ever had a higher score than he did.

So he did. He met me, and at that point he decided to go and get me. So we sang together and practiced together. I felt he was just a nice guitar player, but I loved singing with him and creating songs together. It was an incredibly great musical relationship. I made the best music I think I've ever made in my life. We made what ended up to be about 60 songs together that we created ourselves, so we had a great deal of original material ready to go.

I went—probably every Saturday of this world for years when I was in college—over to Rick Crampton's house, a mutual friend, and practiced with Jim D. Rick had an interest in recording and he recorded us. The early recordings that I have came from Rick recording us at those Saturday rehearsals.

GARY And then you later married Jim D. and he took you away from Louisville. Is this correct?

CARLA Well, we were heard on local TV by a producer who was getting together a tour for Peter, Paul & Mary. It was their very first tour and they had just made a hit with one song or another, and the producer thought that they were going to be big. So he saw Jim and me—originally enough we were called Jim and Carla—and we really impressed the guy, so he asked us to sing for him some more, and we did. We met and shook hands with him, sang for a couple of hours for him, and impressed the heck out of him. He said, "You know, if the rest of the people that are producing this thing agree, you've got a job opening for Peter, Paul & Mary on this tour." He wanted us to tour.

So D. was of the opinion that it was immoral to go out of town with me if we weren't married, so he determined to marry me. I resisted and resisted and resisted. Finally he stopped the car in the middle of Shelbyville Road in rush hour, threw the car door open, and got down on his knees on the pavement and said, "Will you marry me? I'm not getting up until you do."

And I said yes. And so we set our date for the wedding as well as our date to go see these people in Chicago to get the okay for touring with Peter, Paul & Mary. This was in 1964.

Unfortunately, Jim got halfway to Chicago and realized that he did not want to become famous. Unfortunately enough, somebody had asked him for an autograph, and he said, "I don't want to give autographs. I don't want people to get to know me—that makes me feel badly."

So then he wouldn't get out of bed[1] until I said okay. So here I was married to this guy but, unfortunately, no longer going to sing with him. There was no real reason for me to be married to him any longer.

So these two very good friends, who made beautiful music together, became one married person. He distinctly hated being married and wanted nothing better than just his freedom; and I, who did not feel that I should break a promise, stuck with the marriage until he asked me for a divorce years later.

GARY So prior to that point you and Jim D. were participants in Don's channeling group. You attended those, then Jim proposes, and off you go, headed to, at first, Chicago, and then you're stuck in this marriage after he bails on the whole singing venture?

CARLA Right.

GARY Do you return to Louisville or do you go off to—I believe Canada was your next destination.

CARLA Well, I went back to Louisville and enjoyed D. leaving me for a total of seven times in the next three years, and the last time that he left me, the seventh time, he made it. He got all the way to Vancouver, Canada, and set up shop there with his lover.

He said that I was finally free to be free of him. I was thrilled and I was finding a job for myself and letting everything old go away. I was as happy as a clam. Then he called me from Vancouver and said that he needed me. He couldn't find a job, so I would have to come and take care of him. Again, I reviewed the marriage contract—no small print, [it was] "for better or for worse"—so I dropped all my plans and went to Canada and took care of him. And that was finally where he asked me for a divorce.

GARY You were then able to return to Louisville.

CARLA I was then able to divorce him. I did not want to return to Louisville, and I had a good life for myself up in Vancouver. But once more he made one of his famous pronouncements that he would not divorce me unless I came home to "my people," who had never taken care of me a day in my life—I was a little mother and took care of them for the most part. It was ridiculous, but that was D.

GARY So his terms for divorce were that you must return to Louisville?

CARLA I had to return to Louisville. So I returned to Louisville and got the job that I had had before. They were thrilled that I came back. The person that they'd hired couldn't do it and I loved it, so I went back to enjoy my work and not being married to D.

GARY So you get back and you're divorced. Do you immediately resume attending Don Elkins' channeling experiments?

CARLA Well, I attended them when I could. They were having them once every two weeks for a while at Hal and Joe's. But it was pitiful. The group had dwindled to be a very small group. I wasn't a channel myself—I wasn't interested. So the reason I became a channel was that he asked me to continue the experiment: his experiment would die unless I helped him out.

GARY This is a bit further down the road, in 1974?

CARLA Yeah, this was in 1974.

GARY And we're still in 1968, I believe. You've come back to Louisville.

CARLA Right. So I hung out and by the end of 1968 my divorce became final, and, I think the day after it became final, Don asked if he could move in with me.

GARY [*laughs*] Don was waiting patiently.

CARLA Yes he was. As a matter of fact, he asked me to marry him, but I looked at him and saw that he had his hat in his hand and a suitcase. I realized he perhaps did not want to marry. So I asked him to go ahead and go on his trip. (He was a pilot and would be gone for three days at a time, usually). I said, "If you come back in three days and want to marry me, then I'd *love* to—otherwise no," because I'd just gotten out of a difficult marriage.

GARY So my next question was going to be how and when the intimate relationship with Don began, and it seems like right then and there, Don makes it known that he wants to be with you and is interested in you.

CARLA As soon as the divorce became final we became an item.

GARY So at that point, if I understand it correctly, you had six months of attempted intimacy, and then Don opted for celibacy and decided that he did not want to marry. Why did Don decide that he wanted celibacy, and how did this affect your connection?

CARLA In another person it might not have ever affected anything, but I was the kind of person that wanted more clarity. I always wanted more clarity, so rather than just allowing things to dwindle between us, I said, "I'm kind of getting that you don't really want to have sex—kind of getting that you'd like me to not approach you for sex." Because he never approached me, so if we were going to have it, I approached him. So it was easy enough to stop if he wanted me to.

He said he'd like for me to stop and that would be preferable. He never gave me a reason, though I deduced the reason easily enough: He was a very fastidious man—he did not like anything sloppy or messy or that smelled bad or was full of the juice of life the way sex is. I mean you can't help it. It smells questionable: as soon as you have sex, you get male and female mixing together, and their scents mixed together are not wonderful. Then everybody has to go wash, and it's like, [*laughs*] he didn't like any of that. He didn't want to have to go wash. I think that was pretty much it.[2] He wasn't gay in any shape—I never spotted any gay behaviors or leanings in him whatsoever.[3] He was as straight as an arrow, and I was his choice if he was going to have one. He thought I was nice.

At one point he said I was a 9.0 in Louisville and a 5.5 in Hollywood. So I think that was a high piece of praise there. So he liked me just fine, but he just didn't like messiness—he thought it was tacky. I didn't let it affect anything having to do with our relationship, which was metaphysical in nature.

Don never spoke to me much personally at all, but I knew how he felt about me and it was very clear. He took care of me and he loved me dearly, but he didn't speak about feelings to anybody. Not *his* feelings. In terms of being able to talk about sex, to be a regular guy, he was one of the best. But he just didn't share personal feelings.

GARY So as a result, you said you didn't let it affect your relationship because it was a metaphysical one, but you did try celibacy for two years.

CARLA I sure did. I gave it everything I had. [*laughs*] I'm not, by nature, a celibate person. I don't see the benefit of it. I see sexuality as a sacred and wonderful way of expressing love, and I never felt any other way about it. It's just always been very straight with me. I never even dated until I was engaged for the first time at the end of high school. I waited until I felt all the things that you're supposed to feel before I entered into sex for the first time. So for me sex always had all the positive values, and I never had sex with anybody that I couldn't have a positive value with.

GARY It was never just the physical . . .

CARLA Never, not ever. That would have—well, I didn't have to. I had other things to do if that was all it was going to be. [*laughs*] I could take care of myself, no problem—I always had lots of people that wanted to date me, unless I was involved.

GARY So you gave it your best—two years of celibacy—and you concluded that this wasn't for you. What arrangement was made then?

CARLA I went to Don and I told him that celibacy was not for me, and he nodded. He said that he'd noticed that, and I said, "How would it be if I took a lover and you weren't ever involved in having to be embarrassed or anything like that, and I made sure that it was discrete and I would tell you before I took a lover? I would tell you after I dropped him." That was always our arrangement and his only answer to that was a grin and wiggling one ear at me, which was a private signal involving intimacy and love in Don's way, and meaning *have a ball.*

GARY It sounds like that may have been a precursor to the appurtenances of the Ra contact. Ra gave you signals through the incense and the chalice.

CARLA Well, I guess that's the way his mind worked.

GARY So, when you and Don first attempted a physically intimate relationship in 1968, was that also when your work collaboration (that would later evolve into L/L Research) commenced?

CARLA Yes. Everything commenced at once. [*laughs*] And the first thing we did was write a book together. And it was called *The Crucifixion of Esmeralda Sweetwater.*

GARY Which ties right into my next question. So something interesting happened when you two made the commitment to work together. Later on in the Ra contact, Ra spoke to this moment in time (emphasis added[†]):

> **RA** When the commitment was made between two of this group to work for the betterment of the planetary sphere, **this commitment activated a possibility/probability vortex of some strength**. The experience of generating this volume [*The Crucifixion of Esmerelda Sweetwater*] was unusual in that it was visualized **as if watching the moving picture**.
>
> Time had become available in its present-moment form. The scenario of the volume went smoothly until the ending of the volume. **You could not end the volume,**[4] and the ending was **not visualized** as the entire body of the material **but was written or authored**. This is due to the action of free will in all of the creation.
>
> However, the volume contains a view of significant events, both symbolically and specifically, which you saw under the influence of the magnetic attraction which was released when the commitment was made [between Carla and Don] and full memory of the dedication of this, what you may call, mission restored. 68.14

I have a few questions that I'd like to ask about that. Firstly, Ra says, "When the commitment was made . . . this commitment activated a possibility/probably vortex of some strength." Did this happen in a moment,

---

[†] The emphasis in the quoted material throughout this book is an addition of the interviewer.

or over a time, and was it perceived by you?

CARLA It was perceived by us in a general way in that we commented again and again on how easy it was to write, because he would just start talking and we were both seeing these things that were happening. Everything sort of fell into place—the characters, the plot, and . . . Don fiddled endlessly with the plot to make it tighter and so forth. But the story itself was just like, as Ra said, almost as if we'd seen it before.

GARY Did you say that you both saw it? Or just one of you saw it and communicated it to the other?

CARLA Well, the way we wrote was this: Don wrote the first draft. He was just strictly going for plot—he was telling the story. The second draft I tweaked, and I was going for character and for comments and for good communication within the book between the characters and so forth. So I added huge amounts of my own stuff but it wasn't *instead* of Don's stuff, it was embroidered around it. So I was adding to the basic bones—the characters, the way the characters talked and reacted together, and so forth.

GARY So both of you were drawing from this moving picture, this almost complete story, and each of you was drawing from it in different ways, but it was a common vision that was presented to both of you.

CARLA It was. I can still remember—normally I would just lie on the couch with my head in Don's lap while he worked the tape recorder with one hand and talked and then waited and talked and then waited, and it would come pretty quickly. He'd do a whole chapter at a time, and then he'd go off on a trip and I would work on it.

GARY So as he's speaking this into the recorder you're kind of corroborating it yourself in your own mind because you essentially see what he's seeing?

CARLA Exactly. There wasn't a point where I said, "Don, I don't see it that way." It wasn't like that.

GARY That's fantastic. Can you somewhat describe how it predicted the events that would come later on in your life?

CARLA Well, there were a couple of levels to that. One had to do with details of the plot. The space girl and the space man—I think those were pretty clearly our expressions of ourselves being in love with each other and how we saw each other. Pretty idealistic, but he really was that way. He was really a space man, and he thought that I was a really high example of womanhood, and pure. It was the purity of the space man and the space woman that interested him. So those came clearly.

But other things were most peculiar. When we met Andrija Puharich in 1974, we looked at each other and could not believe it because he was Pablo Padeyevsky, a character in the book. And I saw the house that we had seen—I had seen it very clearly, and we had seen it in the book as the result of making a movie about the Old South—and it was a beautiful antebellum-type mansion. And when we drove up to Puharich's house, I looked at Don and said, "That's the house." And he said, "*I know.*" [*laughs*]

And so I said to Andrija, "Andrija, this house . . . everything is the same as in our book, but there's one difference: I saw peonies all around the parking circle." And he said, "Oh, those. Yeah, I had 'em cut down a couple of years ago." Which works: we wrote it before 1970,[‡] and this was in '74, so they would have been there when I saw them.

GARY In the process of giving voice to this vision that you'd both received, and in creating this book, you came up to a certain point where that vision ended, which was the conclusion of the book. Why couldn't you see the ending?

CARLA Well, it didn't make any sense—it wasn't logical, and we were both very logical people. Don was preternaturally healthy. His vision was 20/10. When he was in the Army, he could run rings around his unit all day while he was running them on a ten-mile hike and never run out of breath. He was just so healthy—incredibly healthy—and was never sick. He'd never. been. sick. He'd never had a cold.

I was very, very frail. There was no question about it; I accepted that much myself, although I didn't accept anything more. I was normal. It just took a little bit of skill to stay normal. There was this way and that way I could screw up, and then I would be having a problem because of earlier sickness (kidney problems, rheumatoid problems, that kind of thing). But just seeing that I wasn't long for this world—I was just frail. So it made sense that this person most like me in the book would die, whereas Don's character would not. And we worked with that and

---

[‡] The Crucifixion of Esmerelda Sweetwater was written in 1968, refined in 1969.

worked with that and worked with that, and that's the way we wrote it: the space girl, Esmeralda, dies at the end.

GARY Through the choice of being a martyr?

CARLA Through being a martyr, yes. And Pablo and his friend Josh—Josh was Don's character—are left sitting there watching the dead leaves blow past them.

GARY Were you conscious then that you had the impulse of the martyr within you?

CARLA No, I didn't think about it. I knew that I didn't know anything else but to do the whole hog, that I was always absolutely honest, and that I was always absolutely loyal. I had, for instance, realized that my best friend in boarding school wanted to be first in her class but didn't have a prayer, so I missed my own final, took it late, and made 100% on it; but, because of the fact that I had to take it as a make-up, I got a lower grade and she made it to be first. That kind of thing you can look at in retrospect and say, "Well, yeah, she's got the seeds of that within her. She doesn't care what happens to her as long as somebody she loves is happy." Yeah, that's true. But I never analyzed it or thought about it in any way, no.

GARY Your motivation for martyrdom was pure in that you were willing to sacrifice yourself for the benefit of another?

CARLA Yeah, it wasn't just, "I want to be a martyr."

GARY It wasn't some complex like, "I will achieve glory, if I . . . "

CARLA [laughs] No, not in a million years! I wanted to live a long, long life and have a wonderful time. Fun will be had.

GARY So you just explained why you created the ending the way you did because it logically made sense. You weren't healthy, your body was frail, and Don was extremely healthy. Did you create the ending into a vacuum? Was there nothing for the ending that you had received, or had you received an alternate version, or a muddied version?

CARLA Well, no, we'd received the version that somebody had to die—that was the dictate of the book. It was the way it shaped up, so it was a matter of choosing the person.

We couldn't figure why it was so difficult to do that part. It was peculiar.

GARY You probably saw yourselves in these characters at the time but you didn't know that you were writing about your future in some ways.

CARLA Not at all. It only came to us in retrospect.

GARY In the quote that I had read when Ra is talking about *The Crucifixion of Esmeralda Sweetwater,* Ra says that "full memory of the dedication of this mission was restored." Did you have a sense at the time that you and Don were on a mission?

CARLA Yes. And I was perfectly happy with him dictating just how that would go. I was Don's loyal assistant.

JIM Tell about jumping over the sword and never seeing dry land again.

CARLA Ohhh. I had a dream shortly after Don and I decided that we would jump over a sword together.

Because it meant so much to me to be married, he explained how in Scotland if you jump over a broom (well, it was a sword but we had a broom)—we jumped over that in the hall one day, and I knew and he knew that that was our marriage. And so shortly after that . . . [*turns to Jim*] what's the rest of it?

JIM You'd never see dry land again.

CARLA Oh, yeah, shortly after that I had a very, very real dream, very clear. And it starts out with me going down the river on a great big, four-story houseboat with a paddle wheel. And since I lived by the Ohio River, what could be more natural than seeing that form of transportation? I'm on the top floor and the houseboat starts burning. Don sees me from the shore, jumps in, comes over to the boat, and he grabs me and saves me from the fire. Then we're sailing down the river on his boat, which is not burning, and he looks at me and he says, "Do you want to get off? Because, if you stay on this boat with me, you'll never see dry land again."

And I was sure at that time in the dream that I wanted to stay with him. And that was when I woke up from the dream. So that was my dream.

GARY And that speaks to the situation very powerfully.

So you, in your conscious, waking life, weren't . . . you didn't join Don for the moment but you knew you were committed to something larger and that you and he were doing a Work (with a capital *W*) together?

CARLA I knew that we were working for spiritual reasons rather than for earthly reasons. I didn't really think about how big that was; I just realized that we weren't working towards any earthly goal: no house, no children, nothing to own or have but each other and the work. The work was everything.

GARY Looking back, what would you say was that mission, and do you feel that it was fulfilled?

CARLA I never tried to identify the mission at the time. Looking back on it, I would say that the mission was in two parts which tied into an experience that I had when I was 13. At that time I had what is known as a near-death experience. In the non-physical realm where I found myself, I was given the possibility of allowing my body on Earth to die, and then coming back again in two different lifetimes because I had taken too much on my plate in this lifetime in terms of catalyst. The guidance I received suggested that I would do better if I had two different lifetimes for the two different parts of the mission that I had undertaken.

And I said, "No, I want to go back and do everything now," because I didn't want to die and then have to come back and have another childhood. I was 13 at the time; I was almost done with childhood. One childhood was enough for me. I had had a horrible childhood.

So I knew from the beginning that I had a mission to fulfill and my feeling was—after meeting Don and after all the experiences that I had with him, more and more the feeling continued to grow that my mission would be fulfilled with Don.

So I felt that one part of it was finished when Don died and *The Ra Material* was completed. I felt that the other is still being fulfilled, and that I will continue fulfilling it as long as I breathe—that is to be the spiritual mother of a spiritual home for those who wish to serve planet Earth as wanderers. It's a spiritual place rather than a physical one, but we happen to have a beautiful house that Don bought shortly before he died, so it's nice to have a real house that seems to fill in that. But the actuality of it is that it's a spiritual place.

GARY That's quite the journey. We will explore the art of channeling in greater depth in the section of the same name, later on. For now, I would like to ask at what point you were asked to become involved with the channeling experiment and why was that?

CARLA It was in 1974. Don asked me to begin to learn to channel because otherwise his experiment would die. I just felt that, well, his experiment can't die, so I told him that I had no feeling for it, I don't want to do it, but I'll do it for you. So I was strictly doing it to help him out. I gave it my best shot, and it turned out I had somewhat of a gift for it.

Then, I'd say about the middle of 1975, I had gotten on my feet and was doing a competent job. So it was during that time that all of the channeled information that is featured in *Secrets of the UFO* is taken from. Had I not used the channeled material for *Secrets of the UFO* it would be lost forever because we had a habit of reusing tapes at the time.[5]

GARY That brings up a good point. Don had to have been conducting this channeling years before 1974 when you first learned how to channel, but the L/L Research Transcript Library essentially begins in 1974. I think there are only a handful prior to 1974. Why have no transcripts come to us from that period prior to you channeling?

CARLA I don't believe that he felt the group had produced anything worthy of taping before then.

GARY That is serious dedication on Don's part to continue year after year, hoping for something of greater quality to come through with the faith that it would, eventually, but not knowing how.

CARLA Yeah, his faith was absolute, especially after he knew that I was going to come back and be a part of things. He just had a feeling, I think, that I might be good at it, and it was worth a serious shot by really giving me the old push. [*laughs*]

GARY So, we've already established that Don was very trusting of these sources—at least he found them worthwhile enough that he spent years channeling their messages. How about yourself? Did you have any doubt or skepticism about the sources and what they had to say and who they said that they were?

CARLA Well, ya know, I've been asked that many times. It's not that I don't contemplate things or think about things. It's just that nothing ever sent up a red flag and said, *you don't agree with this, you're gonna have to think about this,* etc.

It was quite beyond me, the stuff that I channeled, so it wasn't like I had it in me just waiting for a reason to pretend that I was channeling. And when you're really channeling, when you're really doing a serious job of it and your tail is hanging right over the line—which is what I've always said was the hard part for people: they don't want to embarrass themselves; they don't want to start channeling and then all of a sudden you're channeling nonsense; and oh, dear, but that only happened to me at various, isolated times and always for a reason—so when you're doing a sincere job, you finish the job, you finish your session, and that's the best you could have done. So what do you have to think about? There it is. It didn't trigger any red flags—you're not unhappy with the session; it's just that it's a peculiar kind of way of gathering information where there's not any way to check it.

So you just have to collect it. Don always believed that the important thing was to collect the material, as much material as possible, because he said it would be the *denseness* of the material and from the things which were repeated that you would get the gist, the heart of the material.

GARY One of the things that most stands out to me and speaks to the integrity of this multi-decade experiment in channeling is its consistency over the years. I think it's very difficult for a person to have a consistent single opinion for that long, much less to have multiple people channeling a variety of sources all conveying an entire cosmology and philosophy of the same internally consistent message over and over across the decades.

CARLA Right, and to respond to your feeling that I could not possibly have generated it myself, I can't remember what I'm talking about half the time.[6] I'm pretty spacey. [*laughs*] The idea that I would be able to retain a huge body of material like that in my head is just ridiculous. That is not part of who I am.

GARY So once your collaboration with Don was formed, where did your adventures take you?

CARLA All over the place. At first we thought, well, we'll write a bestseller. We couldn't get it accepted anywhere. I began papering my bathroom—a small room, mind you—with the rejection slips I got, [*laughs*] and after about a dozen attempts to get the thing published, Don and I decided, "Well, maybe a movie."

I don't know how many versions of *The Crucifixion of Esmeralda Sweetwater* we made in screenplay form, and every time I would finish writing a version up, Don was helpful about it, but then it wouldn't fly. So we'd go back to the drawing board and try to do our best to make it another way that would be more useful to Hollywood. And we'd try again and we'd fail again.

Finally, I think we decided that in order to make a movie, we were going to have to learn the business and do it ourselves. So we did. We made the most ridiculous movie that you could ever imagine.[7] I wrote it with Don's help. I did all the casting, I did all the producing, I did the shooting script, I did everything—the sets, everything to do with the movie I'd done.

But my part was supposed to be behind-the-scenes. The one thing we did not figure was the lady that we had hired as the star, Ruthy, was a woman with an enormous rack and a very small IQ. She read the screenplay the day before shooting began and quit. She said, [*haughty tone of voice*] "I am not a comedian: I am a star." And she quit on the spot and walked off. All of the sudden we needed a topless woman.

I am the most modest of topless women—I had a "rack-let" at the time. It's generally known that as you get older you get larger, but at the time I was tiny. Not *tiny* tiny, but tiny in good proportion to the rest of my body, which was slender. It just seemed like a silly idea to take my shirt off and film me, but we couldn't find anybody else willing to do it.

Of course I did know the lines (having written them), but I did not even have 15 minutes to rehearse. All of a sudden, in addition to being the script secretary and having to write down all kinds of numbers and do figuring in my head going from 90 to 60 (90-something of film to 60-something of time)—I didn't have a stopwatch so I couldn't know how to time it out; I just knew how long, how many, how much film was used, so I figured out the time from that.

So I was figuring that out in my head at the same time I was writing down takes—we did so many takes of this. That's the way the editor edits: you have to write it down every time. If you do 14 takes you have to write every one down. I had writings on my bosom and they could not be messed up because the continuity would have been destroyed, and so I couldn't really put a shirt on, so I walked around topless for days. That experience was one of the more interesting aspects of me being in the movie business. And I was the worst actress you ever saw in your life. But the one thing about the film that you can say is that I got it out of the can and onto the screen and it did play for drive-ins in the South in the summer.

GARY So making movies wasn't exactly your and Don's forte. What were some of the highlights of other areas of your investigation during the '70s?

CARLA Well, it was just mostly investigating hard cases of UFO sightings—talking to the people, the experiencers, writing it down, writing it up—and then sending it to the people like APRO and MUFON.[8] There was a British group we sent it to also—I'm not remembering the name of it.

JIM Flying Saucer Review?

CARLA Thank you. It was *Flying Saucer Review* in Britain, and we sent our reports to those places.

GARY So you and Don were mavericks out on your own, but you also participated in the larger research effort?

CARLA Right. I read a great many of the UFO journals at the time, along with the books of the day, and then would report on them to Don. It was my job as his research assistant to do all the research and then report to him. He would pick the little nuggets that he liked out of them and he would memorize them. That would give him his tools for talking to people and giving them evidence on various subjects. When you read widely, as I did at the time, you have all kinds of nuggets. So he could talk for probably—the longest I ever saw him do it at one time was 6½ hours. But he surely could have talked three times that before he ran out of original material.

He also decided to investigate psychic surgery, including the Philippine psychic surgery. We went there in '75, and I had experiences as one who was operated on. He didn't prefer to be the one. I was the easy one, always, because I had things wrong with me that we could see if the Filipino knew about, and that would be part of the evidence there.

Then in '77 and '78 we investigated a Mexican psychic who used an actual knife and allegedly cut through her patients to excise material that was bad and make them well. That was a lady named Pachita. We went there and stayed there for probably the better part of two months.

GARY And how did that transpire?

CARLA It was very interesting. I had two operations from Pachita, and for the first one she said, "Well, her kidneys are not good, so I will take the two, make one good one, put it back in, and see if it works."

I came back after five weeks and she decided it wasn't working, so she said, "Well, we'll just have a new one." And they had looked all over Mexico City for a kidney and could not find one. It is a huge place. It's like seven million people. Could not find a kidney because there are people—there are waiting lists, and they're assigned to people. Couldn't find one.

GARY She was looking for a physical organ?

CARLA Physical organ. Couldn't find a physical organ so she just opened her refrigerator and pulled out some tissue that looked to Andrija—who was a doctor, medical doctor—like the tissue used for kidneys. Anyway, she held it near the body and it was sucked into my body as if by a magnet. So I had that one. And I will say that I have not had serious problems with my kidneys in all the years since then.

GARY So you travel to the Philippines and Mexico; you travel to speak with abductees and others who have had UFO experiences, and instrumental to all of that was an airplane. Don was a pilot and would fly where you needed to go?

CARLA Right. He didn't have a lot of money in his family. He generated the funds for that by doing work as a pilot. The private airport Bowman Field became a place where you could rent an airplane and go somewhere. So he would take people where they wanted to go and he would never take the money for it; instead, he would put it back as credit, and then spend it out renting airplanes to go wherever he wanted to go.

That reminds me, one other aspect that he investigated was psychic healing, and there was a Kathryn somebody that he was especially impressed by. She had a television show at one time. She would touch people and seemingly the power of the Holy Spirit would touch them and they would keel over, one after the other. So he took me to a great big place in Chicago to one of her meetings, and I was touched. It felt like an electrical charge, but it didn't knock me over, and I didn't feel anything else besides that. It was just like nothing to me, so there you go.

JIM Kathryn Kuhlman?

CARLA That's it, Kathryn Kuhlman.

GARY So your life at this time was anything but ordinary.

CARLA [*laughing*] I really wasn't going for ordinary. After Don I gave that up.

GARY So he's putting together these puzzle pieces as best he can, and channeling seems to be the primary focus or the main avenue through which he's obtaining—

CARLA Right, right. He became more and more interested in channeling, but he wasn't convinced that it was *the* aspect until the Ra contact. When the Ra contact happened, everything else stopped cold, and that's all he wanted to do.

GARY So in your collaboration, as you began to touch on, you did a lot of the writing and the research in terms of reading. What specifically was Don's role in your collaboration?

CARLA I think he was in charge of sharing it and also piloting our ship together, deciding what we were going to do and when we were going to do it. Then he told me—he said, "I want you to do my writing and to create this material and make it available for free, worldwide." At that time we didn't have computers and I was like, "How am I going to do that, Don? I don't know how to do that." But I said I would try, and then he said the other thing was to be the housekeeper for a spiritual house.

So he was still thinking in terms of physical house, but not really—it was a spiritual-physical house. He didn't like the idea of getting a nuclear family going. He wanted a spiritual family, and so I think he got exactly what he wanted.

Anyway, those are my two goals. One of them is finished; you can't do anything more with *The Ra Material.* I can certainly do more channeling when I get done with this health thing, but until then, no outer work like that. But the other is something that I can do all my life, and I will, every day of it. I'm so glad I have the opportunity; so few people have something to do that they love so much.

GARY In your work with Don, at what point did you form the organization L/L Research and why?

CARLA We formed that in 1980 because Don felt that it was time to create a 501(c)(3) tax-deductible-type charity.

GARY You mean 1970? You said 1980.

CARLA Well, 1980 was when we founded L/L Research as a non-profit charity. Before that it had been a partnership. [Somewhere around 1968] Don got me to write up a little piece of paper that said that we were partners and any funds we got from *The Crucifixion* would be split 50/50. So not too long into that we decided to call it the L/L Company. So it was the L/L Company and then, as you noted, there was a changeover to L/L Research, but it was still completely private.

Then in 1980 we created a public entity with Jim McCarty, and we used the papers that Jim had because he had already created a 501(c)(3) organization. We just piggybacked onto that because it had very compatible reasons given in the document of creating that entity, Rock Creek Research & Development Laboratories, as he called it.

GARY The research aspects seem pretty self-evident. What does the "L/L" signify? Why was that chosen?

CARLA That signifies Love and Light, or Light and Love. I've always felt that Love came first just as it does in the Distortions—if you look at the Distortions, Love comes before Light—so, Love/Light.

And the logo that we use, which is Pablo Picasso's drawing of Don Quixote and Sancho Panza chasing windmills—I had it over my desk in college, I had it over my desk all through my marriage, and after my marriage. I love that image and have always felt that was me right down to the ground. I really identify with good ol' Quixote and dreaming the impossible dream. I've always known that was me.

So Don liked it too and decided that we would use that as our logo.

GARY You anticipated my next question which was about the Don Quixote logo. So you felt that was you and that it was emblematic of dreaming the impossible dream. What does it mean to dream the impossible dream?

CARLA Well, I think it means to bring truth, beauty, love, light, and understanding to Earth, and to make it the way people live. It's always felt to me like the right way to live, and I've always tried to live that way—and I know it's impossible.

GARY Is there a reason that that is an *impossible* dream?

CARLA Well, it seems to be impossible in terms of the way the world wags.

If you look at the way the news is organized, for instance, it's always . . . if it bleeds it leads. The bad news comes first. Service to self rules. [*chuckles*] And if you're going to be a clever person and join politics and really make changes in the world . . . I discovered very early on in college you can't do that without learning to lie, which I don't do. I have no capacity to lie. I just don't lie, except for white lies that are necessary, like "what a beautiful hat," or "no, your tail does not look large in that; you look fine." [*laughs*]

Yeah, I had an experience in college with someone who went on to become a prominent politician in which he simply told me, "If you want to join politics, you have to be able to lie." He told me that, and I dropped political science and joined the ranks of arts and became an English major. I was going to be joining those who wanted to help with statesmanship. I wanted to be a statesman, I wanted to make a difference in this world, and then I discovered, "Oh, you can't make a difference in this world." The two things that are apparently the essence, the *essence* of politics, are lying and committee meetings. I do neither well so I had to change my goal. I couldn't work in the world; I had to decide that my kingdom was truly not of this world.

So that's the impossible dream, really. And it's not necessarily a Christian dream, although I am a wholehearted Christian—I love Jesus with all my heart, and I know that my kingdom is not of this world. I identify with that.

GARY Were there any other parallels between Don Quixote's journey in the novel and what L/L Research hoped to stand for or hoped to do in the world?

CARLA I don't identify with the particulars of that story, which is a peculiarly befuddled story of people that are genuinely not seeing what's in front of them. I don't think I've ever fooled myself about anything like that, but it's just that desire to remain pure and true to my standards and not compromise them, regardless of how the world wags. It's often inconvenient to do that.

GARY And the world will tell you otherwise, that what you are doing is foolish.

CARLA The world always tells you otherwise. The world will always tell you otherwise in increasingly strident tones, yes.

GARY And you had to learn to trust yourself and follow your own heart.

CARLA Yes, and that's something that's never been a problem for me. I have always done that since I was a baby. It's the truth.

JIM Tell him what your first words were as a child.

CARLA Yeah, my first words were to my mother and they were "put me down," as Mother wrote in her journal at the time. Not *mama*, not *dada*, but "put me down."

GARY I'm glad, for what it's worth, that you differentiated yourself from the Quixote character because you're not . . . though you want to act in a noble way and though you want to serve others, you're not doing so by being belligerent and seeking fights with people, or by being less than 100% sensitive to other people.

CARLA Right.

GARY So obviously, a little bit further down the road you and Don invited Jim to join you, but prior to that point, had you considered that L/L Research would include other people?

CARLA Yes, we had indeed, and we invited people at various times. For instance, Beth—we invited her to live with us at one time but she couldn't because she was in the middle of having children. All of a sudden she got pregnant. On her way to getting divorced, she got pregnant. It happens. She did not want to bring a baby into our home, and Don was grateful. [*laughs*] I thought it would be a gas! But I like kids. Don did not. So it didn't happen.

Yeah, we had invited her, and Don was always on the lookout for people that he wanted to be part of our household, our spiritual family.

GARY Did he have a certain type of person or certain criteria for whom he would ask?

CARLA I think it was just a matter of who felt right to him. He really trusted his instincts and what he saw in people. He looked right through them. He looked right into their hearts, and he knew them. It didn't take him any time at all. He had a gift that way, and most people simply didn't make it, or they were okay but they weren't people he wanted as part of his household.

Let's put it this way: Every Sunday he would look out the front window to see who was coming to meditation. If certain people were coming to meditation, he went out the back door and he was gone until their car was gone.

And then there were the people he was perfectly happy coming to meditation.

So there were three categories: worthy of being asked to join us; okay, fine, normal people; and those he just didn't want to be with. And most people were in the second category. Jim was the only person in years that made it into the worthy category.

GARY So you began channeling in 1974 and you first received Ra in 1981?

CARLA That's right.

GARY Did the Confederation's message change or evolve during that time? And did Don's questioning evolve?

CARLA Oh, I imagine they evolved in response to what was channeled. But I think that the only other evolution was of my channeling itself. It evolved because I figured out, gradually, how to make a good session. I still feel that I have work to do to become a better channel in terms of how to tune myself and so forth. I'm never satisfied. I always want to be a little bit better, and so I'm always trying to do my utmost to achieve that. But I don't think the message itself evolved too much—maybe in terms of detail, but not in terms of heart.

GARY So the same essential message that was there in 1974 was the same essential message that came in 1980?

CARLA Yeah, I think so.

GARY All right, for our final question in this section: How did the information that you and others channeled affect your own spirituality and Don's (if there was any discernable effect)?

CARLA I don't think it really made any change in either of our spiritualties. I had always been a Christian, and I continued being a Christian to Don's complete befuddlement. He could not understand why I went and spent all this time being a Christian, and being in the choir you spend more time than most people. You don't just go on Sunday. You have choir practice, you have funerals and weddings where the choir is just part of it, so you go in and you do that strictly as a volunteer. All that time that you spend—and of course I was also active in church work, so that was more time.

He was really jealous of it and he was jealous of me singing in the Bach Society, which I did surely for the love of music, to be part of the music. (And I know you'll understand that, Ken.[§] Ken is a trumpeter, a classic trumpeter.) To be part of a classical piece—it's bigger than you could possibly express yourself. It goes beyond your limitations as a singer or as a trumpeter, or as a producer of sound of any kind. All of the sound is all around you and it comes out and it's magnificent. Somebody's written this magnificent work of art and you're part of it and it's just such a joy, I can't express it.

I entered into that for over 30 years. I was a member of the Louisville Bach Society, and Don was really a little bit jealous of that, especially after the Ra contact started. He didn't want me to go to rehearsals, he didn't want me to go on Sunday. He couldn't understand why I spent this time doing something besides the Ra contact, basically, [*laughs*] and yet it was part of my spiritual walk and I stuck to it. It did not make him happy, but my goal was not to make him happy [on this point]; my goal was to follow my bliss, I guess you could say.

GARY So you're receiving this information from these alleged UFO sources, or sources of intelligence not local to Earth, and they're describing this universe built of love and light where free will reigns and the whole function of life is spiritual evolution and—I don't know if the idea of wanderers came through at that time or not. That didn't have much of an impact on your spirituality?

CARLA I thought it was fascinating, and it helped me to shape my goal after Don died, certainly. I could see that what was left for me had to do with making a spiritual home for all these people that felt so isolated and so miserable, and so many wanderers do. I wanted them to know they were not alone, and that somebody loved them very dearly and wanted to support their work wherever it brought them to, that somebody thought they were doing a good job. I think that when you have a homecoming here every year and you see the people that come, filtered through the lens of *The Ra Material,* you see people that are all perhaps isolated in their homes, in their home environment. And in coming here, all of sudden

---

§   Referring to Ken Wendt, our good friend and talented videographer filming the interview.

they have all of these people that are interested in what they have to say, and that don't tell them that they're crazy, and that listen to them and love them, and they love the people so much right back—and it's just an incredibly glorious experience. I wish we could do it 52 weeks of the year.

Unfortunately, as you know from being the producer of so many of these events, it takes a couple of months to prepare for a weekend like that, as far as the logistics of what we do together, how we feed that many people, get the house clean, and all that. (We haven't started getting the house clean yet this year by the way. Time to think about it.)

GARY It would be dramatically simpler if we hosted at a hotel or a conference center, but using your own home as the venue for these . . .

CARLA I've always wanted to open my home and let all that Jim and I have breathed into this home be a part of what we had to offer, because it's part of that little bit that you can manifest on planet Earth. And Jim does the most incredible job of manifesting an atmosphere of wonderful gardens where you can walk and meditate and think and experience—between the water treatments and the fish and the water splashing, and all the meditation you can have with that. And you can look at any one of his rock plantings, how each individual one is built, how the rocks are, how the plantings are, how they've grown up together, and all they have to offer. Or you can just walk along his little paths and use the whole garden at once. It's almost like a feast! And you can get indigestion. [*laughs*] You can't see it all. People's reaction to the garden is, "I've got to come back. I haven't seen half of it." And you haven't unless you've spent a summer or so here. It's following the bloomings and getting to know all the plantings separately.

GARY Yes, this isn't just an empty venue—just four walls and a roof to host an event—it's a character on the stage. It's an active element in the coming together and, like you were saying, people that are sensitive to the energy when they come here—I've heard many speak of how they can sense and feel the joyous energy and the light-filled nature of this particular place and this particular gift that you and Jim have offered.

CARLA Yeah, a lot of people try to create a home that's just a perfect home. They get a lot of antiques and art, and do it that way; or they spend a lot of money and have the latest and make it great as far as what money can buy, and do it that way. Or, what Jim and I do is, we love the things that we have and we don't put them away. They're out where you can grab them and use them, and every book is loved.

I suggested to Ken that he just go around Jim's room—this is the room that Jim and I have been in together for the last three years, more or less? [*Jim confirms.*] I have in this room since 2010's operation. I thought I was going to go back to my own room after it, but I didn't get a chance to because I had something else go wrong. It's been that way ever since I've been here, and I will probably be here . . . So this is a very small example of what you can put into a room if you don't put things away [*laughs*], if you just arrange them neatly and know where they are and can go get any one of them at any time.

GARY Well, that concludes this section coming up to the crossing of paths between Jim, Carla, and Don. That section will be the final one before we dig into the Ra contact itself.

---

1   The manager for Peter, Paul & Mary asked Carla and Jim D. to come to Chicago for an audition to be their opening act. Carla and Jim D. stayed in a motel in Chicago the night before the audition. In the morning D. said that he would not get out of bed until Carla agreed that they would not audition for this job.

2   See page 266 of *A Wanderer's Handbook* for more about this dynamic.

3   A disclaimer, for what it's worth: Carla never exhibited any bias against homo-sexuality. She embraced it as she did everything else, with love. She's stating here simply that to whatever degree Don possessed sexuality, it was of a hetero nature. Though ultimately Don seemed an asexual person.

4   "Indeed, neither Don nor I was subjectively happy with the ending. However, all attempts to rewrite the ending so that *The Crucifixion of Esmerelda Sweetwater* would be an incorrect title were complete failures. After ten tries at rewriting, all of which ended up yielding much the same material as the ending you now see, we decided that the source moving through us to show this point of view was attempting to include within that point of view the acting out of the answer to the question, 'What would happen if two perfectly "good" beings were brought down to this complex and dualistic planet?'"

Don Elkins and Carla L. Rueckert, *The Crucifixion of Esmerelda Sweetwater* (Louisville: L/L Research, 1986), 19–20.

Note: Conceived and written in 1968, the book wasn't published until 1986.

[5]

Much to the dismay of *Law of One* material purists, they had the same habit with the cassettes used for the Ra contact itself. Fortunately, one of the three sets was preserved, but the other two sets were recycled.

Those second and third cassettes used during each Ra session would be helpful to have now, as they recorded portions that were missed during the process of flipping cassette one from side A to side B.

[6]

Fortunately there is no evidence of this in the entire interview. . . . *ahem.*

[7]

Originally titled *The Hidan of Maukbeiangjow,* this movie was written by Don and Carla and directed and filmed by Lee Jones. It was purchased by a distribution company and released on VHS as *Invasion of the Girl Snatchers* in 1985. Carla's assessment of this movie is not far off, though it is rumored to have gained a cult following over the years.

[8]

APRO, the Aerial Phenomena Research Organization, was an UFO research group started in January 1952 by Jim and Coral Lorenzen of Sturgeon Bay, Wisconsin.

The group was based in Tucson, Arizona, after 1960. APRO had many state branches. It remained active until late 1988.

APRO stressed scientific field investigations and had a large staff of consulting Ph.D. scientists. A notable example was Dr. James E. McDonald of the University of Arizona, a well-known atmospheric physicist and perhaps the leading scientific UFO researcher of his time. Another was Dr. James Harder of the University of California, Berkeley, a civil and hydraulic engineering professor who acted as director of research from 1969 to 1982. McDonald and Harder were among six scientists who testified about UFOs before the U.S. House of Representatives Committee on Science and Astronautics on July 29, 1968, when they sponsored a one-day symposium on the subject.

Astronomer J. Allen Hynek cited APRO and NICAP as the two best civilian UFO groups of their time, consisting largely of sober, serious-minded people capable of valuable contributions to the subject.

Wikipedia, The Free Encyclopedia, s.v. "Aerial Phenomena Research Organization," accessed February 15, 2016, https://en.wikipedia.org/w/index.php?title=Aerial_Phenomena_Research_Organization&oldid=704792709.

MUFON, the Mutual UFO Network, is a US-based non-profit organization that investigates cases of alleged UFO sightings. It is one of the oldest and largest civilian UFO-investigative organizations in the United States.

MUFON was originally established as the Midwest UFO Network in Quincy, Illinois, on May 31, 1969, by Walter H. Andrus, Allen Utke, John Schuessler, and others. Most of MUFON's early members had previously been associated with APRO.

The stated mission of MUFON is the study of UFOs for the benefit of humanity through investigations, research, and education. Along with the J. Allen Hynek Center for UFO Studies (CUFOS) and the Fund for UFO Research (FUFOR), MUFON is part of the UFO Research Coalition, a collaborative effort by the three main UFO investigative organizations in the United States whose goal is to share personnel and other research resources, and to fund and promote the scientific study of the UFO phenomenon.

Wikipedia, The Free Encyclopedia, s.v. "Mutual UFO Network," accessed February 15, 2016, https://en.wikipedia.org/w/index.php?title=Mutual_UFO_Network&oldid=698561700.

CHAPTER 3

Meeting Jim

GARY As the biography of L/L Research continues, Jim crosses paths with Don and Carla. Jim, you had been living by yourself on a piece of land in central Kentucky. Can you tell us why you moved there and what you were doing?

JIM Well, I had just come from serving a stint in Teacher Corps where we worked with inner city kids in Jacksonville and Gainesville, Florida. We got kids that were so-called incorrigible. Nobody else wanted them, so we had our own classroom, and we used various resources to figure out what to do with the kids and how to help kids learn who hadn't had a lot of luck with it.

I decided that I didn't want to pursue that any further, so I looked at one of the books that we had used in our classroom, *The Rasberry Exercises: How to Start Your Own School (and Make a Book)*. In the back of that book they used a bibliography that had a fellow in Colorado by the name of T. D. Lingo and the Adventure Trail Survival School. I thought what Lingo had to say sounded really good. So I went to his school two years in a row—the first year I was a student, and the second year I was a teacher.

The whole idea of his school was that the brain is 90 percent dormant, which most of us have heard. Since 1957 he had been living at 10,000 feet up in the Rocky Mountains and had discovered a way of releasing the dormant brain potential in students that came his way. He also worked with inner-city school kids. In the spring and the summer he brought out the rich white kids, like me (if you had any money you were rich in comparison to the kids he usually worked with), and he worked with them as well.

So the whole idea was to use a series of processes: essaying, which in Latin means "to drive out," to drive out understanding; dream analysis; and neuro drama, where you did some work in figuring out what were the problems, or blockages, that kept your energy back in the old brain stem (the part where most of us are) along with the three-eighths of the frontal lobes that are dormant. So the idea there was to figure out a way to release that dormant potential.

After you went through his course and had whatever successes you did, his theory was "each one teach one," which meant *go buy some land and start your own school.* So that's what I intended to do. I looked at—let's see, there were two main catalogs then, for United Farm Realty and Strout Realty. I looked in there. I wanted to be somewhere—being from Nebraska, I wanted someplace that had hills and creeks and had a variety of land instead of being flat like a pool table. So the area around Tennessee, Arkansas, Kentucky, and Missouri looked pretty good to me. I looked into about 50 different places, and I investigated them from a distance. They didn't look so good, so I decided—I found myself in central Kentucky. I looked at the map and I thought, "I'm just going to head back to Nebraska and stop in, unannounced, at every little real estate agent to see what I can find."

So after I made that decision, I came across a fellow who had this piece of land for sale. He was a real estate agent—Eddy Deep, I remember him very well—and he had this 132 acres of land that was available, and at that time it was only $6,000, which was $32 an acre. That was in 1972, and that was a *really* good price, so I took all my savings, and I bought that piece of land and went to the land with the idea of starting my own school.

The first summer there I cut all the logs I would need to build my log cabin because that was what we worked with at Lingo's Adventure Trail Survival School: log cabins and learning how to notch logs and chink logs and cut out the windows and doors and all that stuff—how to make a house out of a bunch of trees. So I did that the first fall and got everything ready to go, got them up on platforms so they could season, and then I went back to Nebraska and got a job.

Let's see, the first job I had was rough carpentry, helping to build grain silos that were poured around the clock. Eventually I quit at 105 feet. It was 20 degrees below zero and it was my job to clean the inside of the places where grain was going to be stored—get the honeycomb out so the grain wouldn't go in there and ferment and ruin all the grain. So that was my job. I was sitting on a little swing—I'd finish one little cubby hole where the grain was going; I'd crawl out and go to another one, and there was just one little light in each one, and I couldn't even see the bottom down there, and it was kind of dark and cold. And I thought I could probably find a better job, so then I got a job as a welder in a farm implement company, and for the rest of the winter I did some welding, which was much warmer.

In the spring I came back to Kentucky, and I skinned all the logs and started putting them up.

I did have two classes that went through the course. I taught the same course that Lingo did, and that's why I was there: to begin a work in helping other people to discover their latent potentials. And that's it.

GARY It's really difficult for me to restrain myself from digging further in. I'm going to allow myself a couple of questions before moving on: Did you feel that you had unlocked the brain's potential—that you had successfully completed his course and achieved that objective?

JIM Yeah. Part of the course was to build your own lean-to at some distant part of the land. He had 270 acres of a mountaintop, and it was rough terrain. It was pretty difficult, so he wanted each person to build his or her own lean-to.

One morning on July 12, 1972, I was in the preconscious state. (The preconscious state is that state where you can receive or send messages telepathically, theoretically. Basically it's the alpha state that meditators find.) That morning before sunrise, I was in that state and I felt my brain circulating. I felt a movement and I felt a *click*, right here [*points to third-eye spot*] between the eyes in the frontal lobes, and when I got down to the camp and told Lingo about that he just kind of smiled at me and said, "Well, that's the beginning."

Since then the frontal lobes have always been active. The most obvious activation of the frontal lobes is in sexual energy exchanges: where most people have an orgasm between the legs, I have one between my eyes as well. And, that's a lot of fun! [*laughs*] But, it also helped me figure out how to use my energies. So I continued the essaying, the dream analysis, and the working with the preconscious state while I was in my cabin on my land.

And I worked with the students that came to Lingo's Adventure Trail School to try to do the same thing. I don't think we had any great successes, but there were a number of interesting contacts that people had in their preconscious with what were very likely extraterrestrials. They had unusual names like Ramordery, Gonodsel, and Bimbleshack,[*] saying that they were in a craft orbiting Saturn, perhaps which all sounds weird and strange until you listen to the messages that they gave through the students that had received them, and it was inspirational. It was much like the Confederation channeling that we've been doing, that Carla and Don started back in 1962.

If you look at life as a wheel and the center being where we're going, it was another spoke in the wheel, another way of getting there. It seemed to be a fairly effective way. So that was what I was doing. That's what happened for me, and I feel that since then I have been more creative, more able to figure out ways of doing things that are outside the box. So it got me out of the box.[†]

GARY And you've stayed out of the box ever since, I would note. So, how would you describe your general spirituality prior to encountering the channeling work that Carla and Don were doing?

JIM Minimal. [*laughs*] I was a late bloomer, I guess you could say. I was about 21 and had already graduated college before I started asking questions. After I graduated I didn't want to do what I was trained to do. I didn't want to pursue business or economics, so I went back for another year of solid sociology, thinking that might be what I wanted to do. But, I also took a course in world religions and became involved with a priest, a Catholic priest, a Fr. John Scott, who had the house where mostly the

---

[*] Spelled phonetically in this transcript.

[†] For more about Jim's experience at the Adventure Trail School and the subsequent six years on his land, see Chapter 29, Jim McCarty Personal Biographical Material.

radicals on campus stayed, though it was supposed to be for the Catholic students. He introduced me to a book called *The Wisdom of Insecurity* by Alan Watts about how to basically begin your own spiritual journey.

So that was where it really started. After that I became familiar with Jane Roberts and her work with Seth—Lingo's course was dealing with the same sort of principles; he was just approaching it from another angle. He was approaching it from the standpoint of the brain's natural ability to circuit its energy forward, once you remove the obstacles that are culturally encoded into each person by schools, by parents, by friends, neighbors, and so forth.

So that, I guess, was the real start to it. And when I was on the land I was listening to WKQQ radio[1] one night (it was put out from Lexington, Kentucky), and they had a couple of folks from Louisville—a Don Elkins and Carla Rueckert were talking about their channeling and their book, *The Secrets of the UFO*, and I thought that was interesting.

In our area there, I was generally part of what was called (then) the back-to-the-land movement[2] in the early '70s: well-educated college kids from the city going back to the land to simplify their lives. "Simplify, simplify"—the Thoreau idea. We got together and had various types of meetings and things, and one of the things we had was a meditation group. It was headed by a group of folks from Louisville, a part of the Eftspan group that Don and Carla had helped to begin, and they were originally pointed towards having their own spiritual community on the other side of the same county that I lived in. At that time they were still meditating and so forth, and I told them that I'd heard this couple on the radio and they said, "Yeah, would you like to meet them?" I said, "Okay, yeah, sure."

So through them, I came up to Louisville and met Don and Carla. I remember walking into their apartment for the first time. Don was at the door and I looked up [*cranes neck up, laughs*]—he was a full foot taller than I was.[3] I remember looking into his blue eyes and thinking, wow. I could see eternity in there somehow. He had this really friendly old rumpled way about him. So I met him and then I met Carla.

After that I started coming every week by myself. And then Eric started joining me—Eric Swan, you remember, who still lives down in Lebanon, Kentucky.[4] So we came up every week after that. It was August 1978 I think I first met you [Carla], and later on, when Carla and Don decided to move to Waterson Trail where we would later have the Ra contact, I helped them move and really got to know them a lot more.

It was at that time that Don invited me to join them, but I'd been taking mailings from Cosmic Awareness Communications[5] out in Olympia, Washington, for a long time. They, through Paul Shockley at the time, were channeling, supposedly, the same source Edgar Cayce channeled, which was the Akashic Records of the planet. I'd been taking their information for about five years and really thought it was good, so I thanked Don and Carla for inviting me, but said that I was heading out to Oregon where they had two centers—Paul lived in Yamhill, Oregon, and then went up to Olympia, Washington, to do the channeling for Cosmic Awareness. The Windsong School of Awareness was in Yamhill, and I moved there—that was in the country and I had my own little trailer. It was a rusty old thing that I called Tootsie Roll because it was the same color as a Tootsie Roll, being full of rust on the outside. I stayed there for a couple of months.

The thing that got me thinking about what I should really do was that, after moving there, I was given a chance to make a lot of money. A fellow who would come down to visit from Vancouver, British Columbia, was part of the group. In his profession he was in charge of the mining of diatomaceous earth, in both the United States and in Canada. Diatomaceous earth is the fossilized remains of various types of sea creatures from millions of years ago, but is found to be very helpful in storing food, such as putting it in your beans so that they won't go bad. You can even brush your teeth with it. It's another one of those things that has got a lot of uses.

Anyway, he offered me a chance to be the general manager for the United States, and he offered me $100,000—a year! I didn't have anything against money, but that wasn't why I went to Oregon, so I took the weekend out to meditate and to think about what I needed to do because I was kind of confused. So 30 minutes—*30 seconds* into the meditation (it didn't take long), there was the answer kind of like a comet across my barren sky: "Go back to Louisville. Join Don and Carla."

So that's what I did, taking their little kitty cat that they gave me. The kids at the Windsong School made money by selling the offspring of these two cats, a big, old Siamese bruiser of a male and a pretty female. The cats came out with long hair—they were Himalayan. So Chocolate Bar came back with me, and I litterbox-trained Chocolate Bar in the truck as I was driving along. I had a litter box over on the passenger side on the floor, and whenever she had to go I picked her up and stuck her over there. So I brought Chocolate Bar back to Louisville and introduced her to Don and Carla. They already had two cats, Gandalf and Fairchild, at the time. Don looked at Chocolate Bar and took the little kitty cat in his hand and he said, "Beautiful."

CARLA That was one of his famous swearwords.

JIM Yeah, that meant *another cat.* [*laughs*]

So that's how I actually did end up with Don and Carla. It was by first traveling 2,500 miles to Oregon and then 2,500 miles back within two months. It was a long trip to go 70 miles total.

GARY Your frontal lobes are too powerful—you have anticipated a lot of the questions I was going to ask.

So, quick one—I think it's a correction. You said in 1972 or '73 you were asked about managing diatomaceous earth—did you mean later on? Am I misunderstanding something?

JIM Yeah, you're right. That would be 1980; 1972 and 1973 was the time that I was with Lingo at the school and had come back and started on my own. Good catch!

GARY I didn't think it took you eight years to drive back from Oregon.

JIM I had to walk. [*Carla chuckles*]

GARY Don said that he had a "knowing" with Carla [that they would be together]. Was there, similarly, a conscious recognition or an inkling within you that this was to be a special relationship?

JIM Oh yeah, there was no doubt. It was odd in that respect. As I was helping them move into the place on Waterson Trail, which was where we had the Ra contact, Carla and I were doing a lot of work together getting things lined up and put in place after we got them moved over. Don was flying so we had some time alone. I remember the hug in the kitchen with Carla—we hugged each other and we knew that neither of us wanted to let go, because it just felt so perfect. It felt like coming home, really.

And from that point on, it was just the same thing. We never had to work at being harmonious. It was just there, and any movement away from being harmonious was *weird*. I was responsible for one or two of those and had to correct it right away because it wasn't right. So, yeah, there was an immediate recognition and a feeling of, *yeah, I want to hang out with these folks*. And it worked out.

GARY Carla, do you remember your and Don's side of that meeting with Jim?

CARLA Well, I can't really speak for Don because, as usual, he was silent on the subject, except for expressing his desire to have Jim join us. I had been resisting liking him because he had a very large beard. I liked his curly long hair, but I was never fond of facial hair, especially on a young man who could look good. I thought it was a waste of flesh, [*Jim laughs*] so I didn't want to like him. He came to the door one time right after he'd worked real hard and was sweating freely, and I thought to myself, "I love the way he smells." [*laughs*] That was it for me. The chemistry just overwhelmed me.

JIM When you find somebody that likes your scent you've got a thing.

CARLA Yeah, I'm a very sensitive . . . my nose is very sensitive, probably the most sensitive of my senses, and if I like the way somebody smells, it's big news. So that, plus of course the fact that I have always been very much attracted to people that have virtue, honor, dignity—doing the right thing. Jim was very high on that. Not that he talked about it or expressed it, but everything that ever came out of his mouth and his decisions all had to do with loyalty, or trust, or just that kind of beauty—it was inner beauty. I saw nothing I didn't like, and I saw so many things I did like.

JIM And she eventually got me to shave! [*laughs*]

CARLA I was really attracted to him sexually, but I was also attracted to his inner character, and all through the years that has only deepened. That was a true, early connection of ours into the deep mind, and we were very compatible there.

GARY Jim, you described hearing Carla and Don on a radio program and how that piqued your interest. Do you remember your reaction when you first encountered their channeled information and what impact it had on you?

JIM Oh, yeah, I really, really felt the message was on target. It was one of those things where that little voice inside that responds to things if you let it, said yeah.

I remember asking a number of questions. They always had a question and answer session after the main part of the message was delivered, and I had some questions that I really needed to ask, because I'd learned a lot of very helpful things at the Lingo Survival School but one of the things that I really didn't like was that he believed in fear—the fear motivation.

One of the reasons he had the class there was to keep planet Earth from "suiciding"—that this was a suicidal culture in which we lived; that human beings were basically glorified "killer apes" that came from the *Australopithecus africanus*, the South African killer ape, the first of its kind to kill its own kind, with a thigh bone or a stick. So it was his feeling that that was the missing link, that we had genes in us that were dangerous, and he, I thought, used fear too much as a motivator in that regard.

So I asked questions of—at that time it was Hatonn that Carla was channeling. And the answer that I got really felt right to me, which was that we basically have to release fear, fear of anything, because we're all one; and if you fear something, you are fearing part of yourself, and you're keeping that part of yourself from giving to you what it has to offer. We all have a dark side—we hide things in there—and things that we fear are especially there.

So that was a message or a response I got that I felt was really on target—it hit home with me and I thought, "Yeah, let's keep going here, let's get some more information here." So yeah, I was in tune right away—they were singing my song.

CARLA He had lots and lots of questions. He was a big questioner for a long time and then that died down after a while—I guess he got them all answered.

JIM Yeah, pretty much. There have been a lot more questions since, but at the time I felt very satisfied.

GARY So, as Jim has described his process, Jim eventually joined you and Don. Why did Don, or why did you and Don in conjunction, issue this invitation to Jim?

CARLA Well, as I said, for years Don had been looking for a way to expand our family, our spiritual family. So it wasn't a surprise to me when he brought it up. It was of a kind with his wanting Beth to join us, with him wanting Morris to join us, and so forth, but none of those had worked out, and that this one did was the big difference.

I was a little bit surprised, because I had told Don that Jim and I were going to become lovers, and I thought that if there was any vestige of jealousy, he wouldn't want Jim to join us. But it didn't matter at all—he never spoke of it. It was just, "Oh, okay." So I don't think that weighed in, for or against—it was not relevant to him.

But I think it was because of Jim's outstanding ability to pitch in and to help without being asked. It was extremely impressive that Jim offered to help and drove so far so many times in order to help us get packed up and moved. Don was gone most of the time, and he wasn't the sort to do any physical labor of any kind—that just wasn't Don. I didn't expect it of him. So it was just me, [laughs] but with Jim helping we knocked it out pretty quick and got it all done, all packed up. We had quite a library. We had a long hallway full of shelving, and that shelving was full of our books at that time, so it was a big job. If I hadn't had Jim I would have been working on it for a long time. Jim was so fast.

But it was more than that. It was his cheer, his easy-to-be-with character, and his desire to be alone. Don had become a person that was very dependent on being with me. When he was off, he wanted to be with me. We had our little thing together and the three of us would get together for meals, which mostly Jim took over the cooking of—Don didn't want me cooking and if Jim wasn't cooking, we went out.

GARY Did you say *Jim* was cooking? [laughs]

JIM Hard to believe, isn't it.

CARLA Well, believe it or not, he was a pretty good cook. I don't think he ever liked it, but he pitched in and did it when it was needed. Jim is just an impressive human being. He was right down Don's alley—the kind of person that Don had been looking for.

GARY So this invitation was given to you and you accepted and moved in with Carla and Don. Did Don describe what your role would be?

CARLA Don't know.

JIM Well, I knew I would be transcribing, typing. What we thought we were going to do right away was to rewrite *Secrets of the UFO*. So for the first three weeks before the Ra contact started, it was my job to read the current literature on UFO investigation to try to update *Secrets*, and so I was reading and taking notes and using Carla's—let's see, at that time it was an IBM electric typewriter. (You've probably never seen such a thing—they came after the manuals.) And then after the Ra contact started, it was my job to transcribe, and everything just seemed to fall into place. I loved being outdoors, so I just took over the mowing of the grass—

CARLA We had 16 acres where we were living at Watterson Trail.

JIM Six. Yeah, and an old tractor there—

CARLA [*laughs*] Really old Ford, like 1953.

JIM Didn't last long, so I took over working the outside, taking care of the grass and the gardens and planting flowers and things like I do here, and transcribing, and taking Carla where she needed to go. We started off pretty much what we're doing now; it just got more intensive over the years.

GARY I'd say so.

Prior to meeting Don and Carla, you created a non-profit that you named Rock Creek Research and Development Laboratories. What was that, and how did L/L become incorporated into Rock Creek?

JIM Well, one of the things that Lingo offered was a chance to use, or to copy, his articles and papers of incorporation. So I used that and I decided to name it Rock Creek because my access road was a running creek with rock all over the place. You'd drive up the creek and you're bouncing around . . .

CARLA More rocks than water.

JIM Yeah, a lot of rocks, and after I named it that and moved to Louisville, I discovered there's a Rock Creek Riding Stable here in Louisville, and our favorite television show, *NCIS*, has a Rock Creek Park in Washington, D.C—I guess somebody else discovered the wheel too. So yeah, the 501(c)(3) was the umbrella which Lingo suggested that we use to start our schools and to be tax-exempt, nonprofit. That came in very handy when I joined in with Don and Carla, because they were in need of such a status, and it was easy to become the umbrella and keep L/L Research as the "doing business as" name because it was known around the world and

Rock Creek was not, except in Washington, D.C.

CARLA I had formed a 501(c)(3) in '73 for Eftspan,[6] doing all the work myself. You're not going to believe it, nobody ever did, but I just went to the law library and poked around, copied things, asked people, and got help here and there, and the third time I went to Frankfort[7] I got it okayed. So Eftspan was what Don thought that we were going to be—a 501(c)(3) so that people could donate money, and that would be our library, and that would be our research, and that would be our name—always doing business as L/L. We had formed Eftspan out of the meditation group that we called the Louisville Group.

So about half of the Louisville Group went south, they got involved in drugs, they didn't want to work; and they decided that they just wanted to live on the land, enjoy the land, and have nature be the reason that we were incorporated. So that got written into Eftspan, and Don discovered that even though it had a large number of acres (I'm not remembering how many), there wasn't any place on it that you could land a small plane, so he wouldn't be able to commute from there.

So things got stacked up against Eftspan, and when people voted not to have new members be required to come to meditation meetings, I was no longer interested in being part of a group that didn't want to meditate, because that was our thrust when we began, and everybody that goes back to the beginning was a meditator.

And so I warned them . . . I shepherded the group. We paid the land off because I made sure that we always had money by nagging people half to death for ten years. I told them that after the land is paid off, I no longer was interested.

I thought that that would make a difference to the group, but they all went, "Okay." [*laughs*] So I made three copies of absolutely everything, copied everything three times over, got redundancy going, and left. Nobody would believe that I couldn't save them when they came to me and said, "We lost all three copies—help us." "I don't have anything—I gave it all to you. I'm out." And I was. I'd moved on to be involved with L/L Research, so that's how come we knew about 501(c)(3)'s and how come we knew how valuable Jim's little thing was, because it was already okayed by the IRS, it was federal, and it didn't matter which state you lived in.

GARY What did Eftspan stand for?

CARLA It was out of *Oahspe*.‡ I found the name. It meant "children of the Creator."

GARY So you've already alluded to the romance that blossomed between you two. Can you describe when and how that happened?

CARLA Well, I'll start first and then you go ahead. I told Jim (like I told the two other people that I'd made love with in that, I guess, nine-year period—I don't know how long), "You know, it can't ever be anything but what it is now, because I am absolutely devoted to Don, absolutely lifetime devoted. He is my life partner." Jim said, "Great, I just want to be by myself. I'm a loner. I love being with you, no offense, but I want to be by myself. [*In a bad German accent*] I *vant* to be alone." So it was well understood. That was the way it was going to be, and everything was sweet between us and everything was sweet between Don and me. Between the two of them, you never saw two guys more totally devoted to each other. Good friends.

JIM That was the summer of '80. Just helping them move, getting to know—

CARLA It didn't take long . . .

JIM It just naturally developed—a magnet and an iron filing.

GARY So you couldn't resist each other. It does seem like a rather perfect fit that you three had—interlocking jigsaw pieces in that respect.

So you described the events that led you three together. A Bring4th member asks if there was anything that you might call dreams, premonitions, or synchronicities that you could identify in the process that led you three together.

JIM Well, I guess you could see the whole thing as being synchronistic, but nothing that really made me go *whoa!* It was just a feeling we had. Just a feeling inside and it was undeniable.

---

‡ Pronounced oh-wa-spee.

[1] In February 2016 Jim re-discovered the cassette recording for Don and Carla's WKQQ radio interview of May 30, 1977. It has since been published to the archive website, LLResearch.org, in the Interviews section of the Library.

To recap, the linkage goes like this: Jim heard Don and Carla for the first time late one night on his battery-powered radio while alone on the land—they were being interviewed on a Lexington, KY radio program. At some point thereafter Jim made mention to his regional food-buying co-op of the radio program he had recently heard. Members of that co-op were also members of Don and Carla's group, Eftspan, so they offered to introduce Jim to Don and Carla.

Eftspan was the group that got the personal growth author Ken Keyes interested in moving his Living Love Center from San Francisco, California, to St. Mary, Kentucky. So it was that Jim met Carla on the front steps of the main meeting hall in St. Mary where all Eftspan members were invited to take a weekend workshop for free at Ken Keyes' new Living Love Center. Jim met Don soon thereafter at a meditation in Don and Carla's Louisville apartment. Jim would subsequently help Don and Carla move to the house where 105 sessions of the Ra contact would later transpire.

[2] A recurring pattern in the twentieth century and into our own, enough people relocated in the '60s and '70s that it is said to have registered on American demographic statistics. With many influences, objectives, and strains, in general the movement was characterized by a desire to live a simpler life in close connection with the land. It seemed a reaction in many ways to the modern ills of urbanism, consumerism, politics, and environmental degradation. Henry David Thoreau was the guiding philosopher of the movement with his dictum, "Simplify, simplify." And the cooperative efforts of all those involved became the counter-culture's answer to the competition that is the hallmark of our capitalistic society. People helped each other build their own homes, plant gardens, raise children, and take part in the local, grassroots political process.

[3] In *The Crucifixion of Esmerelda Sweetwater* Don's height is listed as 6'5". Jim, who was 5'7" at the time Don was alive (but has since shrunk an inch from age), says that there was a question of whether Don was 6'5" or 6'6".

[4] Eric passed away in 2014.

[5] "We are an Organization that has been, for more than forty years, devoted to helping mankind delve deeply within to discover their own divine truth, their own divine cosmic awareness. We have encouraged contemplation on right living, through such cherished notions as universal love, respect and gratitude for all others."

Home page, Cosmic Awareness Communications, accessed February 14, 2016, www.cosmicawareness.org.

[6]

Oahspe is a channeled book from the 1800s which hides really good, solid information in with a lot of seemingly superfluous jargon. In *Oahspe*, Eftspan is the city of the Children of the Law of One.

When the big UFO flap of 1973 came to the Ohio River Valley, a lot of people began attending Don and Carla's Sunday meditations asking questions about UFOs and so forth. After a couple of years those folks who had remained with Don and Carla decided that they wanted to buy a piece of land in the country and build homes and live there. They bought 320 acres of beautiful land on the western side of Marion County. Jim lived on the eastern side and met Don and Carla via the food-buying co-ops that he and Eftspan members belonged to. No homes were ever built there but the group still loosely exists and they still own the land.

In the beginning, Eftspan's policy was that anyone who wanted to join the group had to attend group meditations for a period of time—six months, Jim thinks it was. After a few years, a lot of the original Eftspan members stopped coming to the meditations. The group subsequently removed meditation attendance as a membership requirement. Don and Carla considered this a figurative slap in the face. Carla, as treasurer of Eftspan, bugged them for the next two years for monthly payments until the land in Marion County was paid off. She then gave over all the books and records to the remaining members and, along with Don, bid them farewell.

[7] Kentucky's capital city.

GARY In the story of L/L Research, we come to the Ra contact.

Jim moved in on December 23, 1980. Up until that point all of your channeling, be it from Don, Carla, or other channels, was undertaken consciously; that is, the instrument was always fully conscious and aware of what was coming through them (with one small, brief exception on Carla's part that we will dig into a little bit further on). Then something happened. On January 15, 1981, 23 days after Jim moved in, you were surprised to receive an entirely new contact identifying itself as Ra. Can you describe the events of that day?

CARLA Well, I'll do it because Jim was out getting groceries when it happened. Don was home and he said that he would act as battery. I had a teaching session set up with Leonard, who had been a student for some months and was doing pretty well. He was channeling well and taking it seriously. I was going to teach that day, and I was about halfway through the session when there was a very powerful sort of knock-knock-knock on my inner door. I said, "Is there a spirit that wants to work through me?"

I kept getting, "I am Ra." I'm thinking, "I don't want to talk to a Ra," because the only Ra I knew was from mythology, Egyptian mythology, and it was a fairly negatively oriented entity—it was god of war, Horus the hawk-headed god and all that, not something I wanted to encourage.

So I challenged with every ounce of energy in my little body (at that time it was little), and I kept saying, "Do you come in the name of Jesus the Christ?"

They were indignant. It was like, "Do you think that you're the only people that have Jesus? Do you think you're the only planet that has Jesus? Come on—of course we come in the name of Jesus the Christ. Of course. What else is there when you're talking about love? We come in the name of Jesus Christ, no problem. Get on with it, girl!"

I challenged three times and they were very strongly affirmative: "Yes, of course, we come in the name of Jesus the Christ. We come in the name of love." I thought, "I can't go wrong with that," so I said okay.

I opened up to them and they gave what was for them a fairly long dissertation, at least a page long, typed. It was the longest thing that they ever did, because it wasn't an answer to anything; it was just—I don't think they ever again simply spoke. They always waited for us to ask them. They would say, "We communicate now," and then Don would ask a question, and that's the way they preferred to have it. But this time, to get things started, I guess, they explained briefly who they were and what they wanted to offer us, and I was very impressed. Well, when I read it I was very impressed; I didn't see it right away because I had somehow gone to sleep.

GARY Immediately to sleep?

CARLA I don't know, I guess, yes, and so I was . . . They tried to channel through the others, but they couldn't get anything going, and they would always come back to me. So Don asked a few questions, and when I came to after the session, he was pacing (which he always did when he was excited) and making the sound that he made when he was looking at something particularly good to eat. [*Carla makes the sound.*] He was so excited and he says, "We're gonna have to write a book, Alrac.* This is it!" I said, "Great." [*laughs*] But he wouldn't let me see it right away.

I am told, and you can hear it, that halfway through, Jim comes in manhandling the groceries—the door opening, bags rustling and everything.

JIM It was right at the point that Don was asking about the coming Earth changes when I came in the door. You'll see in the text: "We must pause

---

* Don's affectionate nickname for Carla. It is Carla's name backwards.

and deepen this instrument's contact."[1] That was because I had disturbed the first Ra contact.

CARLA So that was the only one that Jim wasn't right there at the beginning of. After that, he was johnny-on-the-spot.

GARY So Don knew you had something special on the line?

CARLA Absolutely, right away. He was so excited—never saw him more excited.

GARY You just described the way Ra responded to your challenge. Was that unique in the responses you had received to your challenging?

CARLA I never got indignation before, [*laughs*] but I had had the gentle suggestion that Jesus was a galaxy-wide presence and not simply a person on this planet—that the energy of love was the energy of Jesus, and that Jesus was an energy that was elsewhere as well as here.

GARY Beyond their unique response to your challenge, did you perceive them distinctly from the other Confederation sources you had channeled previously?

CARLA Only in the strength of their contact. It was like having a laser go into your head rather than the generalized buzz kind of a feeling that the others tended to give you.

GARY Would you say you felt it in a pinpoint sort of way—very localized?

CARLA Yeah, not pinpoint, but certainly something close to that.

GARY How old were each of you on that day of January 15?

CARLA Let's see, I was born in '43, Jim in '47 . . .

JIM You were 37 and I was 33.

CARLA Thank you. [*laughs*] I'm not that good working it out in my head. Yeah, we were both in our 30s, but I was ending mine up and he was just beginning.

GARY And Don was much older . . .

CARLA Don was 14 years older than me—he was born in '30.

JIM Don was 51.

GARY We know that you slipped into trance. Going into the second session, did any of you know what would happen?

CARLA No. Was it the second session where they set up the routine—the ritual at the beginning?

JIM I believe at the end of the first session they gave the ritual, and we used it for the second session. And it was at that time that we decided to dedicate one room in the house for nothing but the Ra contact. The first contact was in the living room where we always had our Sunday night meditations, so we decided that there was one room that wasn't being used for anything else—it was a bedroom. We decided that would become the Ra room. It had a little bathroom off of it that Carla could use afterward.

No, I don't think we knew exactly what was going to happen. I certainly didn't. I hadn't been at the first one, so I was, "Okay, what are we doing here?"

CARLA No. I didn't realize then that I was going to go to sleep every time, but that's what happened.

GARY So you thought that your slipping into a trance state might have been a fluke or . . . ?

CARLA I thought I just went to sleep, but it was a deep state of concentration, and I just went from there to sleep. That's what it felt like to me—it never did feel any different than that.

GARY Did Don have any sense of alarm that in order to channel Ra you had to be in a trance state?

CARLA I don't remember.

JIM No, he never expressed any.

GARY And this was long before you became aware [of the danger inherent in the process of channeling Ra].

CARLA But he always put me in a bed in the Ra room; there was always a bed that I lay on rather than sitting, so I guess he kind of knew it was going to happen that way.

GARY In the first session (1.11), Ra said, "We have good contact with this instrument because of her recent experiences with trance." Were they referring to the trance channeling that you did for your friend Tom

Flaherty of his recently deceased wife, Elaine?

CARLA That's right. Not too long before she had her final illness. She had been ill for a long time with juvenile diabetes. That's a nasty disease. Not too long after that her kidneys failed, and she went into her final illness and never got up.

JIM And she told Tom that she would give him some indication that she survived death.

CARLA Right. Tom had always been a little panicky, saying, "How am I going to know you're okay?" So she said, "I will let you know." Tom felt—they both felt—that this was time to investigate that.

She might have been already in the hospital . . . do you remember?

JIM That happened while I was in Oregon.

CARLA Ah. I don't remember, but I have a feeling she was already in the hospital. Anyway, I had agreed to do it with both of them and I knew I was set up to do it, so after her passing, Tom asked if I would just go ahead and do it, just one night. I did and I went to sleep.

It was the same feeling, but it was a very heavy feeling, and I just felt awful when I got up. It was like having—I don't know, I've never had a hangover—but my tummy hurt, I felt like I was going to throw up, and my head hurt something fierce. I just didn't want to do it again.

So they got me to do it one more time for, I guess, evidence—Elaine was going to give him evidence, and he hadn't gotten it yet. I think it was in the second time that I was channeling, and I said something, and it was so like Elaine that they both swore that it was like she was in the next room and she was talking to them. And I didn't know that. I didn't know what she said or how she said it—I was just channeling. So they did get their evidence then that she was going to be okay.

He was at peace when she died, and he knew that she was okay. But I did not want to do it anymore, because I felt that he had already gotten his assurances and that was very hard on me. And he agreed. He didn't want to make it hard on me.

GARY So you didn't want to have anything to do with trance after that?

CARLA No, not interested. And then, boom, here it happens again.

GARY One hundred six more times.

CARLA But I did have better support. I don't know exactly—it was hard on me then too. I didn't have any symptoms like I did when I was doing it for Tom, but I had an enormous need to go to the bathroom. I finally got a chance to ask Ra about that: How come, when I wake up from these things, I just have to dash to the bathroom and I pee, and I pee, and I pee, like there was no tomorrow? I'd been saving up![2] [*laughs*]

And they said that I had no understanding of how to produce the ecto-plasm that was necessary. So instead of having a very smooth production of ectoplasm, and then you release the ectoplasm (it looks like cigar smoke), and it comes out of the body, I was using my body to produce it. The by-products of that process were being stored in the body as urine, and that's why I had so much extra. So I was actually using part of my body every time I channeled, and I would lose somewhere between two and three pounds—sometimes it was two and sometimes it was three—but there was an enormous amount of peeing that would produce that much urine. It was amazing. It was just amazing, and I didn't regain the weight: I kept losing and losing and losing. I got down to what, about 80 to 83 pounds?

JIM Eighty-four is what I remember.

CARLA And Don said, "You've got to eat more." I was eating and eating like a mad fool and not gaining, but I stopped losing. I didn't actually look thin, or emaciated, at that weight because I have very small bones. I'm built like a bird. I have flexible, long, thin bones. But I looked slen-der, that's for sure, and the big worry, I think, was that I didn't have a lot of weight that I could lose, say, if I got sick.

GARY Didn't have a big margin for error.

CARLA I didn't have a margin, yeah, of safety. So after I stopped channel-ing Ra, I gained back up to my normal weight, which at that time was between 110 and 120.

GARY Your body, from what I've read, took quite the beating. We'll defi-nitely dig into some of that as we go further on.

CARLA It did, yeah.

GARY How would you define *trance*—at least the trance that you experi-enced during the Ra contact?

CARLA Well, I guess basically what they do is they define it in terms of where your brain is vibrating at—whether it's asleep or whether it's alpha. What do they have, four different states? And I guess *trance* is when you're in one of those two bottom states and you're still able to talk.

GARY Theta or delta are the two deepest—

CARLA I think, but that includes, I think, two different forms of channeling, and yet both of them are unconscious. I would just say that I wasn't conscious, and, unfortunately, we never had anybody there that had a machine on us that could tell us what exactly was happening.

JIM It was a type of trance where the instrument (you) left your body. Not all trances are like that.

CARLA Right. And I never had that happen when I was channeling elsewise. [In conscious channeling] I didn't ever know exactly what had been channeled because you just can't remember that much stuff, but I knew more or less where we'd been, what it was about in general. I remembered doing it, but it seemed like it took much less time than usual. But then, you know how it is to go into a channeling session—you can't believe that that much time has passed when you get the 45-minute signal on the tape recorder, and you go, "Well, I'll be darned, it didn't seem like that long." It never does.

GARY So it felt like going to sleep, and the next thing you know you wake up and have no awareness about what information came through.

CARLA No, I just had Don's voice in my ear going, "Alrac . . . Alrac . . . Alrac . . ."[3] over and over, [*laughs*] trying to make sure I was awake and would respond.

GARY Did you dream at all during that state?

CARLA No.

GARY Did you come to with any impressions?

CARLA I did not have a feeling that I'd been out. It seemed like a moment. I started it, and I conked out, and then I woke up. I had to go to the bathroom, and I knew that the session had ended, but I had no feeling that any time had passed—no dreaming, no sense of time passing, even in that manner.

GARY And it sounds like no sense of resting either.

CARLA No.

GARY As opposed to normal sleep where you wake up and you might feel rejuvenated, you woke up and felt exhausted.

CARLA Right.

JIM Ra said it was the equivalent of a day's work for her.[4]

CARLA Physical labor, he was talking about.

---

[1]
Jim was paraphrasing, actually. It went like this:

QUESTIONER Can you say anything about the coming planetary changes?

[Background noise.]

RA I am Ra. I preferred to wait until this instrument had again reached the proper state of depth of singleness or one-pointedness before we spoke. 1.9

[2]
More information on the physical and metaphysical processes involved in the trance state:

QUESTIONER Is the necessity for the instrument to go to the bathroom several times before a session due to the psychic attack?

RA I am Ra. In general this is incorrect. The instrument is eliminating from the body complex the distortion leavings of the material which we use for contact. This occurs variably, sometimes beginning before contact, other workings this occurring after the contact.

In this particular working this entity is experiencing the aforementioned difficulties causing the intensification of that particular distortion/condition. 63.4

QUESTIONER A question I didn't get to ask the previous session which I will be forced to continue at this time is, is the trance state the only condition from which a mind/body/spirit positive entity may be lured by a negative adept to a negative time/space configuration?

RA I am Ra. This is a misperceived concept. The mind/body/spirit complex which freely leaves the third-density physical complex is vulnerable when the appropriate protection is not at hand. You may perceive carefully that very few entities which choose to leave their physical complexes are doing work of such a nature as to attract the polarized attention of negatively oriented entities. The danger to most in trance state, as you term the physical complex being left, is the touching of the physical complex in such a manner as to attract the mind/body/spirit complex back thereunto or to damage the means by which that which you call ectoplasm is being recalled.

This instrument is an anomaly in that it is well that the instrument not be touched or artificial light thrown upon it while in the trance state. However, the ectoplasmic activity is interiorized. The main difficulty, as you are aware, is then the previously discussed negative removal of the entity under its free will.

That this can happen only in the trance state is not completely certain, but it is highly probable that in another out-of-body experience such as death the entity here examined would, as most positively polarized entities, have a great deal of protection from comrades, guides, and portions of the self which would be aware of the transfer you call the physical death. 69.3

Ra indicated that the instrument stopped relying on the transmutation of physical material into energy for the contact in Session 83:

QUESTIONER Could you please tell me why the instrument gains weight now instead of loses it after a session?

RA I am Ra. To assume that the instrument is gaining the weight of the physical bodily complex due to a session or working with Ra is erroneous. The instrument has no longer any physical material which, to any observable extent, must be used in order for this contact to occur. This is due to the determination of the group that the instrument shall not use the vital energy which would be necessary since the physical energy complex level is in deficit. Since the energy, therefore, for these contacts is a product of energy transfer the instrument must no longer pay this physical price. Therefore, the instrument is not losing the weight.

However, the weight gain, as it occurs, is the product of two factors. One is the increasing sensitivity of this physical vehicle to all that is placed before it, including that towards which it is distorted in ways you would call allergic. The second factor is the energizing of these difficulties.

It is fortunate for the outlook of this contact and the incarnation of this entity that it is not distorted towards the overeating as the overloading of this much distorted physical complex would override even the most fervent affirmations of health/illness and turn the instrument towards the distortions of illness/health or, in the extreme case, the physical death. 83.2

3 Some of the audio recordings of the Ra sessions contain Don calling Carla back to her body at the conclusion of the session by gently repeating "Alrac... Alrac... Alrac... " until Carla vocally responds, her voice heavy with exhaustion.

4 As Jim and Carla mention, the energy drain was so intensive that it was the equivalent of "many, many hours of *harsh* physical labor":

RA The distortions caused by this working (which are inevitable given the plan chosen by this entity) are limitation and, to a degree consonant with the amount of vital and physical energy expended, weariness, **due to that which is the equivalent in this instrument of many, many hours of harsh physical labor.**

This is why we suggested the instrument's thoughts dwelling upon the possibility of its suggesting to its higher self the possibility of some slight reservation of energy at a working. This instrument at this time is quite open until all resources are quite exhausted. This is well if desired. However, it will, shall we say, shorten the number of workings in what you may call the long run. 60.4

CHAPTER 5

Reactions to the Ra Contact

GARY We've already learned that Don was quite excited to have Ra on the line—he was pacing around the room when you came to after the first session, and he saw the possibility of fulfilling the work he wanted to do by creating a book of Ra's answers to his investigative questions. Did Don convey anything else about this new prospect of communicating with Ra?

JIM He always looked forward to the next session; he always loved talking with Ra. He was the one who came up with most of the questions. The night before we would usually have a meditation and talk over potential questions for the next day, and he would write a couple of those down. Frequently, though, he would only get through one or two of them and then Ra would give a response that would be so intriguing that he'd have to go in another direction. All the questions kind of went by the wayside for a while, then, as he followed the new train of thought.

CARLA Yeah, he would get distracted. And he always apologized for it, but Ra never expressed that he needed to, or that it was [not] okay, or anything. Ra just ignored that.

GARY It would have to be so difficult. Any given sentence, much less paragraph or multiple paragraphs that Ra has to offer is rich with so much that can be mined, so many different directions you could explore.

CARLA And I don't know how he understood Ra, because Ra didn't have a lot of expression in his voice—its voice—whatever.

JIM No expression.

CARLA It was just *zzz*—it was like Nebraska.[1] [*laughter*]

JIM You really couldn't tell where the end of a sentence was. You had to listen very carefully. You've heard some of the tape. But he was able to hear and think about it and respond to it, which always amazed me.

CARLA Yeah, and some of those things that Ra said—as you're reading a single sentence you think, *what did he say?* And you're reading it, you're looking at it, you're going back and reading it again, and you're still not there—it takes time to really adjust and process that answer, but not for Don.

He was so intelligent. Now I've aced so many intelligence tests. I've gone off the edge on intelligence tests. They've never been able to give me my IQ because I aced the test: I slid off the end and they couldn't score me. Don was about three times as intelligent as I was. He was a whole other unit going on here. I very much valued and honored and respected that, and that's all that enabled him to keep up because that's what he did: he kept up.

The only thing that Don did that he considered wrong happened when Ra would drop these little gems that would seem to answer something that Don had been asking about on the side for years. Don would *have to ask*, he would have to follow the new lead—he couldn't just stick to his routine and ask the questions that he'd planned. So he kept getting off track.

But he was so excited to be talking to Ra; I've never seen anybody look forward to communication the way Don looked forward to talking with Ra. That was all he wanted was that next session. He really, really wanted that.

JIM When I was transcribing the Ra sessions in the office, Don would be pacing around the office waiting for the next page to come out of the typewriter. [*laughter*]

GARY So he would take his page, and you would continue working, and he'd wait for the next one. He was a junkie for Ra, it sounds like.

KEN * Can I ask a quick question? You mentioned that the pacing was really different from a lot of the other channelings. For those that haven't had a chance to hear some of the Ra contact recordings, can you give a rough idea of how the pacing was so much different than the other channelings?

CARLA Don just didn't express his feelings.

JIM No: Ra. How Ra was different.

CARLA How Ra was different? Ra had quality and depth.

JIM Ra . . . . . . would . . . . . . speak . . . . . . like . . . . . . this . . . . . . and . . . . . . make . . . . . . no . . . . . . in--to--na--tion . . . . . . for . . . . . . any . . . . word.

CARLA Yeah, the expression was—oh, you wanted me to talk like Ra talks.

KEN Just an idea for those who haven't had a chance to hear.

CARLA I . . . . . . am . . . . . . Ra . . . . . . we . . . . . . co--mmu--ni--cate . . . . . . now . . . . . . the . . . . . . reason . . . . . . that . . . . . . you . . . . . . are . . . . . . here . . . . . . is . . . . . . to . . . . . . share . . . . . . love . . . . . . for . . . . . . each . . . . . . other . . . . . . there . . . . . . is . . . . . . no . . . . . .

JIM Actually, you're going too fast. [*laughter*] Really, Ra was very slow—

CARLA And soft.

JIM Yes, and occasionally, the . . . . . . end . . . . . . of . . . . . . words . . . . . . would . . . . . . be . . . . . . ac--cen--tu--a--*ted*. [*Jim accentuates the end of the word "accentuated."*][2]

GARY And no extra spacing between sentences to indicate—

JIM No. It was like they were releasing pulses of energy that happened to be formed in words that we could understand, and they were released at a set pace.

CARLA Yeah, what did they say, "Our information is at a set pace given"?[3]

JIM Right.

GARY There are a few instances in the text where Don interrupts them

---

* The videographer filming the interview, Ken Wendt, occasionally contributed a thought or question.

giving an answer, because he thinks they have completed the answer, and apparently they weren't done.

I've transcribed you guys when you've channeled in a conscious manner; you naturally speak in paragraphs and sentences. It's real easy to tell where a paragraph break should be, or an exclamation mark is, or a period.

I was going to ask you about transcribing the Ra sessions. Did that pose an extra difficulty for you?

JIM No, it made it very easy. They just happened to be transmitting at the same pace at which I could type, which was at that time roughly 40 wpm, I guess.

GARY So maybe had you been faster at typing it would—

JIM Maybe it would have been quicker. It was a happy coincidence. [*laughs*]

CARLA Well, maybe they set the pace of their talking by checking out you typing in the other room.

JIM Possible, but not likely. Carla didn't have much physical energy, so after a while we discovered that if we had sexual relations the night before contact, that contact was longer than if we did not have; so sexual energy exchanges increased the length of the Ra sessions.

CARLA Elkins always made good and sure that we had plenty of time to do that [*laughter*]—to make sure that we were all set up. "Are you ready?"

GARY Carla, you said that you've never seen somebody so excited to communicate. One thing that you didn't specifically say, that I heard previously, was that Don was a very melancholy man, but this was different. The Ra contact lifted Don somewhat out of that melancholiness.

CARLA Oh yeah, he was joyful; he was thrilled to death.

GARY It was the first time that you'd really seen that in the almost 20 years—

CARLA I had never seen him happy until talking to Ra. I was so grateful to be able to give him that. People, through the years, have said to me things like how generous and noble it was of me to channel Ra sessions when I knew I was in a lot of danger of just croaking, and wasn't well at all. I always knew that there was a chance that I could die, and if it gave Don one more session, that was fine with me to give him that happiness. That was the depth of my . . . I adored him.

Our devotion was so deep. Most everything in my life had been heavy on communication. Don never communicated. But I always knew that he was devoted because I knew if he weren't incredibly devoted to me, he'd be out of there. He didn't like a lot of things that had to do with being around women. He didn't like my tendencies to buy clothes. It really offended him that there were things that I *wanted*, and yet he stuck, no matter what.

Now, he never criticized me, and he never praised me. Those were the two things that sort of balanced each other out. He never gave me a hard time, and he never gave me credit.

JIM Up until the Ra contact, his idea of the balanced human being was one who was not swayed by any emotion up or down. He made that choice when he was 26 years old—that basically this world was a crazy place and if you wanted to survive it, you need not to be swayed by it. You needed to look at it with a level mind, a level keel, and keep your emotions at a distance.

It was a spiritual practice for him not to become swayed in any direction, so he didn't give compliments, he didn't give criticism. He was . . . in his own words he was *indifferent*. And later on, during the Ra contact, we discovered that was not the best type of balancing to do; but up to that point, it was a pretty strict and successful spiritual discipline, because he was very wise. He never jumped into anything. You couldn't sway him one way or the other. He needed to gather more data, and he would think about things for a long time, and then he would make a move, and it was almost always the right one.

CARLA Uh huh.

JIM So we really appreciated his nature. But during the Ra contact we discovered the balancing process, which is a more correct way of using catalyst. He *didn't* use catalyst; he just let it slide away.

CARLA His heart was protected in reinforced concrete up until the Ra contact. Somewhere near the middle of the Ra contact he started losing that protection. Oh, I guess I know what it was: it was when we had that unhappy exchange of energy, and he was not ready to have an open heart at all. He was so different. It was scary.

GARY So we know Don was quite excited, and, Carla, you just said that you were happy to make Don happy. So was your reaction to the beginning of the Ra contact similar to his in that this Ra provided a means to fulfill your desire to *know*, or was your reaction more, *Ra provides me a means to make Don happy*?

CARLA It was the second. Don was the one with the burning desire to get all the questions answered and make all the puzzle pieces fit. I was a lot easier going, by nature, than Don. I was interested in all the new information that we got—

JIM But you couldn't read the sessions until like the 21st or 23rd session, because Don wanted to keep it as a scientific experiment. So she didn't know the quality of information coming through. All she knew was that it made Don happy.

CARLA Yeah, but even after I read it I was impressed by it. I was grateful to have it, and I saw nothing to bother my Christianity in it. So there wasn't any reason that I would have any trouble with it. It was all so logical to a person that loves philosophy. It was the only *seamless* philosophy that I'd ever read. There wasn't any reason to say, "Well, there are problems with it in the area of . . ." There weren't any problems—it was logical, all logical. Ra never contradicted himself. It's incredible to have a system that doesn't contradict itself somewhere.

GARY Yeah, it's a pretty amazing feat, considering the scope that it covers.

CARLA Really, yeah. Don had a great ambition, and he really felt that this information from Ra was going to put all the puzzle pieces together. And shortly before he died, during a period when he was definitely sane, he thanked me for helping him achieve his life's work. He was satisfied with it. And I was thrilled to hear that.

GARY How about yourself, Jim: What was your reaction to Ra?

JIM I felt like I was on the mountain top—that all my life previous to that, I'd been climbing this mountain, and now I was there. It was just so obvious. The information was more than I could ever hope for.

GARY So how did that information and the experience of the Ra contact affect the conscious channeling experiment that had been ongoing since the early '60s (and was *still* happening during the Ra contact)?

CARLA It didn't. It didn't as far as I'm concerned, anyway. I was still working with the same skill and art that I had achieved before. I never had any conscious awareness of what was going on in the Ra contact, so it had no effect.

GARY So it just continued on, uninterrupted?

CARLA Yeah. Don didn't understand why I wanted to continue the conscious channeling when I could talk to Ra. We had a big, healthy group and they wanted to get together every week and have a meditation. Did I say, "No, I won't do it anymore"? Of course we continued to meet for conscious channeling.

GARY That was actually a later question of mine I was going to ask: What was your thinking in terms of continuing the conscious channeling when you had Ra? So it was you that wanted to continue the conscious channeling; Don would have otherwise let it go?

CARLA Probably.

GARY And you wanted to do it for reasons of community, to support others who came to the meditation?

CARLA Yeah, plus it continued his experiment on another level. I always valued the conscious channeling more than he did after he got the Ra contact.

GARY Did he still participate in the conscious channeling at that point?

CARLA Yeah. Unless he saw somebody coming in that he had to leave because of. [*laughs*]

GARY Did Don communicate what was happening with Ra to other people, or did he keep a tight lid on it?

CARLA Oh yeah, he'd talk to anybody that wanted to hear it, and we didn't really know how to advertise it, how to publicize it. We were just such innocent babes—we had no idea. We put some ads, some very small ads, in some magazines. We put one in *Fate*—I remember we had one in *Fate* that went on for quite some time. It was just very small and it said, "We have information that you might enjoy as a serious seeker. If you are interested, write us and we'll send it to you for free. If you value it, you can pay us. If not, just send the book back." We seldom got the book back but we often got donations.

GARY Did you receive any responses or feedback from other people who were able to see it prior to the books being published?

CARLA Yes, and if they were people that we respected, oddly enough, they respected the material—they valued the material and could see value in the information.

What kept it from being published for a while—as far as a publishing company buying it—was that it was so different, and it wasn't good English in terms of modern-day English. And we would get these rejections replete with explanations of how we could edit it and make it a lot better, [that] it was basically good material but it was so hard to read and there was no need for all that.

GARY I have the paragraph that you published in Book V, quoting the reviewer or the editor from New York City [coming up] in these questions. It was quite interesting feedback you got there.

JIM He wrote us three pages, single-spaced, telling us why it wouldn't work.

GARY So it had an impact on him too; just not the hoped-for one.

So we'll get into this in more detail later, but for now I'd like to ask briefly: During the first year of your conversation with those of Ra, you had 75 sessions. The following year, 1982, you had 27 sessions. What accounted for the drop-off between the first and second year?

JIM Wisdom. We were going too hard and fast in the beginning. We were so excited about having the Ra contact that we had to learn the hard way that it was wearing on Carla's physical vehicle. So after a while we began slowing down, plus toward the end, both Don and Carla were having more physical problems, and that made things more difficult to take care of in order to have a session. So it was a combination of our desire not to be so hard on Carla's body, as well as both Don and Carla suffering physical difficulties.

CARLA It was just a lot harder for all three of us to come to a session on time, ready to go.

GARY And then the trend continued even more dramatically: The following year, 1983, you had 4 sessions. The final year of the Ra contact, 1984, you had one last session. Did years three and four continue the trajectory of years one and two?

JIM Yeah, pretty much. Carla was having more problems with her body. It was just something that we had to deal with. We had gone too hard in the beginning, sometimes two sessions a day, and her body was just taking too much of a beating.

CARLA A lot of times I'd get right to the meeting time, and I would have been trying really, really hard to allay everyone's worry, and Elkins would take a good look at me and he'd cancel. I guess, in all of his desire to have that conversation, he just didn't want to lose me.

GARY So you would have a session scheduled and he would cancel sometimes.

CARLA He would cancel. Right. Remember that? Right at the last.

JIM A couple of times, yeah.

CARLA That was sad—poignant for me.

GARY Had to be a very difficult for him to do, with his overwhelming desire for contact with Ra.

CARLA Very difficult.

GARY At the time, as this information was coming through, what impact, if any, did you think it might have on the world?

JIM Not a lot. [*laughs*] Even Ra suggested that there were—they gave general figures for about how many people on the planet were interested in Confederation philosophy, in general, and that was about 67 million.[4] But for the Ra contact they said it was about 352,000, which is not a lot.[5]

GARY So you knew from the get-go that this was going to appeal to a very small demographic?

JIM Right.

CARLA I think from the very beginning I realized that the seeking, the search, was a good thing. People found it because they were seeking something; so I knew that if you had something that required you to search for it, it was never going to be a big bestseller because then people wouldn't have to search for it.

JIM I think Ra felt it was a treasure to have the contact—they mentioned that, simply because if one person was illuminated, it was reason enough for the contact, because we're all one.[6] I think the principle there is that once it's been introduced into the consciousness of the planet, maybe it won't be utilized right now, but it will be there for other experiences, other times.

CARLA Yes, and it has turned out to be that way. It's in the general vocabulary and consciousness of people who search out UFO stuff for sure, and spirituality. You see the phrases coming up that people have copped and are using, including "densities."

GARY "Polarity" and the idea of "service to others" and "service to self" being those that you see repeated across the channeled world nowadays. They were probably really introduced through the Law of One.

CARLA Agreed.

GARY Regarding the idea of introducing the ideas into the consciousness, if you see the collective mind as a system that is somewhat closed and self-contained, then Ra was able to inject information into that system from the outside. And once inside, even if it's not used or widely known by the whole, it's available, at least in potential.

And fast forward to now—tens of thousands of people have read this, so each time they read it, each time they internalize and contemplate it, they are bringing it more and more into the collective mind and experience, I would think.

---

[1] Nebraska is a state in the Great Plains region of the United States noted, by some, for being particularly flat and featureless.

[2] Ra's propensity to accentuate the end of some words lead Tobey Wheelock to add grave accents, as they're called, to certain words in the *Ra Contact* text, including "markèd," "wingèd," "blessèd." The accent indicates that instead of pronouncing the word *wingd*, as English dialect typically dictates, Ra pronounced it as *wing-ed*. You may now mark this day upon the calendar as one in which you have learned something important.

[3] About the pace of Ra's replies:

> RA We communicate at a set rate which is dependent upon our careful manipulation of this instrument. We cannot be more, as you would say, quick. Therefore, you may ask questions speedily but the answers we have to offer are at a set pace given. 15.1

[4] In 12.27 of *The Law of One* material, Ra says in 1981 that there were 65 million incarnate wanderers. This would be roughly 1% of the then-total planetary pop-

ulation. This percentage may or may not have increased since that time; though in light of everything Ra said about the harvest, the desire to lighten the planetary vibration, and the intensive, special opportunity available for spiritual evolution at this time, the number of wanderers has presumably increased.

Whatever the number, not every one of those wanderers would be interested in this philosophy. Ra actually guestimates the percentages of wanderers at that time who could, as they say, "make sense" of this material.

QUESTIONER Can you tell me what percentage of the Wanderers on Earth today have been successful in penetrating the memory block and becoming aware who they are, and then finally, is there anything that we can do to make the instrument more comfortable or improve the contact?

RA I am Ra. We can approximate the percentage of those penetrating intelligently their status. This is between eight and one-half and nine and three-quarters percent. There is a larger percentile group of those who have a fairly well defined, shall we say, symptomology indicating to them that they are not of this, shall we say, "insanity." This amounts to a bit over fifty percent of the remainder. Nearly one-third of the remainder are aware that something about them is different, so you see there are many gradations of awakening to the knowledge of being a Wanderer. We may add that it is to the middle and first of these groups that this information will, shall we say, make sense. 36.24

5 The number who, as a result of the Law of Squares, is personally calling Ra. See 7.6 and 14.24.

6 See 2.1 for Ra's verbose explanation about how to serve one is to serve all:

QUESTIONER I'm guessing that there are enough people who would understand what you are saying, interested enough, for us to make a book of communications with it and I wondered if you would agree to this, us making a book, and if so, I was thinking that possibly a bit of historical background on yourself would be in order.

RA I am Ra. The possibility of communication, as you would call it, from the One to the One through distortion acceptable for meaning is the reason we contacted this group. There are few who will grasp, without significant distortion, that which we communicate through this connection with this mind/body/spirit complex. However, if it be your desire to share our communications with others we have the distortion towards a perception that this would be most helpful in regularizing and crystallizing your own patterns of vibration upon the levels of experience which you call the life. If one is illuminated, are not all illuminated? Therefore, we are oriented towards speaking for you in whatever supply of speakingness you may desire. To teach/learn is the Law of One in one of its most elementary distortions. 2.1

CHAPTER 6

Mechanics of the Ra Contact

GARY We resume our interview with "Mechanics of the Ra contact," which concerns some of the nuts and bolts of the contact. To begin, what was the procedure of scheduling the session with Ra? Did you plan sessions for a particular date and time in advance?

CARLA Jim is probably going to be answering more of [these questions] because I was just done unto, and the guys were taking care of everything.

JIM We planned around flights that Don had to make in order to earn a living. And when he was home, then we focused all our energies on when it would be possible to have a session with Ra. Usually Don was home anywhere from five or six days to eight or ten days, so it was possible to plan two or three sessions in advance, keeping two or three days in between. That was after we got going. At the very first, we planned them every day. [*laughs*] And overdid it.

But it was around Don's schedule. He was a pilot for Eastern Air Lines at that time and was frequently flying various locations around the country. When he was doing that, then we were getting Carla in good shape, doing her exercises, thinking about questions for the future, and getting ready for Don to come back home.

GARY So where Don's schedule and Carla's health coincided, a session with Ra happened.

JIM Right. Very seldom was Carla in too bad a shape to have a session, so it was usually Don's availability that determined when we were going to be able to have a session.

GARY Was that the center point of your lives from 1981 to 1982?

CARLA Oh yeah, definitely. And Ra had suggested that exercises be done, and I was already exercising—I did "shapenastics" every day. Or what was the other one?

JIM Jazzercise.

CARLA Jazzercise—I loved Jazzercise.

JIM And walking.

CARLA Yeah, and then also I took a walk—separately from that I took a walk that lasted about an hour, and usually it was at least three miles and sometimes as much as five. I walked pretty fast.

JIM And I had to hustle to keep up with her.

CARLA [*laughs*] So I was very grateful for Jim's company. He's always good company, so we did that usually around the middle of the day and closer to the end of the day for the two exercises, depending on when the classes were held.

GARY So even when not in session you were planning or preparing for the session-to-be?

CARLA There was a good bit that went into the planning of—*let's see if we can do it now.*

GARY Was there ever a session that, upon getting everything in order, Ra failed to speak through the instrument?

JIM No.

GARY Can you walk us through the protocol undertaken before each session, along with the purpose for each step?

JIM Well, as I said, it started the night before. We would have a meditation together, usually in the living room where the public meditations were held (but this was just with the three of us in the evening), and after the meditation we would talk about the previous session and information we got; then logical questions went on from there. And once those were determined, then it was usually time for bed. And when we finally figured out that sexual energy exchanges were helpful to the Ra contact and gave Carla more energy, thereby lengthening them, then Carla and I would do our thing and help out.[1]

CARLA Usually Jim would say, "It's time for that massage." And he would give me a really good massage, and then it would naturally flow into more intimate relations while we listened to our beloved rock 'n' roll. We listened over and over. What were our favorites at that time?

JIM Oh, Rod Stewart, Rolling Stones, the Beatles.

CARLA Yeah, so there was something there, too, that was fun.

JIM And then the morning of the session we would have a light breakfast together, not usually a whole lot—toast, juice, maybe an egg or something. We would then have a meditation in the living room where we would work on any questions that needed to be refined. And then we would retire to the room that was devoted just to the Ra contact, a bedroom off of the living room. And Carla would be in her outfit—after a while it became sort of interesting what she was in. She wore a special white outfit, and as her hands became more delicate and the covers were heavy, we put her hand through a little expandable tubing that is usually used to connect dryers to the vent. So she had her hands through those to keep the weight of the covers off of her hands, and then there was a—I guess it was a white linen over your eyes.

CARLA It was one of Don's—

JIM Shirts.

CARLA T-shirts, yeah, undershirts.

JIM One of his t-shirts over her eyes, and then we covered her with the white cover, the blanket—

CARLA I had little white gloves because my hands were cold.

JIM —to keep warm.

CARLA And then I had shoes, I had white shoes.

JIM Ballet-slipper-type shoes.

CARLA Yeah, little t-strap-type hippie shoes. They did the job.

JIM Once she was in position, then Don would do a measure of the per-
pendicularity of the censor, the chalice, the Bible—all of the
accoutrements—with a yardstick. While he was doing that, then I was
getting the tape deck ready to receive the cassette tapes. We had three recorders going at once because there had been times when one or two
would fail, so we had redundancy. I got those ready to go, got them labeled, and then at that point, Don and I would walk the Circle of One
using the ritual words that Ra gave us to begin.[2]

Then it took probably a minute or two or three before Ra began to speak.
It would take that long for Carla to seemingly go to sleep and apparently
then leave her body. Ra did not enter her body, but used it from what we
would call "at a distance" to make words. That's why if she had a pain
flare it was necessary to move her limb: arthritis requires, now and then,
that you move your limb and get it in another position so that it's more
comfortable, otherwise it freezes there and there is more pain. So it was
difficult for Ra to move, but they, on a number of occasions, did move
one of her limbs in order to reduce the pain. The sessions usually lasted
anywhere between 45 minutes and 1½ hours.

GARY Why the necessity of white?

JIM We just felt that that was a good color, you might say—although
white is all the colors, so it's not one color—but it felt like it was in congruence with the purity of the undertaking which we were experiencing.

GARY You touched on the question formulation. You said the night prior
to a session you would get together and discuss the previous session. So
were you aware of all the questions that Don planned to ask for the upcoming session?

JIM We were aware of most of the questions he was going to ask until the
next morning when we had our final meditation together before the contact started. Frequently, Don would get another question in meditation
and he'd write that down, and we may or may not—

CARLA Yeah, we'd be meditating and he'd write it down, then go back to
meditating, and write it down. It drove me crazy actually, but that's the
way he operated. He would get them by intuition during the meditation.

GARY I recall a few different moments during the Ra contact where Don
states or prefaces the question by saying he got it, or it came to him, during meditation. When he meditated, was he mentally chewing over the

contact to come, that you were aware, or was he . . .

CARLA As far as I know, he just wiped everything out of his mind and hung out in the silence. He loved doing that.

JIM He didn't talk a lot about his technique of meditation.

GARY So Don developed the vast majority of the questions?

JIM Right. At least 90%, I would say. Occasionally either Carla or I would come up with questions— personal questions for ourselves—and we would submit them, and Don would usually try to ask those at the beginning and get them out of the way [*laughs*] so he could get to the real stuff.[3]

CARLA Yeah, he was a little embarrassed. He thought that they were lesser and not very important, so he apologized, but we were grateful that he asked them at all.

JIM Though very interesting information came through frequently. Ra didn't give bad information—it always had spiritual principles as its foundation, so whatever question you asked would be answered from a spiritual point of view.

GARY Don didn't give you any resistance to your questions?

JIM No. We were aware that we didn't want to take up too much time with such things, but it was hard to avoid. He was basically—in the first book especially—he was putting together the puzzle pieces that he had been looking at and thinking about all his life. So he was doing sort of the same thing, it just wasn't real personal as to . . . He did ask a couple of personal questions for himself, but we had some [personal questions about Carla or me] that we eventually did ask.

GARY Yesterday you described how Don would pace outside of the room where you were typing. How and when would you transcribe the sessions? I would imagine that "ASAP" would be your response.

CARLA Immediately, forthwith, yeah.

JIM It was *ASAP*. Got the tape out of the recorder, the session was over, Carla was off doing her thing for a little while, I would do the transcribing; and when the transcribing was done, then Carla and I would take a walk and get her exercise done. She would pester me most of the way: *well, what was in that?* And for about the first 23 sessions,[4] of course, I couldn't tell her anything because Don wanted to keep this as a pure scientific experiment. He didn't want her mind polluted with what had been said.

CARLA [*laughs*] It was very frustrating.

JIM He didn't want her to know anything about what had gone on, but we kind of gave it away and made it impossible for that to continue by asking her, "Is your mind/body/spirit complex distorted towards fullness?" In other words, *you want to go eat?*

GARY That's hard to sit on.

CARLA [*laughing*] I knew something was going on. I didn't know what exactly, but it was different.

GARY So one feeling that is common to those who fall in love with this material, myself included, is a desire to ask Ra more questions. Did you receive questions from outside sources, sources outside of your own group who wanted to ask Ra questions?

JIM Very rarely. Don was good friends with Andrija Puharich. Puharich had been investigating this field for his whole life too, and when he found out we had a contact with Ra and read some of the sessions, he had a couple of questions. That was about it though.

CARLA There was a question from your . . .

JIM Oh yeah, from Paul Shockley, which was very interesting. He was asking about the Law of One and his participation in it, and that's where we discovered that Ra had built the pyramids, and the way they had built them had resulted in their physical vehicle half appearing and half not appearing—visible from the waist up and not from the waist down—as they were using the interlocking dimensions to create what they would see as a crystal, but what we saw as pyramids.[5]

GARY Another interesting tidbit I took from that particular Q&A was that Paul Shockley is asking about . . . Did he have a dream or was it a past life progression?

JIM He had gotten information from the source he was channeling, the Akashic Records, that he had partaken in something to do with the Law of One. Ra mentioned that he was one of those who had prepared the people, at that time in Egypt, for the eventual transmission of Law of One principles and the visit by Ra in person.

GARY Upon commencement of a Ra session, did you sense, perceive, or feel any shift in the room?

JIM Nothing that was particular to the Ra contact. Whenever we entered into meditation I would always feel a great sense of peace, and the enhanced vibrations that you feel when there's a group of people meditating. But it wasn't anything I could identify specifically with the Ra contact. I am not psychic, so I am sure that someone who is more sensitive would have been able to sense what was happening—special vibrations or something like that—but I didn't.

GARY Who, beyond you two and Don, attended an actual Ra session?

JIM There were three people. They were all good friends of Don and Carla and, eventually, of me. There was Sally D., Carla's ex-husband's second wife and Carla's best friend at the time. Sally attended one session. And then there was Leonard Cecil, the fellow who was learning to channel when the first session of the Ra contact happened. He came to two sessions. He was the one who went to sleep later on when Ra spoke about that it would be handy if people didn't go to sleep here[6] (aside from the instrument, of course). And then Tom Flaherty. He had been the one whose wife, Elaine, had died earlier—Carla's first two sessions with trance took place because she was helping Elaine to contact Tom in order to let him know all was well after she died.

So those were the three people who came. We thought that Andrija Puharich was coming at one point, and even George Hunt Williamson, but neither of those did actually come.

CARLA They were trying, but for one reason or another it didn't transpire.

GARY It's incredible how free of outside influence, minus the negative greeting, you three were. You didn't have other people knocking at the door or trying somehow to participate in it.

CARLA Well, we discouraged it. We didn't talk about it. We didn't let people know what we were doing.

JIM The meditation group knew about it, the Sunday night meditation group.

CARLA They knew about it in general, but they didn't know when we were going to have a meeting, and they knew that they were not invited.

GARY Were I a contemporary at the time, I would have a hard time not asking—

CARLA Well, you probably would have gotten to go to one, just to satisfy your—the way—like Tom Flaherty did. Tom was a friend since '75, so, sure, why shouldn't he check it out. Leonard [likewise] was in on the first session, so he wanted to do another one to see how it was going.

GARY Well, beyond Don's opinion and your opinion, I think Ra was the ultimate arbiter there and would have to vet somebody.

CARLA And Jim and Sally worked hard because they didn't meet each other before hand. They meditated with each other's pictures in their hands so that they would be aware of each other and comfortable with each other.[7]

JIM And Sally was the third of the three to come, and when we asked if it would be okay for her to join, Ra said it would be okay, and that this completed the group of those that were able to come to the contact (that we knew).

GARY Nobody else was eligible beyond that point—you'd exhausted the list.

So do you know why Ra virtually always began their response with "I am Ra"?

JIM To let us know who was on the line. It's a formality, but they, I believe, wanted to be very careful that they let us know who they were.

CARLA I think it was a tuning thing too—by saying, "I am Ra," they were tuning, making sure one last time that everything was tuned perfectly, and that I, as a channel, was tuned perfectly.

GARY Do you think a negative entity would find it difficult to mimic that and say, "I am Ra"? So that it turned out to be a safeguard of sorts?

CARLA I do. Very difficult. The energy in the room would have been like trying to get through a brick wall.

GARY So, we'll get more into the psychic attack—or rather, psychic greeting aspect of the work later on in the interview. And I will ask you about standing so close to the light in "The Art of Channeling" chapter.

For now I want to look at the following statement from Ra:

RA This contact is narrow band and its preconditions precise. The other-self offering its service in the negative path also is possessed of the skill of the swordsman. You deal in this contact with, shall we say, forces of great intensity poured into a vessel as delicate as a snowflake and as crystalline. The smallest of lapses may disturb the regularity of this pattern of energies which forms the channel for these transmissions. We may note for your information that our pause was due to the necessity of being quite sure that [the instrument] was safely in the proper light configuration or density before we dealt with the situation. Far better would it be to allow the shell to become unviable[8] than to allow [the instrument] to be, shall we say, misplaced. 64.5

Ra says that "preconditions [are] precise," and says, "forces of great intensity poured into a vessel as delicate as a snowflake and as crystalline," and also adds that "the smallest of lapses may disturb" the contact. This sounds like a real tightrope to walk. Did you feel under sort of a pressure during or between the sessions?

JIM We more had the bliss of the fool. We didn't feel, I didn't feel, and I don't think Don and Carla felt pressure.

CARLA I didn't feel it.

JIM We were aware that harmony was extremely necessary.

CARLA And we entered into that harmony gladly. I felt very protected and ready to work. I did not worry about it at all. We did our work and we tuned. We challenged *beforehand*, of course; I couldn't do it at the time because I was asleep. I was very lucky to have been able to do a physical, conscious, challenging at that first session because that reassured me tremendously. I knew who Ra was; I trusted that.

GARY Otherwise you may have had doubt?

CARLA Yeah. Otherwise I might have, but as it was I felt very secure, I felt very loved, and I felt that all was well—as long as I did the work I needed to do to stay honorable and pure and to do what I had agreed to do. Jim was the same. He was very ethically upright and did everything that he possibly could to enter into the harmony of the group. Don was his own beautiful incredible self and would never have been inappropriate in a million years. He was always just fine—he's quite silent, he didn't say anything, but he was right there.

GARY That sense of confidence and trust and security was also, in and of itself, a protection. Had you given into or dwelled upon the energies of panic or doubt or worry, you would have opened the door, big time, for negative intrusion into the contact.

CARLA That's right. I was not tempted to do that at all.

---

[1] In 16.52 Don notes that the session was longer than usual. Jim writes, "That was our first clue that sexual energy exchanges gave Carla more energy for the sessions so that they were longer. It took us a while longer to figure that out."

[2] Ra's instructions for walking the Circle of One:

> RA The vibrations may well be purified by a simple turning to the circle of One and the verbal vibration while doing so of the following dialogue:
>
> Question: What is the Law?
>
> Answer: The Law is One.
>
> Question: Why are we here?
>
> Answer: We seek the Law of One.
>
> Question: Why do we seek Ra?
>
> Answer: Ra is an humble messenger of the Law of One.
>
> Both together: Rejoice then and purify this place in the Law of One. Let no thought-form enter the circle we have walked about this instrument, for the Law is One. 2.6

[3] A couple of examples of Don getting Jim or Carla's questions "out of the way":

> QUESTIONER The instrument would like to ask a couple of questions of you. I'll get them out of the way first. The instrument would like to know why she smells the incense at various times during the day in various places? 22.1
>
> QUESTIONER I have three questions that the instrument asked me to ask that I'll get out of the way first. She wants to know if the preparation for her hospital experience could be improved for the next experience. 77.6

[4] That would be for about the first four weeks that Carla was not informed of what Ra said.

5
For more information about Paul Shockley's experience and questions, see 27.1–2.

About Jim's statement regarding Ra seeing crystals of (what to human eyes would be) pyramids, see 27.1–2 and:

> RA We attempted to aid [two of Earth's ancient cultures] in technical ways having to do with the healing of mind/body/spirit complex distortions through the use of the crystal, appropriate to the distortion, placed within a certain appropriate series of ratios of time/space material. Thus were the pyramids created. 2.2

It's not entirely clear in Ra's replies that the pyramids were, to their perception, crystals. This assertion may be entirely true but in the absence of definitive testimony from Ra, it is likely conjecture on Jim's part.

6
See 22.29:

> RA I am Ra. The instrument is well. It is somewhat less easy to maintain clear contact during a time when some or one of the entities in the circle of working is or are not fully conscious. We request that entities in the circle be aware that their energy is helpful for increasing the vitality of this contact. We thank you for being conscientious in the asking. 22.29

7
See 53.2:

> QUESTIONER Thank you. I would like to know if [name] may attend one of these sessions in the very near future?

> RA I am Ra. The mind/body/spirit complex, [name], belongs with this group in the spirit and is welcome. You may request that special meditative periods be set aside until the entity sits with this working. We might suggest that a photograph of the one known as James Allen be sent to this entity with his writing upon it indicating love and light. This held while meditating will bring the entity into peaceful harmony with each of you so that there be no extraneous waste of energy while greetings are exchanged between two entities, both of whom have a distortion towards solitude and shyness, as you would call it. The same might be done with a photograph of the entity, [name], for the one known as James Allen. 53.2

8
An unviable physical shell might otherwise be called "death" in our culture.

CHAPTER 7

Your Dynamics

GARY Time to dig into some meatier aspects of the Ra contact. In discussing the qualities of love, wisdom, and power, Ra says of you three:

> **RA** In this particular group . . . each entity manifests one of these qualities in a manner which approaches the archetype. 75.39

Could you elaborate on that?

JIM Well, the three qualities were love, wisdom and power. Those correspond to the 4th, 5th and 6th densities. So beyond the 3rd density, everybody will be going through those densities, but while we're here, each of us can be working on all of those things. It seemed to turn out that—I don't know if it was by chance or pre-incarnative design—our group contained people that had certain propensities that went in a certain direction.

Don, of course, was extremely wise; his years of experience and his intelligence and his intuition were invaluable in being able to formulate the questions that he started the session with, to be able to listen to what Ra had to say, and to respond extremely intelligently.

Carla, with her open heart, was so willing and able to give love that it was just very obvious what quality she embodied—it was a very nurturing type of feeling and vibration that from came her.

And I'm supposedly the one that had the power, which I'm not really sure about. [*laughs*] I like working with big muscles, that's for sure, and I'm certainly not as wise as Don was, and I'm working on opening my heart like Carla was able to do.

So I think what I was able to do, mostly, was provide energy as a battery for the contact. While the contact was ongoing I was doing a certain type of visualization. I visualized pouring light through each of Carla's energy centers to help her and to help energy from the Ra contact come through.

CARLA Yes, I think that there was power too, just the way that you are. There's power in the sturdiness and the steadiness of your being, and you are very strong; you have a very strong will and your discipline is incredible. So all of those things—

JIM Well thank you. [*laughing*] And also extremely humble.

CARLA Yes, thanks for what you said about me. [*laughing*] I just love you so much!

But I think Ra was spot on, as usual. We have a picture* that we took to mock the completeness of that truth, because we knew that we might have some love, power, and wisdom in our group, but we didn't have it all, for sure, so we were laughing at ourselves. Let's see. Don with his wisdom—he had an old army coat and he carried a rifle (for some reason, he thought that was wise), and I put on a leotard and some black high heels—

JIM And a queen's crown.

CARLA Yeah, and carried a little heart balloon. And then, what did you do?

JIM I had on my baseball uniform from high school, and we all had on noses and glasses—

CARLA Noses and glasses that looked like Groucho Marx.

JIM Somebody asked for a picture of us at one point. "Could we have a picture of you?" So we took that picture and sent it to them. We have it in our living room now.

CARLA It's one of my favorite pictures of us.

---

* See Photo Gallery, p. 534.

GARY That's helped to form part of my own policy for this work. In my own role serving as a face for L/L Research, responding to seekers who write L/L Research about this material, there's naturally a certain gravity they assign to this work—a certain seriousness. They elevate it. And naturally so. It's a profound piece of work. At the same time I try to bring some levity to it, in the spirit of that picture, to encourage people to lighten up, because it could be taken too seriously.

CARLA Yes, and I'm glad you do that.

JIM Ra described humor as a sense of proportion (57.1), so I think humor is extremely valuable on the spiritual journey because it's easy to get out of balance.

GARY Yeah, and I've always understood that proportion to mean proportion in terms of comparing whatever happens in this material realm against the backdrop of infinity. However big you think this crisis is in your life, against the infinite universe it's nothing, so stand back and see that proportion—

CARLA I think you're right.

GARY And laughing helps to scale it down—suddenly it's not so traumatic, it's not so dramatic, it's not so life threatening, per se.

This may be more or less a repeat of a previous question, but with a slightly different focus on a slightly different nuance. Ra goes on to say about each of your respective archetypal manifestations of love, wisdom, and power, that "visualization [of these archetypal energies] may be **personalized** and much love and support within the group generated."

Is Ra saying that each of you were so close or pure in these fundamental qualities that to visualize one of you three would be akin to visualizing a face of the archetype?

JIM Well, yeah, sort of, but more or less it would be visualizing that person and how that quality, say for Carla, how the love manifested. If Don and I meditated upon Carla, and upon love, then we would have a greater sense of both who Carla was and what love was. If Carla and I meditated on Don and wisdom, we would do the same thing for knowing more about Don and more about wisdom.

CARLA We were working our way at it, we didn't have it down cold or anything, but we were trying.

GARY Jim, you already began to describe what you did—how you performed the service of being what Ra called "the battery."[1] Could you repeat some of that? I remember asking you that question for the first time, during the weekly radio program, and I thought there was a little more to it, specifically, in terms of what you did.

JIM Well, I was meditating as the session was going on, and the tape recorder only required very infrequent use, so most of the time I could meditate and visualize Carla lying on the bed as she was. And then from the top down, from the violet, through the indigo and blue and green and yellow and so forth, I would see energy, a white light, coming in through her crown and going down all the way through the base chakra and her feet and then out. So I just tried to clear the channel and provide more energy for the Ra energies to come through, to just help them to come through.

GARY And once you'd finished this routine you repeated . . .

JIM Yes, it was continuous.

CARLA At the end of a session he would be sweating. It was really hard on him.

GARY I first learned that just a few weeks ago and it was surprising to me because I had always presumed that your power source was a passive one—just your presence, which I have perceived on my own when interacting with you. You definitely have power emanating, you might say, but it was surprising to me also that you shared that power in an active way.

JIM Right. I think that each of our presences helped, and the presence of anybody who was positively oriented and intended would help, but to also take that vibration that you've got and to consciously use it accentuates it, amplifies it, and makes it more effective.

GARY So prior to the contact with Ra, had you ever had the conscious sense that you possessed or channeled an abundance of power and that this power could be put to service to others?

JIM Only in the physical sense. When I was attending the Adventure Trail Survival School in Colorado, learning brain self-control, part of the work we did there was to help rebuild a section of a mountain road which began at the parking area, 1,000 feet below where Lingo's cabin was. Every now and then he would drive his Jeep up from the parking area, so we needed to get stones put into the ruts where the rain had washed out the road in various places. So we gathered stones, threw them down the hill, placed them, and put dirt over them to repair the road. I was just having a good time throwing stones down, and everybody was amazed how many stones I threw down and complimented me on my work, and I thought, "What? I'm just playing." [*laughs*]

CARLA And he did the same thing when he was cutting tobacco. This one farmer that employed him had never seen anybody that could cut more tobacco. He's very, very quick—very accurate and precise.

GARY So prior to Ra, nobody had called you a *battery*?

JIM & CARLA No. [*laughing*]

JIM When I lived in central Kentucky on the land, I did cut tobacco for various neighbors who were farmers, and they called me "work brickle." That's kind of an odd term. *Brickle* is not actually a word, but in the country it means *tough*—you're tough, you can do the work. So if you're a work brickle, you're a good worker.

CARLA It wasn't too good when he got to the part of tobacco harvest where he had to help hang it, because he was a little guy—being what, 5'8"†?—and not very heavy, and so he had to get all the way up to the top of the barn—

JIM Nobody else wanted to go up to the top of the barn.

CARLA —where everything came up and smelled and it was very intense; tobacco is very strong.

JIM All of it is done by hand. Tobacco is a physically intensive labor. It's a killer. It's always harvested in August and September when it's in the '90s for one thing, and then once you get into a barn and you're hanging it, all the heat, as you know, goes up, so it's even hotter.

GARY So you, who enjoys physical labor—did you find that enjoyable?

JIM Yeah, I enjoyed cutting tobacco. Because it was rhythmic, and I like doing rhythmic things. It was a dance.

CARLA He had a need, for just about everything, he would create a dance.

---

† It seems that Carla so admired Jim that she granted him an extra inch or two. See endnote #3 in Chapter 3 for actual height.

He would just do this dance. It was fun for him—rhythmic. He's just an athlete. Whatever he did, he did it beautifully.

JIM Thank you.

CARLA You're welcome. But it's true.

GARY So the next question I had on the docket was to ask about sexual energy transfer as being vital to supporting and energizing the instrument. You guys touched on that—I think you covered that base pretty well. Is there anything that might be missing?

JIM Well, like I said, we *discovered* that when we finally figured out that there was a correlation between having sexual relations the night before and the length of the session. Then we worked on it, and later on Ra talked about how any sexual energy transfer involves, for the male, transferring what the male has in abundance, and that's physical energy.[2] The female transfers what she has in abundance, which is mental and spiritual energy. I think that the male gets the better of the deal.

So Carla, having a physical vehicle that was somewhat challenged all through her life with medical problems, very much needed, appreciated, and benefitted from a physical energy transfer, which I had to offer, and apparently I had a fair amount of physical energy to transfer. I, on the other hand, certainly appreciated the mental and spiritual energy. I could feel—and always do to this day—the inspiration from an exchange with Carla. Afterwards, I'm buzzing. [*laughs*] The traditional image of the male after sexual intercourse is that he goes off to sleep—not with Carla. *Hmmmm. Let's see, what shall I think about now? [laughter]*

CARLA Well, you know, there wasn't a *wink, wink, nudge, nudge* feeling to it. We were so grateful to have it, and we invested ourselves in it to do the most beautiful job we could of expressing love to each other. And it was a dance too.

GARY As it helped the contact, the sexual energy transfer probably took on a whole new dimension.

CARLA Yes, we always ended by saying, "Thank you, Lord."

JIM It became a sacred activity, and is to this day. Perhaps it is part of what Ra called "high sexual magic," where you can create changes in consciousness by your design of the magical ritual, which in this case is a sexual energy exchange.

GARY And key to that is the open green-ray chakra . . .

CARLA Opening the heart and being pure about it.

JIM Yeah, both people have to be at the green-ray level in order for the transfer to take place.

GARY Quick side question about that: Ra says somewhere that if the act is consciously dedicated to the Creator afterwards—does that also involve *both* entities having to consciously dedicate it?

JIM That accentuates and amplifies the exchange, and also if both have an orgasm it doubles the transfer—fine little details we discovered as time went on and as Ra gave us more information about it too.

GARY Carla, you described that Don and Jim each fit into your life like puzzle pieces. Jim was a loner, wasn't codependent, and didn't have a great need for being with you all of the time. Don, to the contrary, wanted to be with you as much as he could and was celibate, whereas Jim preferred and enjoyed sex. Was that basically how they fit into your life like puzzle pieces?

CARLA Well, that was the beginning of it, certainly—the nuts and bolts, the bones of it, the skeleton of it—but you have to remember the love involved. I was always blown away by the quality and depth of devotion that they both offered me. Anything that I wanted, if they could figure out a way to do it, it was *let's help Carla out*, it wasn't a matter of making fun of me half the time the way a lot of guys do about their women—*oh, the little woman*—you know. No, none of that. There was a value, a respect and honor that each of us was just moved to give each other that was absolutely beautiful.

The physical logic of it is just what you said, that Jim—we got together for meals. A lot of time Jim fixed the meals, otherwise we would go out to the place that Don laughingly called "Eats." He liked little places that were mom-and-pop with blue-plate specials where things were fairly inexpensive. He liked comfort food, and so we would often go to the same place—the Twig and Leaf up at the corner when we were living in that area. And there was a place out near Watterson Trail; I don't remember the name of it . . .

JIM Lindy's!

CARLA Lindy's—and that was the same kind of place. I knew ahead of time what I was going to get because I had memorized the menu—it wasn't that big. I was always hoping we'd go to someplace different—you know how I am about that. And Don and Jim just didn't care, you know, so *let's eat*. So it was always together for meals, and we would watch certain TV things together—we loved *Magnum* and we loved *M*A*S*H*, and . . .

JIM And *The Rockford Files!*

CARLA And *The Rockford Files*. But for the most part Jim spent a lot of time by himself. Don and I were buddies, and I needed to be in the same room with him. It didn't matter—Don didn't want me to talk to him. He would lie for hours on this long couch that we had when he was alive, and he would draw in the air, or write. I was never sure what he was doing, and he never would tell me. But he would just spend a lot of time doing that, and I would be reading or doing stitchery—I loved to do stitchery at the time.

JIM It had to be a pre-incarnative choice, because we didn't have to work at this. This just came naturally.

CARLA It just fell into place.

JIM And I think at one point in the sessions, Ra mentioned that we had previously worked together in other efforts to be of service in other lifetimes,[3] so I think it was cultivated there and brought to fruition here.

CARLA Didn't I tell you, in answer to another question in this series, about Shockley's reading of Don and Jim and me in a previous lifetime?

GARY Not in this interview, you haven't, no.

CARLA Okay, very quickly: It was in the Old West, it was in the Great Plains, and Don and Jim were brothers. I believe I was Jim's child, and Don, as the brother, was very close also to this child. Well, the mother died, so the two men were left to raise this sickly baby—I was a little boy, and I never reached past the age of about five. They were absolutely devoted to taking care of me, but it was very difficult to do, of course, because we were in the Old West. There was little help available, and they had to work for a living cultivating the land. But they took care of me very well. That was a choice of lifetimes in order to set us up for being able to take care of me when I was ill for extended periods of time in this incarnation, which most people just cannot do, and neither of them had any problems whatsoever.

JIM It was déjà vu all over again.

CARLA [*laughing*] So that was a very interesting reading and it felt right.

GARY About your work, Ra mentions:

> RA Each present sacrificed much for no tangible result. Each may search its heart for the type of sacrifice, knowing that the material sacrifices are the least; the intensive commitment to blending into an harmonious group at the apex of sacrifice. 37.3

And then again in a later session:

> RA We thank you for we know what you sacrifice in order to do that which you as a group wish to do. 69.5

So my first question is, what were these sacrifices?

CARLA Well, Don, who didn't want to be responsible for anybody, was taking care of and paying the bills for two other people. That was a big sacrifice for him—huge.

I sacrificed my—there were so many things that I had done to take the high road. I wouldn't break my promise and quit my first husband, Jim D. When he asked me for a divorce, I thought that was okay. Up to that point I had fulfilled all his requests, even though they were ridiculous, and gave up a highly wonderful job that I was really looking forward to up in Vancouver, along with a romance. It was the first romance I'd ever had with a guy that was so in love with me that he would blush beet-red head to toe!

JIM That was your red-haired Scotsman in Vancouver, right?

CARLA That was the Scotsman in Vancouver, and he wanted me to live with him. He said, "I'll pay your bills, I don't want anything from you, I just want to be with you." So I had this $13,000-a-year job in which I was—if I could hold the job for six months, they would double it. And this amount was huge. I was making like $4,000 a year at that time.

JIM In the '60s, that was a lot of money.

CARLA And I had 13 people under me that were librarians, and I was 25 years old.[‡] So it was a wonderful job, it was a wonderful romance, and D. said, "You need to go home and be with your people."

"Noooooo." [*laughs*]

JIM But you always wanted six children too, so you gave up children and a family.

CARLA I always wanted six children, yep. I gave up sex. I wanted to have sex with Don so bad, but it just didn't happen. I gave up marriage. I gave up everything except being and doing what Don needed at the time and doing my very best to take care of him because he desperately needed to be taken care of. He was all alone, and he didn't have a mother anymore. He didn't have a home. He didn't have anything. And when I came into his life he was so incredibly appreciative, and he went from not wanting me to have anything to do with him (except be at home when he decided to come home), to wanting me to be in the same room with him at all times (to the point of not even letting me work in the office when he was in the living room).

I was used to working, but he developed such an incredible devotion. He would call me as soon as he got to the airport, leaving to go to work. He would call me when he got to the motel. He would call me before he left on his flight. He would call me every time he hit the ground. He would call me when he got to the motel. He would call about once an hour just to check in, [*laughs*] and at the end of the day he would just call to say goodnight, and he'd just hang on the line and wouldn't say anything. And I wouldn't say anything. And we'd just listen to each other breathe. It was very, very romantic, and very non-expressed. It was all in here. [*Carla balls up a fist and brings it toward her heart.*]

So I accepted that my gift was going to be from him—it was always going to be that. It was not going to be home, family—things that I had desperately wanted. I didn't think of it as a sacrifice at the time, but when you think back on it, of course it's like an initiation. I had everything stripped away from me, and most women would probably not have stuck under those circumstances. The fact that he wouldn't marry me after he asked me, the fact that he didn't want to make love, the fact that he didn't want to buy a house and settle down—none of that. At some point, I think most women would have moved on. Not me. I adored that man

---

[‡] Carla was probably closer to 23 or 24.

and whatever he needed, I was there to try to give him.

GARY And that he kept you from working while he was . . .

CARLA Oh, yeah. That was another—that was such a bummer. He would talk about, "Well, if you were working, we could buy a house with two incomes." And I said okay, and I'd go out and get this fantastic job.

I got half a dozen of them before I wised up to the fact that he would never let me work. He wanted me home when he was home, and working would cut into that.

GARY You have a genetic need to work, so to override that programming must have been difficult.

CARLA It was so frustrating, yes. But, I figured ways around it to get my needs met, and I focused on meeting his. So I think that's what I gave up. And Jim gave up a loner's life—his own cabin that he'd built from scratch, every board, everything about it.

JIM Up until the Ra contact, that was the high point of my life—I was 6½ years alone on the land.

CARLA And he loved it. He planned on dying there. And then he decided, *well, I need to be of service, and I'm not being of service here, so* . . . Here he came and we formed L and L Research out of that energy between the three of us—we wanted to be of service.

GARY Love and light goes where it's needed.

CARLA So we were working for Don, and as far as we're concerned, we're still working for Don.

GARY In that same quote (37.3) Ra says that the material sacrifices are the least, and that "the intensive commitment to blending into an harmonious group [is] at the apex of sacrifice."

Do you think that such a statement applied only to your group, or do you think that it is a universal property of the human experience—that the toughest and greatest sacrifice is simply learning how to love, how to relate to, how to sacrifice for, and how to operate harmoniously with others?

JIM Yes.

CARLA Definitely. Because there are so many ways that you can fool yourself and say that you are being of service to somebody else, but you're actually trying to control them in one way or another—you know better than them. And, you know, there are so many ways that you can actually try to enslave another human being, and it's all under the—you feel that you're explaining it by saying that you're being of service this way, but you have to get through all of that, be straight with yourself, and realize that you have to love people exactly as they are. Anything that you're doing that has to do with bending them to your will is wrong. No matter how right you think you are, you're incorrect in trying to get somebody else to do what you think is right. You have to help people be who they are.

Loving people as they are continues to be a challenge every day, because you learn a little something new every day and a lot of times it's hard, but it's something that needs to be done.

JIM Uh huh. What she said. [*laughter*]

GARY In 4.22, Ra said:

> RA Further, this instrument's activities must be monitored to pre-vent overactivity, [because acting as the instrument for a Ra session] is equivalent to a strenuous working on the physical level. 4.22

And in 60.4, Ra said of the trance channeling that:

> RA . . . [it] is the equivalent [for] this instrument of many, many hours of harsh physical labor. 60.4

So, as we discussed yesterday, Carla, you woke up feeling tired. What impact did the Ra contact have on your energy levels overall?

CARLA Oh, wiped them out. But I kept getting recharged.

GARY So did you feel tired, day in and day out?

CARLA Pretty much, yeah. But it was a matter of finding so many ways to be enlivened, joyful, and happy—just to enjoy the way the three of us worked together. It was so much fun being with these two people.

JIM Ra said that when she was in trance, she was with them, basically, and that means that she was at a 6th density level which is very filled with light, and when she had to come back to this heavy, dense chemical illusion, it was wearying. And there was a wearying factor that came with the con-tact, and she would bear the brunt of it. Don and I would bear about 10–15% of the weariness that she felt, and this was cumulative, and it would continue for the rest of our lives. But, if we experimented with our physical energy, we would discover that it's still there—even though we're feeling weary, we still have physical energy.[4]

CARLA It's a matter of discipline. Not letting that exhaustion be—all of it going into what is making you happy, what is blessing you. There are so many blessings that you get every day, especially doing work like we were doing, we are doing—blessings abound. And counting them enlarges and enlivens you, and you get your energy back.[5]

GARY I had that quote from Ra where they talk about how it seems like you're experiencing a physical energy loss or deficit, but if you look more closely, or you work with it more, you can differentiate.[6]

So the weariness you're describing—would you describe it as a psychological weariness? A spiritual weariness?

JIM That's a good question. It feels physical. It feels very real in this density, but your physical energy is still there, so I don't know. I guess it must be something that's metaphysical which is translatable to the 3rd density, and the way that it expresses itself is you just feel tired. That's just my guess, I don't know.

CARLA When you're used to 6th density wiring, and you come back into the 3rd density wiring, it's so different, and I was always having to work with that because it bummed me out. So many things about this 3rd density just distressed me tremendously.

GARY Psychologically? Or . . .

CARLA Psychologically, yeah. Look at the evening news. Look at the way people think, the way people treat each other, the way people cheat and lie and justify these things. It's just difficult.

GARY It's surprising for me to hear you say that you are distressed by this Earth world, because it seems you are naturally of a disposition that accepts the darkness and the shadow side of the world.

CARLA I've learned to do that but it just—making that real has taken decades of my life.

GARY You've described yourself as waking up each morning feeling like you're at a party, and your job is to determine the best costume.

CARLA Yeah, that's me. [*laughing*]

GARY It's not that you're unaware of the ills of the world, just that you've made peace with it and determined that you're going to love it, no less, and shine, no less.

CARLA Right.

GARY So we touched on this question also. You lost two or three pounds per session, and then you talked yesterday about how you urinated a lot of that out. So how quickly did that weight dissipate? Say, you went into a session at 85 pounds and then after the session was over, were you 82 pounds?

CARLA Yes, it was that fast. I think it was just the weight of what I lost in terms of urine. That was just a heavy—liquid is heavy. I don't know how much it is per pound, but . . .

JIM A gallon is 7.5 pounds.

CARLA I peed it out. I lost it. It's what was water weight, and the odd thing was simply that I didn't gain it back. I had to work to gain it.[7]

GARY It may have been burnt up in the same way it would be burnt up during exercise: that energy stored is metabolized, or fat is metabolized and is converted into energy, and then you're no longer carrying that physical matter in your body.

So in between sessions, then, you worked really hard to eat and would you incrementally rebuild that weight?

CARLA Yes, it was very strange because I love to eat and I got to the point where I didn't want any more food because I was scarfing it down in such huge quantities. Remember?

JIM Yes.

CARLA I would say I couldn't eat any more and Don would say, "Eat, eat." [*laughs*]

GARY Were I in your shoes, I would be a frequent patron of the buffet.

So during the Ra contact you were in constant pain. The act of your body lying completely motionless for an hour and a half, or longer, during your Ra session caused you to wake in, as you said, "a world of hurt." How did you cope with this?

CARLA Well, you deal with what you've got to deal with. I don't know anything more to say. There wasn't any trick to it.

JIM One foot in front of the other.

CARLA It just hurt. And a lot of times by the end of the day, I'd feel better. Persevere is the secret. Keep at it and keep counting your blessings. And, you know, surf. I learned to surf on top of energy rather than using it.

GARY What do you mean by "surf on top of energy"?

CARLA It's hard to describe. I wouldn't use up my feelings or have any extra concern or get heavy about things that were happening, I would just surf through them and let it all just be and surf on top of that, and it was a joy to learn to do that, and it was definitely an energy-saving device that I use a lot all of the time now.

GARY In the first question of Session 44, Ra said:

> RA We suggest this instrument release the power of judgment to the support group whose interests are balanced far more than this instrument's. Allow decisions to be made without expectation or attachment to the outcome.
>
> Our hopes, may we say, for long-term contact through this instrument depend upon its maturing ability to be of service to other-selves by accepting their help and thus remaining a viable instrument. 44.1

And connected to that one, in 60.2:

> QUESTIONER It is my opinion that the best way for the instrument to improve her condition is through periods of meditation followed by periods of contemplation with respect to the condition and its improvement. Could you tell me if I am correct and expand on my thinking?
>
> RA I am Ra. Meditation and contemplation are never untoward activities. However, this activity will in all probability, in our opinion, not significantly alter the predispositions of this instrument which cause the fundamental distortions **which we, as well as you, have found disconcerting**. 60.2

[*Carla laughs*]

GARY This is a hilarious statement to me, by the way.

Ra expressed multiple times that your untarnished, pure, overriding dedication to the Creator was a key to enabling the Ra contact. Yet, they also describe on multiple occasions your lack of wisdom with regard to serving as an instrument. Can you and Jim speak to this point?

CARLA If you'll look, for instance, at the way I used to cook: I used to cook all day, once a week, and then have everybody eat what I cooked, and it was my joy. But it was too much and everyone would say, "Carla, we only need half of what you're cooking." I wanted to do the bread, I wanted to make the homemade pie, I wanted to do the extra vegetable and an extra salad, and have some fruit cut up. And I just wanted to have a feast, every single meal. It wasn't necessary but I loved to do it.

Whatever was happening, I would look for ways to help, and a lot of times other people could help too. You know, it was, *I'll do this!*

You've seen me, you've seen me through the years, you know what I'm talking about.

JIM She was very pure in her desire to be of service, and occasionally she would go overboard because that's the way the open heart tends to go. If it's balanced by wisdom then perhaps there's not so much food there, and what is needed is cooked, and there isn't so much effort expended.

When I came to the Ra contact she was willing to give all the energy she had, every time, which might not be a good idea if you want to prolong the number of sessions you have. So that's where Don and I came in handy—we were trying to keep the overview so that we could have more sessions and not overuse Carla, which we did in the beginning. Then we learned through trial and error not to do that.[8]

GARY So would you say wisdom provides a sort of breaking mechanism, or a "no" function, or a restraint to love's *I need to give, I want to give, I'm going to give, I'm running out the front door* sort of attitude?

CARLA [*laughs*] Yeah, that's about right. Never is it quite that simple but—

JIM Yes, basically. It's a more balanced way of giving; it's a wiser way of giving. It allows you to give over a longer period of time instead of burning out quickly.

GARY Elsewhere in the Ra contact it's mentioned that Carla needed to be careful how she dedicated herself to having a session because even if a session didn't happen, then she would be as spent energetically as if the session did happen.[9]

JIM Right.

GARY So what was the mechanism there?

CARLA Well, I reserved the energy. I mean I wouldn't know that I did that, but I put the energy aside in my inner self. I'd think about doing the contact; I wanted to do the contact, and I'd get ready to do the contact without listening to the guys telling me, "No, you're not going to do the contact this time."

And unfortunately, in not listening to them, in not being wise enough to do so, I was expending that energy. It was not available for other uses because it was reserved. You know, you cook something and then you put it aside to use later. You don't have it until you get it back out of the fridge and you use it for the reason you fixed it.

GARY Good analogy. I've noticed in my own patterns I have to be careful how I think about doing things because when I *think* of a task that needs doing, I become committed to that task. Then I think of another and another task and there's a sense of weight that happens and energy loss. So I have to pull back when I think about things that need to be accomplished so as to not unwisely drain my energy.

CARLA Jim was just saying the same thing to me: he needed not to be so eager to do what he saw to do that he dropped the other thing that he was already doing in order to do something else that really wasn't appropriate to do it then, but when he saw it, it was like, "Oh, I've got to do that." You don't really—you just have to put it on a list to do when it's convenient or appropriate. So I think that's true of anybody—you have to be more careful about how you push your time and your energy.

KEN A quick question about love and wisdom: Does Ra say that it doesn't always necessitate a movement from love to wisdom or a movement from wisdom to love, but that they're one and the same? Does that happen somewhere or am I thinking of something else?[10]

CARLA Well, then there's also power—the appropriate use, the right use of good power. But I think some people come here to learn how to open their heart more, whereas other people might come here and their lesson for themselves would be more how to put a little wisdom in that heart.

And it's not that they're not two aspects of the same love and light, it's that there are two ways that you express yourself that are fundamentally different enough that there are whole densities involved in learning precisely how to use that beautiful energy.

GARY In 94.7 Ra is responding to Don's question about why he's so tired:

> RA The contact which you now experience costs a certain amount of the energy which each of the group brought into manifestation in the present incarnation. **Although the brunt of this cost falls upon the instrument, it is caparisoned by pre-incarnative design with the light and gladsome armor of faith and will to a far more conscious extent than most mind/body/spirit complexes are able to enjoy without much training and initiation.** 94.7

Before finishing that quote from Ra, I'd like to focus on the latter half of what was just read. The word *caparisoned* is defined as "outfitted with an ornamental covering or rich clothing."

So to re-read their statement with the definition of "caparisoned" included:

> RA Although the brunt of this cost falls upon the instrument, it is [outfitted with an ornamental covering of rich clothing] by pre-incarnative design with the light and gladsome armor of faith and will to a far more conscious extent than most mind/body/spirit complexes are able to enjoy without much training and initiation. 94.7

Is Ra saying that, though you lacked training and initiation, the strength of will and faith with which you furnished yourself prior to incarnation enabled you to carry and bear this heavy load?

[*Carla agrees*]

JIM "Because her heart was pure, she had the strength of ten," is an old saying that I think applies here.

GARY In 30.17, Ra said:

> RA As we scan the instrument we find anomalies of the magnetic field which are distorted towards our abilities to find narrow-band channel into this instrument's mind/body/spirit complex. 30.17

Do you feel, Carla, that there was a pre-incarnational design for the Ra contact? That is, do you feel that you three made agreements before incarnating that would help guide you to this work, and that you constructed the template of your personality to be especially suited for the success of this project?

CARLA Precisely so. I do think that we made agreements with each other. I think that, very specifically, we knew that we were on a mission together in this incarnation, and we were looking forward to blending our energies with each other. That was before we ever got born, you know.

GARY That quote that I just read speaks to that in a very specific sense. We've already been discussing how your, Jim's, and Don's *dynamics* worked together to enable and to allow the Ra contact to happen, but that quote indicates that even the wiring of your physical body was designed to serve as an instrument for the Ra contact.

CARLA I think so. I think that all these things that seem so awkward and useless in earthly terms: my frailness, my sensitivity in so many ways almost to the point of ridiculousness—I'm so sensitive. I'm allergic to everything that the Earth has to—I'm allergic to Earth, one doctor told me. All these things made it possible for me to work with Ra's 6th density wiring, but when you try to live in 3rd density with 6th density wiring you become frail, because it just takes more than you've got. You don't have the proper wiring. You're not vulgar enough. I guess that's what it is. [*laughing*]

I don't mean that I think I'm a miss goody two-shoes or anything like that, I don't think that at all, but I do think that I tend to take the high road to the exclusion of anything else. Things like that—the wiring has to do with ethics and uprightness and living an honorable life, that kind of thing, where you're really basically living in another density in your head, and this world just wags on the way it does. It's a little bit different than that.

GARY And were this world a more peace-filled place, and a more loving place, the difference between the two . . .

CARLA It would be a lot easier, yeah.

JIM Then we probably wouldn't be here.

CARLA Yeah, you go where you're needed. No sense in—what is it Shakespeare said?—"kicking against the pricks," and there are always pricks. [*laughter*] Go look it up. I'm not being crude, nor was Shake-speare.[11]

GARY Ra continually recommended you to operate in harmony, love, praise and thanksgiving, and commended you for doing just that:

> RA Those salient items for the support group are praise and thanksgiving in harmony. **These the group has accomplished with such a degree of acceptability** that we cavil not at the harmony of the group. 103.8

And there are multiple other places where they convey the same sentiment.

CARLA *Cavil* [*pronounces it differently than Gary*] is the word that means argue or criticize.[§]

GARY Side note to readers: Carla has long been an English mentor for me, helping me to pronounce, spell, or *use* the English language.

CARLA [*laughs*] I could be wrong at any time; sometimes I'm in the wrong country.

GARY How would you describe your harmony? You've touched on that. Is there anything more that you could say about your harmony and experience?

JIM You just like being with the people, you miss them when you're not, and it just feels right. It doesn't seem to take a lot of effort.

GARY Ra seemed to indicate that your harmony as a group was somewhat exceptional. How did you succeed in that regard where other groups, presumably, aren't able to hold that level of harmony?

CARLA It's love. It's just an excess of love. Other groups, I'm sure with one guy and two women, or one woman and two men, would fall apart because of jealousy at one point or another, because people go in this world two by two and the other one gets left out, but nobody was left out in our group. Everybody had their place, and we all loved each other adequately and satisfied each other's needs completely.

---

§ Carla's definition applies, but perhaps more precisely, *cavil* is defined as "to raise trivial and frivolous objection" by *Merriam-Webster,* and to "make petty or unnecessary objections" by Google. Let's hope that this footnote does not cavil at Carla's response.

JIM And each of us was pretty well determined in our own being before we'd met each other that we wanted to be of service: that was the foremost goal in our minds. We ran into others that wanted to do the same thing, and *oooh, hey, all right.*

CARLA It felt so good. There are not a lot of people in this world that have that purity of desire.

JIM Having a principle that is more than yourself is very valuable.

CARLA And I'm talking to you, because when I met you, Gary, I thought, "Wow, okay, you may be young, you may need a little bit of buffing up around the edges . . . "

GARY More than a little . . .

CARLA But you're exceptional and you have always been so.

GARY Thank you.

CARLA And when I met you I felt the same way, Ken.

KEN Thank you.

GARY In 99.11, Ra says:

> **RA** We note the relative discomfort of this group at this space/time and offer those previous statements made by Ra as possible aids to the regaining of the extraordinary harmony which this group has the capability of experiencing in a stable manner.

(Apparently Ra referred to themselves in the third person sometimes.) They go on to say:

> We encourage the conscious strengthening of those invisible ribbands which fly from the wrists of those who go forward to seek what you may call the Grail. 99.11

What does that final statement mean to you about strengthening the ribbands in the seeking of the Grail?

JIM The Knights of the Round Table in Camelot had ribbands** (in the colors of their lady, or their house—but usually the lady) that they wore in order to uphold her honor.

** What today we might call a *sash.*

CARLA Their lady was the height of honor—that was one of the rules of the romantic knight thing, the knight errant. He would go looking for the goal of all those who seek truth, which is the grail of spirit, the grail that is Jesus' holy cup that you use at holy communion. It was a reference to all those energies.

In other words: lift up and look up; get a little bit purer than you are right now.

GARY Tune your sense of honor and your sense of being on a quest . . .

CARLA We had problems when we were in Georgia because Don was so incredibly unhappy and didn't want to do anything. Whatever it was we had an idea to do—go to a movie, go out to eat, the simplest things, go for a walk—Don didn't want to do that. He wanted to hide in and be where he [was], but he hated where he was, and he kept saying, "This is our last month here, we just can't stay here, we've got to go someplace else."

And every place that he would find, he didn't like. Every place I would find, he said no to, so we all got more and more frustrated, and it wasn't really anybody's fault. It was a bad situation and it seemed to get worse. Don was absolutely positive that it was getting worse every day, and he was very strong in his belief system, so it was difficult for us . . .

JIM Yes, that was the beginning of his problems back then, and a lot of things were contributing to it.

CARLA So I think Ra was referring to all of that in a gentle way.

GARY So it was the group as a whole, but it was especially pertinent to Don?

CARLA Well, and to us too, because we'd finally go, "Oh for crying out loud, we'll just go out and eat—we'll go to a movie." We left him home. It was not right, but the idea of having yet another time at home—just constantly . . . We really needed and felt that it was a good idea to have some variety, and it was never the right thing as far as Don was concerned, so it was frustrating.

Did we go? Did we stay? We had a lot of problems trying to figure that out. Every time we wanted to do something little, like go out and eat, it got blown up to be a big thing. It had never done that before. We weren't used to it being so difficult just to live from day to day, so we were not that great either.

We were like, "Well, come on"—not very understanding sometimes. Not that we criticized—we didn't go that far, but we were just less *completely* in tune with each other than we had always been before.

GARY Then Ra was suggesting that you fine tune . . .

CARLA Yes and he was right, he was absolutely right. And we tried, we tried our very best.

GARY We'll talk again about the practice of tuning in "The Art of Channeling" chapter. For now, and as it pertains to the Ra contact, how important was both your individual and group tuning in maintaining a contact with Ra and guarding against negative encroachment on the purity of the contact?

CARLA It's always very important. It's never less than completely important.

GARY Doing the research for this interview project, it really was hammered home to me just how vital it is, in a way that wasn't apparent to me before.

CARLA That's good.

GARY And it speaks not to just three people maintaining contact with a 6th density source, but as a way of life.

CARLA Right.

GARY In 69.17, Ra says:

> **RA** Secondly, that which we and you do in workings such as this carries a magical charge, if you would use this much misunderstood term. Perhaps we may say a metaphysical power. Those who do work of power are available for communication to and from entities of roughly similar power. It is fortunate that the Orion entity does not have the native power of this group. However, it is quite disciplined whereas this group lacks the finesse equivalent to its power. Each is working in consciousness but **the group has not begun a work as a group.** The individual work is helpful, for the group is mutually an aid, one to another. 69.17

Considering how tight you three were with common purpose, common work, and common vision, why did Ra say "but the group has not begun a work as a group"?

JIM   They were talking specifically about white ceremonial magical work. We were trying to develop our magical personalities together as a group. We were doing our own meditations and were working individually, and together as a group we were doing the work with the Ra contact and other types of service, but we didn't undertake the ceremonial magic approach. When we finally started touching upon the archetypical mind and studying that, we decided to go the way of the tarot. We had three choices: one was white ceremonial magic, one was astrology, and one was tarot. We chose tarot. But that isn't the same type of power that is available to the individual when you study that as the ceremonial magic.

We didn't think we had the right discipline, or *time*, to undertake ceremonial magical work—that is a work that would take a great deal of energy and might even detract from what we were doing with the Ra contact, in our opinions at the time.

GARY   Yeah, I don't know how most people on this particular planet at this particular time would carve out that sort of space in their busy lives to learn that type of discipline.

In 102.2, Ra says:

> RA   We may note that the instrument has remained centered upon the Creator at a percentage exceeding ninety. This is the key. Continue in thanksgiving and gratitude for all things. 102.2

Carla, how did you achieve this 90% centering upon the Creator? What does this mean? And if 90% was centered on the Creator, what was the other 10% doing?

CARLA   I'm not sure what I did that was . . .

JIM   They were talking about your hospital experience when you went to the hospital and had surgery on your elbow, so I imagine that the other 10% was, "Ow, that hurts! [*laughter*] Where's the nurse!?"

CARLA   In order to focus on service to others, you just focus on, "What can I do to help you?" with everybody that comes into the room. They are people to serve; they're not people to get stuff from. If I had to deal with a difficult landlord (which I did), I still had to see him as my soulmate, to keep my heart open while I was dealing with very difficult financial wrangles.

GARY So this 90% centering upon the Creator, this is manifested in your conscious mind as well as, of course, I'm sure, your deeper self, but . . .

CARLA Yeah. I can't speak to what's going on beneath the level of what I'm aware of. But what I'm aware of was my constant effort to make sure that I was focused on serving others and not on serving myself.

GARY I think that's an important point: that one can so discipline the mind to respond in a certain way or to see a situation in a certain way that they can crystalize their focus upon the Creator. As odd as it sounds, Ra indicates that that focus can even be measured or quantified.

CARLA Thank you, I appreciate that.

GARY I've seen that in both of your lives. You're very much disciplined, I would say.

CARLA Oh, Jim floors me constantly; he amazes me.

GARY Ra identified this multiple times when they say something like "purity of this instrument's dedication to the service of the One Infinite Creator." This again may be a repeat of the previous question, but how would you describe this "purity of dedication"?

CARLA If you want to quantify it, I wake up in the morning and the first thing I do is offer myself to the Creator for the day. Before I get out of bed, before I make a move to do anything, that's my first prayer.

Then Jim and I have, oh I guess it's about a half-hour that we offer to the Creator every morning in doing readings, you know, Bible readings—we've read the Bible every day together since we married, and before that, I've read it every day since I was 12, and made a vow to do that. Then I've read other inspiring works every day. We read the five books of *The Law of One* over and over, just like we do the Bible, both the Old Testament and the New Testament, and when we get to the end, we start at the beginning again, and believe it or not, we finally, after so many years of reading a little bit every day, have started the Old Testament over again. That's a long book. [*laughs*]

Then we read other things that are hopefully inspiring. I sing a hymn every day. We pray together, we meditate, we just offer—we call it a morning offering and it's just the way we want to have our day go, and we try to focus it in the way that will go on.

Of course, by 10:30 am we're completely gone—worried about something or . . . [laughs] it doesn't always last all day—you have to keep working at it. And you do, you keep working at it all day. And I never get tired of it, just like I never get tired of certain prayers that inspire me and rest my soul. I say them over and over, and have all my life. I guess part of that is being an Episcopalian, a cradle Episcopalian. It's a very ritualistic way of worship. And I've been in the choir since I was four, so the singing and the ritual are all very dear to me and make me comfortable.

So I have so many tools in my arsenal because of worshipping that way and the Christian way, and also just my own way of focusing myself on service to my beloved. I call Jesus my beloved. I don't feel that I need to go into it any more. And I love the Holy Spirit. I spend a lot of time with the Holy Spirit, I call her Holly. Spirit does incredible things in my life. It so strengthens and deepens me, I just can't tell you.

So I use the tools that I was given by nature and by going to church and learning stuff in a certain way.

GARY Again to emphasize this disclaimer, I don't want to make sacred cows out of either of you or put you on a pedestal . . .

CARLA Good heavens no, I'm such an idiot.

GARY But, you know, Ra spoke about *your* lives and examined the dynamics of *your* lives, so your lives get to be a means through which spiritual principles are discussed and analyzed. And it seems like your purity of dedication is, of course, an orientation deep within yourself, but it's consciously practiced every day through constant practice of remembrance and recollection and reorienting yourself again and again.

CARLA It's what I want to do: it's not a burden for me; it's the way I want to live. I'm glad when I'm able to recollect and laugh at myself and go on and lift myself up that way. I'm very glad when that happens. I don't just go, "Oh, I've got to be more pure than this. Oh jeez here we go. Lord help me—I've got to be more pure than this." It's not like that at all. It's the joy of my life to rest in Spirit one way or another.

But I'm an idiot too. I have so many obvious faults. I'm often wrong. I remember things incorrectly; you've noted yourself how often I have embroidered a story, and by the time I tell it again it's three different stories all rolled into one. There's nothing accurate in it. I get the tune but not the words.[12] And I have that tendency and lots of other reasons that you'd just run screaming and say, "I don't want to deal with her." [*laughs*] But most people forgive me and just love me as I am. It's a wonderful thing.

GARY Well a lot of these things are surface details. Through your work in consciousness and your open heart—and your heart does shine through—your essence is always there.

Ra mentions in a couple different places about their pairing with you and the group. They say in 69.5, "We **searched long** to find an appropriate channel or instrument." (And they add that "the possibility/probability vortices indicating the location of this configuration again are slight.")

And in 71.21 they say:

> **RA** Consider the process of one who sees the spectrograph of some complex of elements. It is a complex paint sample, let us say for ease of description. We of Ra knew the needed elements for communication which had any chance of enduring. **We compared our color chip to many individuals and groups over a long span of your time. Your spectrograph matches our sample.** 71.21

So as far as we know, Ra hasn't spoken through any other channeling group, at least not the sixth-density social memory complex *Ra* that spoke through your group.

What do you think it was that allowed you three to receive Ra, humble messenger of the Law of One? That is, how, exactly, did your "spectrograph" match theirs?

CARLA I wouldn't touch that question with a ten-foot pole. I've no idea.

JIM We can only guess.

CARLA It's certainly beyond any conscious effort. It's just the way we are.[13]

JIM Well, the harmony was obviously the most important, I think, plus our desire to be of service and our single-pointedness in finding our own way of being a spiritual entity, and wanting to be of service. Then I guess each of us had certain qualities that we've talked about before—love, wisdom, and power—that had some impact on what we were doing, and that those blended together could be harmonious.

CARLA I had such a leg up by having . . . Whether people believe or don't believe that this happened to me, as a child I spent a lot of time in a magic forest where the trees and bushes all could talk to me and all the animals could speak to me. It was a wonderful feeling. And all the colors were alive and moved and flowed. It made this current life look black and white by comparison, it was so vivid. And Jesus was there, and he would hold my hand and look into my eyes. And I would know what love was.

So from about the age of two, I was wanting consciously, as my devotion to this wonderful energy, to serve love, the love I saw in his beautiful golden eyes. I have never varied one iota from that desire. I've always seen my life as service to my beloved, and that being love, love I could not possibly explain or describe because it was the quality in his eyes that was beyond words. But I wanted to be a part of that always. So from baby-hood—imagine this little toddler who was absolutely determined to be of service. [*laughs*] It got me into all kinds of difficulties.

GARY In my experience, most kids don't have that intensive orientation, myself included.

CARLA No, I didn't fit in any of the molds of my peers, so I was always on the far reaches of out—didn't fit at all. It was so difficult to be a child if you were skinny, had really, really thick glasses, crossed eyes, wanted to be of service, wanted to learn stuff, and loved learning stuff more than any-thing. I was so different.

My mother helped me out on that. I remember being, oh, three or four, and her working with algebra. "Okay, Carla, two plus x equals five. What is x?" How many kids get that kind of leg up. My brain was being exer-cised, and my desire to serve was being exercised, and I was a kind of full-service person wrapped in this little tiny kid. It was strange, and I think I finally grew into myself when I got to late high school and college. After that, I had no problems with anybody. Everybody always appreci-ated and liked me.

GARY My next and final question for this section was going to be: Say if in a hypothetical universe, somebody happened upon contact with Ra again, what words of wisdom would you have for that group? But I think your responses to the questions thus far have kind of hit that nail on the head, so shall we wrap up for the day?

CARLA I'm good. Thanks guys.

JIM Good idea. Good job gang!

GARY Thank you both.

1

It was discovered during the editing process that Ra actually never explicitly used the word "battery" in reference to Jim. Ra did however indicate as much when replying to Jim's question about examining body sensations:

> **RA** For instance, at this space/time nexus one sensation is carrying a powerful charge and may be examined. This is the sensation of what you call the distortion towards discomfort due to the cramped position of the body complex during this working. In balancing you would then explore this sensation. Why is this sensation powerful? Because it was chosen in order that the entity might be of service to others in energizing this contact. 64.20

Carla may also be among the sources responsible for the understanding of Jim's role as battery in the interviewer's mind. Reflecting on the Ra contact throughout the years, Carla had often referred to Jim as a battery. Her and Jim's sexual energy exchanges unquestionably supported the instrument and thus helped power the contact itself (see 39.2, 44.1, 44.13, 48.2, 68.2, 72.16, 76.2, 79.2-4, 81.7, 83.2, & 87.27, among others), but it is unknown whether Carla was referring exclusively to the sexual energy exchanges or also to the native power of Jim's physical presence.

About Jim's power, see this instance of Ra's counsel to Jim regarding its use:

> **RA** We may note that the great forte of the scribe is summed in the inadequate sound vibration complex, power. The flow of power, just as the flow of love or wisdom, is enabled not by the chary conserver of its use but by the constant user. The physical manifestation of power being either constructive or destructive strenuous activity, the power-filled entity must needs exercise that manifestation. This entity experiences a distortion in the direction of an excess of stored energy. It is well to know the self and to guard and use those attributes which the self has provided for its learning and its service. 99.5

While Jim undoubtedly provided the strongest input of raw energetic power (through sexual energy transfer, visualization performed during each session, and the power of his physical presence) Ra describes both Jim and Don's ability to energize the instrument and thus the Ra contact in the following Q&As: 11.2, 33.1, 61.12, 76.2, 78.7. And 61.12 speaks to the energizing effect that comes from the proper alignment of the appurtenances themselves.

2

About sexual energy transfers:

> **RA** In green ray there are two possibilities. Firstly, if both vibrate in green ray there will be a mutually strengthening energy transfer, the negative or female, as you call it, drawing the energy from the roots of the beingness up through the energy centers, thus being physically revitalized;

the positive, or male polarity, as it is deemed in your illusion, finding in this energy transfer an inspiration which satisfies and feeds the spirit portion of the body/mind/spirit complex, thus both being polarized and releasing the excess of that which each has in abundance by nature of intelligent energy, that is, negative/intuitive, positive/physical energies as you may call them; this energy transfer being blocked only if one or both entities have fear of possession, of being possessed, of desiring possession or desiring being possessed. 26.38

3

About the group's working together in previous lifetimes:

RA There have been several times when this group worked and dwelt together. The relationships varied. There is balanced karma, as you call it; each thus the teacher of each. The work has involved healing, understanding the uses of the earth energy, and work in aid of civilizations which called just as your sphere has done and we have come. 9.2

4

More on this weariness:

RA Weariness of the time/space nature may be seen to be that reaction of transparent or pure vibrations with impure, confused, or opaque environs.

QUESTIONER Is there any of this effect upon the other two of us in this group?

RA I am Ra. This is quite correct.

QUESTIONER Then we would also experience the uninterrupted wearying effect as a consequence of the contact. Is this correct?

RA I am Ra. The instrument, by the very nature of the contact, bears the brunt of this effect. Each of the support group, by offering the love and the light of the One Infinite Creator in unqualified support in these workings and in energy transfers for the purpose of these workings, experiences between 10 and 15 percent, roughly, of this effect. It is cumulative and identical in the continual nature of its manifestation.

QUESTIONER What could be the result of this continued wearying effect after a long period?

RA I am Ra. You ask a general query with infinite answers. We shall over-generalize in order to attempt to reply.

One group might be tempted and thus lose the very contact which caused the difficulty. So the story would end.

Another group might be strong at first but not faithful in the face of difficulty. Thus the story would end.

Another group might choose the path of martyrdom in its completeness and use the instrument until its physical body complex failed from the harsh toll demanded when all energy was gone.

This particular group, at this particular nexus, is attempting to conserve the vital energy of the instrument. It is attempting to balance love of service and wisdom of service, and it is faithful to the service in the face of difficulty. Temptation has not yet ended this group's story.

We may not know the future, but the probability of this situation continuing over a relatively substantial period of your space/time is large. The significant factor is the will of the instrument and of the group to serve. That is the only cause for balancing the slowly increasing weariness which will continue to distort your perceptions. Without this will the contact might be possible but finally seem too much of an effort. 81.5-8

And regarding Carla's trance experience where Carla was essentially with Ra, in sixth density:

QUESTIONER The instrument has mentioned what she refers to as bleed-through or being aware, during these sessions sometimes, of the communication. Would you comment on this?

RA I am Ra. We have the mind/body/spirit complex of the instrument with us. As this entity begins to awaken from the metaphorical crib of experiencing light and activity in our density it is beginning to be aware of the movement of thought. It does not grasp these thoughts any more than your third-density infant may grasp the first words it perceives. The experience should be expected to continue and is an appropriate outgrowth of the nature of these workings and of the method by which this instrument has made itself available to our words. 88.5

QUESTIONER Well, I will just ask in closing: Is an individualized portion or entity of Ra inhabiting the instrument's body for the purpose of communication? And then, is there anything that we can do to improve the contact or make the instrument more comfortable?

RA I am Ra. We of Ra communicate through narrow-band channel through the violet-ray energy center. We are not, as you would say, physically indwelling in this instrument; rather, the mind/body/spirit complex of this instrument rests with us. 85.20

5

What is vital energy?

QUESTIONER Could you give me a definition of vital energy?

RA I am Ra. Vital energy is the complex of energy levels of mind, body, and spirit. Unlike physical energy, it requires the integrated complexes vibrating in an useful manner.

The faculty of will can, to a variable extent, replace missing vital energy and this has occurred in past workings, as you measure time, in this instrument. This is not recommended. At this time, however, the vital energies are well-nourished in mind and spirit although the physical energy level is, in and of itself, low at this time.

QUESTIONER Would I be correct in guessing that vital energy is a function of the awareness or bias of the entity with respect to its polarity or general unity with the Creator or creation?

RA I am Ra. In a nonspecific sense we may affirm the correctness of your statement. The vital energy may be seen to be that deep love of life or life experiences such as the beauty of creation and the appreciation of other-selves and the distortions of your co-Creators' making which are of beauty.

Without this vital energy the least distorted physical complex will fail and perish. With this love or vital energy or élan the entity may continue though the physical complex is greatly distorted. 63.6-7

6

Weariness of spirit and physical energy:

RA Those of the support group also offer the essence of will and faith in service to others, supporting the instrument as it releases itself completely in the service of the One Creator. Therefore, each of the support group also experiences a weariness of the spirit which is indistinguishable from physical energy deficit except that if each experiments with this weariness each shall discover the physical energy in its usual distortion. 94.7

7 There is indication in 83.2 that Carla is regaining weight for the first time: Don says that Carla "gains weight now instead of loses it after a session."

8

About the instrument not being the best judge of when *not* to have a session and how the support group was critical in exercising that discernment:

RA This instrument is very fortunate in having a support group which impresses upon it the caution necessary as regards these sessions at this time. This instrument is capable of almost instantaneously clearing the mental/emotional complex and the spiritual complex for the purity this working requires, **but this instrument's distortion towards fidelity to service does not function to its best use of judgment regarding the weakness distortions of the physical complex.** Thus we appreciate your assistance at space/times such as that in your most recent decision-making not to have a working. This was the appropriate decision and the guidance given this instrument was helpful. 39.1

9

On the instrument dedicating her energy:

QUESTIONER Could you please terminate this contact as soon as necessary since we are not aware of the vitality of the instrument at this time?

RA I am Ra. In your way of speaking our hands are, to a certain extent, tied. This instrument has called upon inner reserves which are dearly bought. Therefore, we have the honor/duty of using this energy to the best of our ability. When it becomes low we shall most certainly, as always, express the need for ending the working. The only way of avoiding this sharing of service at whatever cost is to refrain from the working. It is a dilemma. 44.2

QUESTIONER I think that it might be a good idea if we terminated the contact at this time to allow the instrument to gain more necessary energy before continuing. This is my decision at this time. I would very much like to continue the contact, but it seems to me, although I can't tell the instrument's level, that the instrument should not use up any more energy.

RA I am Ra. We are responding to an unasked query. However, it is most salient and therefore we beg your forgiveness for this infringement. The energy has been lost to the instrument, dedicated to this purpose only. You may do as you will, but this is the nature of the instrument's preparation for contact and is the sole reason we may use it.

QUESTIONER I'm not sure I fully understood you. Could you say that a little different way? Could you explain more completely?

RA I am Ra. Each of you in this working has consciously dedicated the existence now being experienced to service to others. This instrument has refined this dedication through long experience with the channeling, as you term it, of Confederation philosophy, as you may say. Thus when we first contacted this instrument it had offered its beingness, not only to service to other-selves but service by communication of this nature. As this contact has developed, this dedication of beingness has become quite specific. Thus once the vital energy is dedicated by the instrument to our communications, even if the working did not occur, this vital energy would be lost to the day-by-day experience of the instrument. Thus we indicated the importance of the instrument's releasing of the will from the process of determining the times of working, for if the instrument desires contact, the energy is gathered and thus lost for ordinary or mundane purposes. 44.7-8

[10]

Ken was probably thinking of these two lines:

RA Love and wisdom, like love and light, are not black and white, shall we say, but faces of the same coin, if you will. Therefore, it is not, in all cases, that balancing consists of a movement from compassion to wisdom. 85.16

[11]

Carla was mistaken. The expression "to kick against the pricks" comes not from Shakespeare but from the Bible:

"It is hard for you to kick against the pricks" was a Greek proverb, but it was also familiar to the Jews and anyone who made a living in agriculture. An ox goad was a stick with a pointed piece of iron on its tip used to prod the oxen when plowing. The farmer would prick the animal to steer it in the right direction. Sometimes the animal would rebel by kicking out at the prick, and this would result in the prick being driven even further into its flesh. In essence, the more an ox rebelled, the more it suffered. Thus, Jesus' words to Saul on the road to Damascus: "It is hard for you to kick against the pricks."

Of the better-known Bible translations, the actual phrase "kick against the pricks" is found only in the King James Version. It is mentioned only twice, in Acts 9:5 and Acts 26:14. The apostle Paul (then known as Saul) was on his way to Damascus to persecute the Christians when he had a blinding encounter with Jesus. Luke records the event: "And when we were all fallen to the earth, I heard a voice speaking unto me, and saying in the Hebrew tongue, Saul, Saul, why persecutest thou me? It is hard for thee to kick against the pricks" (Acts 26:14 KJV). Modern translations have changed the word pricks to goads. All translations except the KJV and NKJV, omit the phrase altogether from Acts 9:5.

The conversion of Saul is quite significant as it was the turning point in his life. Paul later wrote nearly half of the books of the New Testament.

Jesus took control of Paul and let him know his rebellion against God was a losing battle. Paul's actions were as senseless as an ox kicking "against the goads." Paul had passion and sincerity in his fight against Christianity, but he was not heading in the direction God wanted him to go. Jesus was going to goad ("direct" or "steer") Paul in the right direction.

"What Does it Mean to Kick Against the Pricks?" GotQuestions.org, accessed September 3, 2015, www.gotquestions.org/kick-against-the-pricks.html.

[12] Carla had a tendency to get creative in the retelling sometimes, but not nearly to the degree she indicates here. Though this could be a case in point . . .

[13] A small window of insight into the *matching of spectrographs*—i.e., how or why Ra was able to contact the group:

> RA This particular instrument was not trained, nor did it study, nor worked it at any discipline in order to contact Ra. We were able, as we have said many times, to contact this group using this instrument because of the purity of this instrument's dedication to the service of the One Infinite Creator and also because of the great amount of harmony and acceptance enjoyed each by each within the group; this situation making it possible for the support group to function without significant distortion. 94.9

CHAPTER 8

Appurtenances

GARY Ra uses the word *appurtenances* 18 different times during the contact. Wikipedia says "appurtenances are things that belong to and go with something else, the appurtenance being less significant than what it belongs to."[1]

Ra describes appurtenances that play an important role in the psychological, mechanical, magical, and metaphysical aspects of maintaining the contact. In 2.6, Ra names the appurtenances and instructs the questioner to *(numbers added)*:

1. Place at the entity's head a virgin chalice of water.
2. To the center, the book most closely aligned with the instrument's mental distortions which are allied most closely with the Law of One, that being the Bible that she touches most frequently.
3. To the other side of the Bible, a small amount of cense, or incense, in a virgin censer.
4. To the rear of the book symbolizing One, opened to the Gospel of John, Chapter One, a white candle. 2.6

What was the history of these particular items?

CARLA They're really part of my Episcopalian heritage. All these items are either on the altar or part of the service. Also, interestingly enough, white magic uses all of these. For instance, the word *virgin* is taken from magic, meaning *unused* or *never used before*. We were so lucky there because my Aunt Tot, Don's aunt, had just given me a chalice, a silver chalice—well, it looked like silver—for Christmas. The Ra contact began the third week in January, and I hadn't used it yet, not even once, so it was completely virgin.

GARY I think that qualifies as synchronicity.

CARLA Yeah, and in terms of a candle, it had never been lit—that kind of thing. It doesn't have any sexual meaning to it; it just means that it's not been used.

I love being as close to the altar as possible. I dressed the altar every week as being part of the altar guild and while being part of the chancel ministry during the actual service. I loved that work, and I think that the Ra group was using my preferences to make me feel reassured and safe.

GARY Further on Ra talks about the nurturing of the instrument.

Why was the Bible opened to the Gospel of John, Chapter One?

CARLA Well, Ra explains it. It was as close as possible to the Law of One: "in the beginning was the Word." That Word is *Logos*. Ra uses the word *Logos* for the one original Thought, which is Love. So if you substitute *Love* for *Logos* you get the Christian meaning very closely. "In the beginning was the Word, and the Word was with God, and the Word was God." And from that, all things sprung.

That's the way the gospel begins, and that's just totally congruent with the Law of One. But it is also my favorite gospel. I love that gospel; it's absolutely beautiful. Unlike the other gospels, it focuses more on the spiritual aspects and less on, *Well, the Tuesday of this week they went here and they did that,* and a lot of detail like that. It is more a kind of defense of the faith. It was written later.

GARY So I'll read Ra's words in their describing of how it nurtures the instrument:

> **RA** We feel that, though this [placement of the appurtenances] is a complex of activity/circumstance and may seem very distorted from a purposeful teach/learning experience, these elaborations on the technique of trance will **ease the mind distortions of those about**

the instrument as they perceive improvement in the instrument's distortions with regard to fatigue. 2.6

RA I was referring to the symbolic objects which trigger this instrument's distortions towards love/light. The placement and loving acceptance of them by all present is **important in the nurturing of this instrument.** 6.3

RA The careful alignment of these is important for the energizing group in that it is a reminder to that support group that it is time for a working. The ritualistic behaviors are triggers for many energies of the support group. . . . This would not aid another group as it was **designed for this particular system of mind/body/spirit complexes and especially the instrument.** 61.12

So, you've already begun to speak to this point, but I'll ask this to get a fuller response, if one is available: were you knowingly, consciously comforted, energized, and supported by these appurtenances and their correct configuration?

CARLA Oh, yes. When you think of how most belief systems—we're going more toward religion here, sort of like shoo everything else out the door—most belief systems say *this is the right way*. Ra was not doing this, but instead they were deliberately bringing in my own distortions in order to help me out in doing the work, and that was tremendously helpful. I was especially impressed with the fact that they let me keep this little metal cross, considering they didn't want anything metal in the room because that would disturb the fine tuning. But they specifically said that I should keep the cross because it was comforting to me.

They were really trying their best to help me. If you'll look at the history of channels, a lot of times they don't care. They get people up out of sleep and say, "Type this book." That was the way *Oahspe* was written.[2] Not get sleep for 10 years because you're doing work on this book?

[*to cat*] Hello Pickwick! This is our little 18-year-old pussycat.

[*to Jim and Gary*] Where other channeled entities have been known to be less than supportive of the instrument's human frailties, the Ra group was endlessly supportive.

GARY So it wasn't just that you felt nurtured due to your personal relationship to these items, but you also felt nurtured by Ra because Ra was encouraging you to use these items.

CARLA I felt both of those things very deeply, yes.

GARY Jim, how about you and Don? How did you relate to these appurtenances?

JIM Well, Don aligned them. And I kept them clean. [*laughs*] I didn't have a particular relationship to them other than that. They were for the instrument and the comfort of the instrument as she was exiting and entering her body.

GARY In 3.4, Ra explains more specifically how the appurtenances function. They say:

> RA We will explain the process by which [the appurtenances] become a significant distortion balancer. **The incense** acts as an energizer to the physical body of this instrument, signifying its humanity. This is, therefore, a necessity that the wafted smoke is perceived from the same relative angle as the instrument perceives the opened **Bible** balanced by **the lighted candle** signifying love/light and light/love and, therefore, give the mental and emotional, shall we call it, distortion complex of this instrument the sight of paradise and peace which it seeks. **Thus energized from the lower to the higher**, the instrument becomes balanced and does not grow fatigued. 3.4

So, the specific items chosen and their particular arrangement seem a means to communicate, not only to your conscious mind, but to your subconscious mind as well.

CARLA Very definitely. Who could consciously be aware of the direction of the wafting of the smoke? That is beyond me.

GARY In the quote I just read Ra begins the final sentence saying, "Thus energized from the lower to the higher . . . " Do you guys have any idea what that means?

JIM Probably from the mundane to the sacred—the lower energy centers to the higher.

CARLA There was always the upward spiraling light, so you're wanting to let that light spiral up.

GARY Ra spoke to the necessity to maintain the proper alignments of these appurtenances. Sometimes they even mentioned when the appurtenances were off:

> RA Remain most fastidious about the alignments of the appurtenances. 71.23

> RA We ward you ware of any laxity regarding the arrangement and orientation of appurtenances. 46.18

Then, about 12 sessions into the contact, you began to become aware that there was a deeper reason that Ra stresses the very, very careful placement and alignment of the appurtenances. Can you elaborate on what that reason was?

JIM Ra mentioned that the Bible was 1.4 degrees out of alignment, and perhaps five-tenths of a degree of the whole layout,[3] so that got us to thinking because there is no way you could get the appurtenances lined up that carefully. So we knew they were talking about something other than the actual physical placement of the appurtenances—they were talking about the alignment of our questions, our *line* of questioning. We had gotten off the track a little bit from what was important to what was transient, and we tried to stay away from what was transient because this was a narrow-band contact.

As Ra said, its preconditions were precise,[4] and in order to keep the contact we would have to continue working in the area of spiritual principles—things that you could use now and 10,000 years from now, now and forever. If we talked about things that were transient and only are of interest now, then we were wasting the great opportunity of the contact. Why should the contact stay around if we were going to do that? So they warned us first: *You're kind of off a little bit—not important for this session. But there's another session today—much more important.* So we figured it out—we had to get our line of questioning straight.

GARY How did you make that leap of realizing that they were not talking specifically about the alignment of the physical objects but about your questions?

JIM Well, it's a spiritual contact, and everything they talk about has a spiritual value or component to it, so what they were saying there about the alignment had to have a spiritual component to it. They're not just talking about a few degrees or tenths of a degree, so what else could it be? It has to be our line of questioning.

CARLA Don and Jim were two sharp cats. If it was going to be figured out, they would. They came to a feeling after they figured it out, that it had taken them far too long. But actually they were pretty quick.

GARY So afterward, after you reached that conclusion, if Ra would later on describe a misalignment, did that cause you to reflect more intensely on where you were going out of line?[5]

JIM Yes. Definitely.

GARY So that was a way for Ra to highlight or point to an error or two?

JIM Yes, to give us a clue. They did that a few times, giving us a clue about something that we needed to consider, but they did not tell us what, because that would be infringing on our free will. Clues were okay. Just laying it out flat—*you need to do this*—was not. The contact was a product of free will, and we had to be able to exercise our free will at all times.

GARY Were the appurtenances also a signal to the group as a whole to begin purifying the desire to serve others and tuning yourselves as a group so as to be in harmony to receive Ra?

JIM In general, yes, but I think more so for Carla than for either Don or me. The whole session—there were a lot of things that had to come together: the bed, the outfit Carla wore, the cover, the appurtenances, the tape recorders, the chair, the path around the bed—all of them were important. Doing all of that got us ready.

GARY So the triggers began even further back into the previous night? You said that you would meditate together, have sexual energy transfer—so there's a sequence of steps where you're getting into the mindset, getting ready for the game, so to speak?

JIM Right. Yeah, that's basically it. Getting ready for the game.

GARY That concludes our chapter on appurtenances.

CARLA And that's the last time you'll have to say that word. [*laughs*]

GARY Yes! I will never have an opportunity to use it again . . . outside of *The Law of One*.

1. *Wikipedia, The Free Encyclopedia*, s.v. "Appurtenance," accessed September 8, 2015, https://en.wikipedia.org/wiki/Appurtenance.

2. Some preliminary research on the topic turned up a slightly different account. Instead of writing *Oahspe* while asleep, its author, John Ballou Newbrough (1828–1891), sat down in front of the newly invented typewriter "for half an hour each morning at which time his hands would automatically type (without his knowledge of what was being written)." This is according to his firsthand reports, which are referenced on the *Oahspe Wikipedia* page.

    Wikipedia, The Free Encyclopedia, "Oahspe: A New Bible," accessed September 8, 2015, https://en.wikipedia.org/wiki/Oahspe:_A_New_Bible.

3. About the alignments:

    > RA I am Ra. We ask you to realign the object upon which the symbols sit. It is not a significant distortion for one session only, but you will find upon measuring the entire assemblage that the resting place is 1.4 degrees from the correct alignment, the resting place an additional one-half degree away from proper orientation. Do not concern yourselves overly with this in the space/time nexus present, but do not allow these distortions to remain over a long period or the contact will be gradually impaired. 12.33

4. About the precise preconditions:

    > RA This contact is narrow-band and its preconditions precise. The other-self offering its service in the negative path also is possessed of the skill of the swordsman. You deal in this contact with, shall we say, forces of great intensity poured into a vessel as delicate as a snowflake and as crystalline.
    >
    > The smallest of lapses may disturb the regularity of this pattern of energies which forms the channel for these transmissions. 64.5

5. To further corroborate the understanding that the alignment of the appurtenances was linked to the alignment of the questions, Ra explains in one particular answer how an alignment had no deeper meaning, implying that, in other instances, there *was* a deeper purpose to their statements regarding alignment:

    > RA The physical appurtenance called the censer was just a degree off, this having no deeper meaning. 77.25

CHAPTER 9

What is Psychic Greeting?

Author's Note: We are about to spend five chapters investigating psychic greeting in general but mostly as it pertains to the Ra contact. This topic merits such focus because, as any reader knows or will soon discover, psychic greeting played a prominent, sometimes even dominant role in the experience of the contact, perhaps even contributing to its end. Indeed it constituted such an important part of the very fabric of the experience that it was inseparable from the journey the group undertook. To neglect this topic would be akin to interviewing Ernest Shackleton and *not* asking him about the Antarctic ice sheets that trapped and crushed his ship on its polar expedition, stranding him and his crew in one of the world's most harrowing and heroic tales of survival.

Unlike the ice sheets, however, psychic greeting also offers an excellent platform for investigating spiritual principles upon the path of self-realization. It brings the polarities (*the axis upon which the creation turns*[1]) into much sharper relief because psychic greeting is a dynamic, intensive arena where the polarities square off, each mode of service forcing the other to be more perfect and pure upon its respective path. Owing to this, the workings of free will are illustrated in vivid, almost tangible light.

Now and then, though, a reader of L/L's work will learn of events during the contact with Ra, and/or learn of the reality of psychic greeting, and become subsequently concerned, even fearful in the worry that similar may befall them. While each path unfolds according to one's free will, it may be well to consider that most spiritual seekers on the planet, in this or any age, will likely never experience these circumstances and intensities, for the same reason most of us will never experience the challenges that astronauts face when blasting through the atmosphere, entering orbit, or traveling in space, like enormous g-forces and zero-gravity environments. It is a circumstance of exceptional, special, and extraordinary nature.

GARY Can you define "psychic greeting"?

JIM An attempt by the loyal opposition to keep you from doing what you're doing, to take your light. If they can't control what you're doing and change it then they attempt to put the light out.

A little more information might be helpful. When contact like this is undertaken by anybody, there is produced a certain metaphysical power or light (it's seen as light on the inner planes). And just like a candle will attract the attention of moths and bugs of various kinds, the light that's produced in a session like this will attract the attention of others. Those of positive polarity will come and rejoice in what's going on and lend their energies and lend their vibrations while those of negative polarity will look for a way to control that light, to get the power, because the light is also a power. They get that spiritual power within their own realm if they can control it in some way. So all the psychic greetings were their attempt to control what was happening or to stop it.

CARLA We get the greetings, we who attempt to serve the light, whenever we attempt to serve. It begins with the elements of our own personality that are resistant to this: don't want to serve the light, want to go off and have a ball, want to do something else. So the shadow side of our personality, as Jung might say, kicks up its heels and says, "Wait a minute."

Beyond that there are a lot of entities in fourth-density negative that attempt to tempt people away from serving the light, usually by invoking the ego: *Don't you want to be famous, don't you want to make a lot of money from this?* And an amazing number of those channels who wish to serve the light are taken away from the light by elements of ego.

Often, they want to answer specific questions posed to them and they can't get it through their tuned contact, so they let themselves be detuned because they want the answer. Then they get an answer and they give it. And the answers start out very close to a positively oriented answer, but if they keep on with that specific questioning, it will get further and further away from love and enter into fear. Then you'll get doom and gloom, and *have cows,[2] stay away from everybody else, and defend your little enclave of like-minded people.* That happens over and over.

It's a shame, but if you resist and keep taking the high road that doesn't need to get the answer, and if the answer received is no, then the answer is *no*. The instrument needs to cultivate an attitude of being okay with saying, "I don't know. I have no idea. I can't answer that."

But eventually, if you keep successfully resisting temptations of that kind, then it gets kicked upstairs to fifth density, which is very rare, actually. Most people capitulate in fourth density and get pulled away by a fourth-density temptation. But if it gets kicked up to where the entities trying to tempt you away are very wise and very clever, then it can be very dicey. It is rare, but it does happen, obviously, and it's happened to us.

GARY Is "psychic greeting" a synonym or euphemism for "psychic attack"?

JIM It's an attitude of how you look at what's occurring. "Psychic attack" is a phrase you would use if you were really wanting to do battle with somebody and feeling that they were your true adversary. "Psychic greeting" is an attempt to make this person or entity the same as the self, to see them as the Creator just as they are the Creator. So by calling it a psychic greeting, we were attempting to downplay the adversarial nature of the relationship, even though that entity itself might feel quite adversarial towards us—

CARLA We wanted to keep our hearts open.

JIM —we did not have to return that same feeling. So that was the beginning of how we dealt with psychic greetings.

CARLA Yes it is a euphemism, and actually it is a synonym.

GARY So the term itself has built into it a prescription for how to appropriately deal with psychic attack in a positive sense.

JIM Right.

GARY So who is susceptible to psychic greeting?

JIM Anybody who is successfully doing service-to-others work of light or power and is generating positive results—

CARLA Everybody.

GARY That work doesn't necessarily have to be on the outer level; you don't have to be out in society causing changes and attracting attention to yourself. This could just be on a level of consciousness itself.

JIM If you're letting your light shine, you will attract attention.

GARY In 80.3 Ra says that the "element of fear" is "a great weapon" in the arsenal of the negative entity undertaking psychic greeting. Can you elaborate on this?

JIM Well, fear is a quality that usually separates us from something. Maybe even part of our self, or a friend, or some activity that we're doing. If you look at things as all being one and seeing that we're all part of the Creator, then there's nothing to fear; it's all yourself, eventually. So fear is something that we need to work on by balancing it with acceptance and love.

That's what we were attempting to do as we dealt with psychic greetings—was to deal with fear, because, of the various types of greetings (I think you're probably going to share some of those later on), some could be fearful. You could feel fear for some of them. And it's a trick sometimes, an act of will and an effort to not fear, but to see it as something that you can send love to and heal.

GARY That goes back to using the term "psychic greeting." Seeing it as a greeting is yet another way to put the foot in the right direction in that you help to remove the fear from it, to make it less threatening.

JIM Right.

CARLA And also seeing that there are fears that are inner: the fear of looking stupid and foolish—you don't want to say, "I don't know," as a channel. You want to have the answer. So there's fear involved in—if your ego comes in and says, "I want an answer," you fear looking stupid, you fear looking like a bad channel.

GARY Right. If you're attached to some image of yourself, then you fear loss of or diminishment to that image.

What are some of the consequences of successful psychic greeting?

JIM Well, most channeling contacts start off very positively. If you're not able to maintain the contact because you aren't aware of things like Carla has discovered—the necessity for tuning yourself before each channeling, the necessity for challenging the entity attempting to contact you each channeling—then it's possible that you could get off the track of what you wanted to do and the contact itself will become mixed. The positive source that began the contact might begin to see that the channel is no longer interested in maintaining the same level of purity in the seeking, or in the tuning, or in the serving. Then the positive source will gently withdraw and be replaced by a negatively oriented entity of roughly the same power which will feel quite similar to the positive entity with which the contact began. Then the contact will begin moving away from the positive concepts which it was sharing, and there would be little turns and barbed hooks inserted in there to begin getting more negatively oriented information where the person's ego, say, may be glorified or gratified with power, or position, or with money, etc.

So very often in channeling, we get mixed contacts. It starts off very positive and then it goes through the process of the positive entity withdrawing and then becoming more negatively oriented. Now there's only so much negatively oriented information that a positive channel, who's really positive, will take before discovering that there is something going on. But, the whole thrust of the effort then has been diluted, shall we say, and may be sidetracked and gotten off in a direction that is of less service than it could have been.

And there are other possibilities. For instance, like the psychic greetings that Carla had where she was given the impression by the negatively oriented entity on her walk that there was no traffic in the road, and that she should step out in front of the traffic.[3] The consequences there are fairly obvious.

CARLA [*laughs*] Mack truck!

GARY So any behavior a human can undertake with a mindset of fear would fall under the consequences of successful psychic greeting?

CARLA Yes.

GARY Ra identifies a group, named the Orion Empire, as being responsible for the psychic greeting you experienced during the Ra contact. Who was this group?

JIM Well, they were entities of a negative nature, apparently, that had been successful in their efforts at control and manipulation of those around them so that they could gather their power and become more powerful. So the entire Orion constellation is not negative; however, the negatively oriented entities from the Orion complex apparently do reside there. That's their home base, apparently. There are plenty of others, but apparently those entities who were visiting our group and had been attracted to it by the light were from the Orion Empire, shall we say.

GARY So Orion is kind of a cosmic geographical location?

CARLA Kinda-sorta. A lot of things get their terms from where they began, and in actuality they've moved on. Or they've collected a lot of different places that have come in under that federation and it's no longer in, say, New York—it's not really the New York Association, but it's called that. Look at the football leagues, that's a perfect example: the East isn't the East and the Big Ten has no geographical location whatsoever and everything's all over the place.[4] It's crazy. But everybody that enters into it knows what they're talking about.

I think the Orion Empire was just like that. It wasn't literal, and it wasn't an empire. It was a confederation of planets in the service of the Infinite Creator by being service to self. Very much like the confederation that Ra belongs to but negative in polarity.

GARY [to Carla] Sounds like you have a husband who watches college football.

CARLA You might think so. [laughs] And you'd be right.

GARY The terms "empire" and "confederation" imply two very different ways to organize and structure and relate to groupings. I would think that the word "confederation" couldn't be applied to "empire" or to a grouping of negative entities. Whereas the negative entities are bent upon conquest and submitting those less powerful to their will, a confederation seeks to share power.

CARLA You're right. You're exactly right.

GARY Which is why Ra describes their own grouping as a confederation and the Orion grouping as an empire.

Doing the research for this interview, I came upon something really interesting that I wasn't aware of previously. There seems to be no mention of the Orion group, psychic greeting or psychic attack in any channeling transcripts prior to the Ra contact. Unless I am mistaken, it seems that Ra introduced you to the idea of psychic attack and the notion that there is this grouping of negative beings associated with the area of the galaxy in or near the Orion constellation. Is this true? If so, how did you react upon learning this?

JIM Well, it caused a reorientation in concept and in thinking, because we weren't aware of psychic greetings before this, and of "negatively oriented entities." We knew, in general, that there were negative entities, but who knows what they were doing and where they were? So we had to try to figure out, *well, how do they evolve? What direction do they go?* I think Don asked a question about that and Ra said that they move through the densities the same as positive entities do, until the negative beings get to mid-sixth density, then there's a change that they have to make because they can't go any further.

So, yeah, it was a new concept and it took a little while to think about it and wrap our minds around it.

GARY So prior to the contact with Ra, polarity wasn't investigated or explored very much then, I presume.

JIM Not so much, though we had been familiar with polarity from a couple of other channeled sources. I'm trying to remember the name . . .[5] Anyway, there were other sources that talked about polarity. Don was aware of the necessity for a 51% positive effort in order to be graduated. But we were not aware of what the negative entities would have to do, that they would have to be much more pure in their efforts to be 95% negative. But we were aware of the concept of polarity before this.

GARY Just hadn't been developed to the full extent that it was during the Ra contact.

CARLA Oh, no. It was something we started thinking about then because of the catalyst of all these things happening.

GARY I feel that *The Law of One* material's treatment of the negative polarity is one of the things that sets it apart, somewhat, from other sources of philosophical or spiritual information.

CARLA Very different.

GARY The sheer abundance of information on psychic greeting in *The*

Law of One is indicative of just how constantly you three, especially the instrument, were under pressure and threat from what you have termed the "loyal opposition."

---

[1] Ra described the choice between STO and STS made in third density thusly:

> RA The choice is, as you put it, the work of a moment but is the axis upon which the creation turns. 76.16

[2] Jim writes:

> I don't believe that Carla had any one group in mind but was putting a number of detuned situations together that she knew of. She was familiar with a few groups that had become detuned and it started for them with asking specific questions about how to survive the "doom and gloom" times that were seen to be coming in the future. The whole idea was to recede into a self-sufficient group and "stay away" from others who might want your things. The "have cows" phrase is another action for such detuned groups to take, in order to be self-sufficient. You could get milk and butter from cows to help in surviving tough times alone.

[3] About the suggestion to step out in front of traffic:

> RA The light [of the negative greeting] would work instantly upon an untuned individual by suggestion, that is the stepping out in front of the traffic because the suggestion is that there is no traffic. [The instrument], as each in this group, is enough disciplined in the ways of love and light that it is not suggestible to any great extent. However, there is a predisposition of the physical complex which this entity is making maximal use of as regards the instrument, hoping for instance, by means of increasing dizziness, to cause the instrument to fall or to indeed walk in front of your traffic because of impaired vision. 67.13

[4] Prior to losing interest in sports altogether after Carla's passing in 2015, Jim had been a dyed-in-the-wool college football fanatic. Though not terribly interested in sports herself, Carla picked up a thing or two.

[5] One source was likely the book, *Oahspe: A New Bible*.

CHAPTER 10
Dealing with Psychic Greeting

GARY In 57.3, Ra says:

> RA The Orion group cannot interfere directly but only through pre-existing distortions of mind/body/spirit complexes. 57.3

As you explained previously, psychic greeting happens only through the function of one's free will. That is, the negative entities can only exacerbate, accentuate, and meddle with one's pre-existing biases and distortions. It stands to reason, then, that the more conscious and aware an entity is of their own distortions, the less likely that the entity's distortions can be used against them.

Ra later conveys this:

> RA The less balanced the distortion by self-knowledge, the more adeptly the [negative] entity may accentuate such a distortion in order to mitigate against the smooth functioning and harmony of the group. 80.4

Why does Ra indicate that self-knowledge makes one less prone to successful psychic greeting?

JIM Well, if you know that any type of movement away from the harmony that you are capable of creates an opening that can be entered, greeted, intensified, and made a difficulty for you, then you work real hard to stay positive. Or if you feel you have a separation that has occurred because of a misunderstanding or some sort of an argument or anger, then you try to heal that as soon as possible, don't let the sun go down on it. Heal it before too long a time passes.

So, self-knowledge gives you the tools with which to deal, knowing where your weaknesses are. If you have a tendency to get upset or disharmonious over certain topics or things, then you work on that.

CARLA We know Ra was always very eager for people to get to know themselves: "Know yourself, accept yourself, become the Creator."[1] Most people do not know themselves. They know themselves as they wish to be, but they have not grappled with certain aspects of their shadow side that constitute the rich, fertile field of what the negative entity can use. If you don't know about it, it will be used, and that right quickly. So it's good to know yourself. Ra has always emphasized that.

GARY Ra gives a basic program for not only protecting one's self or one's group from psychic greeting, but also in neutralizing the power and effect of the negatively oriented entities. I will read several nuggets from Ra in this regard:

> Thus we see protection being very simple. Give thanksgiving for each moment. See the self and the other-self as Creator. Open the heart. Always know the light and praise it. This is all the protection necessary. 32.1

> There is no protection greater than love. 75.2

> Love is the great protector. 63.5

> Sending [the negative] entity love and light, which each of the group is doing, is the most helpful catalyst which the group may offer to the negative entity. 67.8

Also, sending love and light to the negative greeter "neutralizes it" (67.9) and causes the negative entity the need to "regroup" (67.26).

How does meditating on love and light, and sending love and light, provide this protection?

JIM There are two things, I believe. The first thing is it gets your consciousness pointed towards harmonizing and sending love and light to the negatively oriented entity. Now you're not sending it to them in order to make them leave, you're sending it to them because you have honest genuine love and light meant for them.

The technique that I devised over the years was to send love and light: to the entity, to the sending that the entity had made (or the working that the entity was attempting), and then to wherever the working was pointed. If it was me, then I'd send it to me and then to the Creator of all things. And what that basically does is provide a wall of light around you through which the entity cannot move. And it also sends love and light, coincidentally, to the negative entities and they see that as rather sickly.

CARLA Bad taste!

JIM [*speaking for the negative entity*] "Go away, and if you won't go away, then I'll go away." The whole idea is to send love because you see them as the Creator. It has to be genuine and heartfelt. You're not doing, "I love you, I love you, I love you, go away, go away, go away." It has to be, "You are the Creator; thank you for what you have to offer."

CARLA And it takes a lot of work to get to where you genuinely do have compassion and, basically, pity for these poor guys that won't accept that there is any love. They're flogging away at you instead of doing positive things on their own hook. They're spending all of their effort trying to take you down because if they can't have your light, they want to take it out.

GARY Sounds like a miserable existence.

CARLA Yeah, it really does. That was a real help to me in coming to a love of them, a genuine love of them. Here these souls were that were caught in these misunderstandings and having all kinds of troubles. Of course we were given the result of these troubles, and they were troubles to us too. But as far as focusing on them as souls, you had to have compassion for them.

GARY It's a funny position that the positive entity is manifesting what *is*, more and more purely—manifesting love, manifesting beauty, manifesting light—and the negative entity is so perturbed by that, that they don't want to see what *is*. They will go to such great lengths to try to snuff it. But then the protection isn't to fight it like you're describing, but just to love them, to manifest more of what is, and that alone pushes them away, so to speak.[2]

Should one seek to control the perceived negative greeting?

JIM No. Control is their technique. That's their field. Accepting is the positive response. So you accept it as being a portion of yourself and accept them, and you send love to everyone.

CARLA And forgive them. That's the balance between control and forgiveness: judgment and forgiveness, fear and love.

GARY When one feels under threat or under attack, or is just being related to in that way, one of our first instincts as human or third-density entities is to defend ourselves, to strike back or try to control the situation. But you are counseling, and Ra is counseling, and Confederation sources are counseling the opposite of that: loving and accepting. Is there some vulnerability in that, in letting go and accepting and loving?

JIM Well, you have to let go of some of your preconceived ideas that battling another entity that seems to be greeting you or attacking you is the thing to do. So it's all internal. The vulnerability is really to love and to open yourself up to love, and letting it shine through.

GARY So there's a letting down of defenses in a sense and allowing love to do its work, which is its own defense, so you're still defended.

CARLA You just don't defend. You don't see it in those terms. You have an open heart and you're not seeing sides. But, of course, in order to talk about it you really have to talk about it as if there were two sides. In dealing with it you're trying very much to not be a "we/them" but to be an "us."

GARY While still saying no to that portion of us.

CARLA While still not accepting the temptation, yeah. But it's not a no, it's like, "Don't be silly." It's not NO!, it's like, "Of course not."

GARY You're not flipping them the bird, per se.

CARLA There you go.

GARY We actually touch on this in the next question.

In 67.11, Ra is discussing the great saga, and humor, of the way in which those of opposite polarity relate, and how in an infinite creation there are seemingly many different voices saying many different things:

RA Your portion of the Creator is as it is, and your experience and offering of experience, to be valuable, needs be more and more a perfect representation of who you truly are. Could you, then, serve a negative entity by offering the instrument's life? It is unlikely that you would find this a true service.

Thus you may see in many cases the loving balance being achieved, the love being offered, light being sent, and the service of the service-to-self oriented entity gratefully acknowledged while being rejected as not being useful in your journey at this time. Thus you serve One Creator without paradox. 67.11

Ra gave this response because Don was insistent on trying to be of "service" to the Orion entity—

CARLA He was so funny, he was sooo funny. He was just sure that somehow we could make a bargain and get them off our backs.

GARY That was basically my question.

CARLA Give them a lollypop. [*laughs*]

GARY Why was Don going to such great lengths to find out how he could be of service to the negative entity?

JIM We don't know. He never really talked about it. I've thought that was one of the most curious parts of his questioning.

GARY You could definitely see that each time he was trying to get at some philosophical principles there, but it also feels to me (and this is just speculation) that there is some strategizing happening on his part. Maybe he's trying to find a loophole or some way he could undo the situation.

CARLA Exactly.

GARY Then this quote seems to me an excellent elucidation on the principle whereby you embrace everything as the Creator, but you reject the service which is not helpful. To probably oversimplify it, you say yes to the infinite Creation, accepting everything as part of self, but say no to a particular service which is not in alignment with your own polarity. I think it's a point that those of positive orientation get stuck on because they want to say yes to everything, but it's difficult to draw that boundary. Can you comment on this analysis?

CARLA That's it. It's a matter of boundaries. Do you want to be a doormat and just a slave, or do you want to make appropriate boundaries where the two of you have to agree to disagree?

GARY So you can draw a boundary, you can say "no, thank you" while loving the person or the negative entity.

CARLA Definitely.

GARY That has been a very helpful principle introduced to me by Ra.

Ra speaks of the service offered by the fourth-density negative entities (fourth-density as opposed to the fifth-density entities):

> RA The usual attempts upon positively oriented entities or groups of entities are made, as we have said, by [the] minions of the fifth-density Orion leaders; these are fourth-density. The normal gambit of such fourth-density attack is the tempting of the entity or group of entities away from total polarization towards service to others and toward the aggrandizement of self or of social organizations with which the self identifies.
>
> In the case of this particular group [meaning Don, Carla and Jim] each was given a full range of temptations to cease being of service to each other and to the One Infinite Creator. Each entity declined these choices and instead continued with no significant deviations from the desire for a purely other-self-service orientation. 67.7

Okay, multiple questions stemming from this quote. The first is: Were you three aware of any such temptations in your thought patterns?

CARLA Not altogether.

JIM No, not really. I guess they weren't obvious enough.

CARLA They slipped by us, they were so obvious. *No, I don't want to fight with them, I want to find a way to talk things through.* Mostly things like that. Trying to separate two-against-one in one configuration or another but we'd always say, "No, we don't want to separate, we want to find a way to be as harmonious as we always have been."

GARY So I think you've pre-answered the next question which is: Whether or not you were aware that there were "temptations" happening, how did you process thoughts that occurred to you of separation or aggrandizement of yourself? It seems your answer is that you just said no if those thoughts arose, or you just talked it out.

CARLA Yeah, we did. We were never interested in making ourselves anything compared to the material. We felt that the material might be helpful to people and we wanted to make it available to them in case they wanted to see it. So yes, we wanted it publicized. No, we didn't want to become big, and we never did. We never wanted that. It's always been very straightforward: "No, we're just idiots who have this wonderful material, and if it would be helpful to you, here it is. It's for free." And that has always felt right to us.

GARY I want to highlight a point here and that's that . . . not that I feel that this information will ever be popular on this planet, but if you did get big as a consequence of serving, it's not getting big, in and of itself, that leads you astray from the positive path, but rather it's *wanting* to achieve fame or wealth.

CARLA Right. You notice in the Bible it doesn't say, as is so frequency misquoted, "Money is the root of all evil." It doesn't say that. It says *desire* for money is the root of all evil.[3] And it's that desire, it's that greed that is the temptation.

We'd be delighted to have money. We would offer it to the project . . . there are endless ways to help in a project like this—ways to be of service, gatherings we could afford to offer, places we could afford to be and make offerings free instead of having to charge for them because we don't have the money to do otherwise—that kind of thing. Someone might say, "Well, wouldn't it bother you to have a lot of money?" Heck, no. That would be wonderful and we would just find ways to use that budget. But it would always be in service.

GARY Your objective isn't for money itself, it's: *How can we serve? What can we do?*

CARLA Yes. Just take whatever budget we've got and spend it the best way we know how.

GARY So because you had apparently not succumbed to the temptations of fourth-density "minions," a more powerful and skilled negative greeter of the fifth-density variety took it upon itself to visit and greet your group.

Don is asking about this fifth-density negative entity when he says:

> QUESTIONER It seems to me that the fifth-density entity is attracted in some way to our group by [the] polarization of this group which

acts, somehow, as a beacon to the entity. Am I correct?

RA I am Ra. This is, in substance, correct, but the efforts of this entity are put forward only reluctantly. [Because the fourth-density entities failed], one of the fifth-density entities over-seeing such detuning processes determined that it would be necessary to terminate the group by what you might call magical means, as you understand ritual magic. 67.7

Later on, Ra indicates that it was basically through your open hearts that you found some measure of protection against the fifth-density negative entity's greeting:

RA It is not within your conscious selves to stand against such refined power but rather it has been through the harmony, the mutual love, and the honest calling for aid from the forces of light which have given you the shield and buckler. 87.6

When you received information of this sort, did it galvanize you to seek love and harmony ever more strongly?

JIM Sure.

CARLA It was just very encouraging.

GARY I've read *The Law of One* multiple times, of course, but in researching this it spoke to me in that way, reinforcing my faith to love others, to be humble and kind, and to facilitate harmony.

Were you aware that any slip from harmony could have potentially disastrous effects?

CARLA We were indeed. More and more so as time went on, we were increasingly aware of the problems involved in even a tiny lapse in harmony. It was standing close to the light, it became very intense. It was a very intense experience.

GARY In 67.13, the Questioner is asking about the magical or philosophical principles concerning *how* the fifth-density negative entity is able to offer its service of psychic greeting. Ra explains how the entity breaches the quarantine, unnoticed, by using light, and sends forth its consciousness without any vehicle via magical working. Ra then says:

RA The light would work **instantly upon an untuned** individual by suggestion, that is the stepping out in front of the traffic because the suggestion is that there is no traffic. This entity, as each in this group, is enough disciplined in the ways of love and light that it is not suggestible to any great extent. 67.13

They're talking about you being so disciplined that you're not suggestible.

CARLA You're sure? [*laughing*]

GARY Here, as in other cases we will discuss further on, this powerful fifth-density negative entity is essentially trying to kill you in order to stop this contact. Did you believe this? And how did this information affect you?

CARLA Well, it was a little hard to believe at first, but things kept happening. What other explanation was there? So we were logically stuck with this answer. This was the solution; this was what was going on.

How it affected me? Phooey. I was irritated. Rather than making me scared, it made me want to say, "Up yours, Jack!" But who would be so crude? But that was my feeling from deep in the gut. *You're in my way* [*laughs*], *please don't do this.* It didn't make me scared, it just set me down solid; it grounded me.

GARY And fired up your courage even more.

CARLA Yeah.

GARY Ra says that the light that is magically wielded by the fifth-density negative entity would "work instantly upon an untuned individual." I know we discussed tuning, but as it is applied here, how is tuning a protection?

JIM The tuning helps to keep you focused and strong and aware so that when something out of the ordinary happens, you take note of it and the appropriate action.

GARY What you just said hits upon a different aspect of tuning. In that respect, you are, if tuned, simply more conscious of the processes that are happening in the moment—

CARLA And more balanced so that you don't overreact.

GARY Could you discern any perceptible difference between the fourth-density and the fifth-density negative greeting?

JIM I couldn't.

CARLA I never could discern any of that except in terms of results, and looking back knowing, "Oh, that had to be our fifth-density friend again." I was unaware until things happened, and then when they happened, I dealt with it and then afterwards I thought about it.

---

[1] *Know yourself, accept yourself, become the Creator* is Ra's dictum describing what they call the "discipline of the personality":

> QUESTIONER Now, what I am trying to get at is how these disciplines affect the energy centers and the power, shall I say, of the white magician. Could you, will you tell me how that works?

> RA I am Ra. The heart of the discipline of the personality is threefold. One, know yourself. Two, accept yourself. Three, become the Creator.

> The third step is that step which, when accomplished, renders one the most humble servant of all, transparent in personality and completely able to know and accept other-selves. In relation to the pursuit of the magical working the continuing discipline of the personality involves the adept in knowing itself, accepting itself, and thus clearing the path towards the great indigo gateway to the Creator. To become the Creator is to become all that there is. There is then no personality in the sense with which the adept begins its learn/teaching. As the consciousness of the indigo ray becomes more crystalline, more work may be done; more may be expressed from intelligent infinity. 74.11

[2] See the December 23, 2014 episode of *In the Now – Q&A with Carla Rueckert and Crew* for a good discussion on the topic of how love repulses negative entities and protects the self.

Audio currently at www.blogtalkradio.com/llresearch. Transcript soon to be published on the L/L Research podcast page www.llresearch.org/podcast.

[3] "For the love of money is a root of all sorts of evil, and some by longing for it have wandered away from the faith and pierced themselves with many griefs." (1 Tim. 6:10 [NAB])

Why You

GARY We're still in the Psychic Greeting portion and we're now on the sub-section regarding why you three were such a favorite target of negative greeters.

Ra claims that:

> RA This group, as all positive channels and supporting groups, is a greatly high priority with the Orion group. 64.14

Why are positive channels, as Ra says, "high priority" targets for the Orion group?

JIM They have what the Orion group wants: power.

CARLA They're manifesting light, they're giving information which is of a positive nature. That doesn't satisfy the needs of the negatively oriented entity at all. As far as they're concerned, you're trying to take over their territory. If they can't control that light, if they can't bend it so you are actually working for them, then they just as soon [*smacks hands together*] get rid of you and get rid of the light that they can't use.

GARY So it's not just the power in the light, in and of itself, but rather the capacity of the channel to help others, to influence others, to bring others also into the light. It's like you said: it's kind of territorial. The channel, as with others acting in service to others, has the capacity to help awaken others to love and light. The negatively oriented beings don't want that.

As was previously mentioned, your efforts attracted the attention of a negative entity of considerable power—a major leaguer, if you will. The questioner, Don Elkins, wonders why your group in particular would be such targets of intensive psychic greeting considering that you'll reach so few people:

> QUESTIONER As Ra well knows, the information that we accumulate here will be illuminating to but a **very minor percentage of those who populate this planet presently** simply because there are very, very few people who can understand it.[1]

> However, it seems that our fifth-density visitor is, shall we say, dead set against this communication. Can you tell me why this is so important to him since it is of such a limited effect, I would guess, upon the harvest of this planet? Since it seems to me that those who will understand this information will quite possibly already be within the limits of harvestability.

> RA I am Ra. Purity does not end with the harvest of third density. The fidelity of Ra towards the attempt to remove distortions is total. This constitutes an acceptance of responsibility for service to others which is of relative purity. The instrument through which we speak and its support group have a similar fidelity and, disregarding any inconvenience to the self, desire to serve others. . . . **Such purity is as a light. Such an intensity of light attracts attention.** 80.5

And earlier, Ra described how the negative entity operates by saying:

> RA The entity becomes aware of power [the power of the group doing this working]. **This power has the capacity of energizing those which may be available for harvest.** 68.16

So according to this question and answer, it's not necessarily the social or political or cultural impact that this work will have upon the world that attracts potent negative forces who seek to terminate the contact, but rather it is the contact's metaphysical qualities of power and purity that attract this attention.

So, as will happen in the next few questions, we're kind of turning over the diamond to examine a slightly different facet.

What was it about the contact with Ra that made it a source of power in the metaphysical world, and what about it was of some degree of purity?

CARLA Hmmm . . . [*pause*]

I guess it was built into us and manifested in the way we were—essence rather than behavior.

GARY You link the essence of the group to the power it generated?

CARLA Yeah, and all the purity.

JIM The information that Ra had to share was certainly of great value and had the ability to enlighten other folks as well.

GARY Due to its nature, this material must stand out somewhat exceptionally because, in my assessment of this planet (and I could be wrong), there's not a lot of purity on either end of the polarity spectrum. There's not a lot that is purely positive or purely negative. Ra says that most of humanity exists in a "sinkhole of indifference." We're a very mixed people as a whole.

CARLA It's the shades of grey.

GARY When you begin operating strongly and clearly from one end of that spectrum, that work creates a light that is a lot more visible, I would think, relative to this particular planet, given the situation here.

CARLA I would think so, yeah.

GARY According to Ra, this particular work attracted negative attention of what they described as a magical variety. Does that imply that the working you undertook was magical in nature?

JIM Yes, magic being the ability to create changes in consciousness.[2]

CARLA By thought alone rather than by manipulation [of the material world by material means].

GARY Ra goes onto say that:

> **RA** This [fifth-density negative] entity is desirous of disabling this power source. It sends its legions. Temptations are offered. They are ignored or rejected. The power source [of the group] persists and indeed improves its inner connections of harmony and love of

service. The entity determines that it must needs attempt the disabling itself. 68.16

In the same Q&A, Ra mentions that the group actually improved its "inner connections of harmony and love of service." It seems that, daunting though the challenge of the fifth-density negative greeting may have been, as with all challenges it offered equally proportional rewards. That is to say, the intensive psychic greeting provided an intensive opportunity to open the heart, to serve others, to become unified as a group, and to polarize. Can you comment?

JIM Well, what the psychic greeting actually does is to offer a sort of a left-handed compliment[3] that shows you where you have work to do. There may be something you've missed, so if you pay attention to where you're being greeted, you're also seeing things that can help you if you bolster what was weak into a more strong or balanced framework.

CARLA And there's the mentality of the game where you want to get focused in pitch and harmony with your team. It's like, *send me in, coach!* We all were trying to become better team members and more ready to be sent in.

GARY What you describe is an example of the way in which polarities assist one another, what Ra describes as the whole reason the Logos created the experiment of the veil: the polarities act as sort of a battery that moves evolution along. Here it is playing out, in your case, during the Ra contact. The negative polarity was, as you said, in a left-hand compliment sort of way, moving your own evolution along.

This following question is one we've already hit, but maybe we'll get something slightly new from asking it in this way:

The word "aggrandizement," as we have found quoted in Ra previously, is defined in *Merriam-Webster* as "the act of making something appear greater than is actually warranted by the facts." Also: "to enhance the power, wealth, position, or reputation of," and can be synonymous with "glorification."

What is the difference between natural or, you might say, *organic* growth, and aggrandizement?

CARLA The operative word is "natural." If you have to push at it and probe at it, and do something to it to make it happen, that's not natural.

GARY Maybe it's a matter of how and where you're aiming your desires. A thought just came to me from the Christian tradition that goes something like, "Seek ye first the Kingdom of God and all things will be added unto you."[4]

CARLA Yes.

GARY Maybe it's the difference between seeking the Creator, seeking to know yourself and allowing the cards to fall where they may, versus seeking enhancement of wealth and power and position as ends in and of themselves.

CARLA We never kidded ourselves that we were more than the "bozos on the bus," just like everyone else. We knew that we had exceptional material and we really, really wanted to do well by it.

GARY But that was never a stepping stone to—

CARLA No. As a matter of fact, I've been worried a little bit about this interview simply because people might think that, "Well, gosh, these are wonderful people." Well, thank you if you think that. Take a look at the material. Don't keep looking at us, because we will very soon fall on our faces and do something really stupid, like everybody else. And it will be disappointing if you think too much of us, so don't spend that much time, but go back to the material.

Know that we love you, [*laughs*] but then go back to the material.

GARY To conclude this subsection: We've already quoted this, so I won't read it all, but in 67.7, Ra is talking about how the fifth-density negative entity is working to terminate the group, and how you (Carla) are the prime target for that. That and the related Q&As are rather high drama. At least they can be read as such. Yet to hear you guys speak of that time period and the ordeals you endured, you don't sensationalize it, you don't dramatize it, and you don't enlarge the dynamics to inflated proportions. Can you comment on that?

JIM Well, we didn't feel like giving it more importance than it really deserved. If we keep concentrating on something like that, you give it more energy and make it more than it needs to be.

CARLA If somebody is in a horrible crash and they have come very close to death, that is high drama. On the other hand, isn't it good to focus on the healing and let that fade into the past? All that *oh we were driving along* *and they came out of nowhere and we spun and we spun*—all those details. *We're healing, help us to heal, pray for us* would be the better attitude.

---

[1]   Over 30 years later that still seems to be the case.

[2]   Another note about the magical nature or dimension of the contact:

> RA [This instrument is] involved in and dedicated to work which is magical or extremely polarized in nature. This group entered this work with polarity but virtual innocence as to the magical nature of this polarity [which] it is beginning to discover. 75.16

[3]   A "left-handed compliment" is an insult in the guise of an expression of praise; praise that is subtle dispraise; a backhanded compliment.

Jim may be applying the term to psychic greeting because whereas a left-handed compliment is a negative appearing as a positive, psychic greeting is a negative (an attack) appearing as a positive (offering growth). Psychic greeting highlights a weakness or *chink in the armor* where work is needed, and therefore offers the seeker an important service that is, from the greater perspective, helpful. Though on the surface it seems highly undesirable.

Moreover, one would not attract a psychic greeting unless one were making progress, thusly it is a compliment, of sorts.

[4]   "But rather seek ye the kingdom of God; and all these things shall be added unto you." (Luke 12:31 [KJV])

CHAPTER 12

The Brunt
of the
Greeting

GARY You were all targeted with psychic greeting, but the vast majority of that psychic assault was directed at Carla, the instrument. I found six different instances, among others, wherein Ra emphasizes the fact that Carla is taking the worst beating of you three.

> This instrument's bodily distortions are its most easily unbound or unloosed distortion dissolving the mind/body/spirit complex if the Orion group is successful. 62.14

> We have previously discussed the potential for **the removal of one of this group** by such attack and have noted that by far the most vulnerable is the instrument due to its pre-incarnative physical complex distortions. 67.7

> . . . of the [instrument] experiencing the brunt, shall we say, of this attack. 67.21

> . . . constancy of the surveillance of the instrument, for it is the weak link due to factors beyond its control within this incarnation. 67.23

> The free will, pre-incarnative distortions of the instrument with regards to the physical vehicle seem the most promising target for the Orion group. Any distortion away from service to others is also ap-

propriate. 68.16

The [negative] entity hopes to gain a portion of that light; that is, the mind/body/spirit complex of the instrument. Barring this, **the entity intends to put out the light**. 80.6

Carla and/or Jim, can you explain, for the listener or reader, why the instrument was the subject of such intensive psychic greeting?

CARLA They were having no luck with any of us in their usual way, which is internal: the ego, the thinking processes, and so forth. So naturally what was left was trying to weaken the physical vehicle. Well, Jim and Don were two extraordinarily healthy people. They seldom got ill, seldom got a cold even. They didn't have a lot of distortions that they could attack, whereas I was built on such a distorted physical body that I was fat city;[1] you didn't have to search to find a problem that they could intensify. So naturally they were intensifying at will, and I was hurting like a son of a gun. They were just having a good time, hoping that it would become too much for me.[2]

GARY I went hunting for mentions of the many ways that Carla was the recipient of psychic attack and was surprised by the quantity. The following may not be a complete listing but is a fairly comprehensive one. I want to give the readers a sense of what you experienced during the contact.

Instances of the instrument being greeted:

(Direct Ra quotes appear in quotation marks. All other instances are summarized quotes.)

Attempting to interfere with sexual energy transfer. 25.1

Draining the energy. 25.1

"The negative entities are moving all stops out to undermine this instrument at this time." 39.2

"This instrument is under a most severe psychic attack." 57.1

Facilitating a mis-reach, causing "skeletal/muscular deformation" of Carla's arm. 57.3

"This thought-form sought to put an end to this instrument's incarnation by working with the renal distortions." 62.4

Constant psychic attack exacerbating distortions in the pain/discomfort in the area of kidneys, urinary tract, and arthritis. 63.1

Weakening of the physical energy. 67.1

"The psychic attack upon this instrument is at a constant level as long as it continues in this particular service." 67.2

Creating a dizzying effect, loss of balance, and "slight lack of ability to use the optic apparatus." 67.12

Magical use of light to suggest that there is no traffic, thus causing Carla to walk out in front of the traffic; using dizziness in the hopes that she would walk out into, or fall, in front of traffic. 67.13

The Orion's attempt to steal your soul into negative time/space. 68.5

Orion goals to deplete the physical, and then the vital, energy. 70.4

Attempting to create "unconsciousness as in what you would call fainting or vertigo." 72.5

Orion entity hoping to gain Carla's light by enslaving her, or, barring that, by ending her life. In the former, adding to its own power; in the latter, removing a source of light and "radiance."[3] 80.6-7

". . . energizing a somewhat severe complex of imbalances in the manual appendages of this instrument and, to a lesser extent, those distortions of the thoracic region." 88.2

Inciting the instrument's "extreme distortion towards pain during and just after sessions." 94.2

"It is well that this instrument is not distorted towards what you may call hysteria, for the potential of this working was such that had the instrument allowed fear to become greater than the will to persevere when it could not breathe, each attempt at respiration would have been even more nearly impossible until the suffocation occurred which was desired by the one which greets you in its own way. Thus the entity would have passed from this incarnation." 95.2

Attempting to suffocate the instrument through the enabling of fear and hysteria. 96.2

Attempting to "close the throat and mouth" of the instrument by aggravating pre-existing allergies. 98.5

Triggering a "massive allergic reaction" in the "hopes that this entity would wish to leave the incarnation." 105.2

How did you hold up under all of that assault, Carla?

CARLA Well, as it occurred. I tried to stay in the present moment, and I knew that my strong point was faith and fearlessness, and that those were renewable resources, as opposed to my physical, which wasn't as easy to beef up. Faith is absolutely renewable; you just go to spirit and ask. You get a big *woof* and you're fine again.[4]

There's no end to vital energy if you have faith, and I did, and if you have will, and I did, and if you don't tend to worry about the future, and I don't, ever.

So I just stayed in the present moment and dealt with things as they came up. Or went down. [*laughs*]

And I had help, you know—I had physical help. Jim and Don were both right there. Like when I couldn't breathe. I was on a walk, and at first Jim didn't notice it, so I was not having somebody to back me up at that moment, but I just focused on the fact that if I continued not being able to breathe, I would just faint and my body would recover naturally. So I wasn't worried about it. I just made sure that I was in a place where I could fall down and not be in traffic or anything, over at the side of the road. I was off in a subdivision when this happened, so it wasn't a dangerous traffic situation. And after about, I don't know, 30 seconds, just about the time that it let up, Jim became aware of it and he was right there to give me an arm and pat me on the back and make sure that I was okay.

So that was probably the most dramatic of the things that happened to me where I had to consciously invoke fearlessness and the faith that all was well, and that all would be well.

GARY What you said about faith as a renewable resource was a particularly inspiring response. Thank you for that. And what you were describing of the moment when you where you were being suffocated, I wanted to comment that that's an incredible presence of mind to be able to logically think through the situation and deduce that: "Well, if I faint then I'm going to start breathing again, so there is no reason to fear."

CARLA I had a long-standing tendency to function well in a crisis. And then, after it's all over, I just fall apart. [*laughs*] But during the crisis, as long as it's necessary, I'm together and I'm functioning well and ready to react in the most appropriate way.

---

1 "Fat city" here means roughly that Carla was an easy and lucrative target for the negative entities.

2 Jim reflects on this in his Camelot Journal entry for July 15, 2015:

> In the audio book project tonight I recorded Session #62, the one where there was the mis-speaking of one simple word in our ritual of protection that we did prior to all sessions with Ra. After being sure that Carla's spirit was with them, Ra asked that we re-walk the Circle of One and then blow breath across Carla's chest from her right to her left. Don then asked what the problem was, and Ra said that the negative entity that was monitoring our sessions had found a target of opportunity in the missed word to attempt to end Carla's incarnation. It reminded me again of how Carla was willing to give all that she had to be of service. And that was true whether she was in a Ra session or anywhere else. She wanted to serve the One Creator which she saw in all people. After recording the session I could not control the tears of gratitude for her life, nor did I try.

The Camelot Journal of L/L Research, Jim McCarty, July 16, 2015, www.bring4th.org

3 Even if the Orion group succeeded in terminating Carla's incarnation, as Ra indicated was among their objectives, such an outcome would have been the result of extremely clever manipulation of Carla's own free will.

The metaphysics of *where responsibility lies* and *who is responsible* for this or that outcome are challenging and open questions. Ra indicates that everything which transpires to the individual, the group, or the collective happens as a function of the individual's, group's, or collective's free will, even if that free will is misinformed, manipulated, and abridged. Though that general principle of ultimate responsibility is, at times, exceedingly problematic to apply to specific situations.

4 Perhaps in connection to Carla turning to faith as a renewable resource:

> RA This instrument is capable of almost instantaneously clearing the mental/emotional complex and the spiritual complex for the purity this working requires. . . . 39.1

CHAPTER 13

Specific Instances (of Psychic Greeting)

GARY We resume our interview with the final section of psychic greeting that focuses on specific instances of psychic greeting that you guys experienced that were unusual (I guess they're all unusual). To begin with, Ra mentions different times when you were greeted psychically. I would like to ask you about those, beginning with Don's question:

> QUESTIONER I personally have felt no effect that I'm aware of. Is it possible for you to tell me how we are offered this greeting, this negative psychic greeting?
>
> RA I am Ra. The questioner has been offered the service of doubting the self and of becoming disheartened over various distortions of the personal nature. This entity has chosen not to use these opportunities, and the Orion entity has basically ceased to be interested in maintaining constant surveillance of this entity [the questioner]. 67.23

Did you guys see this in Don? That he had some proclivity towards doubting himself?

CARLA Uh-uh.

JIM I never saw it.

GARY So that's how efficiently he chose "not to use" those opportunities.

CARLA He always approached 100% efficient.

GARY And in the same response, Ra talks about psychic greeting that you, Jim, experienced, but Ra was very vague about what that was:

> **RA** The scribe is under constant surveillance and has been offered numerous opportunities for the intensification of the mental/emotional distortions and in some cases the connection matrices between mental/emotional complexes and the physical complex counterpart.
>
> As this entity has become aware of these attacks it has become much less pervious to them. 67.23

Jim, what does Ra mean by "mental/emotional distortions" and "connection matrices between mental/emotional complexes for the physical complex counterpart"? [*Gary laughs at repeating this wagonload of terminology.*]

JIM It's been my incarnational pattern to become angry at myself when I make a mistake, time after time: sawing a line that's crooked, pounding a nail that bends, little things like that. It's part of my trying to get more compassion in my incarnation, and as Ra said, what I've done is program lack of compassion for myself. It's not appropriate to program lack of compassion for another entity if you're positively oriented.

So by trying to get more compassion, I programmed lack of compassion for myself. It comes out as anger at myself when I do something that is so goofy, or at the wrong moment, or whatever reason—one thing after another. So when I would get angry, I would feel that there was an invitation, almost, to get angrier, and that's the connection between the mental/emotional and then the physical counterpart which is to break something. So, [*laughs*] that's what they're talking about.[1]

GARY I've never seen that in you, I don't know what they're talking about. [*everyone laughs at obvious sarcasm*]

That raises an interesting and quick side point in my mind. People not believing in or aware of reincarnation would say that those biases that we develop within the lifetime are developed as a result of interacting with our environment, whether nurtured or something in our genetics; whereas, as you are describing the situation, the entity can program for itself a certain set of predispositions and biases so that it will respond in certain ways. You're contending, then, that you programmed for this incarnation the predisposition to respond to situations with anger in order that you could experience that anger and then balance it.

JIM Right, to eventually feel compassion for myself after having gotten angry and broken something that I really liked, or behaved poorly. Then I think to myself [*in forlorn voice*], *aww. I could have done better.* But, you know, there it is—just accept yourself and go on. And that's hopefully a way of building compassion for myself.

CARLA He's always been able to hide it completely. I remember when I was just getting to know Jim, [*Jim laughs, apparently anticipating what Carla is going to say*] one of the ways it's quickest to get to know somebody is to read their hand, so I looked at his hand and I looked at his thumb, and I said, "You have a really bad temper, somewhere. That's what it looks like anyway." Jim just nodded and said, "Yeah, that's true."

And then I saw it for the first time. He had a little stone that he threw on the driveway right after buying it—I don't remember what he was angry with himself for—but that stone got chipped, and it couldn't be fixed. But he kept the chipped stone as a paperweight on his desk, which is what he had planned to use it for, and I was always amazed at that because obviously he had forgiven himself, and he was quite compassionate about it, and the stone reminded him every time he looked at it, I'm sure. Do you remember that? It had little flowers on it . . .

JIM Yeah, I do. I'd forgotten it, but now that you mention it, I remember.

CARLA I don't know what happened to it but I suppose in one of our moves it got lost.

JIM Yeah, I haven't seen it in years.

GARY Moving on to another specific instance of psychic greeting:

QUESTIONER What has caused the swelling in Jim's body and what can be done to heal it?

RA For the answer to this query we must begin with the consideration of the serpent, signifying wisdom. This symbol has the value of the ease of viewing the two faces of the one who is wise. Positive wisdom adorns the brow indicating indigo-ray work. Negative wisdom, by which we intend to signify expressions which effectually separate the self from the other-self, may be symbolized by the poison of the fangs. To use that which a mind/body/spirit complex has gained of wisdom for the uses of separation is to invite the fatal bite of that wisdom's darker side. 101.2

Can you elaborate more on what is meant by "negative wisdom" and how it pertains to this experience?

JIM Well, the negative wisdom would be some reason that you could give yourself for separating from another person, the rational reasons of *treated me poorly*, or *doesn't like me*, or *doesn't believe what I believe*, or *did something to*—whatever reason you want to come up with. You can convince yourself there's a reason to do just about anything, I guess, but in this case, it's how to separate from another person and why. That was happening at that time.

GARY So you were directing your wisdom in that direction?

JIM Yeah, we'd had a discussion about what to do about the *Law of One* material that we'd collected thus far. I think we were about through Session 75 or 76 or so, and Don wanted to print all 75 sessions in a single book. I was against that because, number one, we couldn't afford it, and two, we weren't done with the Ra contact; there would be more to come which would need to be printed as well. So that's what was happening there. I was allowing a separation to exist between Don and me. And I had to fix that rather quickly.

All that, however, didn't matter as much as the disharmony that I allowed to exist for a day or so. Disharmony in a working with the magical power of the Ra contact needed to be harmonized as soon as possible, so that our friend of negative polarity would not have an opening to energize and further hinder or stop the Ra contact.[2]

CARLA Don could be very frustrating, because he would just say, "No, I don't want to do this thing," and he would get very stubborn and there would be a subtle change in his facial expression. To me, he would resemble a goat, and when I saw the goat expression, I would think, "Oh, dear, there's no use talking to him right now." [*laughs*]

JIM So what had happened there was that one night, before I had healed the rift between us, in my sleep I was bitten by a common wood spider on my arm, and within a week or so I'd gained 30 pounds of water weight, my kidneys had begun to malfunction . . .

CARLA He'd gotten really round. And it was fleshy everywhere. You'd poke him and it would take a while to recover the—

JIM Everything I had except, maybe, my tongue. [*laughs*]

CARLA Water! Water, water everywhere.

JIM And so, actually I did get bitten, and Ra suggested that the bite was intensified by our friend of negative polarity to approximately equal the bite of a cottonmouth snake, a poisonous snake.

GARY And that bite was linked to you . . .

JIM To me due to allowing the difficulty, the poor communication, and the disharmony to exist between me and Don. So the little spider was just the avenue through which the negative entity could intensify the lack of harmony between Don and me at that time.

GARY So had you not been involved with the Ra contact, that sort of in-tensification probably would not have existed for—

JIM No, they wouldn't even notice me.

CARLA It wouldn't have been necessary. Yeah, and that's a good point. I think that all of the energy was focused on us as a group. I might have borne the brunt of it, but I did it for the group. It wasn't me personally. If I had not been doing the Ra contact, I wouldn't have had the problem because I wasn't standing close enough to the light. The Ra contact was dealing with a creature of great light and beauty, and more so than I'd ev-er had before. And it brought the group to their notice. I always think of the negative entity as plural—I don't know if it is or not, but you know—"they are legion," as it says in the Bible.

GARY The next question is about blue-ray blockage. On one level this is—along with other questions that I ask—of biographical interest for the person who wants more background information about the *Law of One* and how it came to be. But on another level, I think it's helpful for the student of this information to see an example of a principle; not to say that the example covers all the bases, but it does help to generate under-standing.

So at one point Ra says:

> RA Again, this group experienced blockage rare for the group; that is, the blue-ray blockage of unclear communication. By this means

the efficacy of the [negative entity's] working was reinforced. 98.5

What was this "blue-ray blockage of unclear communication"?

JIM At that time we were hoping to move down to the Atlanta, Georgia, area where Don was actually based as a pilot for Eastern Air Lines. He had to fly there before he could start his work, and it took about an hour to get there. So we thought it would be a lot handier, with him being based there, if we just moved there. So we were looking for a house and Don had found something that was a possibility, but it was so dirty inside that Carla thought, *we at least need to clean the rugs if not buy new rugs*, and Don wasn't really willing to put out the money necessary to do all the cleaning of the rugs, or get new rugs. But that wasn't clearly discussed on the way home. We flew home together on a plane, and I remember initiating some conversation there with Carla, and then with Don, about that situation, because there was an obvious disagreement as to what we should do about the dirtiness of this place—it's gotta be fixed.

So that was what was happening. For a while, there was a lack of communication.

CARLA I was reluctant to press it beyond a certain point. Again, I could read his face, and I knew that it was no use talking more. But I hadn't expressed myself fully. I hadn't said, "We can't do sessions there unless we get that thing clean." There was one *particular* spot on this rug which had—it was close to the wet bar, and the people that rented it before us were a group of Saints (the football team, the New Orleans Saints) and they were partying hard and drinking too much and they were always high on several substances. It was well known that this was a party place. It was a nice place, but I don't know what was in that one spot on the rug, but it just spoke to me that it was evil. Something was living in that spot. There was enough left of something there for something to gain purchase, and it was alive. And it was malevolent. I really, really wanted it gone in the worst way. Everything else about the place was absolutely wonderful.

So, Don was like, "No, I'm not gonna clean that carpet—that's ridiculous," and I'm like, *Ohhkaay, not today, I'm not going to talk about it.*

And yet I thought about it the whole way back, so it was really bugging me. Jim kept urging me to bring it up and I just didn't feel it was . . . I thought it was potentially harmful to push it at that time. I didn't want to cause disharmony, so, as I sometimes do, I just took it into myself and didn't share it. I thought I would bide my time.*

GARY Knowing you, that had to be difficult, because when something comes up on your radar that's getting under your skin or getting to you in some way, you need to address it *immediately* and work it out.

CARLA I do. Right away. And clearly, yes.

GARY That situation, too, is interesting in how it sheds light on how these mundane situations that we face every day—*cleaning the carpet*—are a platform for the balancing of energy, and working of our chakras, and relating to people.

CARLA We don't have to do unusual things or have great adventures to get the catalyst that we need. We'll get it raising kids and scrubbing the toilet. We'll get it.

GARY This is one that I was puzzled by:

> RA The welting is a symptom of that which has been a prolonged psychic greeting. The opportunity for this entity to experience massive allergic reaction from streptococcal and staphylococcal viruses has been offered **in hopes that this entity would wish to leave the incarnation.**
>
> *The previous occurrence of this state of the mind complex* occurring upon, in your time-numbering system, the ninth month, the twelfth day, of your present planetary solar revolution caught your fifth-density companion unprepared. The entity is now prepared.
>
> 105.2

So the way I read that, is Ra saying that you had wanted to die on September 12th of that year in 1983?

CARLA I don't think so. [*to Jim*] What was he saying, Micky? You get . . .

JIM No, I believe that was about the time we were preparing to move. We'd actually found another house in Georgia and we were about ready to go. And Carla had previously had some symptoms of this welting on her back.

CARLA They looked pretty bad.

---

* This event of seeming little moment had larger metaphysical consequence. See 96.2 for more on this point.

JIM Yeah, it was symmetrical.

CARLA I'd had trouble with that glomerulonephritis when my kidneys failed.

JIM So that was the time, when she was about 12 years old, she had wanted to die because she didn't feel that she could be of service. She'd gotten so much criticism from both her mom and dad over everything she did. When she was given the chance to babysit for her brother—when she was seven years old and the brother was just born. She cooked when she was ten—she had to stand up on a chair to reach the stove. She did all kinds of things to try to be of service, but she kept getting criticism. Her father was this German type of fellow that says, "Well, now, that's good, but you could do that better." Or, "What's the matter with this one B on your report card when everything else was an A?"

So that was the kind of situation in which she was raised, and so by the time she got to be twelve years old, she thought, *I can't be of service and I really want to be of service.* So she prayed to die. Six months later, her kidneys failed. So that's what happened then.

So this situation now, with the welting of a symmetrical nature on both sides of her back, was a possibility of the same thing that had happened to her kidneys, that if she had any desire at all to give up the incarnation now, the entity could intensify that welting, and her kidneys would fail and she would die.[3]

CARLA I'd forgotten that, so I figured he'd bring it back. Yeah, that was scary and, of course, I did not want to die, so that was pretty simple and straightforward once I got the . . . But there was a continuing problem, because I had a tendency to want to jump in and volunteer and do stuff. I remember trying to help pack, and at that point it was not wise for me to pack. Jim had to do everything, and so it was a difficult situation for me. And I, again, had to be reminded that I needed to take care of myself. Do that for the team. That was part of what we did.

GARY You have limitations.

CARLA Yeah, and they were increasing very quickly, so it was hard to be completely aware of just how limited I was getting. It was happening pretty fast. Just like it's happened this time. In the last couple of years it's been amazing how much I've been limited. First, not being able to walk, and then not being able to be free of the catheter, not being able to get out of bed without help—worse and worse and worse as far as being limited—and happening fast enough that it was a challenge to keep up with it, and remember, *this is your situation.*

GARY Yeah, it's kind of been a process of subtraction in your case, just removing one thing you can do, then another thing you can do, and then another.

CARLA Yeah. And it was like that then, also, just not on the same level: *No, you can't drive, no, you can't cook, no, you can't . . .* Just those simple things that everybody does, and I had done all my life. And then all of the sudden, *no, it will not be realized.* I had to preserve my energy.

GARY Especially difficult for someone like you whose whole being is oriented towards, not just doing just to do, but doing to serve. *I want to help, I want to participate.*

CARLA Yeah, I loved it. I loved everything.

GARY During one of your conscious channeling sessions with those of Latwii on August 16, 1981, you had a pretty scary incident. When Don subsequently asked Ra about it, Ra explained how you narrowly avoided a rather undesirable fate:

> **RA** We have instructed this instrument to refrain from calling us unless it is within this set of circumscribed circumstances. In the event of which you speak this instrument was asked a question which pertained to what you have been calling *The Ra Material.* This instrument was providing the voice for our brothers and sisters of the wisdom density known to you as Latwii.
>
> This instrument thought to itself, *I do not know this answer. I wish I were channeling Ra.*
>
> The ones of Latwii found themselves in the position of being approached by the Orion entity which seeks to be of service in its own way.
>
> The instrument began to prepare for Ra contact. Latwii knew that if this was completed the Orion entity would have an opportunity which Latwii wished to avoid.
>
> It is fortunate for this instrument, firstly, that Latwii is of fifth density and able to deal with that particular vibratory complex which

the Orion entity was manifesting and, secondly, that there were those in the support group at that time which sent great amounts of support to the instrument in this crux.

Thus what occurred was the ones of Latwii never let go of this instrument although this came perilously close to breaking the Way of Confusion. [Latwii] continued to hold its connection with the mind/body/spirit complex of the instrument and to generate information through it even as the instrument began to slip out of its physical vehicle.

The act of continued communication caused the [fifth-density negative] entity to be unable to grasp the instrument's mind/body/spirit complex and after but a small measure of your space/time, Latwii recovered the now completely amalgamated instrument and gave it continued communication to steady it during the transition back into integration. 68.5[4]

Ra later explained in that session that, had the Orion entity been successful, your soul, essentially, would have been stolen away to negative time/space. Meaning you would eventually have to relinquish your positive polarity and learn the ways of service to self.[5]

A few questions from that one: So how did you—tell us about this moment. What happened?

CARLA Well, I wasn't aware of it. I was aware of thinking, *gosh, I wish I were channeling Ra, I don't know the answer to this.* And I knew that it wasn't something within Latwii's purview—they didn't know. The answer was going to have to be a simple no.

I was not aware that, within myself, that wish (*I wish I were channeling Ra*) was enough to start the inner processes of getting ready to communicate with those of Ra. I had no idea. To me, I just was getting what seemed to me like normal channeling, although it made less sense than usual, so I just continued channeling, and got it all back together, but it was strange enough to ask about later.

I'm not remembering all the details. Jim, can you fill us in?

JIM Oh, well, I was aware of it even less than you. I was sitting next to you, but I know that you stopped channeling for a moment or two, and then you started channeling—I don't know, it didn't seem to really make sense—they were just trying to generate words through you.

That was about all that happened then, and that was on a Sunday, and I think the next day (or maybe it was Tuesday that we had a Ra session) Don got the chance to ask the question.

GARY It said that the support group was sending support, sending energy . . .

CARLA That would be Jim, gotta be. I must have been drawing[6] for our contact. We always hold hands.

GARY So there was some awareness that there was a basic difficulty there with the instrument, but you had no idea as to . . .

CARLA . . . the depth of the problem. Yeah.

GARY Prior to that point, you were highly cognizant that there were dangers and difficulties associated with attempting the contact with Ra. But at this point, you become aware of a consequence much more grave than any of you had probably imagined. Did this cause you to reassess whether the reward warranted the risk?

CARLA Heavens no! All it caused me to reassess was *The Crucifixion of Esmeralda Sweetwater*, because that was in *The Crucifixion of Esmeralda Sweetwater*—as her danger, or the space girl's danger—I don't remember at this removed time. It's been too long since we read that book, I don't remember much.

Anyway, it was one more thing that was pre-seen in that supposed work of fiction, and we were all fairly amazed: *Oh my God, here's another synchronicity.* And it couldn't be just synchronicity, it was too exact.

JIM Don did everything he could do, to question Ra about what we could do, to be sure that didn't happen. Sessions 68 through 72 are full of questions from Don about that incident and the possibility of losing Carla. *What can we do?*

GARY Ken and I were just talking about that. Don seemed quite baffled by it, but asked questions not only to understand, intellectually, but in order to prevent it from happening.

JIM Yes, that's how we dealt with it, to ask Ra, "Well, what should we do about this? How do we keep this from happening?"

GARY I would be quite disconcerted if I were in those shoes.

CARLA One thing that Ra said at the time was that as long as I was being touched, I couldn't leave my body.[7]

JIM Yes. A simple holding of the hand. That's why, up until this day, I hold her hand when we're meditating.

CARLA Or doing spiritual work like this. We blessed this and tuned for it, so we consider it part of the service to others, so we're holding hands.

GARY Which answered my next and final question for psychic greeting, which was:

What were the lasting ramifications of that moment? And you've held Carla's hand ever since, to make sure that there's no chance that she could leave her body.

JIM ". . . infringe upon her aura so that the spirit does not want, or find it able, to leave."[8]

GARY Good safeguard all these years.

JIM And very simple, and pleasant, and romantic.

CARLA Very low-tech. [*laughs*] Nothing to plug in.

GARY That's a great way to put it. That concludes all the psychic greeting material. Thanks for trudging through all that.

CARLA [*laughs*] Yeehaw. I'm glad it's done.

---

[1] What Ra describes of Jim's patterns is for Jim to know. He reached his own conclusion that works for him. But an alternative interpretation regarding the "the connection matrices between mental/emotional complexes and the physical complex counterpart" may be something along the lines of physical distortions being a result of mental/emotional distortions, and the negative entity intensifying that, as the negative entity did later in the contact with the spider bite. (Thanks to Austin for this insight.)

[2] Half of Jim's thoughts in this Q&A came from Jim's reply to an email seeking further clarification on the point.

[3] Jim writes of this Q&A:

In reviewing this, it does sound like Ra is saying that Carla had wished to die on Sept. 12 of 1983, but I don't remember any mood or feeling like that. What was happening was that she was keeping the feeling of harmony between herself and Don and then herself and our landlord as we were attempting to move. She kept her harmony with both of them even though both of them were giving her a hard time about what they wanted.

4 This question and answer refer to the L/L Research Sunday night meditation of <u>August 16, 1981</u>.

The remainder of Session 68 focuses exclusively on this situation, its practical and philosophical implications. The topic is investigated further in subsequent sessions.

5 Reflecting on the possibility of Carla being stolen away to negative time/space, as it were, Jim wrote in *The Camelot Journal* for June 8, 2015:

> As I was recording Session #68 from the Ra contact this evening I became very emotional at the end. This was the session where Don questioned Ra about Carla's nearly going into trance during a Sunday night meditation and nearly being led away by our negative polarity friend. The tears flowed powerfully because this session reminded me once again how much of a spiritual warrior Carla was in being willing to do whatever was necessary to be of service to others. She was that way all her life, and this session underlined her unbreakable resolve to give of herself until all was given.

The Camelot Journal of L/L Research, Jim McCarty, June 9, 2015, www.bring4th.org.

6 About "drawing," Jim writes: "I was holding Carla's hand while the negative entity [unbeknownst to Jim] was trying to steal her mind/body/spirit away. And she was 'drawing energy' from me as I was her battery."

7 Which is an effective preventative measure and safeguard for conscious channeling, but could not be used for the contact with Ra. While Carla was separated from her body in that peculiar state, her body could not in any way be disturbed by environmental inputs, including physical touch.

> QUESTIONER Thank you. A question I didn't get to ask the previous session which I will be forced to continue at this time is, is the trance state the only condition from which a mind/body/spirit positive entity may be lured by a negative adept to a negative time/space configuration?

> RA I am Ra. This is a misperceived concept. The mind/body/spirit complex which freely leaves the third-density physical complex is vulnerable when the appropriate protection is not at hand. You may perceive carefully that very few entities which choose to leave their physical

complexes are doing work of such a nature as to attract the polarized attention of negatively oriented entities. The danger to most in trance state, as you term the physical complex being left, is the touching of the physical complex in such a manner as to attract the mind/body/spirit complex back thereunto or to damage the means by which that which you call ectoplasm is being recalled.

This instrument is an anomaly in that **it is well that the instrument not be touched** or artificial light thrown upon it while in the trance state. However, the ectoplasmic activity is interiorized. The main difficulty, as you are aware, is then the previously discussed negative removal of the entity under its free will.

That this can happen only in the trance state is not completely certain, but it is highly probable that in another out-of-body experience such as death the entity here examined would, as most positively polarized entities, have a great deal of protection from comrades, guides, and portions of the self which would be aware of the transfer you call the physical death. 69.3

8
About infringing on the aura:

QUESTIONER Then you are saying just by holding the instrument's hand during the channeling sessions that this would prevent trance?

RA I am Ra. This would prevent those levels of meditation which necessarily precede trance. Also in the event that, unlikely as it might seem, the entity grew able to leave the physical complex the auric infringement and tactile pressure would cause the mind/body/spirit complex to refrain from leaving. 69.19

CHAPTER 14

End of the Ra Contact

GARY We'll discuss in detail the events surrounding the attempts at relocating to Atlanta in the personal biography section of Don. In the meantime, this is a question about something discussed in 106.13, the final session of the Ra contact on March 15, 1984. In that session, Ra said:

> **RA** The questioner has, in the recent past, allowed a complete transfer of mental/emotional pain from the questioner to the instrument.
>
> The key to this deleterious working was when the instrument said words to the effect of the meaning that it would be the questioner and be the strong one. The questioner could be as the instrument, small and foolish.
>
> The questioner, in full ignorance of the firm intent of the instrument and not grasping the possibility of any such energy transfer, agreed. These two entities have been as one for a timeless period and have manifested this in your space/time. Thusly, the deleterious working occurred. By agreement in care and caution it may be undone. We urge the attention to thanksgiving and harmony on the part of the questioner. 106.13

Can you describe this incident and why you made this offer to Don?

CARLA Well, he was in great distress while we were in Georgia. He couldn't find any place that was satisfactory, to him, to live, didn't know what we were going to do next, didn't know if he wanted to continue the job at Eastern Air Lines.

He was worried that Eastern Air Lines would go into bankruptcy. It took, I don't know, something like eleven years after Don died, but it did eventually fail.[1] And right along the lines that Don thought. He was always right. So the poor guy was just distressed, very distressed, and very uncomfortable. I'd never known him to be so down. He was normally a very affable, even-level, positive guy who took everything very lightly and nothing made any difference; it was all an illusion, and he was just glad he had a private room. He was on top of it.

Well, all of a sudden, he wasn't on top of anything. The poor guy was just dying, he worried so much, and I was worried for him. So just the way you do, I said, "Look, I'll take this from you if you'll just stop worrying. I'll do the worrying, I'll be the strong one," you know, just like Ra said, "You be the small and foolish person that I am," and Don said, "Oh yeah, right, well let's do that."

He didn't know—we didn't know that it was going to happen on an inner level, but it did. He became the possessor of my inner sensitivity, my open heart. I was open to everything and I wasn't afraid of anything, but he wasn't able to carry the fearlessness, and everything was incredibly moving to him. He would look at a sitcom and he would cry as a result of this switch. His heart had just suddenly opened and he was incredibly ill-prepared to deal with this because his heart had formerly been encased in reinforced concrete. Nothing got to him, whatsoever. So all of a sudden everything was getting to him. So I'd made the situation worse by that offer, not better.

Meanwhile, I got his fear of everything. Don was always very heavily armored. He just thought this world was a dangerous place, and I got that. I was able, for the most part, to ignore that, but that was the situation.

Jim, what am I leaving out?

JIM Well, later Ra mentioned that Don was also going through initiation at the same time. On top of that, Carla, who shared this bond of oneness with Don, had initiated this energy exchange. So that, coupled with the initiation, all made things very, very difficult for Don.

GARY Prior to Ra's confirmation and explanation regarding what happened, did you feel Don's fear within you?

CARLA I didn't identify it as such. I felt an increased level of the potential for the taking of things in a way that I would want to be defended against, and that the world was a dangerous place—things I'd never felt before. But I didn't identify it as that I'd actually received Don's inner mental bias.

JIM The whirlpool activity was an expression of it.

CARLA Well, that one night, I got stuck in a very hot whirlpool for too long before I could get somebody to help me out of it. I couldn't personally get out of it. I was way down and I was so light that I would bob in the whirlpool [*laughs*], and so I had weights around my waist (the kind that divers use) and I was right there: I was grounded in this neck-high whirlpool, and it was really close to bubbling into my nose at all times, and I got really, really dizzy. So when I got out of it, I went psychotic for a little while. I don't remember much about it except that I felt like a cornered animal, and I was ready to charge anybody that got in my way.

GARY And this was subsequent to the deleterious energy transfer?

JIM Yes, the water was too hot for too long, so it put her in a state of shock, and what came out was the feeling that she'd gotten from Don, of his fears, and she went into a psychotic episode which ended as soon as she got back to normal temperature.

CARLA As soon as I cooled off, I was able to get my breath back and everything.

GARY For readers, Carla and Jim are describing what Ra talks about here:

> QUESTIONER Can you tell me what the instrument's difficulty was with her last whirlpool?
>
> RA I am Ra. **The instrument took on the mental/emotional nature and distortion complex of the questioner** as we have previously noted. The instrument has been taking the swirling waters at temperatures which are too hot and at rates of vibration which, when compounded by the heat of the swirling waters,[2] bring about the state of light shock as you would call the distortion. The mind complex has inadequate oxygen in this distorted state and is weakened. In this state **the instrument, having the questioner's**

distortion without the questioner's strength of the distortion one might liken to the wearing of armor, began to enter into an acute psychotic episode. When the state of shock was past the symptoms disappeared. The potential remains as **the empathic identity has not been relinquished, and both the questioner and the instrument live as entities in a portion of the mental/emotional complex of the instrument.** 106.22

So prior to Ra telling you that you had this deleterious energy working, neither you nor Don knew what happened or could explain the strange feelings you were feeling?

CARLA No, it would have been far too bizarre for us to make up. It wouldn't have occurred to us. Stranger than fiction is the way our lives were for a while.

GARY It was a time of mounting bizarre episodes in your lives.

Just a quick detail question on that: How soon after you made this pact together did you begin to feel the other's emotions so strongly?

CARLA Immediately.

GARY Wow. So, I understand you can only speculate, but, had Don *gradually* grown into the open heart, *gradually* had that concrete barrier chipped away, it probably would have been a lot safer for him. Rather than all at once.

CARLA A whole lot safer. When you figure what he did, from a larger point of view, at least my personal opinion is, he spent close to 50 of his 50 years working on his service: the answer to *why*, the filling in of the puzzle pieces, and eventually, the Ra contact. He worked intensively at that and *nothing* else interested him for his entire life, his entire adult life.

Then he spent less than the last year of his life doing his personal work, which he'd probably come here to do as well, which was to open his heart, to balance a little bit more from wisdom to the open heart. And he opened his heart—snap—like that. And then he had to deal with the consequences of everything pouring in and affecting him.

A brave guy—he did a beautiful job of it. It finally killed him. But he got his work done, and he certainly got his service done. Thank God.

GARY In the same session, Ra said of you and Don that:

RA These two entities have been become as one for a timeless period and have manifested this in your space/time. 106.13

I have a hard time trying to wrap my head around that one. Is there any meaningful way to translate that?

CARLA Yeah, what is "a timeless period"? Had we spent some time in the rings of Saturn or something, or in an altered state? I have no idea, I have no idea, I've never been able to . . . Jim, you got a clue?

JIM No, not really. I have a hunch that you have a long relationship—the three of us had times before; you and Don, I believe, had a very special relationship for—

CARLA What was that one reading sent to him, fifteen lifetimes of service together or something like that.

JIM It's in the realms of mystery.

GARY I figured as much. I was just wondering if there was any translation to provide.

CARLA No, I haven't ever figured that out.

KEN Could it have been that you guys were together in a social memory complex in a sixth-density unified space for a while then split down here?

JIM It's possible.

KEN That was the only thing that came to my mind thinking of "timelessness."

CARLA But then that wouldn't be timeless, though. It would still be in time. You don't get into timelessness until the end of the seventh density.

JIM Or the beginning of the first.

CARLA Or the beginning of the next octave.

GARY Logically the term is a paradox: a timeless *period*. *Period* points to the lapsing of time, a beginning and an end.

CARLA Yes, it's completely defying the logical mind. Nothing linear about that.[3]

GARY In the final question of the Ra contact, Don says:

QUESTIONER And we would certainly—I would certainly appreciate the return of the golden hawk. It gave me great comfort. 106.23

What is the incident to which Don refers?

JIM At the house where we were living outside of Cumming, Georgia, which is about an hour north of Atlanta, there was a hawk—it was in the countryside so there was a lot of wildlife around—but there was a hawk in a tree not too far away, and we had, for some period of time, always associated the hawk with Ra, because Ra eventually took the place of the hawk-headed God of the Sun, Horus, in Egyptian mythology. Don saw this golden hawk—not just an ordinary hawk, with grey wings and a white chest—it was all gold. So he took a lot of comfort from that, thinking perhaps he'd made some sort of a contact with Ra, that he was being visited, or there was support; he just felt comforted by it.[4] It was an actual hawk.

GARY That brings up a question I hadn't built into this interview. The long-standing association of hawks with Ra. That was completely your group's invention?

JIM That's what we did.

CARLA But it's historical as well.

GARY I can see why the association was made, I just never understood the genesis of it.

CARLA Well, we just noticed hawks a lot after we got together, and we never had seen them before. Even here, for years, we had a hawk that nested right—I guess up over the next neighbor's door? Overlooking our backyard—raised little hawk families for several years.

GARY It's an association that started with you guys, but because of your creation of it, has extended beyond you. A lot of people who enjoy this material also now see hawks and Ra as being associated. Myself included, I get excited when I see a hawk.

CARLA I'm so glad. [*laughs*]

GARY And in the final response you received from Ra, just before they closed with their customary salutation, they said:

> **RA** We suggest the nature of all manifestation to be illusory and functional only insofar as the entity turns from shape and shadow to the One. 106.23

What does that statement mean to you?

JIM Well, we live in an illusion of shape and shadow, and eventually it's up to us to be able to see through it and to see that it's all part of one being. That whatever we're looking at, we're looking at the Creator. If we see anything other than the Creator, then we're looking at shape and shadow, which is an illusion, and it has a purpose to help us get passed it. Eventually.

CARLA Isn't it a wonderful little phrase? It just puts our humanity right there—the world of shape and shadow and form, physical form—everything that we can see is all illusory. Ra started the contact by saying that we are thoughts.

GARY Dancing thoughts.

CARLA Dancing in the somewhat eccentric pattern [*laughs*] due to our distortion.⁵ So it's a very tidy ending to a long conversation.

GARY And puts the scope of the whole human project into perspective.

So, what would you say brought an end to the Ra contact?

CARLA Don's death.

JIM Don's death.

GARY And I presume that was the same reason why it was never attempted again.

CARLA I was dead set against . . . Ra had warned me specifically against calling for Ra if I didn't have Don and Jim as batteries. It was dangerous to me unless I had Don and Jim. I didn't have Don. Forget the fact that his scope of ability as questioner went far beyond anyone else I knew or have ever known, I just didn't have his physical presence, I didn't have his love. I was not safe and I saw no reason to risk my life if we didn't have the appropriate way to do it. It was hard enough with everything in place, so if I didn't have Don I was definitely going down. [*laughs*] No question about it. And I treasured my little life; I wanted to maintain it and to offer whatever I could. I felt I had more to give.

I had temptations. I had so many people that were very serious about doing whatever, you name it: money, different places to live, different situations that would make it more desirable for me to do this. One guy had a machine that would help me and would take the place of the battery, and all this blah, blah, on and on.

It all just was not appropriate and the only time I had a problem with it was when this one guy was so persistent that it was making me physically ill—the calling and the hounding me—and I can't remember all that he did. Did he sit out at the airport for a while?

JIM Maybe, I don't know.

CARLA Anyway, I felt like anybody that did that—like I was being stalked. You don't know how to remove yourself from the situation and make it stop, and you can't go to the police and say, [*laughs*] "He wants me to channel." The police are going to take a very dim view of the whole thing and just tell me to go see a psychiatrist. So I was very glad when he stopped. I don't know exactly what made him stop.

GARY That's why I remarked earlier about how amazing it is that you guys were kind of insulated from external influence, that there weren't people banging down the door trying to interfere in some way, even in what they perceived would be a positive sense. You guys were kind of on your own in that regard. And it was a blessing, I think.

So, had Don not left this plane of existence, would you have continued the Ra sessions indefinitely?

JIM Oh sure. [*laughs*]

GARY Quite the challenge that would have been.

Do you guys personally have other questions or avenues of inquiry that you would like to have explored with Ra?

JIM Oh, the archetypical mind. We only got through the mind completion, or relative completion. Sure, there are so many things that we didn't get to. Once your circle of knowledge starts expanding, it touches on more things that you don't know—questions just keep coming.

---

[1]

Eastern Air Lines actually declared bankruptcy in 1989, about five years after Don's passing, and was liquidated in 1991.

"Eastern was one of the 'Big Four' domestic airlines created by the Spoils Conferences of 1930, and was headed by World War I flying ace Eddie Rickenbacker in its early years. It had a near monopoly in air travel between New York and Florida from the 1930s until the 1950s and dominated this market for decades afterward. Labor disputes and high debt loads strained the company in the late 1970s and early 1980s under the leadership of former astronaut Frank Borman. . . .   After continued labor disputes and a crippling strike in 1989, Eastern ran out of money and was liquidated in 1991."

Wikipedia, The Free Encyclopedia, s.v. "Eastern Air Lines," accessed June 16, 2016, https://en.wikipedia.org/wiki/Eastern_Air_Lines

2

When queried about the "swirling waters," Jim replied:

If you think back a few years ago you may remember this whirlpool tub being next to the sump pump in the basement. It was white and long and rounded. It was about four feet deep and had a seat on one end on which Carla would sit. The controls were at the other end and would control the amount of air that would shoot into the water and cause a turbulence that came out of two jets on each side of the whirlpool. Carla used that whirlpool at the Watterson Trail location during the Ra contact and also over here for a few years afterward. She had to wear weights to hold her down because she floated so easily.

3

About the issue of existing in timelessness, Ra says:

RA We are not a part of time and, thus, are able to be with you in any of your times. 1.1

Perhaps if Don and Carla were part of those of Ra, they too, then, existed *outside of time,* as it were. Though we can only speculate. In 45.7 Ra indicates that two of the three are sixth density wanderers; the other a fifth density wanderer. Who came from where and from what density is unknowable; also, unimportant. But great endnote material.

4

In the process of recording the audiobook for *The Ra Contact: Teaching the Law of One,* and commenting about that project in *The Camelot Journal,* Jim wrote for the June 23, 2015 entry:

I finished recording Session 106 of the Ra contact today and noted the irony of Don's mention of the comfort he took in the sighting of a golden hawk at our Lake Lanier, Georgia, house. I have a hunch that it was another messenger from those of Ra sent to wish us all farewell.

The date was March 15, 1984, the Ides of March. Upon hearing that I had finished the recording of the last session Gary asked if I would like to do it again to get a more nearly perfect recording as I had gotten much better after 50 or so sessions. I happily agreed as this has been a most healing experience for me. I have felt the presence of both Don and Carla as I recorded and relived our great adventure together. I noted that the first session in 1981 began on January 15, Martin Luther King's real birthday, a fact I always thought to be most promising.

The Camelot Journal, Jim McCarty, published June 24, 2015, www.bring4th.org

5

The exact quote:

> RA You are not part of a material universe. You are part of a thought. You are dancing in a ballroom in which there is no material. You are dancing thoughts. You move your body, your mind, and your spirit in somewhat eccentric patterns, for you have not completely grasped the concept that you are part of the original thought. 1.0

Ra Contact Olio*

GARY Don made inquiries into learning how to heal and received foundational instructions from Ra. Ra indicated that there could be subsequent instruction if you three pursued this path, including instruction in the proper use of crystals for healing. Did you guys ever make serious headway in that regard?

JIM Not really. We got a beginning, Don and I did. Carla was advised to not ever do physical healing; she didn't have enough physical energy to do that. Don and I made a little beginning, and after he died, I continued for a while. But I never felt like it was a natural ability or something that really opened up as an avenue for me, so I eventually let it go.

CARLA I do feel that he has healing hands, but it's not pronounced enough to be an art or to be a gift.

GARY Can you describe, in detail, the cleansing ritual you performed with salt, per Ra's instructions?[1]

JIM Yeah. [*chuckles*] I did it to this house, and I did it to our house in Cummings, Georgia, at midnight. I drove down there with a first load of

---

* "Olio" is one of many uncommon words that Carla, with her expansive vocabulary, knew and used. As she employed the term it meant a *miscellaneous mixture or collection of things.*

things in a U-Haul trailer, and the first thing I had to do was the ritual.

So we got a gallon of distilled water from the grocery store, took it to Father Ben Sanders at Carla's Episcopal church, and he blessed it so that it would become holy water—"blessed by intentions," was what Ra suggested. And using salt, just regular salt (which apparently has an ability to absorb negative vibrations) at the base of every window and doorway, leaving one doorway so I could get in and out, I spread the salt in an unbroken line, and then sprinkled water on it. I'd put it in my hand and sprinkled it like this [*makes repeated motions of flicking his hand downward to distribute water over the salt*]. It didn't have to be totally wet; the water just had to be sprinkled, in general, all along the line of salt. The salt had to be continuous. So that needed to stay—I think it was for thirty-six hours . . .

CARLA Three days.

JIM Three days—72 hours all together.[2] So once that first section was done, then I went back and did the one doorway, after everything else had been cleansed.

CARLA You could go anywhere you wanted except that doorway.

JIM Yeah, I did the one doorway. So, what that is supposed to do is to invite any entities of a negative nature who are inside the dwelling to leave, because they wouldn't find it helpful for their purposes to be in the house, since the entire place had been cleansed and purified. As Carla said, they like dirty places, that junk on the rug. You may remember that at one point there was a smell emanating from the room in which we had the Ra contact, and it was a dead mouse, and an astral entity had taken up residence in it. So we had to be sure to get the mouse out and clean the room, and the astral entity went with the mouse. So that was the whole idea. And then in the boathouse, I believe, we used cut garlic.

CARLA Or was it a cut onion?

JIM It was garlic. I think we got a few cloves that were woven together, and we cut them in half. And garlic also has the same ability that salt does.

CARLA Jim tied it all together. It was like a kabob.

JIM We were trying to get rid of wasps that were living in the boathouse at that time.

CARLA We were all sensitive to any stings. That would have been dangerous.

JIM And then after the garlic has been used, then you burn it, and that was the end of that.

GARY Some technical detail questions: The salt was just on the interior windowsills, or the exterior?

JIM Interior. Didn't matter. Whichever was handiest for me to use.

GARY And the doorway—you're just sprinkling it on the ground of the doorway?

CARLA On the doorsill.

GARY And no invocations were needed or anything?

JIM No, there was a . . .

CARLA There was a little prayer.

JIM Yeah, it's given in the—I don't remember it all right now, but it's given in the book. Ra gives us special words to say when we're spreading the salt and wetting the salt, when we're using the garlic, and when we're burning the garlic. There were words for all of that.

CARLA It was just a little short bunch of phrases that invoked the power of these substances to do their work.

GARY And the garlic—you said you hung it like a kabob? How did you hang it?

CARLA It was supposed to be suspended.

JIM Right. The garlic has a natural leaf on it like onions do. I just braided them together. They come like that from the store a lot, they're already braided together.

GARY And then you cut it in half?

JIM I cut each clove in half so that the garlic scent would come out.

CARLA Did it ever! He would walk through with these kabobs, and the smell— But he was so brave to do that because walking along the boathouse—well of course the boathouse doesn't have a floor because that's where the boat lives when you've got a boat, which we didn't. So he was balancing, walking out on a piece of wood that constituted the structural part of the structure, that part that went along there, so he was balancing on this like a ballerina in the air . . . What do you call them, people that walk tightropes?

JIM A tightrope walker.

CARLA He was like a tightrope walker with these kabobs and then tying them at the end and then walking back, and meanwhile there would be the *buzzzzzz* of the wasps that were still there. He's like, *don't investigate me now, please.* [*laughter*] He's a very brave chap.

GARY In 101.2 on Dec 21, 1982, Ra gave Jim an incredible and accurate medical diagnosis.[3] Did you share this with the doctor, and if so, what was the doctor's response?

JIM Didn't share the whole thing with them—said I'd been bitten by a spider, and it had swollen up fiercely. All of a sudden I started gaining weight. The doctor was fascinated. You could push down on any part of my body and it would stay down for about a minute and then slowly rise.[4]

CARLA This particular doctor was very clever and very sage, and his reaction was to look it up.

JIM Yeah, he looked up in his—I guess they've got a name for it—but he looked up spider bites and saw that there were some spiders who could cause kidneys to go into this type of—it was called "minimal change syndrome" or "nephritis", was the terminology. So he found some basis for it in the medical documents—

CARLA It was rare, but it was that one white crow that shows you that all crows are not black. In other words, it was rare, but it happened. It had been documented.

GARY It's pretty impressive when Ra starts giving these very correct names of anatomy, prescription medication and medical conditions near the end, and I wondered what a medical professional would have to say.

JIM Ra gave one, basically, for Carla too, which was fairly impressive. Don did take that to the doctor and he sort of pooh-poohed it, I believe. Dr. Shane?

CARLA Yeah, when Dr. Shane looked at it—well, he didn't look at it, he just threw Don out. And Don was furious. He kept saying, "You have the answer, and you won't—just give her this prescription and then throw me out." He was so mad. And he stayed mad at that guy. But when I took it to Dr. Blodgett again, he just looked it up and noted that it was accurate. It was amazingly accurate.

GARY You didn't tell either of these doctors the source?

CARLA Only Dr. Blodgett. Dr. Blogett knew everything about me.

GARY And he was willing to go along with it.

CARLA Oh man, he was tough. Very open minded and very understanding.

GARY You reported seeing "silver flecks" during the course of the Ra contact. When Don asks what these are, Ra replies:

> RA These of which you speak are a materialization of a subjectively oriented signpost indicating to one mind/body/spirit complex, and no other, a meaning of subjective nature. 16.47

When and how often did you see these?

JIM Like they did with the hawks, Ra gave us confirmation for the line of thought that we were engaging in at the time, or the plan of action.

CARLA Generally, they were seen on me, mostly around my eyes and my face. Don would carefully go over and he would get it with Scotch tape and then he'd save it so we had all these little pieces of Scotch tape with little dots on it that were the silver flecks. Now somebody took a silver fleck in and put it under a microscope and found that there were crystalline differences between that fleck and, say, glitter that you have on a costume. Nobody had ever made this such as they are.

JIM Suppose they're still in here?

GARY When you said that they were on you, did you mean they were resting on your skin?

CARLA Right on my skin. Smaller than most glitter, but very, very bright. You can't see it on the scotch tape much.

JIM [*Jim retrieves the preserved silver flecks from a box.*] This one is hexagonal.

KEN There's the silver flecks in your box labeled "silver flecks."

JIM Right. [*laughter*]

KEN So you did save them.

CARLA We did. Well Don was ever the scientist, you know.

JIM Probably six or seven in here, I guess, from different occasions. One was in here [*Jim motions toward something else*]—I don't know what happened to it—but at least we do have some.

GARY Did he ever send it off to a lab to get it analyzed to see what its properties were?

JIM No.

GARY That would be interesting. So did this just happen a handful of isolated times? Or was it a frequent thing?

CARLA Yes, for a while there it was constant.

JIM Who was the woman Don met that had them all over her body?

CARLA Somebody involved with Andrija Puharich. I don't remember her name. She was very small, little, petite, and she drew the flecks.[5]

JIM Puharich was familiar with the silver fleck phenomenon.

CARLA It wasn't Anna, was it?

JIM I don't know.

GARY Your group wasn't the only one that experienced silver flecks?

CARLA I don't think so. I think it was this little, petite woman. Puharich and we seemed to be connected in some way. The fact that I got him in the book, and that Don felt that he was his best friend—we were preparing to move up to where he lived, to work with him. We were going to rent the barn on his property, which wasn't a barn, but it was an office and a loft which had been intended for somebody to live and work there. We were going to rent that and live and work with Puharich. Don loved nothing more than talking to Puharich, except, of course, talking to Ra. Puharich and he had long conversations into the night—many, many nights—and they enjoyed each other tremendously.

Puharich was a very misunderstood guy. He was just a hard-working guy. Like Don, he was interested in the paranormal, and once you get hooked by that, you're set for life with more work than you can do. He was up at an early hour working, working, working; and if he got really hungry, he'd stop . . . I've seen him when there was nothing in the house and no-body wanted to cook—I wasn't close enough then to do anything about it. Don didn't want me to cook anyway. (There were people in the house that were capable of cooking, but for some reason they had all rebelled and felt like they were being overworked, which was kind of silly. But they were kids, they were just young kids, and easy to forgive their distortions.)

So there was nothing in the house except some beans that had just been put on to boil and you know what dry beans are like, hard as rocks. I told him, "This has only been boiling for about twenty minutes; it's going to take four hours." He said, "Well, I'm hungry now." So he got this bowl of totally raw beans out of the pot and crunched them down and went back to his work. Mind you, he had plenty of money and there was a diner right down the road from us, from where he lived. He didn't want to spend time filling his belly, he just wanted to have something to eat and go back to work. It would have been very easy to take care of Puharich, I'll say that.

GARY A lot of people of high intellect are like that.[6] They don't pay too much attention to the necessities of life to the extent that they have to wear clothes and they have to put food in their mouths, then otherwise about their business.

CARLA Totally a distraction—they don't want to do any of that.

GARY In the first question of Session 22, Ra says:

> RA Each time, as you would put it, that we perform this working our social memory complex vibrational distortion meshes more firmly with this instrument's unconscious distortions towards service. **Thus we are becoming a part of this instrument's vibratory complex and it a part of ours.** This occurs upon the unconscious level, the level whereby the mind has gone down through to the roots of consciousness which you may call cosmic. 22.1

Was this perceptible to you in any way, and how, if at all, did this manifest? (Ra mentions the smelling of incense as a sign of it.)

CARLA Not really. I was always sensitive. I knew that I was getting more sensitive, especially my ability to smell odor—very sensitive to that. But I didn't chalk it down to anything or make any conclusions, no. [*to Jim*] Do you remember our talking about it at the time?

JIM No. We never really knew how she did what she did. It seemed to be a gift—a very good gift, though we didn't understand it. We were babes in the woods there.

GARY So Carla never appeared from the waist up and then dissolved down?[7]

CARLA [*laughs*] It didn't happen.

GARY When you first sent the manuscript for what would later become the *Law of One* books to a literary agent in New York City, you got an interesting reply back. For the viewers I will read the paragraph of that review, which you quoted and published in Book V:

> No entity that wreaks such havoc with the English language is going to ingratiate himself with the general reading public. This has all the denseness of *The New England Journal Of Medicine*, or the *Journal Of English And German Philosophy* or a Ph.D. dissertation on epistemology . . . and for another thing, the dialogue form gets pretty tedious after a while. It was all the rage in Athens for a while, I know, and its popularity continued all the way through the neo-classic renaissance, but it died out shortly afterwards, and I don't think that it's about to be revived.

The literary agent also included the following points of critique, saying:

- "You're not considering the general reader at all."
- "To effectively hook the reader, you've got to continually work on his credulity, throughout the text, anticipating his questions, and reinforcing your answers."
- That you have to convince the reader "why he should be interested, what should compel him to keep reading."
- That the material is not "persuasive, intriguing, fascinating."
- Ra's dense language creates "an impenetrable barrier to our comprehension and our edification."
- Ra "needs a lot of explaining," and should be "interspersed with your own commentary."
- The book is "rather scattered."[8]

This is a whopper of a review! And it may shine some light on some, but not all, of the more superficial reasons this work will likely not appeal to a broad swath of readers.

Despite receiving this professional feedback, you three didn't reshape the work to improve its marketability. Why did you, for the most part, not seek to mold these books to increase their sellability and appeal?

JIM Well, we thought what we had to offer was a gem, and it was information that was very helpful to people who were really serious seekers. We weren't out trying to convince the world of the validity of the information, or of Ra, or of anything. We were just offering what we had as freely as we could and hoping that those who might benefit from it would find it. To do everything that he suggested would be to try to manipulate your public, which is what business does. That's what his job was. We don't blame him for that; it's not what we do.

GARY Calling it a gem is really helpful to consider, because a gem is already perfect in its own right.

Ra attempted to describe spiritual evolution on the smallest and grandest scale, laying out a rather unique cosmology describing the life cycles of the universe experiencing itself, and addressing the most fundamental questions of this or any stage of evolution.

So, confined as they were by the necessity of strictly verbal communication, why do you think they communicated in such a technical, seemingly left-brained sort of way?

JIM Well, it may seem that way to some people, but to people who really like the material, it makes a lot of sense. To me it was always a combination of being profound and precise. If you look at the language and the way they use it, they use it almost like a mathematical equation. If I try to think, myself, of a better way of expressing what they're expressing, I really can't do it. The way they use the language—they choose the right word at the right time, and they weren't trying to convince anybody else either—they were just saying it the way it was. To people who like this type of material, it's poetic, and it probably is one way of filtering people. If this doesn't appeal to you, there is probably other material that does, and you don't have to worry about this in your life at this time. I don't think it's meant for everybody.

CARLA I think that it was, strictly for Ra, a matter of trying to be as clear and lucid as possible with everything that they said. By calling a person a "mind/body/spirit complex," it expresses, in one phrase, the basic nature of human beings: we have a mind complex, we have a body complex, and we have a spirit (not emotions, not inner insights—we have a *spirit*, and that spirit is of a certain nature, which Ra goes into later). It's a mind/body/spirit complex. So every time he[9] uses that word, he's reinforcing in the reader's mind who the reader really is.

And sometimes, he's trying to move beyond words into myth, using myth and lore to explain the nature of spiritual endeavor. The knight on the quest[†] is about as close as the Ra group could come to that particular mix of linear and dreaming, or right brain/left brain. To me it's great, but then I love philosophy and Ra is a philosopher, there's no question about it. He's a cosmologist, talks about the nature of the universe and what it's made up of, where we came from and where we are and where we're going. Got a whole diagram that you can put down in a linear fashion: the densities, the octaves of creation. I've read a lot of philosophy, and every philosophy I've ever read has its failure, at one point or another, to be internally consistent. Ra is seamlessly, internally consistent, and that is a wonderful thing.

So I rest easy, and I know that this works. Don found out why. All right Don! All right us! [*laughs*]

GARY Don asked Ra about this letter and Ra's response to Don is also a response to the critic:

> RA We found that you had been criticized for the type of language construction used to convey data. Due to our orientation with regard to data, even the most specifically answered question would be worded by our group in such a way as to maximize the accuracy of the nuances of the answer. This, however, mitigates against what your critic desires in the way of simple, lucid prose. More than this we cannot say. 37.4

We're getting close to wrapping up the Ra contact section. I just have five more simple questions to go.

So who was the first publishing firm to publish this material, and what was their assessment of this information?

[†] Ra never spoke specifically of a "knight on the quest," but Carla may be construing such from Ra's statement in 99.11: "We encourage the conscious strengthening of those invisible ribbands which fly from the wrists of those who go forward to seek what you may call the Grail."

JIM I guess that was Whitford Press, which, I guess, is . . . The Donning Company of Virginia Beach. That came because we sent the book off—well, what we had of the book—off to Jane Roberts.[10] She pointed us in that direction, and that's how that happened.

CARLA She was really helpful. There was this one guy . . .

JIM Robert Freedman. You talked to him the other day, didn't you?

CARLA I did.

JIM He was the representative, then, at Donning. He liked the material and he was our editor.

CARLA He dug it. He knew what he was looking at. He was the one guy that would be able to do that, I think, and he got it published by people that really didn't care what the thing was. They just wanted to get a book that would sell in a steady manner. They were very satisfied with us. We've been selling books for, like, 35 years.

GARY Not many, but . . .

CARLA Not many, but very steady, indeed. Well, actually, now we're best sellers . . . if you count it all together. [*laughs*]

GARY If you condense 30 years into one year.

CARLA I don't know how many thousands, but it's up there.

GARY Austin and I crunched the numbers earlier this year, and I think it was up to 56,000 or so of Book I.[11]

CARLA Not bad.

GARY Was Donning the one responsible for naming Book I *The Ra Material*?

JIM Yeah, *The Seth Material* was big at that time and they were trying to ride on its coattails.

GARY Your preferences would have been *The Law of One*?

JIM We asked them to change it after a while, and all they've ever done is put *The Law of One* at the top of *The Ra Material*, and we were still hoping—we still hope that they will change it one day.

GARY What has been your relationship with this material from these humble messengers of the Law of One?

JIM We read it every day as part of our Morning Offering, and we still get new information out of it. It seems like, as time goes on, there's always something that comes up in the life experience that, when you shine a certain phrase from the Ra contact onto it, everything seems new again. So yeah, we're still learning, still reading.

CARLA And we feel like the protectors of it, to make sure that it isn't altered in any way, and it's treated properly and maintained, so we try to do that, and keep it free, globally. That's our goal. Just to make sure that it remains what it is. Nobody puts words that aren't there, or tries to explain it in one way or another that may be true for one person but not another. Just leave it as it is; there's no reason to embroider on it, there's no reason to explain it.‡ In terms of that valuable original material, we're just preserving it, and making it available.

Now I certainly have written about it and quoted from it extensively, and in my book called *Living the Law of One 101: The Choice*, I've tried to go through and explain some of the basic principles of *The Law of One*,[12] in my own way, for the beginning person. If they find *The Law of One* material too difficult to read, they're not going to find my book difficult. I made sure that it was legible and readable by the average guy or the average lady.

GARY It's been very well received and very well loved. You've gotten a lot of positive feedback from it.

CARLA Well, thank you, but I don't value it the way I value the original material.

I realize there are things wrong with the *Law of One* books. It's episodic, because that's the nature of conversation. It picks up, it drops, there's a lull, it starts in a different place. It goes back to the same things half a

---

‡ Likely Carla is intending to convey not that explaining the material should be avoided, but rather that explaining the material in a dogmatic, my-interpretation-is-the-only-correct-interpretation way should be avoided. While there are certainly objective things that can be said about the *Law of One* (e.g., the material is not about migratory bird patterns, or an assembly manual for a trampoline), much of its content is subject to personal interpretation and subjective application. Sharing an interpretation can indeed be helpful, clarifying, and illuminating to an other seeker, so long as it is understood always that *a)* it is one among other possible valid interpretations, and *b)* one person cannot do the learning for another person.

dozen times. It's impossible to rearrange it in such a way that all of a sudden it falls into place. It's a *conversation*. I think it's most helpful to keep it the way it is: this happened in session one, this happened in session two, and just go through those sessions sequentially. There is some slight advantage in reading them as a continuing conversation rather than taking each part of the conversation separately. But the main thing is to have it word for word.

In that aspect, Tobey's been of enormous help at lawofone.info. He's got the *Relistened Version*,[13] where he went back and made absolutely sure that every err, uh, duh, in the thing was accurate, and he found some things that had been overlooked in the typing and so forth, and was able to put them back in where they belong. So the original material has been done a great service by that.

KEN But he has updated that on the lawofone.info, correct? Updated so those changes that he found—so it's up to date as far as he's concerned?

CARLA Well, Gary and I went through it to check and discuss his edits before he was satisfied with the project. Anything that we had a question about, they listened to it yet again, he and his helper, Michelle. Michelle has also done years of volunteer service along with Tobey, being part of The Relistening Project. They're wonderful, and they go back and listen to it for another seven, eight, nine times, just to make absolutely sure that is what Don said, or what Ra said. So as it is written in lawofone.info is the best, most accurate version.[14]

But there's something to be said for the Books I–IV too, because Don personally edited that to just try to focus on the metaphysical material and scratch out the personal stuff. Like the rest of us, he didn't want to put us forward as anything but the people who offered this material.

GARY Readers of this book are probably already familiar with this website, www.lawofone.info, but if not, the notation system that I've been using as I share Ra quotes (when I say, for example, "25.2" or "67.3") comes from a numbering system that Tobey instituted, assigning first the session number and then the number of each Q&A within the particular session, from the first question to the final one. It's provided a great reference system for any student of this material to be able to refer directly and precisely to the particular Ra quote being used.

And Ken, as to your question about what's available at lawofone.info, he has a few different versions. The first is the *Original Version* that's published in the books; then he has the *Relistened Version*, which is an exact, exact, exact transcript of the audio. If it is on the cassette, then it is on the *Relistened Version*—coughs, stutters and all. And then he went through the *Relistened Version* and made the slightest edits to improve readability without changing any meaning.

CARLA He would put a comma in, then take a comma out, that kind of thing.

GARY Yeah. And that's what Carla and I proofread. We went through his edits, working with him and Michelle, and the resulting version is called the *Lightly Edited Version*. That is the default version that you see when you go to lawofone.info.

And then, about what you were saying, Carla, in terms of explaining the material—letting the material sit as it is. That's something I've always enjoyed about L/L Research: they don't seek to get in between the seeker and the material. Certainly, you'll lend a helping hand and say, "This is my interpretation, this is how I've lived it," etc. But your desire and the policy of this organization is to keep this information pure, as it is: let the seeker have at it, let them make their own interpretations, etc.

CARLA Excellent. Yes. Well said. Hear, hear.

GARY To ask a completely objective question without any bias on my part, on a scale of 1 to 10, 10 being the best, how would you rate this information: a 10, or 15? [*laughter*]

CARLA Oh, 50 or 75. [*laughs*] I think it is far and away the best piece of philosophy that we have.

GARY What do you most love about *The Law of One*?

JIM It really seems to speak to my soul. It gets down to where I couldn't go really without it, I think. It just has a familiarity and affinity for me.

CARLA Yeah, I think it hits every single seeker that way. If they're open, if they're listening, it's talking to you, nobody else. It's wonderful that way. It's very personal without trying to develop some kind of relationship. It's just answering the questions, but they're answering them in a way that really does pierce down to your essence. You'd have to read it to see what we're talking about. So many people have said how much it affected them; it's even brought them to tears just sitting there and reading it and feeling, *I'm home at last, this is it, this is what I have felt all my life but couldn't put into words.*

GARY Yeah, that's exactly how I describe my own discovery of it 14 years ago. With little background in metaphysics or spirituality, and lacking a lot of the vocabulary, it nevertheless, somehow, spoke directly to me. I felt that I'd found my philosophical home for the first time. My eyes were just waterfalls. That experience is not uncommon for those who resonate with the material (an exceedingly small demographic, to be sure). They either take that fire from it, or it's kind of inert and they don't have that reaction.

And that's what I wanted to respond to. You had described how, as you keep reading it, you find something new, or it speaks to you in a new way. I found that is true across the board with seekers who enjoy this material. As they grow they find things that they swear weren't there before.

CARLA [*laughs*] Yes. Read that again, I don't remember that.

GARY Yeah, I've read this 15 times and I've never seen this. Or even for that stuff you do remember having read 15 times, it still finds a way to meet you where you are.

CARLA But you still want to hear it again.

GARY Is there anything that you find, to this day, really puzzling about the material?

CARLA Most of the beginning of Book Two [*laughter*] where it gets into the physics of the Big Bang, I guess—when things began. Wooo! I just try and try.[15]

JIM And the archetypal mind is a challenge.

CARLA Yeah, that gets beyond you too. I don't know how long it would have taken us to exhaust that material. We were working so hard trying to get a grip, talking about it, looking at it for hours every day. Still, I don't think the questions did the material justice. We were trying to respond to the Ra's statements and yet the statements themselves were just *ohhkaay*— I don't know, it just gets away from you and yet you do have the feeling that this material is very valuable.

A Fool's Phenomenology, written by a Ph.D. friend of ours who is a philosophy teacher at Southern Illinois University, is a wonderful book on the archetypal mind for people who are philosophers and that are able to follow him. He is somewhat arcane in his references and so forth. It's all in-jokes to him. He gives insight after insight into the archetypal mind.

GARY And for the final question about the Ra contact, before we close up today:

If you two had the opportunity to do it all over again, would you?

CARLA In a heartbeat.

JIM In a minute.[16]

GARY Thank you so much.

JIM Thank you.

---

[1] Detailed, step-by-step instructions can be found in the "Law of One Resources" section of www.llresearch.org, and in the appendix of the upcoming book, *The Ra Contact: Teaching the Law of One*.

[2] There are two principal parts to the salt cleansing ritual. Ra suggests that the salt of each part be left in place for 36–48 hours, meaning that the entire procedure could take anywhere from 72–96 hours, or three to four days.

[3] The accurate and incredible medical diagnosis is as follows:

> QUESTIONER Thank you. What has caused the swelling in Jim's body, and what can be done to heal it?
>
> RA I am Ra. For the answer to this query we must begin with the consideration of the serpent, signifying wisdom. This symbol has the value of the ease of viewing the two faces of the one who is wise. Positive wisdom adorns the brow indicating indigo-ray work. Negative wisdom, by which we intend to signify expressions which effectually separate the self from the other-self, may be symbolized by the poison of the fangs. To use that which a mind/body/spirit complex has gained of wisdom for the uses of separation is to invite the fatal bite of that wisdom's darker side.
>
> The entity has a mental/emotional tendency, which has been lessening in distortion for some of your space/time, towards negative wisdom. The entity being already aware of this causes us not to dwell upon this point but merely to specifically draw the boundaries of the metaphysical background for the energizing of a series of bites from one of your second-density species. In this case the bite was no more than that of one of the arachnids, sometimes called the wood spider. However, it is possible

that were enough work done to test the origin of the pathology of the entity, it is within possibility/probability limits that the testing would show the bite of the cottonmouth rather than the bite of the common wood spider.

The energizing took its place within the lymphatic system of the entity's yellow-ray, physical body. Therefore, the working continues. There is increasing strain upon the spleen, the super-renal glands, the renal complex, and some possibility/probability of difficulty with the liver. Further, the lymphatic difficulties have begun to strain the entity's bronchial system. This is some general information upon what is to be noted as a somewhat efficient working.

The removal of these distortions has several portions. Firstly, it is well to seek the good offices of the one known as Stuart so that harsh chemical means may be taken to reawaken the histaminic reflexes of the entity and to aid in the removal of edema.

Secondly, we suggest that which has already begun; that is, the request of the one known now to this group as Bob that this entity may focus its aid upon the metaphysical connections with the yellow-ray body.

Thirdly, the entity must take note of its physical vehicle's need for potassium. The ingesting of the fruit of the banana palm is recommended.

Fourthly, the links between the swelling of contumely and the apparent present situation is helpful. As always the support of the harmonious group is an aid, as is meditation. It is to be noted that this entity requires some discipline in the meditation which the others of the group do not find necessary in the same manner. Therefore, the entity may continue with its forms of meditation knowing that each in the group supports it entirely although the instinct to share in the discipline is not always present. Each entity has its ways of viewing and learning from the illusion, and each processes catalyst using unique circuitry. Thus all need not be the same to be equal in will and faith. 101.2

4   Known as pitting edema.

5   The name was Betty Andreason.

6   Maybe it's not people of "high intellect" so much as those possessed of purpose who are deeply absorbed in their work.

7   About where that notion came from:

> QUESTIONER The second question is: Paul has also received information that mentions that there were other beings aiding in the construction of the pyramids who were not fully materialized in the third density. They were materialized from the waist up to their heads but were not materialized from the waist down to their feet. Did such entities exist in the

construction of the pyramids, and who were they?

RA I am Ra. Consider, if you will, the intelligent infinity present in the absorption of livingness and beingness as it becomes codified into intelligent energy, due to the thought impressions of those assisting the living stone into a new shape of beingness. The release and use of intelligent infinity for a brief period begins to absorb all the consecutive or interlocking dimensions, thus offering brief glimpses of those projecting to the material their thought. These beings thus beginning to materialize but not remaining visible. These beings were the thought-form or third-density-visible manifestation of our social memory complex as we offered contact from our intelligent infinity to the intelligent infinity of the stone. 27.2

8

The full quote read: "The material is a bit scattered in terms of pursuing meandering lines of questioning; and the reviewer is keen to the need for explanation and elaboration."

An undertaking in which L/L Research has been engaged ever since.

9

Some readers refer to Ra as "he," most refer to Ra as "they." Carla *usually* did the latter.

Ra doesn't identify what role, if any, gender plays in their social memory complex, but they do speak to this point of singular vs. plural here:

QUESTIONER I noticed you started this session with "I communicate now." You usually use "We communicate now." Is there any significance or difference with respect to that, and then is there anything that we can do to make the instrument more comfortable or improve the contact?

RA I am Ra. We am Ra. You may see the grammatical difficulties of your linguistic structure in dealing with a social memory complex. There is no distinction between the first person singular and plural in your language when pertaining to Ra. 83.28

10

Jane Roberts (1929–1984) is the medium who famously channeled a discarnate source of intelligence named Seth. With her husband's aid, Roberts channeled material that would fill over ten volumes of Seth books. This material contributed to and shaped the budding New Age Movement, most notably its foundational principle that *you create your own reality*. When asked, afterward, why Jim contacted Jane Roberts, he wrote:

I had been reading the material that Seth channeled through Jane Roberts, since 1973 or so. It was the first channeled material that I ever read, and I really liked it. I was still reading her book, *Adventures in Consciousness*, when the Ra contact began. After we had completed the first twenty sessions or so of the Ra contact, it became apparent that we wanted to make a book out of this material, but we really didn't know where to go to get the book published, or even looked at. So I got the bright idea to write to Jane Roberts and see what she had to recommend, because I had written her once before, a year or so before I guess, just to tell her how much I enjoyed her books and Seth.

I remember that she sent me back my letter with The Donning Company and Whitford Press' address, hand-written, in the margin on the side. The editor that she recommended was Hank Stein, so we sent the, by this time, first 26 sessions off to him. The Donning Company was located in Virginia Beach, Virginia. I think that both of these companies were already owned by Schiffer Publishing, or were soon to be owned by Schiffer Publishing. My memory is a little fuzzy there. I just checked the *Wikipedia* entry for The Donning Company and it was 1985 when Schiffer bought them.

11 This is an approximation at the time of the interview given numbers from various sources that were a bit difficult to crunch accurately.

12 There is the Law of One, <u>the principle, way, or reality</u> which Ra bent their efforts upon describing and sharing through vocal communication.

And there is *The Law of One* <u>material,</u> which consists of the 106 sessions of the Ra contact that took place between 1981 and 1984.

The latter, being a book title, is italicized.

13 You can learn more about Tobey's work on that project at <u>www.lawofone.info/relistening-report.php</u>.

14 The *Relistened Version*—which is indeed the most accurate rendering into text form of the audio of the Ra sessions—went through several rounds of very light, mostly grammatical editing to form the book *The Ra Contact: Teaching the Law of One.*

15 Sephira Vox wrote an illuminating paper that attempts to tackle some of the most confounding but most fundamental concepts in the *Law of One* philosophy, including the primal three distortions, intelligent infinity, intelligent energy, etc. Titled *Cosmic Genesis*, it should be published in the future *Ra Contact* book, and the website <u>www.llresearch.org</u>.

The following Q&A was omitted from this chapter:

GARY I use this opportunity also to point to the work of Sephira Vox. You named two areas that have been difficult for you to penetrate all these years: the archetypes and the beginning material in Book II (which tackles the very beginning of Ra's cosmology). Seph has, in my estimation, done an excellent job in attempting to help shine some light into exactly those two areas.

CARLA I totally agree with you, and I am so very glad that we were able to give him a place to teach, because this is very specialized material. And I think everybody was so grateful last April when he was able to offer a seminar and workshop. For three days they just immersed themselves in the archetypal mind, and I think everybody felt that he had just opened it up to them. I was so glad to hear that. I'm glad to hear, too, because he's very intelligent and he does not suffer a fool gladly in terms of direct, say, argument or debate, but as a teacher who is endlessly able to encourage people, to meet them where they were, even if the question was not tremendously full of wisdom. He was able to bring out what was in the question that was good, and therefore support all the students, whether they were beginning or advanced. So he did all the things that you're supposed to do as a teacher, and he did them really well. But the main thing is that he studies *The Law of One* to the point where he's able to talk about it.

GARY Yeah, with a fine tooth comb. We will soon be hosting his work to share it with readers as well.

16

Jim answers this basic question in a fuller way in the June 22, 2015 entry of *The Camelot Journal:*

I read Ra sessions #104 and #105 today and felt a lot of sadness as the theme was basically how to help Carla to recover from a very potent psychic greeting from our fifth-density friend. We were struggling to keep the contact going and keep Carla alive. The first year we did 75 sessions. The second year 26. The third year 4. And in 1984 we did 1. We went from as many as two sessions per day to begin the Ra contact to doing sessions two and three months apart at the end because Carla wasn't in good enough shape to do them any more frequently. At the end of session #105 tonight I was once again overcome by tears, but they were an odd combination of sadness and gratitude. If I could chose in my incarnation to do anything that I wanted or which had ever been done on this planet I would chose to do as I did do: to be with Don and Carla and to have the contact with those of Ra as our means of service to others. There is great satisfaction in that choice, and someday I shall die a happy man.

The Camelot Journal, Jim McCarty, published June 23, 2015, www.bring4th.org/

Right: A scene of great purpose and precision, the instrument is carefully positioned in preparation for the coming session with Ra. Carla's energy had an adverse effect upon electronics that necessitated three recorders.

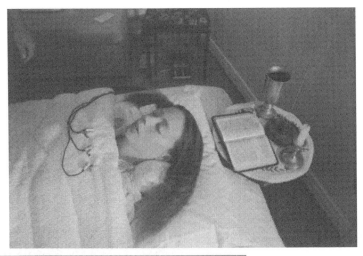

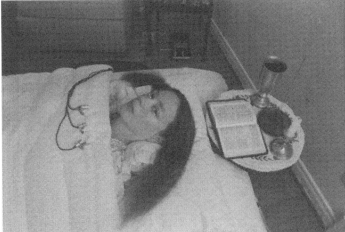

Left: Behind the instrument's head sits the appurtenances: Bible opened to the Gospel of John, Chapter One, chalice, incense, and white candle.
(See Ch. 8.)

Right: Calm, courageous, fearless, serene: Carla awaits the abyss.

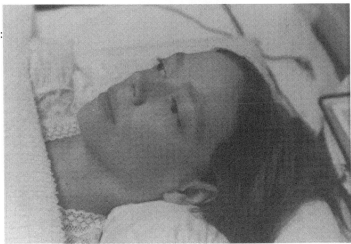

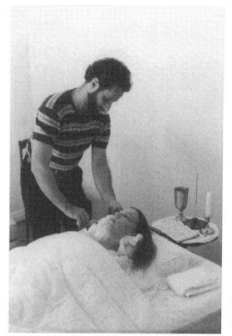

Above: The scribe combs out the instrument's hair. (See 65.0 & 75.33.)

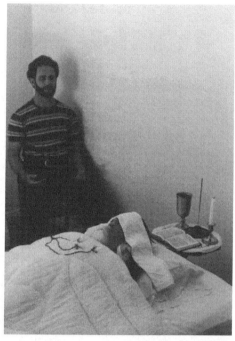

Above: Supporting the instrument, the scribe visualizes light moving through her. (See Ch. 7.)

Above: The questioner rubs the instrument's shoulders after she comes to. Each session took a harsh physical toll on Carla.

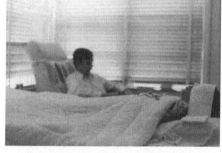

Above: The questioner considers his questions for the upcoming dialogue with Ra.

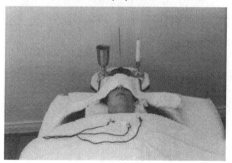

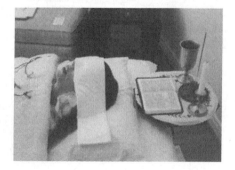

Carla sits outside the group's Louisville home. Her glow subdued by significant fatigue.

Above: Don, Carla, & Jim's home from 1980–83, site of 105 sessions of the conversation with Ra.

Above: Carla meditates, or maybe just relaxes, in the meditation pyramid.

Above: At an Ohio campground, the weight loss of the experience is visible.
Below: Don Elkins

Above: Carla at the Ra contact home with her mother, Jean.
Below: Jim McCarty

Right: The corner room where took place 105 Ra sessions.

Left: The group's home in Lake Lanier, GA, site of Session 106.

Right: Carla standing in front of the lake which their Georgia home faced.

Above and below: The golden hawk whose return Don sought because, he said, it gave him great comfort. (See 106.23 and pages 198 and 201.)

CHAPTER 16

Post-Ra Contact to
LLResearch.org
1984–1996

GARY In this chapter, we focus on the biography of the organization beyond the end of the Ra contact in 1984. To begin, after the dust had settled from Don's death, what did you hope to achieve through L/L Research?

JIM I guess the same thing as we were trying before: to get the word out. We had information—just to keep on doing what we were doing.

CARLA We had our marching orders from the very beginning. We knew that Don wanted to have a spiritual community, that he wanted to make this material globally available, and we assumed he wanted the experiment to continue, and to continue gathering data. So we just kept doing that, and from time to time people would visit us and see if they could live with us (and nobody ever could), but we were still thinking in terms of a physical family. Yeah, just what Jim said: we kept on doing what we were doing.

GARY So that continuity in the mission—was it interrupted at all? Maybe interrupted isn't the word . . . Did you take a moment after Don's passing to reassess your goals and visions—

CARLA No.

GARY —or did you just keep putting one foot in front of the other?

CARLA Yes. That was it.

GARY I presume that you never even considered disbanding or discontinuing your search.

CARLA Good heavens, no.

GARY I was going to ask you if you considered expanding the core group from '85 onward. You said that people tried—you and different people tried to live together. So you had always been open to the possibility and the desire, but it just didn't come to fruition?

CARLA Well, it's funny. Jim was a loner, so he would go through this process of *nobody will ever live in this house again,* and then there would be this person that was so perfect that he'd think *well, let's try.* And we've done this every single time there has been somebody in the house.

GARY In one of the early channelings after Don's passing, you, Carla, with great sincerity and interest asked Latwii about the prospect of regaining contact with Ra. What were your thoughts at that time, and why wasn't that course pursued?

CARLA I just remember I loved life and I thought that it was dangerous. I did not think that I would be able to do it, honestly.

GARY And judging by what I understand, I agree. It was wise not to continue without Don.

CARLA Ra asked me a question, I think it was fairly . . . maybe in the middle of the contact or fairly towards the end, and basically said, "Do you want to be a martyr, or do you want to choose wisdom? Is this your time to go to Jerusalem?" That was in a Christian context: Is this your time to get up on the cross and die?

Jim and I thought about that very deeply, and the result was that we took our first vacation in eleven years.

GARY You held on to the impulse, though, to serve as an instrument for Ra?

CARLA I wanted to serve, but I'd decided to try to cooperate more in cutting back and being part of the team and communicating how I truly felt, and not just going, *send me in, coach. I can do it regardless.*

GARY Personally, I think that your life and your health are worth more than more Ra sessions.

How would you describe your life and your work until the end of the 1980s?

CARLA I was desperately unhappy but I continued. Jim was a wonderful support. We had a nice routine. I went through a period of trying to figure out what I was going to do next. My first attempt was to try to become a librarian again, and I realized that I had to understand computers first. So I went back to school at JCC.[1] I took computer classes for two years, and that convinced me that I was not going to be able to do it. Not because I couldn't understand the computer, but because I never could keep my health together for a significant period of time without it breaking down and my having to have a quiet period. I knew I couldn't hold a job under those circumstances. So that was out.

So then I thought, *well, I'll do church work*, which was great except that it had the same problem politics did. Any organization has politics and committee meetings, lots of committee meetings. If I wanted to serve, for instance, as head of the women of the church, I was expected to give parties. I don't like to give parties. I would prefer simply to scrub down the church, organize the kitchen—that sort of thing. And that's what I did. I was not appreciated by a significant number of the congregation's women who wanted a continuation of the silver tea services and the old fashioned parties that we would give as women of the church. And I just couldn't hack it. I couldn't do it.

So eventually I had to give up the idea of serving as a volunteer in the church. And that made me stop and think, *okay, now what?* So I took a look at Jim. Jim had simply gone on from strength to strength working in the yard, never missing a day, always creating something beautiful in the yard, and making gardens out of every part of the yard. When we came here, the property had been an acre of dead leaves and a house. There was nothing on it and he created place after place after place of beauty, and he had a schedule. His day was very organized and he got a lot done every day.

So I thought, I want to get in on that. I want to learn how to make my schedule, and I want to dovetail it to his so that we have a beautiful life together. But I played a lot of solitaire[2] while thinking about it, and finally it hit me: I need to work for L/L Research. I need to write. I'm a good writer; I have things to say. I had had more and more correspondence with more and more people. About 200 people—when I counted up all the email—had written me asking me questions about how to deal with being a wanderer. So I wrote the Wanderer's Handbook.

That took me years—mostly just gathering my data, writing everybody asking for permission to quote them, and organizing the book in terms of chapters. The writing itself went very quickly. I knew just exactly how I wanted it to go.

So I finally got a handle on it and I've been working for L/L Research as a writer ever since, with the exception of these last few years where I've had to let that go and just basically put myself to finishing up things that I had not been able to finish up because I had too much stuff. I create things, and I don't edit them—they just sit there—so I went back and I started editing things.

That's how the books like *A Book of Days*, and my poetry book, and a coloring book we did for kids happened. *The Aaron/Q'uo Dialogues,* the co-channeling I did with Barbara Brodsky, followed a similar pattern but was initiated on Barbara's end. I went back and edited all my recipes in hopes of doing a recipe book. I have not gotten through with that project by any means, but I have formatted everything.

GARY One of your first book projects after the end of the Ra contact was *A Channeling Handbook* in 1987. Can you tell us something about that?

CARLA Well, Ra had talked a good bit about wanderers and had indicated that there were a certain number of entities that had come to Earth to serve in a certain way, basically by sharing their vibrations with Earth by opening up their hearts and letting the energy of the Creator pour through so that there was more light coming through into the consciousness of Planet Earth.

And the wanderer has a tough job, because the work isn't involved in *doing* so much as *being;* it's involved in essence rather than behavior, and that's very difficult to get. People say, "What do I do? What's my service?" And it's so hard for them to realize: *you* are your service—just keeping your heart open is your service. And yeah, if you want to do an outer work, that's great, what do you want to do? Do you want to raise a kid? Do you want to keep a house? Do you want to teach? Do you want to channel? Whatever you want to do, whether it's dramatic or whether it's seemingly tiny, it's equal. Everything is equal because it's what you're good at and what keeps your heart open. Other than that, it's all inner work—it's all the passive radiation of life.

JIM It sounds like you're talking about *A Wanderer's Handbook*.

CARLA I am. Is that what you asked about?

JIM He asked you about *A Channeling Handbook*.

CARLA Whoops! Okay.

JIM Remember all that for *A Wanderer's Handbook*.

GARY I was eventually going to ask you about *A Wanderer's Handbook*.

CARLA Well, that's good, but I wish you'd stopped me earlier.

Okay, *Channeling Handbook*: I couldn't write at the time, I couldn't even sit up straight, so I did it on tape, and I was never satisfied with it. I'm not satisfied with it to this day, but to go back and redo it is unacceptable. So I'll just leave it as it is because it is as it is. And it's very clear what I wanted to say and what I wanted to get across.

I had done a certain amount of study and research, and I hadn't written it up, so I wrote it up. Simple logic dictated that I would make a report, and this was basically my report. I tried to help anybody that wanted to channel to do it better. I didn't teach people to channel in the book; that wasn't my goal. My goal was to help channels who were doing it to do it better, because there are so many ways you can screw up and fall short. I tried to show the pitfalls.

GARY What about the book are you dissatisfied with?

CARLA Well, if I had been able to write it, it would have been a much smoother book. I'm a good writer; I'm not a particularly good visualiz-er-writer. Some people always write from tape. They can just see it in their head and it comes out perfectly on the tape. Not me. There were things that I would leave out because there is something about the process of seeing it on the screen as you're writing it. There's a feedback that starts happening. It's a very yeasty, fertile feeling. You put in and you take out, and you enlarge, and you play with it. And eventually you get something that you're satisfied with, that is written well, and goes smoothly and all that. I don't think the *Channeling Handbook* has that. Unlike my other writing, it's a little bit less well-done, well-written.

GARY Given your flow when you open up to speak, and your eloquence and depth of thought, I would venture to say that few would notice the difference between speaking and writing, Carla.

Prior to the construction of the archive website, LLResearch.org, how did you guys seek to get the word out; that is, to share and disseminate the information?

JIM Smoke signals. [*chuckles*] We advertised in four or five different journals like the *Yoga Journal*, *East-West Journal*, *Flying Saucer Review* in England, and a couple of others.

CARLA *Fate*.

JIM Oh yeah, *Fate*. That was our first and foremost. That little ad, a little inch ad that offered the book to people, free for the reading: "If you want to keep it, send a donation; if you don't, send the book back." And we spoke here and there when invited, and continued having our Sunday meditations, and people would show up. It was meager, especially compared to what is happening now on the internet.

GARY There were still means for people to come across the material, and they did, and you still had people writing the organization, interested in the work.

JIM Oh yeah. Back in the days of snail mail.

CARLA Yeah, there would be this stack of letters on my desk. I was forever trying to get it down to answering all the letters. But that seldom happened.

GARY I wanted to note here in the interview that what's been remarkable to me is that you continued this work—especially prior to the launch of the archive website—you continued this work without a strong means of sharing it with the world, and with little prospect of any financial remuneration. Nevertheless, you felt the call to do this. You felt you had to perform this service and you wanted to help others. So you just kept on channeling, week after week. I guess I won't turn that into a question, I'll just leave it as a statement.

JIM What else could we do? Go out and sell used cars?

CARLA That's what we did. Don had been very clear in his instructions and we were still working for Don. And, as I said before, we still are, and that satisfies us deeply.

---

[1]   JCC stands for Jefferson Community College, Louisville's local community college.

[2]   All the way to the end, solitaire was one of Carla's favorite and frequent go-to's. It helped her negotiate pain, medical difficulties, and limitations. The other was devouring cheap romance novels.

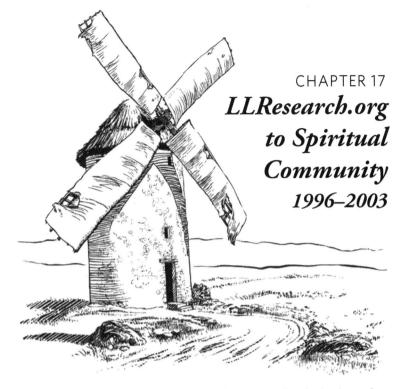

CHAPTER 17

LLResearch.org to Spiritual Community 1996–2003

GARY In 1993 you were first contacted by an individual who, after you two and Don, has arguably done more to connect seekers to *The Law of One,* and to preserve the integrity of the Confederation philosophy, than anyone else. Who was this individual and can you describe what he did to help you?

CARLA When Ian wrote me, he was still working for his own company, which had to do with artistic software for computers. Shortly after he initiated correspondence with us, he sold his company and he was able to retire. So he could spend all his time working on projects that he wanted to work on, and he was very keen on working on this project.

Ian asked if he could read all of our material, and I told him there was a *huge* backlog of stuff that either hadn't been typed up or published. We sent him—clunk—a bunch of hard copies. But at that time they weren't on the computer, so they weren't digital, so they had to be OCR'd[1] and scanned into the computer, and then he had to edit every single one of them.

We, on our part, initiated a year's long attempt to get the rest of the cassettes typed up digitally, and a lot of people took part in that. Judy D. was remarkable in her faithfulness for many years, probably a decade. She typed everything that I channeled through the '80s. And she—I don't know how many she had—she had volumes of them that were digitally recorded by her, and she did a beautiful job—she was very literate and so forth.

And then there was Kim H., also known as Kim [another surname beginning with] H. (She went back and forth on using her maiden name and her married name—she was divorced. I don't know where she settled on that. She's probably somebody else like "Sparrow." She's gone Zen and joined—the last I heard—she had joined a Buddhist-type commune, and she was very happy doing that.) She would sit down and she would whiz through a session almost at the speed at which it was spoken, without having to go back, ever. When she typed you couldn't hear the keys—they didn't go tap-tap-tap, they went whirr—a continuous sound. She was an incredible typist, and she was very faithful. She tried living with us for a while, and it didn't work out. She and Jim had one brangle after the other. They finally figured, *well, it's just a very deep personality problem, nobody's fault.* So we parted as good friends. She continued to come over and work for years after that, but she couldn't live with us.

I can't think of anybody else who spent that kind of time doing it, but one way or the other we had volunteers, wonderful volunteers through the years that plugged away, and, finally, as far as we know, we've gotten everything we have on tape typed up digitally so as to preserve it.

JIM Then Ian did the same thing with our books.

CARLA He did the same thing with our books. But at any rate, he had sent me a thick binder with a proposal of how he wanted to put this stuff on a website. And it involved the OCR and scanning everything that I'm describing. But then he would do the coding, and he would create a website that was a library. I loved the concept—I loved his idea. I had no idea how much it would take, really, even looking at that. The depth of his fidelity was incredible and, oh, how many years? Twenty-some years?

JIM Seventeen.

CARLA Seventeen years he plugged away at that. The amount of work that he got up on that website was huge, absolutely huge. And it's all beautifully done. It's not done in a way that's particularly grateful to the non-scholar, and it's hard for somebody to just pop in and surf their way through the site. We're now trying to make it more accessible.[2]

Ian was so grateful that I did not want to become a personality, that I just wanted to give the material here—me here, yes, I took part in doing it, and that was my part—here's the material. Look at the material, don't look at me.

So he was very grateful for that. He said it was the reason that he stuck for so long, and he so totally agreed with the energy of this group. He didn't come to be part of every gathering. He wasn't that kind of a guy. But we were his go-to volunteer work and he was a worker, just like Jim. He would get up and go to the computer and start his day. A lot of times, we were it, so we were very fortunate in being able to have his volunteer efforts for so very long. He never asked for anything for himself or wanted to have any credit given to him whatsoever. I'm not sure that he'd be terribly pleased with me praising him so lavishly. He thought that what he was doing was not remarkable; it was—it is—remarkable and we're very grateful to Ian.

GARY Being aware of his history as well, he stands out in my mind as one example of a person who, when they come to this material, would *also* like to know more about how the material came into existence, how the people who created the material conduct themselves, what the channel's relationship is to the material, etc.

Some people come straight to the material and don't need to know anything about L/L Research or Jim and Carla or the channels, and that's perfectly fine. But for some people like Ian, it becomes important.

So for those who are of the school of thought that think they would just like to delete, erase, or negate the human element in the equation (which is impossible to separate, I think), I invoke Ian's example, as you were a factor in his decision to serve.

CARLA You're right. That's right. And Jim as well. He thought a lot of Jim.

GARY Oh yeah, absolutely. When I say *you*, I mean the plural. And also, it's been unmentioned in this particular Q&A that Ian also served as the editor for every one of your books beyond *A Channeling Handbook* [all the way until 2012].

CARLA That's right.

GARY And all those years he maintained a consistent standard of professional presentation for L/L Research on the internet.

CARLA Yes. He produced them all.

GARY So I corresponded with Ian on this question just last week, and he thinks that the website first launched in 1996. I assume that at that time there was some measure of jubilation to see your life's work available for anyone the world over?

CARLA Oooh, I knew that Elkins would just have been in alt*—I mean in his way, you know. He would have nodded and said, "Beautiful"—and meant it. This is what he wanted. It was now available globally, for free. Perfect.

GARY Could you describe the effect that the archived website had on the organization or your work?

JIM We started getting orders over the internet! We bought a computer—leading edge, Model D, 1987. I built a little computer station for me on one side, and on Carla's side she had her own computer, so we were looking at each other across the tops of the computer, doing our work together, every day. So we had more orders, and more communication.

GARY Did you look at the new device askew for a while?

CARLA Do you mean askance?

GARY Askance. I imagine it took some time to warm up to it.[3]

JIM No, I didn't have any problem then. It was in the beginning—everybody was in the same boat. I was actually fairly competent at that time.

CARLA The first thing Jim did on the computer—he actually got the computer for this reason—was that he set it to type the— What was it you did that with?

JIM It was The Channeling Handbook.

CARLA *The Channeling Handbook.* In other words, there's a six-number-letter code that you do for a comma, for a period, for a space—that kind of thing. So Jim did that the whole way through with all of those codes and sent it off to Ray Palmer of Palmer Press, which was the old traditional press that had published Gray Barker's books, and we were part of the UFO story that way. Jim didn't make very many mis-

---

* "In alt" means "to be in an exalted state of mind".

takes, so he really liked the computer for that. He had a good relationship with it.

GARY I didn't know that you and the computer were close, ever. That surprises me.

JIM I had to take this little hiatus into cutting grass for a while and everything got away from me in eleven years. Can you imagine?

GARY Yeah, the way things move especially. Spend a few months away and things are different now.

So you met Roman Vodacek somewhere in this period too. What role did he play in L/L Research?

JIM In May, 1992, he was living in Hagerstown, Maryland. He had been a pilot for Pan Am at that time and read our books because his then-girlfriend, Janet Decker, who now works for IMU,[4] had them on her shelf. So he started reading them and got excited. He came to visit us in May and we got along great, so he decided to move to Louisville. Throughout the early '90s, from '92 through '95 or '96, most Sundays he was the only other person there, the third person necessary for a channeling to occur. Carla had never channeled Confederation sources with just the two of us. The contact needed a third person, because it universalizes the material that way. So without Roman, we would not have any of those transcripts from 1992 through 1995 or 1996.

CARLA And those were very fertile years. I was still channeling 12 months out of the year at that time, every week, so I produced 50 or so per year.

JIM He loved our material and the food was great. We served a meal after the meditation on Sundays.

CARLA Well, that was one of the reasons I had Romi over, was that I wanted to feed him.

JIM Yeah, he was a bachelor, and he wasn't a real good cook.

CARLA He was so lonely. He was in a foreign country, he didn't know anybody in town, and he didn't make friends that easily, and everything was high drama with Romi. You know Romi—he was always having pain one way or the other, a lot of angst, and getting over the girlfriend that he'd lost (Janet). She just didn't want to marry him, so that hurt and he would cry and we would comfort him. And we helped him through all the growing pains until he got a decent job and settled down. After that, he was still very faithful, and he took care of our computers from the beginning until he left to take care of his mom last year. Oh, we miss Romi!

GARY So, from 1992, when you said you met him, to 2013, he was here in Louisville faithfully attending meditations and taking care of the computers. A long haul for—

JIM Faithful is a very good word to describe Romi.

GARY You continued to hold your regular public meditations and channelings. Did you do any workshop/gathering sort of events in the '90s?

JIM It seems like we did. We were always doing something.

CARLA We did Homecomings. We were always teaching somebody to channel; usually on Wednesday we'd have a channeling teaching. And remember Mike?

JIM Yeah, from Ohio.

CARLA From Ohio. He would come down, drive all the way down from Cincinnati and maybe stay a couple of days over the weekend and work on his channeling. He and Steve Tyman worked on their channeling together for many a year. Steve driving up four hours from Illinois, and Mike coming down from Ohio. So we did stuff like that. We did whatever was called for. If anybody needed something, we'd try to see if we could do it. And we had Homecomings—not every year, but as often as we could get it together.

GARY You mentioned cooking for Sunday meditations. When I first came to Louisville that tradition was nearing its end, I think. You had some good food!

So your public meditations have always included the ritual of tuning prior to the commencement of the meditation. Could you describe the tuning rituals you've utilized?

CARLA Surely. For myself, I would work on tuning using the prayers of my experience that had stuck with me the longest and given me the most energy—brought me higher than any others—and I would sing to myself or chant or both. I would then meditate for a brief period of time, and then I would set my intention—what I was going to do.

Then I went through a period of preparing myself which involved going to my inner room and asking the Holy Spirit for help and getting all ready to go. Then I would go to the group and tune the group just by having them talk around the circle: "I'm so-and-so and I ran into *The Law of One* in such-and-such a way," or "I'm so-and-so and that's all I want to say," or "I'm so-and-so and here comes a half hour of my telling you my personal problems." And all these things were okay—whatever people wanted to do.

So after we got all that done, then I would go and tune myself. Then I'd come back and we would continue tuning the group by playing music or singing or chanting, "Auming"—doing something that brought us all together and got us to the edge of being ready. Then we would say The Lord's Prayer, and then we would go into meditation. That was the tuning process.

GARY Has it always been pretty much the same structure: the group round-robin, everybody shares around the circle, then the singing or listening to music, then The Lord's Prayer, then off you go?

CARLA I've never found a better way.

GARY So you had two large writing projects between the late '90s and early 2000s. In 1998, you published Book V of *The Law of One* series. Can you tell us about this book and what prompted its publication?

JIM What did prompt the publication?

CARLA Well, it was your [Jim's] idea.

JIM [*chuckling*]

CARLA You said, "You know, Ruck, it's been 15 years since this . . ." Just *so* many people wanted to know: *Give us the rest of the material. We want the rest of the material.* We tried saying, "Well, it's mostly personal stuff, it's not important." But then Jim took a read through it and said, "You know, Ruck, this is pretty good stuff. Some of it is . . . I want to share it."

So, he said, "What if we did it this way? We'll do it by fragment: I'll take each fragment and then I'll write my comments, and then you write your comments." And I said, "Great." So he did his and then handed it over to me, and then I did mine. And I remember doing one a day for quite some time until they were all done. It was just a matter of getting it all done, and then we collected everything and sent it off to Ian.

JIM That sounds familiar.

CARLA A lot of times we'd be working on that and we'd wave at each other.

JIM Yeah, over our computers.

CARLA Every morning we worked together until noon.

GARY So where did the fragments come from to begin with? Why were they fragments?

JIM Well, they'd been excluded from the original publication, basically, by Don's decision. We all supported that because we didn't want people to be looking at our personal lives as being as important as what the material had to offer. So we'd taken it out, and they came from the original transcripts that I transcribed after each session in three-ring notebooks.

GARY So Don was the one responsible for selecting all the omissions?

CARLA Uh-huh. He'd just X it out—*don't want that, don't want that*—yeah.

GARY And then after Book V in the early 2000s, you completed a book you called *A Wanderer's Handbook*. Can you tell us about this book and how it came to be?

CARLA Okay, I started telling you about it before so I won't repeat it. In addition to my getting ahold of everybody that I wanted to quote in the book as "another wanderer," I numbered them and I said, "Do you want to be number 47, do you want to be known as your avatar online, or do you want to be known with your name?" I kept a file at the time—and I'm sure it's still in my files somewhere—of who all these people were, and I used as many of their quotes as was necessary.

Then I just took all the answers that I had given through the years and I categorized them. I found that there were about 107 questions that people asked over and over. So rather than having to repeat my answer over and over, I thought, "Well, I'll write this book, and people can look it up in the book."

So I separated it out into very logically flowing chapters of how the material would fall out: do this, then write about this. And the idea was to help wanderers tell their stories and to come out of the closet with being wanderers and say, "Yeah, that's who I am." Own it, and love it, and use it.

Jim went through all of the sessions (that we had up until that time) with my list of questions, and when he found a session that applied to one of the questions, he excerpted the material and numbered it. Romi set up a database for us, for both of these things. So when I wrote it, it was just a matter of taking the database with numbers for Question 1, then Question 2, and sharing some of the quotations from the Confederation, as well as sharing lots of quotations from the letters I'd gotten from real people who had the same problems that hopefully the reader was experiencing. And then my writing—I did my writing and I wove it all together with my writing. And that was it. The book wrote itself once I got all my data in order.

GARY Do you remember how many pages it clocked in at originally?

JIM [*chuckles*] A thousand.

CARLA Twelve hundred. You took us down to 800.

JIM Further than that. I think we got it down to 650, didn't we? By removing footnotes. There were sometimes four and five footnotes for a point.

CARLA Quotes, you know. I might use five different people saying the same thing. He got it down to three.

JIM I didn't edit any text. Everything she wrote stayed. What I edited was the quotations, the footnotes and things, and duplications.

GARY The abridged version is already a very thick book. It continues to serve as a helpful resource when people write L/L Research, as we can direct them to the book in general, or—because it's, like you said, constructed of chapters answering particular questions—we can direct seekers to particular chapters to help them think about their questions. It's proven enormously valuable in that regard.

Back to Book V: Do you remember reactions to its publication at the time? Were people pretty thrilled to see it?

JIM Yeah, we got a very good response, very positive.

GARY Living as I do on the other side of Book V coming out, I pretty much came into a completed *The Law of One*. I can imagine, if I was told that there are some extra sessions or material I hadn't seen, I would be on the moon with excitement. It had to be a great period for students of the material.

This next question pertains to an event that probably stands out a lot more in my mind because it was a pivotal moment to my life, but I'll ask if you guys have any recollection.

In April 2002, you were invited to participate in Scott Mandelker's "Time of Global Shift" seminar, which he had hosted here in Louisville, Kentucky. There you met a few seekers, some of whom have played important roles in your life in the subsequent years. Any recollections of this event?

JIM [*chuckling*] Well, I think we met Gary Bean there, I'm not really sure. [*laughter*] That wasn't our first meeting with Scott as we'd met him here a couple of times. He'd come to meditation.

CARLA Scott has had us out to California once.

JIM That's right. We went up to his apartment once, didn't we?

Yeah, that "Time of Global Shift" was fun. It was down at the Galt House, and we had a lot of folks there, and the format was pretty nifty. It was, I guess, a tried and true technique for sharing the material that Scott had used around the country. He decided to bring it here to Louisville, Kentucky.

CARLA David Wilcock was part of it. There was a lady who was familiar with the Mayan Calendar—no, it was a gentleman who was familiar with the Mayan Calendar. All of these things fell into the fact that it was time for a global shift—that was the point. Scott had long been a fan of *The Law of One* material, and he just asked me to take part in it. So I sort of was wedged between Wilcock and John Major Jenkins. I couldn't have been in better company.

GARY It was kind of a singular event. There are very few public people out there working with this material, so it was unique in that this grouping of people working with *The Law of One* and the Confederation philosophy are on the same stage, so to speak. It was a most wonderful weekend.

---

[1] OCR (optical character recognition) is a scanning process used to scan the printed channeling sessions and convert the text into a file for a word processing program, like Microsoft Word. Once converted, a human eye is still needed to review the Word document to ensure that all the text was converted

correctly. Many of the channelings now available in the Library section of www.llresearch.org were published to the site using OCR.

[2]   By building a new website! Begun almost two years before Carla passed, it has been a long work in progress and may be launched by the time this book is published. Its objective is to unify the existing archive with community websites.

[3]   Jim is notoriously averse to using new technology or anything overly complex.

[4]   IMU is International Metaphysical University, through which L/L Research offers the Basic Principles of the Law of One course, with *Living the Law of One 101: The Choice* as its textbook. You can find it at http://www.intermetu.com.

CHAPTER 18

Community to Bring4th.org
2003–2008

Author's Note: The following material might be confusing without some backstory. For many years, Carla and Jim had hosted small gatherings and workshops in their home, consisting typically of less than ten people. One such event was the February 2003 Homecoming Gathering. In attendance were two others and myself. All three of us were given an invitation to move in with Carla and Jim and make an attempt at spiritual community. It was a longstanding desire of Don Elkins to have such a community, and Carla and Jim decided it was time to try.

One moved from Minnesota, the other from Virginia Beach, and I moved from Cleveland. Others came and went as time moved on. At maximum there were five or six people besides Jim and Carla in the house. The experiment had ups and downs, and after a couple years everyone had trickled away leaving only me remaining. It was, for me, the opportunity and honor of a lifetime. I've been in Louisville ever since.

GARY As I partition the history of L/L Research into chapters, a new one began at the February, 2003 Homecoming. Can you tell us what happened then?

JIM Everybody stayed. [*laughter*] They wouldn't go home.

GARY It was the cooking. We liked the cooking.

CARLA Suddenly we had seven volunteers in the house and we had a crowded house and a happy house. There were some moments of high drama, but we were all trying to get along and to help out L/L Research however we understood that to be.

The one thing that happened that I didn't expect was that, with people living here, we really needed to have a better basement because it was just a basement. So there was an enormous amount of effort put into rehabbing the basement: making walls, actual walls, closets, ceilings, rooms. It's beautiful down there. We still have places that we can put people when gatherings come. It's not a lot of people because we have people living here, but there are a few extra bedrooms and it's very nice to have them.

And all of this was accomplished by the volunteer efforts of those who were in the house at the time.

GARY So, another way to say everybody "just stayed," was that you also set out to form an intentional community?

JIM Right.

GARY Not the first such time that you'd done so, but the first time on that particular scale. You had three different people that stayed on from the 2003 Homecoming Gathering and then a couple more who came in shortly thereafter.

JIM One showed up about June 21.

GARY Yes, the best one. [*chuckles*]

JIM Not sure who that was. Yes, I wasn't sure about this young fellow. He was the youngest in the group, and I thought, *he's kind of young for this. I wonder what's going to happen.* What happened was he was the only one who stayed, and did a great job. That would be, of course, Gary Bean.

CARLA I felt strongly about you from the very beginning, as you know. There was just something—there was a connection.

GARY You had good soil here, and good nutrition and good sunlight, and good mentorship too. The conditions . . .

CARLA Yeah, and I trusted you. You may have been young, but you had good sense. So when I got to the point where I had to throw up my hands in the air and say, "I need an admin," you said, "I'll take on the job—I'll see what I can do." And you took it between your teeth and ran with it, and you have created your own position.[*]

JIM And you've become invaluable.

CARLA Yeah, you're the one who's out there hoeing, and if you want to use the garden thing as a metaphor, you're the one who's planting and hoeing in the garden of the front office of L/L Research.

GARY Thank you. So when you started out with this intentional community, what did you think would result from the experiment? What did you hope for?

JIM We really had no idea what would happen.

CARLA I was hoping that everybody would get together, get up in the morning and say, "What shall we do today?" And everybody would get together and have a unified idea of what we were going to do.

That did not happen. People got up when they wanted to get up, they did what they wanted to do, and it seemed that everybody had a different idea of what L/L Research should be.

More and more through the next couple of years, people found themselves very dissatisfied with L/L Research as it was. They wanted it to go this way, that way, be a farm, be organized this way or organized that way, and it basically splintered into two main groups: There were those who wanted to work on the farm idea—and we had a farm to work with. Jim and I owned a farm, 93 acres, upriver about 50 miles, and so we had that land. And it was a gorgeous wilderness. And then there were those who stayed in town and worked in the office doing the things that we had been doing all along.

There became more and more of a "we/they" energy, rather than a unified energy, and I never could get everybody to work together. It was impossible. So everybody did what they wanted to do, got what they wanted to get, and then spun out and left.

Over a period of about five years we saw one person after another leaving.

---

[*] Gary did indeed create and develop the role, organizing and coordinating L/L Research over the years, but becoming Carla's administrative assistant was in response to Carla's request and insistence that he give it a try.

So people were here from 2003 through 2005, and then after that people started leaving, and during the 2003 to 2005 period it was mostly construction. That was what we did really well together.

GARY Yeah, I would agree that one of the key issues was lack of common vision and unity.

Then if I were to ask what lessons were gleaned from your attempt at a spiritual community, I presume that would be one of them—the need for unity, for group cohesion?

JIM Yes, yes.

CARLA And I was not willing to put my foot down and be bull-headed about it and say, "Do it my way, or it's the highway." I was more, "Well, tell me about your idea, let's see what we can do with it." That was not a productive way to lead a group. It didn't make for cohesion.

But it was the way I am. I could never be the kind of person that leads a big group and pulls them all together because I'm just me. I don't want to be a leader. I want to facilitate and support people. I was surprised that there were so many different ideas of what to do with L/L. It had seemed obvious to me from the beginning—what to do. And I never heard an idea that was better than mine, in my own personal opinion, so I was never swayed.

GARY I think the situation may have benefitted from a stronger central focus in order to organize and rope in all the cats, so to speak. But I think the differences were fundamental enough that the energy would have dissipated, regardless. I think people just came to the experiment, each wanting different things, and it probably wasn't going to be unified and brought into commonality whatever efforts were made.

CARLA Yeah, and it wasn't that anyone had negative feelings or wished us harm or anything like that. There were strong disagreements certainly, but I think people ended up realizing, *well no, all is well—it's just that I need to do something else.* So people left under very friendly circumstances, but they left.

GARY Moving forward in time and to another subject: in 2004, you gave Tobey Wheelock permission to host your material on his website, www.lawofone.info. He subsequently built that website, dedicated to the study of the *Law of One* exclusively, and it's one of the best possible resources for the study of your work, in my opinion. Can you describe how this came about?

CARLA I think Tobey was one of those who wanted to know about the extra material in Book V. Where did each fragment fit? When Don X'd the stuff out, and then Jim included the omitted fragments in Book V, we didn't maintain an original, unedited manuscript identifying, *okay, it starts here and it ends here, and this is where it fits in.* So we didn't actually know where it fit in after a certain point. We'd lost that information. He wanted to get it further—he wanted to make sure that everything that was transcribed was *accurately* transcribed. So he found that 97% of it was accurately transcribed, and for the other 3%, there was a little tweaking to be done, and in just a few instances, there was material that had been lost, and he found it and restored it to its place.[1] And we're grateful for that.

So through the years—and I'm talking years—he listened to the original tapes, which you [Gary] made available to him. And after he would listen to one, then he would enter the data and have new information. And then years later, when he finished listening to it the first time, he conceived of the idea of listening to it a second time just to make sure he'd not made any mistakes himself—just to check himself.

So eventually, in the fullness of time, he and other volunteers got through all of the tapes again, so it was re-relistened to. So the website recorded all of these changes, small and large, and he created a way to enter the data using a notation of two numbers: one, the session, and two, the question; so you've got 22.15, for example, and you know it's the 15th question Don asked in Session 22, and you can find it just like that in Tobey's search mechanism on his website.

Further, because it's all digitized now, he has a search function which is just crackerjack good, and if you have a key word or phrase that you want to locate, you can locate it in a matter of seconds. So I'm very high on his website, and I use it all the time. It's easier to find things than it is any other way.

GARY And it's been an invaluable ally in my own personal study and in my work through L/L Research, especially when people write in with questions and with just a couple of keystrokes you can get the material for the person, paste it, or link directly to it. It's been amazing, and I'm really grateful for it.

So, in 2005, why did you start something that you named *The Camelot Journal?*

CARLA When I went to Europe on a teaching tour of England, I kept a journal of daily events, and I saw a lot of value in it. It showed that we were very active. It recorded things on many levels, including thoughts on the archetypal mind which occurred during that journey. I thought, *well, you know, I don't want to miss any of this stuff,* so I just continued doing it. And once continued, it had an energy of its own. And as I did more of it I got more good feedback, and so it's a tradition we don't want to quit now. Jim has taken that over and has done a wonderful job with it, as you know, because you [Gary] contribute to it every day—well, every day that you're here.

GARY If any reader is unfamiliar, Carla and Jim keep a daily blog called *The Camelot Journal.* It is currently on the home page of Bring4th.org, but when the two L/L websites merge into a super website it will be available at www.llresearch.org. It reports on our activities every day here at L/L Research.

Also in 2005, one of the community members, moi, produced a Homecoming at Wooded Glen Retreat. That was the first in what has become a long string of L/L Research workshops that he has led in the production of. [*laughs*] I don't know if I should refer to myself in the third person.

So has this new generation of workshops and/or gatherings differed from what you'd done in the past?

JIM Oh, a lot more fun. A lot more activities.

CARLA It's bigger. We never had the number of people all at once that you've generated by opening it up and announcing it on the website. I guess that's the difference, really, from doing it by word of mouth— *By the way, we're having a gathering, you want to come?*—and just letting the people know that we thought might be interested. So before, we'd have maybe five people if it was a big year, to your gatherings which number between 30 and 40.

GARY Yeah, we decided our maximum capacity for Homecoming was 40 people. And when you say "your"— I'm not taking ownership or credit. These people are coming because of the work you guys have done over the decades, but I'm helping to facilitate . . .

CARLA I know, but you're the producer of it.

JIM I think there's a Gary Bean brand on this thing, Gary. The word is out. *Have you been to a Bean party yet?*

GARY I *have* heard people whisper that as I walk by.

In 2006, you created—and you started to get into this—but you created the position of Administrative Assistant for L/L Research. Why was this needed, and how was it fulfilled?

CARLA It was needed because I was going crazy trying to get it all done. I was responsible for getting the books done, which was laughable, but I somehow hacked my way through it.

JIM You created your own technique for bookkeeping.

CARLA I did. [*laughs*] I was only vaguely involved with the actual Quick-Books, but I did my bit. I did the books, did all of the correspondence, did everything that was done, and I was running out of time to the point where I would find myself on vacations answering prisoners' letters because it was the first time all year that I'd had some hours free to do it. I worked from when I got up to when I fell into bed, and I still wasn't getting it all done. I kept falling behind and it was driving me crazy, and of course the idea of doing creative work on top of that was laughable. There was no time, and I really did want to do creative work.

So a fellow named Bill Hay gave me seed money to start up my own office where I could do my own work, and then I could have some help. And I offered the job to Gary Bean, who is you, and as I said before, you took it and leaned on me for about two weeks, got your feet under you, and took off running.

---

[1] By working directly with the audio on the cassettes for the Ra contact, Tobey's efforts produced two versions different from the original published books. The first is the *Relistened Version*, which is an *exact* transcript of the Ra contact audio on the cassettes—stutters and coughs included.

Some of the differences between the *Relistened Version* and the five original published volumes include:

　　1.　Because of its personal, transient, or sensational nature, some material was omitted from Book I through Book IV. (Most of this material was later published in Book V.) These omitted fragments were returned to their respective places within the text of the 106 sessions.

2. In some cases, Don Elkins' questions were edited for the books in order to improve readability.

3. In several cases, material from one session was placed into another for coherence in the published books. For example, session 26, as it appears in the books, contains a fragment from session 31.

4. Each Ra contact session was recorded onto three cassettes, all of which were flipped from side A to side B at different times. During the course of the Ra contact from 1981 to 84, two of the three cassettes were reused for later recording. This means that the remaining, non-reused cassette for each session (which the Relistening Project used) have small sections of missing material where the tape was flipped from side A to side B.

5. In some instances in the original volumes, names were removed (or erased from the audio) to protect privacy. Some of these names have been restored in the new versions (where permission was granted or the person named has passed away, or in the case of prominent UFO contactees).

6. And in some cases, simple errors were made in transcribing or typesetting the original manuscript.

The majority of the changes made were to Don's questions.

From this version was created the *Lightly Edited Version*, as described by Carla.

The *Lightly Edited Version* then met Jim, whereupon it underwent further tweaks to become the version used in *The Ra Contact: Teaching the Law of One*. Even at this advanced stage, the text is still an almost exact facsimile of the audio on the cassettes.

CHAPTER 19

Bring4th.org to the Present[*] 2008–2014

GARY We resume with the final chapter of the L/L Research story. Carla and Jim, in May, 2008, you crossed paths with Steve Engratt. What happened there?

CARLA Well, I had been trying to get an online community going for some time. It had gone through two tries before that; they both failed, and we pulled them offline. I think they exist somewhere in the bowels of old versions of stuff, but we don't have those versions and as far as I know, they're gone. So, Steve was a guy that wanted to do a website too, and his vision was very compatible with mine—of it being a place where we could bring together people who were lonely and who wanted to talk freely in a positive atmosphere.

So we talked about it with you [Gary] and Jim—for the most part you—and we three sort of cobbled together that original vision for the present incarnation of Bring4th.org. We set what it was that we wanted to do and how we were going to try to do it as far as priorities go. I think the first thing was a forum—set the forums up, and then we set up other features. We went online bit-by-bit.[1]

I was really thrilled with Engratt's work. He was very positive, and I was

---

very deeply involved in writing at that point. I believe I asked you to find a way to monitor the communications in the forums to make sure that all the postings were respectful and loving and had a good energy to them. So there has always been oversight there. By necessity, being a dinosaur as far as computers and all things *computer-ese* go, I had to leave the technical aspects in your hands. I've been very thrilled with the results through the years. Seems like it's being of service and that is our goal.

GARY Do you feel that your vision was fulfilled in what we were able to build? It sounds like you're satisfied with it.

CARLA I did feel that my vision was fulfilled because I basically wanted a place where people could go and talk; they certainly can, and they certainly do. I don't know how many thousands of posts we've had on there now, but it's way up there.

GARY Maybe over 100,000 at this point[2]?

CARLA So people are finding good conversations and it has been kept from being ugly. Once somebody starts to be ugly, they're warned and they go through a fairly long process of being warned and being talked to. Almost every case you can work it out and smooth it out. In some very few cases we had to stop the postings from being available with these people, simply because they are going to be ugly, and we don't want that energy online. Nowhere on the site do we want anything except loving energy.

GARY Moderating is not often a fun or rewarding task.[3]

CARLA No, it's a tough job. But somebody's got to do it.

GARY So why was there a necessity to create a separate website for online community and not just incorporate it into the archive website?

CARLA Simply because Ian did not have a vision of that; he wanted a library website. He did not, specifically did not, want a community website. He saw a lot of problems with that, and he didn't want to get involved in that much work. He was already involved in a huge amount of work, translations started pouring in . . . he was putting different translations online and getting each one of those produced, coded, and so forth. The guy was working hard, and he was doing fine at what he did. So we just made another site. But now that Ian has retired and Steve Engratt has taken over the reins for everything, I like your vision of bringing the two websites together so that it's easier to use.

GARY So with the new website also came L/L Research's first online store, the first time that readers could order your books through the internet without using a mail order form.

CARLA Right. And it's the first time that they could easily use charge cards.

GARY Yep. And the online store also had the added advantage of making it easier for the readership to donate to L/L Research. Consequently, for the first time in all the years that you guys have been running L/L Research, you didn't have to fund the organization out of your own pockets. Just enough came in to keep the lights on, as you like to say.

CARLA It was amazing. Sometimes we'd think *there's no way*, and then somebody would send in a big donation and make it just okay, just squeaking by. We've never had a lot over, but we've squeaked by.

GARY That's been my experience of working through L/L Research. We usually start to coast on fumes near the end of the year until enough comes in to keep us running—thanks to the annual fundraiser.

I wanted to note during this interview that you guys have not only performed this channeling service all these years and hosted these workshops and responded to seekers, but you were paying for this whole venture.

CARLA That's true, that's true. And it was very distressing to those who helped me with what Don left me, which I put in trust; my trust officer said, "Why are you taking more and more out of your trust to spend on this—donate to this group?" I said, "Well, they need it. I want to make sure that there's money enough to do this."

JIM We are the "they," and that is our work. What else is there to do? We do whatever we can.

CARLA Yeah, she was somewhat distressed, but I said, "If I pay out all that Don left me, then that is just. Don would have done that." So I was satisfied. And she had to be satisfied.

GARY Among my objectives in having this interview was to communicate to future generations (should L/L Research continue) what the founders' intent was, what your spirit was, how-you-guys-did-things. So whether it's me serving as administrator or somebody else down the line, this is going to be, I hope, part of a policy that stays: that no matter what, we keep L/L Research alive. Even if the donations run dry, then it's up to us to begin chipping in. If I need to get a different job, then I get a different job to make income, but this is primary and this ship stays afloat.

JIM That's the spirit. You've got the spirit.

CARLA You got it, that's right. And hopefully you won't have to do this kind of sacrificing that we're talking about here.

GARY Through the middle of the 2000s up to now, it's been a process of you guys gradually pulling back from some of the front-and-center L/L duties—always remaining, of course, the creative heart and spirit of L/L Research. And as you have done that, I became the de facto direction-setter, policy-maker, and representative of L/L Research, essentially coordinating and managing the entire operation as an administrator. Can you describe this transition and whether I carried forward your work and spirit in congruence with your own heart?

JIM Oh, yeah. We are thrilled to have you there. We've talked about this a number of times over the last, I guess, year or so, and it's a good thing to talk about it in public, I'd say. But it's obvious: you're doing things that we never dreamed of and even if we dreamed them now, we couldn't do them. As Carla said, we've become somewhat of a dinosaur in certain areas, so we are thrilled to sit back and do what we can to be of service to others—communications, meditations, and talking when possible, whatever. But for the sailing of the ship and the steering of the course, there you are, and thank God for you.

CARLA If I had ever seen anything that was questionable, I would have questioned you on it. You've never said, "Well, I'm taking over now, you guys can just go away and retire." It's always been a joint effort, and I think it always will be as long as we're alive. But I don't understand the technical aspects of a lot of things. I can certainly understand the non-technical aspects, and those aspects we've talked about, and they always measure up. So I'm really happy with you.

GARY Thank you. That question could have gone the wrong way. [*laughter*]

JIM The interview could have been over! [*more laughter*]

CARLA Keep your tail up and wagging because you have a right to be cocky.

GARY Thank you for the positive reply. It means the world to me.

In the last self-referential question, during my tenure, as you guys have indicated, L/L Research has grown organically in important ways. L/L is facilitating both an archive and an online community; it's hosting larger workshops; we're doing the weekly *In the Now* radio program. We host a more developed prison ministry, multiple newsletters, a daily blog, social media outlets, a Daily Q'uote feature; we've been working, thanks to Austin, on making audio and e-books of the material available, assisting Tobey's Relistening Project, hosting booths at expos, coordinating volunteer translation projects, etc. Not to reflect on me personally but the *organization*, how do you reflect on this and are you content with the growth that your organization has undertaken?

JIM Oh man, it's amazing. I'm amazed. And astonished. Yeah, just to have it all listed in one place like that, that took a while. It's *wonderful.* It's fantastic.

CARLA And if we could think of any more ways to be of service, we would do it. That's the idea. And any and all ideas that volunteers come up with we'll consider, and the ones that seem good we preserve, and do them.

GARY As we near the end of the L/L Research story, one of its more recent milestones happened in 2013 when you greenlighted my request to bring in Austin Bridges, one of L/L Research's volunteer moderators on the forums, to work alongside of me in the office. Why was this needed, and what have the results been thus far?

JIM Well, we got it on good account from a very knowledgeable person that there was enough work to do that we needed another person because you needed help. You had set out on a bold and brilliant course and discovered that there's a lot to do, and to have a buddy in there working with you would be a real blessing. So of course we said *yes*, and it's been great. I think Austin has done a wonderful job. He's extremely capable, a very gentle soul, very intelligent, wise, and patient. We appreciate his counsel as well, especially talking over what to do about moderator situations. We'd had problems with various people.

CARLA He's very loving and very sensible. Good combination: thoughtful and loving. He seems to either create projects that you hadn't done at all, or manifest projects that were in your head, like digitizing everything on the Q'uo [channeling sessions]. So he just finds more ways to be of service and to make it more possible for people to find us, if they want to. God bless his soul.

I think it's a natural tendency of work to fill the time that you've got, and then to get overfilled. I know that I was overworked for a long time before I finally squawked and we got an admin. And then, for about, oh, fifteen minutes, you didn't have too much to do and you were making lists and then doing stuff on the lists, then coming to me for another list. And *then* you had lists you never finished, and then it got worse and worse. Finally you came to us and said, "Help!"

And it worked out. It worked out with Austin. I was never so happy, and now I hear from his indications that he's getting to the point where you both have too much to do. [*laughs*] It seems like there is an expansion there; it is just amazing. I hope the spirit sends us a third person eventually, because it looks like we'll need one.

GARY It's wonderful that you guys feel that way. It's almost a year; the beginning of August will be a year that he's been with us.

CARLA It doesn't seem like the time could possibly have passed that much, but he's a joy to have with us. He really is.

GARY A really *grounded* individual, a good head on his shoulders, and I knew that would be needed, considering . . .

CARLA And he fit right in, seamlessly. There wasn't an adjustment period that I could tell.

GARY Having seen people spin themselves out in this environment, whether it's because of the metaphysical qualities, or whether because we're just hard people to get along with, whatever the case may be—

CARLA One or the other . . . or both. [*laughs*]

GARY —I knew a strong grounded nature would be needed. And he's rock solid for sure. I agree with the other adjectives that you used as well, including wise and patient and a kind soul.

CARLA My gosh, somebody who comes in and does dictation for me because I can no longer see the computer keys! I can't keep up with my correspondence, so he helps me with that. At the end of it—and you know, talking to friends and stuff isn't exactly high priority for L/L Research—but he helps me out with my personal friends. It's got to be boring—it's got to be very boring—and at the end of it, he thanks *me* that we've been able to work together.

GARY Yes, and you said the word "seamless". That's one word I would have used too. He and I just operate seamlessly, and the four of us do…

CARLA You really do. You're like the Bobbsey Twins, especially when you go into the office and look at the two of you from behind with your curly hair up in your two ponytails that are just alike. I swear to God you look like twins, just going away—clickity-click, clackity-clack. [*laughs*]

GARY Every once in a while somebody will come through here and say, "Are you two brothers?" And I'll answer and say, "We are not of relations." Which is how Forest Gump replies to Lt. Dan when he asks if he and Bubba Gump are related and Forest looks at Bubba confused, not getting that it's not a valid question.

So for our final question regarding the long and rich story of L/L Research's biography: in my own experience over the past eleven years, so much of what L/L Research has been able to accomplish has happened thanks to volunteers. Often those volunteers proactively offer and initiate a specific service of their own design. Has this always been the case, and why do you think this is?

JIM People just want to help out.[4] We've had that happen throughout the years, whatever their talent was. Before the age of the computer, they offered things like artistry—*do you want me to draw something for you?*—or editing—*I can edit*—or—

CARLA Or helping us sort mail when we had a lot of mail to sort.

JIM Yeah, people just want to help. We've always been inspired and amazed by the quality of person that's interested in *The Law of One* information. We just keep seeing that reflected back to us with the offers from folks wanting to volunteer.

CARLA I feel that spirit is sending us that which is necessary. There is an animation of spirit involved in the whole energy of this. People do want to help but I think also there is that feeling of being blessed by spirit that we've prayed for, that we've gotten spiritual, angelic help all along. There are a lot of unseen friends at L&L Research, both from elsewhere and from right here.

GARY I agree on all accounts, especially the type or quality, you might say, of person that is attracted to this material. I've crossed paths with some of the best people in the world thanks to *The Law of One,* thanks to this information.

CARLA It's a wonderful lens that draws people together.

GARY And the volunteer work has been amazing in that sometimes we create a goal for ourselves or have a specific need that we may or may not vocalize, and that specific goal or need is met by volunteers. And then sometimes volunteers come to us with their own projects, and it's something we may not have considered previously. But I think one of the strengths of this organization is that we look at it and say, "That's great, let's do it!" Like, "What do *you* need? How can we assist you?" and then it becomes this collaboration. We become greater than the sum of our parts.

CARLA Right, and we always have been greater than the sum of our parts, even when there were just three of us working, and far greater than that.

JIM We should mention that one of our best volunteers is right here in the room with us, videographing us as we speak and talk.

GARY Off camera I looked up at him.

CARLA Yay, Ken!

KEN You're quite welcome.

GARY The Reverend Doctor, as he's known in some parts. He'll also be the officiant at my wedding, so we've turned to calling him The Reverend. With his Ph.D. he's got the doctor, so he's the Reverend Doctor Ken.

And on that note, we close the biography portion of L/L Research. We've had a long journey: from the Thomas Mantell case and the sparking of Don's interest in the UFO phenomena up to the present moment.

CARLA May it wave as long as there are people that need this energy.

---

[1] To the forums were also added other features, including blogs, a chat room, a map to connect seekers, a subscriptions page for our newsletters, a comprehensive link page, daily revelations of the secrets of the universe, among other components.

[2] 193,920 posts in 10,329 threads, with 6,025 registered members as of February 16, 2016.

3 Empirically speaking, it is the worst.

Fortunately Austin Bridges now heads up the moderator team with the invaluable and intelligent aid of our Australian friend and volunteer, Garry Fung. Username Bring4th_Plenum, Garry is the best moderator an online forum dedicated to the Law of One and spiritual community could have.

4 In calendar year 2014, we received help from about 50 volunteers, including translators.

CHAPTER 20
Vision for L/L's Future

GARY I'm sure that healthy amounts of luck and magic have contributed to the success of L/L Research, but in terms of that which can be identified, what principles do you feel have contributed to L/L Research's ongoing existence and capacity to serve?

JIM Hmm. Desire, I'd say, number one—desire to serve. Perseverance. A little luck in there too. What do you think?

CARLA Well, people find us helpful. As long as we're relevant to the people that are seeking, then that's what we're aiming to do. If this material is helpful, we'll be there with it—offer it for free. It's really . . . it's a very humble aim: just to continue to keep the material available, and to be open always to ways, old and new, that we may help the people who find our material useful.

JIM I think the goal's always the same: to keep the material available, freely. But the way to do it is what's really changed recently with what you've been able to do with the forums, the website, and one thing and another. We hope for more ways.

GARY In Book V you said that as well: that as long as people are interested, as long as people are helped by this, then we're going to answer that call.

CARLA Yeah.

GARY So what principles do you feel are important to any organization that seeks to serve others?

CARLA Purity, humility . . .

JIM Foolhardiness . . . [*laughter*] Don Quixote is the flavor of the thing...

CARLA I think purity in that you maintain a very high road in all that you do and in your ethical stance, and . . . what's the other word that I used . . . oh, *humility*—yeah, it's important to remember that if we find that this material becomes irrelevant, then we quietly shut our . . . you know, we walk away and say, "okay." If we found that this material was not helpful anymore, it's not like we'd find something else to do. This is it, this is the scope and the heart of our service, and we really are very humble about it.* If it's helpful, great. Keep it available.

GARY So, not that this is going to happen anytime soon, at least not until 2100, 2200, but when you do leave your physical body complex behind, what are your hopes and aspirations for L/L Research after you're gone?

JIM It continues to exist and shine and serve and to go forward in whatever ways possible.

CARLA We've changed our Will so that whatever monies that we have had during our lifetimes to spend on L/L Research will now be available to you, so you're sort of our heir. We trust you implicitly to maintain that purity and that humility and that foolhardiness of going forward with flags flying, finding all ways to help that you can.

GARY Dreaming the impossible dream.

CARLA Dreaming the impossible dream. Yes, it would be wonderful if we could be that hundredth monkey that taught the world how to love.

---

* Affirming ones humbleness risks coming across as being not-so-humble. What I think Carla is saying here is that she recognizes her humanity and the inherently flawed, you might say, nature of any effort which attempts to live transparently and walk the high road. Further, she considers her work humble because she, Jim, and her organization are not seeking fame, glory, wealth, or the attention of others. Rather, she and Jim, unknown to most of the world, go quietly about their days living the best lives they know, dispassionately offering their work to the interested seeker, recognizing that it will resonate with only a few but is nevertheless an effort worth the making.

GARY This next question may be a reiteration of what you've already said, but it focuses it in a different way.

I've said before, I'm not placing you two on a pedestal, but for better or worse, I think better, you are the founders of this spiritually-dedicated organization, and those who succeed your generation and my own, and who seek to carry forward your work in their own way, will be operating within a trajectory first put into motion by your efforts and your spirit. Presuming that third density continues, and L/L Research survives, if you could speak to those of succeeding generations who didn't have the benefit of meeting you personally, what would you say to them?

CARLA I would say to them, look at the material. [*laughter from all*] Don't worry about us.

JIM If you're into footnotes, you can check us out later.[1]

GARY Ra says:

> **RA** Nearly all positive channels and groups may be lessened in their positivity or rendered quite useless by what we may call the temptations[2] offered by the fourth-density negative thought- forms. They may suggest many distortions towards specific information, towards the aggrandizement of self, towards the flowering of the organization in some political, social or fiscal way.
>
> These distortions remove the focus from the One Infinite Source of love and light of which we are all messengers, humble and knowing that we, of ourselves, are but the tiniest portion of the Creator, a small part of a magnificent entirety of infinite intelligence. 62.23

As we discussed before, as an individual or organization grows, how do you balance this growth so that the focus, like Ra is saying, is stayed upon the one infinite Source of love and light? How do you grow without removing the focus?

JIM Well, we remind ourselves everyday with our Morning Offering of exactly why we're here and what we want to do and how we want to dedicate our lives. We read from *The Law of One*, from the Bible, Old and New Testament, from other inspirational works, just get the feeling of laying the foundation for the day, and the life over the years just becomes part of the second nature. There it is. It's as much a part of you as the color of your eyes or hair.

GARY Setting your own programming each day . . .

When you did your walking of the circle ritual prior to the Ra contact (a ritual which Ra gave you), Ra has you ask yourselves questions that you then provide the answer for, like, "What are we doing? We're . . ." How does it go?

JIM Oh goodness, it's been years. "What is the Law? *The Law is One.* Why are we here? *We desire to serve the One.*" Yeah, basically that's it.

GARY So you're kind of affirming and restating your intent.

JIM Yeah, it's just like meditation. It takes you back to the heart of who you are. We can travel that same path by the Morning Offering. We meditate then, too—a shorter meditation.

CARLA I have an example of how you keep from being overwhelmed by bigness. I was called not too long after Monica and I started the first generation of the radio show *In the Now*. This guy—his daughter had heard us and she got him to listen to us. He's a producer—big time producer—with several big shows that are doing quite well, and generating a lot of fame and fortune for their hosts. He targeted me as the host even though Monica was actually the one who was doing the intro and the outro and so forth. Anyway, he said, "I want you. I don't need Monica, and I don't need you talking about your show all the time. I want you to have guests on that are really of interest to everybody, and I want you to be direct and angling for the big punch. Make sure you begin with a punch and you end with a punch." He said, "I'll listen, and if you want the job, you're welcome to have a crack at it." And I told him, I said, "Forget it! I'm interested in helping our people, and we're trying to answer questions they might have after reading the material. That goal is very small, and I have no interest in figuring out what's gonna punch, or having guests on that have nothing to do with *The Law of One*." And he said, "You're passing up a lot of money."

And I said . . . "Yeah."

[*laughs*] When I told this to Monica, she said, "Put me in touch with him, would ya?" I would have if she really meant it, but she was just joking.

Anyway, I just passed it up. It wasn't what we're here to do. I didn't want to get big. I have no desire to get big. I just want to serve the material.

GARY You've known what you both wanted to do for a long time and have stayed true to that.

CARLA We're humble instruments.

---

[1] Future generations, hopefully you have not deified or canonized Carla, Don, and Jim, but surely you've given their lives more space than a footnote. Chances are the *Law of One* material is blowing your minds as much as it did ours, and you're amazed that these three very exceedingly human people achieved such a thing.

Unless books have been banned in your post-apocalyptic world, in which case you won't know what a footnote is.

[2] Not the 1960s Motown musical group.

GARY A note before proceeding. The first question seems self-evident to me. However, among the objectives for having this interview was the hope that this material would serve as an internal resource for L/L Research in the future—as a guide, of sorts, for those who will come after you, and me. They will be able to consider your reflections and rationale.

When did you decide that you would make all of your information available for free without charge, and what do you hope to achieve by this policy?

JIM You and Don already had that going, didn't you?

CARLA Right from the beginning, we wanted it to be available for free. There was never any thought of anything else. The material was there. We never had the desire to push it on people, but if they found it helpful, we wanted to make sure they were able to get it. That was Don's policy. We've just not changed.

GARY In a capitalist world, that's not a very smart position.

CARLA "Our kingdom is not of this world." I might use that quote freely.

GARY So you have always offered this information in a spirit of *use what resonates and leave the rest behind*. This basic idea prefaces virtually every

Q'uo channeling, and permeates everything L/L does. How is this helpful?

JIM I think it reaffirms people's free will. There are so many groups around that say they want to help people, but when people get involved with them, they discover that there's some price to pay, that they have to do a certain thing or a certain way, or . . .

CARLA Believe a certain way . . .

JIM Believe a certain thing or whatever. We want people to know that their free will is of utmost importance. That's always the way we've been treated by the Confederation sources, so it just makes every sense in the world for us to treat people that same way too. It lets people know that we value them, and if they have any need for what we've got to offer, we're glad to give it.

CARLA I think it helps people to be supported in their search for their own spiritual path. They're often unable to join the spiritual path of their forefathers, shall we say, or the Christian Church, the Jewish Church, the Buddhist—whatever church it is they were not able to find a home in. They're making their own path, and they have their intuition and good sense, and we want to support that, to let people know that we trust that for them. Whatever is resonating for them is what they need to follow. If it's our work, we're glad to help.

GARY Tackling the same basic question from a different angle, why is it important, in your opinion, to refrain from proselytizing, and to share this information (if you feel called to share it) in a dispassionate manner?

JIM Well, that just seems to be another way of validating people's free will; you wait until you're asked. You might drop a hint somewhere, but there's no need to proselytize. You usually waste a lot of energy doing that, yours and theirs. It's disharmonious to do that. You're trying to manipulate people's free will, that's the negative path. Doesn't feel good.

CARLA And we find we have plenty to do just from people who come to us and ask us about our material. Why waste our energy and time trying to convince people who would never be convinced in a million years? Why do they need that? They're doing just fine without us. It's the people who need our material—find it useful—that we want to support.

GARY Though you've offered plenty of your own reflections and interpretations of this material, you've always, all along, insisted that you are, as Carla says, "bozos on the bus" just like everyone else, and that your opinions are not to be elevated to that of the authority. Can you speak to this?

JIM Oh my goodness, yes! [*laughs*] I mean, we have the same catalyst as everyone else has; it may be tailored in our own way to learn a more specific lesson, I don't know. But we have our own strengths and weaknesses and needs for help, counseling—we do the same thing everyone else does. I mean, it just seems so obvious to me because I live inside my skin—I know what an idiot I am! [*laughs*] But I work with myself too; that's the way I happen to grow. And I think everybody does. All of us have strengths and weaknesses, desires and goals, and we're doing our best. Now and then we need a little help. So we're here for those who need a little help because we've gotten help in the past from others.

CARLA We get by with a little help from our friends.

JIM [*laughs*] We do.

GARY You have sought to foster community among spiritual seekers. Why is this important to you?

CARLA I think people are community-minded. We can do almost nothing alone. We can pretend that we're alone, and we can order out food. We can order things online instead of going out amongst people, but the catalyst is with people. There's a fundamental help that we get from being with other people, especially in terms of talking things over, chewing over things that are on your mind, and not everybody has a chance to do that in their home environment. Many people have expressed to me that they feel so isolated and so miserable in their home environment in terms of not having anybody to talk to about things that matter to them. So let's try to help provide a place like that.

JIM Ra said it really well. "Those who of like mind together seek will far more surely find."[1] It helps to have mirrors. It really does. As much as I love solitude in my life, it doesn't teach nearly as well as being with another person.

GARY You've identified collaboration as an important aspect of L/L Research's operation. Do you see L/L Research as a collaborative effort?

CARLA Oh definitely! From the very beginning it was the group that produced the material, the Ra sessions. It's always the group that asks the questions and produces the tone of the answers received during a session. So even from the heart of it, there's collaboration in the creation of the work. I don't know where we would be if Jim and I were the only ones who worked for L/L Research. It certainly wouldn't be like this. Nothing like this. We don't know half of how you do what you do. We're just thrilled to death that it works so well.

JIM Indeed.

GARY And for my own part, working with and through L/L Research, the teamwork aspect has been prominent. So often I've appreciated and loved that teamwork, and have noticed—you and I have talked about this quite often—how the end product is always better when the whole team is involved, or more than one person.

CARLA Yeah, that second pair of eyes is always helpful.

GARY You've run annual fundraisers and sought to sell hardcopy versions of your material along with other associated things through your online store. Is earning money and paying bills incompatible with spiritual seeking and serving in a spiritual way?

CARLA Heck no! Everybody needs to pay bills. We need to be responsible for what it is that we are buying. I think the concept that *if you do spiritual work you can sort of sit back and get everything for free because it's spiritual work* is not going to work. You have to get down and dig in the dirt just like anybody else.

GARY In the first session, Ra says:

> RA Each of those in this group is striving to use, digest, and diversify the information which we are sending this instrument into the channels of the mind/body/spirit complex without distortion. The few whom you will illuminate by sharing your light are far more than enough reason for the greatest possible effort. To serve one is to serve all. Therefore, we offer the questions back to you to state that indeed it is the only activity worth doing: to learn/teach or teach/learn. There is nothing else which is of aid in demonstrating the original thought except your very being, and the distortions that come from the unexplained, inarticulate, or mystery-clad being are many. Thus, **to attempt to discern and weave your way through as many group mind/body/spirit distortions as possible among your peoples in the course of your teaching is a very good effort to**

make. We can speak no more valiantly of your desire to serve. 1.10

Here, Ra conveys both the ascendancy of the service of *being*—that effortless emanation or radiance of being *who you are* without reference to what you're doing—but they also commend Don's efforts, or the group's efforts, to share this information. Why try to share this information?

JIM Once you gotten the taste of something that's really helpful to you, wanting to share it with other people seems to be a natural outgrowth. If you've got an open heart and you point it towards service to others, it just happens. You want to share it. You've got something good. Little kids discover a new cereal to eat on the shelf, and they go and eat the cereal, see a new show on television—I think it's almost DNA, like it's genetically programmed. *Hey, share it with your buddies!*

CARLA Yeah, we're thrilled to death to be able to help anybody who might be able to find our stuff useful. Why else would we open up like that? Like I said, we're social people. We are *a* social people. And golly, if we find it useful, then maybe somebody else will too.

GARY What are your thoughts on advertising this body of work?

JIM It gets tricky. You have to pay for the ads, so we still use a little of it. Do we still have an ad somewhere in a magazine?

CARLA We tried it. It didn't fly.

GARY Not currently. We're waiting for the launch of the new website and then we're going to try to, smartly, in a limited way, explore some advertising.

JIM I think . . . we've got to think about that. [*laughs*] It's a possibility. It's so widely used in this culture. You advertise what you've got so that people will know about you. Word of mouth has treated us very well in the past. I really lean towards that direction. Every day you hear about things going viral on the internet. I think that when the time's right, people will find out about us. I find myself midstream changing my mind about advertising. [*laughing*]

CARLA Yeah, I'm not a fan of advertising. I like preserving the status of being somewhere between obscure and unknown. I like that people have to search to find us, because I think that spiritual search is all-important. It's intention; it's will that drives desire. It lets spirit know, *hey, I would like this kind of material,* and spirit jumps in and helps. People have found our material in the oddest ways. It might fall on them in a used book store in Athens—very strange ways that historically people told us they found it. But with the internet, it's likely that most people do a search and wind around to finding us that way.

JIM The only time we ever tried advertising, we offered the book free to read, and if you wanted to keep it, send a donation of your choosing—your amount—or send the book back. I guess we probably reached a few people that way, but I don't know how good a way of doing it that was. That's the only way in which we've undertaken advertising.

GARY The thinking that emerged from the staff meeting workshop[2] was that, firstly, if we did engage in advertising, there was no intent to manipulate the psychology of the person or to produce a consumer—like to try to convince them that they need this for any reason or they should buy this, that it will help them to perform better or to score a date or to find salvation, et cetera. And also, if we used paid advertisement, to just plainly and simply state, "This is what it is; this is what we have. If you want it, come check us out; if not, hey, it's all right. Maybe you want something else in that case."

CARLA If you think about it, the culture being what it is, if we try to go big and we try to fly above the radar, it would be 15 minutes before someone who is related to one of the more stringent churches would be pointing at us and saying, "They're of the devil!" I don't see any reason why we want to encourage that. I'm so content to fly below the radar; I think it really serves the spiritual purposes that work to help people, genuinely help people who are seeking to make their own path.

---

[1] Those who together seek may also enjoy the full quote:

QUESTIONER Could you expand on what you mean by that interaction of polarized entities in piercing the veil?

RA I am Ra. We shall state two items of note. The first is the extreme potential for polarization in the relationship of two polarized entities which have embarked upon the service-to-others path or, in some few cases, the service-to-self path. Secondly, we would note that effect which we have learned to call the doubling effect. Those of like mind which together seek shall far more surely find. 83.17

2   A call was issued to every corner of earth for the wisest and most spiritually advanced seekers to convene a Great Council at L/L Research. The goal would be to address the ills that plague this planet and discover a way to bring enlightenment and alleviation of suffering to the great multitudes. When no one responded to that call some of our close friends and long-time volunteers convened at L/L for a staff meeting in 2013 to reflect on L/L Research's work and discuss its path ahead.

GARY What is philosophy, and how is this body of information a philosophy?

JIM A natural philosopher should answer this question.

CARLA Well, philosophy tries to address the questions that cannot be answered in any linear way. Why are we here? Who are we? What do we know? Where are we going?

It is not necessary in order to live a good life to have a philosophical nature. Many people who are not of a philosophical nature are just simple, good, hardworking people, and whatever they follow—their church or whatever—it works for them, and that's all they need to know.

There are lots of other people who wake up intellectually as adults and realize these questions really bother them. They would like to know where we're going, why we're here, what's going on, what's the nature of life? What's the nature of us? How can we know what we know? I mean, these are fascinating questions, and they have their place in the universe of arts and sciences—and always have had since before Greek times—but certainly we are all familiar with the Greek philosophers.

One who seeks philosophically is attempting to answer these questions, and is not necessarily hungering for a religious experience, but simply hungering to find the answer to these questions. Therefore our material would be slotted as philosophical rather than religious, although those two both take a lot of the same questions as their purview. We're not trying to make anybody believe this, or to have faith in this, or worship this. We are trying to engage in finding out what the puzzle pieces are, how they all fit together.

GARY And to provide people with the tools for walking their own path.

CARLA Helping them to seek for themselves.

GARY Would you say that this information, which you guys have spent your lives offering, is infallible in any way? Or free of error and mistake? Is it always *right* (whatever that word means)?

JIM It's an attempt to find the truth, to find the self within, the nature of reality. Ra addresses the notion of right and wrong, saying that there really is no right or wrong; there is unity.

Now, I guess people could say, "Well, is that true?" And I think you have to have the call within your own heart to try to find out the answers here. And together we all help, you know, on that journey. That's the journey we're all on: the pilgrim's journey, the long, dusty road.

And it's more of a *feeling* of rightness than an intellectual, provable rightness. And it's in that inside part of you that vibrates *YEAH!* when you know you've heard the truth; and it says, "Oh, you've got to be kidding me," when you haven't heard the truth.

CARLA But it's not like we've found *the* truth and it's spelled TRVTH like in the comic strip piece, *B.C.*, and we're standing up on a little stool in the park on Sunday and addressing the crowd about truth.

If this material may be helpful to some, we have it available. It's ridiculous to think that there will be one truth that would make sense for everybody. It's not that kind of a world. People are various, people are individualistic; some find comfort in thinking of truth one way, some find comfort in another.

I think that concepts like honor, and ethical probity—uprightness—have a meaning that is eternal. But, I think that it comes out differently for different people. I think it's something you could say for truth forever: that it's good to be honorable. It's good to try to do the right thing. It is worthwhile to behold things of beauty and to have them around you.

But we can't then define what things you have around you or exactly how the truth goes, because you'll fall apart every time. On some level it will not work for one person, whereas it worked fine for another. You have to let people find their own way.

GARY While each seeker will, of course and of necessity, form their own unique relationship with your work, what is the general hoped-for ideal relationship between the information and the spiritual seeker?

JIM That it becomes a part of their seeking; that they incorporate what is helpful in this information into their overall philosophy—I guess you'd say—their reason for living, the thing that draws them forward, the impossible dream.

CARLA [Carla sings the chorus of "The Impossible Dream."[1]]

GARY Is there anything distinct about this channeled and human-authored body of information, the Confederation philosophy? If there is anything distinct, what is it?

CARLA *Je ne sais quoi.* There is a quality to it that is very specific and very memorable in its own way. Whether it's the depth of the information or that it has the tendency to strike at the heart. Some people think that's very notable. It happens again and again. And there's a definite flavor to all things produced by this group, and it's a beautiful flavor! I like it a lot.

GARY Though I and other readers never ceased to be amazed at the profundity and the positivity and the purity and elegance of this information, most on this planet would quickly dismiss this information as invalid. Any speculation as to why this is?

JIM Well, other things are more important in their journey at this time. At some point this may make more sense.

CARLA Yeah. It's not our goal to try to figure out what makes everybody tick. We just want to offer the material—to be redundant in our redundancy—offer the material to those who find it helpful. I don't think we need to think further than that.

KEN Just a quick comment. One thing that I noticed about the material is that it was helpful in reading it to say: even though people may be at a point where this material isn't valuable to them, that's perfectly okay. There's no judgment from you, or shaming of anybody for not being interested in it.

It was like, *you don't want to read it? That's totally okay. Don't read it.* It's perfect, you know. Follow what you want to follow, do what you want to do.

CARLA I remember one very memorable thing: the one time Don was on the television camera. The interviewer said to him, "For the person that says that they don't believe in UFOs, what is your argument?" Don says,"I have no argument. I don't care whether people believe me or not. If they are interested, I'll tell them everything I know." You know? He was totally indifferent. I think it's a beautiful energy there.

It gives people freedom. It gives people dignity. It makes them not stupid, even if they don't agree with you. You don't agree? Fine, it's alright. See ya later.

JIM I think the one thing that needs to be realized is that people are doing what they need to be doing, whatever they're doing. And it may not look like it makes sense, or like it has any value or service to others when you're looking from your point of view. But people are all the Creator. They are all here learning something important. We can't say when a certain step has to be taken. Everything you are doing is important. Do it.

CARLA What he said.

GARY Jim likes to say that L/L Research's work is located somewhere "between obscure and unknown." Why do you think this is, and do you think it will ever appeal to any but a small, niche demographic?

JIM I really don't know why that is . . . and there is not a very big chance it's going to appeal to a lot of people, because of the mystery of why it doesn't. [*laughs*]

GARY Yeah, back to the previous question.

JIM Yeah, see previous.

CARLA Well, it's not useful. It doesn't make anybody money. It doesn't make them prettier or more attractive to the opposite sex. It doesn't have any earthly goals whatsoever. People that don't understand why anyone would study philosophy will have the same problem with this.

And then there are people who are starving for information that really speaks to their soul, and they're thinking on a different level. They're a different cat. If this appeals then great, we've found a match.

But, it's one person, in, probably a hundred who really, really needs this information. And that's the way the world wags. I don't have any argument with who everybody is, or why they are not like me. It's okay.

GARY Those who identify as wanderers seem drawn to this information. Is there any particular reason why the profile we call "wanderer" seems so common among those who enjoy this information?

JIM I think a lot of wanderers have a kind of a soul-memory where this information makes more sense. It has a unifying feel and factor about it that speaks to the wanderer who has come here to be of service. It is sort of like a letter from home.

CARLA Yeah. People remember a better way, and then here, here it is kind of outlined. And that's what they've thought, but they haven't been able to find any support whatsoever. They write in and say finally, you know, this is home. I've found my home, and I'm so glad that that's possible for that one person in a hundred.

GARY L/L Research has received and been honored by many of what you've long called "wanderers' stories," and many other messages from people who have crossed paths with this information. What sort of effect has it had on people's lives?

JIM Oh gosh, people keep writing in saying it has changed their lives, and that's just amazing. That's what we would hope, you know, because it's certainly changed our lives, and to know that other people are being changed too is amazing. Very gratifying.

CARLA Yeah. I think that every time a wanderer tells his story it generates a lot of joy—the joy from the heart of the person telling his story, the joy from people who hear it and are able to go, *yes, yes, I've had that experience myself! I thought I was all alone. But here is somebody else . . .* The joy from all the fellow travelers that we have in unseen worlds, both in our planet's inner worlds and from elsewhere. There is just a lot of joy generated when people open up and say, "This is who I am."

GARY Do you see a certain commonality among those who are drawn to and aided by this information?

JIM Sensitivity, open hearts, intelligence, good will . . . they're really good people. I'm so impressed, some of the niftiest people I've met in the world come through our Homecomings.[2]

CARLA All different kinds of walks of life and ways of expressing themselves and all that, but hey, they all are interested in listening to each other, because they are all good, good people. And that is one beautiful thing about people interested in *The Law of One,* they're just good people. So glad to know them.

GARY Do you think that a dogma can be developed around this information, or does it elude the fundamentalist's mindset?

CARLA Oh, a dogma can and certainly has been generated about this information, and you just gotta watch that, man! [*laughs*] Really, gotta watch that.

JIM Ra said when they walked among the Egyptians there were at least thirty different distortions for every word they spoke. [3]

CARLA Yeah, it's a problem. People want to make a dogma out of things. They want to be right. They want to shrink it down to where—you know, one size fits all. And it just doesn't. Ra made a big barn for all kinds of considerations and ways of approaching the understanding of the Creator, and made all those ways right. We need to preserve that freedom by refusing to accept a dogma.

GARY To your awareness, has anyone tried to build a church, so called, around this philosophy, or turned towards proselytism?

JIM Not to my knowledge. [*laughs*]

GARY Nobody has come knocking on your door to share the good word of Ra?

CARLA No, not to my knowledge.

GARY I think that speaks both to the information and to the seekers attracted to the information.

So among those who study and love this philosophy, there is a tendency to hide this material and their feelings about this material from public view, and if they speak of it at all, they do so only through a veil.

There is, of course, good reason to exercise discrimination and not proactively broadcast one's belief system everywhere and anywhere. As you guys noted, we can only serve to the extent it is requested.

But because this information is seven orders of magnitude outside of the collective box, many who study it hide their love of this material due to fear of rejection, ridicule, or judgment from others.

You two, on the other hand, have always been quite candid and fearless in being open about the work you do as channels and operators of L/L Research. How have you maintained this confidence and relative freedom from concern for the potential ridicule or judgment of others?

JIM Well, we don't advertise it. I mean, in the sense of talking freely with everybody about it. Really, it's just going with feelings when we're with people who may ask a question that could lead to sharing some more information about *The Law of One.* Then drop a little hint. That's what we have done in years gone by. Some of our neighbors are a little more understanding. Some, I have a hunch, really don't grasp at all what goes on here. [*laughs*] *You have these meetings on Labor Day, what is that about?* The Homecomings. [*makes playful sound of confusion*]

CARLA I never did care what people thought. I've always gone my own way.

JIM And Carla talks to spiritual seekers about her Christianity, and talks to Christians about her spiritual seeking. [*laughs*] We don't go into great detail. But we leave a door open and see if somebody may walk through. Very seldom do they walk through. They stand at the doorway and have a conversation.

---

[1] Dale Wasserman and Joe Darion, "The Impossible Dream," in *Man of La Mancha* by Dale Wasserman (New York: Tams-Witmark Music Library, Inc., 1964).

[2] Homecoming is an annual gathering offered to seekers interested in *The Law of One.* It is held at the L/L Research "headquarters," as it were, in Louisville, Kentucky.

[3] In discussing their attempts to answer the call to service in Egypt, Ra says that in one particular instance they manifested in physical form but that:

RA We discovered that for each word we could utter, there were thirty impressions we gave by our very being, which confused those entities we had come to serve. After a short period we removed ourselves from these entities and spent much time attempting to understand how best to serve those to whom we had offered ourselves in love/light. 23.6

CHAPTER 23
Spiritual Principles I

GARY In this section we depart from the biographically oriented questions to explore an area that is very personal to each seeker. Each who embarks upon the quest to seek the truth must find their own answers and find their own ways to live and tackle these questions. We now turn to Jim McCarty and Carla Rueckert to see how *they've* answered and attempted to engage these questions on their own paths.

We'll start with some quotes from Ra:

> The understandings we have to share **begin and end in mystery**. 28.1

> There is a **mystery-clad unity** of all creation in which all consciousness periodically coalesces and again begins. Thus we can only say we assume an infinite progression though we understand it to be cyclical in nature and, as we have said, **clad in mystery**. 28.16

> We must gaze then at the **stunning mystery** of the One Infinite Creator. 97.9

> The rhythms [of intelligent infinity] are **clothed in mystery**, for they are being itself. 27.7

Though certainly English, or any communication of sign and symbol, is completely inadequate to the task of answering this question, I will nevertheless endeavor the query: What, in your opinion, is meant by "mystery" and "mystery-clad"? And why does Ra indicate that all happens in an ultimate context of mystery?

JIM The beginning and the ending, and a whole lot in between, seem to be mysterious. As we progress through the densities, I think some of the mystery falls aside. The veils are taken apart and we're able to see what we couldn't see before, and experience what we couldn't experience. But Ra, being at mid-sixth density, or a little further than mid-sixth density awaiting their seventh density graduation, still says that there's much that they are unaware of. They assume it's an infinite creation. We assume the same thing, but until they are actually into the seventh density, moving into the density of foreverness, maybe until they have again joined the Infinite Creator in what we see as a black hole, perhaps then the mysteries will be revealed.

But there is always mystery—things we don't understand, things that we need to take on faith, things for which we need to continue to exercise our will in order to approach in any way. I think mystery is just part of the infinite creation that each of us is going to continually confront as we move through the densities. Maybe one day the mysteries will all resolve and make themselves known to us, but not any time soon.

CARLA Basically, how do you get from third density, with its very black-and-white, yin-and-yang dynamic, to the density of unity? How do you get all the paradoxes resolved? It's all a mystery. I can answer some questions for readers, but I cannot answer how this particular paradox or that particular paradox is resolved. I don't know. To me, it's a mystery. So I think in some things we abide in the mystery; we take it on faith and put aside the demand to know until a later time.

GARY In connection with the previous question, Ra says:

> RA It is a grand choice that each may make to, by desire, collect the details of the day or, by desire, to seek the keys to unknowing. 84.7

What does that statement mean to you two?

JIM Well, we can continue to seek what we don't know: the keys to unknowing. There seems to be a, what shall we say, *physics* for each level of experience, a way of operating in each level, and in fourth density things will be different than they are here. We'll be aware of each other's thoughts. We can affect things with our mind, and as we go into fifth density, there will be more things that we'll be able to do and think and feel. So we can either continue to seek into the mystery of what we do not know, or we can satisfy ourselves with what is happening in the world around us.

That statement was given in response to Dr. Puharich's tendency toward liking riddles and puzzles, rather than getting information straight out,[1] so we have that choice. We can either satisfy ourselves with what can be known on our third-density level and not try to go any further, or we can seek the keys to unknowing—seek the keys to that place where we don't know and maybe we'll learn more. Maybe we'll expand our natures and our experiences. How about you, Ruck, what do you think?

CARLA I'm happy with what he says.

JIM [*playfully*] And what do you *know*? What level of physics do you have?

CARLA You could look at it precisely the opposite way: the keys to unknowing being the mystery, being satisfied to take things on faith because you simply cannot know everything at this level of understanding, or continue to batter away against the doors of what we don't know with the tools we have at hand, knowing that our third-density tools are pitifully inadequate, even to measure things like our vibrations. What happens when we have telepathy and so forth? I think we'd be fools to expect those tools to be able to answer higher questions.

GARY I hadn't considered the way you just put it. That makes perfect sense, that the next stage will always be unknown to the present stage; that's why it's the next stage. And in order to transcend or move beyond the current stage, we need to, in a way, let go of our attachment to our current situation.

I've always associated *being* with "the keys to unknowing" as well—going beyond the intellectual mind and just abiding in the mystery of being, like you were saying.

There is a notion repeated throughout the massive body of Confederation philosophy that, in short, we can only serve others to the extent that it is requested. Why, according to the Confederation, is this the case?

JIM If we attempted to give people information they did not ask for, we would be infringing on their free will—we'd be forcing something upon them, attempting to control them in some way. *You need to know this, so here, pay attention!* It would be sort of a negative approach to serving, and that's not the way positively oriented entities wish to go about being of service. They need to be asked. There needs to be a request so that there is free will in operation. The person that you're attempting to serve has asked for service with something that maybe you could help with. Then you can give freely. Otherwise, if they don't ask, they don't need you.

CARLA Imagine someone asking you to explain something that you understand but they don't, and yet they still have trouble understanding. Imagine the difficulties involved in saying something to somebody who doesn't give a hoot. Seems to me whatever the person who hasn't asked gets out of that information will be very distorted.

GARY So in this philosophy, there is an absolute necessity for each entity to find their own way, to find their own truth, to determine what is truth for them at that particular—

CARLA In the Ra way of things, yes, free will is always paramount.

JIM In order for whatever you learn to carry any weight in your total beingness, it has to be sought by you. You've got to eventually master it yourself. There are teachers along the way and ways of getting assistance and help in that, but it's got to be the fruit of your own labor.

GARY And the great split of polarity that Ra describes diverges on exactly that point: How do I relate to the free will of others? What is free will? Should it be respected and honored and treated as something that's sacred and inviolable? Or should I infringe on it?

So what, in your opinion, constitutes a *request* for service? And do you think it always needs to be verbalized?

JIM Apparently planet Earth is crying out in agony. The Confederation has mentioned before that when they are tuned in to planet Earth, they are aware of the pain, the sorrow, the suffering—and that is as a great calling. They likened it to one portion of their own body that was injured and cried out for healing.

So no, you don't have to say, "I need your help." You can say *aagghhh!* [*makes noises of anguish*].

CARLA I think we do as teachers need to have the request: *please teach.* Even if the request is somebody showing up at a workshop, that's an implied request—that's enough. They're here at the workshop, they're here out of their free will, they wanted to listen to what was going on. But you can't sense that somebody's in pain and then think that that's the same thing as somebody asking for help. I mean look at girlfriends or . . . I don't know about you guys . . . but a good friend comes to you and goes, "He is the *worst* guy . . . " and she expresses the pain and expresses and expresses and expresses, and you have the answer, you think. Until that person says, "Can you help me with this?" they're just dumping, they're just finding it very helpful to have a listening ear. They may not want to solve the problem at all. They may just want to express the difficulties that they're having.

If you do express your opinion, express it once and then lift up. That's the most that you can press against free will because nobody's asked you, and it won't be taken kindly. So, yeah, you do need—in the sense of us personally—we need to be asked.

JIM There are some planetary entities apparently that do nothing but send love and light to planets like Earth that are in such dire straits, and that service can be used or ignored by those on Earth. It can be used however the entities wish, though they might not even be aware of it.

GARY That's actually a question that I've seen come up among those who study this information: Is it an infringement to send love and light to somebody without it being asked for first? According to that example, it sounds like it's not an infringement because the service of sending of love and light can be used or discarded—

JIM It can be ignored.

CARLA Right.

GARY So what, in your opinion, is the "best" way to serve others?

JIM However you can when you're asked. The best might not be available to you. I don't know what the best is, actually, but you do what you can.

CARLA It depends on the person. Somebody asks you something, you see what you can do to help. If nobody asks anything, but there's implied desire for support, you give what support you can. You just look at the situation at hand and you ask yourself, *what can I do to help?* If what you can do is just rest in love, and love that person, then rest in love for that person, and that's all you can do. That's the amount of service that you can give, and that's good.

GARY I thought this question might also open up the opportunity to dive into the service of "radiation of realization of oneness", the *service of being* that Ra describes.[2]

CARLA Which is more or less what I was saying. If all you can do is rest in love for that person, then let your whole being radiate the love of the Infinite Creator by the simple fact that the spiraling upward light of the One Creator is coming through our bodies at all times; and if we keep our hearts open, our whole being will radiate that love. It's a matter of keeping the heart open and not resting in judgment of that person: *Well what that person needs is—*, or, *What's wrong with that person? You want to know what's wrong with you?*

No, not that kind of feeling, but just thinking, *I love this person, I love this person, I love this person's soul.* A lot of times you don't love their behavior at all.

GARY What is the value of praise and thanksgiving? It's mentioned a lot in *The Law of One.*

CARLA It's personal. The value of praise and thanksgiving is personal to you. If you're resting in judgment and thinking of all the things that are wrong with this world, and you're getting smaller, more and more contracted, then there's no room for the love and light to come through; your heart is closed, closed solid.

But when you start counting your blessings, and resting in joy, and resting in praise, resting in thanksgiving, ah, it feels so good. You're expanding and your heart is opening, and the love and the light have all the room in the world to come through. It's personal to you. It has to do with tuning the instrument, let's put it that way, so that we can be as open-hearted as we possibly can be.

JIM It tunes you up, gets your best energy ready to go. You're affirming what *is*, because you are blessed. It is a blessed creation.

GARY How about prayer? What is prayer and what is its value?

JIM That's a really good way of asking for assistance.

CARLA Help! Help!

JIM If anybody's listening, this is what I need. [*laughs*] I think it also affirms to yourself what you believe in, what you hope for, your highest ideals, your desire to serve others. A lot of prayer is directed for the benefit of others. Carla used to head an intercessory prayer group at her church, and they had people in the group whose job was to pray for other people.

CARLA We would pray for anybody that asked. That was our whole reason for being: to intercede for others. It was a blessing. There are prayers of, "Help *me*, Lord," but in intercessory prayer you are praying, "Help so-and-so, Lord, I'm asking spirit on their behalf." It's a very strong prayer also.

GARY So, it's an activity that can even become a discipline, which helps to further tune and set the intention, and may even have the capacity to create changes in consciousness, whether of self or another.

Do you think anything happens, besides working on yourself, when you pray for the benefit of another?

CARLA You offer an opportunity. That's what healing does in general, at least the kind of healing that Ra was talking about. You see yourself as an instrument that is capable of knowing the truth, and as you know the truth for someone else, you are giving that person the opportunity to know that truth, and, further, to choose that truth over the distortion that he's got going. And then it's up to that other person whether to accept it or not.

But in the case of my intercessory group at Calvary Church, Louisville, we did not pray for someone who we just thought, *put that person on the list, would you?* No, that person had to ask so that we would be sure that we were not simply praying in vain, or against someone else's desire.

GARY What is the "magical personality"?

JIM According to Ra, that's apparently our higher self that exists at mid-sixth density level. Each of us has one, and this higher self has the capability of being of great assistance to us because it knows the path we are on and the potential paths we may travel. It is also the repository of a great deal of information and assistance that we can use as we go through our lives. So the higher self is a resource upon which we can call.

Apparently there's also beyond that—the higher self has a resource upon which it calls: the mind/body/spirit complex totality. I think Ra said that is a collection of all that has been or will be, and is as "the shifting sands."[3] If you try to pin it down and figure out exactly what it is, it's a little harder.

Both of them basically are larger portions of ourselves that are very closely aligned with us and who know what we're doing and what we need. When we are in between incarnations we apparently consult with them very carefully to determine the lessons to be learned in the upcoming incarnations, or even parallel incarnations if that's what we're doing. So they're kind of like teachers, guides, inspiration—the highest and best part of yourself, and also mystery-clad.

CARLA To answer in another way (and probably not as well as Jim), the magical personality has to depend on your definition of magic. In the definition of magic that Don was always using, and that by mutual understanding Ra was always using—that magic has to do with Western white magic, or in other words, positive right-hand path, ceremonial magic. This kind is a lot like the priests expressing, for instance, the rituals involved in the prayers and process of communion. One thing leads to another and another before the ritual is complete.

In this kind of ritual magic there is a simple definition of what constitutes magic. You, as the magician or magical personality, have the capacity to successfully change the direction of your thought by consciousness only—using your thought to change your thought, in other words—the capacity to create changes in consciousness at will.

And that would be the same as a person feeling like he was going down and saying, "No, I call upon all the forces of spirit. I call upon my magical personality to change the force of my feeling right now, and I will now stop feeling that all things are going bad. And I will remember that things are great. I'll remember how terrific things are and that is going to be my state of mind."[4] And being able to switch from the one to the other without negative feelings, like, *oh, darn it, I didn't want to feel this way*. In other words, in the practice there is no internal resistance to the change of consciousness, so that you're capable of honestly being an instrument for the Creator. You're not at the beck and call of your own bad moods.

And that has appealed to me always as something that was very worthwhile doing. I want to be able to create changes in my consciousness at will, and I think it's for my own benefit that I do these things, not just for the benefit of others but beginning with myself. It's a waste of energy. I mean, you're always expressing energy, and that energy cannot be gotten back. You can't get back the energy that you already used up; it's gone forever. It's expended. So don't you want to make the best possible use of your own energy if you know it's limited? I certainly do, and I know mine is very limited, so I don't want to waste any time at pity parties, or feeling sorry for myself, or any of that.

People say that they have an inalienable right to sulk, that it's a good thing to get that out of their system. I'm not sure it always is. It may just be self-indulgent. It depends on your personality and what your needs are. But I don't think I have a need for pity parties; I think my need is to be a servant, and I want to be a good servant, so I want to be able to get myself tuned up again if I'm sliding.

GARY So the magical personality in your case is used as a means to help you meet the challenges of your life with courage and fearlessness, and to open the way for you to serve others.

CARLA That would be the reason that it would be a good thing for me, but in general—Jim is right, Jim is right in all that he said. His is a more general answer and, as I said, the better answer.

But in terms of understanding, *where did that come from? What do you mean, "magical personality"?* Well, it's best to understand what kind of magic we're talking about, because there's ceremonial, negative, left-hand path magic—Satanic magic[5]—which is usually copying the positively oriented magic and then turning something around, like turning the cross upside down, which is one easy example. There's cookbook magic where you create a love spell and all the kinds of magic that go into that. You have little dolls that you stick pins in and things like that, just different ways of creating a curse or a blessing by some kind of a recipe that somebody wrote down; you can look it up and say it again, and it will work. And then there's Wicca,[6] nature magic, and that's really not positive or negative, it includes elements of both, but it's just appreciating Mother Nature, which certainly runs the gamut from awesomely positive to awesomely negative. You can't say that's negative or positive, you just say, well, it pretty much comes out neutral, but it's a beautiful way of worship in that you're worshipping the seasons and the stars and all of those cycles of nature. So all of those are magic, but the one that Ra was talking about is the magical personality in the sense of white ritual magic, in the sense of creating changes in consciousness at will.

GARY So is it fair to say that those changes in consciousness that are created aren't so much a lateral or horizontal change but rather a vertical change in that the perspective or the consciousness is lifted up to a broader point of view, or a truer point of view?

CARLA Not precisely a vertical one, but rather than *linear* you could say, *moves into foreverness.*

JIM Ra made a kind of, I guess you could say, deeper definition of magic, saying that magic was the conscious ability to access the subconscious, which also tells you where the magic is. The subconscious mind is one that is connected to the universe far more closely than is our conscious mind. Our conscious mind has been cut off from everything that exists, including our subconscious, so that we can make choices in, what you might say, a vacuum—make choices all over again, make choices about things we already know in our deeper being. But if we are consciously able to access the subconscious mind then we can make available other energies, opportunities, definitions, and parameters.

GARY Ra also describes a process whereby it can be invoked in a more formalized, disciplined way. How is the magical personality invoked?

JIM Well, there are various rituals that have been set up by, for instance, the Order of the Golden Dawn that have been developed and used over the course of hundreds of years, and I'm sure there are Egyptian rituals as well from way back in the Pharaonic times where certain entities in the court were in charge of doing the magic. You see this in the Old Testament where the Lord God of Israel performs magic or wonders in order to convince the people to do one thing or another, and the court magicians attempt to match it; in many cases they succeed.

But I think the magical personality is invoked through a specific ritual. And you can devise your own. I think in the long run, a ritual you devise yourself and use many, many times is probably more potent for you. But if you want some potency right away it's best to use a ritual that's already been developed. For us, we used the Banishing Ritual of the Lesser Pentagram for a long time in order to clean or clear the place of working—that was the Ra room. I do it every morning in here as well, and the first thing you do is invoke the magical personality.

The way Ra suggested that could be done is by putting on something. Many times a white magician will put on a mantle or a cape or a ring or have a talisman of some kind. We simply make a gesture that suggests that we are putting on something, inviting it to come to us. So we don't actually have a thing that we use, we have a gesture that we use. So you can determine how you want to do it yourself. There are organized ways of doing it, and research into that is very helpful. W. E. Butler is one of the best resources we've ever found. *The Magician: His Training and Work* is probably his flagship and crowning achievement. We've read that a few times. That's where we got the Banishing Ritual of the Lesser Pentagram.

CARLA Just to put it in really simple terms, I invoked the higher self during the tuning that we did before this when I asked for spirit's help in being our highest and best selves, and to keep it that way. That was a way of invoking the higher self. It can be very simple and momentary.

GARY So that invocation—I'm leaning towards the more disciplined, formal way of achieving this—that invocation can be tailor-made for one's own processes and can include, as you said, a simple request. And probably ought to include some gesture or item to indicate that something is being put on.

CARLA And you'll notice that I said, "I want this for the duration of this session," indicating that at the end of the session we were released from that, because you can't keep the magical personality as the default personality. It is *not* your default personality [*laughs*] and never will be. If it were your default personality there'd be no reason for you to incarnate on planet Earth. But you can keep asking for its help as much as you want, as long as you make sure you say: "It's for this moment, it's for this reason." And after the end of that reason then release it, "Leave me and my free will."

GARY So in addition to those things that you've named in your own invocation, are there, in general, other elements that you would encourage seekers to investigate when constructing their own invocation process?

JIM Yes, I would read in the field of magic to start with. If you want to depart from that it's possible, but it's a good idea to start from what's already known and to begin by mastering that. They always suggest that whatever you use, whether it's something you put on, a talisman or ring or a bracelet or whatever, that it be new, that it be virgin, that it be clean and pure and not be used for anything else.

CARLA You can clean something that has been used to the point of making it virgin by putting it in water overnight, salting the water, asking the water to take away anything that is keeping it from being as new in terms of any thing, or any intention, that has been impressed into it. People think that stones are stones and trees are trees and so forth, but it depends on what people have involved them in. The reason that gems are so very impressive as talismans and as things that can be worked with is they have a very specific crystal character, and that is their character, it can't be any other way. They're fit together in a crystalline manner, and no impurities can get into it, or it won't be what it is. It won't be a pure ruby or diamond or amethyst or pearl or whatever.

GARY Are there other elements that go into these invocation processes that you, in general, apply to invocation?

JIM Purity and cleanliness.

[to Carla] So is that why you put so much salt on your food, you're purifying it?

CARLA [laughs] I try to get all that impurity out of myself, that's what it is.

JIM It just came to me. There must be a reason.

GARY Her food is *very* pure in that case.

CARLA I am a salt shaker. [laughs] I represent, I express the salt shaker. We're getting completely silly.

I don't think that, in terms of everyday life, you can go around invoking stuff unless you are very careful about it. As Jim said: do your reading, do your homework, become familiar with what is possible in the natural and appropriate way, not in an inappropriate way, not trying to bend things.

I think your intention is everything. In this world it's your results that count. In worlds that are unseen (time/space) the intention is what counts—it is [as solid and real as] a physical object is here in this world. If you've created a beautiful, perfect intention, in that world it's happened, more or less. In this world it may not ever happen, we may never live up to our intention. In that world, simply having that intention is enough to give us the credit for it. So you can't really mesh the two worlds at all. They don't have the same rules at all.

GARY So I was going to ask if there are any cautions when working with the magical personality. You named the big one—that is the need to release the magical personality when the working is completed. Are there any other cautions to be aware of?

JIM Ra suggested working in a group and not to work by yourself, because if you work by yourself, for only your own self's benefit, it's too easy to get into the negative path—a gathering power for the self's use. So it's a good idea to have as your goal some sort of service to others, and to work with others if possible. It's much like the channeling process. We never channel with less than three people because that's the number that allows the universalization of the information, plus protection of the one serving as instrument.

CARLA And that's not important if you're just praying to the Holy Spirit because praying to the Spirit is protected within the self, you're praying within yourself, so the vast majority of what people intend is within themselves.

Jesus encouraged all to pray, and he wasn't talking about praying to somebody from Hatonn or Latwii or from Ra; he was talking about praying to your own spirit, because the spirit within is that which gives, and that's what, in actuality, I was praying to: the spirit within all of us. I was invoking it for all of us, so that made it a more magical act.

If you're praying within your spirit, you don't really have to have any caution. But as Jim said, if you want to get ahold of a friendly spirit outside of your personal energy system, you want to find out what that being thinks, and whether it comes from Mars or elsewhere—there are so many dangers . . . there are so many dangers that I can't even begin to express them all. And they all have to do with giving over of the will of the self to another will—to another self who may be far stronger than you, and so negative that it beggars the imagination.*

GARY Why does Ra say:

> RA The Law of One blinks neither at the light or the darkness, but is available for service to others and service to self. 7.15

CARLA It has to do with the light. You proceed through the densities because you can use the light. You graduate from density to density because you've demonstrated yourself able to use all the light that a density has to offer, which means that it's time for you to move on in school and go to

---

* Carla has switched gears somewhat in this paragraph. She is talking not about invoking the magical personality, but about channeling outer planes sources. The magical personality *is* you, though a higher you (your mid-sixth-density future you, according to Ra).

the next class and get a higher density more packed with information, packed with light. The denseness has to do with light, and the information is carried by different kinds of light. So in the negative as well as the positive, if seekers can use the light they can graduate.

Now those of the negative polarity are graduating into negative light, negative fourth density instead of positive fourth density because they leave out the heart; and it's the path of that-which-is-not because of this omission. At the point that you can no longer learn anything by having negative beliefs (negative beliefs meaning beliefs in which there is no such thing as love), then the negative path becomes unable to use the light and has to switch polarities in order to be able to use the light again and to continue evolution.

So it's easy to think, *well, you just can't use the light if you're negative.* Well, you can, unfortunately, that's why *The Law of One* doesn't blink at the light or the dark, because it honors all ability to use information.

JIM And it made all the entities, gave them free will, so why would *The Law of One* say, "This child can have the light and this child cannot." They're all the same.

GARY What is initiation? And how, in general, may the seeker skillfully navigate an initiation?

JIM Hmm, that's a really good question. Don was undergoing initiation at his death. Initiation usually involves some type of a challenge. It's an opportunity to become more available to power, you might say, more available to evolution and to the ability to expand your own consciousness. There's usually some sort of a test, some sort of a challenge that you've got to overcome or to meet—to answer the questions, solve the riddles, solve the puzzles—and it usually involves a good deal of effort.

Other than that general description there are apparently all kinds of initiations. One that Don asked about was—he was talking to Ra about an incident many years in the past when his arm began to glow during meditation. As he moved it up and down, there was a blue glow to it.[7]

CARLA He was getting this encouragement to move his arm on the top of a chair—the chair's arm—up and down very quickly [*makes a swishing sound*] like that. It began to glow blue, and he looked at that and watched his arm and he asked the fellow he was meditating with, whose name was Frank, he said, "Frank, do you see this?" Frank said, "You're going blue!"

and Don said, "Frank, I'm sure glad you can see that." [*laughs*]

JIM But when Don asked about it, Ra gave a little description, and then Don asked, "Well, now how could I reproduce it?" Ra said it's an initiation and to reproduce it is to go backwards in evolution. So there was something about it that was an initiation. As to what the initiations are, I do not know. I know there are a lot of them.

CARLA I think they differ from the simpler insight or even epiphany to being that which many have gone through before—which is of a certain kind and can be defined as such. Like the initiation into the Golden Dawn was defined by the Golden Dawn as such-and-such, and then when somebody was able to see what you were supposed to see when you had that initiation, then you had completed the initiation of the Golden Dawn.

So it needs to be part of something that a group defines as such—*this is an initiation*. I think the closest we come to it as regular people is what St. John of the Cross called "The Dark Night of the Soul." Most people have that experience where you're learning, you're learning, you're learning—it gets harder and harder and then finally, *bam!* You run up against what seems to be the end, the absolute end, and you're cast down into the cellar and you're suffering tremendously, and then somehow, there comes to be the light—the dawning of the next day—and everything is clear again, only you've graduated to a new understanding, a new level of understanding.

I think we do that several times in our lives; most people do. It has to do with the spirit, it has to do with a certain amount of things that the spirit learns, and even there, it's very subjective. We all set ourselves objectives in this incarnation, and when we've managed to come to the end of what we've attempted to do, I think we can easily run into a dark night of the soul and then finally the light after the dark, at which it all comes clear: *Ohhh, okay.*

GARY It sounds like initiation sits at the boundary between one stage and the next, one level and the next, and one of its chief characteristics is its difficulty, and that it usually for the entity involves suffering and some kind of releasing of the old in order to step in to the new, to the next level up.

CARLA You got that. Yeah, I think those are all very much part of that phenomenon.

GARY How does one skillfully, in general, navigate an initiation?

JIM Faith—

CARLA Humor, light touch, a refusal to take oneself too terribly seriously, a refusal to be stopped. Absolute stubbornness is a wonderful tool. Say, "No, I won't, uh-uh, I'm gonna keep going, I don't care how hard it is or how long it takes. This is my path and I'm on it, so . . . "

GARY Balanced by a certain amount of surrender too, I would think.

CARLA Well, yeah, definitely, it's the surrender that's there, but it's the surrender into the lesson you gave yourself to learn before you were born, in terms of what the dark night of the soul might be.

KEN Do you think that in studying the information that Ra gave us on the archetypes, specifically the mind cycle, one would set out to do just that in a microcosm/macrocosm to successfully navigate an initiation experience?

JIM To study the archetypes, I think, is to go through a type of initiation. I mean there is so much in the archetypes that unlock parts of ourselves that we've not thought about before—that we're opening up boundaries and expanding possibilities—and that will take some sort of initiation in order to get through it.

GARY What, in your opinion, is the role of discipline along the spiritual path?

JIM Well, it's the way that we get things done. It's good to have a discipline, a ritual, a routine by which you practice your spiritual journey, whether it's meditation at a certain time each day, balancing exercises, yoga, running, jogging, mountain climbing; whatever way you've chosen needs to be done in a regular way, just like exercising your muscles. If you're trying to get stronger to do hiking or do anything, it's a good thing to have a set number of routines that you do every week designed to strengthen certain muscles, and you're doing the same thing when you use a discipline on a spiritual path—you're disciplining your spiritual muscle to meditate, to look at your catalyst around you, and to open your heart.

Also, you're disciplining yourself to assess a situation, hopefully, with wisdom. It helps you use your energy efficiently. If you don't have wisdom, then you're likely to have a big burst of energy at one time. Then it will slack off, and then burst back and forth. You may eventually get somewhere, but it's so much easier and quicker to do it with discipline.

CARLA I tried to help a lot of people who were interested in working with channeling. Through the years I've talked to probably hundreds of people who want help one way or another. At the beginning they all have a great feeling to do these things—a great desire to serve, a great big burst—but if you go at more than a certain level, you burn yourself out. I've seen so many people burn out. They get off the spiritual path and they can't do anything because they've exhausted themselves. They have to sit while they get themselves back together.

So it's better to have a certain amount of self-knowledge, know how much you can do in a day, in a week, at all; know how far you can go with yourself as far as trying to adjust your attitudes; have a lot of respect for yourself in figuring out what "you" is, what the essence of you may be. Then you try to just form the habits that you want to go on with. It's easier to finish your day before you burn out, finish your week before you burn out. It's easier if you don't want to finish it all—if you want the work to be a way of life—to form habits that do take discipline, whatever the work is.

I think it's discipline balanced by a sense of humor and a light touch that will really serve the spiritual seeker.

GARY What's the difference between disciplining the self and the imposing control over oneself?

JIM Nothing. Just different words.

GARY Because Ra says of the two polarities that control is the opposite of love and—

JIM When you're doing it with other people. Self-control and self-discipline are the same thing.[8]

CARLA Knowing yourself. If you know yourself you may have to impose that discipline a couple of times once you're getting the hang of it. But if it's really you, if it's really you and you love it, then you're going to love doing it. If you don't love doing it, you'd better go back and reexamine what it is precisely you wanted to discipline to make sure that it's you and not some idea you have about what you'd like to be. We're all as we are.

We can certainly change a lot; we can eliminate bad behaviors, we can open up new ones, but we can't change our essence. We can't change what's really in our hearts. So if it truly makes us gag to do something, then we shouldn't have to do it.

Some people look at modesty and they see it as an outward behavior. They see a lot of joy, for instance, in clothing themselves the way some Mohammedans do—the covering of the body indicating that only your husband will ever see the you, the outside of you, and that's modesty. But in another person that wouldn't be modesty. That would be not wearing clothes or wearing clothes; it wouldn't have anything to do with modesty. I would never be too skimpy on my outerwear, so I must be somewhat along the lines of people who think that clothing expresses you.

But I think that your words really express you more. A person can be entirely modest simply by choosing to be modest in speech and modest in attempts made to control others, to say, "Boo-hoo, look at me." So there can be a good deal of difference in precisely how you choose your boundaries for yourself, what you choose to change about yourself, and once you've decided *this is what I want to be*, if you can't do it every day then it's probably not you. So try it for three weeks, try it for a month, try it for six weeks, but if you're still hanging up on it, if something about you still wants to take a day off from that, well, it's not really you and you need to think again.

So you need to be very careful about how you discipline yourself. Give yourself the benefit of being in love with yourself and giving yourself the freedom that you need.

JIM What is being disciplined or controlled is the expenditure of energy: in what direction, in what amount, for what reason, for what periodicity. It's just a way of managing your energy.

CARLA That's a good way of putting it. Beautiful.

GARY Why is meditation so repeatedly emphasized in the Confederation's message?

JIM Because it's very helpful. [*laughs*]

Well, meditation seems to be the easiest and quickest and most available way for people to get into that original Self, that Self from which we all sprang; to get in touch with the heart of you in this third dimension; to find out what makes you tick, which is that great inner silence, that unity of all things; to get back down into the silence of the mind so that you can relax into the center of yourself.

CARLA People have talked repeatedly about how they can feel the energy on the tapes, even when the Q'uo aren't saying anything (or whoever I'm channeling). That's a good example of the silence. There's always silence that is used in speech or song or whatever way we have of making noise. There's the silence in between the notes, or in between the words, or in between sentences, in between paragraphs. There are the pauses. So even when we're talking we can make use of silence by being mindful. But when you enter the silence, you are entering a whole kingdom in which you have eternity and you have infinity. It's wonderful rest from our very busy minds and our very busy lives. It is in the kingdom of silence where the spiritual life lies, so you need to become acquainted with the silence.

I don't care how people do it. Some people thrive on very formal meditations, some people thrive on meditating a whole bunch, some others have units of 20-30 minutes where they meditate, or even less, and it works for them. That's certainly true for me. And some people feel that their goal is to meditate all the time, and what would be best for somebody like that would be long walks, especially in a state of nature and without the boombox along or the iPod, no manmade music because the music of nature, the music of silence, is so full of beauty. I've never found an end to the beauty, to the wisdom, to everything—the kingdom of everything that is found in silence. I doubt I ever will. It's an infinite kingdom.

GARY Why does Ra describe the spiritual seeker's path as "strait and narrow"?

JIM Well I guess if you're going to use discipline to take your energy expenditures and use them efficiently, it turns out that it's the shortest distance between where you are and where you want to be, which is, relatively speaking, a straight line.

CARLA Well, strait is s-t-r-a-i-t . . . it's like The Strait of Gibraltar; it's a narrow place. If you've ever done this [*mimics a looking glass with fist*] to focus light in order to see something better, you understand how valuable it is to focus your energies so that you're getting the maximum amount of light into your energy to hit the beam right where you want to hit it and look at what you want to look at. That's why I think it's "strait and narrow."

JIM It's paradoxical too. Ra speaks of the upward spiraling line of light which suggests something like this [*makes a spiral motion*].

CARLA Yeah, you don't go like this [moves looking glass in circles around the eye].

JIM And we're traveling that too. Trying to put "strait and narrow" together with "upward spiraling" is a paradox.

CARLA I love paradoxes. You know you've hit spirituality when you hit paradoxes.

GARY Maybe one way to attempt to understand it is to imagine trying to circumnavigate the globe, heading in what appears to be a straight line to you, but in actuality you're going in a circle.

JIM It's such a large area that you're working with that *you* think it's straight, but eventually—like when you're lost in the woods, you think you're going in a straight line and you come back around to the place you started and you've gone in circles.

CARLA But I think strait is another way of saying narrow. I've always felt that people misunderstand "strait and narrow" to mean "straight and narrow," and it doesn't mean *straight* like a straight line, it means *strait* like narrow.[9]

JIM Which could mean it would meander a little bit. The Strait of Gibraltar isn't straight.

CARLA Well, I doubt that they are, but they are a very thin line where you navigate your ship and we're trying to navigate our ship so it's a beautiful way of pulling that metaphor in. We're navigating a ship, and if it's a spiritual ship our focus is going to have to be strait and narrow in order to maintain maximum focus.

GARY If I had to choose any one word, "focus" would be the one that comes to mind when I think of that phrase. It is an intensive, constantly reinforced focus with less deviation away from that which is sought.

CARLA You can't just be a fly-by-night person and get far. It may feel like far and that's the kind of mind that goes to say, well, "I want to take drugs, I want to have that help." The strait and narrow path doesn't include anything except using the powers of silence and your mind and will, and that is by far the more exciting path.

GARY A concept from Ramana Maharshi that I also associate with "strait and narrow": he says something along the lines that if you were seeking water underneath the ground, you wouldn't go here and there and over there digging holes. You would stop in *one* place and continue boring down in that one place. It's focus in a repeated, determined fashion.

Many who resonate with L/L Research's work feel that they are wanderers, sometimes in the sense of having wandered outside the boundaries of consensus thinking, but more so in the literal sense that their soul came to earth from elsewhere in order to be of service to those of this planet. What is the symptomology of the wanderer profile?

JIM You wrote the book! [*to Carla in reference to* A Wanderers' Handbook]

CARLA Scott Mandelker is actually the one who's done the most careful study of the tendencies of the wanderer and collected them in a wonderful little questionnaire that I have in the *Wanderer's Handbook* that people can take to see how many questions they could answer in the way a wanderer would. The wanderer tends to feel lonely and isolated. He tends not to feel that he came from around here. Sometimes he has feelings of not being from on this planet, sometimes he has feelings he doesn't really come from the parents that seem to be his mom and dad, sometimes he looks up at the stars and feels homesick for home, wants to go home. I think that agony of isolation is very characteristic—that feeling of being tremendously lonely because he has no one to talk to about what's happening to him. That's probably the chief characteristic. Also wanderers tend to be somewhat sensitive to this earth and show up with some kind of allergy, one way or another, to Earth, animals, plants, whatever. What else—what am I missing?

JIM That's a pretty good description. Yeah, there's usually some general alienation. Ra said that wanderers frequently have some kind of a psychological difficulty with blending their vibrations with the planet Earth because this is a very adversarial type of environment; the vibrations are heavy and dense and it's just hard to get to feel at home here.[10] So there's usually some feeling of alienation and a feeling like you're not home.

CARLA My heart just goes out to those who feel this way. That's why I've spent so much time focusing on how to help them. I wrote *A Wanderer's Handbook* for that reason, the whole reason that we're in business. We never ever fail to answer a letter, ever—and that knowledge that there is somebody here, and that they will be heard, and we do care about what they have to say—even knowing that, it makes people feel a little bit less lonely, and I think people do trust us, and thank God.

GARY Those that fit this profile also tend to *care* a great deal, tend to want to better this planet in some way, and tend to be very service-oriented.

CARLA That's true. People have a feeling that they did come here to do something, there's a mission. And what is it? A lot of people are scrambling around looking for the mission that's already right in front of them.

As I said before, it's so hard for people who are oriented towards behavior, towards *doing* something, to just realize that your being, your actual way of being is very, very, very important. If you can open your heart, simply be that much of yourself and rest in the open heart as much as possible, you're already fulfilling your service to planet Earth which was to lighten the vibration.

I can't tell people, "Well, no, you don't have an outer service, just focus on opening your heart," because they may have come to help the planet in a particular way. They may have come to teach. I don't know. I never know. I have to trust the people themselves to start digging these truths out for themselves.

I'll ask things like: "What kind of things to do you like to do to be of service?" If you spend a lot of time volunteering in a certain area, then it's very likely that that's your area of service. That's what interests you—well, go with that. I don't know if you can make a living at it; you may have to stay being a volunteer all of your life. Focus on what you love. And invest whatever you do to make money with all that you can. Sometimes all that you can invest of yourself is to do it the best you possibly can, and that excellence in itself is a gift of yourself.

If your job is to compile lists of stuff and then put the lists against other lists—you know, technical things that people do—it's hard for them to figure, *well how am I of service?* Well, you're of service because you're doing it just beautifully. You're fulfilling that job with all that you can, with your full heart going for it. That's the service.

GARY So you would say to wanderers that you *are* the service, you *are* the mission. It's not what you're doing but *how* you do it, and with what degree of open heartedness and faithfulness, that the wanderer is literally changing the atmosphere of this planet and lightening the vibration, as you said.

Are wanderers alone?

CARLA Not at all. But they are physically. I think in order to sprinkle them around the planet, there had to be a certain amount of division of labor—there's just so many of us, and there's are a lot of mud.

JIM But there are others around. Look, gather together in little communities and help each another out.

CARLA Yeah, I have found no shortage of people that are full of hope and full of desire to do good things. They're wanting to help and it's very reassuring to be with others of like mind, so if you can find a couple of others, then by all means, make sure that you stay in close contact because it's very encouraging to be with others that think like you do.

---

1 About Puharich's love of puzzles:

> **QUESTIONER** Thank you. I'm sure that we are getting into an area of problem with the first distortion here, and also with a difficulty in a bit of transient material here, but I have two questions from people that I'll ask, although I consider especially the first one to be of no lasting value. Andrija Puharich asks about coming physical changes, specifically this summer. Is there anything that we could relay to him about that?

> **RA** I am Ra. We may confirm the good intention of the source of this entity's puzzles and suggest that it is a grand choice that each may make to, by desire, collect the details of the day or, by desire, to seek the keys to unknowing. 84.7

2 On the radiation of realization of oneness with the Creator:

> **QUESTIONER** Is it possible to help an entity to reach fourth-density level in these last days?

> **RA** I am Ra. It is impossible to help another being directly. It is only possible to make catalyst available in whatever form, **the most important being the radiation of realization of oneness with the Creator from the self**, less important being information such as we share with you.

> We, ourselves, do not feel an urgency for this information to be widely disseminated. It is enough that we have made it available to three, four, or five. This is extremely ample reward, for if one of these obtains fourth-density understanding due to this catalyst then we shall have fulfilled the Law of One in the distortion of service.

We encourage a dispassionate attempt to share information without concern for numbers or quick growth among others. That you attempt to make this information available is, in your term, your service. The attempt, if it reaches one, reaches all.

We cannot offer shortcuts to enlightenment. Enlightenment is of the moment, is an opening to intelligent infinity. It can only be accomplished by the self, for the self. Another self cannot teach/learn enlightenment, but only teach/learn information, inspiration, or a sharing of love, of mystery, of the unknown that makes the other-self reach out and begin the seeking process that ends in a moment, but who can know when an entity will open the gate to the present? 17.2

QUESTIONER Well, if an entity wants to learn ways of it, wants to be of service to others rather than service to self while he is in this third density, are there best ways of being of service to others, or is any way just as good as any other way?

RA I am Ra. The best way to be of service to others has been explicitly covered in previous material. We will iterate briefly.

The best way of service to others is the constant attempt to seek to share the love of the Creator as it is known to the inner self. This involves self-knowledge and the ability to open the self to the other-self without hesitation. This involves, shall we say, radiating that which is the essence or the heart of the mind/body/spirit complex.

Speaking to the intention of your question, the best way for each seeker in third density to be of service to others is unique to that mind/body/spirit complex. This means that the mind/body/spirit complex must then seek within itself the intelligence of its own discernment as to the way it may best serve other-selves. This will be different for each. There is no best. There is no generalization. Nothing is known. 17.30

3   See 36.1–14, and 36.22, among others, for more context and information.

4

Author's note: I was a bit confused on the aspect of commanding the self by affirming: "I will immediately stop feeling (insert undesirable feeling)." Such an approach rang to me of control or suppression of "that self which is perfect." A method at odds with balance, acceptance, love, and forgiveness.

Which is not to imply that I have not done similarly, or that in certain pickles sometimes you simply need to assert and demonstrate that level of self-control, just that I'm not sure it is an appropriate application of Ra's teaching.

In querying Jim on the point, he replied saying that he understood and wasn't certain, but he remembers:

When we were discussing with Ra how fasting or the changing of one's diet could aid in changing behavior patterns in the way of purification of the behavior Ra also said that it was possible, by an act of will, to accomplish the same thing. The exercise of will and faith could produce the same results. So maybe Carla was onto something here that is based on what Ra had said.

I think that part of what Carla was saying is that we are responsible for our own thoughts and too often we like to wallow in negative thoughts like self-pity, anger, guilt, despair and it is counterproductive to do that. We can do better just by willing it so. And, maybe, if we are unsuccessful at willing it so, then we will be left with the need to balance the negative thoughts with positive thoughts in our meditative balancing procedures.

On the same question Austin Bridges adds:

Ra says that control may *seem* to be a shortcut to discipline. So when the context is shrunk small enough, the two may look very similar. And in some situations, control and discipline may share similar aspects. The scenario that Carla speaks about is using the will to guide our thoughts in order for us to be our best selves able for service. What she does not speak about is the longer context of dealing with these thoughts:

In a negative context, control over those negative thoughts is sought. The controlled thoughts are then stashed away in a toolbox as aspects of self that may be used to further self-service.

In a positive context, controlled thoughts may be set aside for the moment in order to allow us to serve in that moment, but the controlled thoughts are not forgotten. Ideally those thoughts temporarily controlled would, upon the positive path, be subsequently processed as catalyst: examined, accepted, and distilled to where love may be found until they no longer serve as an interruption to our service, and learning and balance are achieved.

The disruptive emotions or thoughts are controlled for further use in the negative path, but accepted with love and allowed to fall away in the positive path.

I think it is a similar scenario to *experiencing* that which is desired versus *indulging* in that which is desired. There is a point where effort is needed to break habits, thought patterns, and behavior. This effort takes discipline of paying attention to our thoughts and making choices that allow us to move in the direction we wish. In a more general definition, this could be seen as control.

5   It should be noted that there exists a variety of so-called "Satanic" belief systems, each unique in its rituals, beliefs, symbolism, and tenets. Belief systems of this nature may or may not correlate with what Ra describes as the left-hand, service-to-self path.

6   The replies given by Carla and Jim to these questions are their opinions, of course, but in instances like this one where Carla speaks authoritatively on a

subject, perhaps without substantial personal familiarity upon the subject, there exists the possibility of creating significant misunderstanding for the reader. Consequently we add a second opinion regarding the practice of Wicca which states that, according to our limited understanding, prominent early Wiccans explicitly referred to their magic as "white" or "right-hand path," and made the distinction that it was done for positive reasons and with good intentions—they articulated an explicit code to "do no harm." However even this opinion is fairly unfamiliar with the practice of Wicca, so in either event inclusion of salt granules and one's own research is counseled.

[7] Jim wrote of this incident:

> Don was meditating at his and Carla's Douglass Blvd. apartment with a friend. Carla was away. After a few minutes of meditation, Don's arm, which had been resting on the arm of the chair he was sitting in, began moving up and down and glowing blue. The elbow remained on the arm of the chair and the rest of the arm and hand began to raise from the horizontal position to a vertical position and back down to horizontal a number of times, all the while glowing blue. Don opened his eyes to observe the phenomenon and asked his friend if he saw what was happening too. His friend said he did indeed.

Ra speaks about it here:

> QUESTIONER In meditation a number of years ago my arm started to glow, moving rapidly involuntarily. What was that?

> RA I am Ra. The phenomenon was an analogy made available to you from your higher self. The analogy was that the being that you were was living in a way not understood by, shall we say, physicists, scientists, or doctors. 44.12

[8] Where the practices of *discipline* and *self-control* intersect and diverge is a subject absolutely ripe for analysis and consideration. Ra and other Confederation sources generally attribute "control" to the negative polarity, but they have also used the term "control" in positive contexts. In other words, control needn't be strictly an activity of the service-to-self path. For instance, it is well to control one's bowels. Or, more deeply, it is well to control one's impulses if they would result in an infringement upon an other-self.

It is in this author's humble opinion, however, that, in contrast to the replies Jim and Carla gave in this section, self-control and discipline of the self are not precisely equivalent concepts. Though so much depends on how "control" and "discipline" are defined, Ra generally used this terms as if they were *not* one and the same:

> QUESTIONER Am I correct, then, in assuming that discipline of the personality, knowledge of self, and control, shall I say, in strengthening of the will would be what any fifth-density entity would see as those things

of importance?

RA I am Ra. In actuality these things are of importance in third through early seventh densities. The only correction in nuance that we would make is your use of the word, control. **It is paramount that it be understood that it is not desirable or helpful to the growth of the understanding, may we say, of an entity by itself to control thought processes or impulses except where they may result in actions not consonant with the Law of One. Control may seem to be a short-cut to discipline, peace, and illumination. However, this very control potentiates and necessitates the further incarnative experience in order to balance this control or repression of that self which is perfect.**

Instead, we appreciate and recommend the use of your second verb in regard to the use of the will. Acceptance of self, forgiveness of self, and the direction of the will; this is the path towards the disciplined personality. Your faculty of will is that which is powerful within you as co-Creator. You cannot ascribe to this faculty too much importance. Thus it must be carefully used and directed in service to others for those upon the positively oriented path.

There is great danger in the use of the will as the personality becomes stronger, for it may be used even subconsciously in ways reducing the polarity of the entity. 52.7

RA Control is the key to negatively polarized use of catalyst. Acceptance is the key to positively polarized use of catalyst. 46.9

9

Spelled "straight and narrow" in the original publication of The Law of One books, (17.11, 26.38, 27.17, 32.12), it was changed to "strait" for the Lightly Edited thanks to Tobey Wheelock's inspection of the term. Strait was chosen because it seems to be a better contextual fit (the article below sheds some light), coupled with the fact that, as Tobey noted, Ra seemed to love archaic and poetic language.

> "'Straight' is a much more frequently used word than 'strait' these days and so the most common question about this phrase concerns the spelling - should it be 'strait and narrow' or 'straight and narrow'? Well, that depends on just how pedantic you want to be. The source of the expression is the Bible, specifically Matthew 7:13/14. The King James' Version gives these verses as:

>> Enter ye in at the strait gate: for wide is the gate, and broad is the way, that leadeth to destruction, and many there be which go in thereat: Because strait is the gate, and narrow is the way, which leadeth unto life, and few there be that find it.

> That clearly opts for 'strait' rather than 'straight', as it calls on a now rather archaic meaning of strait, that is, 'a route or channel, so narrow as to

make passage difficult'. This is still found in the names of various sea routes, e.g. the Straits of Dover. Such a nautical strait was defined in the 1867 version of Admiral Smyth's Sailor's Word-book as:

"A passage connecting one part of a sea with another."

Smyth also offered the opinion that strait "is often written in the plural, but without competent reason".

The 'confined and restricted' meaning of strait still also lingers on in straitjacket, dire straits, strait-laced and straitened circumstances. All of these are frequently spelled with 'straight' rather than 'strait'. These spellings, although technically incorrect, are now widely accepted and only 'dire straights' comes in for any sustained criticism."

"Straight and Narrow," The Phrase Finder, accessed February 17, 2016, www.phrases.org.uk/meanings/strait-and-narrow.html.

[10]
About wanderers' difficulty adjusting to the planetary vibrations:

QUESTIONER Do any of these Wanderers have physical ailments in this Earth situation?

RA I am Ra. Due to the extreme variance between the vibratory distortions of third density and those of the more dense densities, if you will, Wanderers have as a general rule some form of handicap, difficulty, or feeling of alienation which is severe. The most common of these difficulties are alienation, the reaction against the planetary vibration by personality disorders, as you would call them, and body complex ailments indicating difficulty in adjustment to the planetary vibrations such as allergies, as you would call them. 12.30

CHAPTER 24

Spiritual Principles II

GARY The notion of harvest is a big repeated concept in the Confederation's message, whether via Ra or the consciously channeled sources like Q'uo and Latwii. How does harvest play into your thinking now that we are beyond the date in time so many people targeted? How has your thinking evolved on this particular concept?

JIM Harvest has apparently been going on for a while so it's not something that happens all at once. The common fundamental Christian idea is that there will be a rapture and some people will be taken and others will be left, and it'll all be over in a hurry. I think Ra suggested that it could take anywhere from 100 to 700 years. Considering that we started shortly after World War II we're about 60 years into that then, so 640 years to go.

CARLA The top could have been 700 or 800. Anyway, there's a lot of time. I don't believe our readings ever suggested an all-at-once thing, except in terms of metaphysical things shifting. I think metaphysically there was a big shift at the 2012 deadline, but everybody was waiting for ships to take them away or something to happen—I didn't expect it to happen, I never expected it to happen. I knew that this was not a physical concept. I think the thing that has changed, that has really shifted, is that I see a lot more difficulty that people are running into now, and that's because there's more truth, there's more light; that shift has happened, and people are receiving fourth-density light a lot.

In fourth-density light you have only to ask a little bit and you'll get *such* an answer! You don't want it to be you, you don't want to work with the shadow self—no, no, that's not me—but it is. But then you have to do the work. If you can do the work, sit down and find that part of yourself that was so much in pain that you buried that shadow side. Dig it up and take a look, and see what all needs to be done to heal it. And then go about integrating it into your light side. And that has to be done whenever you see the work to do. We're never quite finished with that.

GARY Anything else you wanted to add?

CARLA I think that a natural harvest also begins when you stop being able to use this physical body. You've shifted. You shifted when you came into this incarnation. Your spirit wrapped itself around this spine and made the chakras. The energy body wrapped itself around the physical body and that was the beginning of this incarnation, as far as you as a creature, as a mind/body/spirit complex, is concerned.

So you accept this gift of a body, and you accept the incarnation that follows and then, when it's over, whenever that is—and the Creator generally has more to say about that than we ever want—you let go. You let go of the physical. You leave that physical body behind again, and you shift into your metaphysical or electrical or spirit body, and off you go, new adventures, new places.

Ra talks about us walking the steps of light. At this time of harvest there's always the chance, and I think it's a reasonably good chance, that everybody that has become aware of these concepts is probably ready to move on. We walk the steps of light, and at some point the steps continue into fourth density, more light. You don't know. You're just walking along enjoying the fuller light, and then at some point it gets to be too much light. You're getting burned, so you stop. You look down and think, *okay higher body, okay higher self, did I make it? Am I in fourth density?* Generally speaking I imagine everybody will be ready to graduate a grade; go from third grade to fourth grade in this school of souls.

GARY I think we would all agree that there are those of the negative polarity on this planet, that they often wield the reins of worldly power, and that, as is characteristic of the negative path, they engage in deceit and manipulation, often cloaking their intentions behind what seems to be service-to-others oriented ideals.

One area of inquiry that seeks to uncover and understand the various schemes and plots of those of the negative polarity is called "conspiracy theory." What has been your relationship to the many conspiracy theories to which you've been privy over the years.

JIM [*chuckles*] And she looks at me. [*referring to Carla*] Yeah, I was fairly heavily involved with various conspiracy theories, having gotten a newsletter from a group in Washington and Oregon. I got very interested in what was going on behind the scenes, and after a while I thought to myself, *you know, this is just normal stuff—this is normal human stuff, and it really doesn't matter.*

If you look at any group, whether it's a family, a church, an office, a team, there are little pairings within the group of people trying to do something behind the scenes; two kids trying to figure out how to extend their vacation so mom and dad will give their blessing, or how to get out of work.

People are always trying to figure out how to get around or to get something done behind somebody else's back or in spite of somebody else. It's just human nature. So it's going to happen everywhere, and of course it's going to happen at the highest levels of government and power. But I finally came to the conclusion that it really doesn't matter because they can't affect my evolution if I am concentrating on what I'm doing and trying to shine my light, and doing what I came here to do. It's just part of the game, and if you get lost in that part of the game it's kind of unfortunate because then you forget what *you're* doing and what you're really here for. So that's my take.

CARLA I think some of them are very interesting. I've always been especially fond of the conspiracy theory having to do with Illuminati and the Emerald Tablets. Some of these are wonderful stories. It's alright to look at them, but I've never taken them seriously. I know that they are going on. I don't doubt that there are people attempting to collect power and are doing so at very high levels and are infiltrating governments and policy. I know any time I want to be entertained I can go and listen to somebody who has been studying some aspect of this. And it's a fascinating couple of hours that you spend in that world, but the truth of it is you have ultimate power over your open heart. That's what our scope of power is. We're not seeking to do anything beyond cleaning up our act and being of service to the Infinite Creator as we came here to do. We can do that without worrying about the conspiracies. We don't have to change the fact that there are a lot of things in this world that are really corrupt. We don't have to fix that, thank God.

JIM The positive polarity does its work in the light, and the negative polarity does its work in the darkness. That's just the way things are.

CARLA There are people who decide they want to fix something and they do wonderful work doing that. I don't want to make them look silly for trying to do something grand, you know, they wear white hats and they do wonderful things. I'm just saying you can wear a white hat and be one of the good guys simply by opening your heart and keeping it open on a continuing basis. It's hard enough, thank you. So to answer your questions briefly, I've never been involved in conspiracy theories.

GARY I note that even in the *Law of One* community, it has a compulsion. It can really catch the attention.

JIM Well, it's fascinating stuff. Great stories.

GARY Yeah, and it provides endless fodder. You can dig into that realm and keep going, and going, and going. There's always some new event and the misinformation and the disinformation is so myriad that who knows where it ends or what's true in that world.

How, in general, do you seek the Creator and seek to serve others in a positive sense on a planet filled with so much confusion and so many horrors, such as ours is; a planet populated with those of a polarity opposite your own?

JIM We do what we've done. Get together with like-minded souls, those here, and do what we can.

GARY I think a smarter way of phrasing that question would be: A lot of people have beautiful ideals in their heart that inspire them to do positive work, and then they turn on the news or look at the world around them and they're discouraged. They can't reconcile the two. *How can I hold on to these ideals and pursue them in an environment like this?* So, I should have asked the question: How do you reconcile, how do you look around you and see that and still continue?

CARLA I think if you never enter the kingdom of silence, you'd be in deep trouble because you can't get away from looking at the way the world wags. It wags the way it does everywhere. But you shut off the mind, you go into the place where there are no words, no time, no space, and you find a whole other kingdom to be explored that has a much different environment. Jesus said: "My kingdom is not of this world." Well, what world was it then? He didn't mean he came from Mars and he was going to go back there; it's the kingdom of spirit, and you need to enter into that spirit however it is you choose to do it. It's really the kingdom of silence. Somebody said, "Well, how do you enter the kingdom of silence?" and I told her, well, stop talking. [*laughs*] It was a particularly apt comment for her. But that's the start.

JIM The Don Quixote ideal, I think. That's why that's our logo. You tilt at windmills, and you go out and uphold the righteous and do your part.

CARLA In college, there was this point where I realized that if you wanted to use words you could make anything wrong or right. You could associate anything together with anything. So words were basically useless. And that ended my love affair with words and opened up a love affair with silence. I'm still an enormous lover of silence. It's the answer to so much in terms of *how do you do this? How do you keep your heart? How do you keep your faith? How do you maintain what you're doing?* Remember it, a couple of moments a day. Just remembering it is enough to strengthen you. Just walk a little ways in the silence—just a few seconds and you remember who you really are, and that's who you bring back and then you sing.

GARY In Book V, Jim writes:

> In order to be of the most appropriate service we must simply desire to serve without any conditions put on that desire.

And later Jim says,

> When that dedication [to serving others] becomes focused on a strong desire that a specific outcome be the result of any effort to serve others, then one is distorting the service with preconceived ideas. *Not my will, but Thy will* is the attitude offering the most efficient service.

Can you elaborate on what this means and how does one serve in this way?

JIM [*chuckles*] That *was* my elaboration. [*everyone laughs*] Should've seen what I started with!

CARLA That wasn't the beginning of it; that was IT!

JIM That's my philosophy: You hope for certain outcomes when you do something, or else you probably wouldn't do it. You have to have a goal and a reason for doing what you do. But in the spiritual realm, if you have too specific an outcome set up in your mind, it would be really easy to get discouraged because things don't always turn out that way. So you have to intend what you want to do, and you have to make the best effort you can. And then at some point you finally say: "Well, I'm not the greatest power in the world, there are greater powers, and I need to give my will over to the Creator or to my higher self or the angelic forces around me, or the forces of right and light, and just say, 'Thy will be done.' Let me do what I can and take my efforts and add them to a whole lot of other efforts that are along the same lines, and let's see what we can do. I'm planting a seed; I know that the path of service to others is the path of that which *is*, so I'm going to keep traveling it."

And eventually we'll realize that we are not only doing what we want to do, but we are the Creator. And everything is available to us.

But it's a way of gaining experience and glorifying the Creator to wend our way through the various confusions, doubts, mysteries, darkness and so forth that *all* people go through. It's just the way things are—keep the faith, keep your intentions, do your part and stay hopeful.

That's elaboration for me, by golly.

GARY I know I kind of began with the answer to that question but I'm very grateful that you took the opportunity to elaborate on that.

Carla, two key things that I've learned from you through your example include: yielding in group work, and your insistence upon always placing relationships first. Can you talk about these two principles?

CARLA Yielding and relationships?

GARY Yeah, how you keep relationships first and, when working in a group, how you have the capacity to yield.

CARLA All right. Well, in the first place, the reason that I put relationships first is that that's where my catalyst, where my service, where my learning is going to be. There's nothing else that is the kind of wonderful teacher that other people are. So whoever is in my life I try to honor as a soul, and whatever they ask of me I really look to see if I can do it. And if I possibly can, I will.

The ones that are very close to me that we work with every day and I know that we'll have a continuing relationship, like a maid or a co-worker—if something's wrong, I want to sit down and I want to talk it out, because I like everything to be sweet between us. And the reason is simply because if you can keep your hearts open to each other, if you're always glad to see each other, then you're going to get the best work done. And I would not be comfortable in any environment that didn't include that capacity to say, "Let's talk."

Jim and I have had almost 30 years of marriage now and more than that of being together, and that has always been our watchword: to sit down and talk if there was anything between us, because we didn't want to go to bed angry and have that be a blockage that would continue until tomorrow. We wanted to get it done now. And we've always been able to do that. We've always been able to go to sleep in good company with each other—happy with each other, satisfied with each other, and feeling loving.

So I know it's possible to do. When two people get together, and they want to solve something, they will. They're going to be able to; there's nothing stopping them. And if you don't do it, then it becomes huge, and then you have a big drama. I don't like drama so I figure—do it for five minutes, get it done [*laughs*], and have a good time. Always enhance your capacity to have fun. If you're laughing this is good.

So that's what I think about relationships. Putting them first is your best shot for having catalyst come to you that you need. They're the mirrors; you need to honor your mirrors. Loving each other and being loved is the joy of my life, and it's just respect for each other; it's just good to honor the people around you.

And as far as yielding when it comes to doing whatever is necessary . . . If I want to stay exactly as I am and have people that admire me exactly as I am, oh, yeah, I can go a long way without allowing anyone to disagree with me. Or I can say, "This is the way I want you all to spend your days," and I can say, "My way or the highway." But it doesn't honor everyone else's desire to get up when he wants to get up and do what he wants to do and have spiritual work be the way he wants it to be. So my attitude is not *let's do things my way, I don't want to hear anything about it,* but *what precisely is it that you want to do that's different from me? Let's see if I can support you*. I see no need for everybody to be like me.

Does that answer the yielding question?

GARY Yes. I've actively learned from both aspects. The relationships first principle—you framed it previously in years past that it's not necessarily about the job, the objective, or the goal, but it's the relationship first and foremost. So set aside the goal for a moment and, if there's disharmony, focus on the relationship. Always the sweetness of the relationship comes first.

CARLA Yeah, I know what you're thinking of, and that was a time when I had to shut down one of the incarnations of Bring4th. I had to shut down two of them. It was because ugliness had entered in and there was no way to make it sweet again. I tried and tried with this one guy who was willing to start a new incarnation of Bring4th but we couldn't ever be sweet together because he was aggravated so much with me over my lack of knowledge of the technical aspects that he was just always mad; he was always angry. So I was trying to make him not angry, and he was trying to make me a person that knew what he was talking about, and he was doomed. [*laughs*] I did make it sweet between us, but it did involve not working together because I would never be the kind of co-worker that he wanted. I could never be a full partner who understood coding and all those things that had to do with technical aspects. I didn't even know the proper use of the word *forum*. I was hopeless.

And so now, when we see each other, it's long lost, and we love each other dearly. But I would not work with him real closely because I know I could never be the person that he would want to work with. He really needs to have people that can be full partners working with the technical stuff. So when Engratt came into my life, he did not need for me to understand the technical aspects. He and I agreed on the metaphysical aspects, and then he just went for it. And I've never seen anything that was a problem in what you two have put together.

You have always had the relationships first and you have always made sure that things stayed sweet on the forums, and that was what I was requiring.

GARY Jim, when working with you one day cutting grass through Jim's Lawn Service, you expressed that above all there is one thing you've learned from life. Do you remember what that was?

JIM Nope. [*laughter*]

GARY I thought we might run into that problem.

JIM One thing? I've only learned one thing? Must have been a bad day. [*laughs*]

CARLA Oh, come on.

GARY It struck me as especially profound because it was very simple—

JIM How profound was it if you don't remember?

GARY Oh, I remember. I was just prefacing it. I was hoping to tease it out of you—

JIM Well, keep teasing.

GARY —for the benefit of anybody that may read this book. It struck me as especially profound because it was something simple coming from a person who has a world of philosophy in his mind, and years of study.

JIM Oh, and my philosophy of life? Always be generous?

GARY Yes! That's it.

[*Jim laughing*]

CARLA Oh, that's wonderful because I have never known another person who does that. No matter how tired Jim was, he would always do a little something extra for the person at the end of all the things he was paid to do, and he would never charge for it. This private generosity of his has resulted in all of his customers—he's been gone for a couple of years now and every time they see him they still say, "Jim, aren't you coming back? Please come back." They adored him and maybe they didn't know why other than that he did a wonderful job with the lawns, but he was always doing something extra.

GARY "Always be generous." I found that an especially beautiful ideal and just wanted to get it on the recording.

CARLA Yeah, it is beautiful.

JIM [*chuckles*] Thanks for helping me remember that.

GARY A Bring4th member asks: "Latwii and Ra mentioned male/female seeking or service to be of significance, namely, an efficient way to seek or to serve. What has been your experience to seek together as a male/female pair only versus seeking together as a three-person group when with

Don?"

JIM Hmm. That's hard to really say because the time we've had together has been mostly without Don. It's been 30 years since he died so we've had a lot of time together, and being able to seek together is invaluable. To be alone on the journey is very hard. I was alone for a while, and like I said, it's a lot harder to learn alone. When you're with somebody else, it just magnifies the ability to learn and serve.

Carla and I have been able to, like she said, talk our way through any misunderstanding or difficulty that's ever come our way. Nothing has ever remained past the day. So when Don was alive, you know the Ra contact was ongoing then too, so it was a golden time.

CARLA Yeah, it was.

JIM We were on top of the mountain, and it was probably overly-colored with rosy hues, even though there were difficulties. So that was a very special time.

Don, though . . . [*laughs in reminiscence*] With his particular way of using, or *not* using catalyst, it was a little different. It was easier to learn with Carla because he had the idea that the world was a crazy place, and in order to keep your balance and sanity, you needed not to let catalyst bother you, either for the ups or the downs—remain even keeled. He did a pretty good job of that.

So with Don it was a little more difficult to learn from communications and so forth because everything was pretty much internalized. But with Carla, it's pretty much externalized.

CARLA But of course with Don, that third person bringing the capacity to do the larger work. That was very invaluable.

JIM Yeah, the third person really helps the outer work in helping form a group to help other folks.

CARLA He was a wonderful leader. Jim and I are both leaders in terms of our genes; we have no problem leading a group. So it's not that we were leaning on him. We were two people who were delighted to give over our will—you know, *what do we do next, George?* and questions of that sort to a boss that was going to tell us a really good thing to do next. We trusted his capacity to lead.

JIM He was definitely the leader but we never felt—I never felt—that he was the boss. He didn't give orders. You just wanted to be around Don. You wanted to do what he wanted to do because he was fun.

CARLA I pattern my boss-ness on his, which was that I never say anything unless there is something wrong. I haven't talked to you, Gary, much over the last ten years as to what you're doing because you're always, as far as I'm concerned, doing everything right. But I don't go around giving you huge compliments all the time; I just enjoy the things that are going on. I might thank you for something, but I don't make you crazy with it.

GARY Yeah, you're not a micro-manager. As I seek to operate in harmony with your interests, and as long as that is met and your spirit honored, then it's full steam ahead.

CARLA Yeah, you've got full freedom to do whatever is in your mind that would never be in mine because I wouldn't know if it was possible.

GARY In Book V Jim writes:

> We also discovered that every person which incarnates brings with him or her certain avenues, preferences, or ways of nurturing its inner beingness. This inner beingness is that which is the true enabler and ennobler of our daily lives.

> When we would ask Ra how best to aid the instrument we would often get more specific suggestions according to the situation, but we would always be reminded of those qualities which were Carla's ways of nurturing her inner beingness.

So what did you each discover which "nurtures your inner beingness"?

JIM Well, I like solitude and I like the primal nature environment. I like wandering out in the woods and just feeling the Creator in the trees and flowers and birds and squirrels. The way things are put together—it's a *wonderful* creation. I mean, it's amazing. So I go out in my yard here and do the best I can to approximate that wilderness and seeing the Creator everywhere. That's what I do.

GARY It's work *combined* with solitude.

JIM Yeah, there always has to be some work in there. I love what the Creator has done, but [*speaking to the Creator*] you know . . . we could do a little better over here. [*laughs*] Just my opinion. Think about it!

CARLA And look what he's been able to accomplish. That's Jim's way. And obviously my way is more taken up in music and ritual and all the joys of *that* kind of sacred environment. I have always wanted to go to church, and be part of the service, sing that sacred repertoire and be part of the music. That feeds me tremendously.[1]

GARY Any suggestions for the seeker looking to discover that which nurtures their own "inner beingness"?

JIM Well, after a few years I think each person kind of has an idea about what he or she likes to do and what really makes a difference with the inner environment, what that little voice inside sings when you do or think or create something or other. Just look. Everybody's got something.

CARLA That's true. I love anything I can do in the way of teaching. When I get to talk about *The Law of One* to audiences and sing a little bit and just make people feel a shift in the way they are, just for a few minutes. I love doing that. That makes me glow. I think I'm full up on glow actually for the incarnation. But I do still enjoy sharing with people.

GARY The word *enlightenment* is of course just a word, just a concept, and like all words, isn't the equivalent of that to which it points. That said, what do you think enlightenment means? To what does the word point?

JIM Well, in the way of Ra's description, the contact with intelligent infinity would be the fully experienced presence of the One Infinite Creator. I think we're all working toward something like that. That would be the epitome of enlightenment. I think most cultures, most religions, have got some word that points you that way, whether it's nirvana, samadhi, kensho or whatever. Everyone has the opportunity to experience that, whatever culture or religion, or whether you see yourself as an expatriate from cultures and religions, make your own path and still get there.

CARLA I think enlightenment suggests more light, so when you run across something that makes you go *oh, now I get it*, that's enlightenment. Whatever degree, wherever we are, I think you can be enlightened about so many things in so many ways, but that commonality of enlightenment is the feeling of almost being lifted up and shown a whole new world. Your eyes get big and you go *wow, this is great*, and you're enlightened at that point. I don't think enlightenment means that you know more because there's so much to know. We need to stay humble with that, but we can become more and more enlightened as we let more and more light into our hearts. That really comes back down to allowing ourselves to take part in that kingdom of silence that is full of light and love, where this environment is so often not.

GARY As Jim mentioned, Ra describes enlightenment both as an opening to intelligent infinity and also as an opening to the "gate to the present."[2]

Why do you think Ra links enlightenment to the present moment?

JIM Well, if you remember *Be Here Now,* the famous book that was written years ago by Ram Das, the moment of now is an infinite moment and continues on. If you can be fully present and aware of what's going on in your life, in your mind, in your heart, then I think that is an enlightening experience. We tend to think towards the future or towards the past a whole lot. *Look what I did back there. Let's see what I want to do.* And we are kind of split. But if you can be right here right now, then it is a whole other world. Those few times that any of us have been able to do that it impresses that point upon us so that we would like to expand the now once again.

GARY In your own journeys have you experienced the energies of self-doubt, and if so how have you related to that?

JIM Oh, no, I've never had any amount of doubt in my life. [*laughs*] Are you kidding? Yeah, sure, self-doubt? Well, I guess for me self-doubt has been a reminder that has honed my energies, my activities, my discipline, because overall I think I've always had confidence, and that has been something that has served me well. Confidence, because things really seem to be working out. I mean, every step of my life has been very well available. I've never had to wonder about it.

Self-doubt has come in more with how do I blend my energies with someone else or with some other group, or in how do I help someone else. For myself though I haven't had that much self-doubt. It's come more in my relationships with others, and it's helped make me sharper to refine what I want to do; refine my thoughts, refine my desires and to get down to it. It reminds me that there's still a distance to go. *We're not there yet—or are we and have I just forgotten?*

CARLA I have had remarkably little self-doubt in my life. I just always feel very grounded in me. I know myself pretty well and haven't had moments, haven't had times where I thought I needed a whole other direction. Now, of course, there are times when you just think you're an idiot—realize you're an idiot— see the fullness of your idiot-ness and you just think, *I'll never ever be able to get rid of it. I'll always be this much of an idiot.* I think when I get fully into that it is discouraging, but there's nothing much you can do with that so I just fall back on . . . whether it's chutzpah or whether it's just self-confidence, I feel that I'm basically right. This is basically what I want to do with my life and I love doing it. So let's just do it. I think we all have these moments—you just get tired, you get very tired and you think *one more effort—I don't know man*, but then you find the space and the time and it's okay again.

GARY And on a related question, how about confusion. What role has confusion played in your life?

JIM Sporadic, I guess. Nothing significant.

CARLA No?

JIM Have I had to worry about confusion—not confusion on a spiritual level, or on a . . .

GARY Well, not confusion like *how do I get to Arby's* but a deeper level of confusion—confused by life, confused by catalyst, what it means, how do you process it?

JIM I've had this little voice inside that's been giving me pretty good counsel over the years, and if I'm uncertain about what to do, I just ask. Sometimes it will give me the answer I don't want to hear, but I know it's right. So I don't stay confused long, but I might procrastinate doing something I don't want to do. [*laughs*] But I eventually get around to doing it, and it's the right thing.

CARLA I loved his answer. I think we're a lot alike that way. I don't think confusion has had anything much to do with my life. I could get confused about that answer. [*laughs*]

GARY I guess both these questions shine a light into both of your characters, and that's the strength that can be perceived in both of you which derives from your foundation in self-knowledge; you know yourselves pretty well.

Regarding confusion, that's something I've always thought, especially in you Jim, was remarkable in that you just seem to know what you want to do, and you do it. And then you don't seem, at least to my eyes, to waste any more consciousness second guessing. Once you do it, it's done and you're ready to move on. That has not been my experience. That's why I find it remarkable in seeing it in you.

CARLA Yeah, I think you're right about it. That is his modus operandi.

GARY How about will and faith: What role have these faculties played on your path?

JIM Pivotal.

CARLA For mine, it's everything.

JIM Crucial.

CARLA Yeah, my faith is number one. All I have to do is remember looking into Jesus' eyes—that pivotal moment when I was two, and the rest of my life just falls into place.

And will—I've been amazed at how strong my will is. I'm very, very focused on using it well. I think the right use of will is a very important thing. I think I did come here to be wiser, to try to learn to be a little bit wiser and not quite so loving—a little more wise, a little discipline in there.

So faith and then secondarily will are two huge aspects of me.

JIM For everything that we've wanted to do, and everything I've wanted to do, whether it was Jim's Lawn Service or working through L/L Research or dealing with difficult people, will and faith have been just the . . . I think that's the rod and the staff that's talked about in the 23rd Psalm: "Ye, though I walk through the valley of the shadow of death I will fear no evil for Thy rod and they staff are with me." I believe that will and faith are the rod and the staff. That's just my interpretation, but they have been just the foundation stones upon which I've built everything that I've done or tried to do.

CARLA There's a wonderful story of Jim in college where—I think it was Jamie who told me this—that you got in between two big people and you were explaining to them why they did not want to beat up on each other, something like that. And Jamie said he'd never heard such eloquence in his life, and Jim said he didn't even remember it, said he must have been in an altered state. He has a wonderfully peaceful way about him, and he's at his very best when he will let himself get in between people that want to beat on each other and explain to them why they don't want that.

JIM That just happened once.

CARLA It's very indicative. [*chuckles*]

GARY My second to final question for this section was originally stated as, "How has this information [the Confederation Philosophy] aided each of you along your journey of seeking?" But I think I'll tweak it so that I tie it into will and faith and ask: How has this philosophy fed your will and faith, or has it?

JIM Well, the will and faith, I guess, and the way I'd previously exercised them was like a skeleton. This information has filled out the flesh on the skeleton and given it a real life in my life so that there's more to look at, more to think about, more to be affected by, more from which to move. There's such a richness that it's added. Everything was black and white before and now it's in color.

CARLA I guess what it's done for me is that it's given me a way to talk to people who are not Christian, and I value that greatly because I have always been a person that would inspire and would love to give inspiration, but before this, if I wanted to give inspiration to people and not use the vocabulary of Jesus, not be a Christian, I was kind of stuck. With Ra's cosmology in mind I can talk about the Infinite Creator and all these various concepts in a way that's neutral and does not bother people in the same way that talking about Jesus and following Jesus bothers people. So I greatly value that. I guess I value the Ra contact in terms of how it's enabled my service, more for that than anything. It's given me a vocabulary.

GARY We'll call it a wrap there. Thank you both so much.

JIM Thank you.

CARLA Yes, indeed.

1

Some of those things which nurture Carla's inner beingness as described by Ra:

> **RA** We have spoken before of those things which aid this instrument in the vital energy: the sensitivity to beauty, to the singing of sacred music, to the meditation and worship, to the sharing of self with self in freely given love either in social or sexual intercourse. These things work quite directly upon the vitality. This instrument has a distortion towards appreciation of variety of experiences. This, in a less direct way, aids

vitality. 44.13

See 99.5 (or endnote #3 in Ch 27) for more about that which feed's Jim's soul, you might say.

2

Can Ra offer a shortcut to opening that gate?

> RA We cannot offer shortcuts to enlightenment. Enlightenment is of the moment, is an opening to intelligent infinity. It can only be accomplished by the self, for the self. Another self cannot teach/learn enlightenment, but only teach/learn information, inspiration, or a sharing of love, of mystery, of the unknown that makes the other-self reach out and begin the seeking process that ends in a moment, but who can know when an entity will open the gate to the present? 17.2

CHAPTER 25

The Art of Channeling

GARY What is channeling?

JIM [*to Carla*] You ought to take that one. You're the channel. I gave it up.[1]

CARLA Channeling is the production of subconscious material in a conscious manner, to be the most general about it and still accurate.

GARY Using the term "subconscious" raises a question. It seems to imply that the source being channeled is derived from within one's personal system, whereas the channeling I'm inquiring about is alleged to be derived from outside of one's personal system.

CARLA Well, you can channel yourself, or you can channel an outside source. But it has to come from within you. So basically, what you're doing is you're getting subconscious material which is not finite, it's infinite. You're getting a concept and then translating it into conscious material words. You basically take a cookie cutter to this infinite concept that you're getting, and you produce words to try to explain what it was that you received.

So it's really almost like the channel is a translator of subconscious material that it's receiving from an outside source. But you can, actually, channel parts of yourself, especially if you have a fragmented personality, or perfectly healthy if you're channeling spirit.

JIM But that was not how it worked for the Ra contact.

CARLA No, in terms of the Ra contact, it was done from within trance so I had no control over the production of material.[2]

GARY So when you say "subconscious material," is it accurate to say that you mean concepts that are outside of the conscious mind that then pass through the conscious mind, which acts as a translator for that material?

CARLA Yes.

GARY Do you remember the first time that each of you encountered channeling? And what your initial thoughts were about channeling?

CARLA Well, my first experiences with channeling were with the Louisville Group in '62 through the next several years as we met every Sunday night at Hal and Jo Price's house, at first in Indiana and later in Kentucky. It seemed pretty silly to me. It was very laborious the way the guys were doing it. They wanted a lot of working of their vocal apparatus to make sure they weren't producing it themselves, so they'd, [*Carla imitating*] "We [*click click sound from the mouth*] are [*click click*]," like that. I thought it was kind of a silly way to gather information, and it didn't attract me. So I enjoyed the messages, such as they were. They were very loving and I respected them. I respected the efforts that the guys were making—all these physics students that were friends of mine, to be accurate. I respected Don once I understood what his goal was, what his experiment was all about, which he didn't tell us for the first few months because he wanted an absolutely pure source of data. He didn't want to mess up the data.

So when this guy came up from the Detroit group and channeled much more smoothly, and said, "Why aren't you guys channeling? Let go and bring it out," Don considered that the experiment was blown. It was no longer pure because it had been diddled with from the outside.* But he

---

* Don had initially launched his experiment without disclosing that its actual aim was to produce telepathic data from ET contacts. His hope, presumably, was that if information was received in this manner, then it would be pure because there would be no chance that the members of his experiment, unaware of the purpose of the experiment, could have intentionally or unintentionally fabricated the received material. The visitor from the Detroit Group, however, let the cat out of the bag, as it were.

still felt that it was legitimate to continue collecting the material as thickly as possible, and that's what he did, constantly.

So at first I wasn't over overwhelmed by this material that was being collected in this way. I had no desire to do it. Didn't think I could do it.

JIM I read *Seth Speaks* by Jane Roberts back about 1970, '71, and I thought it was good material. I still think it's pretty good material. And I was interested in it and wanted eventually to learn how to channel one day.

CARLA Jim is one of my best students. Ever.

GARY We will come to Jim learning to channel in the not-distant future.

So Carla, you and Don developed a unique set of protocols for establishing contact with Confederation sources and channeling their message. How much of that protocol was transplanted from the Detroit Group, and how much did you and Don develop through your own experiment?

CARLA It was all me. I was pretty much on my own. Don was able to teach me the basic heart of channeling, which was to let go and say what was coming through, but he had not been able to get any refinement of that. I refined and refined trying to find out how to be a better channel and how to create a better session. So I observed what worked to make me a better channel and incorporated those things little by little over the years. Around the turn of the century I spent about three or four years practicing the tuning and the challenging process over and over again, every day after morning offering.

GARY So we'll dive more deeply into challenging and tuning later on, but for now are you saying that the challenging and tuning processes were your own creations after Don taught you the basics?

CARLA That's right. And also, the things that I observed that would make a group better were simple. There were just two things: stay away from specific information, anything that would not still be useful in 10,000 years, and let the contact say, "I don't know," rather than trying to get an answer to every question.

GARY Jim, how and why did you become an instrument?

JIM Well, I had the same desire as Carla to be of service. I guess in the beginning it was also sort of an attractive thing to do: *I want to be a chan-*

nel—I want to get my channel stripes. [*Carla laughs*] So I worked at it for 25 years. Clawed my way to mediocrity. Decided, *why bother. I'm sitting next to the best channel I've ever heard. I'll help her out some other way.* So I gave it up.

CARLA And that really bothered me because I don't agree with him, but that's all right. We'll talk about that another time.

GARY I was going to ask about the conclusion of Jim's channeling.

CARLA Oh, he's totally wrong. He's an excellent channel. We all have our gifts. I'm a *blah blah blaher,* and there's a value in that—you get poetry from people who talk a lot; you get depth; you get poignancy; you get nuance. From Jim you get the answer to a question in the shortest possible time. At the end of a session, when everybody's tired, this is wonderful. It's much to be desired. So it just depends on what it is you're looking for: short, terse answer that gives you all the high points, or more of an eloquent answer.

GARY I will say, for the record, that after Jim discontinued his own channeling service based on his assessment that he was mediocre, I gave him the Pepsi challenge. I took channeling from Carla and channeling from Jim, put it on the same piece of paper, mixed it up and removed any identification regarding who was doing the channeling. I then I asked Jim if he could identify who was doing the channeling. Jim indulged me and took the challenge. He had about 50% accuracy.

CARLA [*laughs*] Way to go, Gare!

GARY So his channeling wasn't *that* objectively mediocre. But I guess it comes down to how you feel.

So now we begin diving into first challenging, then tuning. So the practice of challenging is a key aspect of your procedure. What is challenging, and why is it so important?

CARLA In this physical realm we can get by with an amazing amount of B.S. We can lie, we can slant information, we can do all kinds of stuff like that. And people will buy it if we're good at it, if we're clever. In the realm where channeling comes from, the metaphysical realm, there's no fudging, there's no lying, there's no bending the truth. The more you know who you are and can stand on your own two feet, the more you exist in that realm. If you don't know who you are, and are able to say, "This is who I am; this is what I believe; this is the epitome of good qualities for me, and it is this quality which I choose to use as my challenge."

For instance, I'm a Christian and I would naturally be drawn to challenge by saying, "Can you say that Jesus is Lord?" And that's been my challenge from the beginning. That's the depth of who I am as one who follows Christ, so that is very real in metaphysical terms.

I ask people to find out, if they don't really, really know, what is the essence of yourself? What's the heart of it, and then what do you believe? Whom do you follow? Whose are you, if there is an entity that you follow? What quality would you say is that which you believe is the highest and best? So I don't tell people how to challenge. I ask them to find their own challenge.

For instance [*turns to Jim*], when faced with the request what did you choose? You chose things positive. . .

JIM For my challenge? Christ consciousness.

CARLA Christ consciousness. He distances himself a little bit from Christ and uses the consciousness, but that's the heart of who he is so that works for him.

So that's what I mean by challenging. The reason it is so important to use that filter is that it's a very crowded universe. You could get anybody on the horn and you don't want to dial at random and go, "So tell me, what do you think?" You don't know who you're talking to. You need to get the best contact you possibly can. You're expending energy. You need to make the best of it. So basically you're looking for a contact that is in harmony with who you are and how you challenge so that the information that you get is going to be the clearest possible information—the least distorted. Those are very desirable things so that's the reason that you challenge: to eliminate receiving a negative contact, to eliminate getting fooled, to eliminate wasting your time.

GARY So you declare who you are and issue that vibration, that challenge, and any entity—especially those of negative orientation that can't meet that vibration—are thus barred or prohibited from speaking?

CARLA Right. They simply can't function in that environment. It's like they're trying to get through a brick wall—they simply can't do it.

GARY You issue your challenge three times in a row.

CARLA I do.

GARY Would you call that a universal standard or is that just unique to your own processes?

CARLA I recommend redundancy for anybody, whether they want to do it two times or three times doesn't really matter, but are you really doing your highest and best work every single time out of the gate? I just want to eliminate the possibility that I was having a bad day, and so I focus and then I get it together again, and focus, and then I even do it a third time because I want to make absolutely sure that I'm not fooling around with the people that are interested in what I produce. I want my work to be as excellent as I can possibly make it, and I move heaven and earth to do my best because nothing less than that would satisfy me. Once I do that, whatever comes out is what comes out—I can't speak to that, I can just say that I prepared the very best I know how.

GARY So you describe that entities who can meet that challenge are able to pass it and those that are not able to meet it, go away. How do you perceive that process?

CARLA Well, I *feel* it, I think, more than anything else. Let me give you an example: I was in London teaching—what a wonderful thing to say [*laughs*], "I was in London teaching."—and the hostess who was putting me up for the night had a son, and the son, I could tell, was just absolutely hating the ground I walked on. He was very, very jealous, and she took him upstairs to get dressed, and when I got through with the challenging process and I asked my gatekeeper (there's a lot that goes into my process, including working with my gatekeeper), I said, "Is there anything I need to be aware of?" And she said, "Yes, you've got a negative entity that wants to mess you up, so you're going to have to shake him off."

So I think I sang a positively oriented song, and went through that from beginning to end and then I asked the gatekeeper again, "Are we okay?" And she said, "No, you'd better do it again." This is not in words, this is in feelings. So I did it again and the third time that I did it, about half way through the song I felt almost like a snap, and then I felt a release of pressure from inside my head, and I heard this little boy screaming from upstairs—furious, absolutely furious, he was unable to get to me. So I had to shake a very real, very unusually skilled negative entity that just wanted me to go away.[3] It was right there in the physical; it didn't have to be a discarnate entity. It was incarnate.

At any rate, it's that real, it's that specific. You don't want anything that's hanging around the edges of the contact that could misconstrue an answer or something like that so you need to remove anything like that. So you just make sure that you're good and clean before you go into the contact.

GARY So in terms of how you perceive non-physical entities is that you perceive presences—a feeling, a field of an entity.

CARLA Yes. A feeling, usually some kind of internal pressure, like maybe a headache coming on or something like that.

GARY So for those entities who have not been able to pass your challenge, presumably they're of negative orientation, did they *feel* any differently than the positive entities?

CARLA No. All entities that are able to impress others with their messages are using light. Light is light—no difference positive or negative.

GARY Which is another reason to challenge because they can mimic the same field.

CARLA Right, you cannot tell.

GARY Jim, you used a challenging process tailored to your own unique essence. Did you perceive similarly to Carla? How did you know when a challenge had been passed or failed?

JIM Just an inner feeling. I only had one or two times that I felt there was a negative entity that was resisting.

GARY And in those cases you just repeated the challenge until that feeling dissipated?

JIM Yes.

GARY The other key aspect to your pre-channeling procedure is tuning. What is tuning and why is that so important?

CARLA In the process of your own spiritual life, tuning is an internal process which has to do basically with cleaning away negative parts of you that might keep you from having your heart open—like anger, for instance—and then working to release that.

When it comes to channeling, you want to tune your instrument just like you'd take an instrument that, say, has a reed, or something that you can adjust. Come to think of it, the reed is one thing you can't adjust, isn't it?

So anyway, you're tuning to I guess you'd say 440 to concert A. You're tuning to a default vibration which is the one great Original Thought of Love, and the distortions that you have that make your energy less than loving, you're tuning them out. You're letting them fall away, so that you become your highest and best self, so that you can do you're very best work.

It's got to be real though. You can't just say, "I'm going to be positive, damn it!" It doesn't work. You have actually to become more positive. And so you observe what works for you. What works for me is what you've experienced before these sessions. I use very simple prayers that I've known since childhood, and I used them over and over and over again. And they never get stale to me because the ideas are so basic and so loving. The prayer of St. Francis, the prayer of the Holy Spirit: those two are very dear to me. So I use prayer, I use singing, sometimes I use chanting; I use whatever works to lift me up and become my best self for that moment. That is sort of a quick look at tuning.

GARY So tuning not only improves the efficiency of the contact but also serves as a means of protection just like the challenging, because those who don't match your tuning have difficulty relating with you or at least speaking through your instrument.

CARLA Right. Yeah, they need to harmonize.

GARY In Book V, Jim wrote:

> As time and experience with the Ra contact accumulated we be-
> came increasingly aware that the honor of providing this kind of
> service brought with it the need for just as much responsibility for
> providing the service with as much purity and harmony as one was
> capable of producing in every facet of the life experience. What was
> learned needed to be put to use in the daily life, or difficulties
> would result in the life pattern.

So, this is a theme both of you have repeated elsewhere, that is, the need to *live* the message being transmitted through one. Can you expand on this?

CARLA Well, in street talk it's *walking your talk*. You can say all kinds of beautiful things, but if you don't do it, then your kids, for instance, can look at you and say, "Mommy, you told me to do this, but you don't do that." You're caught. So you need to be able to be as close to those things that you've been learning as possible.

JIM Ra calls it the Law of Responsibility. If you stand close to the light you need to be more careful about how you conduct yourself. You have a magnifying glass on you, usually from negatively oriented entities that are willing to accentuate whatever disharmonies that you might allow to creep into your relationships. Always got to be more careful.

GARY What are some of the consequences of not living the message that is being transmitted, or at least not *attempting* to live the message that is being transmitted.

JIM Getting a mixed message—negative entities taking over, positive entities saying, "Oh, well, we tried."

CARLA Basically, if people don't respect your efforts, it reflects on the message, and we wouldn't want to do anything to reflect on this message which we consider to be anything less than very helpful.

GARY So not living the message might be linked to, or connected to tuning. It's a way of losing your tuning.

CARLA Just being *real*, being who people think you might be, being who you might say who you are, being it to your very core, no mixed messages here, a straight message.

GARY That speaks to the responsibility that the instrument has regarding the messages that come through the instrument: their content and spirit have to match the vibration of the instrument. If that instrument lowers its vibration then it can't successfully channel that higher vibration content.

CARLA That's right.

GARY Ra says:

> **RA** We may only suggest that the honor of propinquity [*proximity*] to light carries with it the Law of Responsibility. The duty to refrain from contumely [*insulting treatment/language*], discord, and all things which, when unresolved within, make way for workings lies before the instrument of which you speak. 101.8

What do you think Ra means by "refrain from discord and contumely" as part of the responsibility of the instrument engaging in a channeling practice?

JIM Well, that's again, practicing what you're learning from the contact, putting it in into practice, putting it in your life and not engaging in disharmony that you can avoid.

CARLA Being sweet with each other.

GARY So if you're mistreating other people, it's probably not going to go well for your channeling practice.

CARLA Right. [*laughing*] And a lot of time there is a little ego involved so you have to ask yourself, why do I have this impulse to distance myself by saying something sarcastic, saying something hurtful? Why can't I just support that guy? And then working on yourself until you can support the guy, in all sincerity

GARY And this notion of standing closer to the light, serving the light, serving in the light, implies also that any shadow within you is going to be intensified, energized, and magnified so you have to be extra vigilant and extra mindful.

CARLA We felt like we were standing in full sunlight at just about high noon, and so the shadows were very intense and very short.

GARY During the Ra contact?

CARLA Yeah, during the Ra contact. When the Ra contact started and it settled in, we could feel the tenseness, the intensity mounting daily.

GARY So if you're not attempting to stand so close to the light and you feel, say, anger, that anger might be a more mild version; it might come and go, it might have less consequence, it might grip you less. But when you're attempting to stand in the light, that same anger might be that much more energized, might gain more momentum, might have more capacity to take you over, so to speak, if you're not mindful, if you're not careful.

JIM Right.

GARY So now that I know that you, Carla, were responsible for developing the challenging and tuning aspects, how did you come to develop those? How did you know that that was needed, that that would be of help?

CARLA Well, I just looked at every session after it was done and I was typing it up—for a long time I typed up the session that we had at a 5:00

o'clock meeting, by the next day I would have that done. [These were the conscious channeling sessions that Carla participated in during the 1970s.] While I did it, you know, being very fresh in my mind, I could think about it. I could look at how the questioning went, I could look at the answers, I could look at the dynamic. You can see things if you look closely while it's all still fresh in your mind. You can just penetrate a little bit why this worked or why this didn't work, why this wasn't a good question, why this wasn't a good answer, etc.

I was a researcher—I am a researcher—and I wanted to not just to do it, but to do it as well as possible. A prayer that Jim offers every day really gets to it. Can you repeat that part of it that has to do with, "help me to be as close to you as possible, by doing the things that I do as well as I can".

JIM "Lord, please be with us today which you always are. Help us to see your face in everything that we do, and help us to glorify you by doing everything that we do the best that we can." You know what? I'm going to have to write it down! [*Jim and Carla laugh*] It's the basic thing of: "Help us to do the best we can and to glorify You by doing everything to the highest of our ability." That's not exactly how it goes, but I'm not in the right frame of mind to—

CARLA —to do it, yeah, I know what you mean, but that's the sense of it: honoring and doing the best we can. I wanted always to do the best I could. So I would examine the process to see, well, maybe this is true, and then I'd try it out. Then I could see if it was true or wasn't true. So it was gradual. It was over a period of months, but it didn't take too long be-cause it was so obvious. For instance, when you allowed a specific question, you could feel right away the energy change. And everybody thought, *we're going to get some good stuff now*, but it wasn't the energy that you wanted in a metaphysical session—it wasn't what I wanted. I don't know why other people haven't come to the same conclusion inde-pendently, actually, because it really does work.

GARY Did you see a discernable improvement or change in the channeling once you implemented these measures?

CARLA Oh, yes, I certainly did.

GARY Have either of you ever doubted your own channeling?

CARLA I answered that before. I said you do the very best you can, and then you'd be a fool to doubt that because that's the best you can do. So what are you going to do? It's the best that you can do, that's it. The doubting stops right there. Or you don't do the work. One or the other.

GARY What would you say makes a good channel?

JIM Talent. Natural ability. And Carla has that. Just like anybody can pretty much learn to play chopsticks on a piano, anybody can learn how to channel, but doing it well is the real trick, and using the challenging and tuning are very necessary. But then there's also a talent, and like Ol' Satchmo says, "Some got it and some ain't."

CARLA [laughs] He's so kind to me.

GARY I think, Carla, you already answered this question, so to rephrase and ask if that's correct: in terms of how you perceive what you were re-ceiving, you perceive a "concept ball" that is not given to you in words, precisely, but that you clothe in words. You translate it and give it words.

CARLA Right. A channeling session to me feels like a game of catch—catch the ball, throw it; catch the ball, throw it; catch the ball, throw it. If you don't throw it within seconds after you get it—if you don't speak it out—you lose the contact. You have to keep the energy going—catch the ball, throw it. You can't catch the ball and then give it some words and then contemplate it some more—you don't have that luxury, or you'll lose the rest of the contact. So it feels very patchy. It feels very jerky from the inside out, and on the tape it comes out smooth as silk.

GARY So instead of it being a continuous stream, you perceive it in dis-tinct packets, an on-and-off function. The way you're describing it sounds like there's no time for reflection of the message or analysis of the mes-sage, you just need to let it out.

CARLA Right, none whatsoever. You do not think about it. You catch the ball, you throw the ball. You do not think about it. That would be death to the contact right there.

JIM Analyze it when it's done, later.

GARY Did you guys find yourselves trying to think about it and ask your-selves, as it was coming through you initially: Is this right? Is this wrong?

CARLA That's part of the learning process. Everybody does that. It was a couple of months before I could do the channeling because I got so blown away by the energy. You've done enough trying to do it that you've probably felt that energy come in, right?

GARY I did perceive some conditioning, I don't know about—

CARLA Did it blow you away?

GARY No, I hadn't reached that point.

CARLA When I first got the energy of Hatonn, [*makes a sound of being blown away*], I could not think, I could not speak, I couldn't possibly work with it. I felt it, but it took me a long time to be able to bear it, it was *so* much energy. I was very sensitive to it, it turned out. So it took me a while, and once I was able to receive it, and not get blown away, then I was able to start using it, translating things I got out of it.

GARY So whereas some people feel in channeling like they're flying blind, in a way, in that they don't know if there is something actually there, in your case, you're feeling something very distinct and palpable due to your sensitivities.

CARLA I am. Yeah, and we had a nurse sit next to me one time—this was at Wooded Glen in 1995, was it?

GARY 2005.

CARLA Well I was a decade . . .

GARY You got a five in there.

CARLA And she sat next to me. I don't know if you remember this, but she had a little gadget that she put on my finger that read out some data, and when I got the contact, my blood pressure and everything changed. My body smoothed out actually—it helped—and when I released the contact immediately my body changed back. So there was a perceptible effect that the contact had on me as far as body processes.

GARY Yeah, it would have been so fascinating to have measured your biometrics, your EEG, blood pressure, heart rate, to see measure any changes, and have that documented.

CARLA She just sat next to me. We didn't document it, but she told me that was what happened.

GARY Especially for the materialist. Not that you're setting out to prove anything to anyone, but for the materialists you can say that—

CARLA I have never wanted to try to prove it to anybody. It's not possible, basically, to prove it to anybody. Even though you can be logical and think that you've been very evidential in what you've had to say, a person who doesn't want to believe will not believe and will find all kinds of reasons why. So unless you can prove it with "measure and pen," as Ra said, don't even try. Don't waste the breath, because it's just not possible to convince someone who doesn't want to be convinced about something that cannot be proven.

GARY And that gets to the heart of why channeling is chosen as a means of communication for those higher density entities that wish to offer service to those of Earth: they want to guard the free will of those who receive the messages. Channeling provides a means whereby the content can be evaluated on its own merits, and either accepted or rejected therein.

CARLA Uh-huh. You'd be right.

GARY In the case of *conscious* channeling, I have always perceived the instrument, whoever he or she may be, somewhat as the stained glass window. That is to say, the instrument, as the window, necessarily colors the light moving through it no matter how clear and clean that stained glass window.

To what extent would you say that conscious channeling acts as a filtering or coloring mechanism? That is to say, how much of what comes through is influenced by, or a result of, the instrument?

CARLA Probably a third, something like that. A lot.

JIM Didn't the Confederation say that their ideal was about 70% them and 30% the channel. Because they wanted to use your experiences, your sensibilities and so forth in order to make the message universal *and* human.

CARLA And apt for the group that it's being given to. Every group is different, every day is different, and you can ask the same question lots and lots of times and you'll get a different answer every time because it's a different group every time and they have different needs. They want to hear different things, and you can answer in a million different ways. But as Ra said, it's "always and ever the same,"[4] in terms of what the basic message is: love, love, love.

JIM Again, this is true for conscious channeling. This wasn't the way the

Ra contact worked. No part of that contact was the instrument.

GARY One of the things that made it unique.

CARLA Yes, it was unique to us anyway, for sure.

GARY Yeah, one reaches the conclusion when reading large quantities of the conscious channeling is that it's the same principle; it's just infinitely repackaged in different ways, session by session.

Carla described receiving these packets that she had to translate. Did you perceive the same process or was it different in your case?

JIM Mine seemed to be more a sentence by sentence sort of thing. I was looking for more—we call it *control*, or conditioning, or evidence that it wasn't me, so I wasn't so able to "hang my ass over the line," as she says. I wasn't as fearless. I wanted to make mine more solid and know that it's not me.

GARY So did you perceive that the sentence was almost already formed for you and you just had to relay it?

JIM Sort of, yeah.

GARY I think this question might help illustrate the degree to which the conscious instrument affects the content coming through, so I would ask: What characterizes the differences between Carla's channeling, Jim's channeling, and Don's channeling?

CARLA There's an energy that's unique to each of us. Don's channeling used a lot of repetition and stayed with very simple concepts when he was doing the metaphysical type of channeling. Jim's channeling to me has a tendency to be terser, shorter, clearer, and mine has a tendency to be more poetic.

GARY In examining the answer to that question, it helps one to see just how much a conscious instrument affects the information, what they bring to the table, and it helps delineate the difference between surface features and appearances versus the deeper heart of the message. The heart remains the same, but there are all sorts of surface variability and permutation of that essential message.

CARLA Yes. That is so true. And you can always have your favorite channel and your favorite source.

GARY Listening to Stephen T. channel, one can hear a style that is more philosophical, more elaborate—

CARLA ". . . therefore, and this goes to prove that." Yeah, it's almost a teaching duel.

GARY And that is a consequence of his orientation as a philosophy professor.

CARLA Right, he's been teaching philosophy for 30 years.

GARY So the message is going to be clothed in a particular way that's unique to him.

CARLA It's wonderful, and I'm always thrilled to listen to him. It's a joy. He and Jim are my best students definitely.

GARY There have been a multitude of Confederation groups that have spoken through you and other instruments in a conscious state, including Hatonn, Oxal, Latwii, and Q'uo. Do they have distinct presences?

CARLA They have distinct energies, and then they come into the head in distinct ways.

GARY So say, they didn't identify who they were, you could determine who was coming to you based on how they feel where they enter in?

CARLA You really have a tendency to be able to do that, yeah. [*Carla asks Jim*] Have you ever received Oxal? Zings right in up here at the top, whereas Hatonn I experience as a more general all over, like a big cat.

GARY Just on a whim, Jim, did you feel that there was any connection between your frontal lobe work and channeling?

JIM No.

CARLA That's interesting because they both have to do with feelings that—

JIM Well, there were sensations that come in there in the frontal lobe area, but I think that's true for everybody.

CARLA Yeah.

GARY There's an aspect in serving as an instrument called *conditioning* whereby, prior to receiving information and channeling it, the human instrument feels a conditioning in some sort of way. How have you two experienced conditioning? And what is conditioning?

CARLA Well, you just said what conditioning was. It is some sort of reassuring flip of the tongue or movement of the mouth opening wide. That's very common. It just lets you know that there is a presence there that wants to speak. And some people get the conditioning throughout the message, other people just get it at the beginning. I would get the rush that I was explaining to you before at the beginning, and then it would settle down and that would, I guess, constitute my conditioning. I didn't ever really perceive the need for some kind of reassuring [*makes a sound*]. Don always had that little bit [*makes clicking noise*] before he began, and I don't remember if you—[*to Jim*] what have you done in the way of conditioning?

JIM I would feel it in my jaw, my mouth, sometimes in my sinuses, the frontal lobes area up here would be activated and then I know that it was time for me to speak, that they were there. But again, this is for conscious channeling. There was no conditioning from Ra. Ra said that due to their limitations, they could offer no conditioning. We never questioned as to what their limitations were, but since Carla was asleep it wouldn't do any good to give her conditioning if it were Ra, so that had something to do with it.

CARLA Well, I think Ra's limitations had to do with the narrow band.

GARY Think they could have rung the doorbell or something to give some kind of clue.

CARLA [*laughs*]

GARY During my one attempt to channel at the 2008 Channeling Intensive I did feel pretty intense conditioning, a strong stimulation right around the third eye region. That's as far as I made it in the process.

CARLA Well, good. You were doing a good job then.

GARY What would you say is the difference between channeling and the experience of those people who hear voices in their head, so to speak?

CARLA Well, I guess channeling is much more regularized where you are able to use it for the benefit of others, hopefully.

JIM There's a discipline that goes with channeling so that you use, hopefully, the challenging and tuning, and you're responsible about what you do. People who hear voices probably could speak those voices and they'd probably have something to say. But I don't know if I want to hear it, because they're not usually in control. They're not usually using any kind of discipline, and they're usually at the mercy of the voices that they hear.

GARY So we've talked about entities of the higher densities using the same light regardless of what polarity they are, as mentioned here:

> QUESTIONER This question may be meaningless but would a fifth-density entity of the Confederation who was positively polarized transmit on the same frequency as our negatively polarized fifth-density companion?
>
> RA I am Ra. This is correct and is the reason that the questioning of all contacts is welcomed by the Confederation of Planets in the Service of the Infinite Creator. 89.6

You've seen a lot of channels come and go over the years, and some of their contacts became unwittingly corrupted. How does a channel become de-tuned?

JIM Well, they think they can recognize their contact without doing any challenging or tuning. They may not even know about challenging and tuning, and they think they know the contact just because they've done it so many times; but because a negative entity of the same relative potency or density channels on the same wavelength, you can't tell. You have to say, "Who are you? Do you come in the name of____?" And so forth, every time.

CARLA Every time I have given an honest opinion saying "you need some help" to someone asking my opinion, the channel felt that I was being unduly critical, and that I was dead wrong. Whether it was expressed in tears, or in anger, or whatever, that was the end of our [chuckles] productive discussion of channeling. People don't like being told, "Let's do some work. Let's clean it up."

GARY For those positively oriented channels who intend to channel positively oriented information but eventually get a mixed contact, it seems that mixed, de-tuned contact is a consequence of failing to challenge, failing to tune, failing to live the message, or all of the above.

CARLA There's some sort of ego involvement. One very common theme is the desire to answer every question. If you try to answer specific questions, you're inevitably going to get a service-to-self contact that is very happy to replace the service-to-others contact, because service-to-others sources do not tend to have any interest in specific information or even find themselves able to give it. Their area of expertise is the infinite, the eternal, and not prophecy of the future or something like that.

So what you're doing when you start getting into very specific discussions is you're basically telling the positively oriented source to get lost. You're not going to use that source anymore; you're going to use a source that can answer specific questions.

Or other ego things have to do with, *I always know my source. I'm familiar with my source, I could not possibly be mistaken.* Or, *I want to make money with this contact.* There are all kinds of ways to get tempted, and I think temptation is a good word—to look at what's tempting a person.

Yet another way to mess up a contact is to have fear. People have messed up one contact after another fearing what's to come. *Oh my God, it's all going to splat on the windshield of life. We're bugs, we've had it. Sometime down the road we're toast.* So you ask about that and you start getting information like, *be sure to include a cow among your group so that you'll have a source of milk when everything else falls apart.*

JIM And pack diapers. For the kids.

CARLA Yeah, I've seen both.

JIM Ra said it wasn't the specificity of the questions that was the problem, it was the importance placed on the specificity. Every now and then we got specific information just because we had a question along that line, but we didn't pursue it and think it was really important.

CARLA Very good point.

GARY So, you began to respond by saying that if it's the *desire* to answer those questions, it's the instrument *wanting* to answer those questions. That seems to suggest that there's more human volition, and more human, say, on the part of the instrument than would otherwise seem is the case.

I would think that the human instrument, for the most part, is kind of standing out of the way and allowing the *source* to determine whether or not, and how, the source will answer that question.

Are you saying that in that equation, the human is saying "yes" or "no" to the question as well?

CARLA I think that in a lot of cases, the human is over identifying with the channeled source. When the channeled source says, "I don't know," it has no bearing on the instrument at all, but I think there have been many a channel that felt that it did, and that it would reflect on how good a channel they were. If you were a really good channel, you would always get an answer.

It never bothered me if I got, *I don't know*. I blatted out, "I don't know," and that was the end of it.

GARY So the instrument, hearing the question, can actively and simultaneously desire an answer, even if the source doesn't have it, and thereby—

CARLA Absolutely. And the instrument, when it's got opinions—one particular person I'm thinking of had this problem repeatedly. I was unable to affect it at all. And again, the instrument felt that I was being very critical, and unduly so, when I said that its desire to express its own opinions about politics and the state of the world was getting in the way of his channeling because it came out as channeling, and it never would be. It was not a pure channel at all the way it was coming out. It was almost like a psychic reading on the near future, very specific and very political. It just took away from the purity of the channeling. It lowered the vibration of the channeling overall to the point where I could not work with this person after—I think I tried three times to channel with the person and I had to give it up.

GARY Would you say, during the process of your own channeling, that part of your brain is assessing and evaluating the merit of the question being asked, or are you stepping aside completely and allowing the source to make that determination?

CARLA Oh, honey, I wish I could say I never do that, but I do. I'm such a critic and I really have to watch it every moment of every day to make sure that it's not Carla the Critic that's stepping up to the plate instead of Carla the Supporter, Carla Who Could Channel, Carla Who Could Teach, or whatever. Because Carla the Critic is just mean. I don't mean to be mean, but ruthless.

GARY Say it how it is.

CARLA Say it how I think it is anyway.

GARY So even for a seasoned channel with many years of experience under her belt, there's still difficulty in keeping yourself completely out of the equation?

CARLA Yeah, yeah, absolutely. Not that I don't do it; I think I'm pretty successful, but the temptation is always there.

GARY Have you guys ever knowingly channeled a negative entity?

CARLA No.

JIM No.

GARY In the early 1990s I believe, you initiated a series of Channeling Intensive Workshops designed to teach others to channel Confederation sources, but you brought those to a close for a long time. Why was that?

CARLA [*to Jim*] Why was that? Do you remember?

JIM I think we were having some problems with people not listening to what you had to say: not to try it on their own without any group around, without an anchor channel. You were the one who was the anchor channel, the experienced channel, and we had a couple of people go off on their own and try to do it.

One up in the upstairs room that you used to be in had a fugue and went into this state of consciousness where he was blathering this, that, and the other. We all had to go up there and sit with him and settle him down and calm him down and—

CARLA It was physical—lay hands on him and pull him back into himself. It was a scary half hour or so. It could have gone worse.

Then there was one that committed suicide eventually, and then there was another one that ended up in a mental hospital. And all of these people had started to practice channeling on their own.[5]

GARY The first individual that you mentioned who didn't follow your protocols and channeled on his own and was blathering, what sort of content was coming through him or her.

CARLA Aggrandized to himself, "I will take care of everything, you'll never have to worry again in your life, I will take care of you."

GARY I thought I recall hearing about an incident where someone was saying some really aggressive, negative things.

CARLA Well, that was another case. There was another case that was like that but that's not the one I was thinking of when we talked about the fugue. [*to Jim*] Can you think of anything this guy said other than what I suggested?

JIM No, he was into the Japanese culture so he was trying to mimic the accent that comes with the . . . there was a certain contact that we used to get—

CARLA Oh, you mean Yada! I Yada. Yeah.

JIM Anyway, he was mimicking things that he'd heard.

GARY My memory, and it's been a while since I've heard about that, was that you were a bit spooked by what transpired so you shut down the effort to teach channeling.

CARLA I just felt that if people wouldn't listen to me, that I was introducing temptation into their lives that they couldn't handle, and that it might snap back and hurt them. I did not want to hurt people. It took me a long time to get over that fear and begin to trust again that it was okay to run through my little teaching effort. And it has been okay since then. I've had—how many cycles have I had, four? Four times that I've done the workshop?

GARY At least six or so individual workshops, or seven. I'm not sure how many cycles it was divided up into.

CARLA Anyway, at least four different groups, maybe more.

GARY I asked that question also to highlight that there are very real dangers with channeling with very real consequences when not doing it properly.

CARLA Yeah, I think the guy that you're thinking of was the one that ended up blasting me, right? Messed up the radio, every time he walked past the radio, it'd go *shh*—have all this static.

GARY I don't remember hearing about that. He was the father of a female friend of yours.

CARLA Oh, the father. Yeah, that was the one that was in the fugue.

GARY I thought I remember hearing about somebody writhing around on the living room floor saying, "We're going to get you," or—

JIM It could have been. It's hard to remember after all these years,

CARLA Long life, but this [particular] guy was writhing on the floor but he wanted to take care of us. It's funny, you know, that really is an extremely positive thing—the desire to help somebody, the desire to make things okay, the desire to let somebody know that you think they're worth protecting, that you think their job is good. It ends up being scarily negative simply because it's so out of control and harmful to the person doing it.

GARY It's an enhancement of the instrument's identity. It's saying *I'M* going to do something.

CARLA Right. This source had completely obliterated the person that was channeling. It had taken over completely and that's a scary thing. I'm so glad that we were able to bring him back. He's a wonderful guy. Couldn't be a nicer fellow, couldn't be a more intelligent person, but intelligence has its own problems because then you think, *well, I don't need to listen to what she's saying. She's wrong. I can handle this. I can work on my own. That advice is not meant for me because I am too smart and too clever and too with it to have to be limited like that.* It's not true. No matter how smart you are (and I'm smart enough), no matter how clever you are (I won't say I'm clever), but no matter what wonderful things you've got going for you, the negative entities involved in staying close to a group like this, looking for an opportunity—I would not give that entity opportunities because they can hurt you.

GARY Your intellect is not what's guarding you.

CARLA No. There's a difference between fearing it and acting appropriately, and I think acting appropriately in a world of light and dark, positive and negative, is to follow the protocols that I suggest: stay with a group. Stay with a group with an experienced channel that has a certain measure of protection for you. Any kind of a group evens out your vibrations, makes you all better than you are. That's the beauty of a group.

GARY We probably already covered this question, but in the event that there's anything new to glean here, what's the difference between the "narrow-band" channeling that typified the Ra contact, and the conscious channeling that forms the vast majority of L/L's channeled work?

CARLA Well, as near as I can tell, it's the way that energy comes in. I guess it's characteristic of each density that there would be a certain . . . from here to here [*indicates a distance between her hands*] . . . that much of a difference possible in the bandwidths, and then fourth density like this and fifth density more like this, and then sixth density, narrow. It's just that sixth density is different enough from third density that you have to filter out a tremendous amount of third-density stuff in order to be able to pick up sixth-density information.

GARY In the case of channeling sixth-density entities, at least Ra, the instrument, you, were completely out of your physical body.

CARLA Apparently I couldn't have done it consciously.

GARY So it's essentially as if Ra is in the room with you and you're hearing Ra directly without human interference, without the passing through—

CARLA Apparently Ra was just taking over my vocal apparatus and using it.

JIM They were not *in* her body. They were using it from, what we would say, a distance.

GARY So the body was *very much* an instrument—a radio, a microphone for them. By contrast in the conscious channeling the instrument is *aware* of what's coming through them.

CARLA Yeah, and in conscious channeling you can shut it down at any time if you don't think it's going well. I have been known to do that.

GARY And in both cases there are still the requirements to live what's coming through you and to do the challenging and tuning. Actually you didn't do the precise same methods that you did for the Ra contact.

CARLA I'm not saying you have the responsibility of mimicking them—you just need to be your own self and take in that which you can and express that as it pertains to you.

JIM Whatever your best effort is, is the effort you need to make.

GARY And you should definitely take credit for what is coming through you.

[*laughter*]

CARLA Never.

GARY What is the difference between outer planes and inner planes channeling?

CARLA Well, the difference is between channeling from the Holy Spirit, channeling from the spirit within, inner planes, staying within this density; and outer planes channeling energy from elsewhere, which could be from different densities, probably would be from densities other than our own.

GARY Is internal vs. external applicable?

CARLA Yes, that's fair.

KEN So it doesn't have anything to do with the planet? Like *inner planes* doesn't just mean within the Earth and outer planes means from out—is there a physical boundary to that or is it more of a metaphysical, or both?

CARLA Well, yeah, there's a physical boundary to Earth's inner planes. They're all within third-density Earth.

GARY So inner planes—you can still be channeling outside of your personal mind/body/spirit complex, but still within the Earth's inner planes.

CARLA Oh, very much so. A lot of people channel other entities that have been wonderful and inspirations within their own lives and then they're channeled by someone and that channeling is valued. I'm trying to think of a good example. A lot of Indian gurus are channeled by their students after they die. Is it Maharshi that has had so many that feel that he's been their guru even though he passed on long ago?

JIM You mean Yogananda?

CARLA Yogananda? I don't know. There are quite a few of them that the people that are their students feel that this is their guru and the guru has long since departed the physical. But he's very real on the inner planes to the student and in effect, is channeled.

GARY So you could almost say that there are *inner*-inner planes that include your higher self, maybe your guidance system?

CARLA Yes.

GARY Then there are the inner planes that are part of the Earth's inner planes, but still very local to you, you might say.

CARLA Right, and *safe*, which the outer planes' channeling is not. Safe because you're within the Holy Spirit which protects you as a soul. You have a spirit within—whatever you want to call it. I call it the Holy Spirit because I'm a Christian, and I feel and know that spirit as an individual essence that is able to express very helpful thoughts to me. As a matter of fact, all my channelings from the Holy Spirit are from Holly, my name for the Holy Spirit.[6]

GARY Highlighting another difference: the outer plane contacts require a minimum of three people in the group. Inner planes can be done on your own.

CARLA Yeah. Jim and I did the Holly channeling. That was when I was practicing tuning and challenging and I'd tune and then I'd challenge and then I'd have the Holy Spirit. And it just seemed rude to say, "Well, thanks." So I'd say, "Give me a thought for the day." So the Holy Spirit, Holly, would share a thought for the day, and some of those channelings from the Holy Spirit are really beautiful. So we had, what, close to 500 or 600 of them because I'd been doing this for three or four years before I decided that I'd gotten everything out of it that I could. We picked a year's worth, plus a day because of leap year, so we have 366 readings in that little book—one for each day. So you can take it and start on January 1 and just go through the year letting that be your companion for a year. Many people have told me that's the way they've used it, and they've found it helpful. It's just neat. You can also do an I-Ching and ask, "What's my advice for the day?" And then open it at random and see what you get.

GARY What would you say constitutes transient information?

JIM Material that doesn't have any lasting value. It's only good for the moment. Ten thousand years from now it won't mean anything to anybody.

CARLA Crude examples of it are who's going to win a horserace or who's going to win a football game or where the next Earth change is going to take place—whether it's a tsunami or earthquake or what. All those things matter until they don't matter and they've happened and they're old news. That's transient. Here today, gone tomorrow. Eternally useful wisdom, the eternal wisdom, remains the same always, and that's the realm of Spirit.

GARY And if you find that you have a desire for what is termed transient information you should not be seeking that from outer planes sources.

CARLA I think a person who is really hungry for transient info probably ought to work with the astrology because of the fact that the stars do have an effect on us, and if you're a good astrologer you can really read a lot in a reading specific to one person to one time for that person. You can do readings for people that are very helpful.

GARY In the first question of session 22, Ra says:

> **RA** Each time, as you would put it, that we perform this working our social memory complex vibrational distortion meshes more firmly with this instrument's unconscious distortions towards service. **Thus we are becoming a part of this instrument's vibratory complex and it a part of ours.** This occurs upon the unconscious level, the level whereby the mind has gone down through to the roots of consciousness which you may call cosmic. 22.1

Do you think after multiple decades of channeling these sources that the "meshing" Ra describes continued, creating a blending of identities between the sources you channeled and yourself?

CARLA Yes, I do.

GARY Not of course that you can take credit for that information but there's still that—

CARLA I do feel the presence of unseen friends, let's put it that way.

GARY Do you perceive that you have improved in channeling over the years?

CARLA I've done a certain amount of improvement. I know I've got more improvement to go if I can just open to it.

GARY So you've always maintained a beginner's mind?

CARLA That's right. I've always retained that. I have never been satisfied with my work. Every single time I finish a channeling my first thought is, *I just missed so much.*

GARY So it feels like you're just scraping the surface of what you're receiving?

CARLA Yeah, there are things that are so worthwhile, and I just take the surface up and go on.

GARY If you could plumb deeper into what you're receiving, how do you think you would achieve that?

CARLA If I knew how, I would do it.

GARY So if you guys discovered a genie that could answer any and all questions that you had about how channeling works and what happens during the process of channeling that you haven't previously known, what questions would you two ask about channeling?

CARLA How can I do it better?

JIM Yeah.

GARY What she said?

JIM What she said.

[*laughter*]

---

[1] Jim retired his vocal channeling service on September 7, 2003—in the midst of a Sunday meditation, actually. However, after Carla passed in April, 2015, Jim and a good friend, Stephen T., resumed the channeling service in order to keep the flame alive. And as is discussed elsewhere in this chapter, Jim's assessment of his own channeling was not that, shall we say, objective.

[2] The inability of the instrument to take credit for the working is similar to that of the healer:

> **RA** It is not by example that the healer does the working. The working exists in and of itself. The healer is only the catalyst, much as this instrument has the catalysis necessary to provide the channel for our words, yet by example or exercise of any kind can take no thought for this working. 5.1

[3] Occasionally in this book I supplement Carla's viewpoint with an alternative in order to give the reader more than one perspective to consider. This is one such case. What precisely happened in this situation is completely unknowable to me and is best known to Carla. Yet I wonder if this little boy's effect on Carla may *not* have been a consequence of being a *skilled negative entity*, but rather and simply a concentration, on his part, of intense negative feeling that had some sort of psychic impact on Carla. Food for thought.

[4] The "information which is ever and always the same":

> **RA** We have watched your group. We have been called to your group, for

you have a need for the diversity of experiences in channeling which go with a more intensive, or as you might call it, advanced approach to the system of studying the patterns of the illusions of your body, your mind, and your spirit, which you call seeking the truth. We hope to offer you a somewhat different slant upon the information which is always and ever the same. 1.0

5   Jim believes that the individual who committed suicide and the individual who ended up in a mental hospital happened in the 1970s, before Jim had become close with Carla and Don. He doesn't know exactly what happened, only that he had heard of the incidents. He cannot speak to the strength of connection between their attempting to channel on their own and their eventual fates. Likely attempting to channel unsafely only exacerbated preexisting conditions.

6   Carla stresses how safe it is to channel inner planes entities. To the best of our understanding it is indeed quite safe to channel ones higher self or personal guidance system. In fact many third-density entities likely and often tap into these sources without quite realizing it, whether in moments of creating art, or feeling inspiration, or experiencing a deeper connection. Due to the safety of this type of channeling, the requisite precautions for an outer planes contact (e.g.: a three-person group, challenging, etc.) may not be so necessary.

In Carla's reply, however, she seems to indicate that it is *also* just as safe to channel any source within the inner planes which is outside of one's personal guidance system. Given that the inner planes are populated with a great variety of intelligences, both positive and negative, we would caution anyone attempting to channel an inner planes source to engage in some precautionary safety measures. Always challenge the source. Always tune. And it is probably helpful, if possible, to channel with the support of a group.

GARY We begin the final three sections of our interview of Jim McCarty and Carla Rueckert beginning with a biography of Don Elkins, the person whose desire for the truth and subsequent research efforts set the whole L/L Research project into motion, and set a trajectory that we still walk to this day.

Where and when was Don Elkins born?

CARLA Don was born in Mayfield, Kentucky in . . . wait a minute, wait a minute . . . his mother came to Louisville to give birth. So he was born here in Louisville on the 27th of February, 1930.*

GARY He was born in a hospital in Louisville, but he was taken back to Mayfield, Kentucky to live.

CARLA Well, his family had lived in Louisville and had some good money—good, comfortable . . . when people say of someone else "they're comfortably fixed," that was the way they were. There was a bunch of money in the family which was lost because of the Depression. And so

---

* Carla actually said that Elkins was born on February 28. Subsequent discovery of his birth certificate showed February 27. All instances of the wrong date have been corrected in the second edition of the book.

Sister—the nickname that Don's mother had in the family—Sister moved with her husband, Tully, and with Don to the country.

Don basically grew up to the age of fifteen in the deep country of Mayfield. They made a big garden. They knew how to can and preserve and make the most out of their garden, and they survived the way country people always have. They made enough food to eat, and money was always tight. Tully was always on the road selling something and seldom home. He was a very nice guy and he became, at one point, I think the head of the—what do you call the central council of business people in a town?

JIM Better Business Bureau?

CARLA He became head of whatever that is. Not the Better Business Bureau but...

JIM Like a Louisville marketing association or the . . .

GARY Commerce Guild or . . . [Probably the Chamber of Commerce.]

CARLA You know you focus on welcoming and trying to get new companies to come to town and you try to support the companies that are in town. Anyway, he was well thought of, and he was a really nice guy. But it was very difficult to make money at that time. But they made the little they had go a long way.

Don lived in Mayfield until the age of 15. He became an incredibly good shot. He did a little time behind a mule, plowing, and was part of a farming family, which he did not like. He liked the town, he liked the forests, but he didn't like working behind a mule. [laughs]

GARY He's not one for physical labor?

CARLA Well, he loved physical labor if he got to choose it. Every weekend that he was in Louisville he would take off, and he would be gone from Friday until Sunday night, and he and his best friends would be out hiking down around in the woods, acre after acre, hour after hour. They had a boat that they kept and would row across the river to the Indiana side where Don became an apprentice gunsmith and, by the age of fifteen, was an incredibly good shot. Those were his values at that time: to be a good shot, to be able to spend time with his buddies hiking the woods, and basically to be left alone other than that.

GARY So February 27th he was born, 1930.

CARLA He was born right at midnight, in the first moments of February 27.

GARY This was just a few months into the Great Depression that began on December 29th?

CARLA Well, people say it began then, but there was a deepening of the Depression in '32. He was definitely a child of the Depression.

GARY You began to describe his parents. Did they have any religious or spiritual or philosophical belief system that they imparted to Don?

CARLA They did. Sister was part of the Christian Science Church wherever she was. The latter part of her life she was in Louisville. So from the age of fifteen, they wanted Don to go to Male High School, which his dad had gone to, and so forth and so on—tradition in the family. So they moved up here and, I think, lived with her parents, and Don went to school at Male and graduated from Male. And his best friends did too. So he always had his buds. He was a faithful, loyal friend, too. There was a lot of very real love between those three guys.

GARY You said his mom was a Christian Scientist.

CARLA Yes.

GARY Is that true of his father also?

CARLA His father attended church, went along with things. I don't think he had any really deep beliefs in anything. His father was kind of a [*chuckles*] glib, charming fellow that didn't have a lot of bottom, not a lot of substance. He was a nice guy, but he went along with whatever was going on. He took care of his wife and son and was a good husband and father. And then after his wife died he didn't take much care of anything. Didn't have any money at all for the rest of his life. He dabbled at selling things and he made enough to get by.

GARY So it was his mom who had the higher convictions.

CARLA That's right, she did, and her family had, before that. She was a cradle member of the Church of Christ, Scientist and a reader in the church when she grew up as part of that. She was very highly thought of. And apparently she was an absolute gem, a beautiful woman inside and out. And Don adored her, and she adored him.

GARY You didn't have the opportunity to meet her?

CARLA No, I met Don in something like '65; she died in '63. No, I didn't mean – I meant more like '66.

JIM Didn't you meet him in '62?

CARLA Oh, that's right. I get my decades mixed up.

JIM After so many paths, you know, they just fall off the table. [*laughter*]

CARLA I know [*chuckles*] I'm 70 and I'm just like, *what? What is time?*

GARY 71, actually.

CARLA 71, that's right. I just had a birthday.

GARY Case in point. [*chuckles*]

CARLA There you go! [*laughter*] That's how sharp I am. Anyway, I met his family after she died and became close to the family after she died.

GARY So in order to be a Christian Scientist in the social climate of the time in Kentucky, did one have to stand apart from the crowd? Was that an acceptable thing to be?

CARLA Not at all. It was very acceptable. And they were very, very solid middle class. They had very solid, middle class standards. Sister had taught high school before she married and was a very sharp woman apparently, who was very capable of whatever she'd put her hand to.

GARY Did Don participate in her Christian Science devotion?

CARLA Well, I think in his inner life he pondered the Christian Science dogma and decided that they were as close to right as anything he could come up with; being that everything was an illusion and that spirit was the reality. But he didn't like anything that was formal. He didn't like dressing up to do anything. And so at the age of nine, he bargained with his mom and dad that he would go with them on Sunday if he could stay in the car. Well, they went into service and it's a measure of their relationship that he won his way.

GARY So he probably showed intelligence and responsibility and some self-awareness from an early age.

CARLA Yes, he was precocious in that way. Not in the way of getting As or anything like that, he could care less.

GARY So he didn't apply himself at school?

CARLA Not at all. His mom asked him—she said, "Would you just do it for me one time? Would you just get one good report card?" And he said, "OK," and he did. Once. [*laughter*] Then he went back to tramping the woods on the weekend and not worrying too much about school.

GARY Did he have the sort of personality profile of someone who is very intelligent but doesn't feel quite challenged by school, so he doesn't give it his or her all?

CARLA Right. Nothing ever challenged Don. I remember when he was trying to join Eastern Air Lines, which he did in '65. They had various tests, and one test that they had was supposed to measure how a pilot handled frustration. And so they gave him a little board that had different lights on it and different letters and if you saw this on the board, you hit "A" and "blue"; if you saw that on the board, your response was to hit "B" and "green", and so forth on so on. There were rules, and it started out really slowly so you could check each time. Oh, that's supposed to be "A", "blue"; okay, that's supposed to be "B", "green". And then it started getting a little faster, a little faster and a little faster. Well Don just did it, all the way through to the end. And after a while, it was over, and he had never made a mistake. So they were unable to grade him on that test because he never got frustrated. [*laughter*]

JIM You weren't supposed to pass that test.

CARLA No, you were never supposed to pass it. The idea was to see what happened when you couldn't keep up, how you handled it. And [*chuckles*] they had no idea, but he was remarkably skilled and accurate at anything he put his hand to.

He said of himself that he made a mistake once in 1947, but, he was mistaken. It actually wasn't a mistake. [*laughter*] And that was pretty much true. He didn't make mistakes. He thought quickly, and he thought accurately.

And in terms of knowing people, he could look right through you and see to your heart. It was lovely; I rested in that. A lot of people got spooked: "He can see right through me!" And I'm going, "Yeah, so? Isn't that good? You know, don't you enjoy that?" "No!" [*laughter*] I did.

GARY As it's of a topical association—in terms of Don's grasp of the material world around him and his competency or skill or talent in interacting with that—you also spoke about his sharpshooter skills.

CARLA Yes, like I said, by the age of 15 he was a remarkable sharpshooter. He could throw a bottle cap up in the air, draw, aim, and fire one, two, three times, and make it move in the sky three times.

GARY You also related a story to me once of him at a practicing range?

CARLA Oh, yes. Don was remarkably well-suited to being a non-commissioned officer in the Army. He didn't want to be an officer, and he ended up being the youngest Master Sergeant ever in the history of the Army. He was made a Master Sergeant before the age of 21, which was actually illegal, but he was so good at handling men and making them understand what they needed to understand. And liked doing it. He would make up different ways that they could enjoy it, laugh at it, and still learn it.

This particular day, he was with another couple of his buddies from Male High School who had also joined the Army. This was during the Korean War and in Germany, which was a great place to stay alive. Don enjoyed shooting, so he went his buddies to the range. Well, he wasn't an officer, he wasn't actually allowed on the range, so he asked permission to shoot, to practice with them. And the guy that was running the range said, "Well, we'll try."

And so Don was given a card and was able to shoot one round. He drew, aimed, and emptied his gun very, very quickly and the guy says, "No, no, you shouldn't be doing it that fast." You know, started giving him a lecture. And his friend said, "Uh, pull the card, just pull the card." So he pulled the card to him and you could see his lips moving, the friend reported. [*Carla mimics this.*] And he was counting the little divots; there was only one hole. And he was counting the number of shots that had gone through that hole—nicked a little bit of this or that part of the hole.

JIM It was a scalloped hole.

CARLA Yeah. And all six shots had gone through. So the person in charge stopped the range and he said, "This gentleman is going to give everybody a lesson." [*laughter*] And here he was giving all these officers a lesson. He wasn't even an officer. But that's how good he was. And he was just very, very good at that world of men that includes hunting and shooting and playing poker and laughing and being a pilot and buzzing water towers and having a good time. That was his world for a long time.

He grew out of it. He didn't stay a boy forever. He grew up, but he always enjoyed the company of other men, rather than enjoying the company of women. He did not date; he did not go out with women. He did not take part at all in anything to do with the social rights of the time.

GARY From what do you think that stemmed? Was that a part of his cultural conditioning?

CARLA Well no, I think it was his philosophy. As he grew up, he observed that his father worked very, very hard all the time so that he could put a roof over his mother's and his head, and his father was basically a slave to that, was the way he looked at it.

Don looked around him and he saw all the other guys . . . you know, this was back before women's lib when women stayed at home and the men took care of them and paid the bills and made it possible for them to have children. And the women ran the home and gave them a family, and it was considered a good deal by everybody. But it wasn't considered a good deal by Don.[†] It was considered, by him, that a woman was nabbing the guy when he was in the midst of lust and nailing him down for life to a world of giving the woman a cave and a place where she could raise her cubs, and then becoming a slave to that. And he didn't want to become a slave to that. He didn't want to take care of some family, some bunch of kids. He didn't like kids. [*laughter*] He said if they could be born 17, it would be okay, but younger than that, he wasn't really interested in talking to them.

He was just very cold about it and very judgmental. And I know in his relationship with me, he always kind of wished that I wasn't a woman, and was very grateful to me for not insisting that he step up to the plate and deliver his life to me, so that I could furnish my cave and have some cubs.

GARY So he felt confined and imprisoned by what women wanted.

CARLA Imprisoned and for no good reason. He just didn't see it at all. [*chuckles*] And I could sympathize with the point of view to a certain extent. I think that there was a lot of usage of men by women.

[†] It's a safe bet to assume that Don wasn't the *only* one who didn't think that the traditional, patriarchal arrangement was a good deal.

Manipulation and so forth. Women setting their hats for men and doing it very deliberately, nailing them down. But there are always problems with any arrangement that you have. Now you've got more of an equal situation, but it's still a man's world. There's still a glass ceiling women can't bust through. And women still can't pull down the salaries that men do. And the thinking really goes back to when men had to take care of the family by earning money and women did not.

GARY So, you described how Don joked that if he could have a child that was born 17 years old, that would be okay with him. Was he someone who, like you, was born somewhat of an adult, you might say, in a child's body?

CARLA I guess so, in a way. Although, I always wanted to please the people around me and he really didn't care. [*chuckles*] He didn't give a hoot. Just to give you an example of what I mean, when Don's father died, I went through the whole apartment—bits and pieces of the life that Tully and Sister had lived were still around and had never been thrown out. One thing I found was a little packet of postcards that were stamped and addressed to Sister, and she must have given them to Don when he went to Germany. And he carried them with him, faithfully, the whole time and brought them home and left them in the apartment there. [*laughter*] And there they were when Don's father, Tully, died. Don had never thrown them out. He valued his mother, but he didn't use them.

GARY She had intended that he would use them to communicate with her from Germany.

CARLA She wanted him to communicate. He wasn't a communicator.

GARY He's not the type that's going to call his mom or write his mom.

CARLA No, not at all.

GARY Because that's an obligation, and he doesn't need to fulfill that obligation.

CARLA Yeah, what I faced when he first moved in with me, he said, "Well, I'm going to go." And I said, "Oh, any idea when you'll be back?" I'm planning my day, I need to know.

Well he said, "My mother asked me that once and I told her, 'If you ask me that again I'm going to move out.'" Cold, very cold. Well, I took that in and devised a plan, a plan which ended up working very well. But I had to start where he was.

GARY So just a couple more questions about his boyhood. Did he get into trouble at all, or was he a well-behaved person?

CARLA Never, no. He was not a trouble-maker in any way, shape or form. He was a very polite, courteous young man that knew all the rules and followed them, and knew where the wheels needed to be greased and slid around very skillfully. Everybody thought well of Don.

GARY Was he an avid reader growing up?

CARLA Well, he didn't really much like to read. He liked someone to read to him. His mother read him a lot of books. I read him a lot of books, after we had settled down. He liked knowing things, and the quickest way he could find to get to inform himself on a subject, he would do that. But he wouldn't do more than was necessary.

GARY In the opening section of this interview, you described that he began to become aware that the scientific paradigms of the time, and even the sum of human knowledge, couldn't explain a universe that he had sensed, and was mysterious. So it caused him to begin seeking beyond the boundaries.

CARLA Right.

GARY How old was he at that time?

CARLA 14, maybe 15. Very young.

GARY So he began to become awakened, you might say, around that time.

CARLA Mm-hmm.

GARY Sounds like he was already fairly awakened from early on.

CARLA Right. And he was a very deep thinker. You had only to know Don to realize the depth and the breadth of his intellect. He was a wonderful mind, an extremely capable thinker. Very accurate and very far reaching. I always totally enjoyed Don and respected him tremendously. He was really the only great man I ever knew.

GARY What do you mean by "great"?

CARLA Well, he exceeded all the boundaries of normal human knowledge and he was totally upright, completely ethical, devoted to learning more about *why*, trying to put the puzzle pieces together. Very, very steady. His thinking had a depth and breadth that always took your breath, to me. And I'm a smart cat. There aren't many that are smarter than I am, but Don was maybe three times my intellect.

GARY Don was 18 years old was when the Thomas Mantell case transpired and first set Don on the trajectory of UFOs?

CARLA Is that what you figured out?

JIM Actually it was 17.

GARY 17?

JIM Mantell was in January, Don's birthday was in February; month difference.

GARY So, he joined the military at 18.

CARLA I'm not sure precisely when he did that, but he was, like I said, he was a Master Sergeant before he was 21.[1]

GARY Do you know why he joined the military?

CARLA Yeah, he joined the military so that he wouldn't have to go to Korea. He joined the Reserves.

GARY Was there a draft for Korea?

CARLA Yes, there was a draft, and he was up for it. He was prime. A-1. He wanted to fulfill his service. It wasn't that he was trying to duck out of anything, but he would just as soon not get shot at, he would just as soon not shoot anybody.

GARY How long was his contract with the Army Reserves?

CARLA Gosh, I think maybe 4 years.

CARLA But after he got back from Germany, he became an officer and eventually a captain in the Reserves. He served the Reserves for, I think, 13 years after he came back.

GARY So maybe 17 years in total, ballpark.

CARLA Something like that, yeah. I know he had to quit it when he became an Eastern Air Lines pilot, and that was in '65.

GARY So he was actively engaged in his quest for the truth while in the military, and in the direction of UFOs.

CARLA Yes.

GARY Do you know how he went about his research while in the military, or if those two fields overlapped whatsoever?

CARLA I don't think those two fields overlapped. I know he talked a lot about reading reports. That was his favorite thing to do: just to sit there, as a captain in the Reserves, and read reports of military men in the past, just to see how things transpired. He had wonderful stories to tell about reading those. I think he was just interested in a wide variety of things and just . . . wherever he was, he wanted to know more about it, I guess.

GARY So in trying to put together the social side of Don, I've heard it described that he didn't enjoy humanity and also avoided people, but at the same time he seems kind of gregarious or very able to read and talk to people.

CARLA Well, different people have different reactions to alcohol. Don was a gregarious drunk. [*laughter*] I never saw him *drunk*-drunk; I never saw the man the least bit out of control. The most I ever saw him out of control was one time I noticed he parked a little crooked. He was still between the lines, but the car was just a little bit crooked. [*laughter*] That's the farthest he went out of control, but he would become increasingly charming the more beers he had or the more whiskey he drank. And did he drink because he liked alcohol? No, he drank because he was with his buddies, and they were drinking; he just went along.

GARY So he could be a very social creature.

CARLA A very, very social, charming, wonderful creature that I dearly loved. I loved him to be drunk. [*laughter*] I had no complaints about that at all.

GARY But for all intents and purposes nobody could tell whether he had not had any drinks or whether—

CARLA No, except that he would break out with more stories when he was a little bit soused. It's a lifestyle thing. All his friends were pilots, guys in the army, and there's a certain amount of drinking that goes on. There used to be more than I think there is now. Now there are more acceptable ways of getting high, but in those days it was all alcohol. And so guys met at the bar, and they hung out and they would have one beer and then another beer and then, you know, they would proceed. [*laughter*] And then depending on how long their evening was, they could drink a lot of beer. Or, if they were drinking whiskey, drink a lot of whiskey. But I never saw him have a hangover; never saw him *drunk*. Never saw it interrupt his lifestyle in any way. He didn't have a problem. But he did drink a lot.

GARY Did he have any like minds in his social circle?

CARLA No, not really. Not in terms of people that were interested in pursuing metaphysical interests. He had plenty of friends that tolerated him and thought he was interesting and got him to tell stories. There was a lot of acceptance there, and a lot of just plain old love—the kind of love men have for each other. Good, sturdy, shoot 'em up love. And it was good to be part of that. It was good to see Don with his buddies and feel the energy there of their mutual fondness and affection, respect for each other. They were all good men. They were all worthwhile, upright, trying-to-do-the-right-thing guys.

GARY Did he maintain those connections all way through the Ra contact?

CARLA Mm-hmm. Well, everything went away during the Ra contact. Up until that point, yeah, he would spend time with his friends.

GARY So there were a few different vocations that Don took on beyond being an instrument and a questioner for channeling groups. Among his vocations, how and why did Don become a physics and engineering professor?

CARLA He picked engineering because it seemed more what he might use and be interested in in the long run. He basically needed to go to college because if he didn't do that he would have to work, and he didn't want to work. He didn't want to go get a job 9-to-5 and be in an office. He knew that he wouldn't like that, and he never did it. He was a teacher, and he was a pilot. And neither of those vocations pinned you down from 9-to-5 with a cubicle and so forth.

And once he was in college, he discovered that he was very, very good at it without much effort, and sailed through. All of his professors thought a lot of him. He discovered that he was a natural teacher, and he discovered that it was something that he could do without moving a muscle, without knowing more. But he did constantly read a little of this, a little of that, and was constantly looking for paranormal instances of anything in the newspapers and magazines and so forth. And he shared those with his students.

GARY So he earned two separate degrees? One in physics, one in engineering? And then taught both?

CARLA No, his degrees were in engineering. He earned up through the masters, and then he had a professional degree in addition to that.[2]

GARY But he taught both engineering and physics?

CARLA Yeah. The reason that he taught physics was that nobody else could handle those guys. They were a rowdy bunch. 200 students is a big class. All of the entering freshmen had to take physics, and it had long been tossed from the newest guy, to the next newest guy, to the next newest guy. Nobody wanted the job.

JIM They were all male. There were no females in the Engineering Department at that time.

CARLA Right. And these guys would do lots and lots of little pranks and make the guy look stupid. And most guys can't handle stuff like that. Well, Don could handle that with one hand tied behind his back and his eyes closed. He would turn it right back on them and continue teaching. I've given examples like, one day, all of his 200 students said, "Okay, we're going to throw pennies at him." So they threw this massive bunch of pennies at him. So he spends time and he picks up every single penny, and he says, "Next time, bigger coins," and turns around and starts teaching. So then they leave a dead cat in the lab sink, and he covers it up and continues teaching. They were just trying so hard to get him flustered.

And they arranged with one of the girlfriends of one of the students, who had a job as a bunny at a local bunny club, and she brought her costume from work and dressed up as a bunny and brought in a martini, covered with a napkin, at the beginning of class. So he watches her come in. And she doesn't know what to do, so she finally just sets the thing down and disappears—you know, runs for her life. So he raises the napkin and looks at it and he says, "Too much vermouth." So then [*laughter*] he goes back to working on the board, teaching. He couldn't be flustered! He always had a comeback and his guys ended up absolutely adoring him and doing whatever he said. He was an excellent teacher.

He got all the points across, and he was very conscious of the pressures that men were under at that time. Some of them had to get a certain grade because they were in the Army; if they didn't get that grade they didn't get their scholarship. He would always give them an extra grade: if they were C students they got a B, and if they were B students they got an A. Why? Because they needed it. And that kind of understanding—of how he can best nurture young men . . . he would give them a quiz every Friday. And then he would add up the scores and drop the lowest one. Everybody has a bad day from time to time. And the balance of that would be their grade. And usually you can remember what you've been looking at that week, so it was the best possible chance that the young men had to make a good grade.

And just things like that—the excellent teaching skills, the love of springing one crazy fact on them at the end of every class, so that it wasn't just physics, it was always physics plus an interesting factoid. [*laughter*] Like the inside of a Snapple cap at the end of every class. So his men got through; they knew physics. They passed and they were able to go on. So, he really was valued more for his ability to work with the freshmen than for the mechanical engineering courses that he taught, simply because he could do it so much better than anybody else.

GARY What years did he teach?

CARLA Well, he started after he got back from the Korean War.

JIM '55 to '65?

CARLA Something like that. He left in '65 to go join Eastern Air Lines and be a pilot because they were making roughly three times the amount as a pilot than he did as a teacher, and he could use that money to pay for his research. So it just made sense to him to do that.

GARY Where did he teach?

CARLA He taught at Speed Scientific School,[3] which was the engineering school of the University of Louisville in Louisville, Kentucky.

GARY Both physics and engineering at that school.

CARLA Mm-hmm.

GARY I was going to ask you about that. I recall you speaking previously in this interview of Don learning to fly, and it seemed connected to his research.

CARLA It was.

GARY So all of the motivation for learning to fly and gaining a job as an airline pilot was as a means to an end?

CARLA Yes, but he enjoyed flying too. He just enjoyed it in and of itself. And so he always maintained a healthy amount of flying people around—charter groups—for the various flying services in town. And he kept that up all the time that he was teaching. He was also building up his hours being a charter pilot.

GARY Once he stopped teaching for Speed Scientific School in '65 or thereabouts, did he ever return to being a teacher?

CARLA No. The only thing that he did that was unusual was, one year he went up to Alaska, the University of Alaska in Fairbanks. He had been given the opportunity to be the head of the engineering school and to set their curriculum. And that was a big deal. And he took it. And he said if we had been together he would have stuck to it, but the winters were too long and lonely. He didn't like them. He didn't like the length of the winters and the darkness of it. So he came on back after one year.

GARY What year was he there?

CARLA It has to have been before '65, obviously.

JIM I think it was 1961.

CARLA It was before I was in college. It would have to be before '62.

GARY Okay. So you weren't up there with him.

CARLA No.

GARY It was him alone.

In the recording, "Spiritual Significance of the UFO," Don is giving a talk in what I thought was a classroom auditorium at the University of Louisville, regarding his UFO research. What year was that?

CARLA Oh, maybe something like '77?

JIM No, it was '82 or '83 because we had the Ra contact then.

CARLA Oh, '82, okay.[4]

JIM It was Jefferson Community College. Downtown.

CARLA He was offering it at a sister college that was actually part of the University of Kentucky system, not part of University of Louisville at all. And it was just a one-time thing. One of the students there had asked him if he would give a lecture, so he did.

GARY Oh, he was sort of a special guest.

CARLA Yeah, he was a guest there. He wasn't hired by the college or anything.

GARY Okay. How far did he go flying for Eastern Air Lines? I mean, to what destinations?

CARLA Well, he was based in Atlanta mostly. He was based sometimes in Florida. He went all kinds of places within the United States and then down in the islands. He went wherever Eastern Air Lines had routes that they had paid for and they needed somebody to fill.

GARY He didn't fly internationally then.

CARLA He did not, no. He did not. He was not one of those who did.

GARY And you described that he would use the local airport in Louisville, named Bowman Field, to rent small charter planes and fly to destinations in order to conduct his personal research.

CARLA Mm-hmm. That's right.

GARY At some point Don made an important decision about how he would operate and relate to this world. Can you tell us when that decision happened, and then describe that decision and its implications?

CARLA I'm sorry, what decision was that?

JIM Becoming indifferent to the world. That was twenty—

CARLA Oh. Twenty-six. He was 26 years old.

GARY And what was that decision?

CARLA Well, he decided that he was dead. He no longer was interested in anything the world had to offer, and nothing was ever going to move him again.

GARY So he consciously, basically, said to himself—

CARLA Very consciously released the world and all its strictures.

GARY I am indifferent to . . .

CARLA He didn't want anything to do with it anymore. I'm not sure precisely what brought him to this, but he was a very sharp guy, and the world is as it is. His reaction to it is logical.

GARY So this is long before you met him.

CARLA Yes.

GARY He must have told you about this incident.

CARLA Right.

GARY How did he describe it to you?

CARLA That way.

GARY He said, "I decided to . . . "

CARLA To die.

GARY Did he tell you why he made that decision?

CARLA No. [*laughter*] Don never explained himself. I really don't know what brought him to it, but I think it was simply a logical outcome of his observations up to that point. I think the world basically terrified him and disgusted him. It was rough, it was crude, it was tacky, and nobody kept promises—out there in the world of business and finance and so forth. The higher you went, the more you were going to be lying and cheating and stealing, all in the name of business. He wasn't interested in taking part in any of it.[5]

GARY So he had a very pessimistic view of the world.

CARLA He was a melancholy man.

JIM His famous quote was, "This world is an insane asylum, and the best you could hope for is a private room."

GARY That's funny that he devoted so much—all of his life to this research when he perceived the world that way. He must have perceived that there is some redeeming value in the world nevertheless, or there's some way to uplift the horrible situation that—

JIM This world isn't all there is. There's more, and he was interested in the more.

GARY But he didn't just escape to that more.

CARLA It wasn't escape, it was getting below the surface of things, getting to the essence as he saw it, and trying to find out why things were as they were. *Why are we here? What is the idea? What's going on?*

GARY But not just for his personal individual satisfaction, though that too, but in order to share it with others.

CARLA Well, he was a scientist. If he found something, some result of his research that was worthwhile publishing, he published it. It was not, *all these people have to know this.* It was dispassionate. It was, *time to publish what I've learned.*

GARY So, this decision he made at 26 years old wasn't just a philosophical response to the world, but it was a survival mechanism as well.

CARLA I guess so, yeah. It was—he was, I don't even want to say happy, but he coped better when he had made that decision.

GARY And he stuck by it.

CARLA To give you an idea of how much he did not want to date: I met a woman once—she was close to 50 when I met her, she was his age—and she told me that their parents were friends and they had arranged for him to date her. Well, she was absolutely gorgeous. She was everything you could want: she was sharp, she was intelligent, she was funny, she was beautiful, she was—she was ready to like him, right?

So he's roped in to it. And his mother asked, "Will you please do this?" And he says, "Alright, I'll do it." And he does. Never opens his mouth. Picks her up, takes her where his parents had planned for him to go, gave her a meal, brought her home, dropped her off. Never said a word. His parents did not try to get him to date anymore. [*laughter*] And you can imagine that I was somewhat flattered that he settled down with me. It was a great compliment that he managed to stay with me. Great devotion! He didn't leave. [*laughs*]

GARY I have a vague memory of you describing how he somehow rated or evaluated you. Does that sound familiar?

CARLA You mean my beauty?

GARY You in general.

CARLA He told me one time that I was the best person he knew. That was the nicest thing he ever said about me.

GARY One of just a couple compliments that you ever received from him.

CARLA He was very drunk. [*laughter*]

GARY So you'd see a little bit of the *inside Don* when he drank.

CARLA Yeah, a little bit. Yeah. He let down a little bit. Not all of it. Concrete steel was still reinforced around his heart.

GARY So this decision he made when he was 26 years old carried forward all the way through to the Ra contact until the final couple years when that came undone too rapidly for him.

CARLA Yes, indeed.

GARY So you've described Don as a melancholy man. Was he withdrawn and not engaged or did he laugh or smile?

CARLA Oh, sure. But all the way into his eyes and into his heart? Not a lot. No.

GARY So there's an underlying sadness . . .

CARLA Yes, it was a sadness, a melancholia that was very deep and very, very real.

GARY So on the surface, he would enjoy himself or be sociable or gregarious and laugh and smile, but underneath there was always that melancholia that was always untouched.

CARLA Always, yeah. It was a loneliness, I think, because once he discovered that he could hang out with me, that he didn't have to be lonely, he would call me numerous times a day when he was off on trips. And at night he'd call me, and he wouldn't even say anything. He'd just hang on the phone and listen to me breathe. And that made him happy. Made me happy too.

GARY So you didn't need to talk, you just . . .

CARLA I loved him. I loved him dearly. I just adored him.

GARY It's always problematic to try to answer this type of question, but if there were an antidote to his melancholia, what do you think that would be?

CARLA Conversations with Ra. [*chuckles*] That was the only thing that I ever saw bring him into happiness. He was joy-filled when he knew he was going to get to talk to Ra. It was like before a feast: he would [*makes a sort of tisking sound from the mouth*] do that with his mouth, which he always did before I cooked. He knew I could cook really well, and when it was time to eat one of my meals he'd [*make same sound*] love every bite. And that's the way he was about those conversations.

GARY Speaking of the deliciousness of your cooking, he eventually asked you not to cook, right?

CARLA That's right. Well, he had gained 40 pounds. [*laughter*] He said, "You're going to be the ruin of me if you keep doing this." But it was hard to get me to stop. He eventually made me stop entirely. It was so sad for me because I'd gotten all his mother's recipes and I knew how to make him happy. I knew how to make his tummy happy. [*chuckles*] And it was so much fun to see him enjoy food, and I enjoyed that service very, very much.

GARY I think this question is already answered, but just to be clear: Did Don have any intimate or committed relationships prior to meeting you, with a female?

CARLA No. [*chuckles*] Anything but.

GARY Was Don involved in politics in any way?

CARLA No.

GARY So the Civil Rights struggle and the struggle for social equality across the board was really taking shape and gaining momentum in the mid-fifties—Brown vs. Board of Education[6] time. How did he relate to the social movements of the time? Or was he just as indifferent to that as he was to the rest of the happenings in the world?

CARLA Yes. Yes, he was indifferent. He didn't have anything against those who were fighting for the rights. He respected them, he didn't talk against them; he just wasn't one of them. He wasn't one of the others, either. He just was not involved.

GARY Was this part of the world milieu that he turned an indifferent eye toward?

CARLA Quite. Exactly.

GARY Would you say that Don was single-minded in his research and pursuit of truth, and if so, how did he balance that with the other necessities of living?

CARLA Don paid the bills, and whatever time and money he had leftover was ready to be spent working in this research.

GARY So he wasn't a Captain Ahab in pursuit of the truth, in kind of just becoming overwhelmed and crazy about it.

CARLA [*laughter*] No, he wasn't.

GARY He kept everything in perspective.

CARLA He was very sane. And very effective.

GARY Though each of you three possess strengths not so pronounced in the other, Don Elkins was the leader of your small band. What made him the leader?

JIM Charisma and intelligence. And a great path to follow down the road to the paranormal.

CARLA And neither of us was foolish enough to think that we were better at it than he was. We knew he was a leader among us and we were glad to have him.[7]

GARY This may be already covered, but in the event we can dig something new out of here: What characteristics about Don stand out to you?

JIM Intelligence. Character. Sensitivity. Compassion. Capability. Dedication. Perseverance. And he was tall!

CARLA He was very, very tall. Six-six I think. He always said six-five, because that was the limit for Eastern Air Lines. If he was six-six he couldn't be a pilot for Eastern. As a matter of fact, I think he always said six-four, but I think he was six-six. Anyway, six and a half feet, basically, tall.

GARY In pictures I've seen him in, he looks like he droops a little, leans forward.

CARLA He always did. He was trying to relate to the world below him. *What did you say?* [*laughing*]

JIM When he was in school he was trying to hide behind the fat kid, so the teacher wouldn't see him.

CARLA Yeah, he had no desire to attract attention. He had the gift of being invisible. He could sit there and waitresses wouldn't see him, people would come and go—they didn't see him. I don't know how he did that. But he could choose to become invisible. It was an odd ability.

GARY It sounds like, unless he took a liking to you, he didn't want to be approached or didn't want to be talked to.

CARLA Right. He was a loner through and through.

GARY Is there anything about Don that might surprise people?

CARLA That he was so good with kids, probably.

GARY That would surprise me, too.

CARLA He was wonderful with kids, yeah.

JIM He never talked down to them. He always talked just like he talks to you and me.

CARLA They always adored him, just like everybody else. I think that was the biggest surprise I ever had, was realizing that he had no problem relating to kids. He liked kids just fine. As long as they weren't his.[‡] [*laughs*]

GARY Jim, what kind of relationship did you form with Don after meeting him and Carla, and then living together in community?

JIM Hmm. That was probably one of the most important relationships of my life, but one of the most difficult to describe. It felt like we were brothers, and we had the same basic goals, and we were both dedicated to getting *there* doing whatever is necessary. So we had a shared vision and we both very much wanted to take care of Carla.

And I never felt that I really got to know him the way I wanted to. We were only together for four years, the four years of the Ra contact. So it was a beginning relationship, but it was one that already had taken place elsewhere. It was like renewing a friendship. But in our current personae, [*chuckles*] we had to work our way through what we'd constructed here in

---

[‡] Maybe Don's relationship to the concept or the reality of kids was complex, or ambiguous, or not properly communicated, as this statement from Carla seems *slightly* at odds with her previous statement in this chapter, though not irreconcilable.

this illusion. And we hadn't gotten there yet. I was looking forward to that. I was looking forward to being on, like, some farm someplace and splitting firewood with him. But that didn't happen.

GARY Don felt that he was a wanderer in the sense that his soul incarnated here on Earth from another density in order to be of service. When and how did he become aware of this, and how did he relate to this understanding or belief?

CARLA I think it happened during the Ra contact. When the Ra group introduced the idea of wanderers, he just really related to that, really identified with that. I don't think he specifically thought he was from another planet or anything beforehand. He certainly didn't feel like he belonged anywhere. He was a wanderer in that general sense, but not in the specific sense of feeling he came from elsewhere.[8]

GARY Some wanderers—and I've always found this particularly remarkable—are born knowing that their soul is not of this planet, even prior to encountering any information that might suggest that idea to them. They just know.

So to the best of your awareness, Don didn't have that.

CARLA He wasn't one of them. Hmm. Nor was I, for that matter. That had to be kind of sprung on me in the process of our research.

GARY I was actually going to ask you guys this in your personal bio sections, but, while I'm here: you discovered that through your past-life regression hypnosis—

CARLA Right, which was part of our research together.

GARY So do you know what kind of impact that had on Don, discovering that he was a wanderer?

CARLA I think he was really glad to have found such a good source that was evidential to him about this information being true. He trusted me and he knew that I had had this experience during the session of hypnotism, and I think he was glad that it happened. Glad that I was a wanderer.

GARY When people write to L/L Research on the topic of "Am I a wanderer?" "Is there any value in knowing that I am a wanderer?", etc., I highlight two reasons why I think it is of value to know you are a wanderer, one being that it helps to bring the life into a perspective that might have been unavailable beforehand.[9]

CARLA Mm-hmm. That's true, it does.

GARY All the things you couldn't explain about yourself, especially the sense of alienation, suddenly come into view. So it gives an ordering to the life.

CARLA Right. Plus, for so many people, they have a feeling of having a mission, but that's not a respected idea in our culture. That's considered *maybe you need to have some psychiatry done, a little analysis there to find out where you got this distortion.* But, the Wanderer Syndrome includes that feeling of having a mission, and the thing is, it's very comforting to know that you're not the only one that has this feeling of being under the gun.

GARY Yeah, and that ties into the second thing I highlight, and that's that knowing you're a wanderer helps to underscore the fact that you are here to offer service. The whole reason for your existence on this planet is to help other people.

CARLA Right.

GARY Though if that sense of mission turns into a messiah complex, then maybe there's some ego in there.

CARLA Yeah, you need to stay humble with it. But yes, exactly. You need to keep your proportion—your sense of proportion is very important. Otherwise, you get all emotional and feeling that this is so important, and you burn yourself out, to where you can't really proceed for a while. You have to heal up, sit by the side of the spiritual road and just breathe. And it's better for the long run to always keep the light touch. Always have a sense of proportion.

GARY Yeah, you're still human. You still have human challenges and human lessons to learn. And a sense of wandererhood needn't feed some special sense of identity, like *I am better than others.*

CARLA Mm-hmm. There's that very ticklish characteristic of feeling like the elite, and that's always wrong. Wrong, wrong, wrong.

GARY Returning back to Don. Per the descriptions you've shared with me of Don, he seemed set in some rather peculiar ways. Can you describe any of those?

CARLA Well, he was always heavily armed. I always thought that was a little peculiar. My father wouldn't allow a gun in the house. With Don, we had a gun in every room, tucked in the radiator housing.

You know, he was a loner. He wanted to be celibate. Is that what you're going for? He was peculiar in every single way you want to look at, so it's difficult for me to know where you're going.

GARY Eccentricities and behaviors that one would describe as odd.

JIM When we went out to eat, we usually went out in the middle of the afternoon so the restaurant would be empty. And when we went to a movie, we always sat in the back row.

GARY In order to reduce all social contact?

JIM Pretty much, yeah.

CARLA The most defensible position is in the back row or in the corner, so that nobody could get behind you.

GARY So was he one of those types that kind of had the room mapped out? Mentally he knew where the exit was, he knew how to defend himself should something go south.

CARLA Oh yeah. Definitely. And he wanted to take care of me. It wasn't just to take care of himself, but needed to know how to get *me* out of there. [*laughter*] But he was quite careful to do that everywhere he went, and map the place out, to sit in the most defensible position where nobody could get behind him. And he liked as few people in the restaurant when he ate as possible.

[*laughs in reflection of what she's about to say*] And he would reconnoiter—this used to drive me crazy. He would go into the parking lot, and he would do a reconnoitering walk around the restaurant to see what it was like and if it was acceptable. If there was a place where he could sit that he was comfortable with and so forth, we'd go in. If there was a problem, if there was somebody in there he didn't want to eat with, if there was any kind of a problem, we couldn't go there. We'd move on. So then we'd go to another restaurant—fortunately there were quite a few restaurants in Louisville—and he would repeat the procedure. Sometimes we didn't eat till 10:30 at night. [*laughter*] It was so hard to find a restaurant that he found okay.

GARY You said he wouldn't tell you his reasons for . . .

CARLA [*to Jim*] Do you remember him telling us reasons?

JIM Just wanted to see what the situation was. He had the same behavior as a captain for Eastern Air Lines. He'd walk around his plane and look at everything very carefully. He wanted to be sure that it was, you know, flight-worthy. And that's a really good quality for an airline pilot. But he used that same quality with whatever he did. He was aware of things around him. Potential problems that other people wouldn't think of.

CARLA Yep, that was Don.

GARY Would you say this was a strength or a paranoia?

CARLA Both.

JIM Well, strengths and weaknesses are two ends of the same quality. Just depends on how far you're going and what happens.

CARLA If you were really hungry it was paranoia, and if you were looking at it generally philosophically, it was a great strength.

GARY Carla, you understood Don on a fundamental level, and realized that in order to work with him, you had to release expectations and meet him where he was, not vice versa. You had to make sacrifices and concessions and operate within his parameters. Can you describe that dynamic and why you put his needs before your own?

CARLA I think love has a sacrificial quality to it, or it can have if it's needed. Don was the loneliest man I ever knew. My heart went out to him on so many levels. My poor guy! Everybody else would see this huge, tall, imposing, scary guy, and I would see this little lost boy that was so lonely. And I just wanted to take him, and take care of him, and make it okay. I loved him so much.

And so, whatever it was that he needed I was wanting to do. I wasn't proud. I knew that he couldn't fulfill all my needs. So I figured out what I did need, what I really did need, and then I made sure that I got it. For instance, when he first knew me he asked me to marry him.[§] That was the first night that he moved in, and when he came back after that

---

[§] Carla offers a fuller telling of this story in the chapter of this book where Don meets Carla.

three-day trip, he reneged and said he really didn't want to marry, and so we wouldn't marry. And I was desperately unhappy with that and I cried. Well, he didn't like tears, so he went into his room and closed the door. [*laughter*] And that was going to be the end of it; that was going to be goodnight.

But that was unacceptable to me; that did not meet my needs. So I thought it through (didn't take long), and I went into the kitchen and I got a little juice-glass of water, made sure it was tepid, not too hot, not too cold, and I opened the door to his room and I went in and he was in his bed pretending to be asleep. And I poured it on him.

And he sputtered and sat up and said, "You poured water on me!" I said, "Yes I did. And I will continue to do so until you ask me what it is I need." And he said, "Okay, what do you need?" I said, "I need you—when I cry, I need you to realize that I never use it; it's not a manipulative thing. I'm just desperately unhappy. I need you to pat me on the back, and I need you to tell me that everything is okay, and reassure me until I am over crying, and we're okay again."

And he took it in, and he said, [*Carla gestures a steady patting motion*] "You are on a planet at the very ends of space." (pat, pat, pat, pat) "You're sticking up out of this planet along with everyone else." (pat, pat, pat, pat) And he would continue to tell me what a tiny piece of the Creator I was, and how—[*laughter*] it sounds crazy, but how insignificant we all were, and how tiny our planet was, and how huge the universe was. And he would just continue doing that. And, whenever I cried from then on through the years, then he would very seriously, very conscientiously start doing that. And that was his way of comforting me. And it really, oddly enough, was very comforting, simply because he wanted it to be comforting.

GARY He was trying.

CARLA And it was an effort that he was making. So it worked. It satisfied my need not to be closed off simply because I was crying. He never could understand why I was unhappy. I had told him, "If you don't want to be married, say so, because I don't want another bad marriage."

He took me at my word—why should that make me unhappy? Oh, I don't know! [*laughter*] It did! What can I say? So, it was a matter of: Do I want to take care of this man? Do I want to be with this man? Or, do I want to go back into the world and find someone who will fulfill more of my so-called needs? And he always came out on top. I can't say any more than that. My depth of love for him was enormous.

And so I would figure out—well for instance, here's the way I figured out the problem with his going out of the house and not telling me where he was going or when he'd be back. The next time he went out of the house, I said, "Can I go with you?" He said, "What? You're just going to have to wait in the car. You don't want to go into the flying service with me." And I said, "Okay, I'll wait in the car." So for quite some months, actually, I would take a book with me and I would sit in the car and I would wait for him; it was a big car, very comfortable. And I would read, and if I got sleepy I would sleep. And I would wait for him and eventually he'd come out and we'd have lunch and then he'd go do something else and I would wait and then we'd go to. It was a way of being with him, the only way I had of being with him, and I accepted that.

So, he got used to having me with him, and eventually one of his pilot friends saw me in the car and said, "Well, come on in. What are you doing in the car?" And I said, "Well, Don doesn't think I would be really welcome there; and you know, I'm not a pilot"—blah, blah, blah. So he said, "That's not true! Come on in! You'll see." So I, in fear and trepidation, went with him. And sure enough, everybody was glad to see me. I was well-accepted and one of the gang. Just a little guy with long hair. So it worked out fine. And so Don was able to take me in with him after that, which meant I didn't get as much reading done, but that was okay too.

And once he got used to me being with him, he got used to that feeling of not being alone. Because far below the level of physical nearness or anything like that—you know, like conversation—I was home to him, and he was home to me on a very, very deep level. It was comforting for him to be with me. He was comforted by my presence. And I was very glad that I could do that for him. And of course, he was my beloved, a comfort—it was very comfortable for me to be with him. So, it worked out great and I never challenged him. I just worked around his needs and so that I could fulfill mine without bothering him.

GARY When he was patting you, per your request, and telling you that we live on such and such a planet, we're pretty insignificant compared to the whole . . . it sounds like you were hearing some of his own inner dialogue.

What he must tell himself.

CARLA Mm-hmm. I expect so.

GARY How would Don introduce you to others when you would meet new people?

CARLA My name.

GARY Would he say, "This is my friend Carla. My research associate"—?

CARLA He didn't go into that.

GARY Oh. He just said, "This is Carla"?

CARLA Yeah.

GARY I was wondering if that might give some insight into—

CARLA Oh, no, it was not a matter of avoidance; it was just not part of his dialogue, for people to explain somebody. He was very proud of me, and used to brag on how smart I was, with all the skills that I had, and the things that I could do—that I could sing and so forth. He thought I was a great gal and had wonderful skills and he was pleased with my research for him, and he would talk to people about that. So I guess we related as research partners.

GARY So he, despite his profound loneliness, and the sadness and melancholy that stemmed from the loneliness, and despite his great need for you, he didn't quite know how to let you in. So it was only through you being patient with his own road blocks and working with his blockages that you slowly . . . that he found ways to let you in and bring you closer.

CARLA Yes. Yes.

GARY Was Don someone that allowed or enjoyed physical touch?

CARLA No.

GARY So there was no hugging Don.

CARLA No.

GARY How about shaking hands? He didn't shake hands?

CARLA If he had to.

GARY [*chuckles*] So otherwise he was very cut off from other people in that sense.

CARLA Mm-hmm. Yes. Yes. *I am an island.* Not in a rude way. Some people just don't enjoy touch.

GARY Is there anything else that you could think that you might want to share about Don before—

CARLA Uh, no. Certainly if you look at the way he treated Jim and me, he was always very responsible, and even though he didn't want responsibility, when he felt that he was responsible for our group, for making the money for it, he wrote it—he had a will written out, so that we'd be taken care of if he died. That kind of probity, that kind of care, speaks of very, very deep uprightness and affection and character, that you might not guess looking at the lonely guy, the melancholy man.

GARY Beyond probing the archetypal mind through the tarot, do you know if Don had hopes of exploring other avenues of inquiry with Ra?

JIM I'm sure he did. [*laughter*] We didn't talk a lot about what we were going to do in the distant future, we were focused on the next session.

CARLA Yeah.

GARY You said of Don that he hoped to communicate this information to a large number of people and felt real urgency in getting the word out. Don said to Ra:

> QUESTIONER I personally will not cease while still incarnate to attempt to disseminate this. 37.5

Was it difficult for Don to accept that this information likely wouldn't make a big splash in the Earthly world?

JIM I don't know if it's difficult or not. I know that he was hoping to get it out to as many people as possible, make it generally available. At that time we really didn't know how we were going to do that.

CARLA It surprised him that more people weren't interested. The depth of people's desire to remain ignorant surprised him. It was a very innocent, honest reaction that he had. He was so interested himself that he really didn't see why people were almost allergic to learning the truth about UFOs. Are they here or not? He was glad to tell them anything that he knew! But most people just would say, "I don't believe in UFOs." Well, he never took that as a challenge, he just said "okay" and went on. But it surprised him that people—he could almost bet they would not be interested.

GARY I think people experience echoes of the same feeling when their own world is lit up by this information—they feel it's one of the best things since sliced bread, and they can't understand why others don't feel likewise.

CARLA [*laughter*] Yeah. Yeah, I have to encourage some people that are so excited like that just to lay off, let people indicate their interest. Don't try to influence them.

---

[1] Elkins joined the JROTC at 14 or 15 years old in high school. Upon graduating at 18 years old he immediately moved forward in the National Guard or Army Reserves. Remaining documents issued by the armed services specify that Elkins achieved the rank of Master Sergeant at the young age of 20 years. Whether or not he was the youngest in Army or National Guard in its history at that point is unknown to us and rests on Carla's remembrance.

[2] Don earned his Masters of Mechanical Engineering from the University of Louisville's J.B. Speed Scientific School in 1961 and earned a second Masters of Engineering from the same school in 1972.

[3] The name of this University of Louisville school has since been changed to J.B. Speed School of Engineering.

[4] The date was April 21, 1981, to be exact.

[5] In a transcript of a talk Carla gave at the opening of a Channeling Intensive, she said:

> By the time he was 26 years old he had gotten all the way through his education and was a professor. It came to him that he wanted to dedicate the rest of his life to seeking the truth. He'd already started just desultorily, here and there, investigating this and that. But from that point on it was his life's goal to seek the truth. He said to me several times, "At that time I died to myself. I have no more attachments to any outcome. I just want to seek the truth."
>
> And he never seemed to have highs or lows like most people. Of course he did inside. But he was all about the work, the seeking, the putting the puzzle pieces together, he always said.

Channeling Intensive 1 - Session 1 - Introductory Talk, Carla L. Rueckert, L/L Research, 2008, llresearch.org/homecomings/channeling_circles/cycle_1_channeling_intensive_1/2008_0208_01.aspx

[6]

"Brown v. Board of Education of Topeka, 347 U.S. 483 (1954), was a landmark United States Supreme Court case in which the Court declared state laws establishing separate public schools for black and white students to be unconstitutional. The decision overturned the Plessy v. Ferguson decision of 1896, which allowed state-sponsored segregation, insofar as it applied to public education. Handed down on May 17, 1954, the Warren Court's unanimous (9-0) decision stated that "separate educational facilities are inherently unequal." As a result, de jure racial segregation was ruled a violation of the Equal Protection Clause of the Fourteenth Amendment of the United States Constitution. This ruling paved the way for integration and was a major victory of the Civil Rights Movement."

Wikipedia, The Free Encyclopedia, s.v. "Brown v. Board of Education," accessed February 17, 2016, https://en.wikipedia.org/wiki/Brown_v._Board_of_Education.

[7]

In Chapter 24, page 328, Carla and Jim said:

> CARLA He was a wonderful leader. Jim and I are both leaders in terms of our genes, we have no problem leading a group so it's not that we were leaning on him. We were two people who were delighted to give over our will—you know, "What do we do next, George?" and questions of that sort to a boss that was going to tell us a really good thing to do next. We trusted his capacity to lead.

> JIM He was definitely the leader but we never felt, I never felt that he was the boss—he didn't give orders. You just wanted to be around Don. You wanted to do what he wanted to do 'cause he was fun.

From Book V of *The Law of One*:

> CARLA However, what had always before gone hand in hand with my dependency was his willingness to steer our course, indeed, his insistence upon that. I was glad to give this leadership over to him, and to do what he said. He was far wiser than I was or ever could be.

[8]

Ra was not the first source through which Don was introduced to the notion of *wanderers*. Don likely learned about them from George Hunt Williamson who used the terms "wanderers" and "apples" synonymously. Wanderers are also described rather accurately in Don and Carla's pre-Ra contact book *Secrets of the UFO*, which included citations of several channeled sources outside of L/L work.

About the wanderers in the group:

> QUESTIONER Can you say if any of the three of us are of Ra or one of the other [Confederation] groups?

> RA I am Ra. Yes.

QUESTIONER Can you say which of us are of which group?

RA I am Ra. No.

QUESTIONER Are all of us of one of the groups that you mentioned?

RA I am Ra. We shall go to the limits of our attempts to refrain from infringement. Two are a sixth-density origin, one a fifth-density harvestable to sixth but choosing to return as a wanderer due to a loving association between teacher and student. Thus you three form a greatly cohesive group. 45.5-7

9

In my thinking, knowing that you are a wanderer does not change too much, actually—you are still in a human body living a human life on a human world with human lessons and a human personality—but it is helpful in these two basic regards:

1. It underscores the reason for your incarnation here on planet Earth. The wanderer is literally defined by his or her desire to be of service. In feeling the suffering and the sorrow upon this planet and in hearing the cries for help sounding from every corner of Earth, the wanderer decided to make the sacrifice and take on a body in this illusion, forgetting who they are and risking becoming karmically involved.

    Knowing that you are a wanderer simply connects you with the principal desire at the center of your heart. It is a reminder that the purpose of your incarnation—the very reason of your being—is to be a lighthouse in the darkness. That of course does not necessarily translate into the soup kitchen, social work, or performing some great world service on an outer level. Rather it is a service of *being*, a service of simply being who you are, radiating who you are, and shining the love and the light of the one Creator through your essential vibration. This is perceived by and is helpful to others.

2. It helps one to bring a certain order and perspective to the life that may have been previously unavailable. Many are able to finally make sense of themselves and the patterns of their life when they come to the understanding that they are a wanderer. This can be of tremendous aid in reducing or even eliminating doubt, fear, worry, and stress.

CHAPTER 27

Don Elkins' Final Two Years

Author's Note: In Book V of the original publications of *The Law of One* material Carla and Jim do exquisite and heartfelt work telling the story of the Ra contact, with special focus on one of that story's most important aspects, that which brought the Ra contact to an end: the decline and death of Don Elkins. To the reader interested in knowing more about that tragic episode I would encourage reading Book V and using the following chapter of this book only as supplementary information. Book V is by far the more focused, intensive, comprehensive, and eloquent telling.

Yet, there was more that could be explored than Book V offered. I had had the privilege over the years of hearing stories about the great (and human) Don Elkins, stories that I lamented readers weren't getting the benefit of hearing, including moments in these final two years that weren't explicitly covered in the course of the fifth book. It took me about ten years of being in Louisville before I worked up the courage to sit down with Carla and Jim and ask them for a full account of that final and fateful day.

Carla and Jim were then, as they were with anyone who asked, open books. And just as they had given me the time on that day, they were very open to this particular interview, granting their permission the first, second, and third times I asked if it was okay. Though Don's death represented one of the most traumatic and heartbreaking episodes in their lives—so much so that it broke Carla's incarnation in two and sent her on a journey through a spiritual desert for seven years afterward—they recognize that it was a chapter in a larger book, a chapter inseparable from the story of their journey and inseparable from their extraordinary conversation with Ra.

As such, it has its place, especially, with respect to the reader, in terms of serving as a sign highlighting the dangers and pitfalls of this type of work, about which Ra says, "The missteps in the night are oh! so easy." Hopefully this chapter may offer you a fuller account.

> *We can only say to you that the more you rest in trust and faith, the more room that you give coincidence to work for you. The stronger your belief that all is well, the more quickly patterns will smooth out and reveal that, indeed, all is well. And, conversely, the more a fear is focused upon the more that fear becomes real, to the point where, as each of you has seen in the past, this self-fulfilling prophecy does occur and that which is most feared comes to be because it has been the focus for energy within the self, and it has created its own vortex and started to lay out its talons into your life.* – Q'uo, February 4, 2002

GARY In this section we explore the final two years of the life of Don Elkins, 1982–1984.

I'd like to walk through the onset of Don's descent into mental illness and the eventual end of his life. We can use the attempts to relocate to Atlanta as milestones in Don's final two years.

You pinpoint the beginning of the difficulties that lead to Don's death as happening in the fall of 1982 when you began searching for a house in Atlanta. What happened then?

JIM Let's see . . . that was when we saw the hawk, after we got back from Atlanta, right? And we had seen a house that we thought was the place to be. I'm trying to remember which house that was, though.

CARLA I think it was the one that I wanted to clean up the carpet on. It was only three miles from the airport.

JIM Anyway, when we got back, a *big* hawk with probably a four or five-foot wingspan landed in front of our house just after we had gone into the house from getting out of the car. It landed, and then it got up and took off. And it was just so big and so obvious. And Carla and I took that as a positive sign because hawks had always been confirmations of the line of thought we were on, or the thinking, or action we were anticipating—a hawk was a symbol of, *yeah, that's right.*

But Don took it differently. He thought that since we had already decided that was probably the place we wanted to be, that the hawk for some reason—

CARLA And the hawk had his wings down, Don said, rather than up. We didn't see where the hawk had his wings, but, you know, we didn't understand how it could be anything but confirmation, because that's all it had ever been.

JIM He took it as a warning, though.

CARLA Yeah he took it as, *don't do it.* And he didn't do it. He tried and tried, and he tried to get the Ra group to tell him.

JIM And soon as Ra saw that he wasn't picking up the message, they just backed off, pretty much. They gave him two or three convoluted explanations of the value of the meaning of the hawk, and if you look carefully they were saying, "Yeah, that means *do it.*" But he would never pick up those connotations.[1]

CARLA And they would never interfere with his free will. They went right to the bounds of free will and stopped cold.

GARY They said specifically, didn't they, that any dwelling which this group chooses is permissible to us or can be made able . . . ?[2]

JIM Right.

GARY So you return from Atlanta. You see this hawk. You guys interpret it one way. Don interprets it another way. Was that the first instance that Don read the environment around him with so negative an interpretation?

CARLA Yeah, I think that really marks the beginning of what we noticed as unusual reactions to everything.

GARY Why was it that you were searching for a house in Atlanta to begin with?

CARLA Well, he was tired all the time. There's no question about it—he didn't make any bones about it—he was just flat weary. And Jim and I both felt that if he didn't have this commuting . . . you know, he would get in the car and he would do a half-hour trip to the Louisville airport. He would get in a plane and fly for an hour and be in Atlanta. And then he'd be able to go to work.

JIM He was based in Atlanta. That's where he started his work.

CARLA That's where he worked. So we thought, well, if he didn't have that commuting to do, that would be one less thing.

So we were looking for a place close to the Atlanta airport, but Don always felt that every single house was unacceptable. It was unacceptable for this reason, that reason. He didn't want to bring us into a small or dingy or . . . most houses that are inexpensive are in what Don called "the combat zone" where there's a higher degree of crime than there would be at another place where there is a higher rent. And Don was afraid of putting me into any situation that he considered the combat zone.

And this was very unfortunate, because I have never had any fear in my life. I have walked around in the worst possible places in Louisville, Kentucky, when I was first married, and nobody ever bothered me. And the one time a guy did bother me, he couldn't go through with it, and ended up dropping me at a bus stop and making sure I got home okay.

I was always taken care of. I was always safe, and I did not have any reason to encourage Don in this line of thought. Nevertheless, he had it. And he ended up getting a place that was like that—that was in a higher rent district that was all the way across Atlanta. After the Olympics were held there, everybody found out about how terrible the traffic is in downtown Atlanta. To get from the north side to the south side of Atlanta is excruciatingly hard.

JIM Took as long to fly from Louisville to Atlanta, ironically.

CARLA Or longer. So we didn't get any net gain by moving to Atlanta. In fact we really got a net loss because he was no longer in Louisville where all his buddies were.

GARY So this is a little bit ahead in our chronology. We're still in the fall of '82, the initial search for the house.

So your reasons were that it took him an hour and a half just to get to work: thirty minutes to drive to the Louisville airport, Standiford Field, then another hour down to Atlanta.

Prior to seeing the houses in Atlanta, was he initially enthusiastic about the idea? Or at least in favor of it?

JIM Yeah, he was in favor of it because he was hoping it would make it easier for him. It was obvious that he was worn out by all the travel.

GARY So he was signed on, and you three—as a unified group—thought this would be the best.

JIM Yeah.

CARLA Mm-hmm.

GARY And then after getting there, then he starts showing signs of . . .

CARLA Worsening illness. Yes.

GARY So you go to Atlanta. It doesn't prove fruitful, and you can't find a house that suits Don's needs. This is somewhere in the Ra contact in the late 90s session numbers. So you return to Louisville. He hasn't found a location that works for him, and he has various reasons for that, all of which seem to have a lot of anxiety and fear underpinning them. So you return, and Don sees the hawk that he interprets in a negative light. Can you walk us from that point until June of 1983 when he tried to purchase the house you were renting from its owner?

CARLA I think it was just another attempt to try to buy a house and discovering, in each case after a lot of anxiety and discussion, that it just wasn't going to work.

JIM Our owner of the house where we had the Ra contact wanted an extra $5,000 for the house that Don just couldn't see paying.

CARLA Well, you're jumping ahead there a little bit. Luther wanted to sell the house—he was going to sell it either to Don or somebody else. So they agreed upon a price of $105,000, and $5,000 was put into escrow. Well, Luther wanted that $5,000, so he raised the price to $110,000. And this is after everything had been signed. Don thought that was sneaky and wrong. And it was. But Luther was getting away with it.

Don hired a lawyer and the lawyer did a lousy job, and I ended up, after Don died, having to give Luther $3,000 of the $5,000 just to get him off my back. I could have given him the whole five, but there was something in me that just said *no*. I'll give him what I need to get him gone, but I'm going to keep some—that's Don's money.

Anyway, it was unfortunate in the extreme because that house was *perfect* for Jim, me, and Don. There was part of the house that had Jim's office, Jim's bedroom, and an outside door—so that was basically his little house. He was satisfied with that.

And then you went in to a screened porch that joined the two like an *L*, and the rest of the *L* was Don and me. There were four bedrooms in it, and a great big 32' living room, a great kitchen, a great dining room, and everything that you could ever need for living. And we enjoyed our joined lives, Jim, and Don and me, beautifully, because Jim had a chance to be alone, and Don and I had a chance to be together alone. And then we would get together and be very companionable and have a good time watching TV or eating or whatever we did together—go see a movie. Jim would go back to his and we would go back to ours—it was just so easy and so right. And you don't find too many houses that are organized like that; as a matter of fact, it's hard to find one that is anything like that.

And we also had a huge amount of outdoors, compared to most people's yards, which are less than an acre. We had—how many acres?

JIM Six.

CARLA We had six acres, and it was sort of like shotgun six, which made it bigger, in a way, because you'd go back . . . there was the near garden, and then there was a fence. And then there was a pasture, and then woods, and I think even a creek. It was a quite a ways before you ever saw a neighbor. And Jim *loved* that; he absolutely loved that. He would disappear into those woods and fields, and he loved to take care of all that. It was just perfect for Jim to do hard physical labor, as Ra suggested.[3] There was a lot of hard physical labor to do to keep up a six-acre place that, you know—things would happen to it. Limbs blow down, and trees die and stuff. So Jim was always doing something. And he was content. We were all so content and perfect there we should have just left it alone, but we didn't have the eyesight—the foresight—to see that.

So, we kept thinking that it would be easier for Don in Atlanta. What we didn't realize was that it was very, very expensive to rent or buy things in Atlanta. It was more expensive than here in Louisville. Almost anywhere that you would go was more expensive than what we were paying. Made us look, like, *oh my god, we're really gonna have to take a bite to do this.*

And that was hard for Don. It wasn't that he was a miser, but he always felt like he needed to save as much money as possible. His attitude was that you never knew what was going to happen.

JIM Eastern Air Lines was starting to fail then. He didn't know how long they were going to be in business.

CARLA Yeah, he was worried about even having a job. He was way ahead of his time; it took 11 years for Eastern Air Lines to fail after Don died.[*] But he could just see it coming. He had such clear vision.

So everything worried him. I guess you would say he was paranoid—that was what the doctors said—that he had some paranoid delusions . . .

GARY Later on.

CARLA Later on. So it was a natural element of his personality, but it sort of got out of hand. It got worse and worse and worse and . . . there was no outcome that we could think of that Don felt was a good outcome. Everything was bad.

GARY So everything was going smoothly as far you could tell from outside appearances up to the fall of 1982 and that place on Watterson Trail suited all three of you—it was perfect—but you were willing to let it go in order to try to find some way to maximize Don's experience and comfort.

CARLA Mm-hmm. And when Don couldn't reconcile with Luther over that other $5,000, he wouldn't give it to him. He absolutely refused. So Luther decided he wouldn't sell it to Don at all, he would sell it to somebody else. So he gave us notice that we had to get out of the house. So we had to move some place.

So it got to become a little bit more urgent that we find a good place. And Don was gone a lot besides his working time, just looking up places that might be okay to live and finding them to be unacceptable. It kept on this way for some time.

GARY In this mix there's also the fear that the company that he works for, Eastern Air Lines, is going to go bankrupt and out of business. Why

---

[*] Clarified in Chapter 14.

would that be of such concern to him given his résumé—wouldn't he be able to pick up another job working for another airline?

CARLA You got me, chum. I never could figure it out. It didn't make any rational sense at all. I mean, I never could understand why he wouldn't just accept a job behind a teaching desk. You know, he was so good at teaching, and they were desperate for people to teach pilots. He was perfect but he never would consider that either. I never could figure out why. I think he was just tired of everything.

GARY So between fall of '82 and June of '83 when you attempt to purchase the home you were renting from its owner, was it basically just an overabundance of worry that was showing in Don in terms of outwards sign of something happening?

CARLA Yeah.

GARY Were you concerned at this point?

CARLA No, not really. I mean, it was very characteristic of him to be like this. I don't know about you [*to Jim*] but I didn't really see that it was over the top until quite a ways down the line. It was just Don being Don.

GARY No big red flags?

CARLA No.

GARY And Don being Don, he's not telling you what's happening inside.

CARLA Right, nothing of what's happening.

GARY So you are evicted as a result of this conflict with the landlord and you have to get out . . . do you find some place in Louisville to stay?

JIM No, we continued looking for a place in Atlanta. Eventually we found one.

GARY That doesn't happen until November of '83.

JIM We weren't evicted. He said he was going to sell it but he hadn't sold it yet. So we had time to find a place. And we did.

GARY Okay. How did you land on a place in Atlanta that seemed to satisfy Don?

CARLA He chose it. It was on a lake. It was out in the country. For some reason it suited him when nothing else did. It was expensive. It was fancy.

It was full of stuff we didn't need, had no way to use. [*laughs*]

GARY Would it not have been your first choice?

JIM It was a summer cabin—a glorified summer cabin. 17-foot ceiling in the kitchen, living room; in the winter the heat was all up there. It was chilly.

CARLA Actually I got a couple of places on my toes that were because my feet had been frozen on that cement floor under the carpet. I have a tendency to walk around in my socks and I didn't realize it but my feet weren't just cold, they were frozen. [*laughs*] They were frostbitten. I got ulcers on my feet, on my toes.

GARY So you guys could see the downsides to this particular choice but didn't—

CARLA Yeah even though it was beautiful. We never did unpack. We made a wall out of our boxes—

JIM A pile.

CARLA And we blocked off about half of this *huge* living space so that we could have some feeling of a room—a home, you know, sofas and furniture—a room like we were used to. We coped, you know, but *shoot,* it was out in the country. There really wasn't a good Mom and Pop nearby.[4] We were desperate looking for a place to eat so that Jim didn't have to cook—Don still wouldn't let me cook. And it was not that easy, let's put it that way. I had it the easiest of anybody—I found a place to sing, I found a church, I found a jazzercise group—all in the first week. And that was my life pretty much, you know, going to church, singing in the choir, or creating a choir, as it turned out.

JIM Yeah, you *were* the choir.

CARLA Yeah, I was the choir! I was the member of this little church—

JIM *Little* church.

CARLA —for the time that we were there. Tiny little church. It could hold 50 or 60 people. It was a mission church, and it was a beautiful place to worship out in the country. Anyway, so I just went on with my life, doing my routine, walking my walk, doing my jazzercise, getting my exercise done, going to church and singing in this little singing group, and basically surfing sort of on the surface of things, making all of that be okay.

And it was okay—as long as I was with Don, I was fine. I was with Jim, too, and he was wonderful. And Jim was much more of a companion to me in Georgia than he'd ever been before, because Don hived-in more and more, and the two of us, Jim and me, would want to go out like to eat, or just to drive around, or just to get out of the house, and Don wouldn't want to go. And that was so incredibly unlike his usual behavior—*he* was the one that was restless and would just go out and drive around.

JIM He had to call in sick on some of these trips for the first time that I'd ever seen when we were there.

CARLA And we couldn't really see that he was sick. He didn't act sick, but he acted . . . oh, unhappy in the extreme—just so sure that everything had gone to pot, everything was wrong and never would be right again. It was hard—hard to hear and hard to live with.

JIM So that's when you said that you would be the strong and decisive one, and he could be small and foolish, and that's when the deleterious energy exchange happened.

CARLA Yeah.

JIM Which is very mysterious and quite significant in what happened to Don.

GARY Why is it that your belongings remained all boxed up?

JIM Because we were ready to move at any moment. He said we've got to move as soon as possible.

CARLA Every single month Don would say, "This is our last month. Tell the landlord that we're leaving by the end of the month." I would do so. He was the boss. And then by the end of the month I would have to call the landlord and say, "Well looks like we're not moving yet!" And the landlord is getting *really* tired of this and finally is like, "Look, my family wants to be there in the summer. You're gonna have to move." Here we go again! [*laughs*]

So we were off hunting for houses again to move out of the house we'd moved into four or five months before. So I don't know how fast you want us to go but that continued unbroken until Don picked the house that we were in now.

JIM We had one Ra session there, number 106. Don and Carla both were able to ginn themselves up[†] and get in good enough shape to have a session. We had a really nice room up on the second floor, and we had a session.

GARY So we haven't left your time period in Atlanta yet but to backtrack a moment: The search for the house in Atlanta had begun in fall of '82. June of '83, the conflict with the Louisville landlord began. November of '83 you move to Atlanta, but during the course of 1983 you had five sessions. I know a lot of that was due to the frailty of Carla's health, but did the instability with the housing situation also play a part?

JIM No.

GARY Was it Don's mental situation that played a part?

JIM No.

GARY So it was just strictly Carla's health and—

CARLA They were terribly worried about me, more so than I was, for sure.

GARY So you felt that long spans of time were needed for Carla to recuperate before she had the strength to do another session.

CARLA Yeah, they would make decisions. It would drive me crazy. I didn't want to put off the sessions, but, you know, I wasn't the one who was looking at me from the outside in. Both of the men made that very clear to me that I needed to give to them the power to choose when to stop me from having a session because I had no sense. And it was true! I just wanted to have sessions and see Don happy again. To me that was everything.[5]

GARY Given what you've described of your dynamic and your desire to make a home for him, to make him happy, and here's the single-most thing that brings him totally out of that melancholy, or as much as he can come—

CARLA [*lamentingly*] And I'm not allowed to do it.

GARY So you move down there and discover that you're on the north side of Atlanta, the airport's on the south side, and it takes him even longer to

---

[†] An expression that means, roughly, to get oneself into shape; to motivate or enliven oneself for the task at hand.

commute to the airport from that Atlanta house than it would have from the Louisville house.

CARLA Plus the fact that unlike Louisville, which is almost always drivable, Atlanta was prey to ice storms and there were many a day in the winter that you really couldn't drive on the streets.

JIM And the traffic by itself in the best of weather was just horrendous.

GARY So Don's state of being poised to move at any month caused everything to remain in boxes.

JIM Not everything. Some things we had had to have.

CARLA About half I guess.

JIM But most of it, yeah, it was still in boxes.

CARLA Uh-huh. I got to the point where I was so allergic to the boxes that if I saw one, I freaked out.

JIM Afterward, once we had returned to Louisville, if she saw one of those little blue moving labels on a box it had to go. [*laughs*]

CARLA I said, "Ah! Get it out of my sight!"

GARY This house in Atlanta, is this the same house that you arrived at midnight or so and did the salting ritual, Jim?

JIM In a U-Haul truck, yeah, with our first load.

CARLA It is, uh-huh, with these incredibly high windows that he had to crawl around in at midnight, dark of night.

GARY So even before the deleterious energy transfer, Don is worrying more and more that there's going to be a bad outcome in some way.

JIM Ra mentioned in that one session that we had[6] that Don was undergoing an initiation. I think, just my personal opinion, that the initiation had started a few months earlier judging by his behavior. He was worrying about Eastern Air Lines, worrying about supporting us, and worrying about Carla's condition. All of that was playing on him. I think that it was something to do with his initiation that was causing him to respond as he did.

GARY Speculation only, of course, but could you guess what that initiation entailed, or why it was there?

JIM　No, no, but I know that with the initiation in mind, with the fact that there was this deleterious energy exchange that made it more difficult and probably a lot of targets of opportunity for our negative friend of fifth density. That must have given that fellow all kinds of targets to hit. I just couldn't imagine Don being able to survive that. Looking in hindsight, I think he did well to last as long as he did.

GARY　Was he vocal about his worries at this time?

JIM　Oh yeah.

CARLA　"This is the worst day ever." We heard that every day.

GARY　That was already happening when you were in that house in Atlanta?

CARLA　Yeah, in Georgia.

GARY　You described waking up to him sitting at the end of your bed. That happened in Georgia as well?

CARLA　No, that didn't happen until we got back here in Louisville. I don't know, for some reason that galvanized him—he got back to Louisville and we thought, *oh, this is so great, he's found the best house in the world, it's so gorgeous, it's wonderful, and shoot, we can fix it up, you know, we've fixed up stuff before, it's not a problem.*" And other than that we just thought it was wonderful.[‡]

Well, Don was freaking out, we found out, because he couldn't see out of any of the windows to see who was coming. The only place in the house, you know . . . the only bedroom that he could look out the windows from was the one that looks out over . . .

JIM　Yeah, the one that Austin's in now.

CARLA　Yeah, the one that he stayed in, that David stayed in when he was there, and that you were in for a time. That one. Austin's in it now.[7] And you could see out for some way, but you couldn't really see a satisfactory view there; that wasn't the money view that was looking out on one of the neighbors, but at least it was clear of trees and you know, all the rest of it. I think he had bought it when everything was bare, and when we came back in April, the leaves were all greening out, and he couldn't see

---

[‡]　Carla is speaking of their current home that Don purchased in the fall of 1983.

through the leaves in summer time. I mean take a look out these windows. There's just nothing but green.

I thought that he'd choose this room that we're now in, but he wouldn't have anything to do with it, and I thought, well, then he's bound to pick the one upstairs with that big closet and more room than any other of the upstairs rooms. No, he picked the one where he had a clear view, and it was a small room. It wasn't like him to pick a room that small.

And he wanted to live in it with me. And that absolutely terrified me because that was so unlike him, he always *demanded—must have, absolutely must have—*his own room. Did not want to be in the same bedroom with me. You think it would make me happy, but I didn't want him to change. I wanted my baby back. I didn't care that that was the way he was involved—being a loner and having his own room; that was Don, that was fine! Go get your room. And it terrified me to have him sitting on the bed in my room saying that he wanted to move in with me. That wasn't like him. I didn't see *Don* in there. I was having a whole lot of trouble just making it all okay.

GARY While in Atlanta he's expressing this worry, *this is the worst day ever,* etc., did you guys try to speak to that in any way, and encourage him otherwise?

CARLA Well, sure, we'd say, "We don't see why you see that, we see it differently." And we'd try to get him out of the house and feeling better and pepping up and so forth, and we didn't have a prayer.

GARY So no amount of rational analysis or emotional appeal . . .

CARLA [*to Jim*] Do you remember ever being successful?

JIM No, his frame of mind was not amenable to rational or logical arguments; he had his feeling and his thoughts, and those had always been first and foremost in his mind and actions. In the past it had worked just fine, but now he was, like I said, he was under this initiation. There had been a problem with the transfer; our negative friend was having his way, so it was just harder to communicate anything positive to Don.

CARLA I think he thought in his heart of hearts, too, that I might be drifting towards being fonder of Jim than I had been. I wouldn't go so far as to use the word *jealousy* because he was too noble a guy for that, but I think that that kind of feeling was in there in the mix somewhere. And I never knew about it; I never guessed about it, because it would never occur to me that I would be anything but his baby—that was always our unspoken relationship. I didn't think that you had to speak about it. I didn't know. If I had known I would have been glad to reassure him, but this was Don—he didn't need reassurance. But I have a feeling looking back on it that, somewhere in there, he just started being paranoid about Jim and me, too.

GARY While in Atlanta we haven't discussed *how* your next, and still current, home came to be. You received a surprise call from Don, right?

JIM You got the call, right?

CARLA Yeah, he called and he said, "Well, I bought a house."

JIM [*laughs*]

CARLA And I said, "*Don—!*" I couldn't believe it. Because he had always wanted to live in that area. He had often driven around the streets here and asked me how I felt about it, and I always felt really good about it. I thought it was a very beautiful place, you know, lots and lots of trees—sort of like living in a park. If you had a little house, you still had a lot of land. If you had a big house you might have a farm. There were a lot of wealthy people, and then there were the people who had smaller homes and not so much money, like us, but we all were sort of mixed in there together, and everybody was from the same town. Nobody made any distinction.

GARY So this was completely unlike Don to be so impulsive . . .

CARLA Completely unlike—he had never bought a house in his life.

GARY And there was no consulting with you two prior to—

CARLA Oh no.

GARY —he just all of a sudden, you know, *you've got a new home.*

CARLA It was fait accompli.[§]

GARY According to my memory of your previous description of this in personal conversation, this purchase further accentuated and exacerbated his mental illness because he feared being tied down by a mortgage—he

---

[§] *fait accompli:* noun: something that has been done and cannot be changed.

feared the financial constraint, and feared having others dependent on him. Did all that come into play with the purchasing of the house?

JIM   Yeah. But he went ahead and did it.

GARY   And then immediately afterwards has kind of a buyer's remorse, he's regretting it, thinking, *I've done something terrible I shouldn't have done.*

JIM   Yeah. We're gonna have to move again as soon as possible.

CARLA   Yeah, *we'll fix it up and we'll sell it after we fix it up.* So we were fixing it up to sell. But neither Jim nor I wanted to sell it. We were aware that he had gotten a real deal on the house and that the rent that we were paying was no more than the rent that we were paying in Atlanta and yet we were buying a house. So it was really a good deal.

GARY   So April of '84 you move in, you have this beautiful home . . .

Come to think of it, you must have had the session (#106) in Atlanta *after* Don had purchased this home. Because you're asking about this home and Ra even says to you that it's especially blessed with, for lack of a better term, angelic presences.[8]

JIM   Hm-mm.

GARY   But you get here and he's just—.

CARLA   The first time I ever saw him throw food away, he threw his hamburger in the waste basket in our little motel room and said, "We've made a terrible mistake."

I'm going, *"What?"* And I finally I dig out the reason—that he couldn't see anything but trees, so he didn't feel like it was a good house because he didn't have a good view.

GARY   And you could sense the beauty and the angelic nature—

CARLA   I *saw* the angels! I would sit up there for an afternoon in that little brown loveseat that's up there and commune and just . . . the sun would be streaming through . . . you know how it does late afternoon and, oh, it was just heaven.

[*to Jim*] You remember me sitting up there?

JIM   Mm-hmm. Sure.

CARLA   Having a wonderful moment. And I was very happy there and just, you know . . . I was able to go back to my church and my friends were there. I mean it could have been the same thing with Don. You know all his friends were in Louisville, but somehow he never got out to see them like he always did before. He just stayed at home and moldered. That was tough.

GARY So he wants to move and despite your love of this place, you tried to meet that need.

CARLA Yeah, I was looking for a house that we could move into from this house with every fiber of my being. The paper would come in the morning and I'd be on it. And it would occupy my attention until I checked out every single entry.

GARY And still no matter what alternative home you turned up, he would reject everyone in fear-based, worry-based thinking.

CARLA I never knew why sometimes. There was this one house I remember I found . . . it had two stories and the owners had made the upper story into an apartment and rented it out so it automatically had two places to live—one for Don and me, one for Jim. And it was in Crescent Hill where I had grown up. Lovely neighborhood. And it was $15,000 cheaper than this house, so we would have had a cheaper mortgage most likely. I never knew what was wrong with that house. I never knew what was wrong with half of them. I mean, he'd make something up sometimes, he'd just, "No. No. No. Unacceptable."

GARY I remember you telling me about a moment when, I think he's signing the papers here, and you're trying to communicate with him that it's alright, we don't have to do this.

CARLA Mm-hmm. Yeah, he looked at me and there was such pain in his eyes and I think I even said it aloud, I said, "Don, if you don't want to sign this, let's go, and we'll handle it, it will be okay." Then he went down and signed it.

But it was agony, you could see it. Everything was agony for Don. Nothing was easy. Oh. My heart goes out to him just thinking about it.

Thank God I have spent many, many a time tuning for doing my channeling work. As part of my tuning process, I ask for the Holy Spirit and then I see who comes through the door for the male and female part. And Don started coming through the door soon after he died. So I was able to see him well and still being part of the work, still working with me in the channeling. His mother started coming out too, so I had Don and his mother as the two aspects, male and female, of the Holy Spirit during my tuning process. What could have been more beautiful than that? So I have lots of positive memories of Don that are more recent that reassure me that all is well with Don. But it was a very hard way to live the last year of one's life, as miserable as he was.

GARY To pause for a moment, I'm sensing that the energy of the group is waning. Do you guys want to continue or do you want to split it off and resume tomorrow?

JIM I'm ready to go.

CARLA Might as well finish. I don't know how much more you've got. Might as well finish this part. No, all is well. We're just talking about a really sad subject.

I mean, I'm not *sad*; I'm telling you about a sad subject. I'm okay.**

[*pause*]

I guess I want to make clear to you, because we just paused a minute and you asked me if everything was alright, and I want to reassure that I was telling you about a very sad part of Don's life but I'm okay. I'm happy. I've worked out in my mind the rightness of all that had occurred, and I know that my beloved Don ended his life in the most noble way a person could: really intending to give his life in order to make me safe and happy for the rest of my life. That kind of wholehearted sacrifice is just, oh, it takes your heart, and I look up to this guy more than ever. He's my hero. I just think so much of him; he's a wonderful guy. But I have found a way to lead a wonderful life with Jim, and gone on to the second . . . really, it's a second incarnation of my life. When Don died he really, basically, ended the first, so my life is split into *two* incarnations—very different incarnations.

GARY So you move to Louisville and Don's descent into mental illness accelerates all the way up until November. What sorts of things happen during your time together?

** This is indeed sad even tragic subject matter, but the tone of the discussion itself was buoyed with the light heart despite its seemingly serious presentation.

JIM Well, he did consult a psychiatrist, and he was admitted to the mental ward of Norton Hospital—the seventh floor—and he had a psychiatrist there, Dr. Jess.

CARLA Jessie.

JIM Jess Wright. And he went on vacation as soon Don got there. For the first three weeks of Don's stay there the psychiatrist was on vacation.

CARLA He was gone and nobody else handled it.

JIM So he's just hanging out there. We went up and visited him a few times and eventually, I don't know how long . . . how long was he there, maybe four, five weeks? It's hard to remember.

CARLA He was . . . wasn't he there five weeks?

JIM Something like that. And then he—

CARLA And he gained weight. I mean, prior to entering the hospital he had lost a lot of weight because he wasn't eating.

JIM He realized there was something going on with him, too, so that's why he was amenable to seeing the psychiatrist and checking himself into the hospital.

CARLA But the psychiatrist was a totally null, worthless human being.

JIM But he was *gone* for the first few weeks.

CARLA But when he was there his visits with Don constituted him sitting down and saying, "Well, would you like to talk today?" And Don would say, "No." And he'd say okay, and he'd get up and leave. And that was the session. That was all that ever happened. Don told me that.

So he just hung out. He called me as often as he could. I couldn't call in to him but he could call out to me, and we went to see him whenever we could—we maximized our ability to see each other. But the problem with that was that he was so far gone at this point that he cracked my ribs when I saw him and I had to be more careful after that, because he did have the capacity to hurt me!

JIM He was hugging for the first time, which was strange.

CARLA Yeah, he was hugging me and he didn't know his own strength. And he really hurt me and I just couldn't believe it, but I realized that I had to be a little bit more careful. It broke my heart. I mean, everything about the situation was not my best day. I did not know how to deal with any of it. I was doing my doggonedest, and it was a lousy job. I look back and I think of so many things that I wish I could have done or not done, said or not said. You know, I think we all have that, but I had that in spades, with a take-home bag. I mean it was just . . . it was overwhelming, I think for not just Don but for me too.

Jim maintained his balance throughout. It was remarkable. He just went on doing what he always did: keeping the schedule he always kept and being the Rock of Gibraltar for both Don and me.

So the psychiatrist was making noises like I should stay away from Don because Don had to make this decision to help himself, or it would never work. That was the one thing that broke Don's heart—I was trying to follow the psychiatrist's instructions not to spend a lot of time with him. I had to ask him to do things on his own that the psychiatrist had asked, including stuff like going outside for fifteen minutes at a time and then extending it to thirty and then forty-five, and then being able to go out as he normally did. He wouldn't, and after a while he wouldn't even get dressed.

And he lost so much weight. I didn't realize this but he didn't really have any *clothes*. Why I didn't tweak to that I don't know because I was always very careful to make sure he was dressed. But it just didn't occur to me. I was overwhelmed, let's put it that way. And I wasn't the sharpest cat in the world, at anything! But it was just a tough time, all around. I wrote a lot of poetry at that time. It was the only outlet I really did have.

But I went to church. I sang in the Louisville Bach Society. I did things that made me stay sane and helped me get a sense of what balance I had, but I really didn't know how to take care of Don any more, how to nurture him, how to help him out. I didn't know how to help myself out. I had this horrible feeling that I'd lost him. I looked for him in the person that was . . . I mean, his *eye color* changed, his face changed. He didn't look like himself or act like himself.

I told him once, I said, "Don I really miss you." He said, "I do too."

And that's the situation.

GARY   He really missed you or missed himself?

CARLA Missed himself. It was heartbreaking.

GARY Was he diagnosed with any particular condition?

JIM Let's see what was it . . .

CARLA It was psychotic . . .

JIM Psychotic depression with paranoid features. Something like that.

CARLA Yeah, at one point he became convinced that the CIA was at it, or the FBI—

JIM Some governmental agency.

CARLA Some government agency was spying on us because they thought that he was running coke, or was it—?

JIM Some sort of drug.

CARLA Some sort of drug. Anyway, Don, I, Jim—none of us had ever seen hard drugs.[9] Where he got this I don't know. But it was typical of the kind of thing that was going through his mind. He was totally convinced that our phones were tapped, and we were being spied on and all this totally bonkers stuff, you know. And then he'd turn around and be as sane as you and I, and very much there, very much *in there*.

Anyway, I couldn't put a foot right. I couldn't do anything to make the situation better. I was increasingly ill. This got to my body, naturally.

GARY You had some nervous breakdowns, didn't you?

CARLA I really had a nervous breakdown, but I, unlike Don, I wanted help. I asked for help, and I got help. I had a wonderful psychiatrist who talked with me for I guess about three years, longer than that maybe. And she really stuck with me and helped me to regain my sense of balance and my sense of being me. And of course, you know, when Don died she was especially helpful.

GARY You described once to me a moment where he shows up at your exercise class, or your singing—

CARLA Well, he was supposed to be taking me to and from exercise. It was something that was very odd, another odd thing. He had never wanted anything to do with my daily routine, but he ended up liking taking me places just because we got that time together in the car. But he lost the car in a huge parking lot out at the mall, and it took him forty-five minutes to find the car. I came down with a royal chest cold because I'd been exercising and breathing deeply, and then I was outside without really enough to wear, waiting for the car, not knowing. I couldn't go back in because it was not a glass door; I would have had to close the door and he wouldn't see me then, so I had to stay outside.

So anyway it was borne in on me that, you know, I really couldn't trust him to take me anywhere. I became increasingly distant from him because of the way things happened. After I got sick from waiting for him to find the car, I didn't really want him to take me anywhere because I didn't want to have that happen again.

Whatever the details are, the simple fact was that he was slowly losing his ability to function in the consensus reality world.

GARY Jim, what was your strategy during this time? How did you seek to relate to Don and help Carla?

JIM Well, I tried to talk to him too. I mean there's not much else you can do when talking doesn't work because he doesn't communicate on the same rational level that you do. You just try to make him a meal that he likes. Hang out.

GARY And how about Carla, how did you, what was your relationship with Carla like?

JIM Well, we walked together and talked, tried to figure out what to do. You know we were scrambling, trying to keep up, realizing we weren't really up to the task and didn't know how we could possibly help. But we were going to try for all that we were worth.

CARLA We never gave up, but we never had a clue. I don't think we ever felt like we were succeeding in helping him.

JIM In the last two weeks before he died I think you finally had to move in with your mom and dad because it was just too much for you to hang out here. So I made the trip back and forth between here and where Carla was. And—

CARLA Don was the one that urged me to make that move. He could see that I was beginning to be just too nervous, jumpy, and—

GARY Did you go catatonic sometimes?

CARLA I did, I did once. It was . . . where was I? I was just lying on the couch or something and looking at the—

JIM At the ceiling.

CARLA Looking at the ceiling and neither of the men could get me to react. All I remember was that I was enjoying looking at the way the wood was joined together at that corner of the entry from the office into the living room. I was just looking at it and looking at it and enjoying it, thinking it was beautiful, and I thought my sense of time passing was not much at all, five minutes, but apparently it was over an hour. I snapped out of it after a while. I don't know what caused that, but I mean I was losing it. And I did better over at Mom and Dad's as far as not losing it to that extent, without the catalyst of Don's face at the door saying, "Alrac,[tt] it's worse than ever, this is the worst day ever." And it was always the worst day ever.

GARY It was when he would wait for you to wake in the morning. Sitting on the end of your bed.

CARLA Yes, he would be sitting on the end of my bed waiting for me to wake up, so he could tell me that this was the worst day yet.

GARY So this just overwhelmed your system and capacity to cope?

CARLA Finally it did. Finally it did. I had to let it all go, and you know I didn't want to, but I was falling apart.

GARY Feeling his pain as well.

So the final two weeks Carla moves out and how do events proceed from there?

JIM Well, let's see. In my conversations with Don I knew that he had taken his collection of guns out into the country and thrown them away, so I knew that he was cognizant of the fact that he was a danger to himself and that he was trying to do something about it. But at one point toward the end of the two weeks, he mentioned that he was considering killing himself. And I knew that that was the only way that we could ever have him readmitted to the hospital against his will—if he had mentioned that he was going to harm himself.

[tt] Don's nickname for Carla, her name spelled backwards.

We very much did not want to do that. We don't like infringing on *any-body's* free will, ever. But at this point we didn't see any other way to get any type of help for Don. He wasn't getting any better here. Things were getting worse.

So we went down to the City Hall and up to the sheriff's office, and I signed a "mental inquest" warrant. And that gave them the right to come here and to take Don to a mental hospital. And it was at that point that Carla and I were in the house, they knocked on the door, the police chief at that time—who now cuts grass here, I see him here all the time on the street—was at the door along with the people from the hospital, and he said that they were here for Don. So I went upstairs to let Don know that they were here, and that we were hoping that he would go along and take this one last chance to find his balance again.

He did not want to go at all. He went into the closet and found . . . he had a .38 Special in there in a sack.[10] So he has this gun and he put it to his head and said that he wasn't going to go. So, we came down the stairs, and Carla started to come up the stairs to give him a hug at the landing there.

CARLA Yeah, I thought maybe I could talk to him, and open my heart, and say, "Look, this is our last chance. Just give it a try. I'll wait for you. It will be okay."

Here was this poor, sick puppy of a man who had been such an elegant, wonderful guy, and was reduced to this little wisp of a boy who was so miserable he had a gun to his head. So I got half way up the stairs, and he had the gun to his head at the top of the landing, and it shocked me. I paused, and the police lady came up behind me and dragged me down the stairs. She wouldn't let me go any further.

JIM So we exited the house, and the last I saw of Don alive he was at the door with the gun to his head. There were an increasing number of policemen showing up outside. They had their crime *bus*, their central communications—

CARLA We counted *thirty-nine* who came and answered this call. This poor man, alone in a house—what threat was he to anybody but himself? And thirty-nine guys—and women, police women—swarmed to him.

JIM So eventually we retired to the house next door, which, at the time, was owned by a nice, old lady—she was about 88 years old, I guess—and so her son lived next door. We had a large pow-wow in the kitchen there where the phone was. That was the means of communicating with Don. Don was upstairs in what was now Carla's bedroom, talking on the phone to the police. Carla got to talk to him once, and I got to talk to him once. And we tried to talk him out of the house, and to give himself up, and eventually the police took the phone back and wouldn't let us talk to him again.

CARLA I mean, yeah, they wouldn't let me be real with him. You know, I was saying, "Don, let's put the gun out. Come on out. We'll take a walk. We'll work this out. We'll make our plans." And Don says, "Well, you know I'm gonna have to go to the hospital." And I said, "Well, yeah, that's part of it—" And the phone was grabbed away from me, because I was being real with him.

JIM Don't tell the truth.

CARLA Yeah, don't tell the truth and *psssttt*, that was so silly. I mean he might have been crazy, but he wasn't stupid, I think is the way the cliché goes. But that was so true. He knew that he was in for some therapy back in Norton, and I wasn't going to deny that, but that's where I failed. And they took the phone away, and never would let me talk to him again. That was the last I talked to Don.

JIM So the standoff lasted about five hours. And we're all over at the house there while it's going on, and our neighbor's son was saying, "Well, why don't you just let him go to sleep and sleep it off, and in the morning let's see what happens then. Why do you have to do anything—?" because the police were getting nervous that he wasn't coming out, that he had a gun.

CARLA They were focused on that gun like, you know, *he has a gun!*

JIM So they eventually shot tear gas into the house. That drove Don outside, and he shot himself outside: one shot to the temple and he was immediately dead. The emergency technicians came around and attempted to revive him—

CARLA Half his face was blown off, there wasn't—

JIM Carla's dad and I eventually cleaned up the next day. There were all kinds of syringes and things on the ground there. They were trying to help him, but they couldn't. So they took him down to the morgue and did an autopsy.

He had lost 70 pounds. He was normally 210 pounds. He was 6'6". He actually shrunk some, too; he didn't measure at the same height. Anyway, shot himself and so we were . . . Carla and I were at her mom and dad's that night, comforting each other, and making plans for the funeral. I think it was about two days later, before the funeral, we were in front of the fireplace here one evening—we had just made love, and the fire was burning—and Carla saw Don in a waking vision, and he was golden, and he let her know that all was well, that he was well—

CARLA He was laughing—

JIM And that . . . and he looked at . . . we had just made love, he said, "I can't believe I missed that my whole life long." [*laughs*] He had a different point of view then.

He said things turned out the way they needed to, you're not going to understand why while you're alive. You'll have to have a larger point of view—after you pass from this life as well you'll see.

And I think you [*to Carla*] had another waking vision in which he told you basically the same thing.

CARLA Very reassuring and immediate: I wasn't left thinking that, *oh something terrible had happened to him after death.* Well no, not so, he was just fine—laughing, happy—and I've seen him that way when we do our work together in spirit in my workroom before I finish tuning for a session, that's the part where Don and I work together. It's very reassuring.

JIM And so when they were working on *Esmerelda* and couldn't figure out how to end the book, they knew somebody was going to die. [11]

CARLA Guess what? It wasn't me.

JIM It might have been that you couldn't see the ending because it was going to be Don, and that that would be an infringement on free will for that to be shown clearly. So that's very likely why they couldn't end it.

CARLA We just rejected it. We didn't feel that it was possible. It was silly to think that, of the two of us, Don would be the one that died. But he was the one that, you know, needed to open his heart. He opened his heart in the hardest way a person ever could, and he did get it opened.

JIM He got a short course in the last year.

CARLA He got it opened, and I think he did all the service he came to do. He learned the lesson he came to learn. He had a very successful incarnation. And he was of service to others the most he could possibly be all his life. If he had a relationship with somebody, which he really did with me and almost nobody else. He was very responsible in that. Bless his heart. You know I miss him to this day, Don. Jim and I—I mention it frequently that we miss Don.

JIM Yep.

CARLA We wish that he were here. We look at something, and we'll say, "Don would love that!" You know.

JIM *NCIS*. Don would *love* Gibbs.

CARLA He would love *NCIS*, and Gibbs.

JIM He *is* Gibbs. [*laughs*]

GARY I've heard you express that before.

Final details questions concerning sequence of events, and then a handful of questions reflecting on them.

You had gotten a warrant, was it?

JIM Mental inquest warrant.

GARY Mental inquest warrant as a result of him saying he was going to kill himself, but prior to that point there had been a series of moments where he said *was* going to go get help, but then he would renege on it at the last second. Is that right?

CARLA Do you remember that?

JIM Well, he had a number of times where he talked about dying. He'd once mentioned how he wondered if it were possible to make a deal with our negative fifth-density friend—him for Carla. I have no idea if he ever intended to carry that out, fully, but he didn't mention it again.

He asked me once if I would help him kill himself. I said, "No. Think of something else."

So he had mentioned the possibility, but he had never before said, "I am going to kill myself." So that was the difference, that was the key, and that was the only way a mental inquest warrant could be taken out to have him taken away against his will.

GARY That was the point that led you to that action.

Honest communication from Don may have resolved so much and probably, I should retract the word probably, *may* have prevented the tragic end to his life. But Don was not a communicator of his inner reality, and Don could have only been Don, of course.

Can you comment on how communication's absence affected the situation, and what you would have to say to other groups regarding the necessity of communication?

JIM Well, communication is possible for those who are balanced in their mental capacities; I don't think it was possible for Don then. I think that the initiation, the energy exchange with Carla, and our negative friend intensifying things made clear communication impossible. He was living in a world of fear. He didn't have his native armor because of that exchange of energy with Carla—he didn't have his native armor to deal with psychic greeting of the potency I'm sure he got. He was having to deal with it with Carla's small and foolish attitude of, *what the heck. It's okay, it's gonna be okay.*

So I don't think clear communication was possible. Yet clear communication is *always* recommended; it always helps a great deal, but you have to have the ability to do it. Toward the end of his life I don't think he had the ability to do it. The world he lived in was a very different world—it was one that was very challenging. Just to survive as long as he did was quite a feat.

CARLA Yep, I really don't have anything more to say but how obvious it is that if you can just talk about it you can get through it. You can get through anything if you can talk.

GARY I've worked with and encountered people that have varying degrees of irrational mindsets that don't respond to any amount of rationality, any amount of evidence to the contrary. Maybe even I have encountered people with mental illness. All these years later do you have any insight into helping people with mental illness—reaching in and finding some kind of bridge of connection?

JIM No, I'd have to have special training. No, if it happened again I'd be just as befuddled.

CARLA I don't think so. I have never felt that I gained any insight at all except to realize how noble he was in his own mind.

GARY Befuddlement is my response when encountering people of that nature, because you can't build a bridge in to their world. It's very—

CARLA Right. Just not there.

GARY This is reflecting on what Jim had already mentioned, but with a different question. When you and Don received, as it were, the story of the *Crucifixion of Esmerelda Sweetwater,* the one thing you couldn't see was the ending, and through the function of your own free will, then, you wrote that ending so that the character representing you, Carla, was the one that died at the hands of the bad guys through the choice of the martyr, whereas the character representing Don lived.

Because of that book's ending, coupled with the realistic assessment of your very frail body during the course of the Ra contact, you had assumed that if anyone died as a result of that contact it would be you. As we know, however, the opposite was the case.

CARLA Indeed.

GARY In my limited opinion, so much of this unanticipated twist of fate hinged on the energies of faith and doubt. You clung to the former, and Don to the latter. And you each experienced very different outcomes.

In an intensified situation such as Don experienced—the magical nature of the Ra contact, the fifth-density negative greeter, the initiation he was undergoing, the deleterious energy transfer, the doubts about his connection with you—it seems that doubt was a seed which, when continually watered and energized, warped the situation, and led Don to a negative or self-destructive outcome. [12]

This isn't a qualified psychological analysis of the situation, just a human attempt to gain some perspective. [13]

To leave the memory with you when it was most vivid in your minds, you left yourselves cassette recordings of the events leading to Don's suicide.

CARLA Jim did. I'm not sure, did I say anything? I know Jim made a tape. I don't know if I cooperated in that or if I didn't know about it.

GARY You had a couple of letter tapes afterwards that reflected a bit but that you didn't set out to—

CARLA I didn't sit down and make a tape. Jim did that because he had lived through it and he wanted to get it all down while it was still fresh in his mind. There were so many odd little details so I think that's why he did that.

GARY Back to the point of the question. Those cassettes hardly mention the Ra contact. Rather, they are focused on the health and well-being of your soulmate and friend and companion, Don Elkins. And that's an important point I want to make here. In the readers' minds you may become simply functionaries, existing only insofar as you brought Ra into the world, but while the significance of that contact with Ra can't be overstated for those of us who love this material, the Ra contact was not the end-all-be-all of who you were.

CARLA Not at all.

GARY Can you comment on that statement?

CARLA Well, I remained a woman in love with a very real, a very beautiful man. And the loss of him was almost the loss of me. I didn't know how to live without him. I had given everything up so that I could help him, and I didn't have a lot left. I think *codependent* is what people slap on relationships like that, and you can call it that. It was the only way Don could have a relationship at all, and so that was what we did—that was what I thought was the right thing to do. And I still do. I would do it all again! And the 16 years that I had the care and feeding of Don Elkins were golden in my life. I loved taking care of him, and I loved him. And this was what he needed, so we had 15 wonderful years and one tough one. I'd call that a pretty good deal.

GARY Final two questions, I'll just ask them both at once. What were the short-term effects of Don's passing and the long-term effects?

JIM Well, short-term, the Ra contact ended immediately and we lost a dear companion. We had to regroup ourselves, and get ourselves back together so that we could continue doing what we'd always done which is, you know, the Sunday meditations and channeling and getting the word out. We were still working for Don.

Long-term effects: we became familiar with another path, as a couple, not as a threesome.

CARLA Yeah, it took us a long time to settle down into that, but we eventually became a real couple, realized that we were going to spend a life together. I guess it's kind of obvious when you say it but, you know, to us it wasn't obvious until we accepted it.

GARY Personally, I have undying gratitude for what Don did, what he gave. I wouldn't be where I am without his efforts and his sacrifice. And I've heard many other readers express the same. Even if they don't say it specifically to Don Elkins, any time they express love of this material, they're thanking Don and his pursuit of the truth as well.

I send my thanks to Don Elkins, and I thank you both for allowing me to ask these questions.

> *The energies of reaction to change, which may include much panic, and feeling of loss, and the stumbling effect of not knowing the path ahead, can be mitigated. The simple trust that all is well, and that your experience, whatever it may be, is valuable, worthy of attention, and worthy of your best effort, is very helpful in smoothing and regularizing the process of change that is inevitable and desirable.*
> – Q'uo, September 7, 2003

> *When at last you don't mind free-falling, you shall have arrived at a reasonably comfortable metaphysical stance from which to gain a somewhat more accurate view of the rhythmic beating of destiny. You cannot make a mistake, metaphysically speaking, for your lesson and your destiny shall follow you wherever you are moved to go. Yet to co-operate with that defined destiny is often to allow the little world to die away that the greater self and the greater will might be presented more clearly.* – Q'uo, May 18, 1997

---

[1] Jim wrote in the June 18, 2015 *Camelot Journal* entry:

I did our Morning Offering and then got myself ready for the day. A number of times in the last few days, after I have finished recording a Ra session for our Audio Book Project, I have found myself overcome with tears of gratitude for this contact and for Don and for Carla. This morning, in session #97, I had a very frustrating experience because it was in this session that Don asked about the significance of the large hawk that landed just outside our door after we returned from Atlanta. We had gone there to look at a prospective new home to which we thought to move in order to be closer to Don's work and make it easier for him since he was based in Atlanta as a captain for Eastern Air Lines.

Since Ra was associated with hawks through their Egyptian contact, re-placing Horus, the hawk-headed god of the sun in the eyes of the Egyptians 11,000 years ago, Carla and I saw the hawk as an obvious af-firmation of our move to this new house which was close to the airport in Atlanta. Don, however, felt that the hawk signified a problem with this choice since he was prepared to move to this house before the appear-ance of the hawk.

In the previous session Ra spoke to Don's first question about the hawk with a clear affirmation of the [rightness of the] sign, clear to Carla and me that is. In Don's second question in that session Ra refused to answer because Don was not sure and Ra didn't want to infringe on his free will. Now in this session Don asked twice more about the hawk and Ra tried with every fiber of their light-filled being to give a coded message of the affirmation of this sign regarding our planned move. But Don could not see it, and this session marked the beginning of Don's problems with his job, where we were to live, and how we would continue the Ra contact. This made me so very sad, even after 31 years.

The Camelot Journal, Jim McCarty, June 19, 2015, www.bring4th.org

2

For instance:

QUESTIONER After the suggestions are accomplished with respect to cleansing of the property, does Ra anticipate that our contact with Ra will be as efficient with respect to the location parameters in that particular place as they are in this particular place?

RA I am Ra. All places in which this group dwells in love and thanksgiving are acceptable to us. 95.17

3

The needs of the scribe:

QUESTIONER Finally, of the preliminary questions, one from Jim stating, "For the last three weeks I have often been at the edge of anger and frus-tration, have had a nearly constant dull pain at my indigo-ray center, and have felt quite drained of energy. Would Ra comment on the source of these experiences and any thoughts or actions that might alleviate it?"

RA I am Ra. As in all distortions, the source is the limit of the viewpoint. We may, without serious infringement, suggest three courses of behav-ior which shall operate upon the distortion expressed.

Firstly, it would be well for the scribe to engage, if not daily then as nearly so as possible, in a solitary strenuous activity which brings this entity to the true physical weariness. Further, although any ac-tivity may suffice, an activity chosen for its intended service to the harmony of the group would be quite efficacious.

The second activity is some of your space/time and time/space taken by the entity, directly or as nearly so as possible to the strenuous activity, for solitary contemplation.

Thirdly, the enthusiastic pursuit of the balancing and silent meditations cannot be deleted from the list of helpful activities for this entity.

We may note that the great forte of the scribe is summed in the inadequate sound vibration complex, power. The flow of power, just as the flow of love or wisdom, is enabled not by the chary conserver of its use but by the constant user. The physical manifestation of power being either constructive or destructive strenuous activity, the power-filled entity must needs exercise that manifestation. This entity experiences a distortion in the direction of an excess of stored energy. It is well to know the self and to guard and use those attributes which the self has provided for its learning and its service. 99.5

4 Mom and pop: a local small store or business, often family-run.

5 The instrument's lack of wisdom in offering herself for the contact with Ra was also... *disconcerting* to Ra:

> RA Meditation and contemplation are never untoward activities. However, this activity will in all probability, in our opinion, not significantly alter the predispositions of this instrument which cause the fundamental distortions which we, as well as you, have found disconcerting. 60.2

See the Chapter 7 "Your Dynamics" for more on this interesting subject.

6 Jim is speaking of the final session of the Ra contact, number 106. The only one to happen in Georgia. The first 105 sessions transpired in Don, Carla, and Jim's Louisville home.

7 The room is currently unoccupied. After Carla's passing Jim resumed solitary living.

8 Blessed with angelic presences:

> QUESTIONER How about the metaphysical quality of the house? Could Ra appraise that please?

> RA I am Ra. This location is greatly distorted. We find an acceptable description of this location's quality to elude us without recourse to hackneyed words. Forgive our limitations of expression. The domicile and its rear aspect, especially, is blessèd and angelic presences have been invoked for some of your time past.

> QUESTIONER I'm not sure that I understand what Ra means by that. I'm not sure that I understand whether the place is metaphysically extremely good or extremely negative. Could Ra clear that up, please?

> RA I am Ra. We intended to stress the metaphysical excellence of the

proposed location. The emblements of such preparation may well be appreciated by this group.

QUESTIONER Would the cleansing by salt and water then be necessary for this property? Or would it be recommended, shall I say?

RA I am Ra. There is the recommended metaphysical cleansing as in any relocation. No matter how fine the instrument, the tuning still is recommended between each concert or working. 106.7-9

9
  As the studious reader may recall, Carla twice had the opportunity to take LSD early on during the Ra contact. Carla's statement in this chapter regarding "none of us had ever seen hard drugs," then, may mean one of two things. Either a) she didn't take her earlier two adventures into account when making that statement or b) she doesn't include LSD in the category of "hard drugs." I think *b* more likely. Though it is a very powerful substance, many people would not slot LSD under the "hard drug" category, reserving that title for those substances with little to no spiritual value, those that commonly lead to abuse and self-destruction. Either way her point still stands that the group didn't have contact with, or access to, that which Don had developed delusions regarding.

10
  The following portion of the interview has been allocated to an endnote:

> **JIM** Later on after everything was done and he was dead, I found a . . . it used to be a *Bargain Mart*—before the internet, there was the *Bargain Mart* magazine here in Louisville where people went in and found all kinds of things that you could buy, anything you wanted you could buy there, including guns—and I saw where he had a couple possibilities circled, so I know where he got the gun.

11
  See the Chapter 2 "Don Meets Carla" for more information on *The Crucifixion of Esmerelda Sweetwater.*

See also, The Crucifixion of Esmerelda Sweetwater for more information on The Crucifixion of Esmerelda Sweetwater.

12
  Now and then a reader of L/L's work will learn of events as described in this paragraph, and/or learn of the reality of psychic greeting, and become subsequently concerned, even fearful in the worry that similar may befall them. While each path unfolds according to one's free will, it may be well to consider that most spiritual seekers on the planet, in this or any age, will likely never experience these circumstances and intensities, for the same reason most of us will never experience the challenges that astronauts face when blasting through the atmosphere, entering orbit, and traveling in space, like enormous g-forces and zero-gravity environments. It is a circumstance of exceptional, special, and extraordinary nature.

13

The two paragraphs to which this endnote is connected were added after the interview in order to help clarify the brief reflection on the role of doubt and faith. Don Elkins' diagnosable decline of mental health is a complex and multi-faceted situation beyond my understanding. I don't pretend to encapsulate the entire thing in a pithy summation.

At the same time, I think this general dynamic (between doubt and faith) did play a critical part in his demise.

I don't know what the roots of that doubt were, or how exactly they played out in his mental processes, or whether or how they could have been overcome or balanced, only that constant indulgence of doubt worsened and darkened a situation that desperately needed the light of trusting that *all was well*, trusting that the universe was not conspiring against him, but was ultimately offering Don the material and opportunity for his own growth, even if, on the surface of things, that material was unpleasant, undesirable, or suffering-inducing.

Change is not easy; spiritual death and rebirth is even less easy. Don was undergoing the death of an entire way of life as his heart was cracked so suddenly open for the first time, due in part, or in full, to the deleterious energy exchange he experienced with Carla. After decades of being a rational-minded observer, practiced and skilled at the art of turning off, or armoring against, feeling and emotion, he *felt* emotions and experiences that rushed upon him like a tidal wave. How bewildering and disorienting that change alone must have been. How painful is such a process of transition. But into that recipe were added the other aforementioned elements, including intensive negative greeting (on a level most spiritual seekers will likely never experience) that bred a poisonous doubt.

A healthy dose of doubt, consciously applied, can serve positive functions, of course. If one thinks he has become Zeus, and his decrees have become infallible, or his physical body immortal, perhaps it is well to doubt such grandiose claims. The capacity to subject one's conclusions to scrutiny, analysis, questions and contrary evidence—not protecting them from challenge by assuming one's cherished conclusions are impervious to criticism—is vital upon the path of discernment.

The doubt that Don experienced, however, wasn't a mere matter of scientifically or systematically challenging the veracity of certain truth-claims with contrary evidence, or simply second-guessing his thoughts, it was rather something deeper and corrosive, something beyond his conscious direction that choked out the light and imprisoned his mind in a seemingly inescapable cell of suffering. Moments, events, and situations common to the whole group, which were viewed through Carla and Jim's eyes in a positive light—and thus eminently manageable—were turned into dark and tortured versions when run through the filter of Don's eyes, eyes which were increasingly consumed with fear, worry, and doubt.

Consider a few of Carla's reflections from Book V:

- I cannot express how much agony and suffering he sustained in this time. The concrete walls that were so very strong and had protected him always, fell away as if they were never there, and he felt everything. And how he loved! He could not watch television, even the sitcoms, because there was too much suffering.

- He tried, over and over, to explain to me just how bad the situation was. This one thought was uppermost in his mind, always. The sheer horror of what he was feeling wiped him fairly clean of most other emotion, and he was unable to remain collected for long around me.

- The crises in his head were not real to me, or to Jim. Only he had the awful sense of impending economic doom. Don made a comfortable salary. His expense for all three of us and the kitties cost him about half his check, usually, each month. But Don lost all hope, and truly that being that he became was living in hell.

That's what is meant by stating that Carla and Don experiencing such different outcomes. They both experienced the same basic events. Carla perhaps even more intensely then Don, as Ra indicated she bore the "brunt" of the greeting and the wearying effects of the contact. But her mental health remained clear and joyful. Until, of course, things went south with Don, and she faced increasing challenges to her mental well-being. But even then she never relinquished her backbone of faith, and stood strong in her hopeful perspective and positive interpretation of catalyst.

When, in Chapter 12 of this book, Carla was presented a list of the multiple ways she was psychically greeted and then asked how she held up under the assault, she replied:

CARLA Well, as it occurred. I tried to stay in the present moment, and I knew that my strong point was faith and fearlessness, and that those were renewable resources, as opposed to my physical, which wasn't as easy to beef up. Faith is absolutely renewable—you just go to spirit and ask. You get a big *woof* and you're fine again. There's no end to vital energy if you have faith—and I did; and if you have will—and I did; and if you don't tend to worry about the future—and I don't, ever.

So I just stayed in the present moment and dealt with things as they came up. Or went down. [*laughs*]

If Don's situation had been clarified with the eyes of faith—that faculty which interprets catalyst in a way commensurate with what Ra says in 95.24:

RA The seeker which has purely chosen the service-to-others path shall certainly not have a variant apparent incarnational experience. There is no outward shelter in your illusion from the gusts, flurries, and blizzards of quick and cruel catalyst.

However, to the pure, all that is encountered speaks of the love and the light of the One Infinite Creator. **The cruelest blow is seen with an am-**

biance of <u>challenges offered and opportunities to come</u>. Thusly, the great pitch of light is held high above such an one so that <u>all interpretation</u> may be seen to be <u>protected by light</u>. 95.24

Then he may have been much better positioned to assess the situation, to see clearly, to make discerning choices, to measure things, to root out misunderstanding and falsity... or perhaps to move through and simply *survive* the challenging ocean of confusion and change.

These things can only ever be subjects of conjecture, of course. As with most human situations, there is much more happening beneath the surface, far from view. L/L Research always encourages seekers undertaking metaphysical (and especially magical) work of a positive nature to always do so in a group or a community; one grounded in principles of love and harmony, mutual support, and open, honest, clear communication—one where troubles are shared, support is offered, and the hands linked together in mutual service and seeking.

RA Harmony, thanksgiving, and praise of opportunities and of the Creator: these are your protection. 33.2

RA Continue in love and praise and thanksgiving to the Creator. ... Love is the great protector. 63.5

RA We salute the opening of compassion circuitry in the questioner but note that that which is being experienced by this group is being experienced within an healing atmosphere. The healing hands of each have limited use when the distortion has so many metaphysical layers and mixtures. Therefore, look not to a healing but to the joy of companionship, for each is strong and has its feet set upon the way. The moon casts its shadows. What shall you see? Link hands and walk towards the sun. In this instance this is the greatest healing. 102.21

RA We encourage the conscious strengthening of those invisible ribbands which fly from the wrists of those who go forward to seek what you may call the Grail. All is well, my friends. We leave you in hopes that each may find true colors to fly in that great metaphysical quest, and urge each to urge each other in love, praise, and thanksgiving. 99.11

CHAPTER 28

Carla Rueckert

GARY When, Carla Rueckert, were you born? And where?

CARLA I was born in Lake Forest, Illinois, which is a suburb of Chicago up on the North Shore, on July 16th of 1943, in the hour just at dawn, 6:42 a.m., I think.[1]

GARY You were born with birth defects and suffered from rheumatic fever at two years old. Did your parents think you were not long for this world?

CARLA They were continually told that by the doctors. Doctors were sure I would die before I was a year old—a week old, because of birth defects being in the brain, and the eye being turned so far into the brain, that they didn't think that I could survive. And then the rheumatic fever was a very severe case and affected all the organs in my body, including my heart. And again the doctors said, "She might get over it for a time, but she won't be able to go to school. She'll die before grade school." So, yeah, they kept expecting it to happen. [*chuckles*] Obviously it was somewhat of an exaggeration!

GARY What were those birth defects? You said your eye was turned in on itself.

CARLA My left eye was turned into my brain, and there were quite a few difficulties with it in addition to the extent to which it was crossed. But it was turned in so far you couldn't see the pupil; you could only see the white. So trying to haul it back—you know, haul that muscle to be shorter so that my eye would be straight—was really hard. It was very crossed all of my childhood until I was eleven, and I had an operation that shortened that muscle because the muscles, by that point of my body's growth, had gotten as big as they probably would get. It was possible to do it then because I was closer to adulthood. And they did a pretty good job, but when I'm tired, I still get crossed eyes.

GARY Did that impair your vision up to age eleven?

CARLA Oh yeah, I was legally blind in my left eye for a long time.

GARY Did it affect your image of yourself?

CARLA No. No . . . [*chuckles*] I didn't really think about what I looked like. I was too involved and interested in the process of noticing what was going on and recording everything—it was a fascinating world to me. Everything was fascinating, and I think I was affected most of all by the reactions of my peers in terms of how I looked. And until I went to school, I didn't really think about it. I was never treated as someone who looked unattractive. I was just—I knew that I was odd. My mother used to shake her head at me and say, "I'm so glad you have a good personality!" [*everyone laughs*]

That wasn't something that would add to your self-confidence. [*laughs*]

GARY The birth defects—did the condition have a name?

CARLA Golly, it probably did. It probably had several! [*chuckles*] But I don't remember them.

GARY Did things like the rheumatic fever and the birth defects cause your parents to treat you differently?

CARLA Well, they always treated me as a frail person and were more careful with me. And I was a very sensitive person. I was allergic to the sun, for instance. I couldn't stay out in the sun without sneezing tremendously to the point where they'd have to bring me into the shade. But I was a hardy little thing, and I would get brown as a berry in the summer. I loved to swim, and I was very active and so forth. So that worked against any vision of me as being really frail.

GARY So then, just like now, you had bodily difficulties but you wouldn't let your spirit—

CARLA No, not at all.

GARY —do anything but shine.

CARLA Mm-hmm.

GARY Don asked Ra about an experience you had one time:

> QUESTIONER Can you comment on my and the instrument, if she approves, so-called ball of lightning experience as a child?
>
> RA You were being visited by your people to be wished well. 53.23

Can you tell us what happened in this ball of lightning experience?

CARLA Well, in my case, a ball of lightning, literally, came through the window. My mother and grandmother happened to be in the room watching it as it circled the cradle and went back out the window. [*chuckling*] They thought that was peculiar, and it became part of the family lore.

GARY Did they have a belief system that could—

CARLA No, they had no idea why, and their belief system included the capacity for not knowing.

And in Don's case, I think something similar happened. I think he was in a crib rather than a cradle and it didn't circle the crib but it came in and then went back out after going close to the crib.

GARY Ra said, " . . . visited by your peoples." Do you know what that means?

CARLA [*joyfully laughing*] Yeah, well, one can conjecture! And it's a very pleasant conjecture.

GARY How would you describe your childhood growing up?

CARLA Well, it was difficult. I was always trying to please my parents. They were performance-oriented. My father was a jazz drummer and my mother was a singer, a dancer and actress. They loved and lived for the night life and were not interested in taking care of children. It wasn't that they didn't want to, it was that they didn't think of it. They were pretty much indifferent and just really pretty self-involved. And very, very intelligent; very much a product of that lifestyle of drinking too much, smoking too much, and having a great time staying up until the dawn with jazz sessions and so forth and then barely making it the next morning.

So I was trying to be little mama and take care of the household, and they left me in charge of my little brother who was sickly and very ill, actually, with . . . I guess he'd been hit on the head. His head had a dent in it and when that happens at birth, he became spastic and could only swallow two or three times every fifteen minutes, so that he had to be fed repeatedly all night, all day, twenty-four hours, every day. And this was very difficult. So the little kid was just crying all the time and a difficult child because of the fact that he was spastic, and he was hurting and sick. What did they do but leave me with him. Because I could talk early, I knew what I was supposed to do, but I also couldn't pick him up, so I was, like, really frightened! And Mother kept saying, "Nothing will happen, I'm just next door. I'm just down the road. Give me a call . . . "

JIM You were seven or eight?

CARLA I was seven when this began. Yeah, too young. And, you know, it was a very big burden on me because I was so responsible by nature, and people really valued having home-cooked meals. There weren't such things as take-out and stuff like that back in Louisville, Kentucky in the Fifties. So I would be trying to cook at an early age. I don't mean that anybody held a gun to my head and said, "Cook!" but I was trying to help. But I was, you know, too young to do it.

So, again, it was a matter of asking too much of myself at too young of an age. So when my parents would react to it, they wouldn't react to anything except that I didn't do it very well, and they would be trying to explain to me how I could do it better. So I became convinced that I just couldn't do anything right. I couldn't get it right, and that cast me down. That was difficult.

But then I had wonderful things about my childhood too. My grandmother would take me to dance at Noyes Camp. It was a wonderful form of dancing (it was a modern dance, sort of like Martha Graham), but it had wonderful philosophy behind it, which was very congruent with *The Law of One* actually: that everything was alive in nature, and that you could be anything in nature, because everything had a rhythm, and you could express that. So, even the exercises—instead of having plies and so forth and so on, you had the bear and the horse and the starfish and all these wonderful, evocative animals that you would exercise—that was exercise, but nobody said it was exercise.

I loved the dancing and the course at camp. There was swimming, and I loved to swim. I was just absolutely rubber in the water. You couldn't keep me down; I bounced. I could float on my stomach, which most people can't do, and just be there, on the stomach on top of the water. Most people have to dog paddle to stay on top but I never had to make a move, I was just that buoyant. And everything about camp pleased me down to the ground. I loved to run around and with my feet bare and my arms bare to the sun. And I loved to throw my little crooked pots and make crafts and all that. I loved everything that you could possibly do. I loved drama. I loved singing.

So for two months out of the summer I was just in alt. I was so happy. But then I didn't really know how to get along with my cabin mates, either, so again I was on the outside a lot. And this was a theme throughout my childhood: not being on the inside of any group of my peers. I was thoroughly and universally rejected.

GARY I imagine a rather innocent Carla trying to communicate, trying to relate, but it seems like your classmates shunned you? Or said you can't be a part of our group?

CARLA Well, I guess I just looked different. I acted differently. I was a little spooky maybe. The things that I perceived included a lot of things that nobody else perceived —of any age, you know. [*chuckles*] This has always been so. They didn't cut me a lot of slack, let's put it that way.

I asked somebody once when I was thirteen. She was the leader of a big clique, the ruling clique at the church I went to, and I had a big church life. I went to church a lot. And I said, "Why don't you like me?" and she said, "I don't know." You know, it was like that. There was something about me that ticked people off. I mean, it sounds ridiculous, and it sounds a little paranoid. But it happens to be true.

Now it did turn around the summer that I was sixteen, almost like, *is it . . .? She's sixteen? Okay. That's it. It's the time. Now she can be okay.* And I was alright, and after that I got along with everybody. Everybody loved me. Go figure.

GARY So, while there was some pain involved in that, you nevertheless didn't let that get you down.

CARLA I never did, no. I was too busy having fun. I loved to read. You can always go back inside yourself and have your own life, if you have a lot of internal space, and I did.

GARY And so back at home, you're volunteering, in a way—you want to be of service, but at the same time your parents are thrusting too much on you.

CARLA Mm-hmm. Well they didn't really mean to, it's just that they let me. I would volunteer and they wouldn't say no. They wouldn't say, "No, go have a life." They would be glad to have me. And they expected me to do my part. My father explained to me, whenever I might complain, that other people got so much per hour for babysitting. He would say, "Well, you're part of a family. I work for eight hours a day so that we can pay our bills. What have you done lately?" You know, basically—

GARY Everybody has to carry their own weight.

CARLA That's right. Everybody has to be part of the team. You know, we're a team here, we're a family. And I really had nothing to do but say, "Okay." I knew it wasn't fair, but in terms of what everybody else got and what I was receiving, I wasn't even receiving decent thanks. I was just expected to do this. And other people were "mother's little princess" if they did stuff like that.

GARY Did you feel loved by your parents?

CARLA Not particularly. I was though. I mean, I think I was very deeply loved by my parents. But they didn't really have good ways of showing it. They just didn't think to. My mother especially was perfectly capable of being lovey and huggy and so forth, but it wasn't something that she would do much of.

GARY How about school? How did you do in school?

CARLA Oh, I did great in school, unless the teacher thought that I was acting like a smart-aleck because I was trying to learn too much or trying to go too fast. And I had some teachers that actively slowed me down because I wasn't going at the same rate as the other kids. And I was never allowed to tutor other kids, which I loved to do, and was glad to do, and was asked to do constantly because the other kids knew I could help them out. But the teachers did not want me to do that. They saw that as a form of misbehavior.

GARY You were fairly awake for a child, and that may have played a part in why you were kind of shunned by the main groups or cliques. Did you find yourself at school or in these social situations, explaining world views or explaining a certain magic to the world that they couldn't perceive?

CARLA Well, most people never even asked me about it. And of course I went to church, and in church it was much more acceptable to think about the inner life, and to think about Jesus and salvation and loving Jesus and all that kind of thing. So it wasn't a real problem, except that I never felt that I really could talk to anybody about it. I couldn't even talk to my parents about it, really. It was just something that was inside me, and that was really all I needed, was to know what I was feeling. And I loved the exploration of that feeling. And I had been settled in terms of my loving Jesus ever since I was a very small child, as I have described before.

GARY Did your parents have any kind of religious, spiritual, or philosophical bent?

CARLA No, they were pretty much cultural Christians. I mean, I think later in life both of them tried to deepen their faith very consciously, especially my mom. We went to church every Sunday. It was expected that we would, by both Mom and Dad, so there wasn't a problem between them. It was just what you did on a Sunday morning.

And I remember the joy of—there was this moment when you came home from church, and Mother always saved up so that we could have a roast on Sunday. She would put the roast in the oven on a very low temperature so that it would be cooking the whole morning. You'd come home and she'd flip on the library station and it would have a symphony. It was that time of day—I guess it was twelve o'clock, they would start off the symphony. So, that cluster of memory: the sunlight streaming in the window, the smell of the roast, which was delicious, the sound of the beautiful symphony in the background, and me taking off my treasured Mary Jane shoes—plop, plop on the floor—and loving that moment. Never forgot it.

GARY You described it elsewhere, but not in this interview so far as I remember. Back to your earliest memories, have you always had a conscious sense of being oriented in a religious or in a spiritual direction?

CARLA Well, not really, and when I was oriented in that religious way I didn't see it as religious.

I had never been able to sleep much during the day, and so when I was supposed to be sleeping, I was restless on the bed. And when I was about two, I put my little glasses on the venetian blind prior to getting ready for my nap. I was lying there sort of on the bed looking around, and I happen to notice that the glasses were focusing the sunlight as it came through the window. And there was this beam of light, and I looked at the beam of light, and I seemed to slip out somehow on that beam of light.

And I would be in a magical forest when I could do that. And I would always go to the same place. And this beautiful forest—the colors were very alive. They would flow and be, you know, alive, and the trees . . . all those things were alive and could talk to me. The animals could talk to me, and everybody was full of love, although I didn't describe it that way at the time. But everybody was having a wonderful time. It was like we were all part of this wonderful party.

Well, Jesus was there, and Jesus and I would sit, and we would look into each other's eyes. He never talked, but He would hold my hand. And I would look into His eyes. They were a beautiful golden color. And I would know what love was when I looked into His eyes. I don't know how to say it better than that. And it evoked in me an immediate desire to follow this love, to be a follower, a servant of this love, and to find out and to express that love in my own life. So I was always wanting to be a servant to that love. And so I loved Jesus; it was as simple as that.

And I—mother tells me—told me (she's been gone twenty years now) that she remembered that I told *her* about Jesus; she didn't explain to me. But the problem was, when I told her about Jesus, and she realized that I was having these experiences, she and my father both told me that I was dreaming, that that wasn't real. And after they told me that, I could never go back.

I've heard this from other people who had early childhood experiences. When their parents told them that they were all wet, then they couldn't do it anymore.[2] I guess that doubt had crept in. But from a very, very early age I was totally dedicated to serving Jesus.

GARY Does that experience with Jesus in your memory serve as a reference point for what love is—for setting the direction of your life?

CARLA Yes, definitely. It has never changed. [*pause*] Pretty serious little kid, I know, but I was. That was just me.

GARY How old were you when the experience was happening?

CARLA Two. Almost three.

GARY Two?

CARLA I was a little toddler! And I was very intelligent very early. [*laughing*] I've lost that mind as I've grown older. Think everybody's passed me up now.

GARY When you were thirteen, your kidneys failed. Can you tell us what precipitated this event?

CARLA Well, I can tell you that the doctors never figured it out. There's no medical explanation. They couldn't figure out anything that I'd taken that I could've been allergic to.

But I think, looking back on it, that there was this moment about six months before my kidneys actually failed, where I was so downhearted one day—you know how very serious teenagers can get—it was more intense than they ever get before or after—and I was very downhearted. And I thought I'll never be able to serve anybody, and if I can't serve, what am I doing here? So I prayed to die. I remember the moment, kneeling in the bathroom, putting my head down on the cold porcelain of the bathtub rim and praying: "Lord, just take me, because I can't—I can't serve." And I think that that was very effective in bringing that opportunity to me to go on and leave this incarnation.

GARY What led you to the conclusion that you couldn't be of service?

CARLA Oh, just a constant being informed by my folks that I hadn't done this right. I hadn't done that right.

GARY So your kidneys fail, and what happens during this experience?

CARLA Well, I died for about two minutes. My heart stopped beating, and they were trying to revive me. This happened in the hospital, and people were right there and they responded quickly. But my heart stopped beating, and I went from being in excruciating pain with the glomerulonephritis[3] to having no pain whatsoever, no marks on my body. The glomerulo marked your body terribly with great big welts all over your body, and I had none, and I was completely free of pain and completely free of markings and I was bopping along—I was passing along a park-like rise of hills. And over this one hill I could see the dome of a temple. It was a white marble dome. And I somehow knew all my friends were there waiting for me, and I was just bopping along going for that—couldn't wait to get there, couldn't wait to see my friends.

And all of a sudden this voice speaks to me out of nowhere—it's in the air kind of. I can see this air sparkling with every word. And the voice says, "Well, we don't usually give anyone this opportunity, but you set a very difficult course for yourself in this incarnation, and you took on too much. And really, you could have done two incarnations and not had too much. So we'll give you the chance. You can make your choice: either go ahead and die, and then you can come back for two separate incarnations to get done what you want to do, or you can come back into the life that you are now living and try to do the best you can to fulfill your goals in this incarnation, even though you'll always be frail."

So, I didn't have to think about it ten seconds. I knew I didn't want any more childhood. I was almost over this one and [*laughing*] I figured, *let that be enough!* and I said, "Let me go back and let me try in this life." So once I'd made that decision, I was immediately back on the hospital bed looking up at several faces that were looking down at me because they were trying to get my heart started again.

GARY Is that a similar sort of environment to the one you experienced at age two when you would interact with Jesus?

CARLA Well . . . yes. Yes. The colors were the same, you know, very alive and flowing and yes, it was very, very similar. I noticed more because I guess I was older and I was able to notice more.

GARY Any idea where, so to speak, you were?

CARLA No, I have no idea. But it was a wonderful place. It made this whole experience look like a black and white movie.

GARY So you made a very real decision then, and then it changed the course of your life from then on it sounds.

CARLA Well, it certainly deepened my resolve to serve Jesus. I mean, it didn't change the set-up of my internal psyche, I guess you'd say, but it hardened my resolve. It firmed that up to the point where I would never again consider allowing myself to do anything but just keep on trying, one foot in front of the other.

GARY So, it sounds like it came as a confirmation: you have a service; you are being of service; you have work to do.

CARLA I have work to do, and oh! what a wonderful thing it is to know you have work to do. You know, and that's a marvelous feeling. You're not working in a vacuum and pretty much you have to figure out what that service is. But I mean, that's kind of a game you can play on a very deep level, a good game.

GARY So did this help to liberate you from the need from feedback from your parents?

CARLA I guess so. It would have that effect. Plus, I was getting old enough that I could see that I was doing well whether or not I got the credit from my parents. There's no question in my mind that I was doing well. My brother—and then when my mother had another child when I was four-teen, my two brothers—adored me, and you don't get adored unless you're doing something right.

GARY Did you have a sense of what you would like to do as a career, vo-cation, or passion when you were younger?

CARLA I went around like kids do. I was going to be a statesman and make a difference in the world. I was going to be a nun . . . that was a very short one after I read Albert Schweitzer's book and I thought, *well that's what I need to do: I need to join the religious life*—so I could be supported, you know, while I'm doing this—*then I need to go to Africa and help out there because it's so desperately needed.* Then I thought, *I'll be a doctor.* [*laughing*] You know, I was just going around . . . a lot of times I thought, *well, I just want to be a mom. I want to have six kids and raise them up. That'll be my work.*

Whatever I thought, it was never anything close to what happened in my life. It was an unpredictable one.

GARY So in what direction did you head upon graduating high school?

CARLA I headed in the direction of statesmanship, hoping to work for the government in the state department or maybe politics, and so I went into political science and so forth. And then, I mentioned once before, I had an experience with [a now prominent politician]. He might not appreciate my remembering this. He was having a mock convention for elect-ing—whether it was going to be Barry Goldwater or Johnson for president—it was a Republican convention, of course. And I thought, *well that'll be a good experience and I'll work for him.*

And so, at one point, I realized that he made a decision that allowed us to win, but it also was telling a lie, and I faced him with it. And I said, "You lied!" He said, "Well, yes." He said that's one of the tools you use as a political person, and if you can't lie you might as well forget it. Well, I can't lie. I honestly, physically can't lie, not when it's an important thing. And the more important it is, the less I am able to do it, and the worse I am at it if I try. And also, as I mentioned before, I really, really don't like committee meetings, and there are an excess number of them always in politics. So in between those two things I realized I was going to have to move on. So I changed my major and thought maybe I'd be a college professor, do research into the language or something.

GARY And subsequent to that you determined that you wanted to be a librarian. Is that correct?

CARLA [*laughing*] Subsequent to that, I married and had to figure out how to make a living, and was already working in a library. So my decision was very easy to make. So I just needed to choose a way to earn money at one particular point, and being a librarian was—I could get that job. I had that job, you know, so not a problem as to figuring it out.[4]

GARY Had you been a professor, you would have taught?

CARLA English.

GARY Seems well suited to you. I believe it was during your university years that you were turned on to the theory and practice of silence.

CARLA I wanted to explore silence. I never had, and I became interested in it doing reading. A lot of people that I really respected enjoyed silence. And I thought, *well you know, I never*—The Episcopal Church is wonderful but it's a noisy church. There's a lot of singing and there's a lot of ritual and there's . . . it's all beautiful, but you don't have very many seconds, even, of silence in the service. So I was looking for a meditation group that had silent meditation in it, and that's when Don Elkins was starting his silent meditation group. So I asked if I could be a part of that.

GARY Oh, so it was Don's group that was your first real experience with a more disciplined or formal sort of attempt of meditation.

CARLA Right.

GARY You have identified as a Christian mystic. When did this begin and what does that mean?

CARLA Well, I've been called a Christian mystic more than I've termed myself one.[5] It seems obvious to other people that I'm mystical, and I'm not sure exactly what that means. But I think it means a dependence on your own intuition, your own internal clock, your own guidance system as opposed to being a linear person and wanting to write everything down and make a list of *why*—you know, what this is called and what the scientific name of it is. I'm not a scientist, so mystic seems to fit.

GARY Among the ways to describe mysticism that comes to my mind right now—versus a more traditional, religious mindset—is in terms of where one places authority. The mystic is seeking the authority within, the authority of their connection with the Creator or the source of life. Whereas the person of religious mindset is placing that authority outside of themselves, and investing the priest or the clergy with that authority.

CARLA That never happened to me. I don't think I'm a particularly religious person; I think I'm deeply spiritual.

GARY But you were drawn to the principles of Christianity.

CARLA I was drawn to the principles and the expression of it in the Episcopal Church. There really isn't any more beautiful way to worship than the Episcopal way. It has the very best of the Roman Catholic dogma—not the dogma, but the—what do you call the ritual?

JIM The creed?

CARLA Ah [*apparently dissatisfied with Jim's answer*], not going to get anywhere there . . . anyway, the method of expressing how, how you go about worship. There's no more beautiful way, I don't think, than the Episcopal tradition. It loves the entire range of music—both the older music and the newer. Anything that is oriented towards praising the Creator.

So you have this wonderful, wonderful bunch of music that you have at your fingertips from centuries of the very best composers in the world writing for the church, because, for one thing it's the way they made their money, for another thing it was considered heretical up through the Renaissance for anyone to do any work that didn't have as its aim something within the church. So that's why there's so much religious art and music and so forth; nobody wanted to be a heretic because that really didn't go well.

So you have this incredible body of music, and if you're a singer . . . You know, by the time you get to be a certain age—I'm talking to the videographer [Ken] at this point because he's also a classical musician—and probably through the years you've had lots and lots of experiences with different parts of that great body of music that is of the Christian faith, because so much of that is what people wrote. And so, if you want to do something that's classical, it likely has every chance of being religious.

So you become aware of it, and you're part of that music. And in between being part of the most beautiful rituals in the world, I think—the rituals of the church, holy communion being chief among them—and the being able to sing that Christian music—golly—all kinds of reasons to want to be part of that. So it wasn't just fitting in to the Christian principles, but fitting into the Christian way of worship.

GARY So among that which appealed to you about this tradition was that it offered you a means of praise, devotion, and worship, which is something you really need to do; as we were discussing earlier, it's a means of nurturing your inner beingness.

CARLA Mm-hmm, yeah.

GARY Did you have any difficulties with the content of the Bible itself?

CARLA Well, you know, I did. And I was in an inquirer's meeting at the height of my religious period—so-called, I was about fourteen, I guess—and I asked my bishop, who was holding these inquiry sessions, I said, "I don't know whether I should leave the church, because I don't believe the dogma." I said I had especial problems with the virgin birth, and he said, "Yeah, I've had problems with that myself."

I was really surprised. So I said, "Well, how do you say the Creed?" and he said, "In hope that one day in this life or the next, I will understand more about it." He said up until then, "It's just an article of faith. I take Him on faith. I don't worry about it, and I just go on."

And he said, "Don't ever leave the church! You'll never be able to talk to anybody about Jesus if you leave the church." He was right, and I was very grateful to him. He was also very supportive of my channeling when I began channeling. He was a wonderful bishop.

GARY So that freed you up from the need to interpret the scripture literally.

CARLA Right. I never worried about it one iota of an instant, and fortunately, the Episcopal Church is the haven of all civilized gentlemen, so you didn't have to believe a doggone thing. You could just be inquiring forever, never having to settle on anything.

GARY So they welcome more liberal thinkers.

CARLA It's the haven of liberal thinkers in the church, no question about it. When you find a failed Baptist that's still in the church, he turned Episcopalian.

GARY You mentioned that later on in life you shared your channeling with this bishop. What prompted you to share your channeling with the church?

CARLA I didn't know if I should be in the church. Again, it was a crisis of that nature. I didn't want to shame the church. I didn't want to be keeping secrets. I'm a very open person. So I said, "This is who I am now. This is what I'm doing. What do you think? Should I worry about leaving the church and doing this outside the church?"

And he read it. He took quite a few minutes and just sat and read for a while and he put it down and he said, "I see nothing negative here. I see nothing that would worry me." He said, "Keep me informed. Send me a little sample of your channeling from time to time. And as long as it looks like this, you're fine."

GARY That's remarkably open-minded.

CARLA Remarkably so.

GARY And that wasn't the only time in your life where you've shared your work with the . . .

CARLA I shared my work with every bishop and every priest in my church because I wanted them to know who I was. I didn't want to be a lie.

GARY And they've all, likewise, accepted.

CARLA Well, you know, with varying attitudes of befuddlement or positive acceptance, but never anything less than tolerance.

GARY How would you say you have reconciled your Christian walk with your work through L/L Research?

CARLA Just like that. I've never kept it a secret, but on the other hand, I've never felt the need to tell anybody about my channeling unless they've asked. It's a touchy subject. Everybody knows I'm doing work for L/L Research and it's dear to my heart. If people want to know what L/L Research does, I'll be glad to tell them. Very few have inquired. Those that inquire are almost guaranteed to want to support me.

GARY Have you ever had any trouble, internally, reconciling these two?

CARLA Oh, not at all. I'm a very logical person. I've read a lot of philosophy. There's nothing in the Ra philosophy that wouldn't square with the way I worship. And indeed, Ra specifically supported my way of worship. He called it a distortion—that's fine. "Distortion" is not a nasty word to Ra. It's just a description of something other than total oneness with the Infinite Creator. And the only way you're going to avoid distortions is not to be here.

GARY A quotation just came to mind that I want to ask you about . . . let's see . . . in 60.18, Ra is describing how there's been a negative encroachment on the various religious systems around the planet:

> RA This is in common with each of your orthodox religious systems which have all become somewhat mixed in orientation, yet offer a pure path to the One Creator which is seen by the pure seeker. 60.18

You are in a unique position in that you have continued to work within a religious system. Can you elaborate on Ra's statement about the pure path to the pure seeker that's still afforded in orthodox religious systems?

CARLA Well to the pure, all things are pure, basically. That's the cliché. But more specifically, and, I guess more cleanly answering your question: the things that Jesus actually said are far, far different than the things that the church says in dogma. Jesus was remarkably vague about anything to do with *you will follow me* or *you need to found a church and keep it going through the centuries*. There's no career or corporate-mindedness. His idea was to have churches in people's homes where everybody could gather and worship and also socialize, I think, and take care of the poor among them so that nobody was hungry, so that everybody was taken care of. That was His idea. It was basically communistic, and so everybody runs like crazy, [*chuckles*] including communists, from the Christian dogma or what the Christian message is from Jesus, which is to love each other. And that's pretty much it: love each other. And He finds different ways of saying that.

And so, if you're pure-minded and you simply focus on what Jesus said, and base your worship and Christian life on what Jesus actually said, there's no problem whatsoever being totally pure. And if you try to follow all the dogma, you'll make yourself crazy. I don't know how a person can do that and stay totally pure, because there are some very troubling aspects, mostly including elitism and kicking people out if they don't agree with you. That's not something that Jesus would have ever done, and it's certainly not something that I have a need to do. I'm very inclusive in the way I feel about . . . [*chuckles*] *everybody in*, basically. *Everybody's okay; all ways, they're alright—for them*, you know.

So I think if you're a pure person, and you're following that pure message of love and compassion and loving each other, there isn't a problem being pure and staying religious because that was the epitome of Jesus. So it just needs to be an understanding of Jesus that is not vulnerable to priests explaining to you what Jesus thought. Even Paul re-worked things that Jesus said in order to allow things to be okay, like women being far different than men, and slavery being okay. There are things, even in the New Testament, that one would have great trouble with if one tried to justify them. But if you aren't worried about trying to justify what somebody else said about Jesus, then you just say, "Well, different people have different interpretations of what Jesus said; my interpretation is this one."

GARY So, as Ra is indicating, as is common with all orthodox religious systems, there are negative aspects. Like you were saying: elitism, exclusivity, bellicosity, fundamentalism, et cetera, that are wrapped up in the mix. So for the pure seeker wishing to work within an orthodox religious system, you would recommend not taking a literal interpretation and—

CARLA Right. I'd recommend the mystical point of view rather than the dogmatic point of view.

GARY —finding the essence or the heart of the message, sticking to that, and excluding all the detritus.

CARLA Well, just not addressing it. I mean, it's not your business to address details of dogma. Let somebody else do that. That's a game that is not attractive to the mystic. It's just a distraction.

GARY So the mystic then proceeds forward in a manner that Q'uo would recommend, which is to take what resonates and leave the rest behind.

CARLA Right, right.

GARY Prior to launching into the next type of questioning, is there any-thing you wanted to say in terms of the chronology of your life?

CARLA Well, not unless you wanted me to go from where I was a librari-an . . . well, actually, from where Jim and I started singing together—not *this* Jim McCarty, but Jim D.—and then got distracted from that. And I don't know if I actually covered the fact that, you know, a series of neces-sities brought me back to Louisville, and that here in Louisville, finally, was where I settled on my life's work.

GARY Yeah, those questions about your four-year detour with Jim D. were originally part of this bio section, but then we dug into that when we were talking about events before the Ra contact.

CARLA Okay, so that's all taken care of. No, other than that, there's noth-ing that I would really think is unusual about my life. Really my life has been involved in serving however I could, wherever I was, doing whatever I did.

GARY That you served as a channel for a group of beings who say they came from elsewhere in this solar system, I think that by definition quali-fies as unusual. But I grasp the humility that you are reflecting on your life with.

So, you're a person with many types of gifts and talents, in my opinion, and many roads you could have walked in life, and some you tried. Yet, in each case, life seemed to steer you from one road to the next until you set-tled on working with Don, and then channeling as your primary outer service. Can you talk about the multiple decision points and twist of fate that led you to focus yourself primarily on L/L Research and channeling?

CARLA All of these decision points had one thing in common, and that was that there was an ethical question at the bottom of that decision, as far as I was concerned. I have always been very interested in being a man of honor: that general description of an honorable person, a person who can be counted on, a person who can be trusted, a person who is loyal and who keeps his promises. So there was always a promise to be kept, or loy-alty to pay attention to, or both. And at the heart of why I did what I did. And the other characteristics that the decision points seem to have had in common was that I picked the difficult and unpopular path that no one else in their right mind would have taken [*chuckles*]—according to my family, at least.

GARY What you would also call "the high road."

CARLA The high road, yeah. *Take the high road.* And I didn't need to have to justify that to somebody else, because I knew what I was doing: something that was important enough to me to turn my life upside down to do it. Plus, mother would say, "You're sacrificing everything," being a woman of great drama, "Everything!" And I would say, "Hey! You don't know what's around the next corner. It might be interesting." And off I'd go.

GARY What I didn't ask you when we discussed your four years with Jim D., your journey to Chicago, and then to Vancouver was that during those four years we learned that Don was patiently waiting for you to return—he, possessing a sense that you two would be together. But on your side of that equation, did you have a sense during your four years with Jim D. that you needed or wanted to be with Don?

CARLA Heavens, no. I had no idea. It would never have occurred to me that it would be possible. Don was so far above me. He might as well have been driving his car in some track along the sky, far away.

GARY So when you did return to Louisville, and Don goes from zero to sixty in a couple minutes . . .

CARLA Color me surprised. And delighted! But very surprised.

GARY So, in the sense of being delighted, it felt like a gift, I would presume.

CARLA Well, it took me about fifteen seconds to fall for Don.

GARY You wrote in Book V that, "I had had but one goal for a long time from 1968 onwards, and that was to make a real home, both physical and metaphysical, for Don." I think we've probably hit that, but if you want to touch on that, how did you seek to do that?

CARLA I felt that I needed to be there if he wanted me to be there. I needed to be at his beck and call. I needed to find out what it was that he liked in life, and see if I could do that for him. I took care of his food, and I made sure that he had enough underwear. [*laughing*] You know, I mean, just that the basic nitty-gritty of life. I made him a physical home in this world. He never again had to worry about stuff like that.

GARY You began to touch on this coming topic, but I'd like to explore it a little bit more fully. You've described Don's passing as the ending of one life and the beginning of a new one. Can you explain this?

CARLA Well, when Don died, psychologically I died. I had changed enough of myself that I was unfamiliar to myself unless Don was there. With him gone and the needs that he had for me gone, I had no job description, and so I had to start from scratch. And there was a big question for several years after he died as to whether I wanted to stay here at all. And during that time my body got really, really sick. That's why I couldn't even sit up, and every breath I took was an agony. And the arthritis was working its way through the deeper of my body systems, and it hurt to breathe. It was almost impossible to sit up. My shoulders had crystalized to the point where sitting up was too much for them, and the pain of that was incalculable. And needless to say I just didn't do it.

So, I came close to death physically; I came close to death psychologically. And then one day I read something I had written, and I thought to myself, *I like this person.* And that was very cheering to me, that I actually liked—I had forgotten that I'd written it. And I found it. And I didn't even recognize it when I read it, but I liked it. And I just basically decided I needed to kick myself in the butt and give it a go, you know, so I asked for the rehab, because I knew I could never get back up without it, and I wanted a vertical life if I could do it. So they tested me at—what's the name of the place that I went for rehab?

JIM Frazier.

CARLA Frazier. I went to Frazier Rehab here in Louisville. And first of all they tested me for nine straight days to see what I could and couldn't do in terms of safety. And that about killed me [*laughing*] right there! But after they tested me thoroughly and decided what I could and couldn't do, then I went back for three weeks into hospital rehab training. Training, mostly your thinking processes, but also giving you a lot of tools.

And I worked my way by the hardest: sitting up and getting up. It was very difficult. It was one of the hardest things I ever did. And I can remember sitting up in my wheel chair, just dying. "Jim, is it a half hour yet? . . . Oh." You know, it would be five minutes, [*chuckles*] then ten, but you know, the goal was to sit up for half an hour a day. And I got to where I could do that, and then I used my love of cooking to get stronger. I would hold on to the stove because you can't leave a white sauce before it's done, you know? [*laughing*] *Stir, stir. No, it's not done yet; I can't leave.*

And I got stronger. I just physically got stronger to where I had a vertical life again. And then I had my choice of how to go about things, you know, and I described that before, it seems to me, in this interview. Did I want to be a church person? Did I want to be—? Was I able to take up librarian-ing again and make some money for the family? What could I do? And discovered, well now, I couldn't make money for the family because I could never say I'll be there at five days a week. Sometimes I just had a bad day or a bad week. Nothing I could do about it. So, and I didn't like church work for some of the same reasons I didn't like politics. So then it occurred to me that I could work for L/L Research and write. And so that started me on my course of making a life for myself: writing, teaching, channeling for L/L Research.

GARY So, six to eight years, roughly, that you went through a desert of sorts after Don passed away, thanks to some measure of self-condemnation. And then the transformation was precipitated by forgiveness of self—of falling in love with the self. Would you say that is correct?

CARLA I think that's accurate. It was unfortunate that I did condemn myself so thoroughly, but I'd be surprised if anybody close to a suicide ever escapes self-condemnation. You always think you could have done things better.

GARY When Don was alive he served as the natural leader of your small band. With his passing, you had to take up that mantle and assume those responsibilities. How did you transition into that role?

CARLA Without any difficulty at all. I've never had any trouble leading. Jim has always been a partner that pretty much trusted my intuition and was glad to follow my lead. Jim does not have a desire to lead whatsoever. He just wants to be able to serve, as we've served together for so long. You know: take care of the yard, take care of me, and work for L/L Research. Simple as that. Jim's a simple guy.

GARY People on a spiritual path tend to develop strict rules and ideas about diet. [*Carla giggles*] What role has diet played on your path?

CARLA None whatsoever! I'm a fool for a good—

JIM You've tried them all.

CARLA [*laughing*] Yeah. Give me salt. I have tried them all. And none of them seem to do a lick of good. So why bother? If nothing is going to do me any good, then I might as well enjoy myself, and I have. And mostly by eating comfort food and too much salt.

GARY It's a large topic. In general I think it's safe to say that probably many spiritual seekers feel that spirituality is incompatible with certain diets. That in order to be spiritual you must restrict, and limit, and choose only certain foods.

CARLA Mm-hmm. [*chuckles*]

GARY Each, of course, must walk their own walk, and if they feel called to do so, to eat a certain diet, then by all means, more power to them.

CARLA Yeah, I don't have anything against other people thinking that.

GARY Yeah. But you—in your thinking I would imagine there's no, like, one size fits all, there's no prescription for *you must eat this way* in order to be spiritual.

CARLA No. No, I don't feel that. And nor do I feel that my way is the right way. What I'm saying about myself is that I really, honestly gave a good try to vegetarianism, to the macrobiotic diet. I really liked macrobiotics and I would have gladly stayed on it, but that was the point at which I started having horrible problems with my stomach, having to have operations, and things get taken out. So, macrobiotics—the rice, especially—did not agree with my system. I couldn't eat it; it got stuck in the transverse colon and I ended up having to have parts of the transverse colon removed, along with the rice [*chuckles*], which stayed there and made its home and invited friends. Anyway, so macrobiotics didn't work. I cobbled together a Cayce diet, and this was long before other people had done so, but I had this big thick book of Cayce readings, and I went through the whole doggone thing. And wherever he recommended something for rheumatoid arthritis, I wrote it down. So I had a diet that way. And I did that for about a year and a half. It didn't work at all; I didn't enjoy myself at all. So I let it go. And I tried something else . . . not remembering exactly what, but it was a stricter diet, and it didn't—

JIM Low sediment.

CARLA Well, the low sediment was the one I ended up with, and the one that I've more or less backed away from—not been so careful about. Now I was thinking of one of the diets that people who say things like Gary suggested, you know: well, in order to be a spiritual person, you've got to do something. It wasn't veganism exactly but it was this diet where you had nine different food groups, and you need to have one thing from each of those food groups on the table at all times. Anyway, that was a hard one to follow because there was so much to prepare. But I did follow that for a while, and it did absolutely nothing, again, to help me. So, since it was not doing anything, and—I mean, I gave them at least fifteen months if not a year and a half or two years, each of these diets—I gave them a good try. I let them see if they would work, and they didn't work.

So I ended up just shrugging, and like Jim said, the doctors had recommended low sediment diet, where everything has to be ground up. So I don't eat salad, and I don't eat rice, or especially brown rice, and—what's the other one? I was supposed to stay away from oatmeal. I think popcorn's the other one. I've ignored that. [*laughing*] I love popcorn! But anyway, I have more or less paid attention to that in the extremes, you know: I don't eat big hunks of any red meat. I get it all cut up for me, and so forth. But for myself, I just saw the details as being ridiculous to pay attention to if they weren't helping me. So I just go with my bliss and enjoy what I eat. I think my spiritual principle involved there is to enjoy what I'm doing, and if I'm not enjoying it, don't do it.

JIM　Remember what Jesus said about diet?

CARLA　Um . . . what did Jesus say about diet?

JIM　"Man is defiled by what comes out of his mouth, not what goes into it."[6]

CARLA　That's true. He said that. Good one.

GARY　At one point Ra says:

> RA　This instrument, feeling that it lacked compassion to balance wisdom, chose an incarnative experience whereby it was of necessity placed in situations of accepting self in the absence of other-selves' acceptance and the acceptance of other-self without expecting a return or energy transfer. This is not an easy program for an incarnation but was deemed proper by this entity. 60.8

So my question is: How have you seen this dynamic manifested in your life? And how have you met this incarnational lesson?

CARLA I think there isn't a soul that's not aware how there are some people in your life that just take and take and never give you anything back at all. And perhaps they've had the experience of loving those people and wishing that they were loved back but not feeling loved. And so they probably can identify with my disappointment at having someone in my life that was like that. And I've always had someone in my life that was like that. But as I have learned that lesson, the difficulty has gotten less and less hard, and easier to identify so that I know, *oh, that's the person in my life who's not going to love me back. Okay, I got it.*

So you just love that person and you don't worry about getting anything back. And that is hard sometimes, because everybody wants to have, if not appreciation, at least acknowledgment. And there are people in this world that don't do that.

GARY So, according to Ra, and according to your own understanding of the way your life works, you designed this as a central lesson into your life so that you would interact with this sort of person that wouldn't give you love back, in order to help you meet and learn this lesson.

CARLA Right, and I think that at the point at which I really do love myself tremendously, that, at least for the moment, has not been a big catalyst in my life for a while.

GARY So you've gone through those cycles enough—

CARLA I've gone through a lot of cycles, yeah, and I seem to be at the point where, just a little touch up [*chuckles*] from time to time is enough.

GARY Yeah. So you're not terribly daunted if you give love and there's nothing in return.

CARLA No. No, I'm not.

GARY You can love people as they are.

CARLA I can.

GARY During the Ra contact, Ra describes your "arduous journey of worth in esse." Can you describe this journey and your lessons learned along that road?

CARLA Yeah, well I think that we all have a tendency to identify ourselves with what we do. And get our worth from being a good provider, or a good this, a good that—you know, you name it. And to be worthwhile in esse,* (which is just Latin for in and of yourself; just because you are, you're worthwhile) is difficult to get into your mind, and thank God I had that lesson learned, for the most part, before I became ill enough that I was unable to do much outer work. I would be in a pickle right now if I didn't think that I was worthwhile just sitting here.

But I do—I do realize that we're all worthwhile if we can simply keep an open heart, and that I can. So I focus on the open heart. I let my worth be what it is. I don't worry about it. I don't obsess about it, and I accept the fact that I am worthy. And thank heavens that I have learned that. I would have had no peace of mind as an ill person—you know, what's happening to me right now—if I hadn't done that work beforehand.

GARY So this is a lesson that's universal, it seems, for everybody—

CARLA I think so.

GARY —who measure themselves through all sorts of different ways based on what they're doing or what they're not doing, or what they have, what they don't have, where they're going, et cetera, and the message here is that regardless of anything on the outer picture, you are worthy *because you are.*

CARLA Right.

GARY And it seems you were able to learn this by consciously directing your attention to this lesson, and affirming its value, would you say?

CARLA Well, I used a visual aid to fall in love with myself. Maybe I felt like I hadn't been hugged and loved enough as a child, and that I really hadn't had a childhood, you know, because I'd been working the way an adult works to take care of my brothers, to take care of the house, and put food on the table and that kind of thing since I was a child. And all through my childhood that was a theme, so I really didn't have the kind of childhood that a lot of people had where they had no thought in their mind except to play. I didn't have that, so I thought well, okay, I do feel bereft, I do feel that my inner child was deeply unloved.

So my teacher, Papa—I call him Papa. He's gone from this world now.

---

* Pronounced eh-see.

He sent me a Raggedy Ann doll, and he told me that this was my inner child. He told me to love it until, you know, I'd healed. He said, "Heal yourself up. You don't need this." So I took that Raggedy Ann doll with me everywhere, day and night. I loved on it, I hugged it, I kept it with me, I talked to it. I went with it to lunch with my girlfriends. [*laughing*] I took it to the movies. I was pretty silly, but I was learning a lesson, and I didn't let that silliness get in my way. I just went ahead and did it. I packed it up when I went on vacation. [*giggles*] Raggedy Ann needed to go too! You know? So, I did that for, oh, probably six or seven years, and it took a long time to really feel that I did love myself, and I was not any longer in need of healing.

GARY You had that doll when I moved in, too; I remember that distinctly. That speaks to the creative possibilities that are open to one desiring to learn a lesson. There's no mathematical procedure for it . . .

CARLA No, you need to be creative with it. Figure out what's hurting and how can you heal it.

GARY Another, shall we say, *arduous* aspect of your journey has been the distortions of the physical complex. As you said, you've had a frail body since you were born. And it was that which became the primary target for negative greeting during the Ra contact. Those medical difficulties started at birth and have continued all the way to the present. Do you have any sense of the *why* behind the physical difficulties? Why you programmed this life for them?

CARLA Not really. I sort of think that I felt that this would be a good way to learn to love myself, not to judge myself. And I'm not precisely sure how that works out, you know. I don't know if it works out in any linear sense, but, I don't know . . . [*to Jim*] Have you had a feeling about that? You've lived closely with me for a long time. You know what I'm saying in the first place, and if so, would you agree?

JIM Yeah, I think it had to do with interrelationships with other people, especially with me.

CARLA And how especially with you?

JIM So I could take care of your needs, if possible, and generate a certain sort of love and open heartedness.

CARLA That's true. It's a lot harder to allow yourself to be loved than to love, for me; I think for a lot of people.

GARY Of course you can only conjecture on this side of the veil, but this condition created a situation whereby you could accept the love offerings of others, specifically Jim, and where Jim could learn to give that love, or learn to take care.

CARLA He was trying to open his heart, and so we fit together just like a puzzle. So often I think when there's a relationship that really works, you look at the dynamics and you see that both are teaching both. Each is the teacher of each.

GARY So there's a strong possibility then that, prior to incarnation, both of you got together, and you said, "I'm going to play this role, you're going to play that role, and we're going to work together so we can help each other learn these particular lessons."

JIM Could very well be.

GARY Much encouragement was given by Ra for you to contemplate the acceptance of your physical limitations and medical difficulties, and much has been reflected in your own writing regarding that difficult task. Can you shine some light into this aspect of accepting limitations?

CARLA There are two ways to look at limitation. Either it's a limitation that is agreeable to one (you're just as glad you don't have to do that anyway), or you don't want to accept the limitation. And you feel that you can do better than that, and more than that, and you want to press on. And so you don't want to be limited. And I've always felt strong inside, but then I put my body into it, and I discover I've written checks my body can't cash. [*laughing*] *I'm so mad! No! I'm not going to get to do that!*

That was most especially apparent in things like cleaning and cooking, which has never mentally or emotionally troubled me. I've always gotten quite a bit, actually, out of doing stuff—I mean, people say, "Well, who wants to clean the john?" Well, if you're talking to the john, and you're feeling the john say, "Oh man, you really got me clean! This is so great! I'm just shining!" [*laughing*] You know, and everybody's happy. The john's happy, you're happy—you know? And you got a nice clean john! And I would get down on my hands and knees and do the floor, and it never bothered me. But then, it physically bothered me to where I couldn't do it. And it just was aggravating.

And cooking especially was my dearest love. I loved to cook. I loved to collect recipes and try them out and fiddle with them. Not being able to cook is very frustrating. I still get to cook a little bit in that I pick the recipes and stuff, so I can sort of say, "Well, this would taste good." It's not really cooking. Even if you're collecting a recipe and creating a recipe and changing a recipe, you're thinking of it in your mind, but it's not the same thing as doing it. Getting it all chopped up and ready, and then putting it all together and then watching people go, "Oh, this is so good!" and enjoying them enjoying your food. And really, I think people react to the love in the food. There's something about a food cooked with love that just tastes better. That's always been true of my food.

GARY So accepting your limitations sounds like it has tied into what we explored in a recent question about worth in esse.

CARLA Right. You know, the lesson is not to identify with what you can't do, but to identify with *who you are*. And I've done that. I'd still rather cook, but I've done that.

GARY Yeah, when you've described to it to me personally, before, regarding especially where you are now—three years in a hospital bed, unable to do a lot of what you want to do—you expressed an attitude of surrender, saying, "Well, if this is what the Creator wants, then I'm going to accept this, and love this, and—"

CARLA And explore it. You never know what gifts something like this has in its pockets, so you want to put it on and take a look in the pockets.

GARY As a side question: it just occurred to me as you were describing toilet cleaning that you have had this attitude, when you interact with your environment, that your environment is alive and magical, whether it's food or whether you're cleaning the toilet or whether you're weeding the garden outside. What effect would you say that this attitude has had in your life?

CARLA Why, I think it's improved it immeasurably. I've enjoyed myself more than most people because there's more to enjoy if everything's alive and reacting to you, and you're a part of a dance. You're always dancing. You're always having a good time.

GARY Do you feel that what you're interacting with, whether it is a chair or a flower or the wind, that you are psychologically projecting magic onto it, or that there is inherently aliveness and magic in everything around us?

CARLA Oh, I think I am perceiving something real. I think there is inherently magic in everything, and I wouldn't be a bit surprised if science didn't bear me out on this eventually. It certainly had borne me out on the fact that everything is alive, you know, the string theory of physics and other things that. We're just—this is such an alive universe, and it's reacting to you being part of it. I mean, I can do my dance in bed here. Nothing keeps you from dancing if you're dancing in your heart.

GARY Do you attribute any of the current wear and tear on your body to the contact with Ra itself? If so, what do you think are the long-term repercussions of that experience upon your mind/body?

CARLA I think that there was a definite wearying effect that contact had on me. I wouldn't say there were any specific effects it had on me.

GARY Those that know you are frequently struck by one startling fact: that despite the presence of chronic, deep-level physical pain, your spirit is indomitable. You remain a person of optimism, hope, faith, and good cheer, always seeking to serve others, seldom (if ever) complaining (or if you do it's always with a light touch), and never failing a tuned attitude of praise and thanksgiving. What faculty within you has supported such dogged positivity? In other words, how in the world are you always smiling?

CARLA I think faith is a renewable resource, and I think if you have the wit to go seek it, it's always right there. Spirit is right there waiting for you to ask.[7]

GARY And it sounds like your life circumstances have necessitated that you consciously turn to that renewable resource.

CARLA Yes, but that has been my habit for many years as well. I would be in a pickle of a learning curve if I had to learn it all right now. Uh! It's a lot to learn. But I've had years, so . . . I've had time.

GARY This next question is sort of a reiteration of the previous one. The experts, doctors included, have expected your imminent death since age zero. [*Carla chuckling*] You've defied them and the odds all along. I personally feel that many others in your body wouldn't have made it this far, myself included. To what do you attribute your outstanding longevity, all things considered?[8]

CARLA Taking life easy. I think, you know, the easier you take things, the less stress you put on yourself, the more you're going to be able to withstand the stress of illness. There is a certain stress involved with pain.

GARY You've also had a technique of "finding the caption."

CARLA Yes, I do, and I guess that it's just a tick of mind, you know, but I always am pausing the camera, you know the bio-camera that is running over your shoulder at all times and saying, "Did you get that, George?" [*laughing*] "Wait a minute! Got to put a caption on this one!" [*laughing*] I don't freeze it and then hold it, but I may freeze it long enough to appreciate it.

GARY You feel that you are a wanderer in the sense that your soul came to Earth from another density in order to be of service. When and how did you become aware of this and how have you related to this belief?

CARLA I guess I became aware of it with the hypnotic regression, became aware of this coming from elsewhere. It felt right. I put it on, I tried it on; it fit pretty well. So, I thought, *well, that's probably true.* And I just accepted it for what it was. You know, you can't prove it. You can't prove that it's not so. So why worry about it. It looked like it's true so you might as well just figure it's true for you, subjectively.

GARY Well, thank you very much, Carla Rueckert.

CARLA It's been a blessing . . .

Now I'm going to enjoy listening to Jim! [*chuckles*]

---

[1] Sometime after being born in Illinois, Carla's family moved to Anniston, Alabama. When that happened or for how long she stayed in Alabama is unknown at this juncture, but sometime thereafter her family moved again, this time to Louisville, Kentucky, presumably sometime around 1957 when she was 14 years old. Carla spent the remainder of her years in her beloved Louisville, the city that would eventually become the home of L/L Research.

[2] The full English idiom is: *wet behind the ears*. A phrase meaning that one is immature, unknowledgeable, inexperienced, or just too young to understand. Carla is using a variant of the idiom here. In this case the more knowledgeable parents tell the less knowledgeable child that he or she is too young and/or foolish to know what they are describing and experiencing, thus it cannot be real.

3   "Glomerulonephritis is a group of diseases that injure the part of the kidney that filters blood (called glomeruli). Other terms you may hear used are nephritis and nephrotic syndrome. When the kidney is injured, it cannot get rid of wastes and extra fluid in the body. If the illness continues, the kidneys may stop working completely, resulting in kidney failure."

"Glomerulonephritis," National Kidney Foundation, accessed July 4, 2016, https://www.kidney.org/atoz/content/glomerul

4   Carla had earned her undergraduate degree in English literature from the University of Louisville in 1966 and her master's degree in Library Service in 1971.

5   Over the years Carla had, very deliberately, on multiple occasions, described herself as a Christian mystic.

I emphasize that because it is said of true mystics that they speak the same basic language, regardless of their religious, cultural, or historical background. That language or message is universal and timeless, transcending, as it does, the dogmas of church doctrine. The Persian mystic of the thirteenth century should be mutually intelligible with the Chinese mystic of the sixth century BCE and the American mystic of the twentieth.

"Christian mystic" implies that Carla is rooted in the universal aspects of Christianity: a follower of Christ but not necessarily a follower in the particulars of church dogma.

This is not to denigrate religious ritual and belief. Both can and do certainly serve as a vehicle of worship, a conduit of particulars through which the seeker transcends limited human conceptions of the ultimate nature of things, but more often than not the religious institution or code is opaque to that which it seeks to represent. Dogma tends to add distortion, obscure truth, exclude and separate. Dogma tends to discourage critical thought and genuine self-exploration. It precludes the empowerment that springs from the inherent authority and primacy of the personal connection to the truth within, the truth of oneself.

Mystics see through and beyond this dogma in order to recognize the *essence* of the message contained within. As mentioned elsewhere in this chapter:

> RA This [muddied polarity of religious understanding is] in common with each of your orthodox religious systems which have all become somewhat mixed in orientation, yet offer a pure path to the One Creator which is seen by the pure seeker. 60.18

6   "Not that which goeth into the mouth defileth a man; but that which cometh out of the mouth, this defileth a man."

(Matt. 15:11 [KJV])

7   Jim writes more about this in the August 28, 2015 entry of *The Camelot Journal:*

Tonight I read the November, 2006 entries that Carla made in the Camelot Journal. What strikes me most about all of her entries that I have read so far is her total dedication to being of service to others no matter what difficulties she faced. In tonight's entries she described painful spasms around her GI tract. So she went to her family doctor who referred her to a specialist in that area and they made a preliminary diagnosis of interstitial cystitis. To check this diagnosis they filled her bladder with saline solution and accidentally burst her bladder. Then they apologized for their error, gave her pain meds for the excruciating pain, and said that the test confirmed the interstitial cystitis which has no cure.

This meant that she would have the need to urinate urgently and frequently for the rest of her life. The healing of the burst bladder took much longer than anticipated and needed to be done without the pain meds because they made her stomach very upset and unable to take food. This kind of situation occurred many times throughout her life. It's as if she had pre-incarnatively decided to add a significant degree of difficulty in her ability to be of service to others to increase her polarity, inner strength, will, etc. She never let such physical crises stop her loving and her serving, and, most incredibly to me, they never stopped her happy heart from smiling and loving all those around her. In her frail little body beat the heart of a lion.

The Camelot Journal, Jim McCarty, August 29, 2015, www.bring4th.org

[8]

I've never known another human body so frail and so wracked with difficulties as was Carla's. I had long felt that Carla lived by spirit alone, a supposition shared by others. Ra echoes the same here:

> RA At this nexus it is well to encourage those activities which feed the vital energies as **this instrument lives in this space/time present almost completely due to the careful adherence to the preservation of those mental and spiritual energies which make up the vital energy** complex of this entity. 86.23

> RA The vital energy may be seen to be that deep love of life or life experiences such as the beauty of creation and the appreciation of other-selves and the distortions of your co-Creators' making which are of beauty. Without this vital energy the least distorted physical complex will fail and perish. With this love or vital energy or élan the entity may continue though the physical complex is greatly distorted. 63.17

GARY When and where were you born?

JIM I was found under a catalpa leaf at the age of twenty-seven, fully grown, by my mother and father, in Lexington, Nebraska.

GARY [*laughing*] I knew there was something to the story!

JIM I was born on May 10th, 1947. Kearney, Nebraska. The doctor who delivered me was Dr. Jester.

GARY Is that true?

JIM It is.

GARY That suits the way you have described yourself.

What would you describe of your childhood, growing up in Nebraska?

JIM Pretty normal. Pretty hooked into school, going to school. I was a good student—not great. I always got two As and three Bs no matter whether I was in grade school or graduate school. I went out for sports. That was about the most important thing that attracted me to school. There were sports there. Carla thinks it was my dancing nature that made me go out for sports because there was no place to dance in Lexington, Nebraska, town of 5,000, in the '50s.

GARY I know that you interact with the world, whether in your own bedroom or whether out cutting grass or whether working with stones, in a way that you feel as if you're dancing, moving in rhythm with the world. Was this something you were conscious of at a young age?

JIM No. I just couldn't help it. Everything's got a rhythm. So I just try to keep time with the beat. Everything has a certain pace at which you can do it comfortably. And I've been focused on *doing* things. I've been a do-er, big muscle use, for all my life. So when you're doing things, it's good to get a rhythm. I think that's why the chain gangs and the slaves had the songs and the rhythm to work to, because it was all a hard day of work. And it really does make it easier if you get into a rhythm. Your muscles get where you have an automatic muscle memory that comes back a lot easier than if you're just doing without a rhythm; staccato, shall we say.

GARY Did you find that growing up, as with Carla, that you desired to volunteer, offer your help in some way?

JIM No. As far as helping people out I was pretty unconscious about anything spiritual or service-oriented until about the age of twenty-one. I was a late-bloomer in that regard.

CARLA Tell about what you did, you know, the loner thing, wandering, and arrogance.

JIM Oh! [*chuckles*] When you [Gary] drove past Lexington, Nebraska, last year on Interstate 80, you might have noticed you were following the Platte River. So when I was a kid, I spent a lot of time out at the Platte River. I'd either ride my bicycle out there or my mom and dad would take me out and drop me off and pick me up at the end of the day. They'd drop me off at noon or so and pick me up at five or six o'clock. I'd hike around the river. And then there was a sand and gravel company that was pumping sand and gravel out of the river, and they would create sand pits that were full of fish, carp. I'd go fishing and hiking and looking for arrowheads or fossils or pretty stones. I had a drawer in my chest of drawers at home that was nothing but stones. It got to be pretty hard to get it out after a while because it was heavy. I like rocks. I've always liked rocks.

GARY So before working with stones you were seeking stones.

JIM Yeah! Yeah, I liked their color. I liked their shape.

GARY So your solitary nature showed up all the way back to the earliest stages?

JIM Yeah, well, I was an only child, so I guess it started off there. My mother commented that she noticed when I was a baby that I got along okay with the other kids but I was happiest off by myself.

GARY Did that remain true through your school years?

JIM Oh yeah.

GARY So you didn't have many social activities on weekends either?

JIM No. I never did. I didn't date. I went to my senior prom by myself and came home at nine o'clock after the meal, because I just had a track meet that day, and I was hot and sunburned and tired. So that was my social life. [*laughs*]

GARY Did you get along with the other kids?

JIM Yeah, I got along fine. You know, it's like I said, I was a good student, and I was a likable person. People liked me. And I went out for athletics. I was a big fish in a little pond. Couldn't ignore me.

GARY So how would you describe your parents?

JIM Good people. Simple people. They came through the Depression. Neither graduated from high school because each had to go to work to help support the family. My dad was born in a coal-mining town outside of Birmingham, Alabama, and he quit school, I guess, at his sophomore year in high school and went to work at a grocery store and delivered newspapers to help support the family. His dad had died when he was ten, so he had four other brothers and sisters that his mother needed help supporting. And they worked very hard. She took in laundry and did housecleaning to help support the kids.

My mom was from a similarly poor family in western Nebraska. Dad was raised, by the way, in a log cabin. Mom was raised in a sod house. So she not only had the dirt floor that Dad had, she had dirt walls and dirt ceiling too, and goats on top eating the grass.

CARLA Pioneers in the twentieth century. It was unusual. Both of them grew up in far different places, but had the same pioneer experience and the same values, pitching in to help the family.

JIM Mom rode a horse to school; it was about five miles. All the kids rode horses. If you lived too far away, there wasn't any other way to get there. Either a horse-drawn wagon or a horse. Or you went on a walk, you know, take a few days. It took two days to get to town in the horse-drawn wagon. So, by the time my mom was graduated from the ninth grade, which was the country school, she would have to go to town to go to high school, and they couldn't afford to send her to town, because it took two days to get there and she'd have to have a place to rent. So Mom was sad about that. Her younger sister was fortunate enough they moved after a while and got closer to town so that she got to go through high school and actually went to college, and is a teacher to this day at eighty-four. She's now a substitute teacher.

So when Mom and Dad met and married, they decided that they wanted to give their child everything they didn't have when they were growing up. Which meant [*chuckles*] they were probably trying to spoil me, and they probably did a pretty good job.

But they were very simple people. Mom hardly ever talked much. She still doesn't! Very simple conversation. She's the cowboy. "Yep," "nope," and "maybe." You'd have to pry information out of her.

Dad was more gregarious. When he quit high school he started working in a grocery store and stayed with that profession for the rest of his life. When they were in Lexington, Nebraska, where I was raised, they both worked together in a grocery store called Jack and Jill—you know, like the nursery rhyme characters. But that was part of a chain owned by the Nash Finch company in Minneapolis, Minnesota.

Dad was the manager. Mom was a clerk, and she kept the books. And then when they were home they cooked meals together, they did the housecleaning together, and they did the yard work together. I thought that was the way everybody did it. Turned out it wasn't because Mom was liberated; it was just because that was how they were raised. They had to work together to make it. You know, everybody had to pitch in. The times were just too tough. And that made an impression on the Depression-era children, which is what they were. They were teenagers through the Depression.

And they met in Kearney, Nebraska, where I was born. There was an Air Force base . . . well it was the Army Air Corps at that time[1]. So Dad was a quartermaster. He gave out the uniforms, the shoes, all the equipment. As it turned out, (I think it was probably planned by him before incarnation), a box fell off the top shelf and hit him on his clavicle and broke it. He was deemed unfit for battle, so he never made it out of the United States during the war. And I have a hunch he's a gentle soul that did not want to kill anybody—that's just my guess. So anyway, they worked together all their lives up until the time he died. He was 79 years old. He was still managing a little convenience store.

CARLA He was doing a great job of it. He wasn't just feebly going to work. He managed. He hauled boxes, he made deals. He was wonderful. And they were both healthy as horses.

JIM Yeah, Dad died at 79, and Mom's still alive at 96 and a half.[2] I hope to go back to see her again for her birthday, which is in the first week of December. I always try to go back and see her. And I guess that's pretty much it. They always came to my athletic events. They were big supporters. They always drove a car. We didn't have a bus when we were in high school, so parents would get together and then take four or five kids in the car with them. And we'd go to wherever the game was.

GARY It sounded like you were headed in the direction of describing how your parents met when you were talking about your dad's experience in the military.

JIM There was an Army Air Corps base there in Kearney, Nebraska, and Mom was working as a waitress in The Tasty Tearoom. That was about 200 miles from where she was raised in western Nebraska, because Kearney's in central Nebraska. She and a girlfriend came to Kearney seeking their fortune [*laughs*] I guess, trying to get jobs and also send more money back home. So, she was working as a waitress, and Dad and some of his buddies from the Army Air Corps came in and she was their waitress. And he got to know her and they started dating, and decided to get married, and did.

And then they moved from Kearney to a little town about nine miles outside Kearney called Odessa. It was about 75 people in the town but right then it was on highway 30. That was before the interstate system was built in this country, so it was the main east-west artery connecting Boston and San Francisco. And it was almost exactly in the middle, 1,733 miles from both, which is a curious little fact. And they lived in this combination home, grocery store, and filling station.

So when truckers would come through, they would stop there and get their gas, and they would most frequently pay for their gas with silver dollars. And my mom and dad, whenever they got a silver dollar, would put it aside for my education, my college education. So they got a couple thousand dollars, I guess, that way, which at that time was a lot of money. These days would buy you about twenty minutes of class.

But I remember—I was about two or three years old—my first memories are sitting in the kitchen sink with little dots all over me: chicken pox. And I was getting a bath. And the next memory I have, is—there's a little gravel street on the side there that cut off of Highway 30 and went over to the school yard. I remember little purple flowers that I would pick; I loved these purple flowers. And I remember walking down the road there in my pants and feeling the roughness of the blue jeans against my skin because I just wet my last pair of diapers. So those are my first memories. [*laughing*] Then after that they moved to another town and got to working for this company, Nash Finch. Then they moved to Lexington and started managing the store there.

GARY You had a lot of experiences in the grocery store growing up, didn't you?

JIM I was raised in a grocery store. On Saturday nights when I was in grade school, the store closed at 9 o'clock. After the store closed, I was usually at a movie at the theater across the street. Or I might decide to take a nap in the cardboard boxes that were stacked by the registers to put people's groceries in. Some were large enough for me to fit in.

I went to a movie almost every Saturday night. There were two movie houses, one was right next door to the grocery store, one was right across the street. So I saw all the movies that came through town. And I would sit in row seven, and I would get so totally involved in the movie, with everybody, not just the hero. If there were stressful things happening, I was so engrossed and captured by it—I was taken by it. And I was so glad to get outside and realize it was only a movie, because it would take me away.

CARLA [*laughing*] It's not real, thank god!

JIM And if I'd already seen the movies then I would hang around the store and frequently I'd get sleepy and . . . up front where the checkout registers were they put a bunch of boxes. They get cereal and other things in the store in boxes. They cut them out, stock the shelves, then they would take the box up front and put groceries in it. So you had a big pile of boxes before you went out the door. I would crawl back in there and find a big box and go to sleep in it. So if they couldn't find me they knew where to look for me. I was hiding out in the cardboard boxes.

GARY So, you said when you went to the movies you always chose row seven.[3] So this is—

JIM I've no idea why. [*laughing*]

GARY It's an indicator of your disciplined, habitual, ritualistic way. You chose something and then you tend to do it that way in cycles, again and again.

JIM Yeah, you're right.

GARY So, if I were to ask you what sort of values, you inherited from your parents, I imagine one would be hard work, the need to work hard.

JIM Oh yeah. And it's not that they taught that and said, "Now, you've got to learn how to work hard and be diligent." I just watched. They were both hard workers. They had to be their whole life long. Mom and her dad would hand-milk 27 cows twice a day. I don't know if you've ever milked a cow, but you need a pretty good grip. [*chuckles*] So they were good at working hard and long, so I just did my part. And I didn't realize it—I was a really good worker until I started working with other people.

GARY Would you say you inherited any other values from your parents?

JIM Honesty. They were just as honest as could ever be. They would never do anything that even had the shadow of doubt upon it. They just had high integrity. At the time I thought, you know, I could see their lack of education in their speech patterns. They used incorrect words here and there, tenses on verbs and things. And for a while I was ashamed of that, but I outgrew that. And later as I got older—which happens with most kids, they discover how intelligent and wise their parents were, the older you get. So, yeah, fidelity, faithfulness, and just being good people.

GARY You said that they were very supportive of you, especially given the deficiencies in their own childhood experiences. They wanted to compensate for those and give to you what they didn't have.

JIM Right.

GARY Were you ever in conflict with them?

JIM Not so much as a kid. I remember when I got to be a teenager, it was the time of the hippies and I grew my hair longer when I was in college. My dad and mom really didn't like that very much. I remember my mom saying, "You were a real good kid until you got to be about twelve years old." [*laughing*] But yeah, I really didn't have conflicts with them. I remember maybe two spankings in grade school. And I remember I did something at the dinner table one night and my mom reached over and whapped me. I think that was the only time she ever hit me. She tried one other time but I ducked, I saw it coming. [*laughs*] But, you know, no real conflicts. Just what happened when kids go off to college and become hippies and protest against everything their mom and dad ever believed in. [*laughing*] Not everything, but the government, the war, and so forth. The Vietnam War folks at that time.

GARY Did that sense of support continue when you embarked on this new adventure with L/L Research and you were doing these—

JIM They supported me in everything I did. Even when I lived on the land with no electricity, no running water, kerosene lamp for light, wood stove for heat and cooking, except when it was hot, and I cooked outside over an open fire. You know they grew up under those conditions. They were hoping never to see them again! [*laughing*] They came and visited me and stayed in my little cabin and used my outhouse. And it was fairly familiar to them, but they supported me totally. Didn't understand me a bit [*laughing*], never understood me, but always supported me.

GARY We worked so hard to keep you away from these conditions. And now you return to them.

JIM Yeah. We're trying to give you everything we never had.

CARLA Mmm-hm. The first thing that they ever asked me, or his mom asked me, she says, "What is prompting him to do these things when he can do so much more?"

And I was trying to explain to them that they did really wonderfully, because when you go to college you are furnishing your mind so you can actually think better. And you do: you think more the more you read, the more vocabulary you have, the more different people you've run into that think differently that have new thoughts that you have to grapple with. It all matures your mind, and they gave him that. It didn't matter what he did to earn a living. He was completely using his college. We all use our college regardless of what we do as far as jobs. She never could get that. You know, apart from jobs, what was it, what was the point of going to college? She didn't have the idea of just educating your mind and that being a good thing in and of itself.

GARY In their unconditional support, as you went about your unusual journeys from protesting, to hippie-hood, to being on the land, to channeling with L/L Research, were they ever inquisitive about what you were doing?

JIM Well, they would ask questions, and I would try my best to answer. But I could see that the answers weren't really satisfying them and getting through, so there weren't a lot of questions. They were just very good at just accepting me and loving me no matter what.

CARLA Except for the beard.

JIM Yeah. [*chuckles*]

CARLA It was a small, a very small thing.

JIM When I was graduated from college I had a goatee, and of course with a mortarboard* on top, I looked very Jewish. They didn't have anything against Jews but this kid with a beard, you know . . . Dad was ready to move out of town so he'd never have to be seen again. [*everybody laughing*] If word got around . . .

GARY It was a small town too.

JIM Very small town.

GARY So you described them as simple people. I presume then that they didn't have a strong spiritual or philosophical way of thinking. Did they have a religious belief system?

JIM They went to church every Sunday. We started off I guess as Baptists for a few months till they found the Presbyterian church. And they went until Dad died and Mom would still go if she could. She got her fifty-year membership years ago. So they really didn't have spiritual beliefs. They were, like I said, just good common folks, and they went to church. And Mom was part of a Bible study group, and did things with the ladies.

---

* The academic cap with a square top and accompanying tassel that one wears upon graduation.

They were all ladies in the study group. They went to each other's houses and cooked and brought food and so forth but . . .

GARY This sounds as if it was more of a cultural, social thing than something indicative of strong religious conviction per se.

JIM Yeah.

GARY And you attended church with them on Sundays?

JIM I did. All the way through high school and a little bit in college.

GARY How did you relate to what you were hearing at church?

CARLA [*giggles*]

JIM Didn't really think about it. [*laughing*]

GARY Just went through the procedure and got it done?

JIM Yeah. Like I said, I was pretty unconscious until I was 21. I sang in the youth choir until I was twelve and my voice changed. Then I remember: [*laughing*] I was singing, and this guy in front of me turned around real slowly and looked at me like that—[*Carla laughing*] And I thought, *Oo-oo! Something's the matter with my voice.*

GARY So you leave to go to college upon graduating. What degree did you pursue and earn when you went to college?

JIM My first majors were business and economics. And after four years when I got my degree, I thought, *there's no way in the world I want to pursue these things.* Because that was part of that automatic pattern that I was following. I was expected by my mom and dad, and the company officials from Nash Finch, that I would go to college, get a degree and join the company. They had plans for me. And even through college, I went home in summer, and I worked my dad's grocery store from age of thirteen on, which is a little younger than you're supposed to start for social security. But—[*laughing*] I came home in the summertime, and I worked as a produce manager. I liked the fruits and vegetables; that was about the only thing I could really get excited about in the grocery store.

So the Nash Finch folks figured that I'd be a good candidate for a division manager in their company over produce. And I would go around to the other stores and other towns in the summertime, and fill in for produce managers who were going on vacation. So I got to know a lot of folks in the company that way.

But after the four years, I finally became alive. The hippie generation woke me up. Drugs, sex, rock and roll, and all of a sudden things didn't make as much sense as I'd been taking for granted. And I decided that I didn't want to pursue either business or economics, so I went back for another year. I'd got enough sociology in my undergraduate degree that one solid year of sociology also got me a sociology major. And one of my professors was impressed enough with me that he got me a graduate assistantship at Bowling Green State University in Ohio. And so when I got done with my sociology major, I thought, *no, I don't want to do that either.*

And so I passed up the graduate assistantship and went to Gainesville, Florida to join Teacher Corps, which was a cooperation between Health, Education and Welfare on the Federal level, and the local educational department at the University of Florida. Dr. Leonard Kaplan was the head of the department, and they had a new idea. The Head Start Program had been going on for some years, but a lot of kids that went through Head Start weren't keeping their head start; they were losing it. So this was called a follow-through program. It was for grades one through three. And the idea was to maintain that head start that the kids had gotten. And usually these were—like I say, in Gainesville, and Jacksonville especially, we were working with inner city kids, which were primarily, but not all, black. And they were hoping that we could make a difference.

We got our own classrooms and eventually we got the "incorrigibles": the ones that nobody else wanted. So we were trying to figure out how to do this and—I think it was Jean Piaget who was one of the theorists we were studying. Herbert Kohl and his Open Classroom, Montessori schools—the different ways of approaching education to try to get the educational process more internalized so that the kids are really interested in what they're doing, and they, at some point, can take over more of their direction of learning. So, we did that—and this was also a master's program. Once you finished it, after two years, you got a master's degree. So this was still the time of the Vietnam War and hippies and so forth, and we got to protest what our professors were doing because we had better ideas, we thought, and got a degree and got paid at the same time. It was an ideal situation. [*chuckles*]

So, that was 1972 when I was finally graduated from the University of Florida. And I decided I didn't want to go on with an educational degree. Came to that same point again: that I really didn't like public schools, and I didn't really like working with kids, unfortunately, because they take a lot of energy. If you're going to do it right, they need a lot of energy from you. You can't just get in there and impose discipline and say, "Ok, we're all going to do this at once." It's not that easy, so I thought, *I don't want to do this.*

So one of the books that we used in formulating our setup in our own classrooms was called *The Raspberry Exercises: How to Start a School and Write Your Own Book*, and in the back they had their bibliography of the different sources they used to write their book and start their own school. And one of their resources was a fellow in Colorado: T. D. Lingo and The Adventure Trail Survival School. He was teaching a course of how to really release the dormant brain potential. It was his theory that, if you were able to remove the handful of blockages that are encultured in everybody in almost every culture, the brain would then naturally circuit energy forward into the frontal lobes. There's three-eighths of your brain, from your ears to your eyes, that scientists are only beginning to discover what's there, what it's for, because you can be a normal human being and not use your frontal lobes. Most people don't use their frontal lobes.

There was a book written in 1963 called *The Machinery of the Brain*, by Dean E. Wooldridge. He talks about Phineas Gage. Phineas Gage was a railroad worker back in the 1800s. He set off a dynamite charge as a part of his job that blew a four-foot tamping rod an inch thick through his frontal lobes. He survived! He was more docile afterward, he was more easily manageable, but he was still alive and still kicking and still carrying on. And that's even with his frontal lobes totally destroyed. So the theory that Lingo was following was, if we could just get rid of most of the blockages that people have, that the frontal lobes would be the home of creativity and of contact with, as he called it, *advanced intelligence.* And a lot of times, after the students had been through the course, they began making contact in their preconscious state, which is the state you go through on your way to sleep and come out of on your way out of sleep. It's the equivalent of the alpha state of meditation.

So a lot of the contacts that kids got, or people got, were very interesting, very inspirational; a very high quality of philosophy and ability to write that was beyond what they were capable of previously. One of the techniques we used was essaying. When we discovered there was some sort of a blockage that we knew about in our lives and where it came from we would use essaying as one tool for getting it out, talking about it, discovering it. So we knew what we were each capable of writing because we'd read our essays to each other in the morning around the breakfast campfire. So when they started reporting their contacts with different source of entities—names like [spelled phonetically] Ramord-tary, Ganodzle, Bimbleshack, [*chuckling*]— these contacts were of a very high nature. They were interesting. And so that was part of what came out of the course there with Lingo.

He had been doing this since he got out of college in 1957. (He'd been in World War II and was able to use the G.I. Bill[4] to go to college.) The thing that got him interested in starting the Adventure Trail Survival School was, he served under General George Patton in the Battle of the Bulge at the end of WWII. Sometime after that battle, they got into Germany and began liberating concentration camps.[5] And at that time Hitler was calling up the old men and the young boys, because Germany was obviously defeated but Hitler was not going to give up. So at one point as they were marching through Germany, Lingo came around the corner of a farmhouse, and there was an old German soldier. Turned out it was a grandfather (he didn't know it at the time) so Lingo bayoneted him in his gut, and before the soldier died, he and Lingo sat together on the front porch. The soldier pulled out his billfold, and as he was dying, he showed Lingo pictures of his children and his grandchildren. So the result of this for Lingo was he had to ask himself why he had to kill his brother. You know, why did people kill each other?

So he went to the University of Chicago during what was called The Golden Age. Robert Maynard Hutchins was the university president at that time, and his policy then was to find the best minds in every field of study, and require them to teach freshmen. So they had Mortimer Adler in psychology and David Riesman in sociology. And Enrico Fermi had just split the atom underneath the football stands at the University of Chicago. And one day, informally, Fermi was addressing a group of students outside the classroom, just talking in the hall, and Lingo was on the edge of the group. Fermi said, "I have split the atom and released the energy of the atom. And it is a terrible energy. One day one of you will split the brain atom." And he pointed right at Lingo. So that became Lingo's driving force.

He went back to Colorado. He had a guitar, three chords and six folk songs and he got on the Groucho Marx show. Groucho Marx was a comedian, one of the Marx Brothers. Well, Groucho had a show called *You Bet Your Life* and he had interesting people come on. They had to answer questions, and if you got a number of questions right, you got money. Well, Lingo played his guitar. And some producer in Hollywood saw him and said, "I want that guy." So they did a summer series with Lingo. He got to do eight shows for $2,000 a show. Back in the mid-fifties that was a lot of money. So he took that $16,000, put it in two grocery sacks, gave one to the IRS, and he bought his mountain with the other one.

So he was living at 10,000 feet in the Rocky Mountains outside of Blackhawk, Colorado when I met him. And he started there when he was—I guess he was probably thirty-four or -five in 1957, and he started getting his first classes there. He also worked with inner city kids. He would use the money that he charged kids like me, the fat urban rich kids [*laughter*]—FURKies, he would call them—and he paid for the inner city kids with money from the FURKies. He had a lot better luck with the black kids and the inner city kids than with white kids that were rich because the kids that were poor realized that there may not be another bus that comes along. Whereas white kids had a mindset of, *if I don't make this bus, there'll be another bus.* You know, they were used to luxury.

So, that was what drove Lingo, and he was successful. A lot of students came through there were able to make contact with their frontal lobes, and I was fortunate enough to be able to do that too.

On July 12, 1972 I was in my lean-to—we all built our own lean-tos, that was part of what you did—

CARLA Jim's very good with dates.

JIM Yeah. So, my body was in my lean-to and my mind was in the preconscious state, and it also just happened to be not quite sunrise. The sun was just starting to come up. And I felt my brain—[*chuckles*] Hmm. There was something circulating in my brain. It was like it was made of Jello or something, and all of a sudden, right here [*points to a place on the forehead about an inch above the center point between the brows*] there was a click.

Lingo said it was the amygdala. The amygdala is a little switch in there where, when choices are made, it operates in a different fashion.

CARLA Fight or flight.

JIM Yeah, fight or flight. So, I felt this click, and I felt my frontal lobes come alive and there was—like an orgasm went off in my brain. And after that I guess I had two, three hundred of those experiences while I was on the land. I would feel this pulsing in the frontal lobes. I'd feel that circulation again. And I'd feel that explosion of pleasure and pressure. Frequently there would be visions and voices that I didn't quite understand, never really understood.

But I believe that was the beginning of the work with the indigo ray—the opening of the indigo ray, is what I'm thinking it was. What it did for me was to make me much more creative and be able to solve problems on a basic level.

Lingo had the philosophy—he wanted each of his students that came through there to go out and start your their schools. "Each one teach one" was his saying.[6] This planet needs a little bit of help. We're trying to blow ourselves up with atomic bombs. We need to set off the brain bomb. We need to get people's frontal lobes going. Because once you get that going, you don't want to kill people. You realize you're one with them. You're one with the entire planet.

So I went to Kentucky and found my land and started my own school. And—like I said, there I didn't have any electricity, so I used kerosene lamps for light. And I cooked with wood, and I heated with wood. And in summer when it was too hot to cook inside I went outside and cooked over an open fire. I built a fire pit—a couple fire pits: one for bonfires and one for cooking. And I had a couple of classes of students that came through before I discovered Don Elkins and Carla Rueckert.

Probably other questions in between there too, but I zipped along at warp speed.

GARY I think that's the most I've ever heard you talk at once!

CARLA I asked . . .

JIM I promised Carla I'd go into detail.

GARY [*laughter*] Thank you, Carla.

CARLA You're welcome. I told him it was only the once; we'd never get this chance again, so go ahead. Interestingly enough, when my eye turned into my brain, it was the amygdala into which it was shoving.

JIM She is constantly meditating, I think, with half her—well probably all her consciousness, just half her eyes.

GARY Lingo said that the reason we cannot access our frontal lobes is due to blockages. What are these blockages?

JIM Well it's something that usually gotten in the enculturation process, usually from parents. It can also be from teachers or neighborhood folks; authority figures of one kind or another.

When we are young and impressionable, from zero to seven years old especially, is usually when it happens. We get enculturated with ideas that are—Lingo said they are anti-life, basically. War is one of them. They differ for every person though, and there's usually no more than a handful, three or four large ones. Sex is usually one, self-image is usually one—people lacking in self-confidence because they'd been made to depend upon those outside themselves and they haven't grown their own authentic self.

We used dream analysis to try to figure out what these were. Once you let your subconscious know that you're willing to work with it, and that you want to use dreams to work with it, it'll shoot out a bunch of garbage dreams to start with to kind of get the pump primed, and maybe you won't be able to make a lot of sense out of it. But after a while you'll start giving your dreams in symbolic form. There's a kind of a dream language as Ra started to talk to us about. We just *barely* started asking questions there. But each person can determine his or her own dream language, and once you start working with your dreams, they give you some real good clues as to what your blockages are. Those are the first things I want to do.

The body is a mechanism that heals itself continually on every level, if it's able to, if we give it the ability to do so and make it a good thing to do so. We don't value dreams in this culture. Not many cultures do value dreams. But they can teach us a lot. So once you get your subconscious working with you and feeding you these dreams, then you can find out what some of your blockages are. Once we were able to do that, like I said, we started using things like essaying to get more understanding. While you're writing, a lot of things come to you that you weren't thinking about before you started writing. It's like a channeling, but you're channeling from yourself and your own subconscious.

And once we got a better understanding of that, then we used what are called neurodramas. I think this is sort of like neurolinguistic programming these days. But neurodrama is where you remember specifically where you were and when and by whom you were programmed. And it's usually mom or dad or both. And if you can remember the exact time, then you'd attempt to relive it. When you went through it the first time you were just a kid. You didn't know you had rights. You didn't know you could stand up for yourself. And it would be a good thing if you did overall, but at that time if you stood up for yourself you are liable to get knocked down. So, in the neurodrama, we learned how to stand up for ourselves and to claim our identity, to claim the rights that were taken away from us when we were kids. So it's just—it's another type of therapy. So many of them, then and now, I'm sure, utilize more of a participatory part for the person being therapized, shall we say.

I remember at that time Janov's "Primal Scream" was big.[7] John Lennon was into the Primal Scream with Yoko Ono at that time. Well, we used that too. Whatever would get the energy out, to circuit forward. It was Lingo's philosophy that the neurons in the brain were usually configured in such a way as to hold the energy of that poor programming in place. He called this the energy of neurosis. And once you could free that energy through the dream analysis, through essaying, through neurodrama, Primal Scream, whatever, then this energy of neurosis was released and you had extra energy. This energy could now flow forward in a natural fashion into the frontal lobes. So, that's kind of in a nutshell what I learned and what I went back the second year to teach.

So in '72 I started looking for places. After writing to four or five dozen real estate agencies, I picked out four or five that sounded good and I traveled around in Missouri, Arkansas, Kentucky, Tennessee. I was looking for my piece of land where I could start my school. And I didn't have much luck. Everything I found . . . [*laughter*] . . . this one guy in Liberty, Kentucky, took me out to his place. We were hiking up the side of the hill here, and he was pointing out the boundaries to me. So I said, "The boundary down there is where the hill starts, right?" He replied saying, "Over there, where it starts, and it comes over here, to the south—," "So it's the side of this hill, right?" And he said, "Yeah, that's basically it." [*laughing*] "Okay, thanks anyway."

So I looked at the map, I was in central Kentucky, and Nebraska was a thousand miles away, and I said to myself, "I'm going to stop in, unannounced, to every real estate agent I see." My plan was to tell them what I'm looking for and see if I could get better results. Turned out the first one I stopped into had the piece of land I was looking for.

Eddy Deep took me out to a little place between Gravel Switch, Kentucky, and Bradfordsville, Kentucky, on the Jones Fork—Joner, as it was called by the local people. After you drove down the two-lane blacktop road, it became a one-lane blacktop, then a one-lane gravel, then two ruts [*laughter*] in the road, and it turned off into a creek. And that was my access road, the running creek. And it was rocks all over—you know what creek bottoms look like around here: they're all limestone, their full of rocks. That's why I named my school "Rock Creek." I didn't realize there were other places that were called Rock Creek here in Louisville, like Rock Creek Riding Club.

Anyway, we drove up the creek bottom and it was 132 acres of land. Six acres were bottomland where you could grow crops and you could clear, and I was hoping that eventually I could raise crops there. And on both sides the hills, knobs. They're called 'knobs' if they're too big for hills, too small for mountains in Kentucky. So "knob land" is what I bought; it was unimproved. 132 acres for 6,000 bucks, which was a really good price; nowadays it would be $1,000 an acre.

CARLA At least.

JIM So I bought the land and the first night on the land I had a very unusual experience. It was August, and the creek was dry, which was common for the creeks to go dry in Kentucky in the fall. So I put my sleeping bag in the creek bottom, and it was about twilight; there was still enough light to be able to see fifty or so feet away. I was ready to go to sleep and all of a sudden this gray fox is walking down the creek. He stops at the bottom of my sleeping bag and he looks over at me. I look at him. Outgoing and gregarious, I said, "Hi, how are you doing?" And he grabbed the bottom of my sleeping bag and started shaking it like a dog. And I thought, *this isn't right. Foxes don't do this.* And so I backed off a bit and I got a rock and I threw it and it exploded under him. He didn't move. And I thought, *yep, he's got rabies.* So I just let him go.

And the next day it turned out that a gray fox—it was tobacco harvest season and right down where the road went off into the creek and my land started, there was a barn where they were hanging tobacco. They were up on the tobacco wagon and a gray fox foaming at the mouth came biting their tires. So I got to meet a rabid gray fox [*laughter*] first night on the land. And I never really took any great message from that other than there are going to be challenges and you're going to be dealing with a lot of crazy people [*laughter*] but you're going to come through it just—in good shape, fine shape.

GARY One more question about the T. D. Lingo experience, and that's that, in order to remove these blocks, you did dream work and essaying and neurodrama, which has elements in common with a lot of *know yourself, accept yourself* sort of therapies. But what specifically about that linked that work to the frontal lobes. What caused—

JIM Why did it work? Yeah, I'm glad you asked that question because it's a very important point. It's done in the primal nature environment. Lingo said that the brain gets overloaded in the urban environment. There's too much information. And it begins to back off and to shut down in certain areas, the frontal lobes being one of them. So this type of therapy doesn't work in the city. You have to be in the primal nature environment, because in the primal nature environment you're receiving a normal or an organic level of input. And in this nature environment the brain is able to come out of its shell, shall we say, with a little help from you. So, the reason that it works with the frontal lobes is because of the body and the brain want to work naturally and normally. They just need a little help, and if you can do that in the primal nature environment then success is much more likely.

GARY And perhaps as that was one of, if not the, objective of the whole undertaking, that kind of set an intent, set a framework for precisely that result to manifest.

JIM Yeah, that was the intent for sure. Around the clock. We used our sleep too. [*chuckles*]

GARY You said that one of the reasons for activating and unlocking the frontal lobes was for creativity and communication. Was there any other reason for doing that work?

JIM Well it seemed to be the natural thing, a natural outgrowth of service to others. Lingo looked at the old brain as being the competitive consciousness in our capitalistic society, where a few people are in charge of a whole lot of people and tell them what to do. It's like a corporation or military the way it's formed; a pyramid, from the top down. And it's competitive. But competitive consciousness doesn't produce results as good as cooperative consciousness. Cooperative consciousness is automatically released with the circuiting of energy into the frontal lobes. So he was hoping that if enough people could do that, that we would get away from the type of consciousness that could destroy this planet. And that was his thing, is that he had been to war, he had seen war and he knew the next war could be the last war. So that was his motivation.

GARY So increased awareness, development of consciousness and—he may not have used this terminology, but—opening the heart.

JIM Right.

GARY Any speculation as to the origins of the sources being received and the communication aspect of frontal lobe development?

JIM Are you talking about the people who are doing research into that area or people who are experiencing it or—?

GARY No. You named some like, strange, like, Harry Potter-sounding names.

JIM Oh, the name of the people channeling through; yeah, the contacts. They said that they were extraterrestrials. They said they were in spaceships parked on the other side of Saturn.

GARY [*laughter*] That set the stage.

And a quick question before we return to your experience on the land. You participated in the counterculture while in college. Could you describe a little more about that?

JIM [*laughter*]

GARY In terms of how you participated in newspapers and . . .

JIM Oh. Yeah, well, ok. Where do we start? [*laughter*] In college there was a fellow, a priest, a Catholic priest by the name of Father John Scott. He was the head of the Newman House, which is usually where Catholic students go to live. This particular Newman House is where the radicals went to live. We had a newspaper called *The Scorpion*. (You could see our attitude at the time.) I was the columnist for the paper. We had various demonstrations on campus, everybody did—it was the "in" thing to do!

And we were not about to be left out.

So when the incursion into Cambodia occurred, we had a demonstration. Throughout the country college campuses were being shut down. So we thought, *we need to do that here too.* So that was going to be our goal, but the president of the University—well let's see—now it's the University of Nebraska at Kearney; at that time it was Kearney State College—and the president wanted to see if he could talk us out of it. So he and a couple of the trustees met with us at his house and talked to us about *what did we want?*

The particular thing we were demonstrating about at that time—the Vietnam War and the Cambodian Incursion were certainly the basis for it, but—one of our group from *The Scorpion* was student-teaching at the time and he was dismissed from student teaching altogether because he was participating in writing columns for the paper. We thought that was an abridgment of his free speech rights. So that was the particular reason, in conjunction with the general reason, of why we were there. So we were attempting to get him reinstated and also to see if we could get some classes on educating people concerning the Vietnam War. And so the President said, "It sounds reasonable. We'll see what we can do to help you." And so they did. And from that point on he and I were friends! He handed me my diploma and gave me a good, hearty handshake. And that was what happened at Kearney State College.

Then I went on to the University of Florida and didn't partake in so much structured demonstrations or things at that time—more of the concerts and the happier side of being a hippie: drugs, sex, rock 'n roll. But our activism was—we were expressing that in Teacher Corps, in our classes. We talked to our professors and it got certain things through and done so that we could get our own classrooms. We could try some new ideas and see if there could be another way of approaching the educational system because we had all been part of that educational system. Basically we thought we survived it, we didn't thrive there. We were able to survive it. We were looking for another way of doing things. That's pretty much it. [*laughter*] There were other details but, who cares?

GARY Like Forrest Gump says, "That's all I have to say about that."

So your experience on the land. We know what you did to earn income. You hired out your labor on tobacco farms.

JIM Farm labor in general, tobacco specifically, yeah. That's where I got most of my money.

$1,500 to $2,000 a year was all I needed to support myself. You have to remember this was the seventies! Inflation has taken a toll.

CARLA He ate a great many beans. [*laughter*]

JIM Yeah. Beans. And chapattis. That was pretty much my diet.

GARY How much of what you needed for survival came from the land itself, and how much did you need to purchase with actual money?

JIM Well I did raise my own food, most of my own food—vegetables anyway, and dried what I could. I didn't need to purchase a lot in the way of food. And I think I still have clothes that I wore down there. Gas and insurance, repairs on my truck, and tools are mostly where I spent my money. I did need some canned goods from town, and I needed to buy some of the grains that I couldn't grow, like corn. I could buy corn and wheat berries. So I could grind my own corn and grind my own wheat and make bread. And in the winter when it was cold enough, I could make yogurt and just keep the yogurt starter over in the corner because it never got warm enough for the cabin in the winter to kill the yogurt. I ate pretty simply.

GARY So you had had some preparation prior to going to the land through T. D. Lingo's school because it wasn't just about activation of the frontal lobes, but it was also about learning the skills of survival.

JIM Right. And how to survive on the land long term, not the type of survival Outward Bound taught: *Oh our plane crashed! We've got to survive until we get found.* Not that kind. Long-term survival. Raising your own food. Storing your food. Making your own cabin. Doing it all yourself.

GARY Did that adequately prepare you for your six years?

JIM Oh yeah. Well like I said a few times, I did build my own log cabin. And the last thing I built before that was a shoe-shine kit in 9th grade . . . and I got a B. [*laughter*]

CARLA It was beautiful. And it was so completely useful. Everything that he needed was on a shelf somewhere that was fitted exactly for the can that held it. It was all labeled. It was a librarian's delight. I looked at that beautiful, tiny home that he had and I loved it. Just loved it.

So completely organized. Very clean. And very useful. Everything was useful. And the usefulness was its art. He saw the beauty of all that. So, we were very much in sync.

GARY So you were utilitarian in the construction of everything—

JIM Right.

GARY —and all your possessions had a function.

JIM They were all hanging on the wall, just like here. [*chuckles*]

GARY How would you spend your down time on your land?

JIM My process was to get up in the morning and look beside my bed see if I'd written down any dreams because I may or may not remember doing that. And then the first thing I guess was I'd make some tea. Yes, I was an inveterate tea drinker then, and go over to my easy chair—I had a chair much like that [*points to chair in the room*], over-stuffed and comfortable—and I would look at the dream I had, and I would write, and I would try to figure out what the dream was telling me.

So I'd do some writing, and I'd do some reading, and I'd make some breakfast. Of course I'd meditate. And I did that until noon. I didn't do physical labor until noon. Mornings were sacred time. And I learned that at Lingo's too. When you get up out of bed, you got your best chance at doing your therapy and doing your most creative work, mentally and spiritually. So that's what I did then. Then in the afternoons I worked from about twelve until about eight in the evening—because, in the summer, there's enough light—and put in a good day's work. There's gardening and building other cabins and building the road up out of the creek to my cabin and so forth. There was always work to do.

GARY At then 8 pm onward?

JIM Then I would take a bath. Every day—I had a galvanized steel tub, kidney-shaped, a long tub. And I would cover it with a piece of plastic and a ten-speed bicycle inner tube that held the plastic onto the tub with the inner tube.

CARLA Filled it first from the pump.

JIM And there was water in there. And I'd let the sun heat it up. So by the end of the day it was usually about 105 degrees. So I took a nice hot bath. Even if it was 95 degrees outside, I took a 105 degree bath because I didn't want to get out of that bath—95 degrees felt cool.

GARY How about winters, when you, I presume, couldn't work as much as there was less daylight?

JIM Yeah. Well the morning routine was the same, and I would probably extend it some to the afternoon. But there was still work to do and I had things . . . while I was there I built, let's see, three other cabins and an adult playground—

CARLA And a big root cellar.

JIM Oh yeah, the root cellar.

CARLA Which is very labor-intensive.

JIM So I was working on those things and then I was usually trying to cut some sort of wood. If I needed wood for another cabin I would cut it in the winter when there weren't any leaves on the trees. It was a lot easier to deal with if the sap was down, which meant the logs were lighter, because a whole lot of the weight's in the sap. A whole lot more reading time; a lot more down time. I spent a lot of time reading. Drinking tea.

GARY So you carried forward a lot of that work you had learned from T. D. Lingo in terms of reflecting on yourself, doing dream work, essaying. Did you gain a lot of insight into yourself during that time?

JIM Oh yeah. See those—one, two, three, four, five, six—six three-ring notebooks—yeah, right there. All of those are the essays I wrote while I was there.

GARY Very extensive.

CARLA And they've never been digitized.

JIM And they're not going to be.[†] [*laughter*]

CARLA I've tried repeatedly to get him to.

JIM Those are therapy. Those are . . . to the bone. Those are blood and guts.

GARY So would you say that after six years on the land, you left the experience different than when you began?

[†] Much to the dismay of the interviewer, Jim threw these journals away the following year in 2015.

JIM Oh, yeah. Sure. I mean I'd be different no matter where I was, but the land was a great catalyst. I thought I was going to live there for my whole life and die there and be buried there. But then I met these folks from Louisville, Kentucky who spoke to my heart.

GARY Threw a wrench in the whole program.

JIM [*chuckles*] Yeah.

GARY In what ways would you say that the land changed you, if that can be identified?

JIM Well it gave me a whole lot more confidence. When I bought the land, it was August, and I wanted to explore it some and see if I could find a cabin site. And like I said, my little tent was down in the creek because it was clear. The rest of the bottom land was grown up with weeds; they were eight feet tall! And so, I had to cut a path to where I could see over there on the side of the hill through those weeds about 200 yards, and that was the first thing I had to do, so I knew it was going to be a *lot* of work here. So being able to do the work just gave me a mountain of confidence because I did it by myself.

GARY Did you begin with anxiety, trepidation, fear?

JIM [*Carla and Jim laughing*] Oh yeah!

CARLA Your rating system. Tell them that.

JIM Almost forgot that. Part of my writing in my journal was to give a numerical value to every day. Zero to plus 10 was *I want to stay, I want to be here and I love it.* Zero to minus 10: *I want to leave!* Well I started out minus 9.5. [*laughter*] It was thirty-five days until I got to positive numbers. I had a *lot* of anxiety. I mean, it's the primal nature environment, and you know, there are rattlesnakes and copperheads around. And I saw them. [*laughter*] I took a bath over a couple copperheads—didn't know it until I emptied the tub—there they were! *Sorry! Hope I didn't squish you.* And I didn't because you know, uneven ground underneath. So I knew it was going to be a whole lot of work subconsciously.

So that's where I got—I'm going to blow your order of questioning here again. One night in the tent, I had a friend with me at the time. She had traveled with me from Jacksonville, Florida out to Lingo's, and she took the course too. And on her way back to Colorado she came to visit me, and she had her dog, Sugarbear. He was a three-legged German shepherd.

And in the middle of the night in our little tent there he's eating dry dog food out of a plastic bowl, and it woke me enough to get me into the preconscious state. I wasn't awake and I wasn't asleep. So that's when I got that message from my guide that named itself Angelica. And the message was, "The key to your survival"—and I was very much worried about my survival—"comes indirectly through nervousness."[8] And I always took that, later, to mean that my attention to detail and my fear of failure, the nervousness part, would ensure that I wouldn't fail, that would be my key to survival. And do everything that I could think of doing and anything extra in building a log cabin and building a fire pit and whatever I did, try to do it as well as I possibly could because my survival might depend upon it someday.

GARY So don't let that fear overwhelm you. It's actually of aid to you because it's keeping you moving, keeping you getting the job done.

JIM Right. Yeah. It kept me moving. Doing a lot of moving.

GARY Did that happen within that 30-day window that you received the message?

JIM No, that happened before I moved to the land permanently. It happened in the first visit there. After I bought it I got word to her that I'd gotten land and she came by to see it because she knew what I was looking for.

So I bought the land in August of '72 and then went back to Nebraska to earn some more money because I spent everything I had on the land. It was $6,000 and that was all I had. So I went back to earn some more money and I worked some—yeah, in fact, '72, '73, I'm getting all these dates . . . you know after 40 years you forget things. [laughter] I worked some for my father in the grocery store. That was okay but then I was looking for something that would be—that would pay better, for one thing.

And I found a job working as a rough-in carpenter in construction. In Nebraska a lot of the income comes from grain and growing grain and corn and wheat and barley and rye and oats and so forth. So there are grain elevators in every town. And about 20 miles down the road in Gothenburg, Nebraska, Young Love Construction Company was setting about building new grain elevators. So I got a job with them. $4 an hour at the time was really good. In the grocery store I was only working for $3 an hour.

So I went and worked down there, and after we got the forms made—this was going to be a concrete grain elevator—we had to build wooden forms that would make a wall around all the separate little bins for different types of grain that would be in the grain elevator. There were probably 50 or 60 of these and they were—some of them were about the size of this room, 10 feet by 12 feet, some were maybe 8 feet by 12 feet—generally that shape. So after all of the woodwork was done and the forms were made, then they began jacking it and pouring concrete. They had jacks all the way around it so it could be jacked 24 hours a day. And the concrete could be poured 24 hours a day. So this thing was slowly rising into the air as a mass.

And it was my job to go around to each of these little bins—where there was going to be grain—and to crawl inside and get what amounted to a swing: two rebar came down on the sides, and a piece of wood went across there and I would have to reach out and do the finishing work because when the concrete came out of a form, it was pocked, it was honey-combed. And you couldn't have these honeycombs with grain, or the grain would catch in there and rot and destroy the whole batch, so it had to be smooth. And it was my job to take grout and to smooth all of that around. And even at night there was a little light in there so you could see.

And they were continuing to jack it up and even at 20 degrees below zero they were able to pour concrete by putting enough lime in the concrete that it wouldn't freeze immediately. So they were jacking and jacking, and finally, after we got up to about 105 feet, it was 20 below zero and I was looking down and I was thinking, *I'll bet I can find a better job.* [*Carla laughing heartily*]

So I did. And the end of winter—I guess it was the middle or end of January I got a job with farm implement construction, farm implement manufacturer, and I was a welder. I started off doing stick welding. Welding parts together. They would bring a whole bin of parts with a forklift. There would be, maybe 2,000 of this part over here (all the same), 2,000 of this part over in this bin (all the same). You'd put them in a jig and put them together with a—

CARLA Exactly the same way.

JIM Yeah, put them together, and then weld them together. So, I did stick welding. I did that, and I did that well enough that they put me in wire welding, which is a spool of wire that comes off. And actually I could probably still weld, but I couldn't tell you at what temperature to do that because the foreman did all that. He came by and he set the welder at the right temperature for whatever kind of metal we were using, whatever thickness of metal. So I really would have to have somebody do that for me, but I'm sure I could still weld.

It was really good meditation, because as you're looking through the visor—if you look at the welder without a visor, you'll go blind—so they got the visor there with the really thick glass, and as you're welding you can see the flame. And you see the two pieces of metal and you go very slowly, but all you really see is what's happening right around the flame. It's great meditation! So I'm welding/meditating all day long, eight hours of this.

And after that spring I finally got enough money to move to Kentucky and to cut timbers. That was spring of '73. I was ready to start building right after cutting the timbers. They had to season for over the winter so I went back to Nebraska for another winter's worth of work. I think I worked with my dad then; couldn't find a better job. So, that's how I got the money to pay for the land and live on it.

GARY So speaking of your experience with welding, you describe how you could see the flame, see it melting the metal, welding the metal?

JIM Yes, melting it.

GARY Melting. That implies really intense focus, because there's nothing else you can look at, nothing else you can see, no other sensory input, really, except what's happening right there. That focus and presence of mind is something that you had to exercise also when serving as the battery for the Ra contact.[‡] You were present, and you continually, as you described, visualized energy moving through Carla's system as she's lay unconscious on the bed. Would you say that you've always had presence of mind, free of distraction, which could be brought to such intensive focus?

JIM I'm not really aware of having had that throughout my life.

[‡] Save for moving to flip the cassette at the 45-minute mark, Jim also sat completely motionless throughout each Ra session.

CARLA He's a great focuser. It's deep in his body. He doesn't think about it; it's the way he is.

JIM Well athletics, you know, going out for the various sports was a place where I think I first got my focus, because you have to focus on what you're doing. Especially in pole vaulting: focusing on the runway, planting the pole, and what's happening after that. You have to be paying attention.

I would say that that's where I got my focus. And I didn't learn it as, *I'm going to learn how to focus.* It just happened, because I was doing sports. In various sports you need to learn how to focus. When you're batting in baseball, the ball is coming at you; in high school, probably eighty to ninety miles an hour is as fast as you see it. But that's pretty quick, so you have to focus on that. And in football I would hand the ball off to somebody or pass it down the field. I have to be paying attention to what I'm doing so I have to be focusing.

GARY I think that's a quality or capacity that people possess less and less nowadays due to the great ocean of stimulus bombarding all of us.

CARLA Over-stimulation. Everybody has got ADD.

GARY Yeah. And also I think that capacity for sustained attention is absolutely critical and key if you're going to do the work in the higher chakras of penetrating the veil.

CARLA That's so true.

GARY A quick question or two before we move on from your six years on the land. Did you have much social contact while you were there?

JIM Yeah. Just down the road about half a mile, Eric Swan, the fellow that you know who now lives in Lebanon, Kentucky. There was another couple of folks that lived close. I moved there at the time when the Back to the Land movement was a big deal. Usually college-educated urban kids, hippies usually, were wanting to simplify their lives according to Thoreau's "simplify, simplify" dictum, and so we were moving all over the country to the countryside.

Everywhere people went they wanted to get together and to help each other. So we had a community group. We'd go around once a week to somebody's house that was a member of the group, and do some sort of work. Whatever work they had, we'd do it. And then we'd all bring food and we'd have a meal together. And then some of us got together a meditation group, and we got together to meditate every now and then. That's how I met Don and Carla; a couple of folks on the other side of the county were from here in Louisville, and the Louisville meditation group, and they told me about Don and Carla.[§]

And then there was a food buying co-op. We belonged to a co-op, Federation of Ohio River Co-ops (FORK). It was based in Columbus, Ohio. It covered a five-state area. I think it was Ohio, Indiana, Kentucky, Tennessee, and West Virginia. We would get together at least once a month and place our food orders and then we would—when the truck came in, and it was delivered at a certain location, a centralized location, for each food co-op, then we'd get together and split up the food. So that's where I got a whole lot of food too, rather than at Kroger's or Houchens at the time.

And a funny little aside here. Every two months, FORK would have a meeting somewhere in that five-state area, all of the 150 co-ops that belonged would send representatives, at least two representatives. They would decide on the policy, and it was governed by consensus. And there was a feather, and if you had the feather you could talk; if you didn't have the feather you couldn't talk. So that's how it functioned, that's how we governed ourselves and made the bylaws. It was a very inspiring experience because people here doing that were very far-seeing as far as how to organize socially, and how to get groups of people together to do things for themselves rather than trust the corporate structure that they were raised in and very familiar with.

So, one of those meetings was held on my land, if you can imagine people from 150 different co-ops driving their vehicles—

CARLA Thrump, thrump, thrump.

JIM A Jaguar XKE is the one I remember most coming up out of the creek [*laughter*] and pulling out onto my land. And so for a weekend we had everybody there. And they were gathered in one area where I'd built the adult playground with seesaws that were—a seesaw that was way

---

[§] As discussed in Chapter 3, Jim first heard Don and Carla being interviewed for a Lexington, KY radio program on his battery-powered radio while living alone on the land. Subsequently members of his regional food-buying co-op, who were also members of Don and Carla's meditation group, offered to introduce Jim to Don and Carla.

over-size (so when you're on one end of it up in the air, you're 8 feet in the air) and a huge sandbox and a great big—let's see, what did I have?

CARLA A swing?

JIM A swing, a big swing. Yeah, that was what I had. And your feet wouldn't touch the ground on the swing. It was high enough up that definitely your feet would not touch the ground. So we met over there, and I had the first presentation. There were no outhouses. There were slit latrines. I gave a demonstration of how to use a slit latrine, [*Gary and Carla laughing*] to 150 city folks that had never used one before.

GARY Is this a hole in the ground?

CARLA Slit trench.

JIM Well sort of. It was a *long* hole in the ground, so that as you did your business you covered up that part and kept moving backwards. And there's a certain way you do it. You always point your feet down the hill. Don't put them sideways or up the hill or you're going to tip over. And so forth. So I gave the demonstration and got everybody off to a rollicking beginning.

CARLA Don't use smartweed to wipe!

JIM Oh, yeah! [*laughter*] Smartweed is a weed that's common in Kentucky, and some people just go out in the woods and grab whatever weed. Well if you use smartweed your rear end is going to be burning for a long time. So yeah, we provided toilet paper. They didn't have to worry about running into smartweed.

GARY 150 people. So Homecoming is small potatoes compared to that.

JIM Yeah, we fed them all.

CARLA And everybody cooked over fires.

JIM Everybody in our food-buying co-op helped; and they were all cooking and serving and doing whatever people needed.

GARY So there's co-ops, there's elements of spirituality, there's also some philosophy in the movement of moving back to the land. Did the social movement continue beyond your time on the land?

JIM Yeah, as far as I know there's still a fair amount of people, but you know, I think most of them have moved back to the city, curiously enough. For example, the group that Don and Carla first started, Eftspan, that bought 360 acres on the other side of the county, there were at least 30 or 40 in that group, and I think there may be someone who started a house there and may still be living next to the land. But that's indicative of what really happened. It was a movement. It was a movement that had its beginning and it seems to have had an end, but some folks stayed. Some folks stayed and are still there. But others went on to other things, and we all have steps on our journey and people just keep taking steps. That's a good thing. Although I missed the land a lot.

When I first was here with Don and Carla, I remember having a dream one night. I just *ached* to be back on the land. I hadn't really realized that I missed it that much. But it went away. And now I realize that this is where I want to live for the rest of my life.

GARY You hear Don and Carla speak on a radio program, and through your meditation group you connect with them. Later on you're given an invitation to join Don and Carla after helping them to move and getting to know them, but you don't accept the invitation, you go all the way out to Washington, right? Oregon?

JIM Oregon. Right, yeah, for about five years, the last five years that I lived on the land, I was taking a newsletter from Cosmic Awareness Communications, and they were based in Olympia, Washington. Paul Shockley, who was their channel and who was supposedly channeling the same source that Edgar Cayce channeled—that is, the Akashic records of the planet—lived in Yamhill, Oregon, which is a little town, a little it-ty-bitty town about 30 miles outside of Portland, Oregon. So he would travel the two hours up to Olympia, Washington, on a monthly basis, and stay there maybe for a weekend and do the channelings that they would use in their newsletter. They would invite people to write in with questions and of course they had their own line of questions, and they were very much involved in conspiracy theories as well.

So they kept asking Paul a lot of questions about conspiracies, and they got some very interesting stuff. I got onto people who were into conspiracies on the inside level, that had been involved in the International Monetary Fund, for example, in very high positions, and had the ability to know certain things that other people might not. So there was a lot of interesting stuff that happened, but I think one of the things that also happened was that his information got detuned after a while because he was being asked these questions that were basically transient; they really had only any importance in the moment or for a few years. They weren't dealing with spiritual principles. However, he did have a whole set of channelings that were done on nothing but spiritual principles—that were, I thought, very high quality. And that was what I was really going after.

I got pulled into the conspiracy because it was "in the air." [*laughter*] I was breathing the air, and I was thinking for myself after 21 years of not doing that, and I wanted to know about it. So I investigated it.

Besides Cosmic Awareness Communications—which is located in, like I said, Washington—Shockley also had a group called the Aquarian Church of Universal Service that was located in Portland. I went to their services on Sunday and there was a fellow there from Vancouver, Washington, who was dealing with diatomaceous earth. They were mining it both in the United States and in Canada. It was fossilized remains. Little tiny creatures' fossilized remains that could be used for a number of things. Storing dried foods for example. If you would put that in with your food it would keep much longer. And if you brushed your teeth with it, it was an excellent abrasive. There was all kinds of things you could do with it, so it was valuable.

And he offered me a chance to make a bunch of money; he offered me the position of the U.S. general manager, and offered me a $100,000, which is a lot of money anytime, and back then it was like a million dollars now. And I was puzzled. I didn't have anything against money, but that's not why I went out there. So I decided to take the weekend out. I was staying in this old dilapidated trailer close to the Windsong School of Awareness—called Tootsie Roll because it was all rusted on the outside—and I decided to take the weekend out and meditate and try to figure out what I should do. Because it had me puzzled, and I knew that Don and Carla had invited me to come back to Kentucky. And it was a standing invitation, so I decided to take the weekend out and meditate.

And so, thirty seconds into the meditation I got the very clear message: "Go back to Louisville. Join Don and Carla." So I thought, *well, what shall I do with my weekend?* And I packed up [*laughter*] and I said thanks to folks, and I told them I had a wonderful time. And I did, it was a great time. I enjoyed every one of them, and that's where I brought a kitty cat back with me, Chocolate Bar.[9] I believe [one of our three current cats],

Pickwick,[10] is the reincarnation of Chocolate Bar, who was the reincarnation of the cocker spaniel I had when I was in fourth grade. That's just
my idea. You know I might be all wet, but that's the feeling I've always
gotten.

CARLA I think it's right.

JIM So Chocolate Bar was a Himalayan. The kids at the Windsong
School of Awareness made money by selling the kitty cats that came from
these two Himalayans. A big, old male with long, dark hair and this beautiful female with long whitish hair, colored like Siamese cats. And so
Chocolate Bar had this beautiful long hair and Siamese coloration, and I
litterbox-trained her all the way back, 2,500 miles. Whenever she was
ready to go to the bathroom I'd grab her and put her in the litterbox
which is over on the passenger's side floor.

So I brought Chocolate Bar back, 2,500 miles, introduced her to Don.
He held her in his hand (at that time she was still a kitten) and said,
"Beautiful."

That meant [*unenthusiastically*] *another cat.* They already had two cats.
[*chuckles*]

CARLA That was one of his swear words.

JIM It was "beautiful."

CARLA That and "schmierkase."

JIM Schmierkase. That's German for "pickle."

CARLA No, for cottage cheese.

GARY What would that translate to in the expletive world?

JIM For whatever. [*laughter*] He didn't use swear words, but he liked the
idea. "Oh, schmierkase!"

CARLA He said he didn't use swear words because they were words of
power, and he thought that it was very important to measure your power
and use it only when necessary. He did not feel there were events necessary that called for using words of power. And he never did. I never heard
him swear.

GARY So thirty seconds into your meditation you got that message. Was it
the same type of message receiving that you had experienced when you

first moved to the land?

JIM No. I didn't hear a voice, I didn't see words. I just had the *real* strong feeling: *Go back to Louisville. Join Don and Carla.* It was unmistakable.

CARLA [*laughter*] What a surprise. It was incredible.

GARY You moved out to Washington. You said you wanted to investigate Cosmic Awareness and the Aquarian Church of Universal Service. *That* was the catalyst that prompted you to sell the land? Because you wanted to work with a channeling group?

JIM Right. But I didn't sell the land yet. I still had the land.

GARY So you were undecided about whether you would keep the land but you were taking a hiatus from that.

JIM Yes. I sold it once I came back and joined Don and Carla.

GARY Okay. So what first took you off of the land was desire to work with a channeling group. You just weren't sure which one.

JIM Right. I had been involved with Aquarian Church and Cosmic Awareness Communications for five years. I'd more recently met Don and Carla, and I really liked them. And I enjoyed all the channelings, but I just felt this prior commitment—I had it in my mind I was going to do it that way. And I do a lot of things that way. I discover . . . well I went through college that way! [*laughter*]

CARLA He's an honorable guy

JIM I got this degree, but I don't think I want to use it. I did that three times. [*laughter*]

GARY Well you never know until you try. And then you try and then . . .

JIM Each step was very helpful and necessary along the way. I didn't waste any time.

GARY In the early 2002 you started your own business that you named Jim's Lawn Service. Why was that?

JIM When Don died in 1984, the insurance—life insurance and pension—from Eastern Air Lines provided Carla and me enough capital to invest with a lady who's now become a real good friend, and we're still with her. And we could live on the interest. Back in the late eighties interest rates were between 10 and 13%. So that's probably the best they've ever been. As we moved along through the nineties and into the early 2000s interest rates went down drastically, and we were not able to live on our income anymore. And we were starting to take out of the capital. And if we did that too long we wouldn't have anything left. So Jim's Lawn Service was born utilizing my love of working outdoors, my love of big muscle use, and my love of pretty much working alone, except on Fridays when you, Gary, would help me. I like to use my big muscles and I liked to be in charge of what I'm doing.

So cutting the grass was just perfect because in this town most people—the majority of people pay to have their grass cut. And it's a beautiful area; it's like a park, like Carla said. And so I thought, *hey, let's do that.*

I had been prior to that—I started back I guess in 1992 just working part time because I liked it, I liked doing it. And I had four or five customers: Don's aunt and uncle, and then two of their neighbors over off of Poplar Level Road close to the Watterson Expressway. And then there was a lady out here in Crestwood. You went and helped me out there. She had the family cemetery there that went back to 1804. And there were a couple other folks around that I worked for, and I did that maybe two days a week. Very relaxed and only in the afternoons because I still, at that time, still had my habit of working in the office and doing *inside* work—spiritual, intellectual, mental work in the mornings, and physical labor in the afternoon. So I'd already got a start made on lawn service work and I knew that I could do that and do a good job. So Jim's Lawn Service was just a natural outgrowth of that.

GARY So you carried that scheduling dichotomy through a lot of decades: spiritual, mental, intellectual stuff in the morning, physical labor in the afternoon, beginning with the T. D. Lingo experience.

JIM Right, yeah.

GARY Do you find that your experience with Jim's Lawn Service was a teacher in the way that the land was a teacher?

JIM Well, not so much because I was pretty sure I could cut grass. [*laughter*] I didn't have to worry about rattlesnakes or copperheads.

And you hardly ever see the customers, and when I did I had a good time talking with them because I made them all friends. Most of the time it's a solitary job. I was out there on my mower or with a blower or with trimmers and just working on my own. And I really liked that, and I loved being outside. So it was a teacher in that I needed to keep a schedule. People got cut on a certain day of the week unless there was rain. And then I either cut early to avoid the rain or later to recover from the rain. So it taught me keeping a schedule and getting up earlier than I wanted. And the last couple of years I also needed to blend it in with helping Carla. We were fortunate toward the end to have a lady here to help us so that I didn't have to do as much during the day, so I could go out and work during the day. And what I *learned* from Jim's Lawn Service? I learned how to make money, and—

CARLA Did it really well.

JIM —did a good enough [*laughter*] job of it that it was able to supplement us enough to keep us going. And fortunately two years ago, Larry[11] was a gem in giving us enough of a donation that I was able to retire and take care of Carla full time, which was very handy because starting last year she needed full time. Well she needed full time for a while, but we no longer have our helper/caregiver. So I've been very blessed. Been able to work with Carla and be with her for 24 hours now for two years.

GARY And being able to devote your time to L/L Research has been invaluable.

JIM Yeah, it's great to be here and be able to do whatever we can. We are happy to do whatever we can for L/L Research, but we both realize that you and Austin are now the working part. You're the wheels, you make the ship—no it can't be a ship—you make the car go! [*laughter*] Of course if it's an amphibious car it could have wheels too. We know that the days of us both being in the office are over. Those are halcyon days. We're happy and so thrilled to have you and Austin there because you guys are doing a wonderful job. Whatever we can do to help you do the job or to be here and help others, we're glad to do.

GARY I will note about Jim's Lawn Service as having watched you, for years work though Jim's Lawn Service and having worked alongside of you that it was yet another expression of the way that you see life as a dance, because you saw even the cutting of the grass and the weed-eating and the blowing as a dance.

CARLA Working with nature spirits.

GARY And it was also an expression, among other things, of your rock-solid nature. I would tell people that if Armageddon itself happened and the world was consumed in war and conflict that Jim would not let that alter his grass cutting. [*laughter*] You would be out there; nothing stopped you. Even sickness.

JIM That's right. Lingo tells a story along that line. It's sort of poignant. As they were liberating the concentration camps in Germany they came upon one and as the German guards saw these American soldiers approaching, they all took off, and left only the prisoners there. And when Lingo and some of the other soldiers got into the offices—a lot of the prisoners were used in the office to do work, like sweeping the floor and making food and doing the laundry and ironing and all that—and even though the prisoners knew the guards were gone, and they'd been liberated by the Americans, they *had* to finish their job. Because before, if they hadn't finished their job, they may have died.

[*pause*]

I didn't have that feeling I was going to die. [*laughter*] I'm just dedicated to getting the job done.

GARY Yeah. So we have a couple more questions. You feel that you are a wanderer in the sense that your soul came to Earth from another density in order to be of service. When and how did you become aware of this, and how have you related to this belief?

JIM Well I guess it started back around '78 or '79 when I was in Reno, Nevada with my girlfriend at the time. She was also into spiritual things, and we would go down to Carson City, Nevada to the Family of Man. Marsha Mossman was the channel there, and I think she was a pretty good channel. She was one person that gave me a reading and she mentioned that I was from elsewhere and then went on with some other details about "there are others from elsewhere and they are here to serve." And I thought, *well that's interesting*.

And then when I was in Oregon I got a reading from Paul Shockley that was much more specific, and he used the term wanderer. And then when I came here, I think even maybe before I left for Oregon that we'd had a channeling where wanderers were talked about and it was just you [*referring to Carla*] and Don and me and maybe somebody else and the concept of wanderer came up and mentioned that everyone present was a wanderer. And then of course the Ra contact—we had that confirmed.

So relating to being a wanderer: it was kind of an unreal feeling because I don't think about it. I don't think about my—I think about myself as being a dancer, really. In the heart of my being I see myself as being a dancer. If I'm from somewhere else and I've come here to be of service—great. But whatever the case is, I'm here to be of service. And I'm glad for every step I've made along the way, and I'm looking forward to hanging with Ruckaduck, my nickname for her, for the rest of our lives.

GARY Do you find now that you look back and miss the land?

JIM No. I don't miss the land now. I look back and feel very good about the land and think, *how in the world* [*laughter*] *did I do that?* Good thing I was young and dumb! You know I was 27 years old when I first got to the land, and thought I could do anything. And fortunately I was able to survive on the land, yeah.

GARY You've been a caretaker and support person to Carla since very early on, maybe even in past lives as we've discussed. This role has intensified in recent years as Carla has been bedbound—in what was previously your bedroom—for over three years now with a large open wound on her back from a spinal surgery. How have you processed this catalyst as the years have gone by and would you say that you have grown as a result?

JIM Oh, of course. [*chuckles*] There's no way not to grow, but yeah we've had some great growth together. Look at this room. Imagine this is my heart. I open my room, and my heart, to Carla.

When I first joined Don and Carla, everybody had his or her own room. And we continued that until Carla had surgery. Her bedroom is upstairs on the other side of the house. My room was always right here. So when it became obvious that she was going to need some help, it just made sense to get a hospital bed, and move it in here. So the whole process, since 2010, which would make it four years now, has been making room for Carla and her things. I move my things aside and make room for her in the closet, hanging her stuff up on the doors, whatever she needs for medical supplies are all around. So this is—I do everything symbolically. [*chuckles*] I think everybody does the same thing.

Opening one's heart, for me, is symbolized by opening this room to Carla. And as I've been able to open the room, I've also been able to open my heart. And what has happened is that I feel a great deal more love and absolute, total dedication to taking care of her. And each morning before I get out of bed I pray that I can take care of her to the very best of my ability. Do whatever she needs. And so I know that we're both in *exactly* the same place, learning things that we need to—exactly right here, where we need to be. There is no accident; there's no mistake. The fact that she's having to undergo a wound and a slow healing of a wound in order to bring this all about, is just the means by which it all occurs.

---

[1] Beginning in 1941, the Air Force was a component of the Army known as the Army Air Forces (AAF), a combat arm like the infantry. Six years later, in 1947, it was split into its own branch of the military know from then to today as the United States Air Force (USAF), equal to the Navy and Army.

[2] Jim's mother, Atta McCarty, passed five months after the interview in January, 2015.

[3] Jim didn't mention in this interview that not only did he sit in row seven each time, but always in the same seat.

[4] The G.I. Bill was a law signed into effect by President Franklin D. Roosevelt that provided various benefits to returning vets from WWII, including financial assistance for college tuition. Millions of vets used this to go to earn degrees upon returning.

[5] "My story unfolds with me as a spearhead infantry scout for General Patton's army in World War II. The war was horrible on the front lines. My group was one of the first to arrive at Hitler's death camps to liberate the remaining survivors."

"TD Lingo and The Dormant Brain Research and Development Laboratory," NeilSlade.com, accessed February 17, 2016, HTTP://WWW.NEILSLADE.COM/ART/BRAIN/HISTORY.HTML.

For further reference:

A 1979 documentary about Lingo and his work, *TD Lingo Brain Lab 1979 Documentary*: https://www.youtube.com/watch?v=G1yBWvROBY0

Wikipedia article, "T. D. A. Lingo": https://en.wikipedia.org/wiki/T._D._A._Lingo

[6] About Lingo's life and his "each one teach one" philosophy, Jim writes:

> Lingo was one of the two great men I have known in my life. The other, of course, was Don Elkins. Both wanted with all their being to help save planet Earth. I will always be infinitely grateful for studying with Lingo.

He was a most important step in my own growth.

I looked at some of the other information about Lingo below the Wikipedia entry and was saddened to learn that after he died in 1993 his estate was in such disarray that his 240 acre mountain top retreat was passed on to his adopted, estranged, drug-addicted son who sold the land for $3 million to developers.

His creed for all students who came through his school was "each one teach one." He hoped that each student would find his/her own wilderness land and start a school like his to spread the word about how to do self-therapy in nature and circuit into the dormant frontal lobes. To my knowledge I was the only one who ever did. And my classes only lasted two years—until I met and joined Don and Carla.

I think Lingo would have been amazed at the Ra contact. I made one attempt to share it with him in the early '80s, but it seemed to fall on deaf ears as I believe he was significantly miffed that I was no longer teaching brain self-control. I wonder how he is doing now.

7

"Primal therapy is a trauma-based psychotherapy created by Arthur Janov, who argues that neurosis is caused by the repressed pain of childhood trauma. Janov argues that repressed pain can be sequentially brought to conscious awareness and resolved through re-experiencing the incident and fully expressing the resulting pain during therapy. In therapy, the patient recalls and reenacts a particularly disturbing past experience usually occurring early in life and expresses normally repressed anger or frustration especially through spontaneous and unrestrained screams, hysteria, or violence. Primal therapy was developed as a means of eliciting the repressed pain. . . . "

Wikipedia, s.v. "Primal therapy," accessed July 5, 2016, https://en.wikipedia.org/wiki/Primal_therapy

8

Ra speaks to this moment in the following two Q&As:

QUESTIONER I have a question from Jim about an experience he had when he first moved to his land in which he was told, "The key to your survival comes indirect, through nervousness." The entity was Angelica. Can you give him information with respect to this?

RA I am Ra. Yes.

QUESTIONER Would you please do that?

RA I am Ra. As we have noted, each mind/body/spirit complex has several guides available to it. The persona of two of these guides is the polarity of male and female. The third is androgynous and represents a more unified conceptualization faculty.

The guide speaking as sound vibration complex, Angelica, was the female polarized persona. The message may not be fully explicated due to the Law of Confusion. We may suggest that in order to progress, a state of some dissatisfaction will be present, thus giving the entity the stimulus for further seeking. This dissatisfaction, nervousness, or angst, if you will, is not of itself useful. Thus its use is indirect. 54.2-3

[9] Jim adds:

Chocolate Bar was a Himalayan cat, which means that he had the dark colorations on his nose, ears, tail, and paws that a Siamese cat has, but he had the long hair of a Himalayan. Those dark points are frequently referred to as "chocolate" in color. Rather than call him Chocolate Point and be real literal about his color and name we called him Chocolate Bar, suggesting that he had the dark points of coloration but was a very sweet cat.

[10] To read a short bio of the three cats, see the endnote in Chapter 1.

[11] A generous donor contributed significantly to L/L's budget for two and a quarter years. It was enough that Jim was able to retire from his mostly one-man lawn service outfit, Jim's Lawn Service, and devote himself full time to L/L Research. Which also freed his time to focus on Carla's care during the final two years of her life. Carla and Jim considered it one of the greatest blessings of their lives to have received this gift of being able to be together at the end.

CARLA I wondered at the beginning if we would make through all those questions, a thick sheaf of questions there.

GARY Oh man, yeah, the first obstacle was just getting you guys to accept. [*laughter*] I thought, Jim especially . . .

CARLA It was a while before Jim was even willing to consider it.

GARY Oh, your initial impulse wasn't to go with it.

JIM Well, personal stuff.

CARLA We're not important.

JIM Generally a private person.

CARLA And you know I expressed the concern that if people thought that we were more important than the material, that that would be all screwed up. I did not want that. So you just reassured me and I trust you.

What's your next one, sweetheart?

GARY It's about your marriage, and I'm wondering if I should . . .

CARLA Well, you could use Chloe and Pickwick* as a good visual aid to that. They're so intertwined and comfortable together.

GARY They look like a yin-yang together. I'm going to take a picture.

I would like to ask you about the evolution of your relationship, from its inception, through the Ra contact, to the marriage in 1987, to your unique balance of closeness and independence, to Jim's transformational heart opening at the ocean, and to your current dance.

JIM Oh, that's all one question? [*laughter*] Well, when we first met, the first time at her apartment, with Don there for the meditation, I was very attracted to Carla just as a person. I could tell that she was a really good person. So I was really looking forward to coming to meditations. When it came time to move, I helped them move from that location on Douglas Boulevard out to Waterson Trail where we eventually had the Ra contact. Carla and I were a whole lot more involved with each other, we were much closer. And we had that hug, that memorable hug in the kitchen.

CARLA Mmm. That was transformational.

JIM Yeah, we were over at the new house, moving things in, and we just gave each other a big hug, and neither of us wanted it to end, so we knew that we were . . . together; it felt right. We ought to pursue this. So, we became intimate, and Don gave his blessing, and [*laughs*] when it came time for me to head out to Oregon, they had a housekeeper by the name of Alia, and I came by to say goodbye, and Alia came to let Carla know that I was here. She said, "Ah, come say goodbye to the turkey."

GARY Wasn't happy with you.

JIM Yeah.

CARLA [*laughs*] *I* wasn't happy with him!

JIM Yeah. What was the name of the song you wrote after I drove down the driveway? "Hit and Run Blues"?

CARLA Yeah, I felt like I'd been bowled over by a truck. [*chuckles*]

JIM I went up to Oregon and then when I came back we had a wonderful reunion.

---

* Two of Carla and Jim's cats were lying intertwined together on the bed, one nearly all black, the other an orange-and-white mix.

CARLA Yes, we did.

JIM And then after that we were a group. The three of us were a group, though Carla and I saw ourselves as being intimate lovers—a couple. It was also very obvious that the primary couple was Don and Carla. Always has been, and always would be as long as Don Elkins was alive. There wasn't any problem with that. There wasn't any problem with Don, no problem with me, no problem with Carla. It was just the way things were, and that was indicative of the entire relationship between the three of us. For some reason, it all felt just very right. It felt like it was a culmination of a well-laid plan. So we all just went with it.

And as we progressed and went through the Ra contact we became closer, and then, as Don had his difficulties in the last year of his life, we were thrown together even more trying to figure out the best thing to do for Don—how to help him, how to keep L & L functioning. And that brought us even more closely together. After Don died, it was obvious that now *we* were the couple, and the thing to consider now was what kind of couple. And Carla said, "Well, you know, it makes sense to get married," and I said, "Yeah, I know. If we're going to be together, might as well be together in the most powerful way possible. And that is as a married couple. Let's just take advantage of the situation, of what life has brought us, and let's get married!"

So we got married in '87—May 30, 1987, and Don died in '84—November 7th . . . so it was a couple years, a proper grieving time, and then it was just obvious: *let's get married.* And we did. Carla planned the wedding. She did a bang-up job. You know what goes into that!† [*laughter*]

She did it all by herself. Had a three-ring notebook with contacts, and it's probably still around here someplace, for the various things.

CARLA It probably is, with things taped on the pages that I needed. I didn't do all of it on computer as I would today, it was all . . . If you cut and pasted it was with scissors and glue.

JIM Yeah, you really cut and paste. [*laughter*] So, we got married, and we went on a honeymoon, and Carla got claustrophobia—at first I guess on the plane, and then on the ship. The ship especially. We were in an inner

---

† The questioner was married to the love of his own life three months later.

room that had no windows.

CARLA After I had requested, specifically, not to do that, but to have an outer room.

JIM So we saw the ship's doctor, and he prescribed an outer room and some Xanax. And a lot of trips to the shore. The ship was going around on the cruise to various of the Hawaiian Islands. He said, "Be sure to get off and take the tours. Get off the ship."

So we did, and we had a good time wandering up and down the streets of Honolulu and going to the hotel. Interesting place. It's tropical there all year round so they don't have any need for outside doors. You just walk into the place; you don't open a door, you just walk in. And spent a lot of time sight-seeing with shops of one kind or another, looking for some lit- tle knick-knack or clothes or jewelry or something. Think we might have even gone to the beach one day. [*chuckles*]

CARLA Not sure about that.

JIM Not sure about that, you know, we were in Hawaii and . . . then we came back and set up shop and as they say, the rest is history.

CARLA Made a good life.

JIM Yeah. And various medical problems would pop up from time to time. They've always been there, as you've covered so well. They were there from the birth to the present.

CARLA Now at the beginning, as I've made fairly clear before, there was no romance. There was an incredible amount of admiration, mutual respect for each other's characters, the probity and the uprightness with which each had lived life, and we found great comfort in that. And we're glad to be together, but Jim had no feeling for me, no heart feeling for me. He didn't want to write songs or—

JIM It hadn't skipped a beat yet. [*laughter*]

CARLA Yeah, and I missed that. I missed the romance and sweet talk and just that pull. I'm not talking about the pull from one person to another sexually. That was easy; we were both young and healthy, and Jim was beautiful, and I was relatively pretty, and it all worked out great. But that heart connection that goes beyond those things—*uh-uh*—it wasn't there. He needed his time alone to the point where, if it got really intense like it did during a really sick period where I couldn't get up, I couldn't sit up . . . I've talked about that prior to '92, I think. He went to the country and stayed at the farm for one night, and he really valued that time. He was totally alone in the wilderness, and that was like a prescription for him. *Take two wilderness and I'll see you tomorrow.*

[*laughter*]

And so it was like that until, I guess, '96. And I loved him anyway, so I took it—I accepted it. It was just one of those things. You don't get everything, and I had the best guy in the world, and the best job in the world. So I made a life a life out of that, and was happy to do so.

JIM Well, the crucial point, the point of change, was actually in 1994—

CARLA Oh, '94.

JIM —at Pawley's Island, on the beach. We had been going there since, I guess, the early '80s. Even when Don was alive we went there a couple of times. And they have old cabins, built in the '40s and '50s, that the owners rent out to vacationers on a weekly basis. And it was wonderful; we had a great time. The food was good. There was a place to go shopping, and we went out and jumped the waves. We had a great time jumping waves. We'd have a little place on the beach with our towels and a chair, just hanging out. Then we'd go out into the water, and the waves would be coming in, and we would actually jump them. And sometimes they'd be big enough, you know—they'd wash you back toward the shore, and you'd trudge out there again, jump another wave or two.

One particular day, though, or one particular visit, Hurricane Gordon was close, or coming within the next day. We were going to have to evacuate. But we were out jumping some waves and we got caught in a riptide. The way to get out of a riptide is to swim parallel to the beach, but we didn't know that at the time. We got caught in the riptide and it was taking us out. And I'm not a good swimmer. I even took swimming in college to learn how to swim because, since I had asthma as a kid, the doctor specifically said, "Don't do too much to strain yourself to cause an asthmatic attack." And swimming is one of the most strenuous things you can do, so I didn't learn to swim till I was in college. So I wasn't a good swimmer. And the riptide was taking me out, and Carla was there with me going out too, except she's a fish, and she floats naturally. She has to wear weights to get in the bathtub when it's too full of water. [*laughter*]

Anyway, I was heading out, and she was heading out. She all of a sudden got this image to get behind me and put her feet on my butt. She pushes me with her feet, and pushes me enough that I'm able to find ground down there and wade my way out of the riptide. However, Carla was moving out toward the ocean. And it's a beautiful day: the sun's out, the storm is still way off, you can't see it. And she's thinking, *ah, it's a beautiful day to die.* [*chuckles*] It didn't look like she was going to come back, but somehow, another wave came and deposited her on the shore. And we looked at each other and said, "Phoof! Let's go back to the cabin for a while!" [*laughing*] And all of a sudden I was seeing her in another light. She'd risked her life, willing to give her life for me. And it just seemed like a very—I mean, I didn't have to think about it—*I love this person!* [*laughter*]

You know: *I love you!* And from that point on, there hasn't been any doubt. It's love the hard way: have her save your life.

CARLA Yeah, it was wonderful to have my husband fall in love with me. It's a gift almost nobody ever gets. And I was so grateful. I still am.

JIM Me too.

CARLA I didn't need it to have a good life with Micky but, oh my God, it's been wonderful to have that. So I've never stopped being grateful. And of course I was in love with him all along. He's my cowboy.

GARY Is there anything you would say about your current dance: you taking care of Carla, Carla taking care of you?

JIM Well, it's closer than it's ever been before. I'd imagine it's going to continue that way. I mean, I just feel so much love for her and so much sympathy because she's going through so much and has been through so much. I just want to do everything I can to help her out, and I plan on doing that for the rest of my life, *whatever* condition she's in.

CARLA He's wonderful. What can I say? It may be a little bit challenging to appreciate exactly where I am because it's not what I would have chosen. And I have to call on my faith, which I do. But the one thing I don't have to worry about is my marriage, my closest relationship. I know that it's so full of love it overflows constantly, and I have no doubt it will continue like that.

GARY You said that Don's last work in this world was to select the Louisville home that you have lived in ever since. What has been your relationship with this gift from Don?

JIM   Well, we both love it a lot.

CARLA   We take care of it and we open it up just as he wanted us to, to offer it as a spiritual home for other wanderers. The spiritual home, not the nuclear family. So our family is very large, and I'm grateful for all my children. I love them to death, every one.

JIM   The yard's large enough to play in and make into a pseudo-wilderness environment.

CARLA   Jim just makes every place in the yard a different experience of the spirit, with what he plants and how he uses rocks and plants together. It is very 3D, very organic. He and I have worked on stuff, like it was my idea to put a little path in—you know that—and the way that bricks are in the path, that was my idea too.

JIM   And then the steps up to the gazebo were your idea. I was going to put it on the ground but you said, "Put it up in the air, put some steps there."

CARLA   Yeah, well even having a meditation hut at all was my idea.

JIM   You've ordered all kinds of flowers and perennials to put out there.

CARLA   Yeah, and we've picked flowers together. So it's really his work, and I was chief weeder until I couldn't do it anymore, and it was our mutual concept. But we both feel that this house is absolutely gorgeous. It's wonderful. And we try to treat it with great respect. It's an old lady; she's been here since 1923, so she's coming up on her century. But we keep the roof patched and the eaves painted and the rest—I should say that Jim does—and so that it's a pleasure for people to visit, I think. It's a magical place. We put so much love into all of it. The house loves us back, I think.

GARY   Ra describes a desk or a table or a shelf you were working with and says that it "sang with pride" or "glowed with pride."

JIM   Sang with beauty. Yeah, that was the altar upon which we put all the accoutrements: the candle, the incense, the book (the Bible) and so forth . . . the chalice. It had a bottom that allowed it to be scooted under the bed and be stable, because we had a problem with the room to walk the Circle of One around the bed [*Carla chuckles*] that Carla laid upon for the session. We needed as much room as possible at the head of the bed, so I made a table that could slide under the head of the bed. Carla would be far enough away that it wouldn't be bothering her or take up any walking space. I'm not sure if it's still down in the basement or not.

CARLA He built it and he polished it and rubbed it with oil until it was just, truly, I mean *literally* shining.

GARY And Ra said that it sang with love?

JIM Something like that, yeah. It was singing. [*laughter*]

CARLA It was a beauty, wasn't it?

JIM It was a beauty, yeah.

CARLA We could look it up.

GARY It's a positive quality. I would imagine if they altered . . .

CARLA Somebody will look it up eventually and tell us.‡

GARY Yeah. Where's Austin when you need him? (Anytime he's around, a question that has been asked, whether directed to him or not, he's got the answer for, usually by using his phone.)

So if that one piece glowed or sang love, then I imagine that this house and its grounds do so as well.

CARLA Mmm-hm. Oh, yeah, this house and its grounds I think really do hold a feeling of magic and worship. Isn't that wonderful that we were able to do that.

---

‡ Ra actually said that it "sings with joy":

> **QUESTIONER** I would just ask as a final question, then, if the new table that Jim has built for the appurtenances is satisfactory to hold them since it will give us more room to walk around the bed, and if it is better to leave it in its natural condition as it is, or to coat it with linseed oil or varnish or paint?
>
> **RA** I am Ra. We view this appurtenance. It sings with joy. The pine vibrates in praise. Much investment of this working in wood has been done. It is acceptable. We may suggest it be left either as it is or rubbed with the oil which also is easily magnetized and holds the proffered vibration to a profound extent. 98.16

GARY I think it's spoken to a lot of people over the years, myself included.

CARLA I'm glad. I'm glad. That's what we did it for.

GARY This could be a difficult question to answer. Might be a simple one. How has your spirituality grown over the years?

JIM I guess I think about what I do more than ever before in terms of the spiritual ramifications. Every act, no matter how small, is an expression of my spiritual journey, and every act, in order to be in beauty and love, needs to be consciously undertaken. And I'm *still* working on every act. [*chuckles*] But it's very apparent to me that everything I do needs to be done consciously.

CARLA Me, I think it's just patch, patch, patch, you know. When I see something that needs work, then I'm on it. I remember when you pointed out to me that I constantly interrupt people, and it never occurred to me before. But I thought about it, and it immediately became clear to me: well, that's the way my parents communicated. Everybody talked over everybody. A lot of times when people are explaining themselves, they'll start into it and you get it before they're done, long before they're done. So why waste that time? Why not go ahead with it and say, "Yeah, I understand this," and then you can enlarge the discussion, not just sit there and wait and wait and wait. And really, it's too bad, because this is unusual. I mean, they were two very intelligent people, and they just were impatient and they didn't want to wait. They didn't want to give respect to each other. And I could see that there was a much more gracious way to work on it, to relate. And I wasn't taking advantage of that. So I don't know how—to what extent I've been able to heal that error. Hopefully I've listened better through the years, and you've noticed through the years since you said that, that I'm doing a little bit better and listening a little bit more and letting you finish your sentences. [*Gary chuckling*]

I don't know how much I still interrupt, because when I do it, I wouldn't do it if I saw it. So my spiritual growth is like that. It's a process of taking the catalyst that comes in and learning from it and trying to apply it. But hopefully, *gradually, gradually* climbing that mountain, becoming more mature, more able to love more fully, more able to receive love—that's changed a lot. There was a time not too many years ago when I would not have been able to accept this much love, accept being helped this much. It would have troubled me enormously. And I have gotten to the point now where I'm able to accept love and accept the help without overly feeling inadequate because I can't reciprocate.

GARY　This question is answered least in words. This question is answered in one's heart. But for what it's worth, how do you experience the One Infinite Creator in your life?

JIM　Well, the easiest way for me has been in the primal nature environment. The priest that married us at Carla's church described me as a spiritual pagan. [*laughter*] That's pretty close. He said it positively; he was complimenting me. He says, "You don't need a church. Your church is in the woods!" And that's pretty true. But I guess the more mature I get, I see the Creator in other people. When I really stop to think and I reflect upon somebody that I may end up having a relationship with—you know, customers or people I meet—everybody is the Creator! And that's becoming more and more apparent to me. But the easiest thing, like I said, is for me to be outside. I always take a walk around the outdoors somewhere around 9 and 9:30 in the dim light, and *feel* the place, the presence of the place. It seems to have a lot more magic that's apparent to me in the dim light. I'm not sure why.

CARLA　Well, it's that time of day where it is magical, where it's a switch from day to night or night to day and the nature spirits, some of them are going to sleep, some of them are waking up. So it's very [*sound of relieved exhalation*] psychically exciting.

JIM　Yeah, I think you're right.

CARLA　For me, it was a song "The Cars" sang, "Every move you make, every step you take." And that song is kinda spooky. But, you know, like "I'm stalking you." [*group laughs*]

JIM　I think that was The Police.

CARLA　But it's like, me and spirit are like that. I see it everywhere. I see spirit everywhere, and that's just gotten more profound as I get older. Every day is such a gift, and I almost want to say a redundant gift because, *how can you get more beautiful?* But it does. The flowers Jim gives me—every petal of those flowers. My heart is open to everything. And I'm just—I'm so glad. I think that one blessing of old age—and at 71, I think I could speak at least on the threshold of old age—is that you see . . .

Everything is so distracting when you're young, and it's hitting you so hard and you're trying to keep up. But as you get older you sort of settle in and you see better. You sense better. Spirit is closer. I'm grateful for the age. I hope that I live a long time. You know, 100 would be good. [*laughter*] I'd be glad to do that. And just spend that time keeping my heart open, and doing the job of helping to lighten planet Earth. It's what we came to do. I'm glad to do that job. You know I'd like to get back to writing and stuff, but we'll see what happens. It's not possible right now. I can't even see! I can't type! Right now I can't see well enough to work on writing and stuff. So I have to let that go and just be. And I'm glad to do that.

GARY When you look back and reflect upon your life, what do you see? What do you feel?

CARLA Absolute perfection. I'm so grateful for all of it. I feel so blessed. This has been a wild walk. [*laughter*] And not predictable, but oh, so rewarding. I couldn't possibly have had a better walk through life or known better people or had more wonderful experiences, in all kinds of environments. How about you?

JIM I feel that I've been blessed. A real blessing along the way. The path has always been pretty obvious for me; I haven't had to wonder a lot about what step to take next. I think that's a real blessing. I'm aware of so many people that have written in to us over the years saying that they really didn't know what to do next. You know, I think that's part of figuring out what to do next, but for me it was a process of just taking another step and keeping going. Like Carla says, it does look like, in retrospect, it was perfectly planned and carried out. And a wonderful adventure. An amazing adventure.

CARLA Yeah, yeah. What he said! [*laughter*]

Symphony of Life

"Schopenhauer, in his splendid essay called *On an Apparent Intention in the Fate of the Individual,* points out that when you reach an advanced age and look back over your lifetime, it can seem to have had a consistent order and plan, as though composed by some novelist. Events that when they occurred had seemed accidental and of little moment turn out to have been indispensable factors in the composition of a consistent plot. So who composed that plot? Schopenhauer suggests that just as your dreams are composed by an aspect of yourself of which your consciousness is unaware, so, too, your whole life is composed by the will within you.

And just as people whom you will have met apparently by mere chance became leading agents in the structuring of your life, so, too, will you have served unknowingly as an agent, giving meaning to the lives of others. The whole thing gears together like one big symphony, with everything unconsciously structuring everything else. And Schopenhauer concludes that it is as though our lives were the features of the one great dream of a single dreamer in which all the dream characters dream, too; so that everything links to everything else, moved by the one will to life which is the universal will in nature." – Joseph Campbell[§]

[§] Joseph Campbell and Bill Moyers, *The Power of Myth with Bill Moyers* (New York: Anchor Books, 1988), 283-284.

Clockwise from upper left:
(1) Carla as a toddler. (2) Carla with her parents Jean & Ted Rueckert, and her brothers Jimmy & Tommy. (3) Infant Carla with her mother. (4) Jim & Carla with Atta & Wilson McCarty, Jim's parents. (5) A very happy baby Jim. (6) A contemplative baby Don.

Clockwise from upper left:

1. Don with his mother, Elizabeth, known to most as "sister."
2. Don as a 2nd Lt in his artillery/armor unit.
3. Young Don with his father, Tully.
4. Don Elkins, high school senior.
5. Jim McCarty, high school senior.

Donald Tully Elkins

Below: Don meeting with the original Larsonian physicist, Dewey Larson, about whose work Don would later query Ra.

Next page: Though not mentioned in this book, Don's horizon stopped working during flight. Later in the flight it miraculously, impossibly fixed itself—akin to a flat tire repairing itself while driving, said Don. A few days later he discovered the equally bizarre cause for its repair. Don points to the horizon after landing.

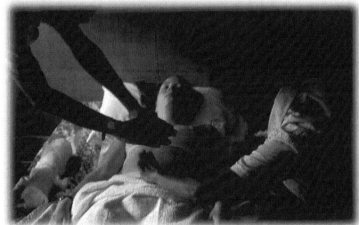

Right: Carla's Philippine psychic surgery.

Carla Lisbeth Rueckert-McCarty

Above: Don and Carla in their Louisville apartment where they lived together for twelve years. Their next house would become the site of the Ra contact shortly after Jim moved in and joined their efforts.

Clockwise from upper left:
1. Interior of Jim's cabin.
2. Jim selling his honey and beets at farmer's market.
3. Jim traveling through Nevada.
4. View of Jim's built-from-scratch cabin.
5. See 99.5.

James Allen McCarty

Above: The only two photos of the whole group. The one in costume was that mentioned on page 110. **Below**: A Carla thinned from the Ra contact offers Jim marigolds in the back yard of their home on Watterson Trail during the Ra years.

Above: Jim and Carla married on May 30, 1987.
Below: Carla spent multiple years of her life confined to a hospital bed, but always cheerful and with an eye toward praise, thanksgiving, and worship.

Above: An image revealing the shining, boundless nature of Carla L. Rueckert's optimism, spirit, and faith.

Clockwise from above: (1) The house that Don purchased in 1984: "the domicile...is blessèd [with] angelic presences," said Ra. (2) One of only a few photos of Carla channeling. Jim serves as battery, in the process holding Carla's hand as he has since 69.18. (3) Jim on his mower starting out a new day for his lawn service. (4) Carla in her living room glowing despite the medical challenges.

Top to bottom:

1. An L/L Research Homecoming Gathering.
2. Austin & Gary with Don Quixote, obviously.
3. Austin cradling a lamb in his farming days.
4. Gary with his wife, Trisha, on Louisville's riverboat.
5. Gary and Trish at the canyon which is grand.

Epilogue

What Don Elkins, Carla Rueckert, and Jim McCarty did with their incarnations was by my measure, and I think by most measures, extraordinary. And to extraordinary things and extraordinary people we turn with questions and desires to know more, to ask of them who they are, what they did, and how we might learn from their successes and their failures.

We also, and perhaps more fundamentally, turn to them to satisfy some basic curiosity. Inbuilt into our natures is the need to look to one another for cues, signals, and information about who we are, how we are, where we have been, and where we are going. So much of what we understand, or think we understand, comes by way of other humans, whether through the physical sciences, religious affiliations, metaphysical studies, literature, arts, culture, or the great tangled morass of opinion that bombards our senses from our first breath outside the womb. Excepting those rare instances in human history and prehistory when our higher-density friends walked the surface, or floated slightly above it, or took one of us aboard their cosmic Cadillac, there is no one here but us to inform (or misinform) each other. Indeed since the dawn of self-awareness we've been incrementally breaking into the unknown, assembling the puzzle pieces, and figuring-it-out *together*.

Not a one of us escapes this context. Even those few among us who reach what's known as enlightenment and transcend the illusion completely (aka: awakening from the dream) do so *through* their local, historical, cultural, and social context, a context into which is packed and embedded millennia of collective unconscious and conscious assumptions and principles; programming that, like it or not, shapes how we see ourselves and the world around us.

It is this same basic drive to learn from one another that motivated this brief [*ahem*], seven-day, 400+ question interview. What did you two do with your time here, Carla Rueckert and Jim McCarty? Why? And, given the unusual nature of your work, *how*? What does this philosophy have to say about the meaning, purpose, and nature of reality? How have you attempted to integrate and live these principles? What about your lives stands out as unique, and what can I recognize in your patterns that is universal to the human path, that tells me about who I am? And as I probe more deeply into what you and I have in common, what do I begin to see of the Creator-awakening-to-Itself peeking through *your* human faces and actions, and my own face and actions?

Two People, Three Words (or more)

Scaling down from the Big Picture for a moment to narrow the focus on these two humans, I asked myself how I would describe Jim and Carla if I had only three words. Immediately I knew that I would say *disciplined, authentic, open-hearted.*

Disciplined is one of the first to come to mind because they were so regular, ritualistic, and reliable in everything they did. I have joked at times how one could set their watch to where Jim was in his day. Any casual observer of modern life will soon recognize the hectic, busy, and variable nature of our days. We certainly have repeat appointments and regularly scheduled activities, but how difficult do we all find it to implement certain disciplines and stick with them. Carla and Jim were amazing in that regard. Though they both felt the stress of too much to do in too little time, they functioned according to consciously chosen rhythms and built their days ensuring that time for the Creator and the spiritual work was included year after year, decade following decade.

The word *discipline* also draws attention to that which they wielded so strongly, that which Ra described as the "great conduit to the Creator": the will. And in that regard the discipline was reserved not just for the day's schedule, but more importantly in disciplining their minds to do the work of processing, analyzing, balancing, and forgiving the day's catalyst. I've never met any others with so crystalline a life of discipline.

Authentic in the sense of being always true to themselves, night and day. I've seen them in nearly every type of setting they entered from 2003 onward, both in and out of Louisville, with and without other people, and in no case were they ever other than themselves. Per my modicum of understanding of psychology I'm sure that they had some layer of persona and mask, but if so it was so subtle, consistent, and not-other-than their spiritual hearts that it was practically invisible to me. They operated with little pretense and great humility, offering themselves as they are regardless of their audience. (When a person is authentic at this level they tend to radiate qualities of light, peace, presence, kindness, etc., so people reliably reacted favorably to them.)

One among many ways I witnessed this authenticity was the way they would so unhesitatingly and unapologetically speak about their shared life's work through L/L Research (including the particular roles they played as channels) to others who had no frame of reference for understanding. When asked, of course. Personally I feel a desire to hide this portion of my life from someone not already interested due to some knee-jerk aversion to the potential of rejection. Not Carla or Jim. They knew who they were and stood strongly but humbly upon that ground. And even in the context of meeting devoted readers of their material, they never elevated themselves to anything but an ordinary fellow human and seeker.

Open-hearted because they did everything they did with basic compassion and kindness, but more fundamentally and philosophically, with a desire to support the free will of others, without, generally speaking, attempting to impose their will. This was borne out countless times in my own relationship with Carla and Jim as they sought to find *my* preferences and, if at all possible, accommodate accordingly. Though not without expectations about the way such and such should be done, by and large Carla and Jim's modus operandi was always to respect and support the free will of others. They were consciously ethical and conscious of the need to make decisions within a framework of the highest ethic they could perceive.

And while the above three qualities speak of great will, they knew and practiced the other side of that coin: faith. Whatever the disciplined activities and intentions enacted by the steady power of will, Carla and Jim chose reliably at the end of the day to surrender that will to the Creator, attempting and usually succeeding to release attachment to outcome and trust that, however the cards fell, all was well.

And then I realized more words would be needed, including *light-hearted, devotional, service-oriented, perseverant, great-with-a-pun, cheerful, optimistic, music-oriented, dancers, lover-of-vodka* (in Carla's case) and so forth before I applied the brakes lest I run out of alphabet letters in my soup.

I will speak to just one more: the quality of perseverance. This was illustrated to me most pointedly when watching Carla type. If you were to see Carla's hands you would notice how very warped they were from decades of very painful rheumatoid arthritis. Her four knuckles were one big undulating bulge, her fingers crooked, and her hands so generally misshapen that she couldn't type on the keyboard with all ten fingers like most people. Instead she had to employ what's known as the *hunt 'n' peck* method whereby she operated two fingers only, one on each hand, to press the keys. Though a fairly slow way of going about things that would frustrate many people, Carla kept at it until she had written her emails of the day and, quite literally, entire books. Will is best expressed, I think, not in a moment of great, grunting strength (though that too), but more so in its steady and sustained application over the long run. Through sheer persistence Carla showed me will at that level.

Yet I cannot release this section without highlighting *one more* quality I admire, this one demonstrated by both Jim and Carla, but most nearly perfectly, I think the word is merited, by Carla: basic cheerfulness. Vibrating an attitude of good cheer, good will, and simple optimism is a difficult virtue to sustain and manifest for even those in perfect physical health. That Carla was able to serve others in this way *while* experiencing profound depths of physical pain and torments of medical hardship continues to astound me. You could walk into her room at any moment (as she lay confined on her hospital bed with an open wound on her back that never healed) and she would greet you with a smile and light in her eyes. In myself I witness daily modes of seriousness, withdrawal, unhappiness, despondency, irritation, and so forth that I absolutely marvel how effectively and potently Carla let no consideration of catalyst or circumstance extinguish her glow. She was so natural in this regard that it would be easy to think it was effortless and subsequently attribute that quality to nature alone, but any investigation into her psyche would show how, through will and faith, Carla *worked* at this mode of being through inner disciplines of prayer, tuning, offering thanksgiving, forgiving, and turning to the Creator through her beloved Jesus the Christ.

These things were important to investigate, also, because it is out of these and other qualities that their organization, L/L Research, grew. These qualities, however, have no copyright claims by Carla, Jim, their organization, or anyone. They are manifested uniquely in these two but are only one example among infinite ways any seeker may make use of will and faith.

Even in light of these glowing terms, their work, as with everyone's work, was and is never finished. This was just a snapshot in time of where they happened to be upon their journey of evolution that has no end. Jim, for instance, lived with a subtle inner armor or barrier that kept others somewhat distant for nearly the entirety of his life. It wasn't until 2015, just months after Carla's passing, that he witnessed those dissolve as a consequence of the transformation we will explore in Appendix B.

A Sunlit Scene

This interview sought to document these sorts of things along with every other that crossed my mind in order to capture a biography, a life story. While I believe it did a fairly comprehensive job, it did not plumb as deeply into the nature of another person as is possible. We didn't dive into what you might call their human flaws or what the Confederation might call the distortions that elicit learning—that portion of experience which, if examined more thoroughly, would have rendered an even fuller, 360-degree picture.

Lest the four people who read this book in its entirety walk away from it with the impression that they have just read about saintly beings, I want to convey that the subjects of this interview, Elkins included, were and are *imperfect,* so far as we would use that term in the relative world. Their natures were all too human, all too *just like you.* Over the years I had witnessed small moments and exhibitions of jealousy, anger, pettiness, hypocrisy, inconsistency, or making what I would call dumb decisions (I would know because I've made a few myself). Seldom were these moments as acute or visible as is the great variety of human drama on this planet—Carla and Jim attempted always to treat others with generosity and compassion, even if that meant keeping opinions to themselves, and Don, as you have learned, hardly expressed any opinion or emotion. But in an interview already a bit big for its britches I chose not to make a focus of basic human shortcomings.

Acknowledging the presence of less-than-ideal behaviors and attitudes, how should they be understood and situated? Picture a beautiful painting of an outdoor scene—country or city, to your preference. However well-lit that scene, and beautiful its proportions and colors, there will be shadows. To remove those shadows would be inauthentic and would diminish the aesthetic and vibrancy of the picture.

Each of us is a natural scene, some of us with more shadow, some with less. Let there be no doubt that Jim and Carla (and Don Elkins) had small shadows around the corner of their buildings, or underneath the awning, or cast upon the ground by the sunlight filtering through the lattice tabletop; but letting the eyes roam the remainder of the painting and, when finished, zooming out to take in the whole picture, at least enough to gain some meaning, it becomes clear what a sunlit scene theirs was; a scene where two people sought and strove <u>always</u> to walk the high road in the face of all distortions, whether theirs or others'.

And gazing upon the painting from that viewpoint, a variety of emotional responses may spring, ranging from congenial respect, to admiration, to awe, to tears, to gratitude, to a sense of love welling within the heart, especially as both the strident and subtle colors of service, sacrifice, and spirit in their lives come into view; especially when realizing that, no matter how extraordinary their work was, they remained remarkably humble people, presenting and sharing themselves as they are with little pretense and great transparency.

But describe that painting as I may, only you can be the viewer. Through their work and communications they have left—and Jim will continue to leave—the world many thousands of words. Through that communication with you and through the accounts of others and the example of their work, you have plenty of material to get a decent sense of who they are—insofar as any expression of the great mystery (such as a human being is) can be understood at a distance—and how this body of philosophy came into being. You can gain an inkling of what they were trying to do, and in that mirror perhaps you might see a reflection of yourself, and be inspired to remember what *you* are trying to do, and with what love you're trying to do it.

And perhaps you will go even further and lift the vision so that your focus shifts from seeing three people, their work, their circumstances, their date in time and their place on earth, to beginning to see instead the only thing we are here to see.

Let us begin and end all our efforts in the One Infinite Creator.

We suggest the nature of all manifestation to be illusory and functional only insofar as the entity turns from shape and shadow to the One.

– Ra, an humble messenger of the Law of One

Dancing in the Fields of the Lord: Sacred Sexuality

What has been your relationship with sex throughout your life?

In my June 26, 2015 entry to the *Camelot Journal*, I think that I summed up the answer to this question with this thought:

> When I was young and carefree in college I had no idea of what sex could be like with a mate of many years. I thought that sex was sex, fun and irresponsible. When Carla and I got together that was the way it started, but as we continued to open our higher energy centers with real compassion and clear communication, I was amazed to the very end of Carla's life how the power and the purpose of sexual energy exchanges continued to grow. It seemed like every date was a step further up the mountain of experience and there was no end to how high we could climb.

When and how did you first realize the metaphysical dimension and spiritual value of sex? [1]

Carla and I always had good sexual chemistry. I think that may have started a few lifetimes ago and perhaps has been going on for a while. That's all hypothetical, but I know that our relationship was something special. It didn't take but a few dates together to know that. You know how the first time with anyone has a unique element of fun and exploration to it; it seemed like that was the situation with Carla and me every time we got together. There was always something new in our experience and in our feelings.

What was Carla's lifelong relationship to this most fundamental aspect of human consciousness, and important of human activities?

Carla was very unusual in that when she was 16 she decided to ask out the most handsome guy in her class. She let him kiss her just to see what it

---

This interview and the next in Appendix B were conducted via email with Jim in March, 2016.

was like. She was not impressed and at that point decided to wait until she was ready for marriage to go any further with sex. So for her the spiritual aspect of sex was always intact. She never entered into any sexual relationship just for the bodily satisfaction of it. There was always recognition that it was a gift of God and should be seen as sacred.[2]

What is a "sexual energy transfer" as Ra defines it?

The energies that are transferred in sharing sex with a mate are of the mind, the body, and the spirit. Together they make up the "vital energies" that fueled the Ra contact. The male usually has a surplus of physical energy and the female a surplus of mental/emotional/spiritual energy and these are the energies that are transferred during a "sexual energy transfer."[3]

The amount of energies transferred is dependent upon the amount of energy stored. Energy is stored by foreplay; the more foreplay, the more energy stored and available for transfer. They are transferred at the time of orgasm. If both partners have the orgasm at the same time the amount of energy that has been stored is doubled in the transfer.[4]

What is the key component that transforms sex from a purely physical, or pleasure-seeking, act, to one in which genuinely mutually uplifting energy may be exchanged?

There are really two key components: First, a mated relationship in which all the chakras or energy centers are clear and open for both partners.[5] Second, both partners dedicate the sexual energy exchange to the Creator. "Soli Deo gloria." This is the phrase that was printed at the end of all of the bulletins for the Louisville Bach Society. Carla sang in it for 37 years and was much fed by this sacred music. The phrase is Latin for "only for the glory of God."[6]

Does conscious intention or dedication play any role in this exchange? Or does it happen automatically as a product of having sex with an open heart?

One must have an open heart chakra before any energy exchange is possible. Conscious dedication of the sexual energy exchange to the One Creator increases the likelihood and purity of the energy exchange. The conscious dedication of both partners of the sexual energy exchange is what makes the experience sacred.

Is there anything two who are aware of this process may do to enhance

and deepen this exchange?

Both partners need to keep all of their energy centers open and clear. Any disagreements between the couple need to be harmoniously resolved before any sexual energy exchanges are attempted. Carla and I never let the sun set on any disagreement. We always harmoniously resolved any disagreement before we went to sleep for the night. This requires a total dedication to each other and to clear communication. The relationship needs to be seen as being more important than either party in it.

Ra says of sexual energy transfer that "in it lies an entire system for opening the gateway to intelligent infinity,"[7] and elsewhere they say of this activity that, at a certain level of expression, it becomes "high sexual magic."[8] What is the highest or deepest possible experience in this particular variety of human intercourse?

The top of the mountain here is the "sacrament of the fully experienced presence of the One Infinite Creator." That would be the violet-ray transfer and would represent contact with intelligent infinity, which is the One Infinite Creator. We never made it that far. I think that the indigo-ray energy exchange was the top of our mountain. That would represent contact with intelligent energy.[9]

What can two seekers do to reach this zenith, if you will, of sacramental, unified consciousness? In other words, how can the Creator be known through sex?

Mates who seek this unified consciousness need to balance their catalyst on a daily basis. They need to meditate and continue to work on any energy center that is not fully activated. Most of the time this work will involve the indigo ray in its activation, then its balancing with all the lower energy centers, and then its use of the spirit as a shuttle to contact intelligent infinity. My indigo ray was activated in 1972, and I have been balancing it with the other energy centers for the last 33 years.[10] This is not a quick process!

Is it necessary in your opinion to be a mated pair to exchange sexual energy of this type? Alternatively, are there benefits to being a mated pair?[11]

It is my opinion that only a mated pair has any chance of using sexual energy exchanges in what Ra calls "high sexual magic" for contact with either intelligent energy or intelligent infinity. Non-mated pairs whose hearts are both activated can, of course, initiate a sexual energy transfer, but for the higher chakra exchanges, it *generally* takes a lot of work, time, intimacy and experience as a couple to master opening the heart to each other, and then being able to clearly communicate to resolve any disharmonies. This is in the positive sense. This is probably not true for negatively oriented entities. [12]

What role does gender or biological sex play? And, in your opinion, can spiritual seekers of the same gender/sex experience the same energy exchange and reach the same potentials?

That's a really good question. Hypothetically I think that it would be possible for the same-sex entities to achieve sexual energy transfers if one of them identified with masculine energy and the other one identified with feminine energy. There would still have to be a sexual polarity for there to be an exchange of sexual energies. [13]

What was your and Carla's relationship with sexual energy transfer?

We always dedicated our sexual energy transfers to the One Creator. In addition I also sought to enhance Carla's vital and physical energies and made a conscious statement of that intention to myself before each love-making. I saw Carla's vital and physical energies being enhanced as helpful in our desire to seek and serve the One Creator, especially during the Ra contact.

Sex, or more specifically, sexual energy transfer, literally helped to power the Ra Contact. Without it there would have been no contact, at least not for long. What an amazing circumstance to be able to fuel your group's work through love power, as it were, and consecration of the sexual act. [14] How did this impact your relationship?

This knowledge gave us a feeling of being very blessed. We felt it an honor to be in the Ra Contact, and a double honor to be able to aid the length and number of sessions with those of Ra by the dedication of our sexual energy exchanges to the seeking and serving of the One Creator.

You and Carla so unabashedly embraced sacred sexuality, writing about it in books, and reporting when it happened *now and then* [15] in the course of your daily *Camelot Journal* entries. Not, of course, in graphic detail. Always euphemistically and creatively, one of the favorite motifs describing some form of movement through the "fields of the Lord":

- "After Mick and I bathed, we came upstairs for a glorious, incredible dance in the fields of the Lord."

- "We danced long and lovingly in the fields of the Lord tonight, and went to sleep in the afterglow."
- "How very fortunate we are that we have moved through all the chakras together to find ourselves in sacred fields of the Lord's blessing. Praise the Lord!"

This suggests a perhaps more enlightened, or, at least *different* relationship to sexuality than historical norms on this planet—a perspective that sees sexuality not as something that must be hidden, or kept private, or discussed only with like-gender companions over a beer. Can you comment on this?

We experienced great pleasure, of course, in our sexual energy exchanges, but we also experienced great joy and a feeling of wholeness and destiny discovered in our experiences together. It felt like the very most natural way that all people should be relating to their mates.

Is it true that Carla felt that sexual energy transfer helped to sustain her, and keep her frail body in this illusion? That is, helped to keep her alive and well.

Carla was very certain that our sexual energy exchanges were responsible for enhancing her health and lengthening her life. That was part of my dedication of each experience that we shared. I was transferring physical energy to her which was like recharging a battery that is low on energy.

Insofar as it can be tactfully described, can you talk about your and Carla's process?

We usually arranged the morning before the date to have the date that night. That gave us the day to enjoy the anticipation of the date. We would frequently bathe together and settle in for slow snuggling and gentle talk and be sure that all energy centers were clear. Then a lot of foreplay and fun.

Due to her daunting and increasingly prohibitive medical condition, Carla's body eventually lost the ability to have physical intercourse with you. Yet you two persisted and found ways to achieve mutual orgasm through energy alone. Can you describe how this was achieved?

I will leave this one to your imagination. Imagine that you are a teenager who is told that you cannot have sexual intercourse, but you still want to have sex. What would you do?

In 54.25, Ra says that the positively oriented entity will be "transmuting strong red-ray sexual energy into green-ray energy transfers."[16] What specifically is red-ray sexual energy, and how, or by what means, is it "transmuted" into green-ray energy transfer?

I can only guess, but my guess is that the positively oriented entities very likely begin their relationship with a very strong physical (red-ray) attraction for each other. But because they are positively oriented they will not just take advantage of that physical attraction as the only reason, or even the basic reason, for sharing sexual energy exchanges. They will look deeper into the nature of the other self and find those qualities that are even more attractive than the physical body. I thought that the sexiest qualities that Carla had were her great intelligence and her very authentic, strong, and independent personality. Having a fearless spirit was also most attractive. She was also quite attractive physically, but that was fourth on my list of attractive qualities that I appreciated about her. The body fades in its attraction as we grow older, but these other qualities tend to increase.

In 32.10, Ra describes something they call "complete fusion nature" whereby two people experience a melding of mind, body, and spirit in what Ra calls a "constant orgasm, shall we say, of joy and delight each in the other's beingness."[17] Is this something that you and Carla ever experienced distinctly? Do you think this might be a description of the experience of a violet-ray transfer?

Again, I am guessing here, but it would be my guess that this would be a violet-ray transfer as a steady state of consciousness. Carla and I had significantly long periods of heightened pleasure and communion with each other, but they eventually did come to an end.

What is most important to consider for the seeker who wishes to likewise engage the gears of sacred sexuality and build their own unique practice and experience?

Find a mate who is as dedicated to the spiritual journey of seeking the One Creator as you are. Share every part of the journey together. Share a ritual of some kind that begins your day with praising the One Creator. End the day in the same way. Work on clearing each energy center with balancing exercises and keep the centers open with clear communication. Never let a disharmony fester. Put the relationship first. Resolve any disharmony as soon as possible, preferably before you go to sleep for the night. Dedicate each sexual energy exchange to the One Creator and thank the Creator often for all of the blessings in your life.

We will close this interview with an excerpt from Carla's *A Wanderer's Handbook:*

In the white ceremonial magical tradition of the west, sacramental sex has sometimes been called "high magic." While I in no way recommend any form of sexual action, whether western or eastern in discipline, that is calculated for effect rather than as a way to share and uplift love, and while I would eschew any sort of "black" sexual activity, involving sadism and masochism in their hurtful, as opposed to playful, form, I can attest to the beauty of this high magic.

> The heart of white magic is the experience of the joy of union with the Creator. This joy will of necessity radiate throughout the life experience of the positive adept. It is for this reason that sexual magic is not restricted solely to the negatively oriented polarizing adepts but when most carefully used has its place in high magic as it, when correctly pursued, joins body, mind and spirit with the one infinite Creator. – Ra, 71.7

This pursuit is not out of the reach of any who finds a good partner. It may be the work of many years to find the springs of love and trust opening in the relationship to the point where such advances are possible. But the work is not arduous, and the results are truly astonishing when one begins to reach these higher energies.

> We ask each to see working on sexuality as a holy occupation and part of a holy life. Let it be wonderful and fun. Free the self to re-joice in the beauty of this energy. This is a long process sometimes;
>
> however, there is much pleasure in the work. – *Q'uo, April 9, 1995*

Yes, there is, and I am most grateful for the passion I have shared in my life. It has been of inestimable benefit. I feel that the nature of sex is play, a divine play that is as rich as the people doing it and the spontaneity of the moment. Treat each time like a new experience, a first time, for it is indeed a first time. And when we have begun to play the old and dear tunes of the body, focus on that note the pleasure sings and the electrical flow and light of it through our body and connecting in its bright loop through our partner's and around again. There is a metaphysical tone and flow of energy that is distinct for each experience, and the moving into the sacramental is done through, first, the dedication of the entire act to the infinite Creator, and the dedication of the pleasure of the act as well; and secondly, the intensity of focus given to the flow of pleasure in the present moment. Give the self completely to and in this most hallowed joining, for it is divine. [18]

1

Ra says that the energies transferred are metaphysical, or of a time/space nature. Those include mental, emotional, and spiritual energies.

QUESTIONER Before the veil, can you describe any other physical difference that we haven't talked about yet with respect to the sexual energy transfers or relationships or anything prior to veiling?

RA I am Ra. Perhaps the most critical difference of the veiling, before and after, was that before the mind, body, and spirit were veiled, entities were aware that each energy transfer—and, indeed, very nearly all that proceeds from any intercourse, social or sexual—between two entities has its character and substance in time/space rather than space/time.

The energies transferred during the sexual activity are not, properly speaking, of space/time. There is a great component of what you may call metaphysical energy transferred. Indeed, the body complex as a whole is greatly misunderstood due to the post-veiling assumption that the physical manifestation called the body is subject only to physical stimuli. This is emphatically not so. 84.17

2

More about Carla's relationship to sex as a function of, and tribute to, spirit:

RA I am Ra. This instrument, though not anomalous, is somewhat less distorted towards the separation of mind, body, and spirit than many of your third-density entities. The energies of sexual transfer would, if run through the undeveloped spiritual electrical or magnetic complex, which you call circuitry, effectually blow out that particular circuit. Contrarily, the full spiritual energies run through bodily complex circuitry will also adversely affect the undeveloped circuit of the bodily complex.

Some there are, *such as this instrument,* **who have not** in the particular incarnation **chosen at any time to express sexual energy through the bodily circuitry.** Thus from the beginning of such an entity's experience the body and spirit express together in any sexual action. Therefore, to transfer sexual energy for this instrument is to transfer spiritually as well as physically.

This instrument's magnetic field, if scrutinized by one sensitive, will show these unusual configurations. This is not unique to one entity but is common to a reasonable number of entities who, having lost the desire for orange- and green-ray* sexual experiences, have strengthened the combined circuitry of spirit, mind, and body to express the totality of be-ingness in each action. It is for this reason also that the social intercourse and companionship is very beneficial to this instrument, it being sensitive to the more subtle energy transfers.

* Ra said "green-ray," but presumably they meant "yellow-ray." 48.2

3

About the types the transfers from the various rays:

QUESTIONER Is there any way to tell which ray the transfer was for an in-dividual after the experience? Is there any way for the individual to tell in which particular ray the transfer occurred?

RA I am Ra. There is only a subjective yardstick or measure of such.

Green: If the energies have flowed so that love is made whole, green-ray transfer has taken place.

Blue: If, by the same entities' exchange, greater ease in communication and greater sight has been experienced, the energy has been refined to the blue-ray energy center.

Indigo: If the polarized entities, by this same energy transfer experience, find that the faculties of will and faith have been stimulated, not for a brief while but for a great duration of what you call time, you may per-ceive the indigo-ray transfer.

Violet: We may not speak of the violet-ray transfer except to note that it is an opening to the gateway of intelligent infinity. Indeed, the indigo-ray transfer is also this but, shall we say, the veil has not yet been lifted. 84.21

4

About stored and transferred energy, and timing of orgasm:

RA The energy transfer occurs in one releasing of the potential differ-ence. This does not leap between green and green energy centers but is the sharing of the energies of each from red ray upwards. In this context it may be seen to be at its most efficient when both entities have orgasm simultaneously. However, it functions as transfer if either has the orgasm and indeed in the case of the physically expressed love between a mated pair which does not have the conclusion you call orgasm there is, none-theless, a considerable amount of energy transferred **due to the potential difference which has been** *raised*—as long as both entities are aware of this potential and **release its strength to each other by desire of the will** in a mental or mind complex dedication.

You may see this practice as being used to generate energy transfers in some of your practices of what you may call other than Christian reli-gious distortion systems of the Law of One. 84.13

QUESTIONER Would you give me an example of that last statement?

RA I am Ra. We preface this example with the reminder that each system is quite distorted and its teachings always half-lost. However, one such system is that called the tantric yoga. 84.14

RA If both entities are well polarized and vibrating in green-ray love, any orgasm shall offer equal energy to both. 84.16

5

In discussing energy transfers before and after the veil, Ra focuses on sexual energy transfers, and alludes to the value of the mated relationship:

RA Let us, as an example, choose your sexual activities of energy trans-fer. In the instance of the sexual activity of those not dwelling within the veiling each activity was a transfer. There were some transfers of strength. Most were rather attenuated in the strength of the transfer due to the lack of veiling.

In the third density, entities are attempting to learn the ways of love. **If it can be seen that all are one being it becomes much more difficult for the undisciplined personality to choose one mate and, thereby, initi-ate itself into a program of service.** It is much more likely that the sexual energy will be **dissipated more randomly** without either great joy or great sorrow depending from these experiences.

Therefore, the green-ray energy transfer, being almost without excep-tion the case in sexual energy transfer *prior to veiling,* **remains weakened and without significant crystallization.** The sexual energy transfers and blockages after veiling have been discussed previously. It may be seen to be a more complex study, but one far more efficient in crystallizing those who seek the green-ray energy center. 83.3

RA The awareness of all as Creator is that which opens the green energy center. Thusly there was no possibility of blockage due to the sure knowledge of each by each that each was the Creator. The transfers were weak due to the ease with which such transfers could take place between any two polarized entities during sexual intercourse. 84.8

And indicates similarly here:

QUESTIONER May I ask if the Logos of this system planned for the mating process as possibly depicted in Card Six— I don't know if this is related— by some type of DNA imprinting as has been studied by our science. In many second-density creatures seem to have some sort of imprinting that creates a lifetime mating relationship, and I was wondering if this was designed by the Logos for that particular mechanism and if it was also carried into third density?

RA I am Ra. There are some of your second-density fauna which have in-stinctually imprinted monogamous mating processes. The third-density physical vehicle, which is the basic incarnational tool of manifestation upon your planet, arose from entities thusly imprinted, all the aforesaid being designed by the Logos.

The free will of third-density entities is far stronger than the rather mild carryover from second-density DNA encoding, and it is not part of the conscious nature of many of your mind/body/spirit complexes to be monogamous due to the exercise of free will. However, as has been noted, there are many **signposts in the deep mind indicating to the alert adept the more efficient use of catalyst**. As we have said, the Logos of your peoples has a bias towards kindness. 99.10

And some of Carla's thoughts from *A Wanderer's Handbook*:

In other words, a bias has been built into our bodies' energy systems by the Creator towards the mated relationship. A mated relationship is work! Guaranteed! But in the school of life, which is a school of love, I feel that the mate is a tremendous prize, easily capable of giving us the catalyst we need to grow more efficiently than anyone else, including ourselves. The mated relationship is a metaphysical fast track. Men, more than women, have traditionally bemoaned the wedded state as that plan which puts him to work for the rest of their lives, paying for the resulting abode, children and life that ensues for their new families. ...in reality, any relationship is an addition of sorts to the responsibility of both people. The more successful mates can be characterized as tag teams, partners, buddies who get it done. And part of the basis of this is a mutual awareness of the body rightness of this mated state that honors the great luck of finding a mate, and sees that there is much to be gained from being true to this mated bond, not only all-important trust, but also pleasure, union and worship.

Rueckert, Carla L., *A Wanderer's Handbook* (Louisville, KY: L/L Research, 2001), 136

6

In keeping with 84.20 (see next endnote), special attention might also be paid to the necessity of the green-ray activation:

RA I am Ra. With the green-ray transfer of energy you now come to the great turning point sexually as well as in each other mode of experience. The green ray may then be turned outward, the entity then giving rather than receiving. The first giving beyond green ray is the giving of acceptance or freedom, thus allowing the recipient of blue-ray energy transfer the opportunity for a feeling of being accepted, thus freeing that other-self to express itself to the giver of this ray.

It will be noted that once green-ray energy transfer has been achieved by two mind/body/spirits in mating, the further rays are available without both entities having the necessity to progress equally. Thus a blue-ray vibrating entity or indigo-ray vibrating entity whose other ray vibrations are clear may share that energy with the green-ray other-self, thus acting as catalyst for the continued learn/teaching of the other-self. **Until an other-self reaches green ray, such energy transfers through the rays is not possible.** 32.5

7

About an entire system for opening the gateway to intelligent infinity:

RA To respond to your query [about sexual energy transfers] we firstly wish to agree with your supposition that the subject you now query upon is a large one, for in it lies **an entire system of opening the gateway to intelligent infinity.** You may see that some information is necessarily shrouded in mystery by our desire to preserve the free will of the adept.

The great key to blue, indigo, and finally, that great capital of the column of sexual energy transfer, violet energy transfers, **is the metaphysical bond or distortion which has the name among your peoples of unconditional love.** In the blue-ray energy transfer the quality of this love is refined in the fire of honest communication and clarity; this, shall we say, normally, meaning in general, takes a substantial portion of your space/time to accomplish although there are instances of matings so well refined in previous incarnations and so well remembered that the blue ray may be penetrated at once. This energy transfer is of great benefit to the seeker in that all communication from this seeker is, thereby, refined and the eyes of honesty and clarity look upon a new world. Such is the nature of blue-ray energy and such is one mechanism of potentiating and crystallizing it.

As we approach indigo-ray transfer we find ourselves in a shadowland where we cannot give you information straight out or plain, for this is seen by us to be an infringement. We cannot speak at all of violet-ray transfer as we do not, again, desire to break the Law of Confusion.

We may say that these **jewels, though dearly bought, are beyond price for the seeker** and might suggest that just as each awareness is arrived at through a process of analysis, synthesis, and inspiration, so should the seeker approach its mate and evaluate each experience, seeking the jewel. 84.20

8

About "sexual magic":

QUESTIONER Would this then be the primal mechanism for the Creator to experience Self?

RA I am Ra. This is not a proper term. Perhaps the adjective would be "one appropriate" way of the Creator knowing Itself, for in each interaction, no matter what the distortion, the Creator is experiencing Itself. The bisexual knowing of the Creator by Itself has the potential for two advantages.

Firstly, in the green-ray activated being there is the potential for a direct and simple analog of what you may call joy, the spiritual or metaphysical nature which exists in intelligent energy. This is a great aid to comprehension of a truer nature of beingness.

The other potential advantage of bisexual reproductive acts is the possibility of a **sacramental understanding or connection, shall we say, with the gateway to intelligent infinity,** for with appropriate preparation, work in what you may call magic may be done and experiences of intelligent infinity may be had. The positively oriented individuals concentrating upon this method of reaching intelligent infinity, then, through the seeking or the act of will, are able to direct this infinite intelligence to the work these entities desire to do, whether it be knowledge of service or ability to heal or whatever service to others is desired .

These are two advantages of this particular method of the Creator experiencing Itself. As we have said before, the corollary of the strength of this particular energy transfer is that it opens the door, shall we say, to the individual mind/body/spirit complexes' desire to serve in an infinite number of ways an other-self, thus polarizing towards positive. 31.3

RA The second energy transfer of which we would speak is the sexual energy transfer. This takes place upon a non-magical level by all those entities which vibrate green ray active. It is possible, as in the case of this instrument which dedicates itself to the service of the One Infinite Creator, to further refine this energy transfer. When the other-self also dedicates itself in service to the One Infinite Creator, the transfer is doubled. Then the amount of energy transferred is dependent only upon the amount of polarized sexual energy created and released. There are refinements from this point onward leading to the realm of the high sexual magic. 73.22

[9]
About indigo- and violet-ray transfers:

RA I am Ra. The indigo ray is the ray of, shall we say, awareness of the Creator as self; thus one whose indigo-ray vibrations have been activated can offer the energy transfer of Creator to Creator. This is the beginning of the sacramental nature of what you call your bisexual reproductive act. It is unique in bearing the allness, the wholeness, the unity in its offering to other-self. 32.6

RA I am Ra. The violet ray, just as the red ray, is constant in the sexual experience. Its experience by other-self may be distorted or completely ignored or not apprehended by other-self. However, the violet ray, being the sum and substance of the mind/body/spirit complex, surrounds and informs any action by a mind/body/spirit complex.32.7

See 84.21 (endnote #2) for a small amount more information on violet-ray transfer. One gets the sense that in a transfer of violet ray, there is a total dissolution of the illusory individual identity, each mate restored to a non-dual wholeness where subject and object collapse, leaving only the All, the One, the I AM.

[10] Jim's experience of indigo-ray activation was discussed in Chapter 28, "Jim's Bio."

[11]

Whether mated or solitary, or somewhere in between, sexuality is a foundational and core component of our natures that can be explored, enjoyed, and integrated into our overall beingness. From *A Wanderer's Handbook*:

> The experience of sexual ecstasy is often our first and sometimes our only experience of the Creator:
>
>> We are not saying that each must have the sex life; we are saying that each must feel good about having a sex life, whether one is or is not in a relationship at the time. One must feel not only tolerant but good when one thinks of one's passion and sexuality, for the passion that one feels at orgasm is one's first experience of the steady state of the Creator. It is brief and fleeting, but it is an indication given as a gift and also as a perfectly practical means of evolving the species by the one infinite Creator. – Q'uo, July 2, 1989

Rueckert, A Wanderer's Handbook, 263

[12]

See 84.20 (endnote #6) for an exception to the necessity of *time* in opening blue-ray transfers.

[13]

See page 268 of *A Wanderer's Handbook* for Carla's take on homosexuality and bisexuality.

Ra speaks to the difference in polarity with regard to sexual energy transfer here:

> RA I am Ra. Energy transfer implies the release of potential energies across, shall we say, a potentiated space. The sexual energy transfers occur **due to the polarizations of two mind/body/spirit complexes, each of which have some potential difference one to the other**. The nature of the transfer of energy or of the blockage of this energy is then a function of the interaction of these two potentials. In the cases where transfer takes place, you may liken this to a circuit being closed.

> You may also see this activity, as all experiential activities, as the Creator experiencing Itself. 31.2

> QUESTIONER In the last session you made the statement that before veiling, sexual energy transfer was always possible. I would like to know what you meant by "it was always possible" and why it was not always possible after the veiling, just to clear up that point?

> RA I am Ra. We believe that we grasp your query and will use the analogy in your culture of the battery which lights the flashlight bulb. Two working batteries placed in series always offer the potential of the bulb's illumination. After the veiling, to continue this gross analogy, the two batteries being placed not in series would then offer no possible illumination of the bulb. Many mind/body/spirit complexes after the veiling

have, through blockages, done the equivalent of reversing the battery. 87.18

[Note: the "blockages" to which Ra refers cover an infinite number of situations, not necessarily situations of gender.]

QUESTIONER Thank you. In the material earlier you mentioned "magnetic attraction." Could you define and expand upon that term?

RA I am Ra. We used the term to indicate that in your bisexual natures there is that which is of polarity. This polarity may be seen to be **variable** according to the, shall we say, **male/female polarization of each entity**, be each entity biologically male or female. Thus you may see the magnetism when two entities **with the appropriate balance, male/female versus female/male polarity**, meeting and thus feeling the attraction which polarized forces will exert, one upon the other.

This is the strength of the bisexual mechanism. It does not take an act of will to decide to feel attraction for one who is oppositely polarized sexually. It will occur in an inevitable sense giving the free flow of energy a proper, shall we say, avenue. This avenue may be blocked by some distortion towards a belief/condition which states to the entity that this attraction is not desired. However, the basic mechanism functions as simply as would, shall we say, the magnet and the iron. 31.7

And in the following Q&A about the archetypes of mind, Ra speaks to the difference in male/female *principles*—not necessarily biological sex—that play a role in energy transfer:

QUESTIONER The Matrix of the Mind is depicted seemingly as male on the card and the Potentiator as female. Could Ra state why this is and how this affects these two archetypes?

RA I am Ra. Firstly, as we have said, the Matrix of the Mind is attracted to the biological male and the Potentiator of the Mind to the biological female. Thusly in energy transfer the female is able to potentiate that which may be within the conscious mind of the male so that it may feel enspirited.

In a more general sense, that which reaches may be seen as a male principle. That which awaits the reaching may be seen as a female principle. The richness of the male and female system of polarity is interesting and we would not comment further but suggest consideration by the student. 92.20

[14] For more information about the way in which the energy transfers supported, energized, and sustained Carla (and thus the contact itself), see: 39.2, 44.1, 44.13, 48.2, 68.2, 72.16, 76.2, 79.2-4, 81.7, 83.2, & 87.27, among others.

[15] Or reliably reported it every time. I have no way of knowing statistically how many acts were reported vs. not. Nor shall I do that research. :)

[16] About that transmutation:

> RA The positively oriented entity will be transmuting strong red-ray sexual energy into green-ray energy transfers and radiation in blue and indigo and will be similarly transmuting selfhood and place in society into energy transfer situations in which the entity may merge with and serve others and then, finally, radiate unto others without expecting any transfer in return. 54.25

[17] On the "complete fusion nature":

> RA I am Ra. The entire creation is of the One Creator. Thus the division of sexual activity into simply that of the bodily complex is an artificial division, all things thusly being seen as sexual equally, the mind, the body, and the spirit; all of which are part of the polarity of the entity. Thus sexual fusion may be seen with or without what you may call sexual intercourse to be the complete melding of the mind, the body, and the spirit in what feels to be a constant orgasm, shall we say, of joy and delight each in the other's beingness. 32.10

[18] Rueckert, A Wanderer's Handbook, 275–76

APPENDIX B
Carla's Passing

Our seven-day interview concluded in mid-summer, 2014. Carla was then, as she had been for over three years by that point, bound to a hospital bed due to a spinal surgery in April, 2011. That surgery produced an open wound that never closed or healed. Even after three plus years in a hospital bed, though, she had had every hope that she would return to full health and resume her creative work of writing and channeling.

After the interview concluded, what transpired in Carla's arduous journey?

She developed anemia. No tests could explain how she was losing blood. But she had to have infusions of blood and iron on half a dozen dates between September 19, 2014 and January 12, 2015. She also suffered increasing nausea, perhaps from the strong pain meds, and her stomach would not tolerate much food. She lost 50 lbs. between the end of the interview and January of 2015. The titanium screws used to fuse her three lower vertebrae also began to show through the wound and there was talk between the surgeons, both plastic and orthopedic, of removing the screws since they had done their job and any foreign object in a wound can cause infection.

Her health began to decline rapidly sometime in winter, 2015. What happened during that period?

A couple of months or so before she passed into larger life her hearing and eyesight were greatly diminished at the same time. An audiologist told us that was a sign of a brain tumor. We never were able to have an MRI to confirm this possible diagnosis. But a brain tumor would account for her frequently feeling distracted and slightly anxious. Her wound began a slow deterioration in the last two weeks of her life. In the last couple days of her life it, and the previously healthy skin around the wound, turned a dark purple, and the wound had a foul smell. It was a massive and rapidly moving infection that eventually ended her incarnation.[1]

A little over eight months after the interview, Carla departed from this plane on April 1, 2015. Can you describe the events of that day?

For the previous two or three weeks she had been sleeping a lot, which made me glad because that was her only escape from the steadily increasing pain. But it also saddened me because I knew that I was losing her slowly as she slept.

On what would be her final night I held her hand and I began to talk to her while she was sleeping. I told her how much I loved her, how much I would miss her, how much she has taught me about being able to open my heart in love, and a lot of things just came rolling out of me. Then she opened her eyes, and I continued talking about the same things, and as it turned out we had a good exchange of love pledges, special memories, and funny stories. We had shared all of these thoughts before but not with such intensity and emotion. It was tremendously therapeutic although I still choke up with tears when I think of her passing on and me being alone. As a spiritual seeker for many years I know that we have been together many times before now and will be together again because we are of the same "clan" or spiritual family. But my third-density, worldly personality needs constant assurance that all of this is true.

So that morning I did our usual morning protocol and gave her a bath in bed. I offered her food, but she had stopped eating the day before. She drank some water a couple of times during the day. She slept most of the day, but at mid-afternoon Helen D. and her husband, Eric, drove down from Vermont to visit her. Helen was her best friend from her senior year at MacDuffie School for Girls in Springfield, MA.

Eric and I walked around the yard looking at the flowers and the stone work as Carla and Helen talked some and Carla napped occasionally. Helen said at one point Carla roused into crystal clear consciousness and said, "This is real. I'm going to die, and I don't know when." Helen, who also suffers from cancer, told her that she was going to die soon too, and also didn't know when.

Helen and Eric left after a visit of about two hours. I took a bath and then took my usual nap around 5:30. I slept for a little more than an hour and when I woke up and looked over at Carla I could see that her eyes were open. That was unusual, so I got up and went over to her to see if I could get anything for her. I asked her if she wanted some pain medication. I thought that she nodded yes, so I put two Dilaudid in her mouth and offered her a glass of water to wash them down.

She gently pushed the water aside with her right hand. Again I offered her the water, and again she gently pushed it aside with her right hand. Then I turned away from her for a moment to replace the glass of water on her bedside table. When I turned toward her again she had a look of shock on her face. I asked her if this was her time. I asked her if she was going to leave me.

Then I took her in my arms and told her that it was okay. I told her that it was okay to leave. I told her that I loved her. She took three long, slow, deep breaths, and she was gone. It was 6:50 pm EDT.

. . .

I immediately called Fr. Michael from St. Luke's Episcopal Church, and he came over and administered the Last Rites. After Fr. Michael left I removed the catheter and changed the dressing on Carla's wound, washed her body, and put oil on it. I removed her jewelry and put a new outfit on her and her favorite socks. Then I called the University of Louisville Medical School to let them know that she had passed away and had donated her body to them for scientific research. Two people from the medical school came within 45 minutes to pick up her body, but we had to wait until the EMS came and certified that she was deceased, and then we had to wait for the coroner to come and issue the same declaration.

In all, the waiting time was about two hours, so I sat on the bed with Carla's body, keeping my hand on her leg, and talked to the two medical school attendants about the books on our walls and the various topics in them, especially the paranormal section. After they left with Carla's body I didn't think that I would be able to sleep that night, but I did eventually go to sleep somewhere around 2 am.

Did you hold a funeral service for her?

She asked that we have the funeral service for her two to three weeks after her passing so friends and family from a distance would have a chance to attend. And she wanted it on a weekend in the evening so people wouldn't have to miss work to attend. We had a beautiful High Mass at St. Luke's Episcopal Church on April 17, a Friday evening at 7 pm. She picked out every part of the service as all choir members had been asked to do, and it was glorious.[2] It included the *Magnificat* which is Latin for "my soul". When Mary visited her cousin Elizabeth, who was pregnant with John the Baptist, Elizabeth praises Mary for her faith. Mary's response is to sing these words which basically say, "My soul doeth magnify the Lord." This was Carla's feeling about her life, that it should magnify the Lord Jesus Christ, her personal savior. I gave her eulogy and felt a great honor to be able to let people know what an amazing person of faith and love Carla was.[3]

How did people respond to her passing?

People were greatly saddened to hear of her passing. I heard from many who offered very thoughtful and loving condolences from around the world. It really made me feel loved and comforted to get such an outpouring of love from so many friends and strangers alike. I don't think anyone can really know how much it means for the loved ones left behind to get condolences and well wishes from people who care about your loved one and about you too. When you lose the person closest to you in the world the sense of incredible loss is almost matched by the sense of now being alone in the world. When people take the time to write a letter, sign a card, or make a phone call to extend heartfelt condolences it brings a little light into a very dark inner life. I was much lifted up by people's love and I would like to thank everyone who sent cards and letters of condolence to me. I love you all.

Do you get the sense that Carla was ready to bring this incarnation to a close?

She had asked me on January 1, 2015 if I thought that she would live to see her 72nd birthday in July. I told her that I really hoped that she would, but that things didn't look good for that possibility. She seemed quite ready to go whenever the time came.

While on this side of the veil we can only ever speculate, do you feel that the soul we know as Carla accomplished her mission, or her pre-incarnational objectives, during her lifetime?

I have no doubt whatsoever that Carla finished her incarnational objectives. We talked a lot about how both of us were learning primary lessons as a result of her needing my attention and help 24/7.

She needed to balance the *learning to give without expectation of return*, that she learned to do in childhood, with *being able to accept the love offerings of others*. In order to be able to accept the love offerings of others she needed to work on strengthening her indigo-ray sense of self-worth.

She did both. And I was able to begin *opening my heart in all compassionate love* by being able to take care of her and do for her what she could not do for herself.[4]

Carla's medical journey was *difficult*, to understate the situation. Most, myself included, would not be able to tolerate that chronic level of physical pain and dysfunction over such a long period of time.[5] Do you feel there was purpose behind the distortions of Carla's body?

Carla was aware that she had programmed physical limitations into her life to keep her from expending her energies all over the place because her personality was like the Tigger in *Winnie the Pooh*. She loved to do everything. The limitations kept her focused on the inner life of prayer, worship, meditation, and channeling. The [mental/emotional] pain of the limitations, according to Ra, didn't have to be there unless she could not accept the [physical] limitations.[6]

How did you respond to, and cope with, your wife's passing in the initial weeks and months?

The day after she passed into larger life we got seven inches of rain, and our basement flooded. I had to clean it all up so her brothers and their families could stay down there when they came for the funeral. It was actually a blessing because it took my mind off of her passing.

During the day I have kept busy doing L/L Research projects that continue to give me the feeling of still being a team with her. At night I would talk to her picture and tell her what I felt and what I was going through. I also read her eulogy every night for a month or so and found unexpected comfort in doing that. Most importantly, I also began to pursue my spiritual journey more intensively, especially with more meditation starting within two weeks of her passing.

We've witnessed you undergo a profound transformation and flowering as a result of Carla's passing. Among other ways that you've changed, your energy is much softer, more open, more approachable, and less anxious, tense, and hurried. You spend more time honoring interpersonal dynamics.[7]

Have you experienced a transformation? Can you talk about that?

While Carla was still alive I was beginning to open my heart in compassion and love more and more for her. This compassion began to be focused on everyone and everything around me after she passed away. On

August 3rd I had a breakthrough when I was able to love and forgive myself for the first time in my life after one of my fits of anger. All my life I have been attempting to generate more compassion by using my pre-incarnative choice to program a lack of love for myself. When I broke my computer on August 3rd I felt horrible, and when I got into bed I told myself that it would be a tremendous breakthrough if I could, at that moment, forgive myself for what I had done. And then I felt a great wave of tears, relief, and love for myself pour through me, and I was able to love myself even in the depths of despair.

It has been almost a year exactly since Carla left us. What effect has her death had upon your spiritual seeking specifically?

Carla's passing into larger life was a trigger for me to get me to focus all of my energy on seeking the Creator within. It is obviously a pre-incarnative plan meant to occur upon her passing. I have done this primarily by meditating many times during the day and by reading all of Carla's works and those of Joel Goldsmith.

What roles did will and faith play in this process?

Exercising my will to grow and my faith that all was well helped, and still help me to make it through each day.

You wrote in your annual Christmas letter later that year that Jesus had come into your heart. Can you describe this moment and its impact upon your life?

In July, while working outside in our gardens, I became aware of silly nonsense ideas going through my mind, as if by their own volition. I decided to replace the nonsense with something helpful. I believe that Carla gave me the inspiration to sing "Alleluia, Alleluia" over and over. It's a Hebrew word that means "Praise the Lord." Within 30 minutes of doing so, and working while singing the phrase, I felt a welling up in my heart and some gentle tears in my eyes.

I incorporated the phrase into our Morning Offering for five to ten minutes before the silent meditation. On August 31st I was singing this phrase, and I got the impulse to ask the Creator to come into my heart. Nothing happened. Then I asked Jesus to come into my heart. Immediately I felt a very strong activation of my heart chakra and a river of tears flowing down my cheeks in joy and gratitude. I knew that He had come. I sat stunned for about ten minutes trying to take in the enormity of the experience. From that point on I have sought to serve with love wherever possible.

How has your relationship with L/L Research changed?

I feel more committed to helping to continue L/L Research activities as we always did as a memorial to Carla and to Don. I feel kind of like a caregiver as you and Austin do most of the actual office work. I am concentrating more on the "hands-on" kind of work—like cataloguing the library, making audio books out of all of Carla's work, editing new books, and continuing on with the channeling meditations.[8]

Insofar as I understand, you have had to undergo a monumental conversion of paradigm. In your many years with Carla, your rules for life boiled down to one: care for and support Carla—in whatever way she needed. I've personally never seen anyone so single-pointed about anything as you were about Carla's care and upkeep. Every other priority, need, and desire in your life was made secondary to, and bent toward, your absolute dedication to Carla.

With Carla's passing you not only had to grieve the loss of your soulmate, but to rediscover who you are and why you're alive. Would you say this is true?

This is definitely true. I was very happy to be Carla's caregiver. I was glad to do whatever she needed me to do. I looked for ways to make her life better or more comfortable. I would awaken in the morning, and before I got out of bed I would offer a prayer to the Creator to help me do my best to help Carla in the upcoming day.

Three of the sweetest words in the world to my ears were "thank you, Micky" when I did something to help her that she really liked. She called me "Micky" because her brother was Jim and her first husband was also Jim, so McCarty was shortened to "Micky" as her name of endearment for me.

When she passed into larger life I was lost as to who I was. For our 34 years together I had become, more and more with each year, her caregiver. And I felt that that was the best job in the world. But it took a few months of re-evaluation for me to get a handle on who I was without her. Then I began to get a feel for my own spiritual journey and how I needed to make that the central focus of my life.

How have you re-oriented your world? What are your new goals?

To seek the Creator within through meditation and to offer myself wherever needed to serve.

I don't wish to make a Virgin Mary of Carla, but she *is* a thoroughly service-oriented soul, and is, presumably, offering what service she is able to from her new location in time/space. Some seekers have reported a genuine sense of feeling that presence, whether for a moment or over time; some describing a feeling that they are being aided by Carla in some way. Do you think this is possible?

It is quite possible and even probable. The Life-Between-Lives work of Dr. Michael Newton, Dr. Brian Weiss, Dolores Cannon, and Rob Schwartz all demonstrate how loved ones check in from time to time with various family and friends to give them comfort and even direction.

What did Carla teach you? What do you feel you learned from her?

How to open my heart in love and how to talk in blue ray to resolve any disharmony. We never let the sun set on a disharmony. We always worked it out before we went to bed.

What is Carla's legacy to the world, and to you, personally?

I think that in general Carla's legacy is the great body of channeled and written work that clearly illustrates the unity of all creation and the fact that we are all made by Love and are all seeking to learn how to love. Her life was an example of these spiritual principles. Specifically, *The Law of One* information that she channeled from those of Ra stands as her great legacy.

Her legacy to me is that she came into my heart, and she left it full of love. She invited me into her heart, and she taught me how to love.

---

[1] Jim reflects in the October 25, 2015 entry of *The Camelot Journal*:

From the time of her lumbar surgery on April 15, 2011 until she passed into larger life on April 1, 2015 she traversed a death-defying gauntlet of medical problems. Seven debridements of infected skin at the wound site created a large open wound, and at three different times wound VAC machines were tried to heal the wound. We rented a Clinitron bed with warm circulating sand under her wound to try to heal it. At one point we even tried a skin graft. We went old school and tried Santyl ointment. And the pain pills would frequently make her so nauseous that she could not eat. But the wound would not heal.

Through it all she somehow kept a happy heart and always had a good word, loving smile, and heart-felt hug for the visiting nurses, friends, family, neighbors and strangers that came to visit her. It took us a while to discover that none of what was happening was a mistake or an accident, that it was part of a carefully made plan. We both were able to learn the most valuable lessons of our lives in this specific situation. She learned how to feel worthy enough to accept the love offerings of others, and I learned how to open my heart in all compassionate love by helping her. Back in the days when she sang in the Louisville Bach Society, at the bottom of the program for the performance always were the words that fit so well the ending of her life, that great symphony of love for the One Creator: "Soli Deo gloria"—Only for the glory of God.

The Camelot Journal, Jim McCarty, October 26, 2016, www.bring4th.org/

2   In the September 2nd entry for the *Camelot Journal,* Jim wrote:

Coincidentally Carla also planned her own funeral service, choosing all the hymns, the readings, the communion, and the time of day to have the service. As a result of Dannah's passing and making her own funeral plans she wrote:

"There is no use in fearing death. We might as well fear our birth. Both are markers in a long journey and constitute the beginning and end of a mysterious side trip into heavier illusion. We wrap the veil of forgetting about us and set sail in our ship of faith. And what a journey! Side trips do end, though, so that we can get back to the main journey. That is all that death is—a transition to the larger road in our soul's journey, from which this incarnation is a diversion, a learning experience and another way to learn to love and be loved."

The Camelot Journal, Jim McCarty, September 2, 2015, www.bring4th.org

3   See the following appendix for Jim's eulogy.

4   About Carla's pre-incarnational programming:

RA I am Ra. As we have said, this instrument, feeling that it lacked compassion to balance wisdom, chose an incarnative experience whereby it was of necessity placed in situations of accepting self in the absence of other-selves' acceptance and the acceptance of other-self without expecting a return or energy transfer. This is not an easy program for an incarnation but was deemed proper by this entity.

This entity therefore must needs meditate and consciously, moment by moment, accept the self in its limitations which have been placed for the very purpose of bringing this entity to the precise tuning we are using. Further, having learned to radiate acceptance and love without expecting return, this entity now must balance this by learning to accept the gifts of love and acceptance of others which this instrument feels some discomfort in accepting. These two balancing workings will aid this entity in the release from the distortion called pain. The limitations are, to a great extent, fixed. 60.8

5

Ra notes similarly back in 1982:

RA This entity has been sustaining a level of the distortion you call pain which few among your peoples experience without significant draining of the energies. Indeed, the stability of the entity is notable. 88.6

6

About accepting the limitations:

QUESTIONER Secondly, she would like to know why she feels more healthy now after she does these sessions. She's generally feeling more healthy as time goes on.

RA I am Ra. [First paragraph removed for brevity] Also, this entity has begun, due to this working, to accept certain limitations which it placed upon itself in order to set the stage for services such as it now performs. This also is an aid to re-aligning the distortions of the physical complex with regard to pain. 22.2

7

Jim's transformation has been palpable to the people around him. His efforts toward spiritual seeking and service have been re-doubled and focused to a fine point, his attitude more lighthearted, and his demeanor more gentle. Prior to Carla's passing I had seen him cry once. Since that date, the tears stand ready, behind the eyes, for a moment of sorrow, beauty, or compassion. He has said that Carla's death is the hardest thing he's ever had to go through, but as he continues walking that difficult road, the catalyst of the loss is removing the hard and rough outer layers, forging a purer version of Jim—more crystalline and shining.

8

Jim wrote in the *Camelot Journal* entry for August 31, 2015:

I continue to record Carla's *Living the Law of One 101* and have decided that the reason it feeds my soul is because it makes us a team again. I am recording her words. It's a team effort. For the last few years of her being bed bound it was totally clear to us that we were a team and always had been. So she is not here physically, but we are still functioning as a team.

The Camelot Journal, Jim McCarty, September 1, 2015, www.bring4th.org

Reflection & Carla's Eulogy

Reflection

Seventeen days after Carla left her body, a small portion of the many people who loved Carla gathered to say goodbye through the funeral service ceremony at her beloved Episcopalian church. Though in the solemnity of the ceremony there were tones of sorrow among those who will not have the pleasure of another conversation with Carla in this lifetime, it was nevertheless a moment of great beauty, celebration, and ultimately joy. Those gathered honored their dear friend and companion, and through the sounds of choir music selected in advance by Carla, they honored the Creator, blessing the soul they called *Carla* as she moved onto her next great adventure.

As the news of her passing spread, an outpouring of love arrived in the form of emails, cards, blog replies, forum posts, Facebook responses, flowers, donations, and in the silent support of love. Each giving meant so much to all at L/L, especially to Jim. It was, indeed, quite amazing to witness people all over this planet express in unison how Carla's life and work affected, informed, illuminated, and even awakened their own desire to seek the truth, often profoundly so. Those who remain at L/L Research feel likewise.

From the small moments in the day-to-day living to the patterns that become visible in the great arc of her arduous incarnational journey, Carla was and will continue to be an exemplar of unconditional love to us. Her physical presence is no longer available to our senses, but the Creator's original light that radiated so effortlessly from her will burn brightly through our own hearts, encouraging us to get out of our thick heads and into the infinite space of the heart where Carla met every soul she encountered.

Special though she was, we're all bozos on the bus, she would say. We, fellow bozos and travelers, are honored to have had the opportunity to ride alongside Carla for a time.

Our Brazilian friend and volunteer, Edgard D., said it wonderfully in his tribute to Carla:

> *We who keep existing in and experiencing the third density have the duty/honor of moving on with the work that she helped to perpetuate, a work that transcends creed, race, geography, time and space—a work that has only one demand: that we seek Truth inside ourselves, and that asks that we materialize this Truth the best way we can, building our own personal myth along the path, aiding in our own awakening and, by example, aiding those around us in their own awakening.*

Jim's Eulogy for Carla

Jim: *I was able to give Carla's eulogy with a strong and clear voice and felt that Carla was steadying my state of mind. This is the full text of the eulogy:*

Carla Lisbeth Rueckert-McCarty was born on July 16, 1943 in Lake Forest, IL. Carla was a child prodigy. At the age of 3 she could read the newspaper, speak French, and read music. She would have started singing in the church choir then, but she wasn't strong enough to hold the Hymnal all the way through the processional, until the next year when she was four years old. She was also the friendliest little girl her mother had ever seen. When they would take the bus to go downtown and shop, little Carla would wander up and down the aisle speaking to everyone who was on the bus. She did not know a stranger. Her mother was mortified.

When she was born her left eye was pointed at her brow, and it was about a year later when surgery was able to correct the defect, and then she started wearing glasses. A fascinating experience occurred because she had to wear glasses at such an early age. One day, when she was 2 years old, and when it was time for her to take her afternoon nap, her mother put her in her crib next to the window and closed the Venetian blinds. Before she went to sleep, Carla took her glasses off and put them between the blinds which were drawn for her nap. Then she laid down and saw that there was light coming through the slit in the Venetian blinds. When it went through her glasses it made a beam of light that she was able to use to slide out of her body and go to what seemed like a magic forest. The animals would communicate with her, colors were more vivid, and when she went to the center of the forest, there she would see Jesus. He didn't look like the paintings you usually see. His hair was long, matted, and dusty from the road. His robe was dusty too, and He never spoke a word. But when He held her hand and looked into her eyes, she immediately knew what unconditional love was. This experience occurred many times over the next few years. When she was five years old she told her mom and dad about the experience, and they told her that it was not real. It was in her mind. That she had made it up. So the experience never happened again. But her devotion to Jesus as her Lord and Savior began then and never wavered throughout her life. And from that point on, love would become her way of looking at the world. Those two parts of this experience never changed for her.

Because of Carla's intelligence her mom and dad gave her more responsibilities at an early age than most kids would ever have. She babysat her younger brother, Jimmy, when she was only 7 years old. When she was 10 she cooked for the family even though she had to stand on a chair to reach the stove top.   Her mom and dad felt that with her high intelligence, she should be pushed to excel more by constructive criticism than by being given praise. So by the age of 13 she believed that she was a failure, and she prayed to die because she felt that she could not be of service. Since her meeting with Jesus, service to others was the way that she believed that she could express the love that she had felt from Him. And if she couldn't serve as Jesus had inspired her to do, then she wanted to die. Six months later her kidneys failed, and she had a near-death experience. She again went to a place where the animals communicated with her. She could see music in the air. A rose twined around her arm, and just over the hill she could see the top of a temple. She knew that her spiritual family and friends were in the temple and waiting for her. But as she proceeded up the hill a clear and heavenly voice told her that it was not her time. It said that she had chosen a great deal to learn in her life, and perhaps she should make another plan that would use another childhood and split the load between two lifetimes. Carla couldn't stand the thought of having to go through another childhood, so she said that she would go back and complete this life. And immediately she was back in her body, which was racked with pain, and there was a circle of doctors' and nurses' faces gathered over her. She chose a hard road in coming back because it offered more chance to serve others, and so she did.

When she graduated from the MacDuffie High School for Girls in Springfield, MA her test scores were so high that she was offered scholarships from all the Ivy League schools and the Seven Sisters Schools as well. But when she went to Wellesley to see the school she couldn't believe how nasty and preppy the parties were that were used to recruit prized students. So she returned home to attend the University of Louisville, much to the chagrin of her mom and dad.

Again, because of her high test scores, she was admitted to the University as a junior, under a program that was used only for a couple of years. Her great love in college was philosophy. She was a natural-born philosopher, so one of the first courses she took was a graduate level course in ethics. After about two weeks of class lectures on various philosophers, the professor gave the first assignment. He said that they had talked about a number of philosophies in the first two weeks, but now he wanted them to write original philosophy on the topic of their choice. He didn't want to hear any other philosopher quoted back to him. He wanted their original work.

So Carla went home, got out her 8 ½ x 11 inch, yellow legal pad, and her pencil, and wrote on the topic of free will. She filled the front of the sheet, turned it over and wrote half way down the back side. When she went back to the next class to hand the paper in, she was somewhat shaken when she saw that her classmates, graduate students all, were handing in 20, 30, and 40 page type-written papers. She thought maybe she had made an error. When the students came back to class the next week the professor walked around the room and handed each student his or her paper, and gave out the grade at the same time. D, F, C, D, etc. until all the papers were handed back, except Carla didn't get her paper back. Then he said, "I gave one A on this assignment, and I'm going to read you the paper." Then he proceeded to read her page and a half paper on the topic of free will. Then he said, "Now that is original philosophy. That is what I was looking for."

Just before she got her degree from the University of Louisville she began dating a fellow who said that she was such a sweet little girl that he wanted to take care of her, because she really didn't know what the world was like. He told her that it was a rough and mean place and that she needed protection in order to be safe. That idea upset Carla greatly. She was sure that if you treated people with love they would treat you with love. So to test that belief, she dropped out of the University and got a job at a sleazy nightclub in downtown Louisville called The Shack. It was a popular hangout for gamblers, numbers runners, pimps, and prostitutes. Her dad was an engineer by day and a jazz drummer by night, and he convinced the owner to give Carla a job, even though she wouldn't be a pro like the other girls she would be working with. When guys would ask her for a date she would politely tell them that she wasn't a pro, but she could get one of the other girls to go out with them. Or she might just listen to their problems, and give them reassurance and advice.

The Shack had live music, and when the band would take a break Carla would get up on the stage and sing folk songs a capella. She became much beloved, and that was demonstrated one day in a potentially dangerous way. A stranger came into the bar and asked her for a date. She told him that she wasn't a pro but that she could get him a date with one of the other girls. But he wouldn't let her go, and he began giving her a hard time. And then the whole place went silent. You could have heard a pin drop. And then what she did hear, was a beer bottle breaking across the room, and then another, and another. Her friends were about to defend her, but the intruder wisely decided to call it a day and quickly left. For Carla that was validation of her belief that if you gave love you got love back, even if it came in the form of a broken beer bottle.

Her first husband, who was known as Dee, was the student of a professor who would become central in Carla's life. Don Elkins was a professor of physics at the University of Louisville, and Dee was taking intro to physics from him. In his off time Don was in the process of starting a meditation group and invited Dee and 11 of his classmates to be part of it. Dee asked if he could bring his girlfriend along. Don said, "Sure." After four years, seven mistresses, and after leaving Carla four times, Dee eventually asked Carla for a divorce, which she happily granted. So when she went back to the meditation group she began to spend time with Don, and they eventually moved in together. When Don told her that he knew that they were going be together after meeting her for the first time she asked him why he didn't tell her that before she married Dee, and Don said, "I knew that you would get a lot of good catalyst and grow from it." To which Carla replied, "Thanks a lot!"

From that point on she began to work for Don as he was a physics professor by day only. On his own time he was very interested in UFOs and the general field of the paranormal, and he needed someone like Carla that could read the existing literature in the field, take notes, and then compare them to the material that he had collected since the mid-50s. Don was also a pilot, and would fly to different parts of the country to investigate close encounters and reports of abduction. Carla would fly along and take notes. They eventually wrote a book called *Secrets of the UFO* which was published in 1977 and is still considered one of the best in the field.

I met Don and Carla in the fall of 1979 when I was living in the woods of central Kentucky and was part of a food buying co-op that met monthly to place orders. I had recently heard Don and Carla interviewed on WKQQ radio in Lexington, KY. The topic was UFOs, and I was very interested in meeting these two folks. Later, I discovered, at one of our food co-op meetings, that there was a group of folks living on the other side of the county who knew Don and Carla. They invited me to attend one of Don and Carla's Sunday meditations that they held in their apartment on Douglas Blvd., here in Louisville. Don and Carla warmly welcomed me to their meditation, and afterward we talked some, and I asked if it would be okay for me to attend the meditations regularly. So for the next year I drove from Marion County to Louisville on Sundays to meditate with Don and Carla.

Eventually I helped them move from their apartment on Douglass Blvd. to a house on Watterson Trail in Jeffersontown, where we would soon live together and join our efforts in pursuing their work in meditation, philosophy, metaphysics, and channeling.

Carla had a gift that is sometimes called mediumship or channeling. She could contact intelligent sources of love and inspiration that some people call aliens and others angels. Carla's real gift, though, was the discernment of spirits. Whenever we meditated and an unseen spirit wished to speak through her she would always challenge that spirit in the name of Jesus Christ, her Lord and Savior. If the unseen spirit could not say that "Jesus is Lord," Carla would not allow the entity to speak through her.

Throughout her life as a Christian mystic, who had this ability to discern spirits, she always asked her priest to look at her work and let her know if he thought it was acceptable. The first priest she asked this question of was Bishop Marmion. He realized that she was serving people who did not go to a church, and so he said to her, "Your work is based on giving and receiving love whether it's done in a church or not. You are Christ to these people. You are their contact with His love. Treat them as sheep of His flock".

Over the next four years we were involved in what came to be called *The Law of One*, or the Ra contact. We completed 106 sessions of this channeled contact, which is the work for which Carla is best known around the world. After Don Elkins died in 1984 Carla and I continued the work of L/L Research with weekly Sunday meditations, further channeling, speaking engagements around the country, and Carla also offered herself as a counselor to those who had questions about their life's path and how they might be aided by the information that we had been privileged to make available.

All totaled Carla either authored or channeled over a dozen books during her life, counseled hundreds of seekers of truth, spoke to thousands of people at spiritual gatherings, and in everything that she did, she happily and naturally shared her love of life and her love of people. In 1987, she and I were married in Calvary Episcopal Church. We were married for 28 years, and together for 34.

Her last five years were spent mostly in a hospital bed at home, attempting to recover from back surgery. Though she experienced a great deal of pain and limitation, she never complained even one time about her situation. She faced all of her life with love and a happy heart that she freely shared with all who came her way. She saw all people as souls, no matter the outer behavior, full of love in their true selves, and she loved them without reservation, without limit, and with all her being, for love was the greatest quality that she could channel through her wide open heart.

The greatest love of her life was Jesus Christ and her spiritual family that lives all over the world, and especially here at St. Luke's. For over a decade she has been a part of the parish of this wonderful church. For the last five years of her life she was unable to attend in person, but she always felt that she was here in spirit sharing her love for each person within the walls of this family church. She was so grateful to Caroline Edelman for bringing her weekly communion that fed her soul. She chose every part of this memorial service as a means by which to glorify God, in the passing of her earthly life, and as a reaffirmation of her belief in Jesus Christ as the Son of God and her personal savior.

Why the Title "Tilting at Windmills"

Carla considered her life's work as one of *tilting at windmills*. Almost since its inception L/L has featured in its logo the ragged but valiant knight errant, his faithful squire, and the windmills at which he tilted.

What does it mean to *tilt at windmills* and why was that phrase chosen as the book's title? That answer starts with the following defining excerpt:

> "To tilt at windmills" is a venerable English idiom meaning to pursue an unrealistic, impractical, or impossible goal, or to battle imaginary enemies. In current usage, "tilting at windmills" carries connotations of engaging in a noble but unrealistic (usually wildly unrealistic) effort.
>
> In Cervantes' story, a retired eccentric obsessed with the ideals of medieval chivalry imagines himself a knight and sets out on a quest for adventure, which is made considerably more dramatic by the fact that "Don Quixote" (as the hero has dubbed himself) misinterprets just about everything he encounters. In the relevant passage early on in Quixote's sojourn, he and his companion Sancho Panza (a dim neighbor he has recruited as his squire) encounter some windmills, which Don Quixote charges on his horse, his knight's lance extended, believing them to be not windmills, but malevolent giants.[*]

L/L Research does not envision itself in precisely the way Quixote envisioned himself: encountering and battling enemies or making right the wrongs of the world for purposes of chivalry, heroism, or conferring glory on Dulcinea. Nor, for that matter, does L/L pursue extravagant and fanciful misinterpretations of *the way things are*. Carla speaks to this point in Chapter 2 of this book:

> **CARLA** I don't identify with the particulars of that story, which is a peculiarly befuddled story of people that are genuinely not seeing

---

[*] www.word-detective.com/2009/03/tilting-at-windmills/

what's in front of them . . . . I don't think I've ever fooled myself about anything like that, but it's just that desire to remain pure and true to my standards and not compromise them, regardless of how the world wags. It's often inconvenient to do that.

GARY So what does it mean to dream the impossible dream?

CARLA Well, I think it means to bring truth, beauty, love, light, and understanding to Earth, and to make it the way people live.[†] It's always felt to me like the right way to live and I've always tried to live that way, and I know it's impossible.

L/L Research's dedicated work might be seen as tilting at windmills be-cause what are we doing? We are attempting to share communication from sources much of the world's people say do not exist. Much of the world would laugh or reject out of hand what we are doing. With good reason. *Truth without proof* doesn't find many an advocate in a scientific paradigm that declares as true only that which can be measured and/or seen by its instrumentation.[‡]

It is not, however, only the communications and their source which high-light our windmill tilting, but also our attempt to live by principles that tend not to be the values of this world; to walk a high (albeit dusty) road of service to others, to seek qualities that many either assign little value to or simply don't recognize. Which is not to commit the error of describing ourselves in glowing and elevated terms that set us apart—for we are most assuredly humble, error-prone, all-too-human bozos on the bus, and there are many people and many sources of light engaged daily in the good

---

[†] "Make it the way people live." That doesn't mean others but rather oneself.

[‡] Further securing our place in the domain of the quixotic: those who call them-selves the Confederation of Planets in Service to the One Infinite Creator cannot themselves be measured by scientific means. This is not to say that there is no set of parameters with which to appraise this situation. These sources of intel-ligence share information, perspective, and wisdom whose substance *can* be evaluated on its own merits—the seeker determining whether and how it may understood and applied—but, these particular beings are not manifest in our physical world or illusion. Moreover, they speak of a multi-dimensional uni-verse, populated by infinite varieties of intelligence, unified by a one infinite creator, built of light made by love operating through free will. Though there are mystical yearnings and perspectives at the frontiers of science that recognize the fundamental oneness of the universe, no such framework as that which the Confederation offers will appear on the pages of any physics book.

work of service to others—it is only to point to a, shall I say, deeper understanding that calls to us, an understanding available always to each and every person but which few recognize or seek in this world.

Indeed it might be said that any who embark upon the quest of self-realization are *tilting at windmills,* or dreaming the impossible dream: the world *clearly* consists of countless separate parts, yet the spiritual seeker seeks unity or oneness; money not love is *clearly* that which makes the world go round, yet the spiritual seeker seeks to know and express the love which made, motivates, and is hidden in all things; disharmony and dispute are the ways that people and nations seem often to relate—barricaded from one another behind layers of legal, geographical, physical, armed, and/or emotional means—yet the student of the open heart seeks transparent harmony and community even, often, at the expense of the self; the world seems to teach the benefit of *self*-gain and the fulfilling of one's private interests, yet the seeker desires to serve and uplift *others* for the gain of all; things have clearly gone terribly awry on this planet judging by the diversity of confusion, ignorance, and frequent cruelty of the world, yet she who consciously walks the road affirms that no matter the surface appearances, there is always cause for hope, there is always something to learn, and, from the greatest vantage point, all is ultimately well. These being several among many ways that conventional wisdom is honored but transcended—sometimes even defied— in the seeking of truth.

In choosing a logo for L/L Research, Carla wrote:

> Don Elkins moved in with me in November of 1968. The drawing [of Picasso's *Don Quixote*] was hanging over my desk and he asked about it. I told him the bare bones of the story of the man of La Mancha and how his skewed vision of the world made it a beautiful place and he, an heroic figure. He mused that it was a perfect image for the work we were then beginning to do, since we were dreaming impossible dreams together.

> Since the beginning of our publishing in 1976 we have used that little image as our publishing logo. And we're still tilting at windmills here at L/L Research with great joy and thanksgiving for the inspiration of that little sketch.

And in Carla's 2002 speech to the International UFO Congress, she said:

Our logo is Don Quixote. Don Quixote tilted at windmills. They were all illusions, but what I care about in Don Quixote is the passion that he had for good, for honor. What I care about is the passion that Jesus had for the beauty in each one of us. He saw all of us as citizens of eternity, and that's the truth of us. We are infinite, magical, powerful, amazing beings. We have connections to each other, to the planet, and to that beyond ourselves which we came to serve, the light.

And the way we do that is to open the heart and let that crystal radio nature work so that as we are getting the unconditional love of the infinite Creator, as the light is flowing into us, we bless it, we consciously encourage it; and we dedicate it not only to our own well-being (although we always need to do that first) but also to the lightening of planet Earth and the healing of the world. There is a tremendous need at this time for healing in this world.

All analogies and metaphors have their limitations—ways in which there is not equivalency between the two things being likened unto each other. There are such limitations in the comparison of L/L Research to Don Quixote. But among the ways that L/L Research draws upon that story (in an illustrative or at least inspiring fashion) is the way in which he uplifted himself by changing his perception and formulating a personal myth. Whether he did so as a conscious choice or as victim of an overtaking madness, the important point is that in so doing Alonso Quixano became Don Quixote and transformed his ordinary, mundane life into a quest—one built upon principles and ideals that invoked a stronger-better-more-noble version of himself—and subsequently committed his will toward that end.

In that journey Quixote's faith informed him of what was real and actual underneath the apparent surface of things, and in that faith he stood true to his vision regardless of what *the world* declared otherwise. Now, the Confederation philosophy never suggests whimsically fabricating things out of thin air, but it does suggest that we generate perception as a function of our orientation (see 33.8). And it also suggests that appearances are illusory—an illusion of intelligence and purpose, but an illusion nevertheless, one that effectively *hides* reality from our immediate vision for the purpose of spiritual evolution.

The Confederation's message (and the teaching of all exponents of the perennial philosophy) simply points behind the illusion to a unified, objective truth undergirding each seeker's subjective journey. And in order to bridge the seeming distance between illusion and the one, ever-present truth, faith is absolutely required; perhaps at times even a quixotic faith. Not a faith in this or any body of material—religious, spiritual, philosophical, or otherwise—but a faith in oneself and to the Creator in all things.

Upon the path of discernment it is, of course, helpful to empirically subject one's conclusions and ideas to scrutiny, analysis, and evidence to the contrary—because there are certainly myriad ways to create more rather than less distortion—but in the more positive and inspiring aspects of Quixote's journey is the indomitable faith that saw something the material world didn't, the will to commit the whole heart to its pursuit, and the inevitable follies and hard knocks upon the head that become contained in an ambiance of magic and adventure.

> RA I am Ra. Your language is not over-strewn with non-emotional terms for the functional qualities of what is now termed the unconscious mind.

> The nature of the unconscious is of the nature of concept rather than word. Consequently, before the veiling the use of the deeper mind was that of the use of unspoken concept. You may consider the emotive and connotative aspects of a melody. One could call out, in some stylized fashion, the terms for the notes of the melody. One could say, "a quarter note A, a quarter note A, a quarter note A, whole note F." This bears little resemblance to the beginning of the melody of one of your composers' most influential melodies, that known to you as a symbol of victory.

> This is the nature of the deeper mind. There are only stylized methods with which to discuss its functions. Thusly our descriptions of this portion of the mind, as well as the same portions of body and spirit, were given terms such as "far-seeing," indicating that **the nature of penetration of the veiled portion of the mind may be likened unto the journey too rich and exotic to contemplate adequate describing thereof.** 86.6

L/L Research Timeline

Date	Event	Notes
1930.02.27	Donald Tully Elkins born	Louisville, Kentucky
1943.07.16	Carla Lisbeth Rueckert born	Lake Forest, Illinois. Family relocates to Anniston, Alabama soon thereafter.
1944/45	Don joins Army JROTC	Louisville's Male High School
1947	Joins Elkins-Mantell Flying School	Don is a student learning to fly at Bowman field in Louisville, KY.
1947.05.10	James Allen McCarty born	Kearney, Nebraska
1948.01.07	Captain Thomas Mantell crashes	National Guard pilot who gained country's attention when his plane crashed in pursuit of a UFO. Incident sparked Don Elkins' interest in UFOs.
1948.07.27	Don enlists (or continues in) the National Guard	Upon graduating Louisville Male High School. Is stationed in Germany at some point.
1949~	Don begins university	University of Louisville's Speed Scientific School
1951.10.	Don earns rank of Master Sergeant at 20 years old	According to Carla, the youngest in US Army (or National Guard?) history. Helped in part by his sharpshooting skills.
1952.05.16	Don receives honorable discharge from National Guard	Goes to officer school immediately thereafter.
1952.07.01	Don receives rank of 2nd Lieutenant	US National Guard, Field Artillery/Armor Division
1955.06.05	Don earns Bachelors of Mechanical Engineering	University of Louisville Speed Scientific School
1955?	Don begins teaching	At The University of Louisville's

	engineering and physics	Speed Scientific School in Louisville, Kentucky.
1955	Don's research into UFOs takes off	Elkins gives this as the year that his intensive investigative efforts began.
1955.07.01	Don earns rank of First Lieutenant	US Army Reserves.* (Don's 2nd Lt commission is listed on the certificate as National Guard. His 1st Lt and Captain commissions are listed only as "Reserved Commissioned Officer." He either rose in rank in the National Guard, or switched to Army Reserves.)
1956	Don goes Vulcan*	Or stoic, if you prefer. Determines that the world is, shall we say, crazy, and in order to survive he must become indifferent, a coolheaded observer who is not swayed one way or the other, especially by emotion.
1956	Carla's kidneys fail, has near-death-experience	Given choice to move on or return. See Chapters 13 and 27 for more info.
1956.07.13	Don achieves rank of Captain	US Army Reserves
1957	Carla's family relocates	To Louisville, Kentucky
1961.06.11	Don earns first master's degree: Master of Mechanical Engineering	University of Louisville
1961	Don moves to Alaska to head new engineering dept.	Arctic cold was not to Don's liking, according to Carla, causing Don to return.
1961	Don meets Hal Price	Receives the Detroit Group material (and *The Brown Notebook*). Visits Walt Rogers' group in Detroit sometime thereafter.
1961.12	Carla meets Don	Through a student in Don's engineering class, and Carla's romantic

---

* Vulcans are a fictional species from the TV series *Star Trek* who are characterized by living according to reason and logic only without interference from emotion. Toward that end they control and suppress their emotions.

		interest, Jim D.
1962.01	First channeling group begins	Don gathers first experimental channeling group. Carla is the 13th member and only female.
1962.07~	Walt Rogers visits Don's experimental physics group	Experiment initially "scientifically clean, but null." Rogers visits the Louisville Group and channels his Confederation contact to the group. Gist of message: "Why aren't you speaking our words? You are receiving them, but you are not saying them." Actual channeling begins soon thereafter.
1963	Don and Carla meet Morris Hoagland	At eight years old due to childhood UFO experience described in *Secrets of the UFO* and referenced in *The Law of One*. Develops lifelong friendship. Eventually becomes VP of L/L Board.
1964	Jim DeWitt proposes to Carla	Says that in order to perform their music on the road, they must be married. See Ch. 2 for more.
1965	Don leaves teaching & the military in order to becomes an airline pilot for Eastern Air Lines	Becomes a pilot to fund his research and devote more time to it. Eventually rises to the rank of a 727 Captain.
1966	Carla earns her bachelors in English Literature	University of Louisville
1967	Jim DeWitt takes Carla to Vancouver, British Columbia	Carla supports her jobless husband, eventually lands a job she loves serving as a librarian at a local university.
1968	Jim DeWitt divorces Carla	Carla returns to Louisville from Vancouver
1968	Don moves in with Carla	They unite immediately following Carla's divorce from Jim DeWitt. Don attempts intimacy with Carla for six months.
1968	Carla and Don write the novel *The Crucifixion of Esmerelda Sweetwater*	They receive or "see" the entire story as if watching a movie, except for the very end, which they have to create

		on their own.
1968–1970	Carla undertakes two years of celibacy	Carla tries celibacy for two years, a result of Don's lack of interest in sex and desire to remain celibate. At the end of which they make a new, mutually respectful arrangement.
1969	Jim earns Bachelors of Business and Economics	University of Nebraska at Kearney
1970	Carla goes to work full time for Don	Leaves librarian position of thirteen-grade private school to devote herself full time to Don's investigation.
1970	Don and Carla form the L/L Company	A private partnership focused on research.
1971	Don and Carla meet Dewey Larson	Arranges for Larson to speak at the University of Kentucky. Don and Carla subsequently join the board of International Society for Unified Science. Remain until publication of *Secrets of the UFO*.
1971	Carla earns her Masters in Library Service	University of Louisville
1972.05	Jim earns Masters of Education	University of Florida/Teacher Corps
1972.05.14	Don earns second master's degree: Master of Engineering	University of Louisville
1972–1973	Jim spends two summers in Colorado	At T. D. Lingo's Adventure Trail Survival School.
1972.08	Jim purchases 132 acres	In Marion County, Kentucky. Influenced by the "Back to the Land Movement," and wanting to follow Lingo's dictum to teach brain self-control, Jim builds his own log cabin.
1973.03	Jim cuts timbers for cabin. Leaves to dry	Has Angelica experience. Gets cabin frame up in October, 1973.
1974.05	Jim moves to Kentucky permanently	Spends first six weeks in a tent before moving into the cabin.
1974	Jim forms the Rock	A 501(c)(3) non-profit modeled after

	Creek Research & Development Labs, Inc.	Lingo's own school. Designed to teach the same methods.
1974	Carla takes up channeling on Don's request	After twelve years of participating in the group but never channeling. She, we now know, was a natural. Likely born for it.
1974	Carla and Don visit Andrija Puharich	And realize that his house was featured in their book, *The Crucifixion of Esmerelda Sweetwater,* and he was the character Pablo.
1974	Don, Carla, and others form Eftspan	Named after a term in the book *Oahspe,* formed as a 501(c)(3) light center with land near St. Francis, KY. Carla and Don eventually drop out.
1975	Carla gains proficiency in channeling	Develops and tests the protocols of tuning and challenging.
1975	Carla undergoes psychic surgery in the Philippines	Don and Carla travel to investigate (and experience) psychic surgery.
1976	Don and Carla change the name to L/L Research	
1977	Secrets of the UFO published	
1977.05.30	Jim hears Don and Carla for the first time	Featured on a WKQQ radio broadcast out of Lexington, KY, Jim hears them while alone on his land, listening to a battery-powered radio.
1977.12– 1978.01	Carla undergoes psychic surgery in Mexico	Don and Carla travel to Mexico to investigate (and experience) psychic surgery for a second time.
1978.08	Jim meets Carla (and soon thereafter, Don)	Meets Carla on the front steps of the main meeting hall at Ken Keyes' new "Living Love Center" in St Mary's, KY. Meets Don at a meditation in Don and Carla's Louisville apartment not long thereafter.
1979.05.03	Don achieves a rank of Captain	For Eastern Air Lines.
1980	Jim moves to Oregon to	Pulled to leave his solitary experience

	join Cosmic Awareness Communications	of six years in order to be of service in a channeling community. Spends two months there.
1980	L/L Research 501(c)(3) created	Becomes a DBA of Jim's non-profit, The Rock Creek Research & Development Labs.
1980.12.23	Jim moves in with Carla and Don	Offered lucrative employment while in Oregon, Jim sets aside weekend to meditate on the question of whether to stay with Cosmic Awareness, take high-paying work, or return to Louisville to accept Don and Carla's offer to live and work with them. Receives answer in a matter of seconds: "Go to Louisville."
1981.01.15	Ra Contact begins	Don Elkins, and universe, jump for joy.
1981	75 Sessions this year	
1982	27 Sessions this year	
1982, fall	Group begins search for a new home in Atlanta	To move closer to Don's work as an airline pilot. First signs of Don's illness.
1983	4 Sessions this year	
1983.11	Group moves to Atlanta	
1984	1 Session this year	
1984.04	Group returns from Atlanta	Moves into new home in Louisville.
1984.11	Don Elkins passes away	Commits suicide after a year of declining mental health at 54 years old.
1986	The Crucifixion of Esmerelda Sweetwater published	18 years after it was written.
1986.01.12	Q'uo first channeled	Hatonn, Latwii, Oxal, and others had been around for some time. Q'uo first appearance on this date.
1987	A Channeling Handbook published	
1987.05	Jim and Carla marry	At Calvary Episcopal Church in

		Louisville, KY.
1987.06	Meet Steve Tyman	A professor of philosophy who would become a dear friend, one of Carla's best two channeling students, and Jim's co-channeler beginning 2015.
1991~	Meet Roman Vodacek	Jim and Carla meet Romi, who will become a longstanding and faithful friend to, and volunteer for, L/L Research, and also the third member who will make possible many of the channelings in the '90s.
1992~	Carla leaves the desert	Roughly eight years after Don died, Carla finally forgives herself and leaves a long spiritual desert experience. Her health rebounds and she regains the ability to be fully mobile again after a grueling physical therapy regimen.
1996~	LLResearch.org launches	Thanks to multiple people but primarily Ian, a professional who volunteers to digitize all of L/L's work, and subsequently builds L/L's first website, LLResearch.org, to share that work with the world. Ian serves as volunteer webmaster and editor/publisher for 17 years.
1998	Book V of *The Law of One* published	
2001	A Wanderer's Handbook published	
2002.04	Meet Gary Bean at the "Time of Global Shift" seminar in Louisville	Produced by Scott Mandelker, Carla and Jim speak at this seminar and meet a young Gary.
2003.04.10	Tobey Wheelock launches Lawofone.Info	A website dedicated to sharing *The Law of One* material. Later will host the *Relistened* and *Lightly Edited* versions, and will become the best study tool for *The Law of One* material.
2003.02	Spiritual community attempted	After group discussion, Carla & Jim invite attendees of Feb, 2002 Home-

		coming to start an experiment in community.
2004.10	Tobey Wheelock initiates the Relistening Project	Re-listens to all 106 sessions of the Ra Contact. Discovers un-transcribed Q&As and other modifications to the text. Begins creation of *Relistened Version*, an actual exact transcript, and the precursor of the *Lightly Edited Version*, that which will be used for *The Ra Contact: Teaching the Law of One* book.
2005~	Initial spiritual community experiment comes to an end	Everyone eventually moves away save for Gary who stays on with Carla and Jim.
2005.06	Carla begins The Camelot Journal	A daily online blog chronicling the life and work of L/L Research, and the personal lives of Jim and Carla. Journal continues uninterrupted into the present.
2005.08	Wooded Glen Retreat	Gary produces his first, and L/L's first, large-scale Homecomings (large by L/L's standards).
2006.02	Gary becomes Carla's administrative assistant	Carla, wanting to be freed to focus on creative work, creates new position and offers it to Gary, who accepts reluctantly but soon embraces it. Several years later becomes L/L's Administrator.
2007	*A Book of Days: Channelings From the Holy Spirit* published	
2008.12	Bring4th.org is born	Steve Engratt had a vision for a community website congruent with Carla's seed idea, and the technical chops to get it done. Signs on as webmaster and together with Gary, builds L/L Research's first community website.
2008.12	First L/L online store launched	As a result of which Carla and Jim do not have to fund L/L Research out of

		their own pockets for the first time in its history.
2009	*Living the Law of One 101: The Choice* published	Carla's attempt to break down the *Law of One* into simpler terms.
2009	*The Light/Lines Newsletter: The First 25 Years* published	L/L's quarterly newsletter *The Light/Lines* features the best of its channeling.
2009	L/L Research Channeling Archives published	An 18-volume set spanning the years 1972 - 2008
2010.08.09	Social media platforms launched	Including Facebook, Twitter, and Tumblr.
2010.09.28	In the Now - Q&A with Carla L. Rueckert launched	Originally hosted by Monica Leal. Will evolve over time to include Jim, Gary, and Austin. Podcast ongoing.
2011.01.17	Basic Principles of the Law of One launched	Carla designs a course based on her book *Living the Law of One 101* and offers it through online school IMU (International Metaphysical University).
2011.04.02	Carla's final Saturday Meditation channeling	Undergoes spinal fusion surgery soon thereafter. Leaves her bound to a hospital bed with an open wound for next four years.
2011.04.13	Audio from the Ra contact published online	Shares audio with the public for the first time, allowing others to hear the slow-moving conversation.
2012	*The Poetry of Carla Lisbeth Rueckert* published	
2012.08	Meet Austin Bridges at Homecoming, 2013	Along with the equally long-haired friend and contributor to L/L Research, Sephira Vox.
2012.12.22	The day after the famously hyped Dec 21, 2012 date...	...is a day like any other.
2013.08	Austin Bridges moves to Louisville	Recognized for excellent volunteer work as a moderator for Bring4th.org, invited to Louisville to work alongside Gary at the L/L helm.

2014.09	Create first L/L Research satellite station	With Jochen Blumenthal for the German translation of all L/L Research material. Soon thereafter incorporates Micheline Deschreider's French translations.
2015.04.01	Carla passes away	After a four-year struggle with an open wound and a lifetime of medical hardship, Carla passes away in Jim's arms in their home at 71 years old.
2015.08	*The Quixotic Quest: The Story & Identity of L/L Research* published	Written initially as a presentation for Homecoming, 2015. Book uses material from this interview.
2015.10~	Gary becomes Director, Austin Assistant Director of L/L Research	Gaining only a formal titles recognizing them for what they had already been doing.
2016	By this year the *Law of One* had been translated into . . .	Portuguese, Chinese, French, German, Hungarian, Romanian, Russian, Spanish, and Turkish. With Italian, Czech, and Bulgarian on the horizon.
2016.08	Publish this book	*Tilting at Windmills: An Interview with Carla L. Rueckert & Jim McCarty*

Upcoming

L/L Research: publishes *The Ra Contact: Teaching the Law of One*, releases first ever audiobooks of all L/L's books, launches a new unified website, assists in creating a documentary about the life and work of Don Elkins, and continues serving seekers and channeling Confederation sources indefinitely into the future.

And then . . . fulfills Smithsonian's request for copies of *The Law of One* books, ushers in new era of world peace using electric guitars and a time-traveling phone booth, welcomes first public contact with ETs, and eventually opens bottle of champagne marked: "Do not open until arrival of fourth density."

Not listed

Individual workshops, speaking events, interviews, individual translations, and the first-time meetings with many dear friends and volunteers (like Terry Hsu) who would become L/L Research family.

Additional L/L Research Publications

The Law of One: Books I – V
Containing the transcripts from an extraordinary conversation with a non-human intelligence, the *Law of One* books explore the blueprint of spiritual evolution of mind, body and spirit, and maps out a cosmology wherein the Creator knows itself.

Living The Law of One 101: The Choice
Written with the intent of creating an entry–level, simple to read report concerning the core principles of the Law of One and Confederation philosophy in general, this book takes the reader through a discussion of Law of One principles such as unity, free will, love, light and polarity.

A Wanderer's Handbook
A reference manual for spiritual outsiders. It explores the alienation that seekers experience, the varieties of the pain of living, the healing of the incarnation, the discovery of the life's mission, and how to live a devotional life in a busy world.

The Quixotic Quest: The Story & Identity of L/L Research
The Quixotic Quest provides a sense of who and what L/L Research is, where it's been, how it came to be, and where it may be headed. It is the first time this has been attempted in a cohesive, streamlined, and integrated fashion. It might be considered a narrated, shortened version of *Tilting at Windmills*.

Secrets of the UFO
A summary of the 25 years of philosophical study that preceded the Ra contact. The progression from physical sightings to metaphysical implications is carefully traced and, in some respects, serves as an introduction to the *Law of One* series.

A Channeling Handbook
Written for channels and those who would like to improve their channeling. Topics include: What is channeling? Why channel? Psychic greetings/attacks. Temptations and the ethics of channeling. Channeling and Christianity.

On the L/L Research Website:
- More publications not listed above
- Over 1,500 channeling transcripts from 1974–Present
- A collection of interviews and speeches including some rare gems w/ Don Elkins.
- The *Light/Lines* and *Gatherings Newsletter*s
- Information from various past L/L Research gatherings and workshops
- An *Origins* section including the *Brown Notebook* which opened Elkins to Confederation channeling.
- Transcripts and audio of L/L Research's podcast *In the Now*.
- Over nine translations and more being added.
- Forums, Blogs, Chatrooms, Seeker Connector, and more.

Tilting at Windmills, Literally
Toner on paper, 300 dpi, grayscale. 2016

Made in the USA
Columbia, SC
30 August 2024